Flow-Control Statements

RETURN [statement number] — Causes a return to the calling program or sub-program. The optional [statement number] is for alternate returns from a subroutine and is not used in this text.

CALL (subroutine name) (argument list) — Transfer of control to subroutine (name).

CONTINUE — Loop terminator or target of a GO TO.

GO TO (statement number) — Unconditional GO TO.

GO TO (statement number list), (arithmetic expressions) — Computed GO TO.

IF (arithmetic expression) sl_1, sl_2, sl_3 — Arithmetic IF statement.

IF (logical expression) (executable statement) — Logical IF statement.

IF (logical expression) THEN — Logical block IF statement.

ELSE — Optional ELSE block.

ELSE IF (logical expression) THEN — Optional conditional block.

END IF — Block IF terminator.

DO (statement number) (name) = e_1, e_2, $[e_3]$ — DO loop. (name) is the name of the loop index; e_1, e_2, e_3, are expressions specifying the index bounds.

File-Directive Statements

OPEN (unit number), FILE='(name)', [options]) — Connects a file to an I/O unit.

CLOSE (unit number) — Disconnects a file.

REWIND (unit number — Positions a sequential file at the beginning.

BACKSPACE (unit number) — Backspace a sequential file one record.

ENDFILE (argument list) — Write an End-Of-File mark on a sequential file.

INPUT/OUTPUT Statements

READ ((unit number), (format), [options]), (in-list)

READ (format), (in-list)

READ *, (in-list) — List-directed READ.

READ (*,*) (in-list) — List-directed READ.

WRITE ((unit number), (format), [options]), (out-list)

PRINT (format), (out-list)

PRINT *, (out-list) — List-directed PRINT.

WRITE (*,*) (out-list) — List-directed WRITE.

FORMAT (format specification list) — I/O editing specifications.

The Order of FORTRAN Statements

PROGRAM/SUBROUTINE/FUNCTION			
IMPLICIT			Comments
Type Specifications (REAL, INTEGER, etc.)	PARAMETER		
Other Specifications COMMON, EXTERNAL, INTRINSIC, etc.		FORMAT	
Statement functions			
ALL executable statements	DATA		
END			

PWS-KENT Series in Engineering and Computer Science

FORTRAN 77
and Numerical Methods
for Engineers

Second Edition

G. J. Borse
Lehigh University

PWS-KENT Publishing Company
Boston

PWS-KENT
Publishing Company

20 Park Plaza
Boston, Massachusetts 02116

PWS-KENT Publishing Company is a division of Wadsworth, Inc.

"CDC" and its computer "CDC-CYBER-730" are registered trademarks of Control Data Corporation. "DEC" and its computers "DEC-20" and "PDP-11" are registered trademarks of Digital Equipment Corporation. "IBM" and its computer "IBM-4341" are registered trademarks of International Business Machines Corporation. "TI" is the registered trademark of Texas Instruments, Inc.

International Student Edition ISBN 0-534-98353-7

Library of Congress Cataloging-in-Publication Data

Borse, G. J. (Garold J.)
   FORTRAN 77 and numerical methods for engineers : G. J. Borse.—
2nd ed.
      p.   cm.
   Includes bibliographical references and index.
   ISBN 0-534-92562-6
   1. Engineering—Data processing.   2. FORTRAN 77 (Computer program language)
TA345.B67   1991
620'.00285—dc20   90-26162
                                                                              CIP

Sponsoring Editor: *Jonathan Plant*
Assistant Editor: *Mary Thomas*
Production Coordinator and Cover Designer: *Robine Andrau*
Manufacturing Coordinator: *Margaret Sullivan Higgins*
Production: *Cece Munson/The Cooper Company*
Interior Designer: *John Edeen*
Cover Photo: *Mark Eberhart*
Cover Printer: *Henry N. Sawyer Company*
Typesetter: *Beacon Graphics*
Printer and Binder: *Arcata Graphics/Halliday*

Printed in the United States of America

91 92 93 94 95 — 10 9 8 7 6 5 4 3 2 1

Contents

A

Programming Assignment   109

4

Elementary Programming Techniques   125

5

Subroutines and Functions   163

B

Programming Assignment   203

6

Elementary Formatted Input–Output   221

7

Arrays and Subscripted Variables   245

D

Programming Assignment   331

10

Taylor Series and Numerical Differentiation   348

11

Roots of Equations   379

E

Programming Assignment   419

G

Programming Assignment 531

14

Numerical Integration 542

H

Programming Assignment 579

Preface

The role of FORTRAN in the education of scientists and engineers has undergone some fundamental changes in the past decade. When the first edition of *FORTRAN 77 and Numerical Methods for Engineers* was written, FORTRAN was almost universally accepted as the programming language of preference among all practicing engineers and the only language familiar to most. Since then Pascal has enjoyed a steep ascent in popularity (and then just as steep a decline), and more recently the language C seems to be enjoying the spotlight.

Simultaneously, ubiquitous spreadsheet programs are being promoted as an easier method of handling numerical computations. Yet, when engineers come across a problem, be it a differential equation or a matrix problem, and for their own amusement wish to see the solution quickly, they invariably use a FORTRAN program. The reason for this, of course, is that FORTRAN was designed to mimic the algebraic formulation of a problem with which engineers are most comfortable.

In the several revisions of FORTRAN, most of the awkward features of the language have been eliminated. Elegant modular programs are now easily constructed and the tedious aspects of FORMAT statements can be almost totally avoided by the use of list-directed output. Thus FORTRAN, the mother of advanced computer languages, will likely remain preeminent among its peers and will continue to be a central element in the training of engineers and scientists.

Objectives

FORTRAN 77 and Numerical Methods for Engineers, Second Edition, is intended to do the following:

1. Present the essentials of the programming language FORTRAN at a level and in a form appropriate to beginning scientists and engineers. Mathematical problems that are solved using computers are often long and complicated; therefore it is essential that procedures for segmenting lengthy problems into manageable subunits be learned from the very beginning, along with the essentials of FORTRAN. Over the last decade a procedure has evolved, called "structured programming," that employs a modular approach

to complex problems and that adheres to the precepts of good programming style. This text offers numerous challenging programming assignments that illustrate the material of preceding chapters and that are intended to test the student's ability to assemble a complicated program from a variety of subunits.

2. Incorporate the concurrent mathematical ability of the student with the problem-solving features of FORTRAN. FORTRAN, like any other language, is of little use if you have nothing of significance to say; programmers must be skilled in mathematics and be familiar with the basic elements of the engineering discipline in which they work. Also, as every practicing engineer knows, a litmus test for the understanding of a mathematical procedure is the ability to program it for the computer. Thus numerical analysis and computer programming strongly reenforce one another. The second half of this text contains most of the common features of numerical analysis found in an advanced undergraduate course. The treatment of each topic, however, has been carefully structured to fit the mathematical level of the beginning student—that is, the student who has taken or will be taking a course in introductory calculus.

3. Illustrate the potential applications of computer solutions and numerical analysis in a variety of engineering and scientific disciplines. Even though each of the programming problems can be successfully solved without a detailed understanding of the engineering principles described in the problem, the incorporation of topical engineering problems in an introductory course provides the instructor with an opportunity to introduce neophyte engineers to ideas and concerns related to their choice of career. Invariably, students at this level appreciate this aspect of an introductory course.

Second Edition Changes

The occasion of a second edition provides authors with opportunities not possible in the original text. Not only can they revise the contents to conform to more modern usage, but they can avail themselves of the valuable comments of hundreds of individuals who have used the first edition.

I appreciate the thoughtful input of numerous colleagues and have tried to implement their suggestions. Primary among these was the wish that subprogram modules be introduced as early as possible. To accomplish this, the introduction of complicated I/O statements was postponed and DO loops were disconnected from subscripted variables (i.e., arrays). This rearrangement results in a sharp change in the order of topics in the FORTRAN section. Less dramatic changes are the rewriting of all the FORTRAN code in the text and the reworking and rewording of programming assignments to make their solution by the student more straight-forward but still challenging.

Other items to note are that the SI system of units is used exclusively, and that sections marked with an asterisk (*) and all of the programming problems are optional and may be omitted without a loss of continuity.

FORTRAN Code

Although the author and the publisher cannot provide a guarantee that the programs contained in this text are free of error, you may find that some of the coded procedures are of use to you and you are free to use and copy any of these routines at your own risk. Copies of all of the procedures in this book are available from the publisher in machine-readable form on floppy disks.

Supplements

Instructors using this text may obtain from the publisher an *Instructor's Manual* containing detailed solutions to all even-numbered problems, complete solutions to each of the programming problems, and over two hundred transparency masters pertaining to material in the text. In addition, two floppy disks will be provided: one contains the FORTRAN code for solutions to all of the programming problems as well as selected even-numbered problems, and the second contains the FORTRAN code for solutions to all sample programming problems as well as copies of the FORTRAN code for each of the mathematical procedures described in the text.

Acknowledgments

I would like to acknowledge the following reviewers for their help and encouragement during the preparation of the first edition of this book:

> Betty Barr, University of Houston
> Tom Boyle, Purdue University
> Bart Childs, Texas A & M University
> Allen R. Cook, University of Oklahoma
> John B. Crittenden, Virginia Polytechnic Institute
> Terry Feagin, University of Tennessee
> Robert Good, Widener University
> Richard C. Harshman, Clemson University
> Linda Hayes, University of Texas at Austin
> William Kubitz, University of Illinois
> Frederick Way, III, Case Western Reserve University
> Glen Williams, Texas A & M University
> Walter W. Wilson, University of Texas at Arlington
> Philip M. Wolfe, Oklahoma State University

In addition I would like to acknowledge the following reviewers of the second edition, whose comments helped shape this edition:

William H. Dodge, Rensselaer Polytechnic Institute
Josann Duane, The Ohio State University
John W. Hakola, Hofstra University
Don D. Hearn, The University of Illinois
Levon Minnetyan, Clarkson University
Howard Pyron, The University of Missouri—Rolla

Computer Operations

1.1 Introduction

The nineteenth century was the golden age of applied mathematics. Many of the great thinkers of that era were interested in solving problems in engineering and physical sciences. Men like Laplace, Gauss, Bessel, and others determined what problems could be solved, and they specified the form of the solutions in elegant mathematical analyses. These men shaped the course of the twentieth century far more than we realize. The methods of approaching almost any problem in engineering today are based on the mathematics developed more than a hundred years ago.

Although the methods of approaching engineering problems may be based on the applied mathematics of a century ago, the tools for implementing those methods have changed dramatically in the last forty years. The current renaissance in applied mathematics, which is certain to define the framework for the solutions to all future engineering problems, is fueled by the phenomenal speed and accuracy of the computer. Problems that formerly were impossible to solve by hand are now often trivial; problems that previously required ingenious approximations and "tricks" are now solved directly on large computers; and problems that most thought were not worth the effort are now solved anyway.[1]

The era of computers has advanced so quickly and the capabilities of the machines are presently progressing so rapidly that mathematical techniques specially suited to large computers are just now being developed. These procedures are generally concerned with special methods for solving extremely long computations, such as tracing the paths of atoms

---

[1] Not long ago, π was computed to an accuracy of millions of digits. Although there have been some applications of this tabulation in testing the accuracy of computer calculations, most would view this use of a computer as an exercise in pure mathematics.

through billions of collisions, or processing a monumental collection of data such as the names in the New York City telephone book. Such techniques, while important in specialized problems, are too advanced for an elementary text. The numerical procedures discussed in this text were originally developed for hand calculations and have been adapted for use on large computers.

The uses of computers can be divided into two classes:

1. Numerical computation
2. Information and data storage, retrieval, processing, and synthesis

Although the first category is the reason for the invention of modern computers, it is the second category that is experiencing the most rapid growth and already dominates all aspects of computer technology. The billing and record keeping of all large companies and many small ones are handled by computers. Most writers, including college students, use computers both to edit text so that it fits neatly into a chosen format and to check the spelling in large blocks of text. There are programs that match a patient's symptoms to a list of diseases and assist in medical diagnosis. The evaluation of huge amounts of data is now done universally by machines. In fact, the Bureau of the Census was among the first users of the early computers. Finally, we are all aware of the enormous popularity of video games and other uses of smaller personal computers.

Today the number and types of computer applications in all aspects of our lives are too vast to catalog. The growth in computer use is expanding at an ever-increasing rate. The variety of uses of computers is limited only by the number of people trained to program them who are simultaneously expert in some discipline of potential application.

This text is concerned almost exclusively with numerical computation. There is an important reason for this. The first two years of an engineering or science program in college are among the most crucial periods in your career. You will be taking physics, chemistry, and calculus along with this programming course. The individual goals of each of these courses are to acquaint you with the important and useful topics that will ultimately become the basis on which other engineering disciplines will build. Viewed collectively, however, these courses have an even more important function: to help you develop an analytic sophistication in the solution of varied problems. Each course is intended to reinforce the other; each course is critical to the other. Physics cannot be adequately understood without calculus, and calculus is more easily mastered with examples from the physical sciences. And, in addition, the best programming of a problem is done by someone who understands both the physical principles of the problem and the mathematics involved.

The first half of this text will help you become fluent in the programming language called FORTRAN. A large variety of programming languages in addition to FORTRAN exists. Each language has its hard core of enthusiastic supporters who claim it is superior in some aspect of its use or ease of learning. Many linguists contend that all human languages are of roughly the same difficulty when they are learned as the first language, and the same can be said of programming languages. As for the relative utility of programming languages, the analogy with spoken languages is again useful. It can be argued that French, for example, is more exact than English, or more poetic, or superior in some other sense. The validity of this type of argument is irrelevant; the essential point is that English is the international language of science and engineering, and every scientist or engineer, anywhere in the world, must have at least a reading knowledge of it. The same is true of FORTRAN. Regardless of its relative merit compared with other programming languages, it is the universally accepted scientific programming language, and the overwhelming majority of scientific and engineering computer programs, both in the United States and elsewhere, are written in FORTRAN.

Since FORTRAN was introduced in the mid-1950s, there have been many attempts to correct some of its failings and limitations, which were generally perceived to be in four major areas:

1. Inadequate ability to read, write, and manipulate textual-type data.
2. Awkward program flow control commands that result in needlessly complex programs.
3. Limited ability to handle a variety of database types. The only way to store large blocks of data in FORTRAN is by a subscripted array such as x_i. (Arrays are discussed in Chapter 7.) Newer languages are more versatile in this regard.
4. Lack of recursive-type procedures. Programs or subprograms in FORTRAN are not allowed to "call" themselves, even though many numerical problems are most succinctly expressed in terms of a recursive-type relation.

The latest version of FORTRAN, FORTRAN 77, addresses the first two shortcomings. The circumstances in which the latter two limitations become serious handicaps are ordinarily quite advanced, and by the time you encounter such problems you will probably be fluent in at least one or two other computer languages and will be able to choose the one that best suits the overall situation.

FORTRAN is relatively easy to learn, much easier than, say, German or Spanish. However, it is essential for efficient and accurate programming to understand that the FORTRAN language is more than simply a mode of communication between humans and computers; it is a set of instructions for a series of computer operations. If you were to prescribe for a friend a set of procedures to follow to solve a mathematics problem,[2]

---

[2] A recipe for the solution of a problem is more formally called an *algorithm*.

a certain amount of ambiguity in your instructions could be tolerated. Depending on the sophistication of the person carrying out the instructions, grammatical errors or trivial assumptions would be overlooked and your friend would interpret what you intended. Because a computer is unable to make judgments like these, all instructions to it must be absolutely precise and complete. A misplaced comma will likely cause the computer either to not recognize or to misinterpret the instruction. Thus, it is important to have a minimum understanding of what is going on inside the computer.

This chapter discusses the principles behind computer operations, the most important of which is the use of base-two arithmetic. The computer's memory, central processing unit, input/output devices, and speed capabilities are then covered. Ways of communicating with a computer are presented next. This is followed by a discussion of how to get started on the computer, which includes some generic information about the system on your local computer. In the final section you will be invited to try running a simple but important program that illustrates the peculiarities of computer arithmetic.

1.2   Operational Principles of Digital Computers

Binary Representation of Numbers and Information

In principle the internal operations of a computer are not very profound. It has long been known that since a switch has two states, open or closed, it can be used to represent the numbers 0 and 1. (It was not until the modern realization of efficient computing machines that this idea was found to be of real significance.) A large collection of switches may then be used to represent or store a corresponding number of 0's and 1's. Ordinary numbers (base ten) can be rewritten in terms of strictly 0's and 1's (i.e., base two) and then represented by combinations of open and closed switches. For example, the number 302 is base ten, which means

$$302 = 3(10^2) + 0(10^1) + 2(10^0)$$

or

$$302 \div 10 = 30 + \text{Remainder of 2}$$
$$30 \div 10 = 3 + \text{Remainder of 0}$$
$$3 \div 10 = 0 + \text{Remainder of 3}$$

Notice that the original number is the sequence of remainders in reverse order.

This suggests that 302 can also be written in base two in the following manner:

$$302 \div 2 = 151 + \text{Remainder of 0}$$
$$151 \div 2 = 75 + \text{Remainder of 1}$$
$$75 \div 2 = 37 + \text{Remainder of 1}$$

$$37 \div 2 = 18 + \text{Remainder of 1}$$
$$18 \div 2 = 9 + \text{Remainder of 0}$$
$$9 \div 2 = 4 + \text{Remainder of 1}$$
$$4 \div 2 = 2 + \text{Remainder of 0}$$
$$2 \div 2 = 1 + \text{Remainder of 0}$$
$$1 \div 2 = 0 + \text{Remainder of 1} \qquad \text{Thus } (302)_{10} = (100101110)_2.$$

You can easily verify this by writing $(100101110)_2$ in terms of ordinary decimal numbers:

$$(100101110)_2 = 1(2^8) + 0(2^7) + 0(2^6) + 1(2^5) + 0(2^4) + 1(2^3) + 1(2^2)$$
$$+ 1(2^1) + 0(2^0)$$
$$= 256 + 32 + 8 + 4 + 2$$
$$= 302$$

Thus, nine switches would be required to represent the decimal number 302 in binary form.

Other forms of data can also be converted to binary code (i.e., written in terms of 1's and 0's), stored, and processed in a computer. For example, each letter of the alphabet can be assigned a coded sequence of 1's and 0's, and ultimately words and sentences can be constructed and manipulated. The information content of a photograph can be (approximately) replaced by a dot matrix, with the location, color, and density of each dot allocated a binary code. The resolution of the photograph may then be computer-enhanced or the entire contents of the picture transmitted to another site by telephone lines or satellite relay. (For visual data, you know these machines as fax machines; for audio data, an analogous transcription is stored on a compact disk.)

For a computer to be able to perform the elementary operations of arithmetic, instructions must be devised for combining two sets of on/off switches representing numbers into a single set representing the sum, difference, product, or quotient of those numbers. Even though it is extremely unlikely that you will need to use binary arithmetic when programming a problem, some familiarity with it will help you better understand the inner workings of computers. This knowledge should reduce the mystery of computers and thereby increase your confidence as master over these machines. To this end you may wish to attempt several of the problems concerned with binary arithmetic at the end of this chapter.

Main Memory

Originally, the actual elements that played the role of switches in a computer were electrical-mechanical relays. They were physically large, consumed significant electrical power, and were very noisy. Over the past several decades, advances in microelectronics have resulted in the replacement of actual switches by small transistor circuits called *flip-flops*. Each flip-flop circuit can be in only one of two states: on (representing 1) or off (0). The state of each circuit can be either sensed (information read from) or altered (information stored into). In the last two decades, methods have been developed that permit the placement of tens of thousands of discrete circuits on a single wafer or chip. The result is called a *very large scale integrated circuit* (VLSIC), although the size is actually about 1 centimeter square. These technological advances have made possible computers that are much faster, more reliable, and considerably cheaper than those of an earlier generation.

The main memory of a large mainframe computer consists of hundreds of millions of such storage elements for 1's and 0's (called *bits*). The main memory capacity of a modern personal computer is about a million or more bits. The bits are arranged in groups of eight (called *bytes*), in which the binary code for a letter, digit, special symbol such as a comma, or a control symbol such as a carriage return may be stored. The memory capacity of a computer is usually expressed in *kilobytes*. One kilobyte is equal to 1,024 bytes. The unit of information that is transferred to and from the main memory is called a *word*. A computer word may consist of from 8 to 32 bits for microcomputers (PCs) or from 32 to 64 bits or more for large computers.

Details about the nature of a computer's main memory are usually of little consequence to a programmer except for the following two features, which will be referred to repeatedly throughout this text:

1. Two items are associated with each element or memory cell in main memory: (1) the contents of the memory cell, which are units of data or some type of instruction written in a binary-coded form; and (2) the address of the memory cell; the cells can be thought of as boxes in a row, with each box labeled by its position in the row.

2. The size of each memory cell, that is, a computer word, is finite. This means that for each number used in a computation, only a finite number of digits can be stored. Thus, numbers represented by nonterminating binary expressions must be truncated before they can be stored in main memory. [The truncation is of the nonterminating fractional part of the number expressed in base two, not in base ten. For example, $(0.1)_{10}$ is a nonterminating fraction in base two. (See Problem 1.1f.)] The length of a computer word will then limit the accuracy of the numerical computations and is an important characteristic of each computer.

The access time (the time required to read the information stored in a particular address) is critical in the operation of a computer. A large computer can ordinarily add two numbers in less time than it takes to find them in main memory. The access time for a large semiconductor main memory consisting of 500,000 computer words is typically 5×10^{-7} seconds.[3] Memory of this type is called *random access memory* (RAM), meaning that the access time for all addresses is roughly the same. The information on a RAM unit is not stored sequentially, but for the time being it is simpler to think of all the information as being stored in order. The main memory of a PC typically has storage capacity for about 100,000 or more computer words.

In addition to main memory, several other possibilities for storing large amounts of data are available. These are called *secondary memory* and usually consist of a magnetic tape or a magnetic disk. A PC may come with a built-in hard-disk memory unit that can hold a few million or more bytes of data. The soft or "floppy" disk can accommodate 350,000 or more bytes of data. The data in secondary memory are not directly accessible but must first be transferred to main memory for processing. Secondary-memory storage is considerably less expensive than main memory, but the price is paid in significantly longer access times on the order of milliseconds or more.

Central Processing Unit

The part of the computer that performs the operations on the data using the instructions stored in main memory is called the *central processing unit* (CPU). The CPU is responsible for two distinctly different functions:

1. Monitoring and controlling the entire system, which consists of all the devices used to get information in and out of the computer, and controlling the associated traffic of information flow between the various elements of the computer
2. Processing the binary-coded instructions transmitted to it from main memory

The CPU may be thought of as two submodules performing these operations. The control unit executes the necessary control functions, whereas the data and instruction processing unit is responsible for executing the elementary commands of a program. The functions consist primarily of performing the operations of arithmetic as well as comparing two data items. This data and instruction processing unit is called the *arithmetic-logic unit* (ALU). (See Figure 1-1.)

The control unit is responsible for fetching the next instruction and the address of the required data items from memory and temporarily

---

[3] Even this incredibly short time can be reduced by temporarily storing the recently used data and instructions in a smaller, even faster memory device called *cache memory*. The idea is that the recently used items are likely to be used again shortly, and if so, they can be more quickly accessed if grouped together.

Figure 1-1
Block diagram of
the functions of a
computer

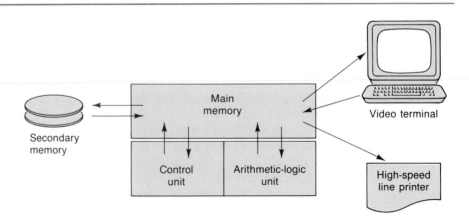

storing them in local fast memory registers. The instructions are retrieved
from memory in the order that they are stored in the program, and the required data items are then likewise fetched from memory. The two data
items are then transmitted to the ALU along with an instruction to add,
subtract, compare, or whatever is desired. The control unit is then responsible for moving the result back to main memory.

Recall that all the items processed by the CPU, including data and
instructions, are written in binary code—the only form of communication
a computer understands. Programs written in this manner are called *machine-language* or *microcode programs.* It is unlikely that you will ever
have to concern yourself with microcode programs. However, computer
programs that will be executed millions of times or that will be running
continually, such as a program to monitor the operations of a machine,
can be made somewhat more efficient if written in microcode. This task is
primarily the concern of the computer engineer. This text is exclusively interested in using the computer to solve numerical problems—classical
number-crunching—which is a distinctly different task from that faced
by the computer engineer or systems programmer and as such requires a
different approach to the use of the computer. This text's primary task is
to develop your skills in writing easily readable computer code that follows as closely as possible the ordinary algebraic solutions to a problem.
These are the formulations with which scientists and engineers are most
comfortable, and this is the reason that your instructors have chosen
FORTRAN and not microcode as your introduction to computers.

Input/Output Devices

Two common and rather embarrassing errors in computer programming
are to instruct the computer to execute some operation on data items that
were never stored in memory and to complete a computation and forget to

print the result. The mechanism for reading data and the instructions for processing that data and displaying the results in a useful form are obviously important concerns. The most common input devices include video terminals and magnetic-disk or tape-reading devices. The results generated by the computer can then be displayed on the same video terminal, printed on a high-speed line printer, or written on magnetic tape or disk. This book is concerned primarily with input via the terminal and output either at the terminal or on a line printer. In Chapter 4 the use of magnetic disks is described in more detail.

All the machinery comprising the CPU, the main and secondary memory units, and the various input/output devices is called *computer hardware*. The set of coded instructions or programs available on the computer is called *software.*

Computing Speed of a Large Computer

Basically, what a computer does is rather trivial. It simply manipulates 1's and 0's, nothing more. Its claim to fame rests on the fact that it can do the elementary operations on hundreds of thousands of stored numbers at an absolutely incredible speed. The time it usually takes a computer to add two 60-bit numbers (about 14 decimal digits) is about 1-millionth of a second. To appreciate the enormous consequences of this fact, consider that it would take you about 10 seconds to add two 12-digit numbers, and there is a fair possibility that you would make a mistake. The computer adds the two numbers seven orders of magnitude faster, with the likelihood of an error being extremely small. Not only that, but if you were paid $10 per hour to do this operation (perhaps because you are very accurate in addition and can do hundreds of thousands of these additions without becoming bored—in short because you have many of the attributes of a computer), the cost would be about 3 cents per addition. A large mainframe computer typically works at $500 per hour, or 1.3×10^{-7} cents per addition. Thus, the machine not only is faster by a factor of 10^7 but cheaper by roughly the same factor.

These two factors, speed and cost, are the main reasons for all the excitement about computers. The tremendous advances in computing have taken place in a period of about 30 years. Consider for a moment an analogy with the advances in transportation over the years. For untold centuries, humans were limited by the fact that getting around meant walking, which meant a speed of about 5 miles per hour. The domestication of the horse revolutionized civilization but was only a change from 5 to about 20 miles per hour—not even a factor of 10. Modern automobiles, which have a top legal speed of 55 miles per hour, represent a tremendous advancement (one factor of 10), and airplanes that travel at about 500 miles per hour are a further advancement (two factors of 10). Most of these changes took place in the course of one century. Imagine what the consequences would be if the achievements in transportation could match those in computing (an increase in speed by 10^7, a decrease in cost by 10^{-7}, in 30 years). You could travel from New York to Los Angeles in less than 1 second, and the total cost of your trip would be less than 1 cent. Clearly, such dramatic changes in the field of computational mathematics will profoundly affect society.

1.3   Communicating with the Computer

In the early days of computing, programming a computer to do calculations was extremely tedious. The difficulty was that the programmer was forced to communicate with the machine on its terms. If a program required the product of two numbers represented by the symbols A and B, the programmer would have to code binary instructions to accomplish the following operations:

> Recall number A from address X
>   Transfer to arithmetic unit
> Recall number B from address Y
>   Transfer to arithmetic unit
> Multiply the two numbers
>   Transfer the result to address Z
>   .
>   .
>   .

All of this work had to be done just to multiply two numbers. Also, the machine-language code written in this fashion would work only on the machine for which it was originally intended and on no others. The use of computers, therefore, was limited to only those brave souls who had mastered this monotonous skill. The first significant step in broadening the pool of potential computer users occurred in 1955 at IBM when the first version of FORTRAN was developed. The idea was to write a program in machine language that would take a set of instructions written in a form resembling ordinary algebra and translate these instructions into all the transfer-here-store-there instructions required by the computer. Thus, a statement like

$$X = 7.0*A + 3.0*B$$

which, of course,[4] represents

$$x = 7a + 3b$$

---

[4] The instructions to the computer to carry out the operations of multiplication and division are effected by the symbols * (asterisk, as in 7.0*A) and / (slash, as in B/2). Two side-by-side asterisks, **, are used to designate the operation of exponentiation as in X**2, which represents x^2. A complete description of how a sequence of arithmetic instructions is written in FORTRAN is discussed in Chapter 2.

would be read off a punched card. A program permanently residing in the computer would then translate this into terms understandable to the machine, that is, the binary instructions for the operations:

Fetch the number in the location allotted to symbol A
  Transfer it to the arithmetic unit
  Multiply by 7.0
  Temporarily store the result
Fetch the number in the location allotted to symbol B
  Transfer it to the arithmetic unit
  Multiply by 3.0
Add the result to the previously stored multiplication
Store the result in a location allotted to symbol X

The program that translates the FORTRAN equation into machine language is called the *compiler*. The set of instructions written in FORTRAN is called the *source code*, and the machine-language translation is called the *object code*. Because machine code is written to conform to the specific features of an individual computer, an object-code program will run only on the machine for which it was intended. The expression that is to be translated is, on the other hand, universal—that is,

$$X = C - D$$

would look the same in any program run on any machine. FORTRAN compilers were the first to appear and are still among the most commonly used. Programs written in FORTRAN closely resemble ordinary algebra plus some simple English key words. (FORTRAN stands for FORmula TRANslator.) It is one of many so-called higher computer languages (i.e., above machine language) and has undergone several revisions. The form used in this book is FORTRAN 77.

Since the introduction of FORTRAN, numerous other programming languages have been developed. Each of those listed here can very likely be compiled on every large computer in the world.

Common Higher-Level Computer Languages

ALGOL ⎤
Pascal |
PL/I   ⎬   General-purpose languages
C |
APL   ⎦

COBOL   Designed for application in business

BASIC   A simplified language, similar to FORTRAN, commonly used on microcomputers

The universal nature of these programming languages has resulted in very rapid growth in computer usage and also in collaboration among individuals working on different machines.

▬▬▬▬▬ 1.4   **Computer Operating Systems: Getting Started on the Computer**

There are two modes of communication with a computer: batch processing and interactive computing. *Batch processing* generally refers to the execution of computer programs that have been previously stored in a file on magnetic tape or disk. The instructions encoded in the files will be carried out in sequence by the computer, and ordinarily, once the computing job begins, the programmer cannot correct or alter the program until the job has passed through the machine. The programmer then checks the printed output for errors, corrects them, and resubmits the program. Batch processing is basically a "hands-off" computing mode.

Conversely, *interactive computing* is "hands-on" computing. The program is composed, edited, executed, and corrected at a video terminal connected to the computer. The computer may be in the same room, as with a PC, or it may be across campus and linked to the terminal via telephone lines with a modem.

Both forms of computing have certain advantages. Batch processing allows you to see the entire printed listing of the program and to make changes at your leisure. Interactive computing at a terminal allows you to see only 20 lines or so at a time, and program surgery frequently tends to be somewhat hectic. In addition, the execution cost of a program run in a batch mode is considerably lower than the cost of the same job run interactively. In spite of these disadvantages, the last few years have seen a tremendous growth in interactive computing and a consequent reduction in demands for batch processing. Card punches and readers have all but disappeared from college campuses, a result of the increased ease of computing via conveniently located terminals. It is assumed throughout this text that you will be communicating with the computer by means of a cathode-ray tube (CRT) terminal. The response of the computer will usually be on the terminal screen, although computed results may also be sent to a high-speed printer.

▬ Interactive Processing

Interactive processing, also called *time-sharing* on large multiuser computers, allows you to monitor your program as it compiles and executes and to correct errors or alter the program immediately. The program is typed in at a terminal, the appropriate system commands are entered to execute the program, and the output is displayed on the terminal screen. The terminal either may be wired directly to the computer or it may use an audio link by means of telephone lines. You may also have the computer produce a printed copy of the program and its results. There is a wide variety of interactive computing environments, and the operational procedures for running FORTRAN programs vary considerably from one computer to the next; thus, only general instructions can be given here. For detailed instructions, you should obtain a *FORTRAN User's Guide* or its equivalent from your computing center if you are working on a large mainframe computer connected to many terminals or the owner's manual if you are working on a PC.

Three levels of procedures must be learned to execute a FORTRAN program at the terminal:

1. The system protocol, or system control language (SCL), defined by your computing center. This protocol will include a set of instructions for performing five operations:

   Accessing the computer through your terminal

   Translating (compiling) the FORTRAN code into machine-language object code

   Executing the program

   Saving the program

   Printing the results on a printer

   None of these instructions are in FORTRAN, and the precise forms of the SCL commands differ considerably from site to site. You will need to determine how to accomplish each of the five operations before even the simplest FORTRAN program can be attempted. The general structure of some elementary SCL commands will be discussed shortly.

2. Program composition and editing. Each FORTRAN program that you will be executing must first be written and typed into a file. To create the file containing the program, you will be using an editor program. Many (but not all[5]) of the editor programs that you have been using to write term papers can also be used to write files containing FORTRAN programs. The basic elements of using an editor program to write, correct, and save a file need to be mastered before you can learn the details of FORTRAN programming.

3. The FORTRAN program itself.

---

[5] If you are using a multipurpose editor program to write FORTRAN programs, you should make sure that the editor produces ASCII files. Basically, ASCII files do not contain strange-looking characters representing carriage returns, margin settings, and the like. Of course, many of the features used in a term paper, such as underlining, boldface type, and so on, cannot be used in a FORTRAN program. You are limited to upper- and lowercase plus the normal characters that appear on a typewriter keyboard.

▮ Format of FORTRAN Lines

When entering FORTRAN code, you need to follow some general rules regarding the positioning of various types of information on each line. The characteristics of a FORTRAN line are shown in Figure 1-2.

- The entire line is 80 columns wide.
- The FORTRAN statement must appear in columns 7 to 72. The compiler ignores blank columns, so the FORTRAN statements may appear anywhere in this field.
- Columns 1 to 5 are available for supplying an identifying statement number to a particular line of FORTRAN.

Thus, a FORTRAN statement like

    731   STOP

which will result in termination of the program's execution, can be referenced by means of its statement number, 731. Again, blanks are ignored and the 731 could appear anywhere in the statement number field (columns 1 to 5). Modern programming style attempts to avoid, as much as possible, using statement numbers.

Column 6 is called the *continuation field*. If a FORTRAN statement is too long to fit on a single line, it may be continued on the next line by including any symbol other than 0 in column 6. Either a plus sign (+) or a dollar sign ($) is commonly used to indicate that a line is a continuation of a previous line. The maximum length of a single FORTRAN expression is 20 lines (1 plus 19 continued lines). A statement number is not permitted on a line that is a continuation of a previous line.

Figure 1-2
Placement of information on a FORTRAN line

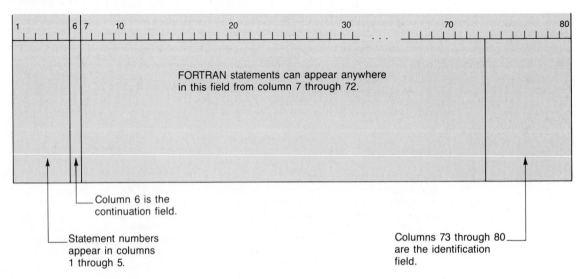

FORTRAN statements can appear anywhere in this field from column 7 through 72.

Column 6 is the continuation field.

Statement numbers appear in columns 1 through 5.

Columns 73 through 80 are the identification field.

From the discussion thus far, we would conclude that all of the following FORTRAN statements would be translated identically:

1	2	3	4	5	6	7	8	9	10	11	12	13	14	15	16	17	18	19	20	21	22	23	24	25	26	27	28	29	30	31	32	33	34	35	36	37	38	39	40	41	42	43	44	45	46	47	48	49

```
731     STOP
7 31          ST     OP
  731   S
        + T
        + 0
        + P
```

Columns 73 to 80 on the FORTRAN line are called the *identification field*. Anything that is entered in this part of the line is ignored by the compiler but does appear on the listing of the program supplied by the compiler. Usually the identification field either is left blank or is used to add sequencing numbers to the FORTRAN lines.

If a C (capital) or an asterisk (*) appears in column 1, the entire contents of the line are ignored by the compiler, but, as with the identification field, the information contained on the line is included with the listing. These lines are called *comment lines,* and they constitute a very important part of a program's documentation. Comment lines are used to explain to someone reading the program what each element of the program is attempting to do. Even if you are the only one who will ever read a particular program, it is still a good idea to sprinkle comment lines amply throughout your program. Few tasks are more frustrating than trying to understand the operation of an undocumented code that you wrote six months ago. Most installations of FORTRAN permit the use of either lower- or uppercase letters within a program. If this is the situation on your computer, enter the comment lines in normal lowercase English and use uppercase only for the FORTRAN. An example of possible use of comment lines is shown in Figure 1-3.

Getting Started

The steps necessary to initiate a program at a terminal or a PC can be summarized as follows:

1. "Wake up" the computer. On a PC this is called *booting up* the computer, or loading the system programs. On a terminal connected to a mainframe computer, you will have to *log on* to the machine by supplying your name, a password, and possibly some additional information.
2. Enter the system commands to call up the editor program that will be used to write the FORTRAN program. The FORTRAN code to follow will be stored on what is called a *file,* which has to be given a name.

Figure 1-3

Example of the use
of comment lines

```
        PROGRAM ZERO
*
* This is a demonstration program that illustrates the various arithmetic
* operations in FORTRAN and some of the odd features of INTEGER and REAL
* arithmetic on the computer.  It is also an exercise in learning the pro-
* cedures necessary to enter and execute a FORTRAN program at the terminal.
*
*  Programmed and          In partial fulfillment
*  submitted by            of the requirements of
*
*  |=================|  |========================|  |=======================|
*  | Joe Student     |  | Comp.Sci     --    201 |  |Source code - FORTRAN  |
*  | Room 6-C        |  | Section      --     11 |  |Compiler    -- WATFOR  |
*  | North Quad.     |  | Instr. - Prof. Babbage |  |Computer    -- VAX 8530|
*  | City College    |  | Due Date     --   10-3 |  |=======================|
*  |=================|  |========================|
*
* The input parameters A,B are assigned values by entering the numbers,
* separated by a comma, upon execution of the READ statement in the program.
*
        READ *, A, B
```

3. Type in the FORTRAN program correctly positioned on the screen according to the rules given in the preceding section. When finished, save the file containing the FORTRAN program and exit the editor program.

4. Enter the system commands that instruct the computer to compile and execute the file containing the FORTRAN program. If during execution the program is to read data, the program will stop and wait for you to enter the data at the terminal. If either compilation or execution-time errors occurred, you can correct them and try again.

5. If all was successful, instruct the computer to produce a printed copy of both the program and its output.

This list may appear to be a formidable collection of procedures, but with practice these tasks can be quickly mastered. During your first few sessions on the computer, make a short list of the instructions required to create, execute, and print a program. Use this list until these instructions become automatic to you. In addition, determine what some of the "panic" buttons are for your computer—that is, find out how to stop a program if it seems stuck in an endless loop and how to save a program for another try on another day. On many computers, simply entering the word "HELP" will call up a short tutorial session that may clarify a confusing point. Also, do not be afraid of inadvertently entering some instructions that will cause the machine to grind to a halt. For the novice, this is next to impossible to do.

Even though you have not begun studying the FORTRAN language, you are probably eager to try writing and executing a simple program. Once you have determined the required log-on procedures, try to execute the following simple programs. You should have no difficulty reading and understanding the FORTRAN code.

1. Simple arithmetic

| 1 | 2 | 3 | 4 | 5 | 6 | 7 | 8 | 9 | 10 | 11 | 12 | 13 | 14 | 15 | 16 | 17 | 18 | 19 | 20 | 21 | 22 | 23 | 24 | 25 | 26 | 27 | 28 | 29 | 30 | 31 | 32 | 33 | 34 | 35 | 36 | 37 | 38 | 39 | 40 | 41 | 42 | 43 | 44 | 45 | 46 | 47 | 48 | 49 | 50 | 51 | 52 | 53 |

```
A = 2.5
B = 3.5
C = A + B
PRINT *,A,B,C
STOP
END
```

The PRINT statement instructs the computer to display the numbers A, B, and C, which will then appear on the terminal screen.[6]

2. Printing text

| 1 | 2 | 3 | 4 | 5 | 6 | 7 | 8 | 9 | 10 | 11 | 12 | 13 | 14 | 15 | 16 | 17 | 18 | 19 | 20 | 21 | 22 | 23 | 24 | 25 | 26 | 27 | 28 | 29 | 30 | 31 | 32 | 33 | 34 | 35 | 36 | 37 | 38 | 39 | 40 | 41 | 42 | 43 | 44 | 45 | 46 | 47 | 48 | 49 | 50 | 51 | 52 | 53 |

```
A = 100.0
B = A*A
PRINT *,A,' squared equals ',B
STOP
END
```

The three items to be printed are separated by commas, and in this case include the two-word phrase, "squared equals," which must be enclosed in apostrophes. The symbols between the apostrophes are printed as is, including blanks.

---

[6] The mechanisms in FORTRAN for having a program display results obtained at any particular point in that program are easy. The word PRINT followed by an asterisk and a comma

```
PRINT *,
```

simply precedes the list of variables or constants to be printed or displayed on the terminal screen. These are in turn separated by commas. Upon execution of this line of the program, the values associated with the quantities in the list will be displayed. This manner of printing results is discussed in more detail in Section 2.9. Some programmers prefer the equivalent statement "WRITE(*,*) ⟨list of variables⟩." The WRITE statement is discussed in detail in Chapter 2.

3. An infinite loop

| 1 | 2 | 3 | 4 | 5 | 6 | 7 | 8 | 9 | 10 | 11 | 12 | 13 | 14 | 15 | 16 | 17 | 18 | 19 | 20 | 21 | 22 | 23 | 24 | 25 | 26 | 27 | 28 | 29 | 30 | 31 | 32 | 33 | 34 | 35 | 36 | 37 | 38 | 39 | 40 | 41 | 42 | 43 | 44 | 45 | 46 | 47 | 48 | 49 | 50 | 51 | 52 | 53 |

```
*   This program contains an infinite loop.
*
      X = 100.
  12  PRINT *, ' x = ',X
      X = X*X
      GO TO 12
      END
```

This program will first print the current value of X, that is, 100., and then replace the current value of X with the value of X squared. The GO TO 12 statement is a FORTRAN transfer statement that causes the program to branch directly to the FORTRAN line that bears the statement label 12. GO TO statements are discussed in more detail in Section 3.4. For now its meaning is rather transparent and you should have no trouble understanding the effects of GO TO statements. In this instance, the effect is to branch back to the PRINT statement and continue with the calculation from that point. There is no way out of this loop, and the values of X will grow without limit. Of course, there is a limit to the size of the numbers that can be stored in the computer, and the program will terminate when this number is exceeded. An error message will also be generated on the terminal screen.

4. Reading data

| 1 | 2 | 3 | 4 | 5 | 6 | 7 | 8 | 9 | 10 | 11 | 12 | 13 | 14 | 15 | 16 | 17 | 18 | 19 | 20 | 21 | 22 | 23 | 24 | 25 | 26 | 27 | 28 | 29 | 30 | 31 | 32 | 33 | 34 | 35 | 36 | 37 | 38 | 39 | 40 | 41 | 42 | 43 | 44 | 45 | 46 | 47 | 48 | 49 | 50 | 51 | 52 | 53 | 54 | 55 |

```
      PRINT *,'Input x and y, separated by a comma,
      READ   *,X,Y
      Z = X*Y
      W = X/Y
      PRINT *,X,'  times     ',Y,' equals ',Z
      PRINT *,X,' divided by ',Y,' equals ',W
      STOP
      END
```

This program will execute the first PRINT statement, and then the program will pause at the READ statement and wait for you to enter the values of X and Y at the terminal. The program will then resume after you enter the values (and after you strike the "ENTER" key).

■ A Typical Terminal Session

Figure 1-4 illustrates the dialogue required with the computer to execute program ZERO of Section 1.5. This program was run both on an IBM PC and on a VAX mainframe computer. Except for the FORTRAN itself, all of the SCL and edit commands will differ from those on your computer. The general structure of the commands will be similar, however. Once you

Figure 1-4 _____

Sample dialogues
with the computer

Example of program execution on a VAX computer

Log on to the VAX mainframe computer. You will need to enter a user
name and a password.

Call up an editor to write the FORTRAN program. Save the program
on a file called ZERO.FOR for example.

Compile the program by issuing an SCL command to execute the
FORTRAN compiler. On a VAX this command would be

    FORTRAN ZERO.FOR

The compiled program must then be linked with various subprograms
it will be using. On a VAX this linking is accomplished by the
SCL command

    LINK ZERO

Finally, the program is executed by issuing the SCL command

    RUN ZERO

The program then executes and produces the following output:

A listing of the Program

```
0001        PROGRAM ZERO
....           ...
....           ...
0054        END
```

Output from the compiler program. This information usually supplied by the compiler includes:

1. The size requirements of the program.
2. A list of all variable names used in the program along with
   their addresses.
3. A list of the locations of all statement numbers in the
   program.
4. A list of all the library subprograms referenced by the
   program.
5. A list of the locations of all statement numbers in the
   program.
6. The time required for compilation and the time required for
   execution of the program.
7. A summary of all fatal and non-fatal compilation errors and
   their locations.

Figure 1-4
(continued)

The results of the execution of the program

```
c1 = a(1/a - 1)    c2 = a(1/a - b/ab)
Input values for A, B separated by a comma
Input values      a =    4.000000
                  b =    9.000000
Arithmetic checks:
                  c1 =   0.0000000E+00
                  c2 =   0.0000000E+00
 Try again
Input values for A, B separated by a comma
Input values      a =    3.000000
                  b =    55.00000
Arithmetic checks:
                  c1 =   0.0000000E+00
                  c2 =   8.9406967E-08
Computed Values:  g =    3.0517578E-05
                  q =    0.0000000E+00
```

The program then attempts to divide by zero and generates the
following execution-time diagnostics:

```
%SYSTEM-F-FLDIV_F, arithmetic fault,
floating divide by zeroat PC-0000939, PSL = 03C00020

%Traceback, symbolic stack dump follows
module name routine name    line    rel PC     abs PC
ZERO          ZERO           29      0000339   0000939
```

Example of program execution on an IBM PC

Insert a bootable disk, that is, one containing the system in
drive A, and issue the commands to wake-up the computer.

Next replace the system disk with a disk containing the editor
program. Call up the editor program to create a file containing
the FORTRAN program. On an IBM PC this would resemble

```
->EDIT B:ZERO.FOR
```

which means that the FORTRAN program will be written and saved
on a separate disk in drive B. (-> is the system prompt.)

After typing in the program and saving it on the file named
ZERO.FOR, replace the disk containing the editor program with a
disk containing the FORTRAN compiler.

Enter the command to execute the FORTRAN compiler. This command
will likely produce a compiled image of the program in a new file
called ZERO.OBJ. The command will resemble

```
->FORTRAN B:ZERO.FOR
```

Next, enter the command to link the program to the various subprograms that it will be using. This command will likely resemble

```
->LINK B:ZERO.OBJ
```

and will finally produce an executable program named ZERO.EXE.
This program can then be executed as

```
->B:ZERO
```

Figure 1-4 _____
(concluded)

The program then executes and produces the following output:

A listing of the Program

```
0001        PROGRAM ZERO
....            ...
....            ...
0054        END
```

Output from the compiler program. This information usually supplied by the compiler includes:

1. A list of all variable names used in the program along with their addresses.
2. A list of all the library subprograms referenced by the program.
3. A list of the locations of all statement numbers in the program.
4. The size requirements for the program
5. The time required to compile the program.
6. A summary of all fatal and non-fatal compilation errors and their locations.

COMPILATION COMPLETE

    The results of the execution of the program

```
c1 = a(1/a - 1)    c2 = a(1/a - b/ab)
Input values for A, B separated by a comma
Input values      a =   4.00000000
                  b =   9.00000000
Arithmetic checks:
                  c1 =   0.000000000E+00
                  c2 =   0.000000000E+00
 Try again
Input values for A, B separated by a comma
Input values      a =   3.00000000
                  b =   55.0000000
Arithmetic checks:
                  c1 =   0.00000000E-01
                  c2 =   2.98023224E-08
Computed Values:  g =   2.77555756E-17
                  q =   5.95022627E-08
      Finally,  a/q =   5.04182501E+07
```

have mastered the procedures for getting started on your computer, try to execute the simple examples in the preceding section. Again, be sure you know how to write, edit, save, and print a file.

1.5 Program ZERO

As a more demanding test of your abilities to execute a program, try to run the program listed in Figure 1-5. Enter the FORTRAN code exactly as it appears, execute the program, and obtain a printed listing of the program

Figure 1-5 —————————————————————————————————
Program to
demonstrate
arithmetic
operations

```
            PROGRAM ZERO
            REAL A, B, C, C1, C2, D, E, F, G, H, P, Q
            INTEGER IB
     *
            PRINT *,'c1 = a(1/a - 1)     c2 = a(1/a - b/ab)'
     *
     1      PRINT *,'Input values for A, B separated by a comma'
            READ  *,A,B
            PRINT *,'Input values      a = ',A
            PRINT *,'                  b = ',B
     *
            C1 = A*(1./A) - 1.
            C2 = A*((1./A) - B*(1./(A*B)))
     *
     * The values computed for c1 and c2 should be identically zero for
     * all values of a and b.  If we find non-zero values it is a test
     * of the accuracy of this machine.
     *
            PRINT *,'Arithmetic checks: '
            PRINT *,'                   c1 = ',C1
            PRINT *,'                   c2 = ',C2
     *
     * If the computed values for c1 and c2 are zero, we will continue
     * to search for values of a and b that yield non-zero c1, c2
     *
            IF(C1.EQ.0 .AND. C2.EQ.0)THEN
               PRINT *,' Try again'
               GO TO 1
            ENDIF
     *
     * Once a problem of real arithmetic has been isolated (non-zero
     * c1,c2), we then attempt a variety of additional operations.
     *
     *
     *  Arithmetic Operators
     *
            C = A+B
            D = A-B
            E = A/B
            F = A*B
            G  = C*D/(E*F) + (B/A)**2 - 1.
     *
            PRINT *,'Computed Values:  g = ',G
     *
            IB = B
            C  = A**B
     *
     *  <NOTE: The next line involves mixed-mode arithmetic>
     *
            P  = LOG(ABS(C))/IB
            Q  = EXP(P) - A
            PRINT *,'                   q = ',Q
            PRINT *,'   Finally,     a/q = ',A/Q
            STOP
            END
```

and its output. Because this program is more complicated than those described earlier, you may not be able to completely understand the FORTRAN. The code will be discussed line by line in Section 2.7.

If you spot typing errors after the computer lists the FORTRAN code, correct them before you attempt to execute the program. If undetected typing errors remain, the computer will likely indicate them as errors in FORTRAN grammar and will give some indication of the location and nature of the error. You should then have no trouble correcting them.

The purpose of the program is to illustrate some of the quirks associated with ordinary arithmetic when it is executed on a computer. Once all the typing errors have been eliminated and the program is finally running, it will repeatedly ask you to enter pairs of numbers until it finds a problem with the simple arithmetic involving a particular pair. It may take a bit of searching before a problem is found. If you cannot seem to get the program out of a loop, try entering one of the pairs $[(3, 55), (7, 13), (5, 3)]$. They seem to cause problems on a variety of computers.

■ Error Diagnostics

Once the entire program in Figure 1-5 has been typed and the code for compilation and execution has been submitted, the computer will first attempt to translate the FORTRAN into machine language. If there are typing errors, the compiler will endeavor to diagnose the nature of the error. For example, if the line C = A + B were typed C = A # B, the output would indicate something like:

```
FATAL ERROR -- line 14 --- ILLEGAL USE OF OPERATOR --- A #
```

This output indicates that the compiler was unsuccessful in translating the statement. The symbol # is not an allowed symbol in FORTRAN.[7] This error produces a line of code that does not satisfy the rigid rules of FORTRAN grammar and results in a compilation-time error. No object code is generated, and there can be no attempt at execution.

But beware. Frequently, typing errors will result in a FORTRAN line that is grammatically correct but that has a meaning significantly different from the one intended. For example, leaving out the addition

---

[7]The only symbols allowed in FORTRAN are the letters of the alphabet, the integers, and the following special characters:

+	plus	·	period	(	left parenthesis	$ dollar
−	minus	,	comma	)	right parenthesis	' apostrophe
/	slash	*	asterisk	=	equals	: colon

Lowercase letters may be used in FORTRAN statements on some compilers, but this is not standard and will usually result in a "WARNING" diagnostic being displayed. Of course, lowercase as well as any other characters on the keyboard may be used freely in COMMENT lines.

operator in the line C = A + B results in C = A   B, which is the same as C = AB. Since no value has been assigned to a variable named AB, the value assigned to C will be meaningless and will likely cause the program to "die" during execution. (See Problem 1.9.)

Frequently, when a compilation error is encountered, the messages supplied by the compiler are extremely cryptic and may not be readily understandable to the novice. In such cases you can consult the reference manual that describes the features of the FORTRAN compiler in use on your computer or seek help from your instructor. (Reference manuals are usually available in the computing center.) Ordinarily, merely knowing which line the error is located in is sufficient information to find a simple typing error.

Elimination of errors in programs is called *debugging,* and the correction of compilation-time errors is the first and easiest stage of debugging a program. After all the FORTRAN has been corrected so that it satisfies the grammar rules, the compilation of the FORTRAN can be completed and the program may then begin execution. However, the program may still die during execution—for example, if division by zero is attempted. An error such as this is called an *execution-time error.*

The second stage of program debugging consists of eliminating all execution-time errors; these errors are usually much more difficult to find and correct. Most modern compilers have special commands that will attempt to trace an execution-time error such as division by zero. These debugging programs will locate the general region of the program in which the error occurred and will print the values of the variables in the program at the time of the error. You should familiarize yourself with the instructions necessary to implement these features if they are available on your machine.

After these hurdles are passed and the program runs to completion, the final and most difficult phase of debugging a program begins— to verify the validity of the results. For example, even a perfect FORTRAN code will not produce valid answers if the results depend on the value of π and π was incorrectly entered as PI = 3.4416. As with any algebraic or numerical problem, care must be used in writing equations and entering numbers. Before you begin writing a program to solve a problem, you should have some approximate idea about the magnitude of the result to be obtained. Every well-constructed program should then have some form of check to ensure that the computed results are within expectations.

■ Additional Information Supplied by the Compiler

The example listing in Figure 1-4 is for a successful compilation and execution of program ZERO. The output was then sent to a tabletop printer. The printed output you receive from the computing center or from your own printer may look different, but the overall features should be similar. First is a complete listing of the FORTRAN program submitted—that is, the source code. The compiler will generally add sequenced line numbers off to the left and will insert error diagnostics if required. Next comes the output of the compiler program, usually giving some details concerning the translation of the FORTRAN code. This output is called the *load map* and may include such things as a list of all variables used in the program and all library functions required by your program (such as the FORTRAN function for computing e^x, which is called EXP). The load map often contains additional information such as the size of the program and the time for compilation.

Following the load map is the computed output of program ZERO, which is discussed in Chapter 2. The last item on a listing is usually the dayfile, which includes several bookkeeping items such as the time and date of program execution, central processor time used, main memory requirements, and, of course, the cost of the job. In addition, if execution-time errors are encountered, they are listed in the dayfile.

Summary

Perhaps the most difficult step in learning how to use a computer to solve numerical problems is the initial one. Before you can begin your study of FORTRAN and numerical analysis in earnest, you must first become familiar with the rudiments of the operating system of your computer. You should know the following information:

1. The essential commands to initiate communications with your computer. If the computer is a mainframe, you should know how to log on, create, save, and print files. If the computer is a PC, you should know how to boot up the system, write to and read from floppy disks, and print a file on a floppy disk on your printer.
2. The basic steps required to access a special text-editing program to write, correct, and save documents. You will be using this editor program to write and correct FORTRAN programs.
3. The system commands required to translate (compile) a program written in FORTRAN into an executable object-code program.

Several examples of very simple FORTRAN programs were given in this chapter. These programs are intended to aquaint you with the above operating procedures as well as to introduce some elementary features of the FORTRAN language. You should execute each of these programs, including a printed listing of the programs as well as their numerical output. Make notes of the problems you encounter as well as their resolution. Finally, you should construct a detailed outline of all the steps involved in executing a FORTRAN program on your computer, from turning on the machine to getting a printed copy of the program and output. As you learn more system procedures, you can add to this outline. You may even wish to use the computer's editor program to write the outline.

Problems

1.1 Rewrite the following base-ten numbers in binary (base-two) form.
  a. 11   **d.** 2.5   Use 0.5 = 2^{-1}.
  b. 33   **e.** 12.625
  c. 100   **f.** 0.1   This will be a nonterminating fraction.

1.2 Rewrite the following base-two numbers as base-ten numbers.
  a. 1011.0   **c.** 0.11
  b. 110011.0

1.3 Perform the following base-two arithmetic operations. Verify your answers by converting them to their equivalents in base ten.
  a. 1011   **b.** 1010
      + 11   − 11

1.4 Convert the following base-ten arithmetic operations to binary form, and compute the results in binary arithmetic. Verify your answers with a base-ten calculation.
  a. 3 + 3 + 3   That is, 3 × 3   **c.** 10 × 0.1
  b. 11 × 33

1.5 As a rare example of the utility of binary arithmetic that is not related to digital computers, consider the following description of the ancient Oriental game of nim: One player arranges in rows any number of markers. The number of rows and the number of markers per row are left to the discretion of the player. The two players then alternately remove markers from the arrangement, taking any positive number from any one row. Either player may begin. The one removing the last counter is the winner. If you go first and if the initial arrangement is not a trivial one, you should be able to win almost every time. Consider the initial arrangement

$$\square \; \square \; \square \; \square \quad (4)$$
$$\square \; \square \; \square \quad (3)$$
$$\square \quad (1)$$

The game-winning strategy is most easily explained by writing the number in each row in base two:

$$\square \; \square \; \square \; \square \quad (110)$$
$$\square \; \square \; \square \quad (011)$$
$$\square \quad (001)$$

The correct next move is to remove enough markers from some row so that the base-two numbers of those remaining add up to even numbers when each column is added (base ten) separately. Since the opponent's next move will remove markers from only one row, some of the columns will then unavoidably add to an odd number. Continuing the strategy will ultimately leave us with the final arrangement

$$\square \quad (001)$$

for the winning move. Thus, the correct first move with the given arrangement is to remove two markers from row 1 to obtain

☐ ☐ (010)
☐ ☐ ☐ (011)
☐ (001)

(even-even-even)

a. If you were playing against a computer and, in response to the preceding first move by the computer, your move was to remove one marker from the first row, what would be the computer's optimum next move?

b. Is there any other first move by the computer that will guarantee a win?

1.6 Explain the significance of the following columns on a FORTRAN statement line.

a. Column 1   **b.** Column 6   **c.** Columns 73–80

1.7 This question is for those running FORTRAN programs on a PC.

a. List the procedures for booting up your computer.

b. What are the commands to accomplish the following?

  (1) Display a list of all files on drive B.

  (2) Display a list of only the FORTRAN program files on drive B.

  (3) Print a file.

  (4) Delete a file.

  (5) Copy a file from a disk in drive A to a disk in drive B.

  (6) Create a directory or a subdirectory.

  (7) Print a file.

c. What is the name of the editor program you will be using to write programs?

d. List the steps required to load the editor program into the computer and then to use the editor to create and save a file of text.

e. List the steps required to load the FORTRAN compiler into the computer and then to compile and execute a previously saved program on a file called ZERO.

1.8 This question is for those running FORTRAN programs interactively on a mainframe computer.

a. List the complete procedures for logging on to your computer.

b. How do you leave the system—that is, log off?

c. What are the system commands to accomplish the following?

  (1) Display a list of all files currently in your account.

  (3) Print a file.

  (4) Delete a file.

  (5) Copy an existing file named ZERO to a new file called ONE.

  (6) Create a directory or a subdirectory.

  (7) Print a file.

d. What is the name of the editor program you will be using to write programs?

e. List the steps required to use the editor program to create and save a file of text named ZERO.

f. List the system commands required to use the FORTRAN compiler to compile and execute a previously saved program on a file called ZERO.

1.9 The following short programs contain several grammatical errors. Enter and run the programs as they are. What error diagnostics are supplied by the compiler? Use these clues to correct the FORTRAN as best you can and try again. Were there any obvious errors that the compiler missed?

a.
```
PROGRAM OPPS
PRINT *,'Enter values for a,b,c separated by commas'
READ   *, A, B  C
D = 2A + BC
E = D/-A
B = F
PRINT *, ' a = ',A
PRINT *, ' b = ',B
PRINT *, ' c = ',C
PRINT *, ' d = ',D
PRINT *, ' e = ',E
PRINT *, ' f = ',F
STOP
END
```

b.
```
PROGRAM TYPO
X = 0.
X + 1 = Y
PRINT X,Y
This is a Comment!
STOP
```

1.10 Determine the answers to the following questions for your computing environment.

a. What is the size of the central memory of your computer in bytes? in words?

b. What is the length of a computer word in bits? What is the corresponding number of decimal digits?

c. Where are the public-access terminals that are connected to this machine, and what hours are they available?

d. Where is the reference manual for the FORTRAN compiler located?

Fundamentals of FORTRAN

2.1 Introduction

The data types that can be processed by a FORTRAN program come in a variety of forms. The two most commonly used types for numerical values are integer and real. Textual items (symbols) are character type. A few additional data types are available, and they are described in Chapter 6. The three data types discussed in this chapter are sufficient for most problems.

The arithmetic involving the numbers used in FORTRAN differs in many ways from the arithmetic you have previously used. Moreover, in most cases in which a seemingly valid program gives incorrect results, the wrong answers are the result of the odd features of computer arithmetic. The purpose of this chapter is to show you how to translate algebraic expressions into FORTRAN code so that the computer will evaluate the expressions in precisely the manner intended. Computers are designed to store and manipulate textual or numerical information. And numerical values may either include a decimal point (defined as real constants) or be whole numbers without a decimal point (integer constants). The basic features of these three types of data items are described in Section 2.2. How FORTRAN permits the symbolic manipulation of data items by ascribing values to variable names analogous to ordinary algebra is then discussed. The operations of computer arithmetic on FORTRAN variables or constants often yield results at variance with ordinary arithmetic. This phenomenon is explained in Section 2.4 and illustrated with a detailed analysis of program ZERO of Chapter 1. A description of how to translate an algebraic expression into FORTRAN code, and vice versa, follows. The last section of this chapter extends the input/output capabilities of programs by showing you how to read from and write to a stored data file.

2.2   Constants in FORTRAN

A FORTRAN constant is a fixed quantity that may be either in numerical form or in a specified collection of symbols. The numerical constants used will be one of two types: integer or real.

Integer Constants

An *integer constant* in FORTRAN is any number that does not contain a decimal point. It can be positive, negative, or zero. If it is positive, the plus sign can be omitted. For example,

+3
−17
999999999

Embedded commas are not permitted (e.g., 999,999,999), but since FORTRAN ignores blanks, large numbers can be written in groups of three digits, as in 999 999 999.

The computer stores each of these numbers in main memory in a computer word of from 4 to 8 bytes in length. The largest allowed integer depends on the word length, which varies from machine to machine but is finite in every case. (The finite nature of the number set in computer arithmetic has some odd consequences, which are discussed in Section 2.4.) Some examples of the maximum number of decimal digits allowed for integers for a variety of computers are listed in Table 2-1.

Real Constants

The numbers most often used in computation are those with decimal points. Numbers with a decimal point are called *real numbers*.[1] Real numbers can be written either with or without an exponent.

Table 2-1

Maximum number of decimal digits permitted for integers for selected computers

Type of Computer	Maximum Number of Decimal Digits
CDC-Cyber	14
IBM-4341	10
PDP-11	11
DEC-20	8
Typical PC	8

---

[1] A somewhat older terminology calls numbers with a decimal point *floating-point numbers*, and numbers without a decimal point *fixed-point numbers*. The FORTRAN definition of the word *real* is different from and should not be confused with mathematical terminology, in which *real* is used to characterize all numbers that are not complex or imaginary.

Real Numbers without Exponents

Again, if the number is positive, the plus sign may be omitted.

Valid

3.0   This is *not* the same as integer 3.
-3.14159259

Invalid

1,000,000.0   Embedded commas are not allowed.

Real Numbers with Exponents

The exponent consists of the letter *E* followed by a positive or negative integer and corresponds to the power of ten used when the number is written in scientific notation. If the integer exponent is positive, the plus sign may be omitted. The base of the number—that part of the number that precedes the exponent—should contain a decimal point.

Valid

1234.56E-3   This is the same as 1234.56×10^{-3}; that is, 1.23456.
0.123456E+1   That is, 1.23456
1.E10

Invalid

123.45E-5.5   A decimal point is not allowed in the exponent.
123E+45   The base should have a decimal point.
123.E-456   On most computers the exponent is limited to two digits.

Once again, the maximum allowable real number is determined by the word length of the particular computer. For example, on a computer with an exceptionally long word length of 64 bits, the limits are

$$10^{-294} \quad \text{to} \quad 10^{+322}$$

On most other 32-bit machines, the limits are typically

$$10^{-78} \quad \text{to} \quad 10^{+75}$$

On a typical PC the limits are approximately

$$10^{-37} \quad \text{to} \quad 10^{+38}$$

You should determine the precise limitations on the size of integers and real numbers for your computer. (See Problem 2.1.)

■ Character Constants

A *character constant* is a string of any of the allowed symbols in FORTRAN (see footnote 7 in Chapter 1) that are enclosed in apostrophes. The string of characters is stored in memory exactly as it appears, with blanks included. The minimum number of symbols in a character constant is one, whereas the maximum is at least several thousand and depends on your local compiler. We will use character constants primarily to label the output of the program using the PRINT statement.

Valid

```
'NOW is the time for all good ...'
        'X = ',
          ' '        A single blank space
        '4.2'        The symbols for four-decimal point-two, not the
                     numerical value
```

Invalid

```
Now is the time    Apostrophes missing
'End of run''      Too many terminating apostrophes²
```

The values of constants are printed in a FORTRAN program by means of the PRINT statement. The form of the PRINT statement is[3]

```
PRINT *,    A list of constants or variables separated by commas
```

This is an executable FORTRAN statement. All FORTRAN lines can be classified as either executable or nonexecutable. An *executable* FORTRAN line ordinarily calls for some action on the part of the computer; *nonexecutable* FORTRAN lines are used to set various attributes in a program, such as declaring which variables are integer and which are real, prior to execution. (Type-declaration statements are covered in Section 2.3.) Most nonexecutable statements are positioned at the very beginning of the program and are followed by the main body of the program, which consists of executable statements. The PRINT statement may be placed anywhere among the executable statements and may be used to display the value of integer, real, or character constants or variables that have been assigned

---

[2] If the character constant itself contains an apostrophe, the single apostrophe in the string is represented by two consecutive apostrophes in the character constant. Thus, the expression "That's all, folks" would be written as a character constant as

```
'That''s all, folks'
```

[3] In many of the examples of FORTRAN statements in this text, the correct form of the FORTRAN expression will be given in capital letters and a description of the remainder of the FORTRAN statement will follow, in colored type.

values. For example, the three types of constants are all present in the statement

```
PRINT *, 100,' squared = ',1.0E+4
```

The output that results from this statement is

```
100 squared =    10000.0000000
```

The PRINT statement is explained in more detail in Section 2.9.

2.3 FORTRAN Variables

As in ordinary algebra, quantities may be associated with symbols or variable names, and these names may then be symbolically manipulated according to the rules of arithmetic. Each variable name identifies an address in memory, and whenever the variable name is referenced, the current value in that location is used in its place. Variable names in FORTRAN must satisfy two rules:

1. The variable name may be any combination of letters or numbers, but it must begin with a letter. No special symbols are allowed in a variable name.
2. The number of symbols in a variable name is limited to six or fewer.

Variable names may be declared as containing a constant of type character, real, or integer.

Default Typing of Variable Names

Unless the FORTRAN code explicitly states otherwise (see the next section), the type of the number that is associated with a given variable name is determined by the following default-typing rule:

> All variable names that begin with the letters
>
> I J K L M N
>
> refer to integers. All others refer to real numbers.

A few examples of valid and invalid FORTRAN variable names are listed in Table 2-2.

Table 2-2
Examples of valid
and invalid
FORTRAN variable
names

Integer Names			Real Names		
Valid	Invalid		Valid	Invalid	
I	X	[Real]	X	IDIOT	[Integer]
K27B	K-8	[Only letters	XK57	ENGINEER	[Too many
INTGR		and numerals	ANSWER		characters]
KOUNT		allowed]			
	INTEGER	[Too many			
		characters]			

Explicit Typing of Variable Names

A sound procedure in every FORTRAN program is to invent variable names that have a clear meaning when the code is read. For example, if your program is concerned with printing the current date, integer variable names will be needed to store the values of the month, day, and year. The variable names IM, ID, and IY could be used, but the meaning of the FOR-TRAN code would be much more apparent if MONTH, DAY, and YEAR were used instead. However, the variables DAY and YEAR would be default typed as real and thus could not be used to store integer values. The method provided in FORTRAN to override default typing is called *explicit variable typing* and involves using the following FORTRAN statements:

> **REAL**   List of variable names
> **INTEGER**   List of variable names

These statements are called *specification statements* and should appear at the top of the FORTRAN code. They are nonexecutable statements—they do not call for any action by the computer. The variables in the list are any valid FORTRAN names and are separated by commas. A variable name declared to be real cannot also be declared to be integer. Attempts to do so will result in a compilation-time error.

The following variable names are explicitly typed:

> REAL COST, LENGTH, MASS
> INTEGER DAY, YEAR, MONTH

The REAL and INTEGER statements can be in either order, and one or both may be absent from the program. All variables that are not explicitly typed will follow the default-typing rule.

To avoid confusion, it is generally suggested that all variables that appear in a program be explicitly typed. This suggestion is often relaxed for simple variable names that are always used for the same function, such as a subscript or counter (I or J); variables in an equation, such as X; or common fixed constants such as PI.

Default typing can be used only for real and integer variable names. To declare a variable to be character requires an additional statement. This statement is slightly more complicated because the length of the character string that is to be stored in the variable must also be specified. The form of the CHARACTER specification statement is

CHARACTER name₁*⟨sl₁⟩, name₁*⟨sl₁⟩, . . .

where name₁, name₂, and so on are the names of the variables, and ⟨sl₁⟩, ⟨sl₂⟩, . . . are positive integers corresponding to the length of the string stored in the corresponding name. For example,

CHARACTER NAME*10, STREET*12

If all of the variables in the CHARACTER statement are to be of the same length, the statement can be shortened by attaching the common string length to the word CHARACTER, as, for example,

CHARACTER*10 NAME, STREET, CITY

The two forms of the CHARACTER statement can be combined. For example, in the statement

CHARACTER*10 NAME, STREET*12, CITY

the variables NAME and CITY are of length 10, and STREET is of length 12.

2.4 Arithmetic Expressions

An *arithmetic expression* in FORTRAN is an instruction to perform one or more arithmetic operations on constants or variables that previously have been assigned values. An expression can be quite simple, such as A + B, or complicated, extending over several lines. The expression is evaluated and then the entire expression is replaced by that value. The operations that are to be carried out in the expression are determined by both the operators that it contains and the sequence in which they appear.

Arithmetic Operators

The ordinary operations of arithmetic are effected in FORTRAN by means of the following symbols:

+   Addition
−   Subtraction
*   Multiplication
/   Division
**   Exponentiation

The symbols for multiplication, division, and exponentiation were chosen because they are available on every typewriter. The exponentiation operator is defined to be a single symbol.

The rules for constructing arithmetic expressions in FORTRAN are fairly simple:

1. No two operation symbols may occur side by side.
2. The multiplication, division, and exponentiation operators must appear in conjunction with two numbers or variables, for example,

    A*B   D/2.0   F**2

   The addition and subtraction operators may appear with a pair of numbers or variables,

    A + B   D - 2.0

   or with a single variable or number, as in negation:

    +A   -B   -7.0

Keep in mind the following points when translating algebraic structures into FORTRAN:

1. Multiplication can never be implied, as it often is in ordinary algebra. Thus, $a(b + c)$ must be written as A*(B + C), not A(B + C).
2. The rule about side-by-side operators must be carefully adhered to, even in cases where there appears to be no ambiguity.

Invalid FORTRAN	Valid FORTRAN	Algebraic Expression
X**-2	X**(-2)	x^{-2}
A * -3.0	A * (-3.0) or -3.0*A	$-3a$

   The entries in the first column will result in compilation-time errors.
3. Just as in ordinary algebra, terms may be grouped by using parentheses. The expression within a pair of parentheses is then evaluated before any operations outside the parentheses are executed.

Integer Arithmetic

Arithmetic expressions involving only integers will always result in a number that is an integer. This is especially important to remember when the expression involves division. If the result of the division of two integers is not an integer, the computer automatically truncates the decimal fraction:

$$6/2 = 3 \quad 6/3 = 2 \quad 6/4 = 1$$
$$6/5 = 1 \quad 6/6 = 1 \quad 6/7 = 0$$

Because of this odd feature, integers should never be used in arithmetic expressions in which physical quantities are computed. They should be used exclusively as counters or indices.

■ Real Arithmetic

The actual computation in a FORTRAN program is done with real numbers and variables. Because the result of any arithmetic expression containing real numbers is a real number, the problem with integers does not occur.

$$6./2. = 3. \quad 6./3. = 2. \quad 6./4. = 1.50$$
$$6./5. = 1.2 \quad 6./6. = 1. \quad 6./7. = 0.857142\ldots$$

However, real arithmetic has peculiarities all its own that are a consequence of the finite word length of the computer. For example,

$$1./3. = 0.3333333333\ldots$$

where ... means that the decimal expression continues indefinitely. The decimal answer stored in the computer, however, cannot repeat indefinitely but is limited by the number of significant figures in a computer word. A typical size for a computer word is about 10 significant figures, so in real arithmetic,

$$1./3. = 0.3333333333 \quad \text{No} \ldots$$

or, put another way, the result of 1./3. is slightly less than one-third. Thus

$$3.*(1./3.) - 1. \neq 0.0$$

whereas

$$2.*(1./2.) - 1. = 0.0$$

Of course, the numbers stored in the computer are stored in base-two notation. In base two,

$$1/2 = (0.1000000000\ldots)_2$$
$$1/3 = (0.01010101010\ldots)_2$$

and

$$[2(1/2) - 1]_{10} = (10. \times 0.1 - 1.0)_2$$
$$= 1. - 1. = 0.0$$
$$[3(1/3) - 1]_{10} = (11. \times 0.0101010101 - 1.)_2$$
$$= 0.1111111111 - 1.0$$
$$= -0.0000000001$$

Similar consequences of a finite word length are always present on all computing devices.[4] (Try it on your pocket calculator.)

2.5 More Complicated Arithmetic Expressions

Hierarchy of Operations

The sequence in which the computer processes a series of mixed arithmetic operations is determined by a set of rules that have been formulated to remove potential ambiguities. Understanding these rules is essential to read and program code successfully in FORTRAN. This ordered sequence or hierarchy is listed in the following box.

Order in which arithmetic operations in an expression are executed		
First: ( )	Clear all parentheses (innermost first).
Second: **	Perform exponentiation.
Third: * or /	Perform multiplication and/or division (equal priority).
Fourth: + or −	Perform addition and/or subtraction (equal priority).

These rules are effected by successive scans of the expression, looking for each of the preceding elements in turn from left to right.[5] Some examples follow.

---

[4] Many modern compilers and even pocket calculators have cleverly hidden this problem by always rounding up after arithmetic operations. On these machines the result of $3.*(1./3.) - 1.$ is always zero. If your computer gives a zero result for this computation, try running the following program:

```
PROGRAM TEST
PRINT *, 1./3. - .33333      ,'5  digits'
PRINT *, 1./3. - .333333     ,'6  digits'
PRINT *, 1./3. - .3333333    ,'7  digits'
PRINT *, 1./3. - .33333333   ,'8  digits'
PRINT *, 1./3. - .333333333  ,'9  digits'
PRINT *, 1./3. - .3333333333 ,'10 digits'
PRINT *, 1./3. - .33333333333 ,'11 digits'
STOP
END
```

Since 1/3 has a nonterminating decimal fraction, none of these results should be zero. But you will find that once the number of digits exceeds that stored in a computer word, the result will be exactly zero for the last several PRINT statements.

[5] Unfortunately, successive exponentiation is an exception to the left-to-right rule. FORTRAN compilers are written to evaluate A**B**C as A**(B**C), that is, right to left. For operators of this type, it is always best to avoid confusion and include parentheses to force the sequence of operations to be what you intended.

1. A + B + C is evaluated as

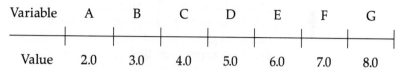

2. $4*3/2 \rightarrow 12/2 \rightarrow 6$
but
$3/2*4 \rightarrow 1*4 \rightarrow 4$

3. $2.**3 - 1. \rightarrow 8. - 1. \rightarrow 7.$

Consider how the machine would process an expression like

`A**B/C + D*E*(F-G)`

Assume that the variables A through G have been previously assigned the values

Variable	A	B	C	D	E	F	G
Value	2.0	3.0	4.0	5.0	6.0	7.0	8.0

The first scan is to clear all parentheses, and thus the first operation is to evaluate (F − G) and temporarily store the result in, say, R_1 $[(7. - 8.) = -1. = R_1]$. The expression now reads

`A**B/C + D*E*R₁` $R_1 = -1.$

The next scan looks for exponentiation, replacing A**B with the temporarily stored value R_2 $(2.**3 = 8. = R_2)$. We next have

`R₂/C + D*E*R₁` $R_2 = 8.0$

The third scan carries out all the multiplication or division found, proceeding left to right

`R₂/C  =  R₃` $8./4. = 2. = R_3$
`D*E  =  R₄` $5. \times 6. = 30. = R_4$
`R₄*R₁  =  R₅` $30. \times (-1.) = -30. = R_5$

and we are left with

`R₃ + R₅`

The final scan executes all addition or subtraction proceeding left to right to obtain the final value of the expression

`R₆ = (2. + (-30.) )  =  -28.0`

Of course, additional parentheses could be inserted to alter the order of operations and perhaps the result. You should verify that the slightly changed expression

`A**B/(C + D) * (E*(F - G))`

has the value −5.3333333. A beginner's rule is, *When in doubt, always add parentheses.*

■ Mixed-Mode Expressions

All of the arithmetic expressions discussed so far have been carefully constructed to contain only elementary operations between the same types of numbers—integers added to integers, real numbers multiplied by real numbers, and so on. The reason for this is that the ALU of the computer is set up to execute the operations of arithmetic or comparison only between numbers of the same type. It does not know how to multiply a real number by an integer. To carry out such an operation, the numbers must first be converted to the same type.

All modern compilers are written to handle an arithmetic operation between two numbers of different types by first converting the numbers to the same type and then carrying out the operation. To accomplish this in an unambiguous manner, levels of dominance are assigned to the number types real and integer, with reals having dominance over integers. Thus, an expression like

        3.0*I

is evaluated by first converting the integer I to a real number and then multiplying by 3.0. The result of the operation is then real. This type of expression is called a *mixed-mode expression.*

Mixed-mode expressions often cause considerable confusion among both beginning and more experienced programmers. This confusion often results when the expression involves division. The presence or absence of a decimal point can dramatically alter the result.

Mixed-Mode Expression	Is Evaluated to Be
1. + 1/2	1.0 {1/2 → 0}
1 + 1./2	1.5 {1./2 → 1./2. → 0.5 1 + .5 → 1. + .5 → 1.5}

Even though mixed-mode expressions can serve very useful functions in programming, they should be avoided by beginners. Numerical computations should involve real numbers only, with integers used primarily as counters. If you do find it necessary to use mixed-mode expressions, for a while every FORTRAN statement you write that employs mixed-mode arithmetic should be preceded by a comment line like

        *   Intentional Mixed Mode Follows

which will serve both as a reminder and as an announcement to others.

2.6   **Assignment Statements**

Although the assignment operator (=) in FORTRAN looks like the equals sign in ordinary algebra, it has a significantly different meaning. A FORTRAN expression like

```
X = 14. - 4.**.5
```

is a set of instructions to the computer to complete the arithmetic computation on the right and to assign that value to a variable called X. An important feature of higher computer languages like FORTRAN is that this statement will automatically determine and remember a storage location in main memory for this number. Subsequent access to this number is obtained simply by using the variable name, as in

```
Y = X**3.
```

Because what was stored in X is 12.0 (i.e., $14. - 2.$), the value stored in Y is 1728.0. With this understanding of what the = operator does, FORTRAN statements like

```
I = I + 1
X = X + DX
```

make sense, whereas in algebra they would be nonsense; that is, in FORTRAN the statement I = I + 1 means, Take the value assigned to I, add 1 to it, and store the result in the location allotted to I.

Character Assignment Statements

Variables that have previously been declared character type may be assigned "values" by means of the assignment operator =. The value of a character variable is not numerical but is a string of symbols. For example,

```
CHARACTER  NAME*6, STREET*6, CITY*7
NAME   = 'Miller'
STREET = 'E.Main'
CITY   = 'Chicago'
```

In each case the character constant on the right of the assignment operator is assigned to the variable on the left. Previously defined character variables may also appear on the right of the expressions, as

```
NAME   = 'Miller'
STREET = NAME
CITY   = 'Chicago'
```

The variables NAME and STREET now contain the same string of characters.

If the length of the string on the right of the expression is not the same as the specified length of the variable, the expression is altered to fit the length of the variable. If the expression is longer than the length of the variable, the expression is first truncated from the right until the lengths match:

```
CHARACTER NAME*6
NAME = 'Williams'    Stored in NAME is the string  W i l l i a .
```

If the expression is shorter than the length of the variable, it is padded with blanks on the right:

```
NAME = 'Doe'         Stored in NAME is the string  D o e     .
```

Mixed-Mode Replacement

Consider the consequences of statements like

```
I = 14./3.             The integer 4 is stored in I.
N = 3.*(1./3.) - 1.    The integer 0 is stored in N.
R = 4/3                The real number 1.0 is stored in R.
```

In each case the expression on the right of = is first evaluated as either a real or an integer value, and then the assignment is made to the variable on the left, which here requires that the mode of the result (i.e., integer or real) be converted. Thus, 14./3. = 4.666666667, and the assignment to I automatically converts this to an integer by truncating the decimal part. The preceding statements illustrate what is called *mode conversion,* that is, an integer (or real number) is converted automatically into a real number (or integer) by the assignment operator. The reason for this is that the number stored in the address allocated to I, for example, must be an integer, and so the number must be converted to an integer before it can be written in location I. One of the most common errors made by novice FORTRAN programmers is that of unintentional mode conversion, which occurs when integer variable names are used for quantities that were intended to be real numbers. Mode conversion can be an extremely useful feature of FORTRAN if used with care. As with mixed-mode expressions, while you are learning FORTRAN, every statement you write that employs mode conversion should be preceded by a comment line like

```
*      Intentional mode conversion follows
```

Expressions or assignment statements that mix character variables or constants with numerical values will always result in compilation errors. Thus, the code below will result in two fatal compilation-time errors:

```
CHARACTER NAME*5
REAL X,C
X = 2.0
NAME = 'Jones'
B = X + NAME    Error: Character and other type values may not be
                       mixed in an arithmetic operation.

C = NAME        Error: Character values cannot be converted to
                       real numbers.
```

2.7 **Program ZERO**

FORTRAN, like any skill, is best learned by doing. So before introducing any more rules and features, we will carefully go over program ZERO, which was executed in Chapter 1. The rest of this section discusses the program in Figure 1-5 line by line. (To get a better sense of how each line fits within the program, have the complete program listing in Figure 1-5 handy as you read this section.)

The first FORTRAN statement in the program is

```
PROGRAM ZERO
```

which simply gives this program a name of ZERO. This line is optional; if it is omitted, the compiler will assign a name.

The next two lines of FORTRAN code

```
REAL A, B, C, C1, C2, D, E, F, G, H, P, Q
INTEGER  IB
```

explicitly type the variables as either real or integer. If these two lines were omitted, the variables would have been default typed exactly the same. However, as was discussed in Section 2.3, it is usually good practice to explicitly type all variables that appear in a program.

The first executable statement in the program appears next.

```
PRINT *,'c1 = a(1/a - 1)    c2 = a(1/a - b/ab)'
```

prints the algebraic expressions between the single quotes exactly as they appear on the screen and indicates the type of calculation that will be performed on the constants a and b. The next PRINT statement bears a statement number in the statement number field and directs that the phrase

```
Input values for A, B separated by a comma
```

be displayed on the screen. This is then a "prompt" for the READ statement that follows:

```
READ *,A,B
```

This statement is an instruction to read the values that will then be assigned to the variables A and B. When the program is run at the terminal, this statement will cause the program to pause and wait for you to enter the numbers. The values entered are separated by a comma (or optionally a blank space), and since A and B are associated with real values, they should contain a decimal point. If we had neglected to insert the previous PRINT statement, the program would still stop at the READ, and we could easily be confused about why it stopped. Inserting this form of prompt before each READ statement is essential if the program is to be run interactively. The READ * statement is an example of list-directed input and is discussed in more detail in Section 2.9.

The next PRINT statements,

```
PRINT *,'Input values   a = ',A
PRINT *,'               b = ',B
```

are called *echo prints* and simply verify that the numbers you intended to enter are indeed what the computer read. In every program you write there should be some form of check like this on the input data to a program.

The next two arithmetic statements,

```
C1 = A*(1./A) - 1.
C2 = A*((1./A) - B*(1.(A*B)))
```

represent calculations that should yield zero for any values of A and B. The parentheses were added to make the statements more readable. Using the rules for hierarchy of operations, the first statement could be rewritten in an equivalent fashion without parentheses as

```
C1 = 1./A*A - 1.
```

To rewrite the second statement without parentheses would require two separate statements:

```
T  = 1./A - 1./A/B*B
C2 = A*T
```

Recall that 1./A/B*B is executed as

$$\underbrace{\overbrace{\underbrace{1./A}_{\dfrac{1}{a}}\ /B}_{\dfrac{1}{ab}} *\ B}_{\left(\dfrac{1}{ab}\right)b}$$

If the computer simply truncates the decimal fraction, the result of both operations will not be zero. [Recall that $3(.333) - 1 = .999 - 1 = -0.001$.] If, as is likely, your computer "rounds up" the result of arithmetic operations, the computed result will be precisely zero, thus concealing the inherent inaccuracies associated with finite word length. To uncover the nature and magnitude of the problem, we must first search for numbers that will not give a precisely zero result for C1 and C2. After printing the values computed for C1 and C2, the next sequence of FORTRAN statements illustrates a very useful construction in FORTRAN: the IF test.

```
IF(C1.EQ.0 .AND. C2.EQ.0)THEN
   PRINT *, 'Try again'
   GO TO 1
ENDIF
```

The description of the grammar rules associated with the IF test appears in Chapter 3. At this point, however, the close connection between FORTRAN and ordinary English should make this set of statements fairly transparent. The idea is, *if* the condition in the parentheses is satisfied, *then* the next set of commands is executed. If not, the commands are skipped over and the program continues. The ENDIF marks the end of the block of commands to be conditionally executed. The placement of the periods in the test condition is critical. There must be periods at the beginning and end of the symbols AND and EQ. The condition reads, if both C1 = 0 and C2 = 0 then.... The effect of either C1 or C2 being other than identically zero will cause first the phrase "Try again" to be printed and then a jump back to a previous statement in the program labeled by the statement number 1. This is the original PRINT statement, and so the program will start over again by asking you to once more enter two numbers for A and B. This is an example of a *loop* in a program. There is only one way out of this particular loop, that is, if either C1 or C2 happens to be other than zero. Program loops constructed using the GO TO statement are frowned upon in modern programming usage. The preferred alternatives are described in Chapter 3.

Once an offending pair A, B has been found, the program continues by executing a series of elementary arithmetic statements.

```
C = A+B
D = A-B
E = A/B
F = A*B
G = C*D/(E*F) + (B/A)**2 - 1.
```

Notice that by using the hierarchy rules and the earlier assignments for C, D, E, and F, the assignment for G can be translated into ordinary algebra as

$$g = \left[\frac{(a+b)(a-b)}{\frac{a}{b}ab} + \left(\frac{b}{a}\right)^2 - 1 \right]$$

$$= \left[\frac{a^2 - b^2}{a^2} \right] + \left(\frac{b}{a}\right)^2 - 1$$

$$= 1 - \left(\frac{b}{a}\right)^2 + \left(\frac{b}{a}\right)^2 - 1 = 0$$

The computed value for g should be identically zero for any values of a and b. The next statement prints the computed value for g. Notice that the PRINT statement has been set up so that the printed values for g will line up with the earlier PRINT statements for C1 and C2. This alignment is not required, but such efforts will make the output of the program easier to read.

The operation of exponentiation that appears in this statement, (B/A)**2, requires some explanation. To execute the exponentiation, the computer first determines a value for B/A and temporarily stores it in, say, R_1. The computer then calls up a special program stored in main memory whose assignment is to take a base, here R_1, and raise it to an integer power, here 2. Then the base is multiplied by itself the appropriate number of times, and if the exponent is negative, the result is inverted. The base and/or the exponent may be positive or negative. However, an operation like

```
(B/A)**2.3
```

requires special care. The subprogram that calculates this quantity must use logarithms, and since the logarithm of a negative number is undefined in our number system (it is actually an imaginary number), we must take care that if the exponent is not an integer the base must always be positive. For example,

```
(-3.)**3        Works      Gives   -27.
(-3.)**(-3)     Works      Gives   -1./27.
(-3.)**3.       Will not work
```

If the exponent is real, then the base must be *positive.*

You may have noticed that we have been mixing modes without including the appropriate comment lines. Exponentiation is an exception to the previously stated mixed-mode rule. From the explanation given for the execution of the operation

```
X**7    Real base, integer exponent
```

we can see that at no time are two quantities of differing mode involved in an elementary arithmetic operation (addition, subtraction, multiplication, division). In fact, whenever possible, exponentiation should be of the form

```
X**I
```

rather than

```
X**R
```

since the former is much faster and safer.

After the exponentiation is completed, the value of G is computed and printed. The next several lines in the program employ intentional mixed-mode replacement and mixed-mode arithmetic.

```
        IB = B
        C  = A**B
    *
    *    <NOTE: The next line involves mixed-mode arithmetic.>
    *
        P  = LOG(ABS(C))/IB
        Q  = EXP(P) - A
```

It is not difficult to predict the result of the statements IB = B and C = A**B; however, the P and Q statements are probably confusing. They both use *intrinsic functions,* which are subprograms stored in main memory that can be used by a FORTRAN program to calculate several common mathematical functions. Thus, LOG(X) computes the natural logarithm of x, that is, $\ln(x)$, and EXP(X) computes e^x. For both of these intrinsic functions, the argument should be real. The operation of these functions is very similar to operations on your pocket calculator when you push the appropriate key (e.g., $\ln(x)$ or e^x). These functions are only two of a long list of intrinsic functions available to FORTRAN programs. A few of the more commonly used functions are listed in Table 2-3. (A more complete list can be found in Tables 9-2 and 9-3.)

Now let's return to the assignment statements for P and Q. Once the $\ln(h)$ and e^p have been calculated, the first statement involves authentic mixed-mode arithmetic, which should be avoided. However, in this instance it is easy to figure out how the machine handles it. As mentioned earlier, before the division is executed, both numbers involved [i.e., LOG(C) and IB] are converted to the dominant mode, in this case real. In order to see the effect of all these statements, they are rewritten in algebraic notation:

$$c = a^b$$

$$p = \ln(a^b)/b \qquad \textit{Note:}\ \ln(x^y) = y\ \ln(x)$$

$$= (b\ \ln(a))/b = \ln(a)$$

$$q = e^p - a$$

$$= e^{\ln(a)} - a \qquad \textit{Note:}\ e^{\ln(x)} = x$$

$$= a - a$$

$$= 0.0$$

Table 2-3

Some intrinsic functions available in FORTRAN

FORTRAN	Algebra	Description	Argument	Result	Example
LOG(X)	$\ln(x)$	Natural log	Real	Real	Y = LOG(3.1)
EXP(X)	e^x	$e = 2.71828\ldots$	Real	Real	P = EXP(1.5)
SQRT(X)	$\sqrt{x}$	Square root	Real	Real	R = SQRT(4./7.)
SIN(X)	$\sin(x)$	Trigonometric sine	Real (radians)	Real	S = SIN(3.14)
COS(X)	$\cos(x)$	Trigonometric cosine	Real (radians)	Real	T = COS(0.0)
ABS(X)	$\lvert x \rvert$	Absolute value	Real	Real (positive)	W = ABS(−5.5)
ACOS(X)	$\cos^{-1}(x)$	Inverse cosine, if $x = \cos\Theta$ then $\Theta = \cos^{-1}(x)$	Real	Real (radians)	PI = ACOS(−1.)

To see the results of the calculation thus far, the program next prints the current values of some of the variables.

```
PRINT *,'                           q = ',Q
PRINT *,'      Finally,     a/q = ',A/Q
```

The computed values for both G and Q are expected to be exactly zero, and thus the value for a/q should be undefined. The output from the two computer runs illustrated in Figure 1-4 is given in Figure 2-1.

Compare this output with the results you obtained on your computer. The computed values of c1, c2, g, and q are all expected to be zero. Yet when these variables are printed, some are, some are not. Why does this happen? The answer once again is caused by the fact that the machine, when working with real numbers, only carries about eight significant figures, so

$$B/A = 55.0/3.0 = 18.333333$$

and also that the computer will round up the results of arithmetic operations. In short, computer arithmetic is not exact. It is only reliable to eight digits or so.

The final calculation in the program is to print a/q, which should be 3/0, that is, an undefined quantity for all cases, thus generating an execution-time error. In the VAX mainframe computer run, q was precisely zero and a/q caused an error. Notice that the nature and location of the error are indicated on the output in Figure 2-1, and it is not difficult to track down the offending operation. However, in the IBM PC run, the

Figure 2-1
Program output from two computers

Program Output from a run on a VAX mainframe	Program Output from a run on a PC

```
c1 = a(1/a - 1)    c2 = a(1/a - b/ab)          c1 = a(1/a - 1)    c2 = a(1/a - b/ab)
Input values for A, B separated by a comma      Input values for A, B separated by a comma
Input values     a =    4.000000               Input values     a =    4.00000000
                 b =    9.000000                                b =    9.00000000
Arithmetic checks:                              Arithmetic checks:
                 c1 =    0.0000000E+00                           c1 =    0.000000000E+00
                 c2 =    0.0000000E+00                           c2 =    0.000000000E+00
 Try again                                       Try again
Input values for A, B separated by a comma      Input values for A, B separated by a comma
Input values     a =    3.000000               Input values     a =    3.00000000
                 b =    55.00000                                b =    55.0000000
Arithmetic checks:                              Arithmetic checks:
                 c1 =    0.0000000E+00                           c1 =    0.00000000E-01
                 c2 =    8.9406967E-08                           c2 =    2.98023224E-08
Computed Values: g =    3.0517578E-05          Computed Values: g =    2.77555756E-17
                 q =    0.0000000E+00                            q =    5.95022627E-08
                                                    Finally,   a/q =    5.04182501E+07

%SYSTEM-F-FLDIV_F, arithmetic fault,
 floating divideby zero at PC-000939, PSL = 03C00020

%Traceback, symbolic stack dump follows
 module name routine name line   rel PC    abs PC
 ZERO         ZERO          29   0000339   0000939
```

computed value for q was extremely small but not precisely zero and so no error occurred. Thus, the same program run on two different computers produces different results. It is important to be aware of the computational limitations that are the result of the manner in which computers execute arithmetic.

The last two lines of the code in Figure 1-5 are essential to the execution of a FORTRAN program. The statement

```
STOP
```

will cause the program to terminate. This is an executable statement because it calls for some action on the part of the computer. Other examples of executable statements that we have seen so far are the simple arithmetic assignment statements.

The last line in the program,

```
END
```

is also executable and can be used to terminate the program. However, the principal use of the END statement is as a marker to inform the compiler where the program ends and where to stop the translation into machine language. You should use the END statement only for this purpose. Every FORTRAN program or subprogram must have an END as its last line.

2.8 Translating Algebra into FORTRAN

To develop a facility in using the hierarchy rules, you should translate several moderately complicated algebraic expressions into FORTRAN, and vice versa. A few examples follow.

1. It is an axiom of programming that good FORTRAN code is easily readable. "Easily readable" usually means that expressions resemble as closely as possible the algebraic formulas they came from. Thus, an equation like

$$x = \frac{rP}{1 + [1 + (r/100)]^{-n}}$$

which represents the size of the loan payment when borrowing P dollars for n years at an interest rate of $r\%$, would be transcribed into FORTRAN as

```
X = R*P/(1. + (1. + R/100.)**(-N))
```

As a test of your understanding of the hierarchy rules, try to rewrite this equation into FORTRAN without using any parentheses. The result might resemble

```
TERM = 1. + R/100.
TERM = TERM**N
BOTTOM = 1. + 1./TERM
X = R*P/BOTTOM
```

2. The following code represents a translation of a single equation into FORTRAN without using parentheses. Transcribe it back into an algebraic equation, and then rewrite it in a more readable form using parentheses.

`TERM1 = 1. + C`	$t_1 = 1 + c$
`TERM1 = A*B/TERM1`	$t_1 = ab/(1 + c)$
`TERM2 = 1. + R`	$t_2 = 1 + r$
`TERM2 = TERM2**N`	$t_2 = (1 + r)^n$
`TERM2 = TERM2 - 1.`	$t_2 = (1 + r)^n - 1$
`TERM2 = TERM2/R`	$t_2 = \dfrac{(1 + r)^n - 1}{r}$
`T = X*TERM1 - P/TERM2`	$t = \dfrac{ab}{1 + c}x - \dfrac{rP}{(1 + r)^n - 1}$

Thus

```
T = A*B*X/(1.+C) - R*P/((1.+R)**N - 1.)
```

3. The simplest use of a FORTRAN program is to duplicate the operations of a pocket calculator: take an algebraic expression, insert numerical values for the various quantities in the expression, and compute the result. For example, the velocity of very small water waves is given by the expression

$$v = \sqrt{\frac{2\pi t}{\lambda d} + \frac{g\lambda}{2\pi}}$$

where t is the surface tension (N/m), d is water density (1,000 kg/m^3), g is the gravitational acceleration (9.8 m/sec^2), and λ is the wavelength (m) of the wave. The computed velocity will be in meters per second.

A program to read t and λ from a terminal and compute the wave velocity would then be as shown in Figure 2-2. This FORTRAN program has three points of special interest:

- Since the variable names were not explicitly typed as integer or real, using the names L or LAMBDA for the wavelength would have been incorrect and might have resulted in error.
- Unlike most pocket calculators, the computer has no stored value for π. A somewhat more accurate assignment is obtained by

  ```
  PI = ACOS(-1.)
  ```

- The successive divisions at the end of the expression for V are equivalent to

  ```
  G*WAVLTH/(2.*PI)
  ```

Figure 2-2

Program to
compute the
speed of water
waves

```
        PROGRAM WAVES
*
* Variables:
*        G     -- Gravitational acceleration (9.8 m/sec^2)
*        D     -- Water density (1000 kg/m^3)
*        PI    -- 3.1415...
*        T     -- Surface tension of water (N/m) [INPUT]
*    WAVLTH    -- Wavelength of water waves (m)  [INPUT]
*        V     -- Computed velocity of the wave (m/sec)
*-------------------------------------------------------------
        D  = 1000.
        G  = 9.8
        PI = 3.14159265
        PRINT *,'Enter values for surface tension and'
        PRINT *,'      wavelength (separated by a comma)'
        READ  *,T,WAVLTH
        V = 2.*PI *T/(WAVLTH*D) + G*WAVLTH/2./PI
        V = SQRT(V)
        PRINT *,'If surface tension = ',T      ,' N/m'
        PRINT *,'and the wavelength = ',WAVLTH,' m'
        PRINT *,'the wave velocity  = ',V      ,' m/sec'
        STOP
        END
```

Table 2-4 lists several common examples of incorrect transcriptions of algebra into FORTRAN along with the corrected versions.

Table 2-4

Common errors in
translating algebra
into FORTRAN

Algebra	Incorrect FORTRAN	Comments	Corrected FORTRAN
$a(b + c)$	A(B + C)	Compilation error	A*(B + C)
$2a + 4$	2*A + 4	Legal, but mixed mode is not appropriate for beginners	2.*A + 4.
a^{n+1}	A**N+1	Legal, but results in $a^n + 1$	A**(N+1)
$a^{(1/n)}$	A**(1/N)	Legal, however (1/N) is likely zero (integer arithmetic)	A**(1./N)
$\dfrac{ab}{cd}$	A*B/C*D	Legal, but results in $\left(\dfrac{ab}{c}\right)d$	A*B/(C*D) or A*B/C/D
$(-x)^n$	-X**N	In FORTRAN, exponentiation precedes negation, so this results in $-(x^n)$.	(-X)**N
$t = 3. \times 10^6$	T = 3.*10.**6	Legal, but needless arithmetic. The corrected version requires no arithmetic operators at all.	T = 3.E6

2.9 Elementary Input and Output in FORTRAN Programs

Every FORTRAN program, no matter how simple, can be expected to obtain a result that has to be printed or displayed on the terminal screen. Many programs will require a number of parameters to be assigned values each time the program is run. Thus, it is essential that from the very beginning the user has some familiarity with FORTRAN statements that permit interaction with an executing program by either reading in data for parameters or printing out results. If your program is to produce a table of numbers with perhaps several entries per line, there are many decisions to be made, including where on the line the numbers are to appear, how many digits are to be displayed, and what text is to accompany the numbers. All of these editing decisions are handled in FORTRAN by means of FORMAT specifications, which are discussed in Chapter 6. Any set of editing instructions will be fraught with innumerable details concerning the positioning and presentation of the printed results, and this is doubly so in FORTRAN. For this reason, we will delay the discussion of FORTRAN FORMAT statements and instead describe some temporary alternatives that can be used for most elementary programs.

List-Directed Input/Output Statements

READ *, Statement

The FORTRAN programs discussed up to this point have used list-directed input statements of the form

> **READ *,** A list of variables

The values entered at the terminal must agree in number and type with the variable names in the READ statement. The values should be separated by commas.[6] For example, the statement

```
READ *, X, IA, Y, KOUNT
```

when used to enter the values

```
5, 72, 4, 3.E6, 10002
```

is equivalent to the assignments

```
X     = 5.72
IA    = 4
Y     = 3000000.0
KOUNT = 10002
```

---

[6] You may alternatively separate the numbers by blanks. However, since it is easy to accidentally introduce an extra space in a number, especially when many long numbers are entered on a single line, I would suggest using commas to explicitly delineate the items in a string of input items.

If the data were entered as

```
5.72, 4, <CR>
3.E6, 10002
```

where ⟨CR⟩ stands for carriage return, exactly the same assignments would be made. The input

```
5.72, , , 10002
```

would read zero (0) for IA and 0.0 for Y.

The list-directed READ statement can also be used to read values for variables of type character, provided the character strings that are read are enclosed in apostrophes.

PRINT *, Statement

The list-directed output statement

     PRINT *,   A list of variables, arithmetic expressions, or character strings

operates in a similar fashion, with the additional features that arithmetic expressions may be included in the list and strings of characters may be printed if they are enclosed by apostrophes. The number of digits that will be displayed and the precise positioning of the numbers on the line are not adjustable. Thus, it may take a bit of experimenting to obtain printed results that are acceptable. For example, blank lines can be inserted in the output by repeated use of PRINT *. With no list of variables to be printed, a single blank line will result. By inserting blank character strings between the items in the output list, the position of these items on the printed line can, to some extent, be adjusted. In this manner you can arrange for the column headings of a table to roughly line up with the table's contents.

A few examples of list-directed output are given in Table 2-5. The ability to print character strings as well as numerical values can be used to facilitate data input at a terminal. As suggested earlier, including an explanatory PRINT before each READ will eliminate a great many mistaken

Table 2-5
Examples of
list-directed output

FORTRAN	Output

```X = 5.```
```Y = 8.```
```I = 6```
```J = 12```
```PRINT *, X,Y,I,J```
```PRINT *, Y/X, I+J+2```
```PRINT *, I + SQRT(X/Y)```
```PRINT *```
```PRINT *, 'x = ',X,' i-j = ',I-J```
	
	```5.00000 8.00000 6 12```
	```1.60000 20```
	```6.79057```
	```<a blank line>```
	```x = 5.00000 i-j = -6```

variable assignments. It is also a good idea to use echo prints (defined on page 44). For example, the water-wave velocity problem in the previous section would be incomplete without the addition of the PRINT/READ lines

```
PRINT *,'Enter T(surface tension) and the wavelength'
READ  *, T,WAVLTH
PRINT *,'Input values  t = ',T,' wavelength = ',WAVLTH
```

Alternative List-Directed Input/Output Statements

The significance of the single asterisk in statements like PRINT * and READ * is to inform the compiler that default formatting is to be used for the positioning of the numbers read or printed. In addition, it is assumed that the output will be displayed on the default output device, which is usually the terminal screen, and that input will be read from the default input device, which is usually the keyboard. Two alternative FORTRAN statements that accomplish the same thing but are a bit more explicit are

READ(*,*)   Input list   is equivalent to READ *,   Input list

and

WRITE(*,*)   Output list   is equivalent to PRINT *,   Output list

In the new forms, the first position in the parentheses designates the input device that is to be used for the I/O. In this case an asterisk specifies that default input (keyboard) or default output (terminal screen) devices will be utilized. The second asterisk characterizes the format specifications used to control the form of the I/O, and again the asterisk indicates that default or list-directed format will be used. Thus, the FORMAT statements themselves should be read as

READ(*,*)   "Read from the keyboard, according to list-directed format, the variables..."

WRITE(*,*)   "Write to the terminal screen, according to list-directed format, the variables..."

The advantage of the longer forms of the I/O statements is that they can be used to direct the output to devices other than the screen and read input from locations other than the keyboard. The FORTRAN statement that is used to specify the target of these I/O operations is described below.

Additional Specification Options in READ( ), WRITE( ) Statements

In addition to designating the location of the I/O file and the format specification, two other fields may appear in READ( ) and WRITE( ) statements.

If the parentheses in either the READ( ) or the WRITE( ) contain the expression

ERR = ⟨err.−sl⟩

where ⟨err.−sl⟩ is the statement number of an executable statement in the program, then if there is an error when executing the READ or the WRITE, the program will branch to that statement rather than terminating via an execution-time error.

If the READ( ) statement contains the expression

END = ⟨end.−sl⟩

where ⟨end.−sl⟩ is the statement number of an executable statement in the program, then if the end of the data file is encountered while executing the READ, the program will branch to that statement rather than terminating via an execution-time error. Examples of these extensions of the READ( ), WRITE( ) statements are

```
WRITE(*,*,ERR = 99)
WRITE(12,*,ERR = 98)        Writes to file number 12
READ(13,*,ERR=99,END=98)    Reads from file number 13
```

OPEN Statement—Naming Data Files

The OPEN statement in FORTRAN is used to connect a disk file to a program and to define various attributes of the file. Two of the common disk-file specifications that are prescribed in an OPEN statement are the UNIT number and the NAME of the file.

UNIT Number

A positive integer (less than 100) may be associated with a disk file and is then used to identify that file in all READ( ) and WRITE( ) statements. For example, if a data file exists on the disk and it contains numbers that are to be read by the program, the OPEN statement could be used to associate the integer 12 with the data file. The integer 12 would then replace the first asterisk in the READ statement, and all READ(12,*) statements would read from the file identified as 12 (and not from the keyboard). Or the output from the program could be directed to a file associated with unit number 13, and statements like WRITE(13,*) would print the results in that output file (and would not be displayed on the screen).

File NAME

Files stored on the disk must have a name. The rules associated with naming disk files are system dependent, but a few general guidelines might be helpful:

- The name usually cannot include any characters other than letters and numerals.

- The maximum length of a name varies, with a common limit being 12 characters.

- On many systems, the name may include the identification of the "path" to the file as well. Thus

  ```
  \COMPSCI\PROGS\NEWDATA
  ```

  would identify a file called NEWDATA, which is in a subdirectory called PROGS, which in turn is part of a larger directory called COMPSCI.

- Some systems permit a "suffix" that can be used to characterize the contents of a file to be attached to the file name. For example, the suffix .FOR on a file named PROG1.FOR might be used to identify it as a FORTRAN program, while GRADES.DAT could be a data file containing course grades.

The form of the OPEN statement that accomplishes the association of a name and unit number with a disk file is

```
OPEN(UNIT = un, FILE = flname)
```

where un is the integer that specifies the unit of the file to be opened and flname is the name of the disk file (perhaps containing a path and/or a suffix). Note that since the name of the file will be a character-type constant it must be enclosed by apostrophes, for example, FILE = 'OLDDATA.' An example of an OPEN statement used to connect the program to a file called RESULTS, which will contain the printed output, might be

```
OPEN(UNIT=33,FILE='RESULTS')
```

The expression UNIT=33 may be shortened to simply

```
OPEN(33,FILE='RESULTS')
```

Numerous other attributes of the disk file can be specified by means of the OPEN statement; these will be discussed when we return to this statement in Chapter 4.

The OPEN statement is an executable FORTRAN statement that may appear anywhere after the type-declaration statements in the program, but it must precede any reference to the associated disk file by means of READ( ) or WRITE( ) statements.

■ Using Text Editor Programs to Refine and Print Output Files

As mentioned earlier, since the user has limited control over the positioning of printed output when using list-directed PRINTs and WRITEs, it is often difficult to obtain output in a form that is neat and attractive. FORTRAN provides extensive editing commands for printing output, but they are sufficiently complicated that their description will be delayed until

Chapter 6. At this stage it is more important to develop an understanding of the construction and implementation of elementary programs than to get bogged down in all the details of formatting output. Thus, in this section a temporary alternative is suggested.

While you are learning FORTRAN, you are also extending your skills in the use of a text editor. The FORTRAN programs you create are written with the aid of this text editor. No doubt you have also used it to write papers for other courses and for personal correspondence. If this editor reads and writes ASCII files (see footnote 5 in Chapter 1), it can be used as well to improve the appearance of the computed output. The idea is quite simple: after you have finally gotten the program to execute successfully, you add an OPEN statement near the beginning of the program to identify the output file. Next, in addition to having the results printed on the terminal screen, you could add WRITE( ) statements in the program to have the same results stored on the disk file. The alignment of the numbers and accompanying text is likely to be less than perfect. After executing the program and writing the output file, you then use the editor program to further edit and refine the appearance of the output file. The editor program can be used to print the final version of the output.

You should know how to use the editor program to edit a specific named file (here the output file); delete and add both single characters and entire lines; copy a line or line segment to a different point in the file; save the latest version of the file; and print the file.

Summary

The material in this chapter will enable you to transcribe algebraic expressions into FORTRAN. This transcription is always a key element of any numerical program.

The computer stores constants in its memory. The constants may be of type integer, real, or character. Because of the finite word length of the computer, the size of the stored constants is limited. Integer constants contain no decimal point; real constants may be truncated when they are stored, and they may also be written in scientific form (with an exponent); character constants are stored in a string of symbols.

Constants may be associated with variable names. The type of the constant stored in a variable name must be predetermined. This is done either by default typing or by explicitly declaring variable names to be one of the three forms of FORTRAN constants. Variable names are limited to six symbols, must begin with a letter, and may contain only letters and numerals. Storing an integer in a real-type variable name (or vice versa) will cause the type of the numerical value to be altered to fit the variable name. This is called mixed-mode replacement.

Arithmetic operations are effected in FORTRAN by means of the symbols +, −, *, /, and ** (exponentiation). To avoid possible ambiguity, a strict hierarchy code is used for the sequence of these operations (** first, then * or /, finally + or −). Expressions are evaluated by first clearing all parentheses, innermost first, by evaluating the operations within the parentheses according to the hierarchy rule for arithmetic operators. Keep in mind that the computer knows how to add, subtract, multiply, and divide only integers with integers or reals with reals. To multiply an integer by a real, the integer is first converted to a real and the result is then a real number. This is known as mixed-mode arithmetic.

Computer arithmetic differs from ordinary arithmetic in two important ways:

1. Arithmetic operations involving only integers will result in a value that is an integer. This fact is especially significant when dividing one integer by another integer.
2. Real numbers stored in the computer are first converted to a binary form, usually a nonterminating binary fraction. Because the computer has a finite word length, the stored number is often truncated. Thus, real arithmetic is always approximate and prone to round-off error.

Many common mathematical functions are available in FORTRAN programs (see Table 2-3). Although their use is usually obvious, they do provide new sources of potential problems if they are used without care. For example, SQRT(negative number), COS(angle in degrees, not radians), and LOG(integer) are examples of errors in the use of FORTRAN intrinsic mathematical functions.

The READ(*,*)⟨list of variable names⟩ command will read a sequence of values separated by commas and entered at the keyboard and associate those values with the variable names listed after the parentheses. The values entered must match the type of the associated variable name in the list. Constants of type character must be enclosed in quotes when entered. The WRITE(*,*)⟨list of variable names⟩ command will display on the screen the values associated with the variables in the list.

The OPEN (#, FILE='file name') command is used to connect the FORTRAN program to a separate file that has the name of ⟨file name⟩ and that will be identified by the integer (#) within the FORTRAN program. After this command in the FORTRAN program, the file may be read from or written to by replacing the first asterisk in READ(*,*) or WRITE(*,*) by the file identification number. Thus, a program's output may be saved on a permanent file and later printed, edited, or perhaps graphed.

Problems

2.1 What are the limits for numerical values on your computer? From the results of program ZERO, determine the maximum number of digits allowed for a real number. Use a similar procedure to determine the maximum number of digits used by your pocket calculator.

2.2 Execute the following program on your computer:

```
      I = 1000
   1  PRINT *,I
      I = 10.*I
      GO TO 1
      END
```

From the output, determine the maximum number of digits permitted in integer constants. (You cannot use your calculator for this problem; calculators do not have integer arithmetic.)

2.3 **a.** Execute the following program on your computer:

```
      X = 10.
   1  PRINT *,X
      X = 10.*X
      GO TO 1
      END
```

From the output, determine the maximum integer value permitted in the exponent of real constants.

b. Execute a similar program to determine the minimum integer value permitted in the exponent of real constants.

2.4 From the definition of the assignment operator, determine the errors in the following FORTRAN statements.

a. 3.0 = K   **d.** X = 1.0
b. A + B = C   X = Y
c. X = 3.0 = Y   PRINT *, X,Y

2.5 For every computer the arithmetic

$$1000. + EPS \rightarrow 1000.$$

is true provided that the chosen EPS is small enough.

a. If the maximum number of digits on a computer is six, what is the largest value of EPS for which the preceding statement is true? (*Hint*: Write 1000. as 1000.00 and note that EPS = 0.1 means 0.100000.)

b. Use the result from part a to determine the result of

$$EPS + EPS + EPS + \ldots + EPS \quad \text{100 million terms}$$

when EPS = 0.1.

c. Is the result from part b the same as 100 million times EPS (i.e., 10^6*EPS)?

2.6 Identify and correct any FORTRAN grammatical errors (i.e., compilation errors) in the following terms. If there are no errors, write "OK."

a. REAL IJKLMN   **f.** INTEGER X
b. INTEGER REAL   X = 17
    REAL INTEGER   REAL Y
c. INTEGER*5 X,Y   Y = 4.
d. REAL X, Y, Z   **g.** CHARACTER NAME*N, SEX*M
    INTEGER IX,Y   **h.** N = 7
e. INTEGER IX, IY   M = 6
    REAL IX IY   CHARACTER NAME*N,SEX*M
                     i. INTEGER X, REAL Y

2.7 Identify and correct any FORTRAN grammatical errors (i.e., compilation errors) in the following terms. If there are no errors, write "OK."

a. X = 1,000,001.2   g. I = 7./7.1
b. Y = -1.73E-6.2   h. S = X**-2.
c. Z = 61E-06   i. U = (-3.)**.5
d. W = 7   j. V = 16/2./2./2./2.
e. R = 2.E2   k. A = I
f. 6XA = 12.   l. X = X

2.8 Determine the output of the following programs (use your calculator if necessary).

a. I = 2   b. R = 0.07/12.
   J = 3   P = 8000.
   K = I + J   N = 36
   L = I + L + 1   T = 1. + R
   L = L/J/J   T = T**N
   PRINT *,I,J,K,L   T = 1. - 1./T
   STOP   X = R*P/T
   END   PRINT *,'Car Payment = ',X
                                STOP
                                END

c. I = 2   d.   X = 3.
   J = 3   1   Y = 5. + X
   K = I**4   Z = X/Y
   L = 4**(-I)   W = (Y + X)*(Y - X)/Y/Y
   M = (J**I)**4   PRINT *,'x = ',X,' W = ',W
   N = J**(I*4)   PRINT *,'Loan Cost = ',N*X-P
   I = J**(I**4)   STOP
   PRINT *, I,J,K,L,M,N   END
   STOP
   END

2.9 Assuming mixed-mode arithmetic is, for the moment, acceptable, determine the value of the following arithmetic expressions.

a. 1 + 1./5.   e. 28/3/2/3   i. 9.**1./2.
b. 5*4/5   f. 28/3/2./3   j. 3.**9**.5
c. 4/5*5   g. 28/(3/2)/3   k. 27/3**3
d. 4./5*5   h. 4/1+1

2.10 Translate the following algebraic expressions into FORTRAN expressions. Use FORTRAN intrinsic functions where indicated.

a. $\sin[\cos^{-1}(\beta)]$ e. $\tan^2(x/\pi + y)$
b. $e^{\alpha+\beta} - \sin(\alpha - \beta)$ f. $\cos^{-1}(x + |\ln(y)|)$
c. $|a + b|^{-1}c + d$ g. $(x/y)^{n+1}$
d. $\dfrac{x/y + \pi}{\pi - y/x}$

2.11 The following translations of algebra into FORTRAN are incorrect. Write
the correct FORTRAN expressions.

a. $\dfrac{xy}{z+1}$ $\quad\rightarrow\quad$ XY/Z+1

b. x^{n+1} $\quad\rightarrow\quad$ X**N+1

c. $x^{1/2}$ $\quad\rightarrow\quad$ X**1./2.

d. $\cos^{-1}(|\ln(x)|)$ $\quad\rightarrow\quad$ ACOS(LOG(ABS(X)))

e. $x^a x^b$ $\quad\rightarrow\quad$ X**A**B

f. $(x^a)^b$ $\quad\rightarrow\quad$ X**A**B

2.12 The equation for the height of a falling object is

$$y(t) = y_0 + v_0 t - (g/2)t^2$$

where y_0 is the starting height at $t = 0$, v_0 is the starting velocity, and g is
the gravitational acceleration (9.8 m/sec^2). Write a program to read positive values for y_0, v_0, and a value of y that is less than y_0, and then to print
the value of t that satisfies this equation. (You will have to use the
quadratic equation.)

Flow-Control Structures and Program Design

3.1 Introduction

A program normally proceeds from one statement to the next. FORTRAN flow-control structures that may be used to alter this progression in a number of ways include decision structures and loop structures. *Decision structures* compare the values of two quantities and, based on the result, branch to a variety of points in the program. *Loop structures* return to a previous statement and repeat the calculation using different numbers.

This ability to follow diverse paths through a code helps make the computer the useful computational tool that it is. If the program requires only one straight-through pass, the computer is merely duplicating the operations of a simple calculator. In almost all cases it would be more efficient to do the calculations by hand on a calculator.

The step-by-step recipe for solving a problem is called an *algorithm.* Clear, concise, and effective algorithms are the keystone of computer programming. Once an algorithm has been designed, constructing a FORTRAN code to implement it is usually straightforward. A variety of mechanisms are used for preparing computational algorithms. The two most common schemes presently in use, flowcharts and pseudocode, are discussed first. Almost every computational algorithm will involve some form of repetitive calculation built around standard decision structures and loop structures. The details of these two types of procedures are discussed next along with the new FORTRAN statements for their implementation. Since repetitive programs usually have numerous alternate paths, the structure of the program's flow can become quite complicated. A variety of systematic procedures for designing clear and efficient programs have evolved over the last decade in the form of programming style guides. These guidelines are next outlined and suggested to help you maintain clarity and simplicity in your programming. Finally, some alternative forms of FORTRAN flow-control statements are described.

3.2 Using Flowcharts and Pseudocode in Program Design

Constructing programs that employ complicated branchings requires significantly more forethought than was required in the program examples in Chapters 1 and 2. Frequently both reading and writing such code can create considerable confusion, even in the best programmers. The difficulty in such a project is that the computation can no longer be traced straight down from the first line to the END statement: two or more possible alternatives must be considered simultaneously. If faced with similar problems in developing a complicated essay, you would resort to an outline. The outline of a FORTRAN program has been standardized and is called a flowchart. Flowcharts are not always easy to read and are often difficult to alter, especially if the program is quite long; their popularity among professional programmers and engineers has diminished considerably in recent times. An alternative to flowcharts is pseudocode.

Flowcharts

Before you begin to write any moderately complicated program, some sort of flowchart is essential as a guide to the construction of the code. Preparing a neat flowchart is an excellent way to organize your thoughts on a computational algorithm. A flowchart can also be an important part of a program's documentation and is especially useful if you intend to discuss your code with colleagues or your instructor. It is usually much easier to read someone else's flowchart than his or her FORTRAN.

A *flowchart* is a method of diagramming the logic of an algorithm using a standardized set of symbols to indicate the various elements of the program. The most common symbols used in flowcharts are shown in Table 3-1. In a complete flowchart, short messages are ordinarily written within each symbol to explain the current activity. A flowchart should have one *start* and preferably only one *stop*. The logical flow of the algorithm is from top to bottom; alternative paths are indicated by flow lines with arrowheads to indicate the direction of the calculation. You should avoid crossing the flow lines. The merging of two or more computational paths at a point in a program is indicated by the connector symbol, which may also include the statement number of the junction point of the lines in the program.

As an example of a flowchart representation of a simple program, consider the problem of computing the wages for a worker who has worked a given number of hours in a week and is paid at a rate of PAYRAT

Table 3-1
Symbols used in
flowcharting
FORTRAN programs

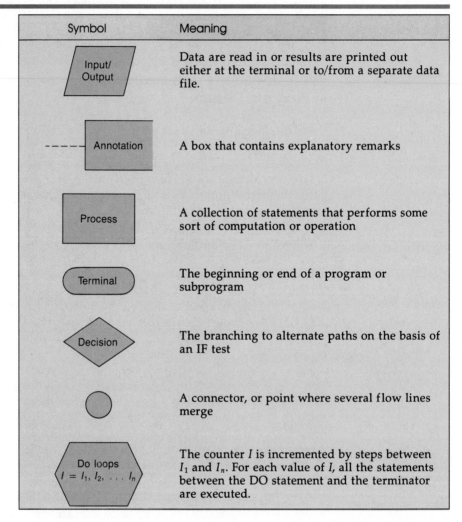

Symbol	Meaning
Input/Output	Data are read in or results are printed out either at the terminal or to/from a separate data file.
Annotation	A box that contains explanatory remarks
Process	A collection of statements that performs some sort of computation or operation
Terminal	The beginning or end of a program or subprogram
Decision	The branching to alternate paths on the basis of an IF test
(connector)	A connector, or point where several flow lines merge
Do loops $I = I_1, I_2, \ldots I_n$	The counter I is incremented by steps between I_1 and I_n. For each value of I, all the statements between the DO statement and the terminator are executed.

in dollars per hour for the first 40 hours and at a higher rate of OVTRAT for time exceeding 40 hours. The flowchart for this rather simple problem is shown in Figure 3-1. The key element of the algorithm is the decision structure represented by the diamond-shaped symbol. At this point the program is expected to compare the value read for hours worked with the number 40. If the hours are more than 40, a calculation of the overtime pay is executed and this result is added to the base pay; otherwise the program skips the overtime computation. In FORTRAN, decision structures are implemented by IF(...)THEN statements, which are discussed in Section 3.3.

More complicated flowcharts are illustrated after the discussion of pseudocode, another method of outlining an algorithm.

Figure 3-1
Flowchart for a
simple program

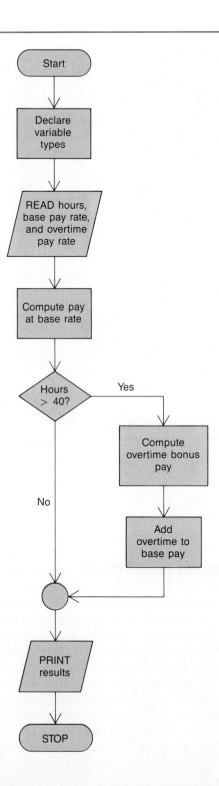

■■■■ Pseudocode Outlines of Computational Algorithms

Before a program can be written, the problem to be solved must be mapped out and some form of outline constructed. One procedure for doing this is the flowchart. However, a great many scientists and engineers who write complicated programs feel that flowcharts are too formal and artificial for a preliminary draft and resort instead to a highly informal procedure called *pseudocode*. The idea is to describe the operation of the program using a simplified mix of FORTRAN and English. Because pseudocode is a response to the rigidity of flowcharts, few rules govern its use. Basically, you write out the operation of the program using minimal English and FORTRAN phrases, which are capitalized. A separate line is used for each distinct segment of the code. It is also a good idea to indent subsegments as in an ordinary outline. A pseudocode outline of the salary problem follows:

```
READ in hours worked, base pay rate, and overtime rate
Echo PRINT
Compute pay using base rate
        PAY = PAYRAT*HOURS
IF (hours worked > 40) THEN
        Multiply excess of 40 by overtime bonus rate
                (HOURS − 40) * (OVTRAT − PAYRAT)
        Add to base pay
ELSE
        Skip overtime computation
PRINT pay
STOP
```

In this form of outline, the decision structure in the program is indicated by the English words IF and ELSE. This form closely resembles the actual FORTRAN implementation of the algorithm, as described in Section 3.3.

■■■■■■■ **3.3 Decision Structures in FORTRAN**

In addition to the elementary arithmetic operations, the ALU in the computer is designed to compare two items and execute instructions based on that comparison. In the most elementary type of comparison, the two items are either the same or not the same. To facilitate the construction of comparison tests that are easy to read and understand, a new form of expression, in addition to arithmetic and character expressions, has been added to FORTRAN. It is called the *logical expression,* and it constitutes the central ingredient in decision structures. Logical expressions are employed in logical IF tests and logical block IF structures. The logical IF test, a short form of the logical block IF structure, is discussed in Section 3.6.

Logical Block IF Structures

The FORTRAN structure that is the keystone of all decision procedures is the logical block IF structure, which takes the following form:

IF (⟨logical expression⟩) THEN

> This set or block of FORTRAN statements will be executed only if the logical expression is evaluated as true.

ENDIF

IF the logical expression is true, THEN
the block of FORTRAN statements is executed.

IF the logical expression is false, THEN
the block of statements is ignored and the program proceeds to the next statement after the ENDIF.

The IF(...)THEN occupies one line, and the FORTRAN statements that constitute the execution block appear on subsequent lines. The block of statements to be executed conditionally must be followed by the statement ENDIF. The ENDIF statement should not have a statement number. Also, for every IF(...)THEN there must be a corresponding ENDIF. To improve the readability of the code, the block of FORTRAN statements is usually indented from the IF(...)THEN and the ENDIF.

Logical Expressions

The action of the IF statement depends on the definition of the logical expression. A logical expression is built up from combinations of one or more relational expressions of the form

$$a_1 \, op \, a_2$$

where a_1 and a_2 are arithmetic expressions, variables, constants, or character strings; in short, things that have values that can be compared. The "op" is a relational logic operator belonging to the following set:

Relational Logic Operator	Meaning
.EQ.	Equal to
.NE.	Not equal to
.LT.	Less than
.LE.	Less than or equal to
.GT.	Greater than
.GE.	Greater than or equal to

The periods are part of the operator and must always be present. A relational expression must have a value of ⟨true⟩ or ⟨false⟩.[1] The simplest logical expression consists of a single relational expression like

    12 .GT. 6   This expression has a value of ⟨true⟩.

A logical expression may then be incorporated in an IF block structure, as in

```
IF(TEMP .GT. 450.)THEN
    PRINT *,'Steam temperature dangerously high'
    STOP
ENDIF
```

More complex logical expressions can be built up by combining two or more relational expressions by means of the following combinational operators:

Combinational Logic Operator	Meaning
.OR.	Or
.AND.	And
.NOT.	Not (Changes a value ⟨true⟩ into a value ⟨false⟩ and vice versa)

The evaluation of logical expressions is fairly transparent, as can be seen from the following examples.

1. If the variable SIZE has previously been assigned the value 12.0, then the expression

    SIZE .LT. 100.0

has a value of ⟨true⟩.

2. All arithmetic operations are processed before the logical expression is evaluated. Thus

    SIZE .LT. 10.*SQRT(100.)

has the same value as the previous expression.

3. Parentheses may be added for clarity or to alter the value of the expression.

    (SIZE-6.) .LT. (10.*SQRT(100.) - 50.)

---

[1] In addition to the data types real, integer, and character, FORTRAN permits values of type logical. Logical variables may only have a value of .TRUE. or .FALSE. (Again, the periods are part of the expression.) The FORTRAN values are indicated in the text as ⟨true⟩, ⟨false⟩. Logical variables are described in more detail in Section 9.1.

4. Logical subexpressions may be combined by using the operators .AND. and .OR. and are then evaluated according to the following rules:

⟨true⟩.AND.⟨true⟩ = ⟨true⟩

⟨true⟩.AND.⟨false⟩ = ⟨false⟩

That is, the entire expression is ⟨false⟩ if either side of the .AND. is ⟨false⟩.

⟨true⟩.OR.⟨false⟩ = ⟨true⟩

⟨false⟩.OR.⟨false⟩ = ⟨false⟩

The entire expression is ⟨true⟩ if either side of the .OR. is ⟨true⟩. For example, if the variables A and B have values 2. and 8., respectively, then

```
A.GT.6. .AND. 2.*B.LT.20.
```
Is evaluated as ⟨false⟩ .AND. ⟨true⟩, which is then ⟨false⟩

```
A*B.EQ.0. .OR. A.LT.0.
```
Is evaluated as ⟨false⟩ .OR. ⟨false⟩, which is then ⟨false⟩

A New Hierarchy Rule

Because processing complicated logical expressions can lead to ambiguities, another hierarchy rule is required in addition to those used in ordinary arithmetic (see Section 2.5).

> A logical expression is evaluated by first processing all arithmetic expressions. Then the logic operators are processed scanning left to right. The subexpressions are combined (the .AND. and .OR. operators processed) from left to right, with the .AND.s processed *before* the .OR.s.

Consider the meaning of the following rather complicated logical statement:

```
I.EQ.10 .OR. X.LT.1. .AND. Z.GE.0.0
```

This statement could also be written as

```
(I.EQ.10) .OR. (X.LT.1.) .AND. (Z.GE.0.0)
```

and has the same meaning as

```
(I.EQ.10) .OR. ((X.LT.1.) .AND. (Z.GE.0.0))
```

That is, .AND. is done before .OR. If the values assigned to the variables are

```
I = 10
X =  0.
Z = -1.
```

the expression reads

⟨⟨true⟩ .OR. (⟨true⟩.AND.⟨false⟩))

Since ⟨true⟩.AND.⟨false⟩ = ⟨false⟩, this expression is equivalent to

⟨true⟩.OR.⟨false⟩

which has a value of ⟨true⟩. The expression forcing .OR. before .AND. has a different meaning:

```
((I.EQ.10) .OR. (X.LT.1.)) .AND. (Z.GE.0.0)
```

Using the same values for the variables, this expression is equivalent to

(((⟨true⟩.OR.⟨true⟩) .AND. ⟨false⟩))

or

(⟨true⟩ .AND. ⟨false⟩))

and in this case the expression has a value of ⟨false⟩.

Potential Pitfalls

When using logical IF tests, two "rules" will help you avoid some commonly made errors:

1. Never test for the equality of real numbers obtained from computation. The reason for not doing this is because of the approximate nature of the arithmetic operations involving finite word length representations of real numbers. For example, if

   ```
   A = 2.
   B = SQRT(2.)
   B = B**2
   IF(A .EQ. B)THEN
        STOP
   ENDIF
   ```

   the test may possibly fail since B could have been assigned the value 1.9999999.

2. If it is necessary to test whether a quantity is smaller than some very small number, say EPS, the form of the test should never be

   ```
   IF(X .LT. EPS)THEN
   ```

but rather

```
IF(ABS(X) .LT. EPS)THEN
```

The point is that X might be negative, and any negative number, regardless of size, would satisfy the first IF test. The test for the equality of the two reals, A and B, should then possibly read

```
IF(ABS(A-B) .LT. EPS)THEN
```

Several other forms of IF statements are discussed in Section 3.6. However, all of the additional features they represent can be duplicated by combinations of block IF structures. And more important, these alternate forms of the IF test date from earlier versions of FORTRAN and are partly responsible for generating FORTRAN code that is difficult to read and even more difficult to change or correct. Whenever possible the decision structures in a program should employ IF(...)THEN statements.

Examples of IF(...)THEN–END IF Structures

An important part of any program is the error diagnostic. As will be discussed in Section 3.4, many programs are designed to monitor the behavior of some function and, if the calculation proceeds as anticipated, print the result. If problems develop during the calculation, the program should be written so that it will flag the error and take some action. For example,

```
IF(VOLTGE .GT. 125. .OR. VOLTGE .LT. 105.)THEN
    PRINT *,'Danger Warning'
    PRINT *,'Voltage outside acceptable limits'
    STOP
ENDIF
```

This test could not be written as

```
IF(VOLTGE .GT. 125. .OR. .LT. 105.)THEN      Incorrect
```

Because the logical expression has two operators side by side (.OR. .LT.), the statement will lead to a compilation-time error. An analogous statement that will not lead to compilation errors but that is also incorrect is to write the test for I = 0 or I = 10 as

```
IF(I. EQ. 0 .OR. 10)THEN      Incorrect
```

Both sides of the .OR. operator must have a value of either ⟨true⟩ or ⟨false⟩; in this case the value of the expression on the right is 10.[2]

---

[2] The results of this statement are unpredictable. In a proper logical expression, both sides of the .OR. operator must be either ⟨true⟩ or ⟨false⟩. Here, one side is "10." Because most compilers will not permit mixing character variables and real numbers in a comparison, this statement will lead to a compilation error. However, other compilers may first check only one side of an .OR. and if it is ⟨true⟩ ignore the other side. (If either side is ⟨true⟩, the expression is ⟨true⟩.) A similar operation will occur if either side of an .AND. is ⟨false⟩.

Another alternative is simply to flag the errant condition and continue:

```
REAL BALANC, WITHDR
INTEGER FLAG
FLAG = 1
IF(BALANC - WITHDR .LT. 0.0)THEN
     FLAG   = 0
     WITHDR = 0.0
ENDIF
     ...        ...
     ...        ...

IF(FLAG .EQ. 0)THEN
     PRINT *,'Insufficient funds'
     STOP
ENDIF
```

The FORTRAN code for calculating the overtime pay discussed in Section 3.2 may now be constructed by using the IF block, as illustrated in Figure 3-2. Notice the similarity between the actual FORTRAN and the pseudocode version of the program.

The block IF could also be used to convert a number in radian measure to an angle θ between 0 and 360°. The number must first be scaled

Figure 3-2

IF block used to calculate overtime pay

```
PROGRAM PAY
REAL PAY, PAYRAT, OVTRAT, OVRTYM, HOURS
READ *, HOURS
*
*  First compute the base pay based on the base hourly pay rate
*
   PAY = PAYRAT*HOURS
*
*  If more than 40 hours, compute overtime bonus at higher rate
*  for excess hours
*
   IF(HOURS .GT. 40.)THEN
*
*              Add overtime pay to base pay
*
       OVRTYM = (HOURS - 40.)*(OVTRAT - PAYRAT)
*
*              And add overtime pay to base pay
*
       PAY = PAY + OVRTYM
ENDIF
PRINT *,'Hours worked       = ',HOURS
PRINT *,'Base pay rate      = ',PAYRAT
PRINT *,'Overtime pay rate  = ',OVTRAT
PRINT *.'        Net pay    = ',PAY,' dollars'
PRINT *,'of which ',OVRTYM,' dollars was overtime pay.'
STOP
END
```

so that it is between 0 and 2π by subtracting integer multiples of 2π. (See Figure 3-3.)

IF(...)THEN–ELSE Structure

Frequently, an algorithm will have two computational branches as a result of a logical IF test. If the condition is ⟨true⟩, a complete block of statements is to be executed; if ⟨false⟩, an alternate set of statements is to be executed. You could easily accomplish this operation using two block IF structures. However, an additional option in the block IF structure enables you to construct a code that is easier to read and, more important, ties together the two related branches into one structure. This option is the ELSE statement, which is placed between the IF(...)THEN and the ENDIF.

IF(⟨logical expression⟩)THEN

      This block of FORTRAN statements will be executed only if the logical expression is evaluated as true.

ELSE

      This block of FORTRAN statements will be executed only if the logical expression is evaluated as false.

ENDIF

Figure 3-3
IF block used to convert a radian measure to an angle

```
      REAL THETA, RADIAN, PI
      INTEGER MULTPL
      PI = ACOS(-1.)
      PRINT *,'Enter angle in radians'
      READ  *, RADIAN
*
*  The variable MULTPL is the integer number of 2 PI multiples
*  in RADIANS.  This next statement involves intentional mixed-mode
*  replacement.
*
      MULTPL = RADIAN/(2.*PI)
      IF(MULTPL .GT. 0)THEN
*
*         Subtract this multiple of 2 PI's from the angle
*         RADIAN.  The next statement employs intentional
*         mixed-mode arithmetic.
*
          RADIAN = RADIAN - MULTPL*2.*PI
      ENDIF
*
*  Convert the radian measure to degrees.
*
      THETA = RADIAN*360./(2.*PI)
      PRINT *.RADIAN,' radians = ',THETA,' degrees'
      STOP
      END
```

As with ENDIF, the ELSE statement occupies a line all by itself and should not have a statement number.

Consider the problem of writing an algorithm to find the smallest-magnitude real root (if any) of the quadratic equation

$$ax^2 + bx + c$$

The nature of the root depends on the value of the discriminant, $\Delta = b^2 - 4ac$.

If	Then

$\Delta > 0$ Two real and distinct roots:

$$x_+ = \frac{1}{2a}(-b + \Delta^{1/2})$$

$$x_- = \frac{1}{2a}(-b - \Delta^{1/2})$$

$\Delta = 0$ Two real roots, both identical:

$$x_- = x_+ = -\frac{b}{2a}$$

$\Delta < 0$ Two complex and distinct roots:

$$x_+ = \frac{1}{2a}[-b + i(-\Delta)^{1/2}]$$
$$i = (-1)^{1/2}$$
$$x_- = \frac{1}{2a}[-b - i(-\Delta)^{1/2}]$$

To compute the smallest-magnitude real root of a quadratic with coefficients a, b, and c, the program will have to first compute the discriminant Δ. If Δ is negative, the program will print a message (complex roots) and stop. If Δ is not negative (including the case $\Delta = 0$), the smallest-magnitude root is

$$\frac{1}{2a}(-b + \Delta^{1/2}) \qquad \text{if } b \text{ is positive}$$

$$\frac{1}{2a}(-b - \Delta^{1/2}) \qquad \text{if } b \text{ is negative}$$

The flowchart for this problem is shown in Figure 3-4, and the FORTRAN program is given in Figure 3-5. This code contains two nested IF blocks. The inner IF block is completely contained within the outer IF block, and for each IF(...)THEN there is one corresponding ENDIF. IF blocks may be

Figure 3-4
Flowchart for
computing the
smallest-magnitude
real root of a
quadratic

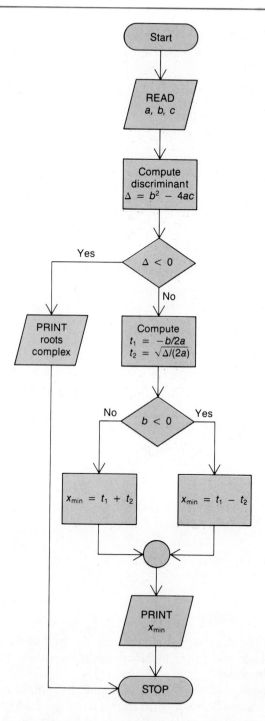

Figure 3-5
FORTRAN program
for computing the
smallest-magnitude
real root of a
quadratic

```
      PROGRAM QUAD
      REAL A,B,C,DISCR,T1,T2,XMIN
      PRINT *,'Enter the coefficients of the quadratic: a,b,c'
      READ  *,A,B,C
*
*  Compute the discriminant
*
      DISCR = B*B - 4.*A*C
*
*  Test for complex roots
*
      IF(DISCR .LT. 0.0)THEN
         PRINT *,'Both roots are complex'
      ELSE
*
*         If not zero, define the two terms t1, t2
*
         T1 = -B.2./A
         T2 = SQRT(DISCR)/2./A
*
*           The minimum root depends on the sign of b
*
         IF(B .LT. 0.)THEN
            XMIN = T1 + T2
         ELSE
            XMIN = T1 - T2
         ENDIF
         PRINT *,'Smallest-magnitude real root = ',XMIN
      ENDIF
      STOP
      END
```

nested in this manner, one inside the other, but they must never overlap.

```
      IF(A .LT. 0.)THEN
         . . .
         . . .
      IF(B .GT. 0.)THEN
            . . .
            . . .
   ENDIF
            . . .
            . . .
      ENDIF
```

In spite of the suggestive indentations, the first ENDIF is paired with the inner IF block, and thus the code will not execute in the manner that was probably intended.

The algorithm used to determine the roots of a quadratic has three natural branches depending on the value of the discriminant $b^2 - 4ac$, and even though the program will correctly handle the third possibility, that of $\Delta = 0$, to avoid confusion it is best to use a decision structure better suited to a situation with more than two alternatives. A further option available in the block IF structure is designed to handle multiple paths as the result of an IF test: the ELSE IF structure.

ELSE IF Statement

Frequently, the possible branches of a computational algorithm are more numerous than the two permitted in a true-false test. To accommodate these cases the ELSE IF structure is used. It is best explained by an example. The code for the roots of the quadratic may be written using the ELSE IF structure in the following way:

```
READ *,A,B,C
DISCR = B**2 - 4.*A*C
IF(DISCR .GT. 0.)THEN
    ...
    ...

ELSEIF(DISCR .EQ. 0.)THEN
    ...
    ...

ELSE
    ...        These statements are executed only if both IF tests fail.
    ...

ENDIF
```

Notice that the ELSEIF(...)THEN is not paired with an ENDIF. Also, as with the simple ELSE, the ELSEIF(...)THEN is on a line by itself. An unlimited number of ELSEIFs may be placed within the block IF structure.

As a second example of nested block IFs with multiple alternatives, consider the problem of determining whether three lengths a, b, and c can form a triangle, and if so, whether the triangle is isosceles or equilateral.

Three lengths a, b, and c can form a triangle if

$$|a - b| < c < a + b$$

The triangle is isosceles if

$$a = b \quad \text{or} \quad a = c \quad \text{or} \quad b = c$$

The triangle is equilateral if

$$a = b \quad \text{and} \quad a = c \quad \text{and} \quad b = c$$

The program for this problem will have to make multiple comparisons and account for several possibilities. The flowchart for the solution is shown in Figure 3-6, and the FORTRAN program is given in Figure 3-7.

Figure 3-6
Flowchart to
determine whether
three sides can
form a triangle and
then if the triangle
is isosceles or
equilateral

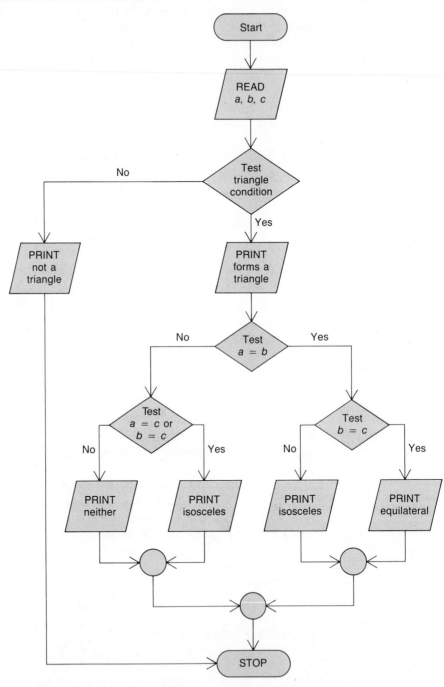

Figure 3-7
Program to
determine if a
triangle is isosceles
or equilateral

```
PRINT *,'Enter test sides a, b, c'
READ  *, A, B, C
PRINT *,' Sides a = ',A
PRINT *,'       b = ',B
PRINT *,'       c = ',C
IF((ABS(A-B) .LE. C) .AND. (C .LE. A+B))THEN
     PRINT *,' can indeed form a triangle that is'
     IF(A .EQ. B)THEN
          PRINT *,'   Isosceles'
          IF(B .EQ. C)THEN
               PRINT *,'   and equilateral'
          ENDIF
     ELSEIF((A.EQ.C) .OR. (B.EQ.C))THEN
          PRINT *,'   Isosceles'
     ELSE
          PRINT *,'   neither isosceles nor equilateral'
     ENDIF
ELSE
     PRINT *,' can not form a triangle.'
ENDIF
*
     IF(B .LT. 0.)THEN
          XMIN = T1 + T2
     ELSE
          XMIN = T1 - T2
     ENDIF
     PRINT *,'Smallest-magnitude real root = ',XMIN
ENDIF
STOP
END
```

3.4 Loop Structures in FORTRAN

Perhaps the most common and useful computational structure in programming is the *loop structure,* wherein a block of statements is executed and the block is then simply repeated with some of the parameters changed. The formal construction for operations of this type is a loop structure called a *DoWhile* loop structure. DoWhile loops have four characteristics:

1. An entry point (the top) labeled as DoWhile(...).
2. An execution block. The body of the loop containing the block of FORTRAN statements to be conditionally repeated.
3. A normal exit point (the bottom) labeled as EndDo. [In some cases it may be necessary to leave the loop before completion. This exit is accomplished by means of an IF(...)THEN and a GO TO structure. However, because all uses of the GO TO statement are contrary to modern programming guidelines, this alternative should be avoided if possible.]
4. Loop control specifications. Conditions on a parameter that determine when the cycling of the loop is to be terminated. These conditions will be part of the specifications required in the DoWhile entry point statement.

FORTRAN 77 does not currently contain specific DoWhile or EndDo statements for constructing loop structures. At present, loop structures in FORTRAN are constructed by using three new FORTRAN statements: the DO loop, the CONTINUE statement, and the GO TO, which are explained in the next section. Even though a program cannot be written in standard FORTRAN 77 using DoWhile and EndDo statements, loop structures are more easily understood when expressed in terms of these ideas. For this reason these statements have become more or less standard in pseudocode outlines of a program even though they do not exist as actual FORTRAN statements. Fortunately, it is easy to combine existing FORTRAN statements to accomplish the objectives of the missing statements. Future revisions of FORTRAN will almost certainly add the DoWhile and the EndDo to the vocabulary. A substantial number of local installations of FORTRAN 77 have augmented the language to include the DoWhile/EndDo statements. In these situations the FORTRAN employed is usually called "Extended FORTRAN." (See also Section 9.4.)

FORTRAN Implementation of DoWhile Structures

DO-Loop Structure

Loop structures are currently implemented in FORTRAN by means of a DO-loop structure. A *DO-loop structure* is a block of statements with an entry point (the top) and a normal exit point (the bottom). The beginning line of a DO loop has the following general form:

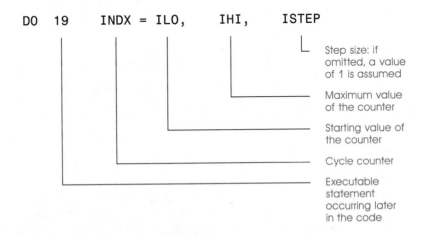

```
DO   19    INDX = ILO,    IHI,    ISTEP
```

Step size: if omitted, a value of 1 is assumed

Maximum value of the counter

Starting value of the counter

Cycle counter

Executable statement occurring later in the code

All FORTRAN statements beginning with the DO statement down to and including the DO terminator (here statement 19) are executed first with the index INDX = ILO. The loop is then repeated with INDX = ILO + ISTEP, and so on until the maximum value is reached. The terminal statement of the DO loop must be an executable statement, but it cannot be any of the following:

```
GO TO    Unconditional
IF       Arithmetic
ELSE
ELSEIF
STOP
END
DO
```

If the terminator is a logical IF, it must not contain a DO, another IF (block or logical), ELSE, ELSE IF, END, or END IF. Rather than attempt to remember these rules, you can use a FORTRAN statement whose primary purpose is to serve as the terminator of DO loops. This statement is the CONTINUE statement, which has the simple form

⟨statement number⟩   CONTINUE

CONTINUE Statement

The CONTINUE statement in FORTRAN is an executable statement that performs no operation and is used primarily as a marker for the end of a DO loop. It may also be used as the target of a GO TO (see the next subsection). The CONTINUE statement should have a statement number label. Because FORTRAN 77 does not have an EndDO statement in its vocabulary, the CONTINUE statement is used in its place. An example of its use in a DoWhile structure is given below.

Pseudocode	**FORTRAN**
Print a table of x, sin(x),	PROGRAM TABLE
and cos(x) for $0 \le x \le \pi$.	REAL X
First print table headings	PRINT *,' X SIN(X) COS(X)'
	DX = 0.1
DoWhile($0 \le x \le \pi$)	DO 1 X = 0.0,3.14159, DX
PRINT *, x,sin(x),cos(x)	X = INDX*DX
Increment x by 0.1	PRINT *,X,SIN(X),COS(X)
EndDo	1 CONTINUE

This program will produce 31 lines of values for the sine and cosine. The calculation starts with x = 0 and prints a line of the table. The value of x is then incremented by the step size, 0.1, and the next line is computed and printed. This operation is repeated until the specified limits in the DO-loop statement are satisfied.

```
    X          SIN(X)       COS(X)
0.0000000    0.0000000    1.0000000
0.1000000    0.0998334    0.9950042
0.2000000    0.1986693    0.9800666

2.8999999    0.2392499   -0.9709580
2.9999999    0.1411207   -0.9899924
3.0999999    0.0415815   -0.9991351
```

The index range parameters, ILO, IHI, and ISTEP, may be either integer or real constants, variables, or expressions. The indexing variable INDEX may also be integer or real; however, whenever possible, integer values should be used exclusively. In the output above notice that the values of X printed at the end of the calculation are not precisely multiples of 0.1. This result again is because of the approximate nature of real-type arithmetic on a computer and illustrates the reason for using only integer variables for the cycle counter.

The DO-loop structure has a built-in test for completion of the loop.[3] After completing the DO loop, the index parameter is officially "undefined" in standard FORTRAN, but with most compilers it will retain its most recent value. A few examples of DO statements are given in Table 3-2.

Table 3-2
Examples of DO
statements

DO Statement	Number of Cycles Executed	Comments
DO 44 I = 1,5	5	
DO 73 K = 5,1	0	
DO 73 K = 5,1,-1	5	Negative steps
DO 11 M = 1,9,3	3	
DO 15 X = 1.,4.,0.8	4	
DO 15 M = 1.,4.,0.8	None (execution-time error; zero step not allowed)	The loop limits are first converted to the type of M, so this statement is the same as DO 15 M = 1, 4, 0
DO 91 R = SQRT(2.),5	4	

---

[3] The test for completion is at the beginning of the loop in FORTRAN 77. The compiler will compute how many cycles will be required to complete the loop conditions and will execute this many cycles even if the loop conditions are changed within the loop itself. Thus in DO 4 I = 5,4 zero cycles will be executed. The program will skip the DO loop. See the second example in Table 3-2.

The following list contains some examples of DO-loop structures:

1. Factorials, $n! = n(n - 1)(n - 2)\ldots2 \times 1$

```
INTEGER N, FACT
READ *,N
FACT = N
DO 2 I = N-1, 1, -1
    FACT = FACT*I
2   CONTINUE
```

2. Binomial coefficients. The expansion of $(a \times b)^n$ can be found in any book of numerical tables under the binomial theorem.

$$(a + b)^n = a^n + na^{n-1}b + \frac{n(n - 1)}{2!}a^{n-2}b^2$$

$$+ \cdots + \frac{n!}{(n - s)!\,s!}a^{n-s}b^s + \cdots + b^n$$

For example,

$$(a + b)^5 = a^5 + 5a^4b + 10a^3b^2 + 10a^2b^3 + 5ab^4 + b^5$$

The coefficient of the general term

$$C_i = \frac{n!}{(n - i)!\,i!}$$

can be determined as follows. First show that the ratio of successive coefficients, C_{i+1}/C_i, is given by

$$\frac{C_{i+1}}{C_i} = \frac{n!}{(n - i - 1)!\,(i + 1)!} \times \frac{(n - i)!\,i!}{n!} = \frac{(n - i)}{(i + 1)}$$

[*Note*: $(i + 1)! = (i + 1)i!$] Thus, if we know one of the coefficients, C_i, we can obtain the next, C_{i+1}, by

$$C_{i+1} = \frac{(n - i)}{(i + 1)}C_i$$

The FORTRAN code to determine the binomial coefficients is then

```
PRINT *,'Enter Degree = '
READ *,N
C = 1.
PRINT *,'Binomial Coefficients for N = ',N
PRINT *,'  i          C-s'
DO 1 I = 0, N-1
    C  = C*(N-I)/(I+1.)
```

```
      *
      *     What is the purpose of the period after the 1?
      *
                IC = C
                PRINT *,I+1,IC
   1        CONTINUE
```

The output of this program for $n = 15$ is then

```
            Enter Degree N =
            Binomial Coefficients for N =   15
                 i            C-s'
                 1              1
                 2             15
                 3            105
                 4            455
                 5           1365
                 6           3003
                 7           5005
                 8           6435
                 9           6435
                10           5005
                11           3003
                12           1365
                13            455
                14            105
                15             15
```

3. A table of the speed of sound in air. The temperature dependence of the speed of sound in air is given approximately by the expression

$$v = 331(1 + T/273)^{1/2} \qquad \text{(m/sec)}$$

where T is expressed in °C. If we are interested in obtaining values for the sound velocity for temperatures in the range $20° \le T \le 35° \text{C}$ in steps of $1° \text{C}$, the FORTRAN code would be

```
PROGRAM SOUND
REAL T, V
*
PRINT *,'  Temperature        Sound '        First print a
PRINT *,'    (deg-C)       speed (m/sec)'     heading for the
*                                             table to follow.
DO 1 T = 20., 35., 1.                         The PRINT for the
    V = SQRT(1. + T/273.)                     table heading
    PRINT *,T,V                               must be outside
1   CONTINUE                                  the loop.
STOP
END
```

Abnormal Exits from a DO Loop: GO TO Statements

Frequently, you may wish to terminate a loop structure before the total number of cycles is executed. This termination is usually done with a logical IF and an unconditional GO TO.

Unconditional GO TO

The form of the unconditional GO TO statement is

GO TO ⟨statement number⟩

where ⟨statement number⟩ is the statement number of an executable statement. The effect of this statement is to transfer control of the program to the statement bearing the indicated statement number, which may be any executable statement in the program, coming either before or after the GO TO. (See Figure 3-8.)

Figure 3-8
Program using
GO TO statements
to alter the flow of
a program

```
* A program to count the number of students who pass a quiz,
* that is, score 60 or above.  The total number of quiz scores
* is less than 100.  The end of the list is marked by entering
* a negative value for the latest score.
*
          NTOT  = 0
          NPASS = 0
     1    DO 3 I = 1,100
             PRINT *,'Enter next quiz score'
     2       READ  *,SCORE
             NTOT = NTOT + 1
             IF(SCORE.GT.100.)THEN
                PRINT *,'Input Error'
                PRINT *,'You entered a score greater than 100'
                PRINT *,'Re-enter the correct value'
                NTOT = NTOT - 1
                GO TO 2
             ELSEIF(SCORE .GE. 60.)THEN
                NPASS = NPASS + 1
             ELSEIF(SCORE .LT. 0.)THEN
                GO TO 99
             ENDIF
     3    CONTINUE
    99    PRINT *,'The number of students who passed was ',NPASS
          PRINT *,'out of ',NTOT
          STOP
          END
```

> Unrestrained use of the GO TO statement is the primary cause of FORTRAN code that resembles spaghetti: numerous branchings up and down in a program that result in code that is unreadable and unalterable.[4] Be extremely conservative in using this statement.

The code in Figure 3-8 can be easily rewritten without any GO TO statements, as shown in Figure 3-9. The improvement to this program is minimal, but for larger programs the effect can be significant. Notice in Figure 3-9 that there are two distinct terminal paths: one for a successful calculation and the other for a program failure. Upon execution of the corresponding STOP statement, the program will additionally print either of the words "success" or "failure."

Figure 3-9
Program in
Figure 3-8 rewritten,
eliminating all
GO TO statements

```
* A program to count the number of students who pass a quiz.
* It is assumed that there are fewer than 100 students taking
* the quiz.  This program avoids using GO TO statements.
*
          NTOT  = 0
          NPASS = 0
          DO 2 I = 1,100
             PRINT *,'Enter next quiz score'
             READ  *,SCORE
             NTOT = NTOT + 1
             IF(SCORE.GT.100.)THEN
                   PRINT *,'Input error'
                   PRINT *,'Entered score out of range 0 - 100'
                   PRINT *,'Re-enter the score carefully'
                   READ  *,SCORE
                   IF(SCORE .GT. 100.)THEN
                       PRINT *,'It is still out of range'
                       PRINT *,'Two tries is all you get'
                       STOP 'Failure'
                   ENDIF
             ELSEIF(SCORE .GE. 60.)THEN
                NPASS = NPASS + 1
             ELSEIF(SCORE .LT. 0.0)THEN
                PRINT *,'Number passed was ',NPASS,' out of ',NTOT
                STOP 'Success'
             ENDIF
       2     CONTINUE
             END
```

---

[4] A word of explanation about this criticism of GO TO statements: The objection is not primarily with the GO TO statement itself but rather with the targets of the GO TO, which are labeled statements distributed anywhere in the code. When reading the code there is no ambiguity as to the progression of the program following a GO TO. However, when you come across a labeled FORTRAN statement other than a CONTINUE, you are forced to assume that it is the target of a GO TO located somewhere else, and thus you must search the entire program to determine exactly how the program got to this point. In a long or complicated program, this can be extremely difficult and frustrating.

Keep in mind the following points when using DO-loop structures:

- When exiting a DO loop before completion, the value of the index parameter is the last value assigned.
- Never branch from outside a DO loop to statements within a DO loop. The counter will most likely not have an assigned value.
- Never redefine the DO-loop index within the loop. Also, it is not possible to alter the DO-loop limits from within the loop.[5]
- To improve the readability of DO loops, indent the body of the loop in a manner similar to block IF statements.

Nested DO Loops

When one DO loop is entirely contained within another DO loop, the grouping is called a *DO-loop nesting*. Nesting of DO loops to any depth is permitted, provided each inner loop is entirely within the range of the next-level outer loop. Basically, this rule ensures that the execution of the inner loop is completed before moving on to the next step of the outer loop. An inner loop and an outer loop may, however, share a terminal statement. A few examples of allowable nestings are shown in Figure 3-10.

Figure 3-10
Examples of allowable nested DO loops

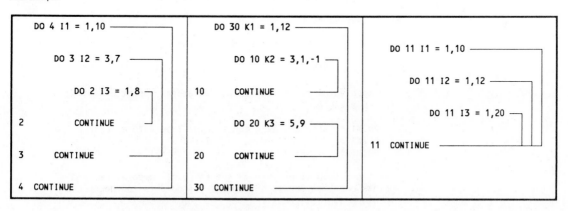

```
DO 4 I1 = 1,10

    DO 3 I2 = 3,7

        DO 2 I3 = 1,8

2           CONTINUE

3       CONTINUE

4   CONTINUE
```

```
DO 30 K1 = 1,12

    DO 10 K2 = 3,1,-1

10      CONTINUE

    DO 20 K3 = 5,9

20      CONTINUE

30  CONTINUE
```

```
DO 11 I1 = 1,10

    DO 11 I2 = 1,12

        DO 11 I3 = 1,20

11          CONTINUE
```

---

[5] The potential number of cycles of the DO loop is ordinarily computed by the compiler at the very beginning of the loop from the index range parameters in the DO statement. And, except for abnormal exits from the loop, that many cycles are executed even if the index range parameters are changed within the loop. Attempts to change the index parameter itself will result in a compilation-time error.

For each cycle of an outer loop, the inner loops are completely executed. Thus

```
DO 2 I = 0,9
    DO 2 J = 0,9
        PRINT *,J + 10*I
2   CONTINUE
```

will print the integers from 0 to 99 in order.

A common use of nested DO loops is to compute and print a series of tables; that is, for each value of the outer-loop parameter, a table of values is computed, one line of numbers for each value of the inner-loop parameter. This process is then repeated for the next value of the outer-loop parameter. For example, the equation of state for an ideal gas is $PV = nRT$, where P is the pressure (n/m^2), V the volume (m^3), T the temperature (K), n the number of moles, and $R = 8.3144$ (J/mol K). [*Note:* Temperature in degrees Celsius is related to the Kelvin temperature by $(T)_K = (T)_C + 273$.] The program to print a sequence of tables of pressure for various ranges of volume and temperature for a fixed number of moles of ideal gas is shown in Figure 3-11.

Figure 3-11 _____

Program to produce a sequence of tables of ideal gas pressure as a function of temperature for a variety of volumes

```
        PROGRAM GASTBL
*
        INTEGER TC
        REAL P,V,T,R,N
        N = 1.0
        R = 8.3144
*
*   Print overall headings outside of all loops
*
        PRINT *,'Pressure of a container of ',N,' moles of ideal gas.'
*
*   Outer loop is the volume of the container, from 0.1 to 0.5 m^3
*
        DO 2 V = 0.1, 0.5, 0.1
*
*       For each value of the outer loop parameter, print a heading
*       for this table.
*
            PRINT *,'Pressure as a function of Temperature for V = ',V
            PRINT *,'    P (n/m^2)        T (K)  '
            PRINT *,'  -------------    -------------'
*
*       The inner loop steps through the range of temperatures and
*       prints one line for each value of T from 0 to 100 degrees C
*       in steps of 10 degrees.
*
            DO 1 TC = 0, 100, 10
                T = TC + 273.
                P = N*R*T/V
                PRINT *,P,T
1           CONTINUE
2       CONTINUE
        STOP
        END
```

■ Further Examples of Loop Structures: Repetitive Programs

Sample Program: Auto Loans

When buying a new car, some of us must borrow money. If the amount of money borrowed is P, the yearly interest rate is R for Y years, and the payments are monthly, then the amount of the monthly payment, PAYMNT is given by

$$\text{PAYMNT} = rP\frac{l}{1 - 1/(l + r)^n}$$

where r is the monthly interest rate ($r = R/12$) and n is the total number of installments ($n = 12Y$).

The problem is to write a program to calculate the PAYMNT and the total cost of the loan for all possible combinations of

$$Y = 2, 2\tfrac{1}{2}, 3, 3\tfrac{1}{2}, 4 \text{ years}$$

$$R = 10, 11, \ldots, 18\%$$

with $P = \$9,500$. The pseudocode outline of this program is shown in Figure 3-12, and the complete flowchart is given in Figure 3-13. This program requires that two independent loops, one for the values of R and one for the values of Y, be nested, one completely inside the other. For each value of Y, the term of the loan, a complete cycle of interest rates is executed. The R loop is the inner loop, and the Y loop is the outer loop. The complete FORTRAN program is given in Figure 3-14. Notice that the output

Figure 3-12
Pseudocode version of auto loan payment program

PRINT overall table headings

DoWhile (2. ≤ Y ≤ 4.)

    PRINT table headings for
        current value of Y

    Compute number of payments
    N = 12*Y

    DoWhile (10 ≤ R ≤ 18)

        Compute PAYMNT
        PAYMNT = ...

        PRINT line of values
          in table

        Increment R by 1.0

    EndDo ⟨R loop⟩

    Increment Y by ½

EndDo ⟨Y loop⟩

Figure 3-13

Flowchart for
calculating auto
loan payments. This
program has two
nested loops.

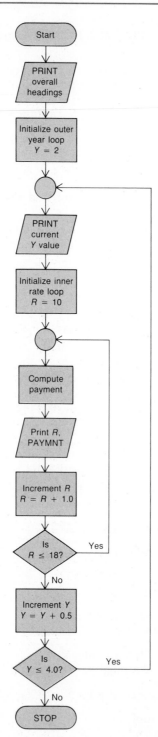

Figure 3-14

FORTRAN code and
results for the auto
loan program

```
      PROGRAM CARS
*
* This program computes the amount of the monthly payment for auto loans
* of 2 through 4 years in half year steps and for interest rates from
* 10 to 18 %.  The program illustrates nested loops.
*-------------------------------------------------------------------
* Variables
*
      REAL P, YMAX, R, X, Y
      INTEGER N, RMIN, RMAX, RATE
*
*      P      -- Principal, the amount of the loan      [INPUT]
*      YMAX   -- Maximum length of the loan in years    [INPUT]
*      RMIN   -- Starting value of interest rate (%)     [INPUT]
*      RMAX   -- Maximum interest rate (%)               [INPUT]
*      Y      -- Current value of loan length in years
*      RATE   -- Current value of interest rate (%)
*      R      -- Current interest rate per month as decimal
*      X      -- The computed value of the monthly payment
*      N      -- The number of payments (12*years)
*-------------------------------------------------------------------
* Initialization
*
*  Read in the principal, the limits on interest rates, and the
*  time frame of the loan.
*
      OPEN(22,FILE='CARS.OUT')
      WRITE(*,*)'Enter principle of loan'
      READ  *,P
      WRITE(*,*)'Enter the maximum number of years of the loan'
      READ  *,YMAX
      WRITE(*,*)'Enter the minimum, maximum interest rates (%)'
      READ  *,RMIN,RMAX
      WRITE(22,*)
*
*  Next, print overall headings for each set of calculations.
*  This is done before entering the loops.
*
      WRITE(22,*)' '
      WRITE(22,*)'The principle of the loan = $',P
      WRITE(22,*)' '
      WRITE(22,*)'   The calculation limits are:'
      WRITE(22,*)'        Years:  from ',2. ,' to ',YMAX
      WRITE(22,*)'        Interest:  from ',RMIN,'% to ',RMAX,'%'
      WRITE(22,*)' '
*
*  Start the outer loop (i.e., for each value of y = years, from
*  2 to YMAX in steps of 0.5 years).
*
      DO 2 Y = 2, YMAX, 0.5
*
*  Next, print the table headings, that is, one for each year calculation
*  Each cycle of the outer loop will print the next set of lines.  (You
*  may have to run the program again to get things to line up.)
*
      N = 12*Y
      WRITE(22,*)
      WRITE(22,*)'The results for a loan of ',Y,' years '
      WRITE(22,*)'            (or a total of ',N,' payments)'
      WRITE(22,*)' '
      WRITE(22,*)' Interest    Payment       Total cost'
```

Figure 3-14 _____
(continued)

```
        WRITE(22,*)'   rate    (dollars)      of loan '
        WRITE(22,*)'   ------   -------       ---------'
*----------------------------------------------------------------
* Computation
*
*    The current monthly interest rate is computed.
*
        RATE = RMIN
        N    = 12*Y
*
*    The next statement is the top of the inner loop; that is, for each
*    year, step through all the interest rates from RMIN to RMAX in
*    steps of 1.  The inner loop will be indented.
*
        DO 1 RATE = RMIN, RMAX
          R = RATE/100./12.
          TOP = R*P
          BOT = 1. - (1.+R)**(-N)
          X   = TOP/BOT
*
*     Print the current table entry
*
          WRITE(22,*)RATE,N,X,N*X-P
  1       CONTINUE
*
*         The inner loop is completed for this value of y.
*
  2     CONTINUE
*
*   This is the end of the outer loop.  The calculation is finished.
*
        WRITE(22,*)'  Calculation completed'
*
        STOP
        END
```

The principle of the loan = $ 9500.0000000

    The calculation limits are:
        Years: from   2.0000000   to   4.0000000
        Interest: from   10% to   18%

The results for a loan of 2.0000000 years
            (or a total of   24 payments)

Interest rate	Payment (dollars)	Total cost of loan
------	-------	---------
10	438.3770000	1021.0480000
11	442.7723000	1126.5350000
12	447.1984000	1232.7610000
13	451.6455000	1339.4910000
14	456.1228000	1446.9460000
15	460.6216000	1554.9190000
16	465.1498000	1663.5950000
17	469.7003000	1772.8070000
18	474.2792000	1882.7010000

Figure 3-15
Flowchart for
square roots via
Newton's algorithm

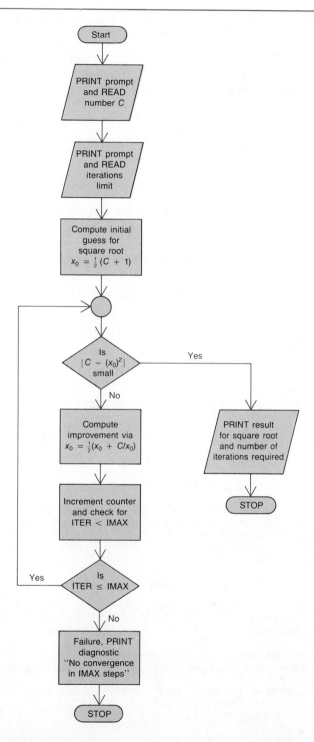

Figure 3-16
FORTRAN code for
calculating square
roots via Newton's
algorithm

```
      PROGRAM ROOT
*
*  Demonstration program illustrating Newton's iterative
*  algorithm for computing square root of a number C.
*------------------------------------------------------
* Variables
*
      REAL X,C,EPS
      INTEGER ITER,IMAX
*
*   C  -- The number whose square root is desired[INPUT]
*   X  -- The computed square root
* EPS -- A small number used for convergence tests
* ITER -- Iterations counter
* IMAX -- Limit on iterations                      [INPUT]
*------------------------------------------------------
* Initialization
*
*  Print prompts and read number C and iterations limit
*
      PRINT *,'Enter number whose square root is wanted'
      READ  *,C
      PRINT *,'Enter maximum number of iterations'
      READ  *,IMAX
*
*  Assign small value to EPS, convergence criterion
*
      EPS = 1.E-6
*------------------------------------------------------
* Computation
*
*  Determine value of initial guess
*
      X = 0.5*(C + 1.)
*
      DO 1 ITER = 1, IMAX
*
*      Test current value of X
*
      IF(ABS(C - X*X) .LT. EPS)THEN
*
*          Success, print result and stop
*
          PRINT *,'After ',ITER,' iterations the'
          PRINT *,'program successfully found the'
          PRINT *,'square root of ',C, 'to be ',X
          STOP 'success'
      ELSE
*
*          Not yet converged, improve x and continue
*
          X = 0.5*(X + C/X)
      ENDIF
    1 CONTINUE
*
*  Failure path -- exceeded iterations limit and no
*  square root was found within the required accuracy
*
      PRINT *,'FAILURE -- After ',IMAX,' no root was'
      PRINT *,'found within an accuracy of ',EPS
      STOP 'failure'
      END
```

```
Enter number whose square root is wanted
200
Enter maximum number of iterations
10
After    8 iterations the
program successfully found the
square root of   200.0000000 to be    14.1421400
```

3.5 Good Programming Style

Every so often we hear of an individual who has been classified as "dead" by the Social Security Administration showing up in person to request that the error be corrected, only to be told that the mistake is irreparable, the computer code has no entry for "resurrected." Stories like this point out the problems that can be caused by poorly documented computer programs, assembled piecemeal over many years by numerous individuals. These codes are often a mysterious black box to those who use them and are almost impossible to modify. These undocumented, patchwork programs are a serious problem everywhere computers are used. It cannot be stressed too strongly that the programs you write must be understandable, now and anytime in the future, to any potential user.

Comment lines inserted throughout the code will help explain the operation of the program. Several additional steps can be taken to improve a program's readability:

1. Segment the program into a sequence of blocks or modules such as the following:

Variable dictionary:	A list of all the variables in the program and an explanation of their meaning (perhaps including units).
Initialization block:	A segment of the program where the constants are assigned values and the data are read in.
Computation block:	Contains the body of algorithms used in obtaining the numerical results.
Success path:	After a successful completion of the program, it branches here and the results are printed.
Failure path:	If problems are encountered during execution, the program branches here and some form of diagnostic message is printed.

2. Explicitly declare each variable in the program to be either integer, real, or character.
3. Echo print all numbers read in to verify accurate assignments. This recommendation usually means that a corresponding PRINT statement should immediately follow each READ statement. This practice is often relaxed if every value read in is eventually printed somewhere later in the program.
4. Before you begin writing the program, outline it using a simplified flowchart or pseudocode description. After the program has been tested and successfully executed, prepare a detailed flowchart as part of the program's documentation.
5. The fundamental commandment of structured programming is, Spend time on the design of the program *before* you begin to write the code. You may think you can sit down at a terminal and compose a program, and often you can. But 90 percent of the time you will end up frustrated. Write out the program first, in block form, using either a flowchart or pseudocode. Include ample comments in the program and liberally add error diagnostics.

3.6 Additional Control Statements

Several alternative forms of the FORTRAN control statements are described in this section: the logical IF test, the computed GO TO statement, and the arithmetic IF statement.

Logical IF Test

Frequently, the block of statements that is to be executed as a result of a single-option IF(...)THEN–END IF structure will consist of a single executable FORTRAN statement. For example,

```
IF(ASSETS .LT. BILLS)THEN
    PRINT *,'Stop payment'
ENDIF
```

FORTRAN permits simple block IFs of this type to be written as a single line with the executable FORTRAN statement following the IF test, as

IF(⟨logical expression⟩)⟨an executable FORTRAN statement⟩

If the logical expression is evaluated as ⟨true⟩, the FORTRAN statement is then executed.

If the logical expression is evaluated as ⟨false⟩, the FORTRAN statement is ignored and the program proceeds to the next line of code.

The FORTRAN statement can be almost any of the executable statements that have been discussed up to this point, such as READ, PRINT, assignment, GO TO, STOP. It cannot, however, be another IF-type statement or a DO statement.

It is usually acceptable to replace single-option–single-statement block IF structures by a one-line logical IF statement. However, if you find your program contains numerous statements of the form

        IF(...)GO TO

you are probably creating a code that contains excessive branchings. Structured programming means that you should, whenever possible, be constructing all computational algorithms out of the basic decision and loop structures discussed in this chapter. If the logical IF statement is part of one of these larger structures, it is acceptable; if not, it probably violates the normal style considerations of structured programming.

Computed GO TO Statement

The form of the computed GO TO statement is

        GO TO $(k_1, k_2, k_3, \ldots, k_n)$, Iexp

where $k_1, k_2, k_3, \ldots, k_n$ are statement numbers of existing executable statements and Iexp is an integer, integer variable, or integer arithmetic expression. This statement transfers control to one of the statements in the parentheses depending on the value of Iexp.

If Iexp = 1, the program branches to statement k_1.

If Iexp = 2, the program branches to statement k_2.

$$\vdots$$

If Iexp = n, the program branches to statement k_n.

If Iexp > n, no transfer is made, and the next statement is
        executed.

If Iexp < 1, no transfer is made, and the next statement is
        executed.

For example,

        K = 15
        I = 6
        GO TO(4,83,15,1,9,15,6),K/I + 1

has the same effect as GO TO 15. The comma after the parenthesis is optional.

Arithmetic IF Statement

The form of the arithmetic IF statement is

        IF(exp)k_-, k_0, k_+

where k_-, k_0, k_+ are statement numbers of executable statements existing somewhere in the program, and exp is an integer or real constant, variable, or expression. The arithmetic IF transfers control to one of the three statements depending upon the value of exp.

If exp < 0.0, the program branches to statement k_-.

If exp = 0.0, the program branches to statement k_0.

If exp > 0.0, the program branches to statement k_+.

For example,

```
X = 2.
IF(X**2 - 3.)17,35,108    Transfer is made to statement 108.
```

But beware of the following improper code:

```
X = 2.
Y = SQRT(X)
Z = Y**2 - X
IF(Z)7,8,9
```

This code will probably cause a transfer to statement 7, not statement 8, illustrating once again the recurring problem of approximate arithmetic when using real numbers.

In the earliest versions of FORTRAN, the arithmetic IF statement was the only comparison statement available, and as a consequence many of the "old-timers" use it almost exclusively. In modern usage it has been replaced by IF(...)THEN structures or the logical IF test. The trend in computing is, as much as possible, to eliminate completely the use of statement numbers.

Summary

The elementary procedures for translating a prescription for a numerical calculation, an algorithm, into an easily readable and efficient FORTRAN program have been described in this chapter. The first step is to highlight the essential elements of the algorithm by means of a program outline, which may be either in the form of a flowchart or in terms of the less rigid requirements of pseudocode. A flowchart diagrams the flow of the program using standard symbols to represent various program functions such as looping, input/output, decision structures, and branching. A pseudocode description of a program replaces the standard symbols of a flowchart by FORTRAN keywords and simple English phrases and is constructed in a form similar to an ordinary outline, indenting subordinate elements of the algorithm from the principal functions.

A FORTRAN program assembled from either a flowchart or pseudocode outline will invariably contain sections of code that repeat a calculation over and over again, with slight changes in the parameters in each pass, until some specific conditions are met. Repetitive operations of this type are realized in FORTRAN by means of decision structures and loop structures.

The basic unit of a decision structure in FORTRAN is the logical block IF(...)THEN–END IF structure. The logical expression in the parentheses is evaluated, and if it has a value of ⟨true⟩, the block of FORTRAN statements, down to the first END IF statement encountered, is executed. Multiple alternatives to the comparison are accommodated by using the ELSE and ELSE IF(...)THEN statements. If the logical expression is ⟨false⟩, the block is skipped over and the program proceeds with the statement following the ELSE IF(...)THEN statement (if the latter comparison is ⟨true⟩), the statement following the ELSE statement (if present), or the statement following the next END IF statement encountered. The body of the IF(...)THEN–END IF structure is usually indented with respect to the IF, END IF, and ELSE statements.

`IF (`⟨logical expression a⟩`) THEN`

> FORTRAN block executed if expression a is ⟨true⟩

`ELSEIF (`⟨logical expression b⟩`) THEN`

> FORTRAN block executed if expression a is ⟨false⟩ and expression b is ⟨true⟩

`ELSE`

> FORTRAN block executed if both expressions a and b are ⟨false⟩

`ENDIF`

A logical expression is an operation of comparison of two quantities or arithmetic expressions. The operators that effect comparisons are .EQ., .NE., .LT., .LE., .GT., and .GE. (The periods are part of the operators.) Additionally, logical expressions may be combined by using the operators .AND. and .OR. or reversed in value by using the operator .NOT. The evaluation of a logical expression, as with an arithmetic expression, proceeds from left to right. All subexpressions are first evaluated to have a value of either ⟨true⟩ or ⟨false⟩ and are next combined using the rule that .AND. operations have precedence over .OR. operations.

A loop structure in FORTRAN is a set of statements that consist of a start, a test for completion, a body of the loop containing FORTRAN statements to be repeatedly executed, a terminus line, and some form of instruction to return to the start of the loop. Although loop structures can easily be constructed using a combination of logical IF blocks and GO TO statements, FORTRAN provides a special set of statements that are ordinarily used for this function. In most installations of FORTRAN, the DO-loop structure is used to perform all repetitive program functions. A DO-loop structure consists of a DO statement that defines the limits of a loop counter, a body of FORTRAN statements that is to be executed for each value of the counter, and a terminus statement, which is usually the CONTINUE statement:

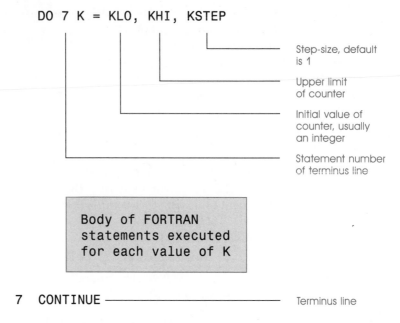

DO 7 K = KLO, KHI, KSTEP

Step-size, default is 1

Upper limit of counter

Initial value of counter, usually an integer

Statement number of terminus line

```
Body of FORTRAN
statements executed
for each value of K
```

7   CONTINUE —————————————— Terminus line

DO-loops may be nested, one entirely within the body of another, with the inner loop being completed before the next repetition of the outer. The loop limits and the loop counters may not be redefined within a loop, and a loop may be entered only through the DO statement. You should be familiar with the use of DO loops to produce a table of results or to iteratively refine a computation. The body of a DO loop is usually indented from the header and terminus line of the DO loop.

In some installations of FORTRAN, the DO loop is replaced by a DoWhile(...)–EndDo structure. In this case the block of FORTRAN statements within the structure is repeatedly executed so long as the logical expression within the parentheses remains ⟨true⟩.

The ability to implement a complicated computational algorithm by means of easily readable FORTRAN code using basic loop structures is the single most important skill a scientific programmer can acquire. Programs should be refined until the number of alternative branches is reduced to a minimum and a logical structure that is as clean and clear as possible is created. Some ways to improve a program's readability include inserting comment lines, segmenting the program, explicitly declaring all variables, echo printing all input values, and using a flowchart or pseudocode to design the program before you begin writing the code.

Additional statements to control or alter the flow of a program include the single-line logical IF test, the computed GO TO statement, and the arithmetic IF test. These statements merely duplicate functions available in the standard loop and decision structures and are included only for completeness.

Problems

3.1 Identify the errors in the following code as grammatical (compilation) or execution errors. If there are no errors, write OK.

```
a. IF(A .EQ. 5)
        THEN STOP
   ENDIF
b. IF(A .LT. 5.)THEN
        A = 5.
   ELSE
        A = 5.
   ENDIF
c. IF(I.GT.10 .AND. X.LT.1.)THEN
        X = X/2.
        I = I + 1
   ELSEIF(I.LE.10 .OR. X.GE.1.)THEN
        X = 2.*X
        I = I - 1
   ELSE
        PRINT *,'How did we get here?'
   ENDIF
d. IF(X .AND. Y .EQ. 1.5)GO TO 5
e. IF(C .LT. 5 .AND. C .GT. 5)C = 5
f. IF(GE .GE. LE)PRINT *,GE,LE
g. IF(A .EQ. 0.)A .EQ. 0
h. IF(ABS(X-Y) .LT. 1.E-5)Z = 0.0
i. IF(R)1,1,2
j. IF(DISCR < 0.)THEN
        PRINT *,'Complex roots'
        STOP
   ENDIF
k. IF(A .EQ. B)THEN
        IF(B .EQ. C)THEN
            PRINT *,'Equilateral'
   ENDIF
l.  IF(I .LT. IMAX)DO 2 I = 1,IMAX
        PRINT *,'Iter = ',I
   2 CONTINUE
m. IF(A = 0.)THEN B = 5.
```

3.2 The following code will print how many of the values A, B, C match. Simply by indenting portions, rewrite the code in a more readable form.

```
        IF(A .EQ. B)THEN
        IF(B .EQ. C)THEN
        PRINT *,'All three match'
        ELSE
        PRINT *,'Two match'
        ENDIF
        ELSEIF(B.EQ.C .OR. C.EQ.A)THEN
```

```
PRINT *,'Two match'
ELSE
PRINT *,'None match'
ENDIF
```

3.3 Write a program that will read a person's age and print "Teenager" if $13 \leq AGE \leq 19$ or "Retired" if $AGE \geq 65$.

3.4 Write FORTRAN logical expressions that are ⟨true⟩ when
a. $a > b \geq c$ **d.** $c < d$ or $a < b$, but not both
b. $|x - y| < \epsilon$ **e.** $n = $ an odd integer
c. $x = y = z$

3.5 Determine whether the following logical expressions are ⟨true⟩ or ⟨false⟩. Use the following values for the variables: $I = 2, K = 4, X = -2., Y = 1.,$ $E = 3., Q = 2.$
a. `(I**4.NE.2*K .AND. K/I.EQ.I*I .OR. Y.GT.X)`
b. `( I.GT.K .AND. Y.GT.X .OR. K-I*I.EQ.0)`
c. `((I.GT.K).AND.(Y.GT.X .OR. K-I*I.EQ.0))`
d. `E*3.3E-3*EXP(E).GT.Q**E*1.E-1/E/Q/Q`

3.6 Write a pseudocode description of the program in Figure 3-3.

3.7 Write a program that will read an angle θ in radian measure and determine in which quadrant the angle lies. (Assume θ is positive and less than 50π.)

3.8 Write a program that will determine whether
a. Four sides that are read in could form a polygon. If the sides are labeled a, b, c, d, the following conditions must be satisfied:

$$a \leq b + c + d \qquad c \leq a + b + d$$
$$b \leq a + c + d \qquad d \leq a + b + c$$

b. If a polygon can be formed, whether it could be a rectangle or a square.

3.9 The commission earned by a used-car salesman is determined by the following rules. If the amount of the sale is

Less than $200 there is no commission.

Between $200 and $2,500, the commission is 10% of the sale.

Greater than $2,500, the commission is $250 plus 12% of the amount above $2,500.

The amount of the sale is the price of the car sold less the value of any trade-in. Write a complete program that reads the price of the car sold and the value of the trade-in and then computes the commission.

3.10 What is wrong with the following program segments? Rewrite the code using a block IF structure to accomplish what the programmer probably intended.

```
a. IF(X .LT. 0)TIME = 0.
   TIME = 10.
b.    IF(A .LT. B)GO TO 7
      IF(A .GT. B)GO TO 8
      IF(A .EQ. B)GO TO 9
   7  X = B-A
   8  X = A-B
   9  X = 0.
c.    IF(DISCR .LT. 0.0)GO TO 5
      X1 = (-B + SQRT(DISCR))/2./A
      X2 = (-B - SQRT(DISCR))/2./A
      PRINT *,'The two roots are ',X1,X2
   5  PRINT *,'The roots are complex'
      STOP
      PRINT *,'Calculation completed'
```

3.11 An algorithm to compute the inverse of a number C without using any division is

$$x_{new} = x_{old}(2 - Cx_{old})$$

provided that the initial guess for the inverse (x_{old}) is chosen so that $(2 - Cx_{old})$ is greater than zero.
  a. Write a pseudocode outline of a program that will
  (1) Prompt and READ a positive number C.
  (2) Specify an initial guess x for the inverse of C.
  (3) Check that $(2 - Cx) > 0$. If $(2 - Cx) \geq 0$, reduce x and try again.
  (4) Prompt and READ the iterations limit, IMAX.
  (5) In successive iterations improve the guess by the given algorithm. The test for success is $|1. - Cx| < 1 \times 10^{-6}$.
  (6) If successful, PRINT the number C and its computed inverse; if not successful, PRINT a diagnostic.
  b. Write and execute a FORTRAN program corresponding to your outline. Also carry out the calculation on your pocket calculator for a variety of numbers.

3.12 The roots of a nonlinear equation can sometimes be solved by an iterative procedure called the *method of successive substitutions,* provided the equation can be written in the form

$$x = f(x)$$

The procedure is to guess a value for the solution, say x_{old}, and compute a new value for the solution via

$$x_{new} = f(x_{old})$$

This process is repeated until the difference between successive values of x is smaller than some prescribed small number or until it is clear that the procedure is diverging (i.e., successives x's differ by more than some prescribed large number). Write a complete program to solve for a root of the following functions (i.e., find an x such that $F(x) = 0.0$). The program should have safeguards to handle a diverging solution.

a. $F(x) = x/3 - e^{-x^2}$

First write the equation $F(x) = 0$ as $x = [\ln(3/x)]^{1/2}$ and then try writing it as $x = 3e^{-x^2}$. The root is near $x = 1.0$.

b. $F(x) = x^{10} + 5x^3 - 7$

First write the equation $F(x) = 0$ as $x = (7 - 5x^3)^{1/10}$ and then try writing it as $x = (7/5 - x^{10}/5)^{1/3}$. The root is near $x = 1.0$.

c. An approximate equation for the velocity of a falling object that includes the effects of air drag is

$$v(t) = v_t(1 - e^{-(gt/v_t)}) \qquad (\text{m/sec})$$

where t is the time in seconds, $g = 9.8$ m/sec^2, and v_t is the terminal velocity. (The speed of an object falling from rest will continually grow until the increasing drag force balances the gravitational force. At this point the velocity will no longer increase, and the object will fall at a constant velocity equal to its terminal velocity.) If the velocity 1 second after release is measured to be 9.34 m/sec, write a program to determine the ultimate terminal velocity by the method of successive substitutions. (The answer is near 100 m/sec.)

3.13 What is wrong with the following program segments? Rewrite the code in a form that will accomplish what the programmer probably intended.

a.
```
    DO 2 I = 1,IMAX
       X = C/2.
       X = .5*(X + C/X)
    2 CONTINUE
```

b.
```
    DO 2 THETA = 0., 45., 5.
       PRINT *,'Table of cosines'
       PRINT *,'Angle    Cosine'
       PRINT *,THETA,COS(THETA)
    2 CONTINUE
```

c.
```
    DOLLAR = 1.0
    RATE   = 0.05
    PRINT*,'A 1991 dollar was worth'
    DO 2 YEAR = 1991,1971
       DOLLAR = DOLLAR*(1. + RATE)
       PRINT *,'DOLLAR,' in ',YEAR
    2 CONTINUE
```

d.
```
    DO 3 I = 1,IHI
       IF(I/2*2 .NE. I)THEN
          PRINT *,'Only want even I-s'
          I = I + 1
       ENDIF
       PRINT *,'Even Nos. = ',I
    3 CONTINUE
```

3.14 If the present population of a country is P and if the population is known to increase at a constant rate of RATE (in percent/year), then the population next year will be $(1 + RATE/100)*P$. Write a complete program to produce five separate tables for rates of population increase of RATE = .5, 1., 1.5, 2.0, 2.5 (%/year) to cover the population projections over the next 25 years. The tables should be clearly labeled and should include the year and the projected population for that year. Use $P = 1,000,000$ for the present population.

A

Programming Assignment

A.1 Introduction

To learn FORTRAN, you must write programs. The short programming exercises in the problem sections at the end of each chapter are meant to illustrate specific elements of FORTRAN. To really develop skill in FORTRAN programming, you must construct more complicated programs. A moderately long program is usually much more challenging than several short programs. Eight major programming assignments are included in this text. Each is designed so that it can be completed in about a week and is challenging enough to be interesting.

These programming assignments will also be used to familiarize you with some of the methods of engineering analysis associated with the subfields of engineering. Each branch of engineering uses the computer to solve a variety of problems, many of which can be understood by a novice and can provide a good illustration of the ideas used in that area of engineering. Each programming assignment is constructed in such a way that understanding the background material concerning engineering concepts is not essential to solving the problem. Also, each major programming assignment begins with a sample problem similar to the assignment. The sample problem is completely solved and can be used as a model for constructing your programs.

A.2 Sample Program

Civil Engineering: Pressure Drop in a Fluid Flowing Through a Pipe

Background. When an incompressible fluid is pumped at a steady rate through a pipe from point 1 to point 2, the pressure drop is given by

$$dP = P_1 - P_2$$

$$= \rho(gh + W)$$

where W is the energy lost per kilogram due to internal friction in the fluid and with the pipe walls. The fluid density is ρ, the gravitational acceleration is g, and h is the difference in height between the two points. All units are SI (i.e., meters, kilograms, seconds). The expression for the energy loss is

$$W = \frac{4fv^2L}{D}$$

109

where f = Friction factor
   v = Velocity of fluid flow (m/sec)
   L = Pipe length (m)
   D = Pipe diameter (m)

The fluid flow velocity is related to the volume flow rate, Q (in m^3/sec), by

$$v = \frac{4Q}{\pi D^2}$$

For smooth pipes the friction factor f depends only on the Reynold's number R:

$$R = \frac{\rho v D}{\mu}$$

where μ is the viscosity of the fluid.

   If ($R \le 2{,}000$), the flow is laminar and $f = 8/R$.
   If ($R > 2{,}000$), the flow is turbulent and $f = 0.0395/R^{1/4}$.

Problem Specifics. Write a complete program to perform the following operations for each of four separate liquids:

1. For each liquid, read in the name and parameters, which will include D, h, σ, and μ. Use a constant pipe length of $L = 100$ m for all calculations.
2. Echo print the data.
3. Read in the limits on the flow rates for the table: Q_{start}, Q_{top}, and Q_{step}.
4. Print, as neatly as possible, the headings for the table.[1] Perform the following operations for each value of the flow rate Q:
   a. From the values of Q and D, compute the fluid velocity.
   b. Compute the Reynold's number and from it determine the friction factor, f.
   c. Compute the frictional energy loss, W, and the pressure drop, dP.
   d. Print as one line of the table the values for Q, v, R, f, W, and dP.
5. At the completion of the entire job, print a statement indicating that the program has successfully accomplished its task.

The data to be used in this problem are contained in Table A-1.

---

[1] It may take several runs to finally line up the numerical output with your table headings.

Table A-1

Fluid parameters used in sample program

Liquid	ρ (kg/m³)	μ (kg/m-sec)	h (m)	D (m)	Q_{start} (m³/sec)	Q_{top}	Q_{step}
Ethyl alcohol	789.4	0.00120	10.0	0.01	.00002	.00004	.000005
Benzene	899.0	0.00065	10.0	0.01	.00002	.00004	.000005
Glycerin	1260.0	1.4900	3.0	0.30	.005	.01400	.001
Water	998.0	0.0010	10.0	0.02	.00002	.00004	.000005

Sample Program Solution

The complete FORTRAN program for this problem is given in Figure A-1. Notice in particular the following points in the program:

1. The name of the liquid is read in as a character constant. The name must be enclosed in single quotes when it is typed at the keyboard.
2. A prompt is issued before each READ statement.
3. All variables in the problem are explicitly typed as either real, integer, or character.
4. The program consists of two nested loops. For each value of the outer-loop parameter (IRUN), a complete table of values is computed. For each value of the inner loop (Q), a line of the table is computed.

```
DO 4 IRUN = 1,4

    Print liquid name and input parameters
    Print table headings

    DO 3 Q = Qstart, Qtop, Qstep

        Compute Reynold's number, friction
        factor, and pressure drop for this
        value of Q

        Print one line of the table

3   CONTINUE
4 CONTINUE
```

Figure A-1

FORTRAN program for the pressure drop in a fluid flowing through a pipe

```
        PROGRAM FLUID
*--
*-- This program computes the pressure drop for a fluid flowing
*-- through a pipe.  The flow is either laminar or turbulent,
*-- depending on the Reynold's number.
*--
*-- The program executes a separate run for each of four separate
*-- liquids. For each run (the outer loop) the program first prompts
*-- and reads the liquid and pipe parameters. It then prompts and
*-- reads the limits on the loop for the flow rates.
*--
```

Figure A-1 _____
(continued)

```
*-- Before the flow rate loop is started, a list of the parameters
*-- is printed along with table headings for computed quantities.
*--
*-- The main features of the program are two nested DO loops and the
*-- use of a block IF structure to determine the friction factor.
*-------------------------------------------------------------------
* Variables
*
      REAL DENSTY,VISCOS,HEIGHT,DIAM,FRICT,L,Q,QSTRT,R,W,VEL,DP,
     +     QTOP,QSTEP
      INTEGER IRUN
      CHARACTER NAME*13
*--
*--    IRUN   - Run number
*--    NAME   - Character variable containing liquid name   [INPUT]
*--    DENSTY - Fluid density (kg/m**3)                     [INPUT]
*--    VISCOS - Fluid viscosity (kg/m-sec)                  [INPUT]
*--    DIAM   - Pipe diameter (m)                           [INPUT]
*--    HEIGHT - Height fluid is pumped above original       [INPUT]
*--             position
*--    QSTRT  - Limits and step size in the flow rate loop. [INPUT]
*--    QTOP
*--    QSTEP
*--    Q      - Current flow rate
*--    L      - Pipe length
*--    VEL    - Velocity of flowing fluid
*--    FRICT  - Pipe friction factor (dimensionless)
*--    W      - Energy loss/kg due to friction
*--    R      - Reynold's number
*--    DP     - Pressure drop
*-------------------------------------------------------------------
* Initialization
*--
      PI = ACOS(-1.)
      L  = 100.
*-------------------------------------------------------------------
* Outer Loop Start
*--
*-- The outer loop is the Run-No. loop
*--
      DO 4 IRUN = 1,4
*--
*--   For this run, prompt, read and echo print the input parameters
*--
      PRINT *,'For run No. ',IRUN,' enter the following',
     +        'parameters:'
      PRINT *,'Enter name, viscosity, density, diameter, height'
      PRINT *,'Enter diameter, height, density, viscosity'
      READ  *, NAME,VISCOS,DENSTY,DIAM,HEIGHT
      PRINT *,'Enter the limits on the flow rate:',
     +        ' Qstart,Qtop,Qstep'
      READ  *, QSTRT,QTOP,QSTEP
      PRINT *,' '
      PRINT *,' '
      PRINT *,'-------------------------------------------------'
```

Figure A-1
(continued)

```
                    PRINT *,'The parameters for run No. ',IRUN,' are:'
                    PRINT *,'  For liquid ',NAME
                    PRINT *,'    which has a density = ',DENSTY,' (kg/m^3)'
                    PRINT *,'    and a viscosity      = ',VISCOS,' (kg/m-sec)'
                    PRINT *,'  Flowing through a pipe of'
                    PRINT *,'              diameter = ',DIAM,  ' (m)'
                    PRINT *,'              length   = ',L,     ' (m)'
                    PRINT *,'    and pumped a height = ',HEIGHT,' (m)'
      *--
      *--        Print table heading for Q-loop here.
      *--
                    PRINT *,' '
                    PRINT *,'----------------------------------------',
          +                 '----------------------------------------'
                    PRINT *,' Flow         Fluid       Reynolds   ',
          +                 ' Friction     Energy      Pressure   '
                    PRINT *,' Rate         Velocity    Number     ',
          +                 ' Factor       Loss        Drop       '
                    PRINT *,'----------     ----------  ---------- ',
          +                 '----------     ----------  ----------'
      *--
      *--
      *--       -----------------------------------------------------------
      *--       Beginning of the inner loop in flow rates
      *--
                    DO 3 Q = QSTRT,QTOP,QSTEP
      *--
      *--            The velocity of flow is determined from Q, L,
      *--            and DIAM by
      *--
                    VEL = Q/(PI*.25*DIAM**2)
      *--
      *--            Next compute the Reynold's number
      *--            and friction factor
      *--
                    R = DENSTY*VEL*DIAM/VISCOS
                    IF(R .LT. 2000.)THEN
                        FRICT = 8./R
                    ELSE
                        FRICT = 0.395/R**.25
                    ENDIF
      *--
      *--            Compute energy loss (W) and the pressure drop (DP)
      *--
                    W = 4.*FRICT*VEL**2*L/DIAM
                    DP = DENSTY*(9.8*HEIGHT + W)
      *--
      *--        Print results for this line in the table
      *--
                    PRINT *,Q,VEL,R,FRICT,W,DP
      *--
         3          CONTINUE
                    PRINT *,'----------------------------------------',
          +                 '----------------------------------------'
      *--
      *--        The calculations are complete for this run.  The next run
      *--        is started with a new set of data.
      *--
         4   CONTINUE
      *--
```

```
*--    At this point, the entire job is completed.
*--
       PRINT *,'Calculation Completed - Job Terminated'
       STOP
       END
```

As mentioned in footnote 1, you will undoubtedly spend a considerable amount of time rearranging the table headings to line up with the numerical output. It is also likely that you will be unsuccessful in getting the output to be as neat as you would like. These problems will be addressed in Chapter 6, when formatted output is discussed. The output from this program is shown in Figure A-2.

The FORTRAN solution to this problem may look intimidating for your first major assignment, but most of the program listing is explanatory comment lines and numerous PRINT statements used to construct a table. Once you have read this program and compared it with the printed output, you should attempt to understand the listing in Figure A-3. This

Figure A-2

Portion of output
from the sample
program

```
For run No.  1 enter the following parameters:
Enter diameter, height, density, viscosity
Enter the limits on the flow rate: Qstart,Qtop,Qstep


-------------------------------------------------
The parameters for run No.  1 are:
  For liquid ethyl alcohol
    which has a density    =    789.0000 (kg/m^3)
    and a viscosity        =      0.0012 (kg/m-sec)
  Flowing through a pipe of
            diameter    =      0.0100 (m)
            length      =    100.0000
    and pumped a height  =     10.0000 (m)


-------------------------------------------------
```

Flow Rate	Fluid Velocity	Reynolds Number	Friction Factor	Energy Loss	Pressure Drop
2.0000E-05	0.2546479	1674.3100	0.0047781	12.39351	87100.480
2.5000E-05	0.3183099	2092.8870	0.0583997	236.68510	264066.500
3.0000E-05	0.3819719	2511.4650	0.0557976	325.64030	334252.200
3.5000E-05	0.4456339	2930.0420	0.0536882	426.47640	413811.900
4.0000E-05	0.5092959	3348.6200	0.0519255	538.74220	502389.600

```
-------------------------------------------------
For run No.  2 enter the following parameters:
Enter diameter, height, density, viscosity
Enter the limits on the flow rate: Qstart,Qtop,Qstep
```

Output continues for three more runs

Figure A-3 _____

```
PROGRAM FLUID
REAL DENSTY,VISCOS,HEIGHT,DIAM,FRICT,L,Q,QSTRT,R,W,VEL,DP,
+     QTOP,QSTEP
INTEGER IRUN
CHARACTER NAME*13
PI = ACOS(-1.)
L  = 100.
DO 4 IRUN = 1,4
    READ(*,*)NAME,VISCOS,DENSTY,DIAM,HEIGHT
    READ(*,*)QSTRT,QTOP,QSTEP

    PRINT *,  | Table headings and input parameters |

    DO 3 Q = QSTRT,QTOP,QSTEP
       VEL = Q/(PI*.25*DIAM**2)
       R = DENSTY*VEL*DIAM/VISCOS
       IF(R .LT. 2000.)THEN
           FRICT = 8./R
       ELSE
           FRICT = 0.395/R**.25
       ENDIF
       W = 4.*FRICT*VEL**2*L/DIAM
       DP = DENSTY*(9.8*HEIGHT + W)
       PRINT *,Q,VEL,R,FRICT,W,DP
3      CONTINUE
4   CONTINUE
    PRINT *,'Calculation Completed - Job Terminated'
    STOP
    END
```

figure shows the same program but without all the comment lines and
PRINT statements. If this were the only description you had for the operation of the program, it would probably be confusing. But after you have
studied the details of the long version, you will be better able to appreciate
the overall purpose of the program in terms of the basic features of nested
DO loops and table construction.

A.3 Programming Problems

Engineering Career Choices: Mechanical Engineering

Generally speaking, mechanical engineers are concerned with machines
or systems that produce or apply energy. The range of technological activities that are considered part of mechanical engineering is probably
broader than in any other engineering field. The field can be roughly subdivided into four categories:

1. *Power.* Design of power-generating machines and systems
   such as boiler-turbine engines for generating electricity, solar
   power, heating systems, and heat exchangers.

2. *Design.* Innovative design of machine parts or components from the most intricate and small to the gigantic. For example, mechanical engineers work alongside electrical engineers to design automatic control systems such as robots.

3. *Automotive.* Design and testing of transportation vehicles and the machines used to manufacture them.

4. *Heating, ventilation, air conditioning, and refrigeration.* Design of systems to control our environment both indoors and out and to control pollution.

Mechanical engineers usually have a thorough background in subjects like thermodynamics, heat transfer, statics and dynamics, and fluid mechanics.

Programming Problem A-A:
Mechanical Engineering: Most Cost-Effective Steam Pipe Insulation

When deciding how much insulation to install on a long steam-supply line (see Figure A-4), the amount of money to be saved from lower fuel bills must be compared with the initial insulation purchase and installation costs; too much insulation can be just as wasteful as too little. This problem will allow you to determine the thickness of the insulation that will give the greatest savings for the least cost. The heat flow through the insulation is given by

$$Q_1 = 2\pi kL \frac{(T_a - T_b)}{\ln(b/a)} \quad \text{(watt)} \tag{A.1}$$

Figure A-4
Insulated steam
pipe

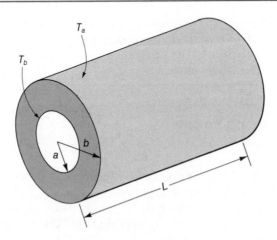

a = Outer radius of steam pipe (m)
b = Outer radius of insulation cover (m)
T_a = Temperature of pipe surface (°C)
T_b = Temperature of outer surface of insulation (°C)
T_{air} = Air temperature (°C)

The heat transfer from the insulation to the air is given approximately by

$$Q_2 = 2\pi bF(T_b - T_{air})L \qquad \text{(watt)} \tag{A.2}$$

where k = Thermal conductivity of the insulation
$\quad$ = 0.1 watt/(m °C)

F = Convection coefficient for the air-insulation interface
$\quad$ = 3.0 watt/(m² °C)

In a steady-state situation, $Q_1 = Q_2$, so T_b can be eliminated from Equations (A.1) and (A.2). By combining the two equations we obtain

$$Q = \left[\frac{2\pi bkFL}{k + bF \, \ln(b/a)} \right] (T_a - T_{air}) \tag{A.3}$$

(Verify this equation.)

$\quad$ Now for the costs. The pipe insulation costs \$325.00 per cubic meter (C_{vol} = 325.0), and the installation costs amount to \$1.50 per meter of pipe (C_L = 1.50), independent of thickness. The cost of heat is 0.4 cents per kilowatt-hour or \$1.11 × 10^{-9} per watt-sec (C_{heat} = 1.11 × 10^{-9}). Assuming a pipe of length L, the volume of the insulation used is $\pi(b^2 - a^2)L$ and the total insulation cost is

$$C_{insul} = \pi(b^2 - a^2)LC_{vol} + LC_L \tag{A.4}$$

$\quad$ To obtain the amount of fuel savings, we need the difference between the heat loss with no insulation, that is,

$$Q_3 = 2\pi aF(T_a - T_{air})L \tag{A.5}$$

and the heat loss with insulation [Equation A.3)], that is, $dQ = Q_3 - Q$, or

$$dQ = Q_3 \left[1 - \frac{b/a}{1 + (bF/k) \, \ln(b/a)} \right] \tag{A.6}$$

(Verify this equation.)

$\quad$ The fuel savings over a five-year period (1.578 × 10^8 sec) is then

$$C_2 = dQ(1.578 \times 10^8)C_{heat} \tag{A.7}$$

The outer radius of the pipe is 5 cm (a = 0.05 m), and insulation is available in thicknesses t ranging from 1 to 10 cm in 1-cm steps (i.e., $b = a + t$, $t = 1, 2, \ldots, 10$). For air temperatures of T_{air} = −10 °C, 0 °C, and +10 °C, determine the most cost-effective thicknesses of insulation.

Details. Write a program that will perform the following operations:

$\quad$ **1.** Read the REAL variables

A = Pipe radius		= 0.05 m
L = Pipe length		= 100.0 m
TP = Pipe temperature		= 150.0 °C

$$
\begin{aligned}
\text{RK} &= \text{Insulation conductivity} & &= 0.1 \text{ watt/m } °C \\
\text{RF} &= \text{Convection constant} & &= 3.0 \text{ watt/m}^2 °C \\
\text{CVOL} &= \text{Cost per volume of insulation} & &= 325.0 \text{ \$/m}^3 \\
\text{CL} &= \text{Cost per meter for installation} & &= 1.50 \text{ \$/m} \\
\text{CH} &= \text{Cost per kilowatt-hour for heat} & &= 0.004 \text{ \$/kw-hr}
\end{aligned}
$$

and neatly echo print them with appropriate labels.

2. Use an outer DO loop to step through the three values of the air temperature. For each value of T_{air}, produce a table of insulation cost (COST) and net savings over a five-year period (SAVE) computed for insulation thicknesses $t = 1$ cm to 10 cm in 1-cm steps. Thus, first print table headings (including T_{air}), then use an inner DO loop to step through the range of insulation thicknesses. For each value of insulation thickness, compute the cost of the insulation (COST) [Equation (A.4)] and the fuel savings over a five-year period (SAVING) [Equation (A.7)]. (*Note:* Be sure to convert CH to cost per watt-second.) Print one line of this table.

By inspecting the printed output from your program, determine the most cost-effective insulation thickness for each of the three air temperatures. Indicate this optimum thickness in pencil on your output. Include a flow-chart with your program.

Engineering Career Choices: Civil Engineering

The field of civil engineering is concerned primarily with large-scale structures and systems used by a community. A civil engineer designs, constructs, and operates bridges, dams, tunnels, buildings, airports, roads, and other large-scale public works. Civil engineers are also responsible for the effects these large-scale systems have on society and the environment. Thus, civil engineers are involved in water resources, flood control, waste disposal, and overall urban planning. The field can be subdivided into three categories:

1. *Structures.* Design, construction, and operation of large-scale edifices such as dams, buildings, and roads. The properties of materials, geology, soil mechanics, and statics and dynamics are important elements of the background training. For example, how tall a building can be constructed before it will buckle under its own weight is a question involving all of these subjects.

2. *Urban planning.* Planning, design, and construction of transportation systems (roads, railroads, river development, airports) and general land use. Surveying and mapmaking are necessary skills.

3. *Sanitation.* Waste treatment, water supply, and sewage systems. Fluid mechanics, hydrology, pollution control, irrigation, and economics are important considerations.

Programming Problem A-B:
Civil Engineering: Oxygen Deficiency of a Polluted Stream

Because the amount of dissolved oxygen present in a stream is a critical factor in the vitality of the stream, understanding how various pollutants affect the oxygen content is of concern to a water resources engineer. Organic matter in sewage decomposes through chemical and bacterial action, consuming oxygen in the process. A standard procedure for determining the rate at which sewage reduces the free oxygen in a stream involves diluting a sewage sample with water containing a known amount of dissolved oxygen and measuring the loss in oxygen after the mixture has been maintained at a temperature of 20 °C for a period of 20 days. This loss is called the biochemical oxygen demand (B_{20}). The subscript refers to the temperature. For any temperature T, the oxygen demand B_T can be computed from

$$B(T) = B_{20}(0.02T + 0.6) \tag{A.8}$$

Of course, while the oxygen is being consumed by the sewage, fresh oxygen is continually being absorbed from the air but at a different rate. Usually, the sewage will initially consume the oxygen at a rate much greater than it can be replenished by the air. Eventually, the oxygen appetite of the sewage will be satiated and the oxygen content of the stream will cease to decrease and will begin to heal back to its original value. An equation that approximately characterizes the oxygen deficit of the stream as a function of time is

$$D(d,T) = \frac{\alpha(T)B(T)}{\alpha(T) - \beta}(e^{-\alpha(T)d} - e^{-\beta d}) + D_0 e^{-\beta d} \tag{A.9}$$

where d is the elapsed time in days and T is the temperature in °C. The units of the oxygen deficit are in kg/m^3. Also,

$\alpha(T)$ = Rate of oxygen consumption by the stream (a function of the temperature)

β = Rate of oxygen replenishment by absorption

D_0 = Initial oxygen deficit (kg/m^3)

$B(T)$ = Biochemical demand of the stream at temperature T (kg/m^3)

The constants D_0 and β have been measured and tabulated for this stream. However, $\alpha(T)$ depends on the amount and type of sewage dumped into the stream as well as the temperature. If α_{20} is the measured rate of oxygen consumption at 20 °C, then the value at a temperature T is given by

$$\alpha(T) = \alpha_{20}(1.047)^{T-20} \tag{A.10}$$

Finally, the biochemical oxygen demand of the mixture of stream plus pollutants is given by

$$B_{20} = \frac{B_{20}^{\text{upstream}} Q_{\text{stream}} + B_{20}^{\text{sewage}} Q_{\text{sewage}}}{Q} \tag{A.11}$$

where B_{20}^{upstream} = Biochemical oxygen demand of the stream above the point at which the sewage is discharged

B_{20}^{sewage} = Biochemical demand of the sewage itself

Q_{stream} = Flow rate of the stream (m^3/sec)

Q_{sewage} = Flow rate of the sewage (m^3/sec)

Q = Net flow rate of sewage plus stream $(Q_{\text{stream}} + Q_{\text{sewage}})$

Thus, for a given value of temperature T, we first determine B_{20} from Equation (A.11) and then compute $\alpha(T)$ from Equation (A.10) and $B(T)$ from Equation (A.8). The oxygen deficit for this temperature may then be calculated as a function of time (d) by using Equation (A.9). [*Note:* When $d = 0$, the oxygen deficit of the stream starts out at $D(0) = D_0$.]

We are particularly interested in the amount of time it takes for the stream to begin healing. We anticipate that the oxygen deficit will initially increase and will continue to increase for a period of time. Eventually, though, it will turn around; that is, the deficit will start to decrease (i.e., the oxygen content will increase). We wish to compute the amount of time this process takes using Equations (A.8) through (A.11).

Details. Write a FORTRAN program to compute the amount of time it takes for the stream to begin healing. The overall structure of your program should follow the outline below:

1. Read in the stream and sewage parameters listed in Table A-2 and neatly echo print them. Compute and print the quantity B_{20}.
2. For a range of temperatures from 4 °C to 32 °C, in steps of 4 °C,
   a. Compute $\alpha(T)$ and $B(T)$.
   b. Start with $D_{\text{old}} = D_0$.
   c. Print table headings for the table of turnaround times and the corresponding maximum oxygen deficit.
   d. For a range of time in days from $d = 0$ to 4, in steps of 0.1,
      (1) Compute the oxygen deficit and call it D_{new}.

Table A-2
Input parameters for the pollution problem

$$Q_{\text{stream}} = 150 \text{ m}^3/\text{sec}$$
$$Q_{\text{sewage}} = 9 \text{ m}^3/\text{sec}$$
$$D_0 = 1.3 \text{ kg/m}^3$$
$$\alpha_{20} = 0.23 \text{ sec}^{-1}$$
$$\beta = 0.45 \text{ sec}^{-1}$$
$$B_{20}^{\text{upstream}} = 0.8 \text{ kg/m}^3$$
$$B_{20}^{\text{sewage}} = 145 \text{ kg/m}^3$$

(2) If the deficit is still increasing, that is, if $D_{new} > D_{old}$, then redefine $D_{old} = D_{new}$.
(3) Otherwise, print one line of the table, which should include the current value of the time at which the deficit is a maximum and the maximum value of the deficit, then exit the time loop.

From your printed table, determine the approximate temperature at which the healing time for the stream is a maximum.

If there are errors in your coding of the several equations in this problem, it is possible that the oxygen deficit will never reach a maximum. Thus, it would be prudent for the first several runs of your program to print each value of $D(d,T)$ as it is computed. In this way you can monitor the progress of the program and more easily isolate the source of any errors. For the final "production" run of the program, all these test prints should be removed.

Engineering Career Choices: Industrial Engineering

Each of the traditional engineering disciplines (civil, mechanical, electrical, chemical, and metallurgical/mining) relies on a particular area of natural science for its foundation. Industrial engineering, however, incorporates the knowledge of the social sciences into designing improvements in human-machine systems. Industrial engineers are responsible for designing, installing, and evaluating machines and systems and also for monitoring their interface with people to improve overall productivity. This job may involve understanding human behavioral characteristics and their effects on the design of machines or the workplace. Industrial engineers draw heavily on knowledge in economics, business management, and finance, as well as in the natural sciences. The areas of specialization of the industrial engineer may be divided into four categories:

1. *Operations research.* This area involves the application of analytical techniques and mathematical models to phenomena such as inventory control, simulation, decision theory, and queuing theory to optimize the total systems necessary for the production of goods.
2. *Management or administrative engineering.* The increasingly complex interplay of management and production skills in modern industrial operations has resulted in a need for technically trained managers. These managers evaluate and plan corporate ventures and interact with labor, engineering departments, and subcontractors. A management engineer may also participate in the financial operations of a company, drawing on knowledge in economics, business management, and law.

3. *Manufacturing and production engineering.* Before a product is produced, the complete manufacturing process must be designed and set up to optimize the economics involved and the final quality of the item. This task requires a broad knowledge of process design, plant layouts, tool design, robotics, and human-machine interactions.

4. *Information systems.* This area involves the use of computers to gather and analyze data for decision making and planning and to improve human-machine activity.

The following list includes the most common responsibilities of industrial engineers who responded to a recent survey by the American Institute of Industrial Engineers:

Facilities planning and design	Cost control
Methods engineering	Inventory control
Work systems design	Energy conservation
Production engineering	Computerized process control
Management information and control systems	Product packaging, handling, and testing
Organization analysis and design	Tool and equipment selection
Word measurement	Production control
Wage administration	Product improvement studies
Quality control	Preventive maintenance
Project management	Safety programs
	Training programs

Programming Problem A-C:
Industrial Engineering: Cost Comparisons for Purchasing a Fleet of Cars

The increasing cost of automobile fuel has caused a surge in the demand for smaller cars with greater fuel economy. A counterargument being used for larger cars with greater fuel use is based on the economics of a lower long-term maintenance cost for the larger automobile.

The executive officer of a large company must decide between two automobiles that will constitute a fleet purchase of over 8,000 cars to be used by the company over the next four years. He turns to the engineering department for guidance. To provide a recommendation, the group must first restate the problem in mathematical terms amenable to a computation. Because different user groups in the company will drive different distances, it is necessary to estimate the annual cost for a variety of cars as a function of the distance driven.

The annual cost (A_{cost}) of a car is composed of three parts: loan repayment (L_{cost}), operating costs (O_{cost}), and maintenance costs (M_{cost}).

$$A_{cost} = L_{cost} + O_{cost} + M_{cost} \qquad (A.12)$$

The loan payment depends on

P = Amount borrowed (principal)
r = Yearly interest rate
n = Number of years of loan ($n = 4$)

The equation for the total amount of the loan repayment is then

$$L_{cost} = nP\frac{r}{1 - (1 + r)^{-n}} \qquad (A.13)$$

The operating cost of a car depends on

d = Distance driven (km/yr)
F_c = Fuel cost ($/l)
Q = Fuel use rate (km/l) (The fuel use rate for city driving will be labeled Q_{city} and that for highway driving, Q_{hghw}.)

From reviewing company records and from surveys, it is known that the first 10,000 km (labeled d_0) of annual driving is about 70% city and 30% highway. Any additional distance ($d - d_0$) is about 20% city and 80% highway. The fuel operating costs are then expressed as

$$O_{cost} = \frac{d}{0.7Q_{city} + 0.3Q_{hghw}}F_c \qquad \text{if } d < d_0$$

$$\qquad (A.14)$$

$$= \left[\frac{d - d_0}{0.2Q_{city} + 0.8Q_{hghw}} + \frac{d_0}{0.7Q_{city} + 0.3Q_{hghw}}\right]F_c \qquad \text{if } d > d_0$$

The average maintenance costs for a large fleet of automobiles generally increase dramatically with distance driven and are essentially zero while the car is under warranty ($d < 20{,}000$ km). For distances beyond the warranty limit, the following expression roughly summarizes the maintenance costs:

$$M_{cost} = M_0(d - 20{,}000)^{\beta} \quad \text{(for } d > 20{,}000 \text{ km/yr)} \qquad (A.15)$$

The two parameters M_0 and β are known for each type of car.

Annual distance driven by automobiles in the company fleet ranges from 10,000 km to 25,000 km. The problem is to determine the annual cost for each of three cars for the first through fourth years and the total four-year cost for each car. This cost is to be computed for a range of annual yearly driving distances. The parameters to use in this problem are given in Table A-3.

Table A-3
Values of
parameters for the
annual car-cost
problem

Variables	Automobile Type		
	Volkswagen Rabbit	Pontiac Grand Prix	BMW
P = Original cost ($)	8,750.00	14,625.00	34,500.00
r = Annual interest rate	0.12	0.12	0.12
n = Length of loan (yr)	4	4	4
Q_{city} = Fuel use rate (city) (km/l)	12.6	10.3	7.6
Q_{hghw} = Fuel use rate (highway) (km/l)	17.0	13.6	11.9
F_c = Fuel cost ($/l)	0.26	0.26	0.34
M_0 = Maintenance cost coefficient	0.95	8.45	16.55
β = Maintenance cost exponent	0.70	0.42	0.31

Details. Structure your program using the following steps:

1. Declare the type of all the variables used in the problem.
2. Prompt and read the parameters common to both calculations, for example, r, n, d_0. Echo print them neatly, with labels.
3. Use the outer loop for the three separate cars; that is, for CASE = 1, 2, 3 the program should perform the following operations:
   a. Prompt and read the data associated with each automobile (including the name).
   b. Echo print with appropriate labels.
   c. Compute and print the total cost of the loan for this car.
   d. Print the headings for the table of the total four-year fuel costs, maintenance costs, and overall costs versus distance driven per year. For yearly driving distances d = 10,000 km/yr to 60,000 km/yr, in steps of 5,000 km/yr, compute the yearly operating costs using Equation (A.14). The four-year cost is then four times this amount. Then compute the four-year maintenance costs in the following way: The distance driven in the first year is d. Thus use Equation (A.15) to determine the first-year maintenance cost. The odometer distance after the second year is $2d$. Compute the yearly maintenance cost using this value in Equation (A.15) and add it to that of the first year. Repeat for the third and fourth years to obtain the total four-year maintenance cost. Finally, add all the four-year costs and print one line of the table.

After a successful computer run, inspect the printed output and determine the range, if any, in the annual driving distance where a lower-priced car is actually more expensive over the four-year period.

Elementary Programming Techniques

Introduction

The flow-control structures introduced in Chapter 3 make it possible for us to analyze a vast array of problems. This chapter concentrates on a few elementary techniques that form the basis for many of the computational algorithms used in solving actual engineering problems. As the programs implementing these algorithms become more elaborate, the importance of simplicity and clarity of the code increases.

This chapter begins with a discussion of FORTRAN statement functions that replace complicated algebraic expressions in much the same way that ordinary functions are used in algebra. Using statement functions can significantly reduce the clutter of a typical program, thereby improving the program's readability and reducing the potential for errors. The first computational algorithm considered is that of scanning a list or monitoring a function to determine a minimum or a maximum of the list or function. Although the procedure is trivial, the manner of progression from operational algorithm to actual FORTRAN code is instructive and can be used as a model for more complicated procedures. The process of summation on a computer is described next. Because summation is probably the single most important computational procedure and is central to many programs, several examples are described in detail. The third computational process described is the search for the roots of a function by the method of bisection. In this procedure the sign of a function will be monitored by the computer as the program steps through values of the independent variable. When the computer detects a change in sign of the function, a root has been located within the most recent step and the program will then narrow in on the root. The idea of having the computer monitor some feature of a function, taking some specified action when a particular condition is found, is the basis for a wide variety of programs in engineering.

More complicated programs generally require more complicated input and output. It is not uncommon for a program to require that hundreds of variables be assigned values before the program can begin. Such programs may produce many pages of numerical output. The use of data files for controlling the input and output of a program can greatly reduce the complexity of program execution. Several FORTRAN statements useful in specifying and manipulating data files are described as well as the characteristics of both sequential and random-access data files.

4.2   Statement Function

The form of the FORTRAN statement defining a statement function is

FNC(A,B,...,X)   Any algebraic combination, even including intrinsic functions, of the variables in the argument list (A, B, ... , X) and constants.

The name of the function (here FNC) may be any valid FORTRAN name. Although it is not required, to avoid confusion any and all variables that appear on the right side of the replacement operator should also appear as one of the variables in the argument list [here (A, B, ... , X)].

Two examples follow:

1. The function $f(t) = 35t^2 - \sin(\pi t) - \sqrt{t}$ would be written as a statement function of the form

   F(T) = 35.*T*T - SIN(3.14159*T) - SQRT(T)

2. The cubic expression $x^3 + ax^2 + bx + c$ could be represented by

   CUBIC(A,B,C,X) = X**3 + A*X**2 + B*X + C

The type of the value returned by the function is determined by the type of the name of the function. Thus, with default typing, F(T) would be real and N(X) would be integer. The function name can also be explicitly typed by including it in a prior type-declaration statement.

> A statement function definition is not considered an executable statement. It must appear *before* the first executable statement and *after* the type declarations (i.e., integer, real, or character).

Using the Statement Function

The statement function allows almost limitless possibilities for constructing a set of intrinsic-like functions in addition to those listed in Table 2-3. Statement functions are often used to reduce long and complicated pro-

gram statements, resulting in a code that is easier to read. And a code that
is easier to read is much less prone to error. A statement function is used,
or referenced, in the same way that intrinsic functions are referenced.
After the function has been introduced in the defining line, the name of
the function, along with its argument list, can be used in any arithmetic
expression or executable FORTRAN statement.

For example, when you need to calculate the square root of a number in a program, you could insert the line defining a statement function called SQROOT that employs one iteration of Newton's algorithm to compute $\sqrt{C}$ using an initial guess X0 (see Section 3.4):

```
SQROOT(C,X0) = 0.5*(X0 + C/X0)
```

The code using this function to obtain a rough value for $\sqrt{7}$ then might be

```
X = SQROOT(7.,2.)
```
  [x = 2.75]

A better value would be

```
X = SQROOT(7.,2.)
X = SQROOT(7.,X)
```
  [x = 2.6477]

A much simpler and more accurate approach would be to use
the intrinsic function SQRT(C), which, incidentally, also uses Newton's
algorithm.

When the compiler encounters a FORTRAN name followed immediately by a parenthesis, as in SQROOT(C,X0), a search is initiated for
the definition of the name SQROOT. The compiler has been written to recognize that a "name-left parenthesis" structure like FA(C + D) does not
imply multiplication but instead indicates that the name FA must have a
special meaning. To determine precisely what FA represents, the compiler
looks at the beginning of the program to see if this name has been defined
as a statement function. If it has, a value is computed for FA as specified by
the code in the statement-function definition and is then returned to the
line in the program that contained the reference to FA. The program then
continues from that point. If FA is not found at the top of the program, a
search of the library is made; if a function named FA is found, it is linked
with the main program and that function is used whenever the name is
referenced. If the function is not found among the intrinsic functions, an
execution-time error results.

This process implies that if you had named the square root function SQRT, the program would use that function and not the intrinsic
function, since it finds your function first.[1] Obviously, to minimize confu-

---

[1] A word of caution: In some installations of FORTRAN 77 it is forbidden to define statement functions that have the same name as existing intrinsic functions; in all circumstances it is flagrantly poor programming style.

sion you should try to avoid defining functions with names identical to intrinsic functions.

■ Argument List

The interpretation of the variable names that appear in the argument list of a statement function depends on whether the function is being defined or simply used.

Dummy Variable Names

The variable names in the argument list of a statement-function definition are called *dummy arguments,* meaning that they do not represent numerical quantities in the same sense as ordinary FORTRAN variable names; that is, instead of designating a location in memory for a numerical value, a dummy-argument name merely reserves a position in the arithmetic procedure defined in the statement function. Only later, when the statement function is referenced in the program, will an actual numerical value be inserted in the function expression. This use of symbols to represent as yet unspecified numerical values is analogous to the ordinary symbolic manipulation of variable names in algebra.

Actual Variables

When the function is referenced, the names, numbers, or arithmetic expressions that appear in the argument list are called *actual arguments,* implying that they are then expected to have numerical values at that point in the program.

Consider the following program segment:

```
F(A,B) = (A**2 - B**2)*PI
PI = ACOS(-1.)
X  = F(3.,2.)      The value of x here is 5π = 15.708.
Y  = F(X+1.,X)     The value of y is (2x + 1)π = 10π² + π = 101.84.
PRINT *,'      x = ',X,' y = ',Y
PRINT *,' and a = ',A,' b = ',B      The output is unpredictable.
```

The variables A and B were never assigned values in this program. The statement-function definition merely defines a procedure for symbolically manipulating the variables in its argument list. Thus, in the first reference the value of F will be determined after replacing the symbol A by 3.0 and B by 2.0. Notice that at this point in the program, PI has been assigned a value and since it will not be changed it need not appear in the argument list. The value used for PI will be whatever value currently resides in that memory location. In the second reference to F, the arithmetic expressions in the argument list are first evaluated before the function expression is actually used.

Actual arguments represent numbers that are transferred to the dummy arguments in the statement-function definition. The transfer is determined by the position in the argument list, not by the name of the variable; that is, in the example above, the value associated with B is whatever number appears in the second position when the function F is referenced. In addition, the argument list in any reference to a statement function must agree in number and type with the argument list in the function's definition. In our example this means that any reference to function F must have two numbers, variable names, or expressions representing numbers in the argument list, and both must be of type real. Dummy and actual arguments are considered again in Section 5.3.

4.3 Finding the Minimum and Maximum of a Set of Numbers

A common and useful programming procedure is a code that will scan a list of numbers and determine the minimum and/or maximum number in the list. The basic algorithm simply mimics the steps you or I would follow in scanning a list of numbers. Starting at the top of the list, we define the current maximum to be the first number. We then check the next element in the list. If this number is larger than the current maximum, it becomes the current maximum and we discard the earlier value. If not, the current maximum is still valid and we proceed to the next number in the list. We could easily construct a FORTRAN code to duplicate this procedure. The program segment in Figure 4-1 is designed to continually repeat the comparison of numbers read with XMAX until a negative value is entered. The most important statement in the program is the IF test, where the current maximum (XMAX) is compared with the most recently read value of X. If X is greater than the current maximum, the current maximum is redefined.

This method can also be used to find the maximum or minimum of a function of a single variable x over some interval, $a \leq x \leq b$. A program to accomplish this is illustrated in the following example.

Example of Minimizing Costs

In an automobile manufacturing plant, door handles are made in large lots, placed in storage, and used as required in assembling the cars. A common problem is determining the most economical lot size, x. The following parameters must be considered:

$$w = \text{Workdays per year} \qquad\qquad = 242 \ (\text{days/yr})$$
$$s = \text{Setup cost to produce one} \qquad = 547 \ (\$/\text{lot})$$
$$\qquad \text{lot of door handles}$$
$$u = \text{Usage rate (door handles/day)} = \ 90 \ (\text{no./day})$$

Figure 4-1 _____

Program to
determine the
maximum of a
sequence of
numbers entered at
the keyboard

```
        PRINT *,'Enter first value'
        READ  *,XMAX
   1    PRINT *,'Enter next value'
        READ  *,X
        IF(X .GE. 0.)THEN
*
*           Compare current x and xmax.
*           If necessary, redefine xmax.
*
            IF(X .GT. XMAX)
                XMAX = X
            ENDIF
        ELSE
*
*           A negative x indicates the end of the list.
*           Print the maximum x and stop.
*
            PRINT *,'Maximum value in list = ',XMAX
            STOP
        ENDIF
*
*       Return to the beginning for the next x
*
        GO TO 1
        END
```

$$m = \text{Material + labor costs per door handle} \quad = 2.05 \ (\$)$$

$$a = \text{Annual storage costs per door handle} \quad = 0.55 \ (\$/\text{yr/door handle})$$

Thus, the number of lots used per year is

$$\frac{w(\text{days/yr})u(\text{no./day})}{x(\text{no./lot})} = \frac{wu}{x} \ (\text{lots/yr})$$

and so the yearly equipment setup cost is

$$\frac{swu}{x} \ (\$/\text{yr})$$

Adding all the costs, we obtain the following expression:

$$c(x) = \frac{swu}{x} + umw + ax$$

We next turn to the computer to find the minimum of this expression as a function of the lot size x. The procedure will be built around the algorithm given earlier for finding the minimum and/or maximum of a list of numbers.

The FORTRAN program to determine the lot size that corresponds to a minimum overall cost would be constructed along the following lines:

Pseudocode description of optimum-lot-size code

Type all variables as they are encountered in writing the code

REAL X,W,S,U,M,A,COST,CMIN,XBEST

Statement function for COST

COST(X) = ...

Prompt and READ the values for the parameters
Initialize:

XBEST = 1000.

CMIN = COST(XBEST)

Loop through x values

```
      DO 1  X = 1000., 10000., 10 (i.e., 900 steps)
          IF(COST(X) .LT. CMIN)THEN
              XBEST = X
              CMIN  = COST(X)
          ENDIF
    1 CONTINUE
      STOP
      END
```

The results of a FORTRAN program constructed from this outline are shown in Figure 4-2.

Figure 4-2
Output of a
program that
computes optimum
lot size

```
Enter workdays/yr (W) and usage rate (U)
242., 90.
Enter costs for setup (S), material (M), and annual storage (A)
547., 2.05, 0.55

    A Computation of the Optimum Lot Size

       Input Parameters

            Workdays/year       ---  242.
            Usage rate per day  ---   90.
            Setup costs         ---  547.   ($/lot)
            Material + Labor    ---    2.05 ($/item)
            Annual storage      ---    0.55 ($/item)

The optimum lot size is 4650.0 door handles.
Annual costs for this lot size are $49768.58.
```

■■■ Reconsidering the Optimum-Lot-Size Problem

The program in Figure 4-2 is an example of one of the most common errors made in programming: computing without first carefully thinking the problem through. Even though the program finds a valid estimate of the optimum lot size, and does so with relative ease, the speed and accuracy of the calculation can be greatly improved by introducing more intelligence into the algorithm. The expression obtained for the cost was a simple function of the lot size and is graphed in Figure 4-3.

At the lot size corresponding to the minimum cost, the curve has a horizontal tangent line; that is, the value of its slope is zero. Since the slope of the tangent line at a point is equal to the value of the derivative at that point, the requirement for the minimum point on the curve is

$$\frac{dc(x)}{dx} = 0$$

$$= swu\frac{d}{dx}\left(\frac{1}{x}\right) + 0 + a\frac{d(x)}{dx}$$

$$= a - \frac{swu}{x^2} \qquad \left(\frac{d}{dx}x^{-1} = -x^{-2}\right)$$

Solving for x yields the optimum lot size, x_{best},

$$x_{best} = (swu/a)^{1/2} = 4654.159 \rightarrow 4,654 \qquad \text{Truncated to an integer}$$

with no need for a computer at all. This example illustrates the fundamental tenet of all numerical analysis on a computer: Intelligence is more

Figure 4-3
Annual production
costs (*c*) as a
function of lot
size (*x*)

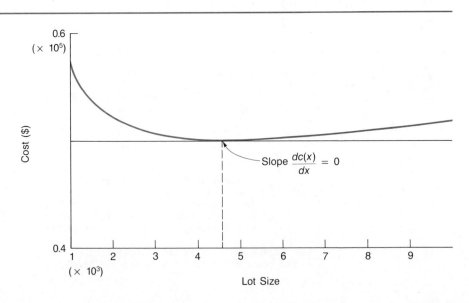

important than computing power. It is not at all rare to replace a computer program that costs thousands of dollars per run with an improved version that obtains more accurate results for only pennies. This replacement is done by programmers experienced in analyzing problems as well as in writing FORTRAN code.

4.4 Performing a Summation

Perhaps the single most useful task a computer is called upon to handle is to quickly perform a summation. The ability to transcribe the algebraic equations for summations into FORTRAN code is an essential element in developing programming skills.

Structure of the Summation Algorithm

If the current value of the sum is represented as SUM, the current value of an individual term in the sum as TERM, and the loop counter as K, then the FORTRAN code for executing a summation consists of four parts.

1. *Initialization.* The variables SUM, TERM, K, and the maximum of the loop counter, KMAX, are first assigned values.[2]

   ```
   SUM  = 0.0
   TERM = ...
   K    = 0
   KMAX = ...
   ```

2. *Summation.* The operation of summation in FORTRAN is affected by the replacement.

   ```
   SUM = SUM + TERM
   ```

3. *Redefine TERM.* The value of the next element in the summation is computed. The loop counter is then incremented as well.

   ```
   TERM = ...
   K = K + 1
   ```

4. *Test for completion.* The sum is terminated when the loop counter exceeds the limit or when an individual term is less than some small tolerance EPS.

---

[2]Some installations of FORTRAN preset all memory locations to zero before the program begins, but most do not. If a variable that has not been assigned a value within a program is used in an arithmetic expression, the result will be unpredictable. Thus a fundamental commandment of FORTRAN is, *All* variables that are used in a program *must* have been assigned values earlier within that same program.

```
IF(K .GT. KMAX)THEN
       GO TO ...
ENDIF
```

or

```
IF(ABS(TERM) .LT. EPS)THEN
       GO TO ...
ENDIF
```

A summation loop is usually written using a DO loop or a DoWhile structure, in which case it becomes

```
SUM  = 0.0
TERM = ...
K    = 0
KMAX = ...
DoWhile (counter K ≤ KMAX and TERM ≥ EPS)
    SUM  = SUM + TERM
    TERM = ...
    K    = K + 1
EndDo
```

■ Examples of Summations

In Figure 4-4 the FORTRAN code that will compute the sum of the squares of the integers from 1 to 100 (called ISUM) and the sum of the square roots of the integers from 1 to 100 (called XSUM) is illustrated. The algebraic notation for these quantities is

$$I_{\text{sum}} = \sum_{i=1}^{100} i^2 = 1^2 + 2^2 + 3^2 + \cdots + 100^2$$

$$X_{\text{sum}} = \sum_{x=1}^{100} \sqrt{x} = \sqrt{1} + \sqrt{2} + \sqrt{3} + \cdots + \sqrt{100}$$

■ Infinite Summations

Many functions in mathematics are represented in a form involving the summation of an infinite number of terms. For example, the series expansion for the exponential function can be found in any book of mathematical tables:

$$e^x = 1 + x + \frac{x^2}{2!} + \frac{x^3}{3!} + \cdots + \frac{x^n}{n!} + \cdots = \sum_{n=0}^{\infty} \frac{x^n}{n!} \tag{4.1}$$

where $n!$ (n factorial) means

$$n! \equiv n(n - 1)(n - 2)\ldots2 \times 1$$

Figure 4-4
FORTRAN program
for summations

```
          PROGRAM SUMS
*--
*-- This program performs two summations, one using real arith-
*-- metic, the other integer arithmetic.  There are 100 terms
*-- in each sum.
*------------------------------------------------------------------
* Initialization
*--
      REAL X, XSUM, XTERM
      INTEGER I, ISUM, ITERM
*--
      XSUM = 0.0
      ISUM = 0
*--
*-- Loop through the integers from 1 to 100
*--
      DO 1 I = 1,100
          X = I
*--
*--       Define individual terms in each sum for this value of I.
*--
          XTERM = SQRT(X)
          ITERM = I
*--
*--       Summation consists in the replacement SUM ==> SUM + TERM.
*--
          XSUM = XSUM + XTERM
          ISUM = ISUM + ITERM
    1 CONTINUE
*--
*-- At this point, both sums have been completed.
*-- Print the results.
*--
      WRITE(*,*)
      WRITE(*,*)'The sum of the square roots of the integers'
      WRITE(*,*)'from one to one hundred is'
      WRITE(*,*)'                              ',XSUM
      WRITE(*,*)
      WRITE(*,*)'The sum of the squares of the integers'
      WRITE(*,*)'from one to one hundred is'
      WRITE(*,*)'                              ',ISUM
      STOP
      END
```

```
The sum of the square roots of the integers
from one to one hundred is
                      671.4628471

The sum of the squares of the integers
from one to one hundred is
                      338350
```

That is, $2! = 2$, $3! = 6$, and so on. Also, $0!$ is defined to be unity. Equation (4.1) is exact only if an infinite number of terms are included in the summation. However, eventually the terms in the sum will become extremely small (i.e., $n!$ will be very large), and we may be justified in terminating the summation when this happens. (The tricky question of deciding whether dropping an infinite number of small quantities is justified is left for you to ponder for now but is considered in more detail in Chapter 10.)

The relation between successive terms in this sum can be expressed in terms of their ratio:

$$R = \frac{(\text{term})_{n+1}}{(\text{term})_n} = \frac{x^{n+1}}{(n+1)!} \frac{n!}{x^n} = x \frac{n!}{(n+1)!} \tag{4.2}$$

Since $(n+1)! = (n+1)n!$, this equation can be simplified to

$$R = \frac{x}{n+1} \tag{4.3}$$

This ratio approaches zero as $n \to \infty$ for any finite value of x. The key step in the algorithm to compute the sum is then the line that calculates the next term in the series by using Equations (4.2) and (4.3).

$$\text{TERM} \to \text{TERM}*\text{RATIO} = \text{TERM}*(\text{X}/(\text{N}+1.)) \tag{4.4}$$

The FORTRAN code to calculate e^x for a specific x by summing the series expansion until the absolute value of a term is less than 10^{-6} is given in Figure 4-5. However, this program will have difficulty obtaining accurate results if x is large and negative (see Problem 4.4).

As a final example, consider the problem of finding both the maximum and minimum values and performing a summation in the same program. Here is the problem:

> A data file called GRADES contains a list of the following information: The first line contains the number (N) of students who took a one-hour quiz. Each subsequent line contains the student's last name, ID number (e.g., Social Security number), and the student's score on the quiz. Write a program to compute the average exam score and the name, ID, and exam score for the students who did the best and the worst.

The program is given in Figure 4-6. This program will not handle tie scores. Try to modify the program to cover the situation of a few students tying for the best or worst scores. You will notice that the program will get complicated very quickly.

Figure 4-5
FORTRAN code to
evaluate e^x

```
          PROGRAM ETOX
*--
* This code evaluates the series expansion for EXP(X).  The sum-
* mation is terminated when ABS(TERM) .LT. 1.E-6.  Each term is
* is related to the previous term in the summation by
*--
*--            Term(n+1) = Term(n) * Ratio
*--
* where Ratio is an algebraic expression for the ratio of terms.
*----------------------------------------------------------------
* Variables
*--
          REAL X, TERM, SUM, RATIO, EPS
*----------------------------------------------------------------
* Initialization
*--
          WRITE(*,*)'Enter value of x'
          READ (*,*)X
*--
          SUM = 0.0
          EPS = 1.E-6
*--
*  Sum the first 100 terms in the series for e^x. The index n will
*  correspond to the power of x in each term.  Thus the n = 0 term
*  corresponds to x**0 = 1.  The first term is then term = 1.
*--
          TERM = 1.0
          DO 1 N = 0,100
             SUM = SUM + TERM
*--
*--          Redefine Term by using the ratio of terms
*--          (Note the intentional mixed-mode arithmetic)
*--
             RATIO = X/(N+1.)
             TERM  = TERM*RATIO
*--
*--          If the value of Term < eps the summation is terminated
*--          and the result printed.  This is the success path.
*--
             IF(ABS(TERM) .LT. EPS)THEN
                WRITE(*,*)'The computed value of EXP(',X,') = ',SUM
                WRITE(*,*)'and ',N,' terms in the series were used'
                STOP 'success'
             ENDIF
        1 CONTINUE
*--
* The program executed 100 terms and still did not successfully
* obtain a sufficiently accurate value for EXP(X).  This is the
* failure path.
*--
          WRITE(*,*)'-----FAILURE in Program ETOX------'
          WRITE(*,*)'The series has not converged after 100 terms'
          WRITE(*,*)'The size of the most recent term = ',TERM
          STOP 'failure'
          END
```

```
Enter value of x
2.2
The computed value of EXP( 2.2000) =  9.0250120
and   13 terms in the series were used.
```

Figure 4-6
Program to
compute the best,
worst, and average
exam scores

```
      PROGRAM EXAMS
*--
*-- This program will read a data file called GRADES that in-
*-- cludes a set of student names, ID's, and exam scores.  The
*-- first line of the file contains a number that indicates how
*-- many lines of data are included in the file.  The list is
*-- scanned for the minimum/maximum scores.  The ID and name of
*-- the students with these scores are then printed.
*-- Also, the scores are summed and an average is computed.
*-------------------------------------------------------------------
* Variables
*--
      REAL AVG
      INTEGER EXAM, BEST,WORST,SUM,ID,IDBEST,IDWRST,N
      CHARACTER*12,NAME,NBEST,NWRST
*--
*--      EXAM    -- Current exam score
*--      BEST    -- The maximum exam score
*--      WORST   -- The minimum exam score
*--      ID      -- Current Student ID
*--      IDBEST  -- The ID of student with best exam
*--      IDWRST  -- The ID of student with worst exam
*--      NAME    -- Current Student name
*--      NBEST   -- The name of student with best exam
*--      NWRST   -- The name of student with worst exam
*--      SUM     -- Sum of all exam scores
*--      AVG     -- The average of all exams
*--      N       -- The total number who took the exam
*-------------------------------------------------------------------
* Initialization
*--
      SUM   = 0
      BEST  = 0
      WORST = 100
*--
*-- Note: Start with impossible values for best/worst scores.
*-- Next, OPEN the data file and read the number of data lines.
*--
      OPEN(11,FILE='GRADES')
      READ(11,*)N
*-------------------------------------------------------------------
```

4.5   Bisection Technique for Finding Roots of Equations

A common feature found in almost every program concerned with numerical analysis is to have the computer repeatedly monitor some property of a function and to take some action when a particular condition is satisfied. An example of this process is found in the determination of the roots of an equation by the bisection method.

Roots of Equations

Engineering and scientific problems often require the calculation of the roots of a function or equation for their solution; that is, those values of x such that $f(x) = 0$. The function may be a polynomial like

Figure 4-6
(concluded)

```
* Computation
*--
*-- A DO loop is used to step through each of the data lines.
*-- Each line is of the form 'last-name',123456789,72
*--
        DO 2 I = 1,N
            READ(11,*)NAME,ID,EXAM
            SUM = SUM + EXAM
            IF(EXAM .LT. WORST)THEN
                WORST  = EXAM
                IDWRST = ID
                NWRST  = NAME
            ENDIF
            IF(EXAM .GT. BEST)THEN
                BEST   = EXAM
                IDBEST = ID
                NBEST  = NAME
            ENDIF
    2   CONTINUE
*--
*-- Compute the average score taking care to note that both SUM
*-- and N are integers.  (Again, intentional mixed-mode arith-
*-- metic is used.)
*--
        AVG = (1.*SUM)/N
*-------------------------------------------------------------------
* Output Section
*--
        WRITE(*,*)'The average of the ',N,' exams = ',AVG
        WRITE(*,*)
        WRITE(*,*)'The students at the extremes were'
        WRITE(*,*)'          Name        ID        Score'
        WRITE(*,*)'  Best  ',NBEST,IDBEST,BEST
        WRITE(*,*)'  Worst ',NWRST,IDWRST,WORST
        STOP
        END
```

$$p(x) = x^7 - 5x^5 + 6x^4 - 2x^2 + 1 = 0$$

or a more complicated expression involving transcendental functions, like

$$t(x) = e^{-x} - \sin(\tfrac{1}{2}\pi x) = 0$$

Depending on the nature of the function and on the demands of the problem, any of a number of calculations could be required:

Since the polynomial is of degree 7, find all seven roots of $p(x)$.

If the polynomial $p(x)$ has less than seven real roots, find only the real roots or perhaps only the positive real roots.

The second equation, $t(x) = 0$, has an infinite number of positive roots. Find only the first five, or perhaps only the first.

Given an approximate value for a root, find a more precise value.

For the moment, we will concentrate on the last, least ambitious project.

As with any program, we begin by gathering as much information as possible before trying to construct a FORTRAN code. In functional analysis this step almost always involves making a rough sketch of the function being considered. The second equation above can be written as

$$e^{-x} = \sin(\tfrac{1}{2}\pi x)$$

A root of the equation then corresponds to any value of x such that the left side and the right side are equal. If the left and right sides are plotted independently, the roots of the original equation are then given by the points of intersection of the two curves (see Figure 4-7). From the sketch we see that the roots are

Roots $\approx 0.4, 1.9, 4.0, \ldots$

And since the sine oscillates, there will be an infinite number of positive roots. We will concentrate first on improving the estimate of the first root near 0.4. We begin by establishing a procedure, or algorithm, that is based on the most obvious method of attack when using a pocket calculator; that is, we begin at some value of x just before the root (say 0.3) and step along the x axis, carefully watching the magnitude and particularly the sign of the function.

Step	x	e^{-x}	$\sin(\tfrac{1}{2}\pi x)$	$f(x) =$ $e^{-x} - \sin(\tfrac{1}{2}\pi x)$
0	0.3	0.741	0.454	0.297
1	0.4	0.670	0.588	0.082
3	0.5	0.606	0.707	−0.101

The function has changed sign between 0.4 and 0.5, indicating a root between 0.4 and 0.5. Thus, for the next approximation we use the midpoint, 0.45:

4	0.45	0.638	0.649	−0.012

Figure 4-7
Intersection of e^{-x}
and $\sin(\tfrac{1}{2}\pi x)$

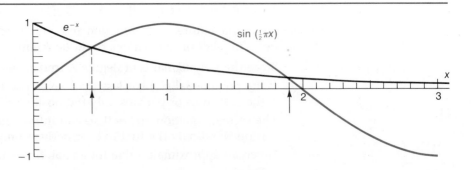

The function is again negative at 0.45, indicating that the root is between 0.4 and 0.45. The next approximation will therefore be the midpoint of this interval, 0.425. In this way we can proceed systematically to a computation of the root to any desired degree of accuracy.

5	0.425	0.654	0.619	+0.0347
6	0.4375	0.6456	0.6344	+0.01126
7	0.44365	0.6417	0.6418	−0.00014

The key element in the procedure is the monitoring of the sign of the function. When the sign changes, specific action is taken to refine the estimate of the root. This change in sign of the function, indicating that the vicinity of a root has been located, will also form the key element of the computer code.

You should try this rather unsophisticated root-solving method on some simple equation. For example,

$$f(\alpha) = \sin \alpha - \alpha/3 = 0 \quad \text{The } \alpha \text{ is in radians.}$$

This equation may be written as

$$\sin \alpha = \alpha/3$$

Again plotting left and right sides independently (see Figure 4-8), we see that the first positive root is near 2.2. The answer you should get for the root is $\alpha = 2.2788626602\ldots$.

Bisection Method

The root-solving procedure illustrated in the preceding section is suitable for hand calculations; however, a slight modification will make it more "systematic" and easier to adapt to computer coding.

Figure 4-8
Intersection of sin α and $\alpha/3$

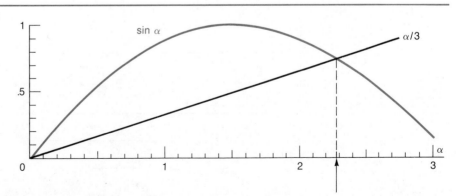

Suppose we already know that there is a root between $x = a$ and $x = b$; that is, the function changes sign in this interval. For simplicity we will assume that there is only one root between $x = a$ and $x = b$ and that the function $f(x)$ is continuous in this interval. The function might then resemble the sketch in Figure 4-9. If we next define $x_1 = a$ and $x_3 = b$ as the left and right ends of the interval and $x_2 = \frac{1}{2}(x_1 + x_3)$ as the midpoint, in which half-interval does the function cross the axis? In the drawing, the crossing is on the right, so we replace the full interval by the right half-interval

$$x_1 \rightarrow x_2$$

$$x_3 \rightarrow x_3$$

$$x_2 = \tfrac{1}{2}(x_1 + x_3)$$

and ask the question again. After determining a second time whether the left half or the right half contains the root, the interval is once more replaced by either the left or right half-interval. This process is continued until we narrow in on the root to within some previously assigned accuracy. Each step halves the interval, and so after n iterations, the size of the interval containing the root will be $(b - a)/2^n$. If we are required to find a root to within a tolerance δ, that is, $|x - \text{root}| < \delta$, the number of iterations n required can be determined from

$$\frac{b - a}{2^n} < \delta$$

For example, the initial search interval in the example in this section was $(b - a) = 0.1$. If the root was required to an accuracy of $\delta = 10^{-5}$, then

$$\frac{0.1}{2^n} < 10^{-5} \qquad \text{or} \qquad 2^n > 10^4$$

Figure 4-9
Root determination
by the bisection
method

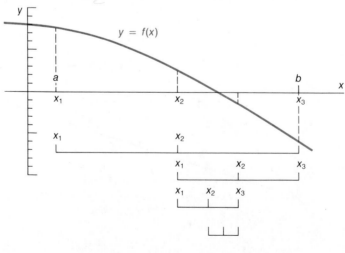

So,

$$n > \frac{\log(10^4)}{\log(2)} > 13$$

The only element of the bisection method that has been omitted is how the computer is to determine which half of the interval contains the axis crossing. To that end, consider the product of the function evaluated at the left, $f_1 = f(x_1)$, and the function evaluated at the midpoint, $f_2 = f(x_2)$.

If	Then
$f_1 f_2 > 0.0$	The f_1 and f_2 are both positive or both negative. In either case there is no crossing between x_1 and x_2.
$f_1 f_2 < 0.0$	The $f(x)$ has changed sign between x_1 and x_2, and thus the root is in the left half.

The program to compute the root of an equation using this procedure is given in Figure 4-10. This program illustrates most of the ideas of this chapter and should be studied carefully. Notice especially the following features in the program:

- In each iteration after the first, there is only one function evaluation. It would be highly inefficient to reevaluate $f(x_1)$, $f(x_2)$, and $f(x_3)$ for each iteration since two of them are already known. If the function were extremely complicated, redundant computations like this could be a serious problem. A great deal of computer time is wasted every day by carelessly written programs that contain unnecessary function evaluations.
- The program contains several checks for potential problems along with diagnostic messages (e.g., excessive iteration, no root in interval, etc.) even though the programmer may think these possibilities are remote. Generally, the more of these checks a program contains, the better. They take only a few minutes to add to a code and can save hours of debugging time.
- The criterion for success is based on the size of the interval. Thus, even if the function were not close to zero at this point, x is changing very little, and continuing would not substantially improve the accuracy of the root.

One final comment: This method is an example of a so-called brute force method; that is, it possesses a minimum of finesse. Although it is an excellent example of FORTRAN techniques, much more powerful and clever procedures will be found when we discuss numerical analysis.

Figure 4-10

FORTRAN program
for the bisection
algorithm

```
      PROGRAM BISEC
*--
*-- The interval a<x<b is known to contain a root of f(x).  The
*-- estimate of the root is successively improved by finding in
*-- which half of the interval the root lies and then replacing
*-- the original interval by that half.
*------------------------------------------------------------------
* Variables
*--
      REAL X1,X2,X3,F1,F2,F3,A,B,EPS,D,D0
      INTEGER I,IMAX
*--
*--     X1,X3,X2  --  The left, right, and midpoint of the
*--                        current interval
*--     F1,F3,F2  --  The function evaluated at these points
*--     A,B, D0   --  The left and right ends of the original
*--                        interval and its width (b-a)
*--       EPS     --  Convergence criterion based on the size of
*--                        the current interval
*--        D      --  The width of the current interval (x3-x1)
*--       IMAX    --  Maximum number of iterations
*--        I      --  Current iteration counter
*------------------------------------------------------------------
* Statement function for the function f(x)
*--
      F(X) = EXP(-X) - SIN(.5*PI*X)
*--
*--          (or any other function)
*------------------------------------------------------------------
* Initialization
*--
      PI = ACOS(-1.)
      WRITE(*,*)'Enter limits of original search interval, a,b'
      READ (*,*)A,B
      WRITE(*,*)'Enter convergence criterion (EPS) and ',
     +          'max. no. of iterations (IMAX)'
      READ (*,*)EPS,IMAX
*--
      WRITE(*,*)'The original search interval is from ',A,' to ',B
      WRITE(*,*)'The convergence criterion is (interval) < ',EPS
      WRITE(*,*)'The maximum No. of iterations allowed is  ',IMAX
      WRITE(*,*)
*--
      X1 = A
      X3 = B
      F1 = F(X1)
      F3 = F(X3)
      D0 = (B-A)
*--
*--      First verify that there is indeed a root in the interval.
*--
      IF(F1*F3 .GT. 0.0)THEN
          WRITE(*,*)'No root in original interval. It is possible'
          WRITE(*,*)'that the function is incorrectly coded.'
      ELSE
```

Figure 4-10
(concluded)

```
*       Begin Iterations loop
*--
          DO 3 I = 1,IMAX
*--
*--         Find which half of the interval contains the root
*--
            X2 = .5*(X1 + X3)
            F2 = F(X2)
            IF(F1*F2 .LE. 0.0)THEN
*--
*--           Root is in left half, so
*--
              D  = (X2 - X1)/2.
              F3 = F2
              X3 = X2
            ELSE
*--
*--           Root is in right half, so
*--
              D  = (X3 - X2)/2.
              F1 = F2
              X1 = X2
            ENDIF
*--
*--         Test for convergence
*--
            IF(D .LT. EPS)THEN
*--
*--           Success path
*--
              WRITE(*,*)'A root at x = ',X2,' was found'
              WRITE(*,*)'in ',I,' iterations'
              WRITE(*,*)'The value of the function is ',F2
              STOP 'success'
            ENDIF
 3        CONTINUE
*------------------------------------------------------------------
*       Excessive Iterations Path
*--
          WRITE(*,*)'After ',IMAX,' iterations, no root was found'
          WRITE(*,*)' within the convergence criterion'
          STOP 'failure'
        ENDIF
        END
```

```
Enter limits of original search interval, a,b
 0.4, 0.5
Enter convergence criterion (EPS) and max. no. of iterations(IMAX)
 1.E-5, 25
The original search interval is from 0.400 to 0.500
The convergence criterion is (interval) < 1.000E-05
The maximum No. of iterations allowed is  25

A root at x = 0.4435669 was found
in 13 iterations
The value of the function is 1.215935E-05
```

4.6   Using Data Files and Data Statements

Most likely the programs you will be writing in the future will be designed to execute at a terminal and will require numerous variables to be assigned values by reading data. Every time the program is executed at the terminal, the data will have to be reentered and correctly positioned. During the debugging stage of a program's development, this task can be an extremely annoying interruption to your work. As was pointed out in Section 2.9, it is possible to use an editor program to create a data file that will include all the numbers to be read by the program. The data file is then connected to the FORTRAN program by means of the OPEN statement and is read from by using the READ( ) statement. This section will explain how to take advantage of your increased facility with file manipulation and text editors. The discussion of data files, begun in Chapter 2, will be expanded, making possible the routine use of data files for both program input and output.

Disk Data Files

As mentioned in Section 1.2, a computer has two types of memory: main memory (or fast memory) and secondary memory (slower). Data files are always stored in secondary memory. In order to visualize the structure of data files, it is useful to have some familiarity with the operation of two secondary-memory devices: magnetic tape and magnetic disk.

One of the first devices used to store large amounts of data was *magnetic tape.* On the tape each line of data or code is called a *record,* and the information is copied onto the tape sequentially. The end of the data or program is then marked with an END-OF-FILE mark. These files are called *sequential-access method* (SAM) files. Sequential files can also be written to magnetic disk and are by far the most commonly used by FORTRAN programmers. The information contained on a SAM file can be read only in the same order it was written. Thus, it is not possible to skip to the middle of a large SAM file. This feature can be a significant disadvantage when huge data files are being used and manipulated.

A second type of file in FORTRAN uses the properties of a magnetic disk. The magnetic disk, like magnetic tape, stores information compactly in terms of magnetized bits. The physical structure is similar to a phonograph record, and the information is read from the disk by an access arm. The information recorded on the disk can be written in normal sequential order (a SAM file), or it can be placed in random order with each line (or record) assigned a sequencing record number. Such files are called *direct-access method* (DAM) files. Each record or line on a DAM file must be of the same length. The records on the file can be read in any order. This feature is especially useful when you are reading or updating large data files such as personnel records or inventory lists. Although sequential files may be easily created by using a text editor program, as was discussed in Chapter 2, direct files can be created only by means of a FORTRAN program.

Either type of file may be connected to the FORTRAN program via the OPEN statement.

■ OPEN Statement Specifications

As described in Section 2.9, the OPEN statement can be used in FORTRAN to assign a name and a unit number to a file. Several additional file attributes can be specified by the OPEN statement:

> Whether the file is sequential (SAM) or direct (DAM)

> Whether blank spaces in the file are to be interpreted as zeros or as blanks

> Whether the file already exists in the system (like a data file) or is to be a new file (e.g., results)

The complete form of the OPEN statement to accomplish all this is

```
    OPEN(UNIT = ⟨un⟩, FILE = ⟨flname⟩, ERR = ⟨sl⟩,
+        STATUS = ⟨stat⟩, ACCESS = ⟨acc⟩,BLANK= ⟨blnk⟩)
```

where

> ⟨un⟩ is a positive integer (< 100) that specifies the unit of the file to be opened (e.g., UNIT = 33).

> ⟨flname⟩ is a name (perhaps including a "path" and/or a suffix) that identifies the file. Because this name is ordinarily a character expression, it must be enclosed in apostrophes (e.g., FILE = 'NEWDATA').

> ⟨sl⟩ is a statement number of an executable statement to which the program will branch if there is an error encountered while opening the file. (Perhaps the data file is not present in the system.) The ERR = ⟨sl⟩ field is optional.

> ⟨stat⟩ is a character expression that specifies whether the file already exists or is to be created. The valid values are

> > 'OLD'   File ⟨flname⟩ already exists in the system. (The apostrophes must be included.)

> > 'NEW'   The file does not yet exist in the system.

> > 'SCRATCH'   The file must not be named. The file will be deleted at program termination or upon execution of a CLOSE statement (see the next section). This is a method to provide temporary files.

The STATUS = ⟨stat⟩ field is also optional; if it is omitted the value of STATUS is 'UNKNOWN'.

⟨acc⟩ is a character expression that specifies whether the file is sequential or direct access. The valid values of ⟨acc⟩ are

> 'SEQUENTIAL'   File ⟨flname⟩ is SAM.
>
> 'DIRECT'   File ⟨flname⟩ is DAM.

The ACCESS = ⟨acc⟩ specification is optional; if it is omitted the file is assumed to be sequential.

⟨blnk⟩ is a character expression used to specify whether blanks are to be interpreted as zeros or as blanks. It may have only the values

> 'ZERO'   All blanks, other than leading blanks, are treated as zeros.
>
> 'NULL'   Blanks appearing in numbers are ignored, except that a line of all blanks is treated as zero.

If this field is omitted, a value of 'NULL' is assumed.

Because of the default assignments listed above, the OPEN statement

```
OPEN(UNIT=9, FILE='MYDATA', STATUS='UNKNOWN',
     ACCESS='SEQUENTIAL', BLANK='NULL')
```

is identical to the shortened statement

```
OPEN(9,FILE='MYDATA')
```

A few additional attributes of a data file may be specified by means of an OPEN statement; these will be described when direct-access files are discussed in Section 4.7.

Additional File-Manipulation Statements

CLOSE Statement

After you are finished with a file, the file may be disconnected from the program with the CLOSE statement. The specification options are similar to those for the OPEN statement. Thus, after reading data from the data file opened above, you could close the file with

```
CLOSE(9,STATUS = ⟨stat⟩)
```

where the value of ⟨stat⟩ is either of the character expressions 'KEEP' or 'DELETE', indicating that the file is or is not deleted upon execution of the

CLOSE statement. If the STATUS = ⟨stat⟩ field is omitted, 'KEEP' is assumed. A simplified form of the CLOSE statement is

```
CLOSE(9)
```

Because all files are automatically closed when execution of the program is completed, using the CLOSE statement to close a file is not required.

REWIND Statement

When you use a disk data file it is always a good idea, after opening the file, to make sure t at the computer is positioned at the beginning of the file. (It probably will be but it does not hurt to make sure.) This check is done with the REWIND statement, which is of the form

```
REWIND (UNIT=⟨un⟩)    or    REWIND ⟨un⟩
```

For example, REWIND(UNIT=9) and REWIND 9 are equivalent.

BACKSPACE Statement

A statement similar to the REWIND statement but that backspaces only one line at a time is the BACKSPACE command. The form of this statement is

```
BACKSPACE(UNIT=⟨un⟩)    or    BACKSPACE ⟨un⟩
```

where ⟨un⟩ is the unit number of the file to be backspaced. Only sequential files (SAM) can be backspaced. If the file is already positioned at the beginning, a BACKSPACE statement has no effect.

An obvious application of the BACKSPACE statement might be to read a data file down to a particular line, backspace, and then rewrite the data line with corrected information back into the same file. Unfortunately, this is not possible with SAM files. You cannot both READ from and WRITE to the same file in a program.[3] Thus, SAM files cannot be easily updated using the BACKSPACE statement. In applications where updating large files is important, direct-access (DAM) files should be used (see Section 4.7).

The only real utility of the BACKSPACE statement is as part of a diagnosis of data-reading errors. The idea is to include an "ERR = " option in the READ statement (see Section 2.9); then, if an error is detected during the read, instruct the program to branch to a section that backspaces and rereads the entire line as a character variable of width, say, 72. The line is then printed as is, and perhaps the problem can be identified.

---

[3] Technically, writing to a SAM file is always possible. The difficulty is that all the information on the file that follows the just-written line is destroyed. This feature is acceptable if we are always writing information sequentially but could be disastrous if an attempt is made to alter a line in the middle of the file.

ENDFILE Statement

The END-OF-FILE mark is useful when the "END = " option is employed in READ statements (see Section 2.9). An END-OF-FILE mark can be written on a SAM file with the FORTRAN statement

ENDFILE ⟨un⟩

Since an END-OF-FILE mark will automatically be placed on the file after it is written and disconnected from the program used to create it, it is not required to specifically mark the end of a data file.

Creating a Data File

The steps involved in creating a data file at the terminal are similar to those used in setting up a FORTRAN program; that is, an editor program is used to write, name, and then save the data file. The file is then accessible to FORTRAN programs. For example, the file below was entered and saved as a data file with the name GRADES. The information on each line consists of a student's last name (enclosed in apostrophes), class (1 = freshman, 2 = sophomore, etc.), college (1 = Arts and Science, 2 = Business, 3 = Engineering), three one-hour quiz grades, a homework grade total, and the final exam score. The first line of the file contains a single integer indicating how many students are in the class.

```
14
'Wilson    ', 2, 3, 71, 65, 82, 80, 77
'Greeley   ', 2, 1, 95, 92, 91, 30, 85
'Novak     ', 3, 1, 66, 50, 59, 66, 62
'Chen      ', 2, 3, 77, 75, 80, 86, 83
'Strauss   ', 1, 1, 91, 96, 93, 88, 94
'Reeves    ', 2, 2, 71, 65, 80, 80, 72
'Hunsicher ', 2, 3, 82, 89, 91, 75, 84
'Levy      ', 2, 3, 61, 68, 60, 42, 57
'Brown     ', 2, 3, 71, 80, 77, 65, 73
'Cassidy   ', 2, 3, 82, 71, 88, 56, 71
'Taylor    ', 3, 2, 66, 75, 77, 67, 82
'Stephenson', 2, 3, 45, 60, 62, 21, 51
'Nelson    ', 2, 3, 91, 86, 94, 92, 91
'McDermitt ', 2, 1, 71, 65, 66, 61, 69
```

The program ASSIGN (Figure 4-11) reads the file GRADES (several times) and computes a final score (the sum of the quizzes plus homework plus three times the final exam score) for each student. It rereads the file once for each college and lists the students in that college and his or her final grade. Rereading the data file in this manner is extremely inefficient.

More efficient methods for problems of this type are presented in Chapter 7. A pseudocode outline of the problem follows:

```
PROGRAM ASSIGN
OPEN data file
OPEN file for results
PRINT overall headings
For each college k = 1 to 3
        PRINT table headings
        REWIND data file and read N = No. of lines
```

Figure 4-11

FORTRAN program for computing student grades

```
         PROGRAM ASSIGN
         CHARACTER GRADE*1,NAME*10
         INTEGER CLASS, COLEGE,KOLAGE,Q1,Q2,Q3,HW,EXAM,TOTAL
         REAL PERCNT
*--
         OPEN(22,FILE='GRADES')
         OPEN(33,FILE='RESULTS')
         WRITE(33,*)'The final grades for students arranged by college'
         DO 3 KOLEGE = 1,3
             WRITE(33,*)'-----------------------------------------------'
             WRITE(33,*)'For students in college No.-',KOLAGE
             WRITE(33,*)'           Hour quizzes  Home Final  Tot.     '
             WRITE(33,*)'Name       1    2    3   work Exam   Pct.  Grade'
             WRITE(33,*)'--------- --   --   --   ---- ----   ---   -----'
             REWIND (22)
             READ(22,*)N
             DO 2 I = 1,N
                 READ(22,*)NAME,CLASS,COLEGE,Q1,Q2,Q3,HW,EXAM
                 IF(COLEGE .EQ. KOLEGE)THEN
*--
*--              Compute letter grade for this student in college = KOLEGE
*--
                     TOTAL  = Q1 + Q2 + Q3 + HW + 3*EXAM
                     PERCNT = TOTAL/700.*100.
                     IF(PERCNT .GE. 90.)THEN
                         GRADE = 'A'
                     ELSEIF(PERCNT .GE. 80.)THEN
                         GRADE = 'B'
                     ELSEIF(PERCNT .GE. 70.)THEN
                         GRADE = 'C'
                     ELSEIF(PERCNT .GE. 60.)THEN
                         GRADE = 'D'
                     ELSE
                         GRADE = 'F'
                     ENDIF
                     WRITE(33,*)NAME,Q1,Q2,Q3,HW,EXAM,PERCNT,GRADE
                 ENDIF
2            CONTINUE
3        CONTINUE
         CLOSE (22)
         CLOSE (33)
         STOP
         END
```

Figure 4-11
(concluded)

```
(The numbers in this file were repositioned by using a text editor.)
The final grades for students arranged by college
--------------------------------------------------
For students in college No.-    1
            Hour quizzes  Home Final  Tot.
Name        1    2    3   work Exam   Pct.   Grade
---------   --   --   --  ---- ----   ---    -----
Greeley     95   92   91   30   85    80.42    B
Novak       66   50   59   66   62    61.00    D
Strauss     91   96   93   88   94    92.85    A
McDermitt 71     65   66   61   69    67.10    D
--------------------------------------------------
For students in college No.-    2
            Hour quizzes  Home Final  Tot.
Name        1    2    3   work Exam   Pct.   Grade
---------   --   --   --  ---- ----   ---    -----
Reeves      71   65   80   80   72    73.14    C
Taylor      66   75   77   67   82    75.85    C
--------------------------------------------------
For students in college No.-    3
            Hour quizzes  Home Final  Tot.
Name        1    2    3   work Exam   Pct.   Grade
---------   --   --   --  ---- ----   ---    -----
Wilson      71   65   82   80   77    75.57    C
Chen        77   75   80   86   83    81.00    B
Hunsicher 82     89   91   75   84    84.14    B
Levy        61   68   60   42   57    57.42    F
Brown       71   80   77   65   73    73.14    C
Cassidy     82   71   88   56   71    72.85    C
Stephenson45     60   62   21   51    48.71    F
Nelson      91   86   94   92   91    90.85    A
```

For each line of data, i = 1, N
    IF(student is in college k)THEN
       Compute total score and from it letter grade .
    PRINT a line of table for this student
    ENDIF
  End i-loop
End k-loop
CLOSE input and output files

■ DATA Statement

Most programs require the initialization of numerous constants before the computation can commence. These assignments differ from the initialization of the variables of the problem, which will be changed from one run to the next by reading input data from a file. A simple assignment statement at the beginning of the program could be used to assign the appropriate values to these constants; however, each FORTRAN assignment or READ statement is, of course, an executable statement and as such adds to the execution time of the program. For cases such as this and for those cases where the amount of the input data is small enough to make the creation of a separate data file inconvenient, FORTRAN provides an alternative: the DATA statement. The form of the DATA statement is

DATA ⟨namelist⟩/⟨valuelist⟩/

where ⟨namelist⟩ is a list of FORTRAN variables to be initially assigned a corresponding value in the ⟨valuelist⟩. The values in the ⟨valuelist⟩ must agree by type to the corresponding name.

DATA PI,ILOW,IHI,/3.1415926,0,50/

Notice that the names and the values are separated by commas and that the ⟨valuelist⟩ is enclosed with slashes. Also, the constants in the ⟨valuelist⟩ can be repeated by including an unsigned positive integer as a replication factor.

DATA SUM,TERM,I,J,K/2*0.0,3*1/

Parentheses are not permitted in the ⟨valuelist⟩.

The DATA statement is a nonexecutable statement and may appear anywhere in the program after the type-declaration statements. It is advisable though always to place the DATA statement immediately after the type declarations. It is important to remember that the DATA statement assigns values to parameters before execution of the program begins, that is, during compilation of the program.

4.7 Using Direct-Access (DAM) Files*

Sequentially accessed (SAM) files are the most common type of data file used in a typical engineering application. With a SAM file the information is read from or written to just as you would with a list—in order, one line after another. There are, however, two applications in particular for which the properties of SAM files are not well suited. The first is reading information directly from the middle or end of a very large data file. The second is reading a line of information and then correcting and rewriting the same line on the file—that is, updating the file. If these two types of tasks are or will be an important part of your work, you should be familiar with the manipulation of direct-access (DAM) files.

Records on DAM Files

On a SAM file, a record is simply a line of information that may be of any length, limited only by the associated I/O devices. Ordinarily, the data lines or records will not have explicit line numbers, and to read the

---

*This section contains more advanced material and may be omitted without a loss of continuity.

information on the 13th line we have to first read through the preceding 12 lines.

On a DAM file, each record (or line) must have a corresponding record number (or line number). These records are then positioned on the file in random order. A particular record may then be accessed directly by specifying its record number. This process is illustrated in Figure 4-12.

From the way information is stored on a DAM file, we see that a command to REWIND the file would have no meaning. A DAM file does not have a conventional beginning or end. Attempts to write an END-OF-FILE mark on a DAM file will cause an error.

An important constraint on the use of DAM files is the requirement that all records on the file have the same length. For this reason, list-directed I/O is not possible with DAM files. The record length is specified when the file is created and is ordinarily expressed as the total number of computer words (or, on some computers, bytes) to appear in a record.[4] To determine the maximum record length you will need when creating a direct-access file, simply count the maximum number of numerical values to be included in a record. Each numerical quantity of types real and integer occupies one word (or perhaps 4 or 8 bytes). Character variables are a bit more troublesome. Depending on the computer, from 4 to 10 charac-

Figure 4-12 _____

Comparison of the structure of SAM and DAM files

Sequential arrangement
of data on a SAM file

Random arrangement of
records on a DAM disk file

'BANK BALANCE'
'ARRON', 322.55
'BAKER', 1044.20
'SMITH', 2.78

_____

[4] A DAM file must be specified as either FORMATTED or UNFORMATTED. If the file is of type FORMATTED, the record length is given in terms of the maximum number of spaces or characters to be stored in each record. The DAM files described in this chapter are of form UNFORMATTED. Reading from or writing to a FORMATTED direct-access file is less efficient and requires using the FORMAT statement, which will be described in Chapter 6. Additionally, list-directed I/O (for example, PRINT *) is actually formatted in the sense that the appropriate format specifications are supplied by the compiler rather than by the user.

ters are stored in a computer word. Thus, if the variable NAME is of type CHARACTER*17, it would occupy from two to five computer words. If you do not know how many characters are in a computer word, assume there are four for safety. Obviously, execution-time errors will be caused by writing beyond the specified length of a record. Also, each record need not be filled.

Creating a DAM File

Whether you are creating a new file or reading from an existing data file, the OPEN statement must first be employed in the FORTRAN program to establish a link between the program and the file. The form of an OPEN statement used to access a DAM file is similar to that used with a sequential file. The differences are that for a DAM file the argument of the OPEN statement must include the following additional information:

1. *ACCESS type of the file.* Since the default is type sequential, the argument list for a DAM file must contain the phrase

   ```
   ACCESS = 'DIRECT'
   ```

2. *FORM of the formatting specification.* The arrangement of the information must be specified as either FORMATTED or UNFORMATTED. So, for our applications, the OPEN statement should contain the phrase

   ```
   FORM = 'UNFORMATTED'
   ```

3. *Record length.* As mentioned above, the required record length will depend on the problem at hand. Be sure that ample room is provided on each record. The record length is specified by including a phrase of the form

   ```
   RECL = 100
   ```

   This specification must be included when opening a DAM file.

   A typical OPEN statement to connect an existing data file of type DAM named MYDATA and associated with unit number 43 would be

```
OPEN(43,FILE='MYDATA',ACCESS='DIRECT',FORM='UNFORMATTED',RECL=100)
```

The procedure to write information to this file is now rather simple. In addition to the unit number, all READ( )/WRITE( ) statements for DAM files must also include the record number of the associated line of information.

```
READ (<unit>,REC = <integer>,...)
WRITE(<unit>,REC = <integer>,...)
```

For example, to write names and bank balances to a DAM data file after they are entered at the terminal, the code in Figure 4-13 could be used.

▉ Reading and Correcting Information on a DAM File

As indicated above, the only information that must be added to an ordinary READ statement when you are reading from a DAM file is the location (record number) of the line containing the data. The information must be read from the file in exactly the same manner in which it was written. The variables in the READ list must match the variables in the WRITE by type. Also, a DAM file cannot be edited with a text editor. The primary advantage of DAM files, at least for our purposes, is that the READ can be followed by a WRITE to the same file. (Recall that with sequential files a WRITE statement will destroy all subsequent lines in the file.)

As an example, suppose you wish to correct the bank balance of Jane Smith. If we kept a list of the names and associated record numbers on file BANKBL, we would first scan the list and perhaps find that Smith's data line is on line 3017. After the bank balance file has been opened (on unit = 88), the code to correct Smith's balance would simply be

```
READ *,BAL
WRITE(88,REC=3017)'Smith, Jane          ',BAL
```
This character constant must be of length 20.

DAM files are a relatively new addition to FORTRAN. Engineers and scientists are just beginning to realize the advantages and convenience of DAM files for some applications.

Figure 4-13

Program to create a DAM data file of names and bank balances

```
        CHARACTER NAME*20
        READ      BAL
        INTEGER   LINE,N
*
        OPEN(16,FILE='BANKBL',ACCESS='DIRECT',FORM='UNFORMATTED',
       +       RECL= 50)
        PRINT *,'Enter the total number of data ',
       +       'lines you wish to correct'
        READ *,N
        PRINT *,'Enter name (enclosed in single quotes)'
        PRINT *,'and bank balance (separated by a comma)'
        READ *,NAME,BAL
*
        DO 1 LINE = 1,N
             WRITE(16,REC=LINE)NAME,BAL
      1 CONTINUE
        STOP
        END
```

Summary

Most numerical analysis programs will use one or more of the elementary programming techniques described in this chapter. These techniques are the basis for the "bag of tricks" that every programmer must have at his or her disposal. A well-written program will usually contain one or more of these procedures constructed with easily recognizable variable names and in a form similar to that given in this chapter. Since the goal is to create clear and accurate programs, replacing complicated algebraic expressions by FORTRAN statement functions is always recommended as a first step in removing program clutter.

A statement function is simply a replacement for a single FORTRAN assignment statement containing an arithmetic expression. There are several rules for constructing statement functions:

- Other than assignment statements, no other FORTRAN statements are permitted in a statement function [e.g., IF( ), DO, READ( ), etc.].
- The statement-function definition line must precede all executable statements and follow all nonexecutable type-declaration statements. If a statement function refers to another statement function, the latter must have been defined in a previous line.
- The variables in the argument list of a statement-function definition line are called dummy arguments and are assigned values (by position in the list, not by name) when the function is used in an arithmetic expression later in the FORTRAN program.
- The type of the numerical value returned by the statement function is determined by the type of the name of the function. Statement-function names should be different from common intrinsic library functions. In the case of a conflict of names, the program will use the user-defined function.
- The definition of a statement function remains valid only within the program or subprogram in which it is defined.

The three computational algorithms discussed in this chapter can serve as prototypes for programs to solve a wide variety of engineering problems. These three procedures follow:

1. Scanning a list to find the minimum or maximum of the list. The essential elements of the algorithm follow:

```
READ ( * , * ) XMAX
```
Define top of list to be temporary value of maximum.

```
      DO 1 I = 1,IMAX
        READ(*,*)X
        IF(X .GT. XMAX)XMAX = X
    1 CONTINUE
```
Scan down remaining list. If current value is greater than temporary maximum, redefine temporary maximum.

2. Performing summations with the use of DO loops.

```
      SUM = 0.
      DO 2 K = 1, KMAX
        TERM = ...
        SUM  = SUM + TERM
    2 CONTINUE
```
Initialize SUM.

For each term in the sum, compute the value of the next term and replace SUM by SUM + TERM.

For infinite summations, the DO loop is terminated when $|\text{term}| < \epsilon$, where ϵ is a user-supplied convergence criterion.

3. Monitoring the progress of a function until a particular condition is met. This computational procedure, in one form or another, is present in a majority of programs and is most clearly illustrated by the algorithm for finding roots of a function by monitoring the sign of the function as the program progresses through a range of the independent variable.

```
      DX = ...
      X0 = ...
      F0 = F(X0)

      DO 8 I = 1,100
        X = X + DX

        IF(F(X)*FO .LT. 0.)THEN
            A = X-DX
            B = X
              etc.
        ENDIF
    8 CONTINUE
      WRITE(*,*)'stepped too far'
```
Initialize the starting values and the step size.

Step along the axis in small steps of size DX.

Monitor the function. If the function changes sign, a root is contained in the most recent step.

The use of data files both for input to and output from your FORTRAN programs will significantly reduce the potential for errors and greatly enhance the ease of running a program and obtaining suitable output. Data files used for input will replace repeated typing of numerical values on subsequent runs; used for output, they can then be read by editor programs for printing or by graphics programs for plotting. The principal points to remember about creating and manipulating data files follow: The OPEN statement is used to connect a FORTRAN program to other new or existing files. The shortened form of the OPEN statement is

```
      OPEN(#,FILE = 'filename')
```

where # is a positive integer <100 that is used to identify the file in subsequent READ/WRITE statements, replacing the first asterisk in READ(*,*) or WRITE(*,*). The file name must be enclosed in quotes and may require a "path" designation. Data files may be rewound, read, or reread by your program. In addition, data files created by a FORTRAN program may be read by an ordinary text editing program and may be used as input to a variety of spreadsheet programs or to graphics programs that can be used to produce a plot of the results.

The DATA statement is used to initialize variables at the time of compilation and is of the form

DATA⟨namelist⟩/⟨valuelist⟩/

where ⟨namelist⟩ is a list of FORTRAN variables to be initially assigned a corresponding value in the ⟨valuelist⟩. The DATA statement is a nonexecutable statement and may appear anywhere in the program after the type-declaration statements.

Direct-access data files may be useful in situations where individual lines of a data file must be frequently accessed or altered. The principal attributes of a direct-access file are that each of the individual lines (or records) of the file are limited to the same maximum length specified in the associated OPEN statement, that the lines are placed randomly on the disk and are located by their line number, and that the information on a line will be read in exactly the same form in which it was written.

Problems

4.1 Write statement functions for the following expressions:
 a. $f(x) = 3x^2 + x - 1$
 b. $g(x) = ax^2 + bx + c$
 c. $r(a,b,c) = (-b + \sqrt{b^2 - 4ac})/2a$
 d. $h(y) = e^{-ay} + \ln[\sin(\pi y)]$

4.2 A data file with the name GRADES contains the results of an examination in a class of 65 students. The data on each line includes the student's name (CHARACTER*15) and the exam score. Write a complete program to read the data file and perform the following operations:
 a. Write the names and exam scores of students who have failed (score < 60) as they are encountered.
 b. Count the number of students receiving each letter grade A–F, determined by

$$F < 60 \le D < 70 \le C < 80 \le B < 90 \le A$$

 c. Determine the names of the students with the maximum and minimum exam scores.
 d. Determine the average exam score.
 e. Determine the class grade point average (GPA) on the A = 4.0, F = 0.0 basis.

4.3 Write programs to evaluate the following expressions, terminating the sums when the absolute value of a term is less than 10^{-4}. Use a DO loop by first determining the upper limit of the loop from the given convergence criterion.

a. $\dfrac{1}{1^2} + \dfrac{1}{2^2} + \dfrac{1}{3^2} + \cdots + \dfrac{1}{n^2} + \cdots \left(= \dfrac{\pi^2}{6} \right)$

b. $1 - \dfrac{1}{3} + \dfrac{1}{5} - \dfrac{1}{7} + \cdots \left(= \dfrac{\pi}{4} \right)$

c. $1 + \dfrac{1}{2} + \dfrac{1}{4} + \dfrac{1}{8} + \cdots + \dfrac{1}{2^n} + \cdots (= 2)$

d. $\dfrac{1}{4} + \dfrac{1}{16} + \dfrac{1}{64} + \cdots + \dfrac{1}{4^n} + \cdots \left(= \dfrac{1}{3} \right)$

4.4 In each of the infinite expressions below, relate the $(n + 1)$-st term to the nth term. Then write a program to use a DO loop to evaluate the expression, including terms until $|\text{term}| < 10^{-5}$. Print the result and compare it with the exact answer.

a. $1 + 2 + \dfrac{4}{2!} + \dfrac{8}{3!} + \cdots + \dfrac{2^n}{n!} + \cdots (= e)$

b. $1 + 1 + \dfrac{2}{4} + \dfrac{6}{27} + \dfrac{24}{256} + \cdots + \dfrac{n!}{n^n} + \cdots (= 2.879853862175\ldots)$

4.5 Adapt the algorithm for infinite summations to handle the infinite product below. How will you have the program decide on when to terminate the calculation?

$$\left(\dfrac{2 \times 2}{1 \times 3} \right) \left(\dfrac{4 \times 4}{3 \times 5} \right) \left(\dfrac{6 \times 6}{5 \times 7} \right) \cdots \left(\dfrac{(2n)\,(2n)}{(2n - 1)\,(2n + 1)} \right) \cdots \left(= \dfrac{\pi}{2} \right)$$

4.6 The FORTRAN program to sum the series for e^x given in Figure 4-5 is likely to fail when the magnitude of x is large. Since the general term in the series is $x^n/n!$, the terms will continue to grow until $n!$ finally becomes larger than x^n, and many terms will have to be included to obtain an accurate result. For x large and negative, the situation is much worse. Not only will many large initial terms have to be accumulated, but since the result is nearly zero (e.g., $e^{-10} \approx 0.000045$) the near cancellation of large terms will introduce considerable round-off error. Rewrite the program to read a value of x, and if $|x|$ is larger than 1.0, first scale x to a value x' such that $0 < |x'| < 1$ and evaluate $e^{x'}$. Then scale the result back up to equal e^x. Test the program for $x = 50$ and $x = -50$.

4.7 Write a program that creates a data file of 101 lines. The first line contains values for dt, v_x, and v_y, and the numbers on successive lines are the values of t_i, x_i, and y_i, which specify the trajectory of a projectile, namely,

$$x_i = v_x t_i$$
$$y_i = v_y t_i - \tfrac{1}{2} g t_i^2 \quad (g = 9.8 \text{ m/s}^2)$$
$$t_i = i\,dt \quad \text{for } i = 0, 100$$

and

$$v_x = 10.5 \qquad v_y = 51.0 \qquad dt = 0.1$$

a. Write a separate program that reads and scans the data file to find the value of t_i that corresponds to the maximum height (y_i) on the trajectory.

4.8 Write a program that will read a file called ROSTER. The first line of the file contains the total number of data lines that follow. On each of the subsequent lines is a student's name, current GPA, and credits earned to date. The data file is then to be completely rewritten. If the number of credits ≥ 125, the student has graduated and should be deleted from the list. If the GPA is ≥ 3.25, the student has made the dean's list. If the GPA is ≤ 2.0, the student is on probation. The rewritten file should first list all the dean's list students, followed by all students on probation, followed by all the remaining students. (Your program will have to read the data file several times. Do not use arrays.)

4.9 This problem illustrates the use of direct-access data files.
a. Write a program that will read the SAM file used in program ASSIGN of Section 4.6 and write a more accessible DAM data file containing the same information. In addition, the program should count and include in the DAM file the total number of students in each college. The information should be written to the DAM file so the record numbers on the file are of the form

```
Rec. No. = 1000(COLLGE - 1) + I
```

where COLLGE = college (1 = Arts and Science, etc.) and I is a counter from 1 to 999. Thus, Rec. No. = 2006 includes the information for the sixth student in the engineering (3) college.
b. Rewrite the program ASSIGN to accomplish the same results using the newly established DAM data file.

4.10 Consider the iterative procedure defined by

$$x_{n+1} = \frac{a}{b + x_n}$$

where a and b are positive constants.
a. Write a program to read in constants a and b and to obtain a solution to the procedure such that the difference between successive results is $< 10^{-5}$. For the starting value in each case, use $x_0 = 1.0$. Limit the number of iterations to 500.
b. Show that if this procedure converges, that is, if $\lim_{n \to \infty} x_n = r$ then the exact result of the procedure is $r = \frac{1}{2}(-b \pm \sqrt{b^2 + 4a})$.
c. Run your program and compare it with the exact result for the following choices of (a,b): $(1,1)$, $(8,3)$, $(10,0.1)$. (*Note:* The procedure may converge very slowly for some of these choices.)

4.11 Use the bisection procedure for finding roots of an equation. First construct a table of the following form:

							Crossing	
Step	x_1	x_2	x_3	f_1	f_2	f_3	Left	Right
0	a	$\frac{1}{2}(a+b)$	b					
1								
⋮	⋮	⋮	⋮	⋮	⋮	⋮	⋮	⋮

Next use the bisection procedure and a pocket calculator to obtain the roots of the following functions to an accuracy of five significant figures.

a. $f(x) = x^2 + 2x - 15$
($a = 2.8$, $b = 3.1$, exact answer = 3.0)

b. $g(x) = \sin(x)\sinh(x) + 1$
[Elliptic gear equation, the hyperbolic sine is defined by $\sinh(x) = \frac{1}{2}(e^x - e^{-x})$ and is available on most calculators. Also, x is in radians. Use $a = 1$, $b = 4$.]

c. $e(x) = \sqrt{R^2 - x^2} - x\tan(x)$
(Equation for quantum energies of a particle in a box. Use $R = 10.$, $a = 4.0$, $b = 4.7$.)

d. Predict the number of steps needed to obtain the answer to the specified accuracy in parts a through c.

4.12 Adapt the FORTRAN code in Figure 4-10 to solve for the indicated roots of each of the functions of Problem 4.12. Execute the program and produce a table similar to that in Problem 4.11.

4.13 Write a program to find the maximum of a function $f(x)$ over an interval $a \le x \le b$ by starting at $x = a$ with a step size Δx. Evaluate $f_1 = f(x)$ and $f_2 = f(x + \Delta x)$. If $f_1 < f_2$, replace $x \rightarrow x + \Delta x$ and continue; otherwise, reduce the step size by half and repeat the comparison. The program should terminate successfully when $\Delta < 10^{-6}$.

Subroutines and Functions

5.1 Introduction

Newton once said that if he had achieved much, it was because he had stood on the shoulders of giants. In science and engineering today, progress is still dependent on the discoveries of those who have gone before us. However, it is important to realize that science is structured so that the cumulative effect of centuries of discoveries is not a house of cards. Each discovery of the past can be duplicated and understood by those in the present. Yet each time we differentiate a function we do not rederive the definition of the derivative. Once we have satisfied ourselves that a procedure is correct and well understood, we will thereafter use it without hesitation. These same ideas are in force in FORTRAN programming. Whenever possible, each distinct element in a set of procedures that make up a complicated program should be separately coded, refined, and tested in the form of FORTRAN subprograms. A well-constructed program will be modular, with separate subprogram modules used to perform most of the computations. These subprogram modules may then be easily reused in subsequent programs.

For example, in subsequent engineering courses or in your career, you will be solving problems by using a computer. These problems will probably be much more complicated and involve much longer FORTRAN code than has been presented so far. Suppose you wanted to compute a very complicated function, $y = f(x)$; determine the maximum and minimum of the function over some range; find the zeros of the function by the bisection algorithm; and then graph the function on an automatic plotter. Since it is likely that some or all of these procedures will be used again in future programs, it would be a waste of effort and time to recode and retype those elements of the program that remain basically unchanged from earlier programs. FORTRAN allows the segmentation of a long program into subprogram blocks that are compiled separately. These blocks are called *subroutines* and *functions*, and almost every computer solution to a problem would benefit from their inclusion in the FORTRAN code. The idea behind program segmentations is quite simple: Each computational problem is broken down into its elemental parts, and a separate FORTRAN module (i.e., a subroutine or a function) is written, edited, and tested to handle just that task. Constructing complicated FORTRAN code in terms of smaller program modules serves two very important purposes:

1. The modules can be separately compiled and tested. Thus, debugging a very large program can be addressed in manageable stages.
2. The modules can be used subsequently in other programs. Thus, if considerable effort is expended in designing a reliable function that finds the roots of an arbitrary function, this module can be inserted, *without alteration,* in any later program that requires the roots of functions.

The ability to assemble previously tested FORTRAN code instead of reprogramming the same elements over and over again saves time and effort and frees us from the frustration of making the same dumb errors repeatedly. Indeed, the characteristic feature of modern programming style is the drive toward modular programming.

The definition of subroutines and functions and their use in FORTRAN programs are quite similar to the operations of a simpler but related structure, the statement function. FORTRAN statement functions were introduced in Section 4.2, and since they share many of the features of subroutines and functions, the basic elements of statement functions are reviewed in the next section. This is followed by separate sections detailing the rules pertaining to FORTRAN subroutines and functions, along with a discussion of the distinction between *dummy* and *actual* variables in an argument list. Several examples will illustrate the use of and the distinction between subroutines and functions. Because the majority of large programs consist of a variety of standard or routine operations (represented by subprogram units) on *generic* functions, the assembly of modular units into a complete program is an essential skill and is described in Section 5.6. The final section of this chapter introduces two new FORTRAN statements—the SAVE and COMMON statements—that may be of use in modular programs.

5.2   Review of Statement Functions

Before describing subroutines and functions, let's quickly review the general properties of statement functions. Recall that the rules relating to statement functions pertain to their definition and use.

Definition

1. A statement-function definition must precede the first executable statement and must follow all type-declaration statements in a program.
2. All variables in the statement-function expression should appear in the argument list of the function. For example,

$$\text{FNC(A,B,T)} = \text{A} + \text{B*SIN(T)}$$

Use

1. The statement function is called up simply by using the function name followed by its argument list in any arithmetic expression or FORTRAN statement.
2. When using the function, the variables or numbers appearing in the argument list must agree as to type (integer, real, character) with the variable names in the function definition.
3. The order or sequence of the variables in the argument list is critical. An example follows:

```
X = 2.
A = 3.
B = 4.
W = FNC(A,B,X)        X, not T, is used in the reference
                      to the function.
Y = FNC(3.,4.,2.*A-B)  Y has the same value as W.
```

5.3 Subroutine Subprograms

Frequently, the operations we want the program to execute are too extensive to be represented by a statement function and yet too distracting to the logical flow of the program to include in the body of an otherwise clear algorithm. For example, if in the middle of a program we find that we need the minimum and maximum of a function $f(x)$ over some range $a \leq x \leq b$, it would be very helpful if we could simply instruct the computer to

> Go off to the side, find the minimum, f_{min}, and maximum, f_{max}, of the function for x's in the range $a \leq x \leq b$, and when they have been found, return the values and we will continue from there.

The mechanism for doing this in FORTRAN is the subroutine. As with statement functions, the rules for subroutines relate to their definition and use.

Defining and Referencing a Subroutine

Defining Subroutines

A FORTRAN *subroutine* is a complete, self-contained subprogram that can be initiated in a main program or in other subprograms or functions. The subroutine is compiled separately from the main program and all other subprograms, and the beginning and end of this compilation unit are delimited by a special header line at the beginning and closed with an END statement. Subroutines appear after the END statement in the main program. The form of the first line of a subroutine is

SUBROUTINE ⟨name⟩ (argument list)

The name of the subroutine may be any valid FORTRAN variable name; however, since it will designate a procedure, not a variable, it cannot be assigned a value or used within the body of the subroutine. In short, the subroutine will not have a value for "name." All computed quantities are passed to and returned from the subroutine via the argument list.

It is not required that a subroutine have an argument list, although most will. The parameters in the argument list of a subroutine definition are called *dummy arguments,* meaning that they will be assigned specific values only when the subroutine has been called by some other program unit. (Review the discussion of dummy arguments in Section 4.2.) For example, the subroutine VECTOR in Figure 5-1 computes the length r and angle θ associated with a two-dimensional vector with components x, y (Figure 5-2). When the subroutine is compiled, the variable names X and Y have not yet been assigned values and are dummy arguments.

Figure 5-1

A subroutine to determine in which quadrant a point lies

```
SUBROUTINE VECTOR(X,Y,R,THETA)
REAL X,Y,R,THETA,PI
PI = ACOS(-1.)
R = SQRT(X*X + Y*Y)
THETA = ATAN(ABS(Y/X))
*
*     The point is in the 1st, 2nd, 3rd, 4th quadrant
*     depending on whether (x,y) is (+,+),(-,+),(-,-),(+,-)
*
      IF(Y.GT.0) THEN
          IF(X.GT.0)THEN
             THETA = THETA + 0.0
          ELSE
             THETA = THETA + PI/2.
          ENDIF
      ELSE
          IF(X.LT.0)THEN
             THETA = THETA + PI
          ELSE
             THETA = THETA + 3.*PI/2.
          ENDIF
      ENDIF
RETURN
END
```

Figure 5-2
The relation between the Cartesian (x, y) and the polar (r, θ) coordinates of a point

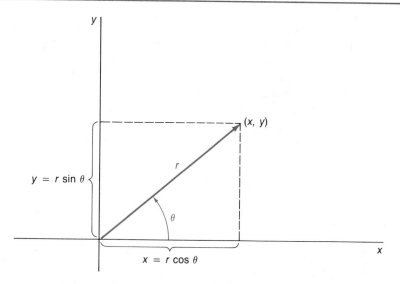

Subroutines usually contain at least one RETURN statement. When this statement is encountered during execution, the operation of the program transfers back to the line from which the subroutine was called and continues from that point. The END statement marks the end of a compilation unit and should not be used to terminate the operations of the subroutine. (If, however, the END statement is encountered during the operation of the subroutine, the program will return to the statement from which the routine was called.)

All variables and statement numbers defined within a subroutine are only locally defined and will not conflict with variable names or statement numbers used in the main program or other subprograms. This feature is important since it would detract considerably from a subroutine's portability if such potential conflicts had to be eliminated every time a subroutine was used in a large program. The calling program can communicate with the subroutine only by means of the argument list, which can be thought of as the only "window" in the structure.

Referencing Subroutines

A subroutine is accessed by means of a CALL statement,

   CALL⟨name⟩ (argument list)

where the "name" agrees with the name in the subroutine definition and the variable names in the argument list agree in number and by type (real, integer, character) with the dummy arguments in the defining argument list. The number of variable names in the argument list of the subroutine CALL must agree with the number of arguments in the subroutine definition, or an execution error will result. Ordinarily, when a subroutine is called, the computation proceeds from the first line of the subroutine until a RETURN, STOP, or END statement is encountered. Additionally, in FORTRAN a subroutine may not directly or indirectly call itself.

A program employing the subroutine VECTOR from Figure 5-1 is shown in Figure 5-3. The parameters are transferred to and returned from the subroutine by position in the argument list. Thus, if the values read for RX and RY were 5.0 and 12.0, the values assigned to X and Y within the subroutine would be 5.0 and 12.0, and the subroutine would compute values of R = 13.0 and θ = 1.176 radians. When the subroutine returns to the main program, these values are then assigned to the variable names in the CALL statement (i.e., 13. → LENGTH, 1.176 → ANGLE); that is, the input to the subroutine is the pair of numbers 5.0 and 12.0, and the output is the pair 13.0 and 1.176. It is the numerical values associated with variable names that are transferred back and forth, not the variable names themselves.

Consider the following incorrect use of a subroutine:

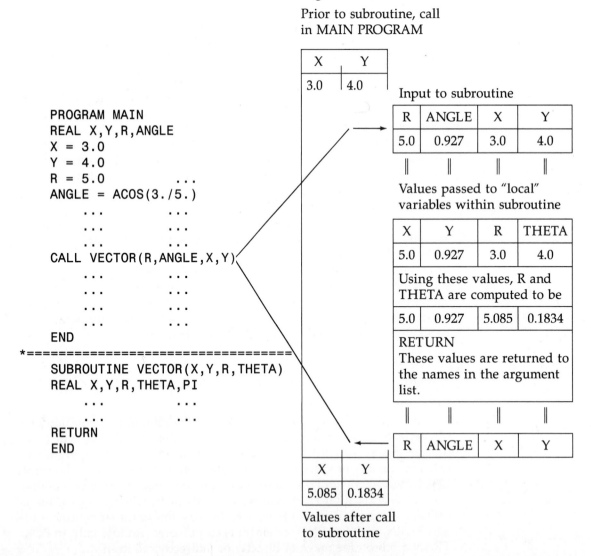

Prior to subroutine, call
in MAIN PROGRAM

X	Y
3.0	4.0

```
PROGRAM MAIN
REAL X,Y,R,ANGLE
X = 3.0
Y = 4.0
R = 5.0              ...
ANGLE = ACOS(3./5.)

      ...             ...
      ...             ...
      ...             ...
CALL VECTOR(R,ANGLE,X,Y)
      ...             ...
      ...             ...
      ...             ...
      ...             ...
END
*==================================
SUBROUTINE VECTOR(X,Y,R,THETA)
REAL X,Y,R,THETA,PI
      ...             ...
      ...             ...
RETURN
END
```

Input to subroutine

R	ANGLE	X	Y
5.0	0.927	3.0	4.0
‖	‖	‖	‖

Values passed to "local"
variables within subroutine

X	Y	R	THETA
5.0	0.927	3.0	4.0
Using these values, R and THETA are computed to be			
5.0	0.927	5.085	0.1834
RETURN These values are returned to the names in the argument list.			
‖	‖	‖	‖
R	ANGLE	X	Y

X	Y
5.085	0.1834

Values after call
to subroutine

Figure 5-3

A program that
uses subroutine
VECTOR to produce
a table

```
PROGRAM LIST
REAL RX,RY,ANGLE,LENGTH
OPEN(12,FILE='VECTORS')
WRITE(*,12)'Table of Vectors'
WRITE(*,12)' Rectangular        Polar'
WRITE(*,12)' Coordinates       Coordinates'
WRITE(*,12)'   x     y          r      theta'
WRITE(*,12)' ----- -----       ----- -----'
DO 1 I = 1,5
  PRINT *,'Enter x, y components of vector'
  READ  *,RX,RY
  CALL VECTOR(RX,RY,LENGTH,ANGLE)
  WRITE(*,12)RX,RY,LENGTH,ANGLE
1    CONTINUE
STOP
END
```

By entering the variables in the wrong order in the call to the subroutine, we have not only obtained incorrect results for R and THETA, but we have overwritten the original values of X and Y.

Transferring Information into and out of a Subroutine

When a subroutine is referenced by a CALL statement, the input variables in the argument list are assumed to have been assigned numerical values. After the CALL, the output variables will also have numerical values. These variables are called *actual arguments*. The assignments to the dummy arguments in the subroutine definition are made by position in the argument list when the subroutine is entered and when it is exited. Since all the variables in the argument list, including those representing input variables, are subject to change, there is a potential for inadvertently altering input variables that were intended to remain fixed. For example, the subroutine in Figure 5-4 will compute the root of a function $f(x)$ by using the bisection algorithm of Section 4.5. The function F(X) must be included elsewhere in the code as a separate FORTRAN FUNCTION subprogram (to be discussed in Section 5.4) and, at this point, must be named "F." The root of the function is known to be in the interval

$$x_1 \le \text{root} \le x_3$$

The input to this subroutine is the interval X1, X3; the convergence criterion, EPS; and the maximum number of iterations, IMAX. The output is the actual number of iterations, I, and the answer, ROOT. This code is nearly the same as the program BISEC of Figure 4-10. The conversion of that tested program to a portable version in the form of a subroutine was easy. In the future, whenever a root of a function is required, we need only to insert this subroutine after the main program, code the function $f(x)$, and insert an appropriate "CALL" in the main program.

Figure 5-4 _____

Subroutine for roots
of a function by
bisection

```
        SUBROUTINE BISEC(A,B,EPS,IMAX,I,ROOT)
*--
*-- The interval a<x<b is known to contain a root of f(x).  The
*-- estimate of the root is successively improved by finding in
*-- which half of the interval the root lies and then replacing
*-- the original interval by that half.  The function f(x) must
*-- have only x in its argument list and must be coded elsewhere
*-- in the program and named FUNCTION F(X).
*-------------------------------------------------------------------
* Variables
*--
        REAL X1,X2,X3,F1,F2,F3,A,B,EPS,D,DO
        INTEGER I,IMAX
*--
*--     X1,X3,X2  --  The left, right, and midpoint of the
*--                       current interval
*--     F1,F3,F2  --  The function evaluated at these points
*--     A,B, DO   --  The left and right ends of the original
*--                       interval and its width (b-a)
*--     EPS       --  Convergence criterion based on the size of
*--                       the current interval
*--     D         --  The width of the current interval (x3-x1)
*--     IMAX      --  Maximum number of iterations
*--     I         --  Current iteration counter
*-------------------------------------------------------------------
* Initialization
*--
        X1 = A
        X3 = B
        F1 = F(X1)
        F3 = F(X3)
        DO = (B-A)
*--
*--     First verify that there is indeed a root in the interval.
*--
        IF(F1*F3 .GT. 0.0)THEN
            WRITE(*,*)'No root in original interval. It is possible'
            WRITE(*,*)'that the function is incorrectly coded.'
        ELSE
*-------------------------------------------------------------------
* Iterations loop
*--
        DO 3 I = 1,IMAX
*--
*--     Find which half of the interval contains the root.
*--
            X2 = .5*(X1 + X3)
            F2 = F(X2)
            IF(F1*F2 .LE. 0.0)THEN
*--
*--             Root is in left half, so
*--
                D  = (X2 - X1)/2.
                F3 = F2
                X3 = X2
            ELSE
*--
```

Figure 5-4
(concluded)

```
*--                    Root is in right half, so
*--

                      D   = (X3 - X2)/2.
                      F1 = F2
                      X1 = X2
                 ENDIF
*--
*--          Test for convergence
*--

                 IF(D .LT. EPS)THEN
*--
*--              Success path
*--
*--

                 ROOT = X2
                 RETURN
            ENDIF
      3     CONTINUE
*--------------------------------------------------------------
*          Excessive Iterations Path
*--
            WRITE(*,*)'After ',IMAX,' iterations, no root was found'
            WRITE(*,*)' within the convergence criterion'
            ROOT = X2
            PAUSE 'To continue anyway, enter return key'
         ENDIF
         END
```

Protecting Dummy Input Arguments

Even though A and B are input to the code, all the variables that appear in the argument list will have values upon a return. These values will replace the values in the originating CALL. If you check the listing of the subroutine, you will notice the two lines

X1 = A   and   X3 = B

Couldn't we shorten the code slightly by removing these two lines and changing the definition line to read

SUBROUTINE BISEC(X1,X3,EPS,IMAX,I,ROOT)

while using A and B, as before, in the referencing statement

CALL SUBROUTINE BISEC(A,B,EPS,IMAX,I,ROOT)

When the subroutine is called, there will be a transfer of the values of A and B to the parameters X1 and X3, and thus the subroutine will execute exactly the same. However, there is subtle but significant difference. Within the subroutine, the values X1 and X3 are the limits of the search interval, which is continually shrinking until a root is found, at which point $|x_3 - x_1| \approx$ EPS. The final values of X1 and X3 when the subroutine returns to the calling statement will be very different from A and B, and these are the values that will be returned in the position for A and B, overwriting the previous values. If A and B are needed later in the program, their values would have been lost. To avoid this, the following safeguard is recommended.

> Within a subroutine, all dummy input variables should be replaced by locally defined variables. If a dummy input variable appears to the left of = in the subroutine, it is likely that the value of the variable after the call will be different from the value that went into the subroutine.

Remember, the only access the main program has to parameters in the subroutine is via the argument list. Thus, the only changes that can take place in parameter values before and after a call to a subroutine are to those parameters named in the argument list, including those intended only as input values.

How to Handle Subprogram Failure

Throughout the remainder of this text we will be constructing numerical subprograms that will generally have one of two results: success or failure. If a subprogram succeeds in its assigned task, a normal RETURN will be executed, the appropriate values returned, and the program will continue from that point. However, if for any reason the subprogram fails, it is unlikely that you would wish the program to continue. The subprogram should print a diagnostic message indicating the reason for the failure, and in almost all cases the program should then be terminated until the problem can be corrected. But in the interests of subprogram portability, the decision about whether to terminate a program should usually be in the hands of the main program. There are two common ways to accomplish this: SUCCESS/FAILURE flags and the PAUSE statement.

SUCCESS/FAILURE Flag

A common method to monitor the success or failure of a subprogram is to include a special variable in the argument list, called, say, FLAG, which will be assigned a value of 1 or 0 within the subprogram depending on whether the subprogram succeeds or fails. Then, after the call to the subroutine, the main program will either continue or stop depending on the value of the error flag.

PAUSE Statement

The form of the PAUSE statement is

PAUSE ⟨a single real, integer, or character constant or blank⟩

The operation of the statement is similar to the operation of the STOP statement; that is, upon execution of the statement, the program stops and the constant is displayed. Unlike the STOP statement, however, the program can be continued from this point by pressing the return [or enter] key. Thus, when a serious error is encountered in a subprogram, the nature of the problem would be printed and followed by a PAUSE statement. If the program is being executed at a terminal, the user would then decide whether or not to continue.

Using a PAUSE statement is not appropriate for batch computing modes. If you are submitting your programs as files to be executed by someone else and then have the results returned to you, never include a PAUSE statement in your code. In this situation all the PAUSE statements that appear in the remaining programs in this text should be replaced by STOP statements.

5.4 Function Subprograms

Another form of FORTRAN subprogram is the *external function*, which combines the features of the statement function and the subroutine. Like a subroutine, it is a complete program, separately compiled from the main program and other subprograms. The rules for passing information to and from the function via the argument list are the same as for subroutines. Like a statement function, it is referenced simply by using the function name followed by its argument list in any FORTRAN arithmetic expression or statement. FORTRAN functions are used most often when a single value is to be computed and returned to the calling program. The principal differences between functions and subroutines are a consequence of the fact that a function returns a value associated with its name and a subroutine does not. The name of a function is important; the name of a subroutine is usually not. The rules relating to the definition and use of a FORTRAN function follow.

1. A function has one of the following header lines

```
FUNCTION           (name)   (argument list)
REAL FUNCTION      (name)   (argument list)
INTEGER FUNCTION   (name)   (argument list)
CHARACTER FUNCTION (name)   (argument list)
```

Unless the type of the function is explicitly declared, as in the latter three cases, the type of the result returned is determined by the default typing associated with the function name; that is,

FUNCTION KOUNT(A,B,C)   Would return an integer value
                         for KOUNT

FUNCTION BGGST(X,N)   Would return a real value
                         for BGGST

It is usually recommended that, along with all other variables in a problem, function names be explicitly typed in their definition lines. If you choose to type-declare all functions when they are defined, the function names must also be type-declared in the calling program.

2. Because the function is expected to return a value associated with the name, it is crucial that before any RETURN is encountered in the body of the function program, an assignment of the form

⟨name⟩ = ...

be present.

3. Although a subprogram is not required to have an argument list, a function subprogram must have one (though it may be empty); that is, the compiler has been programmed to recognize that a name followed by a left parenthesis represents something other than a simple variable.

Referencing a Function

A FORTRAN function is accessed by its name, not with CALL, in precisely the same way as a statement function.

As a simple example, consider the program in Figure 5-5, which sums the series for e^x by employing a function subprogram to compute the factorials of integers, $n! = n(n - 1)(n - 2)...2 \times 1$. (Recall that 0! is defined to be 1. and that $n!$ is undefined if n is negative.) It is permissible to print (or to read) data from either a function or subroutine subprogram.

Even though functions can return values in addition to their name by means of the argument list in the same way as subroutines, this practice should be avoided. If the subprogram is to return one value, use a function; if it is to return more than one value, use a subroutine. Using a function structure when a subroutine would be more appropriate results in a very confusing logical flow to a program.

Finally, none of the dummy arguments in the argument list of a function should be altered within the body of the function. This suggestion is most easily adhered to if you agree never to use variables in the argument list as output from a function. Also, just as with the arguments in a subroutine argument list, function variable names should always be protected by introducing local replacements.

Figure 5-5 _____
Program to sum the
series for e^x

```
           PROGRAM ETOX
 .*
 *   Read a value for x and sum the first 25 terms in the
 *   series for exp(x) where
 *
 *   exp(x) = 1 + x + x^2/2! + x^3/3! + ...
 *-----------------------------------------------------------
           REAL X,SUM,TERM
           INTEGER I,NFACT
           PRINT *,'Enter x'
           READ  *,X
           SUM  = 1.0
           DO 1 I = 1,25
               SUM = SUM + X**I/NFACT(I)
       1   CONTINUE
           WRITE(*,*)'exp(',X,') = ',SUM
           STOP
           END
 *===========================================================
           FUNCTION NFACT(N)
           NFACT = 1
           IF(N .LT. 0)THEN
              PRINT *,'Error in NFACT, (Neg)! is undefined'
              PAUSE
           ELSEIF(N .EQ. 0)THEN
              NFACT = 1
           ELSE
              DO 1 I = N,1,-1
                  NFACT = NFACT*I
       1      CONTINUE
           ENDIF
           RETURN
           END
```

5.5   Sample Programs Using Functions and Subroutines

Essentially all of the procedures discussed so far could be recast in modular form using functions and subroutines. The result would be a code that is much more portable, efficient, easier to read, and less prone to error. In addition, when constructing a program that will read extensive data lists or print elaborate tables, you may also find it useful to employ subroutines to separately handle the input/output. In the future your main programs may consist of little else than CALLs to subroutines to read data, print output, and execute the computations. The sample programs in this section illustrate how functions and subroutines can be used in a variety of situations.

Fractions

You certainly remember, perhaps with some pain, the rules for adding fractions and reducing them to simplest form by dividing both numerator and denominator by common factors. Adding a large number of fractions exactly, that is, to express the answer as a fraction rather than a decimal, usually involves a considerable amount of tedious arithmetic. Thus the evaluation of

$$1 + \frac{1}{2} + \frac{1}{3} + \frac{1}{4} + \cdots + \frac{1}{25}$$

is easily done on a pocket calculator if the numbers are expressed as decimals. (The answer is 3.815958177....) If you attempt to add the fractions exactly, you will see that the problem quickly becomes hopelessly complicated. But hopelessly complicated and terribly tedious arithmetic is the computer's strong suit. To code this problem we will have to construct the following main program and subprograms:

1. Function IGCF(ITOP, IBOT). An integer function that determines the greatest common factor contained in both the numerator, ITOP, and the denominator, IBOT, of a given fraction.

2. Subroutine ADD(A1, A2, B1, B2, C1, C2). A subroutine to add two fractions represented as a_1/a_2 and b_1/b_2 where a_1, a_2, b_1, and b_2 are the integers representing the numerators and denominators of the two input fractions and c_1/c_2 is the fraction representing the sum, defined by

$$\frac{a_1}{a_2} + \frac{b_1}{b_2} = \frac{c_1}{c_2}$$

where $c_1 = a_1 b_2 + a_2 b_1$ and $c_2 = a_2 b_2$. The fraction is then reduced to lowest terms by using the function IGCF.

3. Program SERIES. A program that will sum the series by repeatedly calling the subroutine ADD.

The main program is similar to an ordinary summation and is given in Figure 5-6. The subroutine to add two fractions and reduce the result to lowest terms is fairly simple and is shown in Figure 5-7.

The algorithm to determine the greatest common factor in two integers was developed by Euclid and consists of dividing the first integer (the larger, P) by the second (the smaller, Q) and determining the remainder, R. If the remainder is not zero, the pair (P, Q) is replaced by the pair (Q, R) and the process is repeated. If the remainder is zero, the greatest common factor (GCF) is the last value of Q. For example, starting with $P = 221$, $Q = 91$, Euclid's algorithm yields

P	Q	R
221	91	39
91	39	13
39	13	0

Figure 5-6
Main program to
add a series of
fractions

```
      PROGRAM SERIES
      INTEGER A1,A2,TERM,SUM1,SUM2,LIMIT
*
*  The terms in the series are 1/term where term = 1,2,...
*  up to 1/limit.
*
      PRINT *,'Enter limit of terms in series'
      READ  *,LIMIT
*
*  Initialize the sum  (Note: The fraction for zero is 0/1)
*
      SUM1 = 0
      SUM2 = 1
*
      DO 1 I = 1,LIMIT
*
*     Summation consists of Sum ==> Sum + term
*
      CALL ADD(SUM1,SUM2,1,I,SUM1,SUM2)

  1   CONTINUE
      WRITE(*,*)'The sum of fractions 1/n for'
      WRITE(*,*)'n = 1 to ',LIMIT,' is'
      WRITE(*,*)
      WRITE(*,*)'    ',SUM1
      WRITE(*,*)'    -------------'
      WRITE(*,*)'    ',SUM2
      STOP
      END
```

So the GCF is 13. The function to execute this algorithm can also be found in Figure 5-7. By the way, the result of the problem with LIMIT = 15 is

$$\frac{1{,}195{,}757}{360{,}360}$$

Satellite Orbits

The period or time for one revolution of a satelite in a circular orbit about the earth is given by

$$T = 2\pi \sqrt{\frac{R_e}{g}} \left(1 + \frac{h}{R_e} \right)^{3/2} \tag{5.1}$$

where $R_e = 6.378 \times 10^6$ m is the radius of the earth, $g = 9.8$ m/sec^2 is the gravitational acceleration at the earth's surface, and h is the height in meters of the satellite's orbit measured from the earth's surface. The reciprocal of the period is the frequency,

$$f = \frac{1}{T} \tag{5.2}$$

Figure 5-7

Subprograms
required by the
program in
Figure 5-6

```
      SUBROUTINE ADD(A1,A2,B1,B2,C1,C2)
      INTEGER A1,A2,B1,B2,C1,C2,ID
      C1 = A1*B2 + A2*B1
      C2 = A2*B2
*
*  Use the funcion IGCF to determine the greatest common
*  factor in the fractional sum c1/c2.
*
      ID = IGCF(C1,C2)
      C1 = C1/ID
      C2 = C2/ID
      RETURN
      END
*=============================================================
      FUNCTION IGCF(ITOP,IBOT)
      INTEGER IGCF,ITOP,IBOT,P,Q,R
*
*  Local variables, (P,Q), are introduced so that the
*  dummy variables, (ITOP, IBOT), remain fixed.
*
      P = ITOP
      Q = IBOT
*
*  The remainder is r.  Note the use of integer arithmetic.
*
    1 R = P - (P/Q)*Q
      IF(R .EQ. 0)THEN
           IGCF = Q
           RETURN
      ELSE
           P = Q
           Q = R
      ENDIF
      GO TO 1
      END
```

Thus, the period for a satellite in an orbit 100 km above the earth's surface is easily computed to be $T = 5188.5$ sec $= 1$ hr $26\frac{1}{2}$ minutes, and the frequency is one revolution per 5188.5 seconds, or 0.694 revolutions per hour. But this calculation ignores the fact that the earth is itself revolving underneath the satellite's orbit with a frequency of $f_{earth} = 1/24$ hrs $= 1.1574 \times 10^{-5}$ sec^{-1} in the same direction as the satellite. Thus, the apparent frequency of the satellite with respect to points on the earth is

$$f_{app} = \frac{1}{2\pi}\sqrt{\frac{g}{R_e}}\left(1 + \frac{h}{R_e}\right)^{-3/2} - 1.1574 \times 10^{-5} \tag{5.3}$$

and the effective period is $T_{app} = 1/f_{app}$.

The velocity of the satellite in its orbit is $v = 2\pi(R_e + h)f$. The apparent velocity with respect to the earth's surface is $v_{app} = 2\pi(R_e + h)f_{app}$.

It takes a considerable amount of energy to accelerate the satellite to sufficient speed and raise it to a sufficient height to remain in orbit. The equation for the energy required for each kilogram of payload, ignoring the energy required to lift the booster rockets part way, is

$$E = gR_e\left[0.9966 - \frac{1}{2}\left(1 + \frac{h}{R_e}\right)^{-1}\right] \tag{5.4}$$

A subroutine that will compute the absolute velocity, v, the effective velocity, the apparent period, and the energy required for an orbit of height h is given in Figure 5-8.

This subroutine was used to generate a table of these quantities for values of h from 0 to 40,000 km. The results are given in Table 5.1. The

Figure 5-8

A subroutine to compute the absolute and apparent period of a satellite orbit

```
SUBROUTINE ORBIT(H,VABS,VAPP,TAPP,ENRGY)
FREQ(H) = .5/PI*SQRT(G/RE)*(1. + H/RE)**(-1.5) - 1.1574E-5
PERD(H) = 2.*PI*SQRT(RE/G)*(1. + H/RE)**1.5
V(F)    = 2.*PI*(RE + H)*F
E(H)    = G*RE*(.9966 - .5/(1. + H/RE))
PI = ACOS(-1.)
RE = 6.378E6
G  = 9.8
*
F = FREQ(H)
PERIOD = PERD(H)
VABS    = V(1./PERIOD)
VAPP    = V(F)
TAPP    = 1./F
ENRGY   = E(H)
*
RETURN
END
```

Table 5-1

Orbit characteristics for a range of circular satellite orbits

Height (km)	Velocity (m/sec) Absolute	Apparent	Apparent Period (hrs)	Energy/kg (mega-J)
0	7906.0	7442.2	1.5	31.0
2,000	6898.1	6288.8	2.3	38.5
4,000	6197.8	5443.1	3.3	43.1
6,000	5675.1	4774.9	4.5	46.2
8,000	5265.6	4220.0	5.9	48.4
10,000	4933.6	3742.6	7.6	50.1
12,000	4657.5	3321.0	9.7	51.4
14,000	4423.0	2941.1	12.1	52.5
16,000	4220.7	2593.4	15.1	53.4
18,000	4043.9	2271.1	18.7	54.1
20,000	3887.6	1969.3	23.4	54.7
22,000	3748.1	1684.4	29.4	55.3
24,000	3622.6	1413.4	37.5	55.7
26,000	3508.9	1154.3	49.0	56.1
28,000	3405.3	905.3	66.3	56.5
30,000	3310.4	664.9	95.5	56.8
32,000	3223.0	432.1	155.0	57.1
34,000	3142.1	205.8	342.5	57.4
36,000	3067.1	−14.7	−5031.5	57.6
38,000	2997.2	−230.1	−336.7	57.8
40,000	2931.8	−440.8	−183.6	58.0

Figure 5-9

Absolute and apparent satellite velocity as a function of the height of the orbit

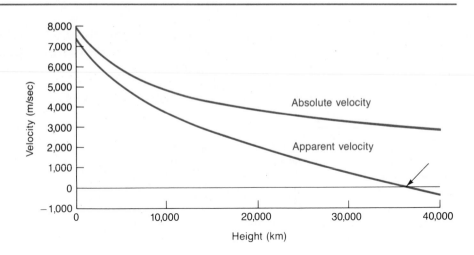

absolute and apparent velocity are plotted in Figure 5.9. Notice that at a height of approximately 36,000 km the apparent velocity is zero; that is, the satellite will appear stationary over the equator and the apparent period will be infinite.

Function to "Round" Numerical Values

In many situations, particularly when plotting a graph, it is useful to be able to round a numerical value. Thus, if you were plotting a graph and the data along the x axis extended from −14.32 to 102.77, it is very likely that you would automatically select the limits of the x axis to be from −15 to 105 or −20 to 110. But to instruct the computer to accomplish the same thing is not quite so easy. Basically, if we wish to round a number up in magnitude so that the first two digits are divisible by 5, we would begin with a sequence of statements like

```
                              for X =
                          [5.645   5.21  −1.43]
IX = 2.*(ABS(X) + .5)     [  12     11      3]
X  = .5*IX *ABS(X)/X      [ 6.0     5.5   −1.5]
```

These two statements cleverly employ mixed-mode arithmetic to accomplish the task, provided that the number X is in the range 1 to 9.999.... If X is outside this range, the above procedure will not work. For an arbitrary X, the computer code will have to first scale down the number so that it is in the 1 to 10 range, round it, and then scale back up. This task is accomplished in the code in Figure 5-10 by using the $\log_{10}(x)$ function, which in FORTRAN is LOG10(X). Also, with minor modifications, the function can be made to "round down." (See Problem 5.10.)

Figure 5-10
Function to round
numbers

```
      FUNCTION ROUNDR(X)
*
* Roundr will round the real number x up in magnitude so that
* the result will have the first two digits divisible by 5, i.e.,
* 771.3 becomes 800.0 and -0.08341 becomes -0.085.
*
      A = ABS(X)
*
*           The input dummy variable X is protected.
*           The sign of X is x/|x|
*
      B  = LOG10(A)
      IB = B
      B  = B - IB
*
*           If b is positive, it is the magnitude of the mantissa
*           and Ib is the characteristic; e.g., if x = 15.0,
*           log(15) = 1.1761, so Ib = 1, b = 0.1761.  IF b is
*           negative, the log is expressed as 0.xxxxx - 1.0, so
*
      IF(B .LT. 0.)THEN
          B  = B + 1.
          IB = IB - 1
      ENDIF
*
*           Thus if x = 0.8, then Ib = 0, b = -.0969 are replaced
*           by b = 0.903, Ib = 1, i.e., log(0.8) = 0.9031 - 1.0.
*
      C = 10.**B
*
*           C is X without its sign or exponent. (Do not
*           omit the decimal point on the 10.)
*
      IC = 2.*C + 1.
*
*           This line does the actual rounding.  Next reattach
*           the correct power of 10 and the sign.
*
      ROUNDR = 0.5*IC * 10.**IB * A/X
      RETURN
      END
```

5.6 Constructing Modular Programs

There is one minor problem with the subroutine BISEC of Figure 5-4. This subroutine will find the root of a function $f(x)$ only if the name of the function is "f." Thus, within the subroutine there are statements of the form F1 = F(X1), which, as we know, cause the computer to search for the definition of the function named F, which must be included elsewhere in the complete program. If at some later date we wish to find a root of a function named $g(x)$, we will either have to replace F( ) everywhere in BISEC by G( ) or rename the function, that is, unless we can transfer the name of the function along with its numerical parameters through the

Figure 5-11

The structure of a program that uses a subroutine to find the root of an arbitrary function

```
PROGRAM XXX
   ...        ...      ...
   CALL BISEC(0.1,0.4,1.E-4,20,ITER,ANSWER)
   PRINT*,'After ',ITER,' iterations, root = ',ANSWER
   ...        ...      ...
END
*==============================================================
SUBROUTINE BISEC(A,B,EPS,IMAX,I,ROOT)
   ...        ...      ...
   F1 = F(X1)
   ...        ...      ...
   RETURN
END
*==============================================================
FUNCTION F(X)
   ...        ...      ...
   F =
   ...        ...      ...
   RETURN
END
```

argument list. That this transfer is indeed possible in FORTRAN is one of the most attractive and useful features of the language in constructing modular programs. To understand how a transfer of name is accomplished, consider again the definition and use of a subroutine like BISEC (see Figure 5-11).

Clearly, if we wish to transfer into BISEC the name of an arbitrary function we could do so by adding the name to the argument list in the subroutine definition,

$$\text{SUBROUTINE BISEC(A,B,EPS,IMAX,I,ROOT,F)}$$

where F is now a *dummy* name of a function; that is, nowhere in the complete program is there a function named F. The actual name of a function will be transferred into BISEC when the subroutine is called,

$$\text{CALL SUBROUTINE BISEC(A,B,EPS,IMAX,I,ROOT,COST)}$$

where COST(X) is a function we have coded and whose root is desired. We expect then that when the subroutine is called the actual name COST will be transferred to BISEC and will replace the dummy name F everywhere within the FORTRAN code for the subroutine. Or, if we wanted the root of the cosine, we could use

$$\text{CALL SUBROUTINE BISEC(O,PI,EPS,IMAX,I,ROOT,COS)}$$

There is however, one problem.

When the above lines are inserted into the main program and the main program is compiled, there is no way for the compiler to determine which of the names in the argument list for BISEC refer to numerical quantities and which refer to complete "procedures" like a function or another subroutine. Recall the method used up to this point by the compiler to identify a function: When the compiler encounters a name followed by a left parenthesis it searches first the beginning of the program for a statement-function definition, next the remainder of the code for a function definition, and finally the library for an intrinsic function by that name. Thus, the compiler has been written to recognize that name(will characterize something other than a simple numerical variable. The solution cannot be to attach parentheses to the function name in the CALL and subroutine definition since it is forbidden to have any parentheses in the argument list of a subroutine definition line. In situations like this, when the name of a function appears in the argument list of another function or subroutine and the compiler is thus unable to recognize it as the name of a function, new FORTRAN statements are needed to assist in the recognition: EXTERNAL and INTRINSIC statements.

EXTERNAL and INTRINSIC Statements

The form of EXTERNAL and INTRINSIC statements is

```
EXTERNAL   ⟨name₁⟩,⟨name₂⟩,...
INTRINSIC  ⟨name₁⟩,⟨name₂⟩,...
```

where $name_1$, $name_2$, are names of functions or subroutines that are not called directly but that appear in the argument list of referenced subroutines or functions. The EXTERNAL statement is used to identify a name as that of a user-written function subprogram that appears elsewhere in the code; the INTRINSIC statement identifies a name as a library function.

The EXTERNAL and INTRINSIC statements are required only in the program unit that makes indirect reference to the function through the argument list of a referenced subprogram. They are not required in a subprogram that makes a direct reference to the function. Thus, in the previous examples, the statements

```
EXTERNAL COST
INTRINSIC COS
```

would be required in the main program that calls BISEC (which in turns calls COST and COS) but would not be needed in BISEC itself. By inserting these statements in the main program, we are telling the compiler two things: (1) the names COST and COS that appear in the calls to BISEC are not variables but correspond to entire functions; and (2) these functions can be found elsewhere in the complete program (COST) and in the library (COS).

The names of statment functions, which are defined internally in a program, can never be included in an EXTERNAL or INTRINSIC statement. The EXTERNAL and INTRINSIC statements are nonexecutable and must appear before the first executable statement in a program.

■ Sample Program Illustrating EXTERNAL and INTRINSIC Statements

The theory of probability is concerned with describing the results of measurements that contain a degree of randomness. This theory has applications in a variety of fields. For example, suppose you want to determine whether investing in a gas station on a new interstate highway is a good idea. The most important factor in the decision is the volume of traffic passing the station. The traffic flow can be characterized by n, the average number of cars that pass during the daylight hours. To aid in your decision, you set up some expensive electronic equipment to measure how many cars pass in each 10-second interval during the day; that is, the equipment counts how many times five cars pass in 10 seconds, six cars in 10 seconds, and so on. From these data you are able to determine the total number of cars that passed and the average number per time interval. But when you return in a few days, you find a problem. The electronics could not keep up with the counting when the flow was extremely heavy. Whenever 20 or more cars passed per 10 seconds, the counting apparatus malfunctioned and registered "tilt." This "tilt" occurred in 70% of the measurements. The incomplete data are shown in Figure 5-12. From these incomplete data it appears that we cannot even estimate the total number of cars that passed the station. The measurements seem worthless.

However, with a bit of work, a knowledge of probability theory, and some computing skills, we can at least salvage an approximate value for the average number of cars passing per 10-second interval.

First of all, probability theory says that if α is the average number of events (i.e., n cars passing) in an interval, the probability of k events in a given interval is given approximately by the Poisson function:

$$P_k(\alpha) = \frac{\alpha^k e^{-\alpha}}{k!} \tag{5.5}$$

where $P_k(\alpha) \approx 1$ implies near certainty that k cars will pass in any 10-second interval.

Figure 5-12

The results of the monitoring of traffic flow. The occurrence rate, X_n, is the number of times n cars were observed passing the observation point in a 10-second interval, for $n = 0, 1, \ldots$

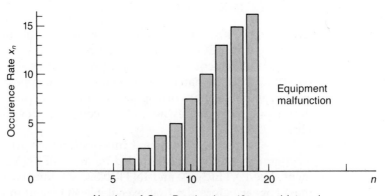

Number of Cars Passing in a 10-second Interval

Now, our faulty measurements tell us that the probability of 20 or more cars per 10-second interval is 70%; in other words,

$$0.70 = \sum_{k=20}^{\infty} P_k(\alpha) \quad \text{Sum from 20 to } \infty \tag{5.6}$$

This equation must be solved for the average α.

We first express Equation (5.6) as a FORTRAN function called, say, TILT(α) to sum the Poisson functions, which are in turn coded as a FORTRAN function P(K, ALPHA). The subroutine BISEC of Figure 5-4 will then find the root α of Equation (5.6) once an initial search interval has been specified. The main program then initializes the parameters and calls BISEC. (See Figure 5-13.) Notice the following items in this program:

- TILT must be declared EXTERNAL in the main program.
- The Poisson function P(K, ALPHA) is not declared EXTERNAL since it does not appear in an argument list.
- The subroutine BISEC has been made "portable" by using a dummy name for the function whose root is desired.
- Since BISEC has already been coded and tested, the actual amount of FORTRAN coding in this problem is quite minimal.
- The setup for this program would have the main program first, followed by the subprograms in any order. The subprogram should be ordered in relation to the sequence that they are called; that is, BISEC calls TILT, which calls P(K, ALPHA).

Floating-Point Overflow/Underflow

If you try to execute the program CARS of Figure 5-13, there is a good chance, depending on the word-length characteristic of your machine, that the program will fail. The FORTRAN code is valid; however, the function P(K, ALPHA) requires the calculation of very large factorials (e.g., $50! = 3.04 \times 10^{64}$), and these may easily exceed the capacity of a typical computer. The maximum real number on a computer depends on the word length of the machine and varies considerably. A typical maximum real number might be as large as 10^{375} on a large mainframe computer or as small as 3×10^{38} on a personal computer. A similar limit exists for the smallest-magnitude real number. If any computed quantity in your program falls outside these limits, the program will fail because of an execution-time floating-point overflow or underflow condition. On some computers the maximum possible real number may be increased by using variables of type DOUBLE PRECISION, to be discussed in Section 9.2. If the change to double-precision variables does not effect the maximum computer number or if the program failure persists, correcting the problem can be extremely difficult and often will require rewriting the entire code to avoid the problem. This revision usually requires considerable ingenuity.

Figure 5-13

FORTRAN code to
find the average
number of cars
passing

```
          PROGRAM CARS
*
*  Based on the information that the probability of 20 or more
*  cars passing per time interval is 70%, the average number of
*  cars passing per time interval is estimated by assuming a
*  Poisson distribution and solving the equation
*
*              Sum[P(k,avg)] = 0.70
*
*  where the sum is from 20 to infinity and avg is the root of
*  the equation.
*------------------------------------------------------------------
*  Declare the function TILT as external
*
          EXTERNAL TILT
*------------------------------------------------------------------
*  Initialization
*
          A    = 15.
          B    = 24.
          IMAX = 20
          EPS  = 1.E-3
*------------------------------------------------------------------
*  Computation
*
*  The only function of the main program is to call BISEC to
*  find the root of TILT.
*
          CALL BISEC(A,B,EPS,IMAX,I,AVG,TILT)
*------------------------------------------------------------------
*  Output
*          And print the results
*
          IAVG = AVG
          WRITE(*,*)'Average number of cars/10-sec    = ',AVG
          WRITE(*,*)'Probability of this No. cars/10s = ',P(IAVG,AVG)
          WRITE(*,*)'Probability of zero cars/10-sec  = ',P(0,AVG)
          STOP
          END
*==================================================================
          SUBROUTINE BISEC(A,B,EPS,IMAX,I,ROOT,F)
*--
*--  The only change to Figure 5-4 is to include the dummy
*--  name F in the argument list.
             ...          ...          ...
             ...          ...          ...
          END
          FUNCTION TILT(X)
*
          IF(X .EQ. 0.)THEN
              TILT = 0.
              RETURN
          ENDIF
*
```

Figure 5-13
(concluded)

```
*     Sum from k = 20 until terms are smaller than 1.E-6.
*
          SUM  = 0.
          DO 2 I = 20,100
             TERM = P(I,X)
             SUM  = SUM + P(I,X)
             IF(ABS(TERM) .LT. 1.E-6)THEN
                TILT = SUM - 0.70
                RETURN
             ENDIF
    2     CONTINUE
          WRITE(*,*)'In Tilt, excessive No. of terms'
          STOP
          END
*==================================================================
          FUNCTION P(K,X)
*
*  P(k,x) is the Poisson distribution which gives the approximate
*  probability that k events occur in a time interval if the aver-
*  age in that interval is known to be x.
*------------------------------------------------------------------
* Variables
*         REAL X,FACTK,P
          INTEGER K,I
*
*         X     -- The average number of events/interval
*         K     -- Events per time interval
*         FACTK -- K factorial
*         I     -- A counter
*------------------------------------------------------------------
*  The case k = 0 must be handled separately
*
          IF(K .EQ. 0)THEN
             P = EXP(-X)
             RETURN
          ENDIF
*------------------------------------------------------------------
          FACTK = 1.
          DO 1 I = K,1,-1
             FACTK = FACTK*I
    1     CONTINUE
          P = X**K * EXP(-X)/FACTK
          RETURN
          END
```

```
Average number of cars/10-sec   =  22.0829
Probability of this No. cars/10s =   0.08472
Probability of zero cars/10-sec  =   2.5675E-10
```

For example, in the car-counting problem the error occurs in the computation of the function $P_k(\alpha)$, which is called from the function $\text{TILT}(\alpha)$,

$$\text{TILT}(\alpha) = \sum_{k=20}^{\infty} P_k(\alpha) - 0.70 \tag{5.7}$$

and as k becomes large will require the evaluation of very large factorials. However, from the definition of the probability function, we know that

$$\sum_{k=0}^{\infty} P_k(\alpha) = 1 \qquad\qquad (5.8)$$

Equation (5.8) is a statement that the sum of the probabilities of all possibilities must be 1. (It is a certainty that either zero or some cars pass in each time interval.) Combining these two equations, we obtain

$$\text{TILT}(\alpha) = \left[\sum_{k=0}^{\infty} P_k(\alpha) - \sum_{k=0}^{19} P_k(\alpha) \right] - 0.70$$

$$= 0.30 - \sum_{k=0}^{19} P_k(\alpha) \qquad\qquad (5.9)$$

and thus the function TILT may be rewritten without any infinite summations. Once again, carefully analyzing the problem before attempting to write FORTRAN code can often enormously reduce the time spent in later patching up a poorly thought out and casually constructed program.

5.7   Additional Features Available for Subprograms

SAVE Statement

Occasionally, when a subprogram is called more than once, we may wish to use a locally defined variable that was computed in an earlier call. Ordinarily, all values associated with variable names within a subprogram that are not also in the argument list are lost after leaving the subprogram. To preserve the value associated with a variable from one use of a subprogram to the next, the SAVE statement is inserted before the first executable statement in the subprogram. The form of the SAVE statement is

$$\text{SAVE} \ \langle \text{name}_1 \rangle, \langle \text{name}_2 \rangle, \ldots$$

For example, if we wanted to find the root of the function $g(x) = (\sin \pi x - \pi x \cos \pi x)/x^2$, it is likely the FORTRAN code for this function would include a statement like PI = ACOS(−1.) for the computation of π. Each time this function is called, which could be hundreds of times, the value of π is recomputed. In some cases, unnecessary recomputations of this type can cause the running time (and thus the expense) of a program to be excessive. It would be preferable to compute π the first time the function is called, SAVE this value, and in all subsequent calls to the function skip the calculation of π. The manner in which this might be done is illustrated below:

```
FUNCTION G(X)
INTEGER FLAG
SAVE FLAG,PI
DATA FLAG/0/
```

```
IF(FLAG .EQ. 0)THEN
    PI = ACOS(-1.)
    FLAG = 1
ENDIF
G = (SIN(PI(X) - PI*X*COS(PI*X))/X**2
RETURN
END
```

In this function we have inserted a variable called FLAG, which is initialized to zero at compilation time by means of the DATA statement. The first time this function is referenced, FLAG is thus zero, the value of PI is computed, and FLAG is assigned a value different from zero. These values are then saved, and in all subsequent calls to the function the computation of PI will be skipped.

In Section 5.6 the function TILT sums the Poisson functions, which are reevaluated each time it is called. And each time the Poisson function is called, it computes many factorials. Thus, these factorials are recomputed perhaps hundreds of times in finding the root of TILT. Chapter 7 explains how to store all these values in an array that can then be saved, avoiding the inefficient recomputation.

There is never a need to explicitly SAVE variables in the argument list of a subprogram. Attempts to do so will result in compilation errors. Saved variables may, however, appear as actual arguments in the argument list of a subprogram that is called from the current subprogram.

If the SAVE statement appears without a list of variables, then all the locally defined variables in the subprogram are saved from one call to the next.

COMMON Statement

Up to this point the only communication that subroutines and functions have had with each other and with the main program is via the variables that appear in their argument lists. One additional mechanism for transferring information is available: *common blocks*. The idea is to reserve special blocks of memory that may be accessed by one or more program units. The form of the statement that assigns variables to these blocks is

> COMMON /⟨blockname⟩/⟨variable list⟩

or

> COMMON ⟨variable list⟩

In the first example, called *labeled common*, a block of memory is assigned a name, "blockname," which is any valid FORTRAN name and is set off by slashes. The list of variables contained in this block then follows, separated by commas. The variables may be a mix of integers and real numbers, but the list may not contain any function names. Additionally, if any of the variables in the block are of type character, all the variable names in the block must be of type character. The second example is called *blank common*. The only difference from labeled commons is that the reserved block of memory has been left unnamed.

Examples of labeled COMMON statements follow:

`COMMON/ABLOCK/X,Y,J,K`   Block ABLOCK consists of four memory words, two containing real numbers, two containing integers.

`COMMON/W/W`   Block W is one word and contains the value of the variable named W. There is no conflict of names since the name of a block cannot be used in any executable statement.

The two statements could be combined as

`COMMON/ABLOCK/X,Y,I,J/W/W`

But in the interests of writing code that is easily readable, each common-block declaration should be allotted a separate statement. In this text labeled common blocks are used exclusively.

The following rules govern the use of COMMON statements:

1. A pair of slashes is used to separate the name given to a group of variables, all stored together in a block.
2. A COMMON statement is nonexecutable and must appear before the first executable statement.
3. A similar FORTRAN line, with the same block name, must appear in both the program units that share the use of some or all the variables in the block.
4. The assignment of values to variables in the block proceeds in the same manner as for argument lists—that is, values are assigned by position in the list, not by variable name.
5. Variables in a labeled common block may not be assigned values by means of a DATA statement.
6. Only names representing variables, not functions or procedures, may be included in a common block.
7. Common blocks with the same name referenced by two program units must be of the same length.
8. Once outside of the two (or more) program units sharing the variables in labeled common blocks, the variables become undefined. Of course, if one of the program units is the main program, the variables always remain intact.
9. All of the entries in a labeled common block can be saved by including the common-block name in a SAVE statement in each of the program units accessing the block. The names of individual entries in a common block are not permitted in a SAVE statement.

10. If a variable is in a common block, it cannot simultaneously be in an argument list. Such an arrangement would require two distinct memory addresses for the same variable. For example,

```
SUBROUTINE PRODCT(X,Y,N)
COMMON /AAA/X,Z                    Incorrect
```

You will have no difficulty understanding COMMON statements if you recognize that they are simply a replacement for an argument list. Thus,

```
                                    PROGRAM MANE
PROGRAM MANE                        COMMON/COEF/D,E,F
READ *, D,E,F                       READ *,D,E,F
Z = 2.3                             Z = 2.3
T = F(D,E,F,Z)                      T = F(Z)
  .                                   .
  .                                   .
  .                                   .
STOP                        and     STOP
END                                 END
FUNCTION F(A,B,C,X)                 FUNCTION F(X)
  F = A*X**2 + B*X + C              COMMON/COEF/A,B,C
  RETURN                              F = A*X**2 + B*X + C
END                                   RETURN
                                      END
```

are essentially interchangeable.

Common blocks are most often used in two frequently occurring situations in FORTRAN: eliminating long argument lists and matching the argument list to a dummy function.

Eliminating Long Argument Lists

If a subprogram is referenced many times and if the argument list of the subprogram is long, it is easy to make errors. The order of the variables or their type may be entered incorrectly, or some accidentally omitted. It is therefore tempting to use a common block to pass the variables to the subprogram. The COMMON statement can then simply be copied into each subprogram that uses it. This arrangement may also make the program easier to read. However, COMMON statements are frequently misused in this regard. If numerous variables are in the block and the block is shared by several subprograms, it is likely that some of the subprograms will only use a few of the variables in the list, leaving the reader confused as to the meaning of the remaining names. This practice should be avoided.

Matching the Argument List to a Dummy Function

Frequently, a subprogram module will refer to a function of a single variable F(X), whereas the particular function in question requires several parameters in addition to X. The only recourse is to pass the additional parameters through a common block. Thus, if we wished to use the subroutine BISEC to find the root of the quadratic function in the above FORTRAN code, the representation on the left would not be suitable.

Summary

This chapter has described methods for constructing modular programs. That is, the distinct parts of an algorithm are isolated, and for each element, separate subprograms are written, compiled, and debugged. These subprograms are then assembled along with a main program into a complete code in which the main program will sequentially call on the subprograms to perform their assigned tasks. The subprogram modules in FORTRAN are called subroutines and functions.

A subroutine is generally a procedure that will generate more than a single number. Subroutines can be constructed to plot graphs, read data files, or compute a set of numerical results. The definition line of a subroutine is

SUBROUTINE ⟨name⟩(argument list)

The subroutine name must satisfy the ordinary rules for FORTRAN names. It is the name of a procedure and may not be assigned a value or conflict with any other name in the subroutine. The argument list is optional but is usually present and represents the primary window of communication of the subroutine with other program units. In the definition-line argument list, variable names are dummy arguments. They are assigned values, by position in the list, not by name, only when the subroutine is accessed. All subroutine variables not in the argument list and all statement numbers are only locally defined within the subroutine. No parentheses are permitted within the argument list of a subroutine definition line.

A subroutine, like every other FORTRAN procedure, must have as its last line an END statement. If this statement is encountered during execution of the subroutine, the program will return to the statement following the line in which the subroutine was referenced. A normal return from a subroutine is effected by means of the RETURN statement.

A subroutine is initiated by means of the CALL statement of the form

CALL ⟨name⟩(argument list)

where ⟨name⟩ is the name of the subroutine and the variables in the argument list are actual variables that are expected to be either input to or output from the subroutine.

Another type of subprogram is the FORTRAN *function*. A FORTRAN function is generally a procedure that will generate a single numerical value as its primary output. The definition line of a function is

⟨type⟩ FUNCTION ⟨name⟩(argument list)

The function name is significant; before any return from the function, a value must be assigned to the function name. A function may be typed as REAL FUNCTION ⟨name⟩, INTEGER FUNCTION ⟨name⟩, or CHARACTER FUNCTION ⟨name⟩. If the function is not explicitly typed, the default typing rules apply.

A FORTRAN function is referenced in the same way that intrinsic or statement functions are referenced. Simply use the function name along with its argument list in any executable statement. If the function contains READ or WRITE statements, it may not itself appear in the input/output list of a READ/WRITE statement. The interpretation of the argument-list variables as actual or dummy is identical to that of a subroutine. Indeed in all other respects, the properties of a function are the same as those of sub-routines. Local variables and statement numbers are defined only within the function; a normal return is effected by a RETURN statement; and the last line of the function must be the END statement.

Several new FORTRAN statements that pertain to functions and subroutines were introduced in this chapter.

The PAUSE statement, of the form

PAUSE ⟨a single numerical or character constant⟩

will cause the program execution to be interrupted and the optional number or character string to be printed. This statement is used to halt the program in the event of a user-defined error condition. Program execution will continue if a return key is struck.

The EXTERNAL/INTRINSIC statements, of the form,

EXTERNAL ⟨function name⟩
INTRINSIC ⟨function name⟩

are used to facilitate the transfer of the names of functions or subroutines between program units. When the name of a function appears in the argument list of another function or subroutine, the name of the function must be identified as either a user-defined function (EXTERNAL) or a library intrinsic function (INTRINSIC) name, in order for the compiler to distinguish it from ordinary variable names. These statements are nonexecutable and must appear before all executable statements.

The SAVE statement, of the form,

SAVE ⟨variable list⟩

is a nonexecutable statement that must appear before all executable statements. It will cause the local variables in the list to retain their values after leaving the function or subroutine. If the variable list is absent, all local variables are saved.

The COMMON statements, of the form

COMMON/⟨blockname⟩/⟨variable list⟩   [labeled COMMON]
COMMON ⟨variable list⟩   [blank COMMON]

are nonexecutable statements that must appear before all executable statements. If two program units (programs, functions, subroutines, block data) each contain similar COMMON statements, with the same (optional) (blockname), all the variables in the list are then defined in both units. In this regard it is similar to an argument list; variables are assigned values by position in the list, not by name. Variables in a labeled common block may not be initialized in a DATA statement; however, a BLOCK DATA subprogram may be used for this purpose. (BLOCK DATA subprograms will be discussed in Section 9.2.)

Problems

5.1 a. Construct a subroutine that will return the coordinates of a point in Cartesian coordinates, (x, y), computed from the polar coordinates of that same point (r, θ) by means of the equations

$$x = r \cos \theta$$

$$y = r \sin \theta$$

b. Write a program that will read values of x and y; then use subroutine VECTOR in Figure 5-1 to compute the polar coordinates r and θ; and then use the subroutine of part a to return to Cartesian coordinates comparing the initial and final values of x and y.

5.2 Give an algebraic example of the distinction between dummy variables and actual variables. Give a similar illustration of the distinction between the use of a dummy function and an actual function.

5.3 a. Write a subroutine that does something useful and has no argument list.
b. A subroutine will compile without a RETURN statement. Can you think of any use for such a subroutine?
c. Is it possible to do the following from a subroutine?
   (1) STOP
   (2) Call a different subroutine
   (3) Call a different subroutine and from the second subroutine return directly to the main program
   (4) Open and write to a file
   (5) Open and read from a file

5.4 Redo Problem 5.3 applied to function subprograms.

5.5 Write a subroutine that takes two real variables (a, b) and returns the values interchanged, that is, (b, a).

5.6 Write a subroutine called BANNER that will produce a neat heading for your program output. You may want to include your name, address, problem title, course, instructor's name, and so on.

5.7 A rather famous infinite series for early computations of π is

$$\frac{\pi}{6} = \frac{1}{2} + \frac{1}{2}\frac{1}{3 \times 2^3} + \frac{1 \times 3}{2 \times 4}\frac{1}{5 \times 2^5} + \frac{1 \times 3 \times 5}{2 \times 4 \times 6}\frac{1}{7 \times 2^7} + \cdots$$

This series converges quite rapidly.

a. Determine an expression for the general term in the series.

b. Write a subroutine TERM to compute an individual term in the series as a fraction reduced to lowest terms by using the function IGCF of Section 5.5.

c. Write a program that will sum the first four terms in the series as a fraction reduced to lowest terms. *Answer:* $\frac{\pi}{6} = \frac{112{,}579}{215{,}040}$

5.8 The two linear equations in two unknowns x and y,

$$ax + by = e$$

$$cx + dy = f$$

are easily solved by solving the first for x and then substituting this result into the second and solving for y. The result is

$$x = \frac{ed - fb}{ad - bc} \quad \text{and} \quad y = \frac{af - ec}{ad - bc}$$

a. Write subroutines PROD, DIVD, and MINUS that will, respectively, multiply, divide, and subtract two fractions and use function IGCF of Section 5.5 to reduce the result to lowest terms.

b. Write a program that will read six pairs of integers representing the numerators/denominators of the fractional parameters a, b, c, d, e, and f. The program will then solve for x and y as fractions reduced to lowest terms.

c. As a test case try

$$\left. \begin{array}{l} \dfrac{1}{3}x + \dfrac{2}{5}y = \dfrac{3}{8} \\[2mm] \dfrac{7}{9}x - \dfrac{6}{7}y = \dfrac{-1}{11} \end{array} \right\} \quad \text{The solution is} \quad \begin{array}{l} x = \dfrac{3{,}951}{8{,}272} \\[2mm] y = \dfrac{8{,}925}{16{,}544} \end{array}$$

5.9 Write a subroutine called CHANGE that will determine the appropriate change to be returned when an amount PAY is submitted for an item that has a price COST. Assume that PAY is less than $100 and that there are no $50, $20, or $2 bills. The subroutine should return integer values for

```
(TENS,FIVES,ONES,HALFD,QUARTR,DIMES,NICKL,CENTS)
```

To get you started, note that if CHANGE is a positive real number less than $100 and TENS is an integer variable, then the number of tens to be returned is

```
TENS = CHANGE/10.
```

and the remaining change is

```
CHANGE - TENS*10.
```

The subroutine should minimize the amount of small change.

5.10 Rewrite function ROUNDR to:

a. Round an arbitrary number down. Thus, if $Q = 0.16731$, then ROUNDR(Q) = 0.15.

b. Round an arbitrary number up so that the first two digits are divisible by 10.

5.11 If a function can be represented by a single algebraic equation, it is perhaps most conveniently coded as a statement function. However, this is not always possible. Give an example of a function that cannot be coded as a statement function.

5.12 Write a function subprogram that returns the cube root of a real number x. (*Note:* x may be negative.)

5.13 The combinatorial function is defined as

$$C(n,p) = \frac{n!}{(n-p)!\,p!}$$

and represents the total number of combinations of n objects taken p at a time. Note that $C(n,0) = 1$.

a. Show that the ratio of successive C's for a given n is given by

$$\frac{C(n,p+1)}{C(n,p)} = \frac{n-p}{p+1}$$

b. Write a FORTRAN function that uses the ratio of successive terms obtained in part a to compute the combinatorial $C(n,p)$ for an arbitrary n and p ($p \le n$). The function should start with

$$C(n,0) = 1$$

$$C(n,1) = nC(n,0) = n$$

$$C(n,2) = \tfrac{1}{2}(n-1)C(n,1) = \tfrac{1}{2}n(n-1)$$

$$\vdots$$

c. Use the function in part b to produce a table of all combinatorial functions for $n \le 10$. Such a table is known as Pascal's triangle. The first few lines of the triangle are

n	$C(n,p), p = 0,\ldots,n$				
0			1		
1		1		1	
2		1	2	1	
3	1	3	3	1	
4	1	4	6	4	1

5.14 A vector **a** can be represented in terms of its components along the x, y, and z axes; $\mathbf{a} = (a_x, a_y, a_z)$. The dot product of two vectors is then a number defined by the equation

$$\mathbf{a} \cdot \mathbf{b} = a_x b_x + a_y b_y + a_z b_z$$

and the cross product is a vector whose components are defined by

$$\mathbf{c} = \mathbf{a} \times \mathbf{b}$$

$$c_x = a_y b_z - a_z b_y$$

$$c_y = a_z b_x - a_x b_z$$

$$c_z = a_x b_y - a_y b_x$$

a. Write a function for the dot product and a subroutine for the cross product of two vectors.

b. Write a main program that tests whether the identity

$$(\mathbf{a} \times \mathbf{b}) \cdot (\mathbf{c} \times \mathbf{d}) = (\mathbf{a} \cdot \mathbf{c})(\mathbf{b} \cdot \mathbf{d}) - (\mathbf{a} \cdot \mathbf{d})(\mathbf{b} \cdot \mathbf{c})$$

is correct for values of $\mathbf{a}, \mathbf{b}, \mathbf{c}, \mathbf{d}$ that are read in.

5.15 Find any compilation errors in the following expressions:

```
a. SUBROUTINE AB(X,I+1,EPS,ANSER)     h. SUBROUTINE DIFF(X,Y)
b. CALL CD(X,I+1,EPS,ANSER)              DIFF = X-Y
c. FUNCTION EF(X,A(X),I)                 RETURN
d. Z = GH(Y,A(Y),I)                      END
e. FUNCTION F()                       i. FUNCTION Z(T)
f. SUBROUTINE G()                        T = 2./Z
g. FUNCTION SUM(X,Y)                     RETURN
     X = X + Y                           END
     RETURN                           j. FUNCTION X(W)
   END                                    X = 2.
                                          STOP
```

5.16 a. The largest integer on your computer is very likely of the form $2^k - 1$. Write and execute a program that will print k and $2^k - 1.0$ for $k = 1$ to 100. From the results, estimate the maximum integer available on your computer.

b. Write and execute a program that will print $(11.0)^k$ for $k = 10$ to 100. From the results, estimate the maximum real number available on your computer. You may wish to refine your estimate by rerunning the program using a base slightly different from 11.0.

5.17 A point on a sphere can be characterized by two angles, the polar angle α and the azimuthal angle β, as shown in Figure 5-14. Locations on the earth, however, are ordinarily expressed in terms of latitude and longitude measured in angles north or south of the equator or east or west of the Greenwich meridian, respectively. The angles α, β are related to latitude and longitude as follows:

$$\alpha = 90° - \text{latitude} \quad \text{(if north)}$$
$$\alpha = 90° + \text{latitude} \quad \text{(if south)}$$
$$\beta = \text{longitude} \quad \text{(if west)}$$
$$\beta = 360° - \text{longitude} \quad \text{(if east)}$$

a. Write a subroutine that will convert the coordinates of a point on the earth given in terms of longitude and latitude in degrees into coordinates in terms of the angles (α, β) in radians. The input angles should be in the form:

Figure 5-14

Relation between latitude/longitude coordinates and the polar/azimuthal angles α, β on the earth's surface

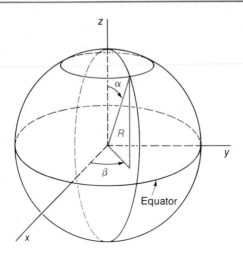

Latitude

If north (e.g., dd°mm′N) use → +dd.mm
If south (e.g., dd°mm′S) use → −dd.mm

Longitude

If west (e.g., dd°mm′W) use → +dd.mm
If east (e.g., dd°mm′E) use → −dd.mm

Thus, 45°21′S would be entered as −45.21, representing a latitude of 45 degrees, 21 minutes south, and would be converted to $\alpha = 90° + (45 + 21/60)° = 135.35° \rightarrow (135.35°/180°)\pi$ radians.

b. If two points on a sphere are specified in terms of their polar and azimuthal angles, (α_1, β_1) and (α_2, β_2), the angular separation between the two points is an angle θ_{12}, which can be determined from the equations

$$C = \cos(\theta_{12}) = \cos(\alpha_1)\cos(\alpha_2) + \sin(\alpha_1)\sin(\alpha_2)\cos(\beta_1 - \beta_2)$$

and $\theta_{12} = \cos^{-1}(C)$

Write a function subprogram that will compute and return the angular separation of two points on a sphere, θ_{12}, from (α_1, β_1) and (α_2, β_2).

c. The surface distance between points on a sphere is given by $d = R\theta_{12}$, where R is the radius of the sphere and θ_{12} is the angular separation between the two points. Write a program that will read in the latitude and longitude of two cities on the earth and compute the surface distance between the two cities. Use $R = 3958.89$ miles for the earth's radius.

d. Create a data file containing the following names of cities and their location.

City	Latitude	Longitude
Chicago	41°49'N	87°37'W
Los Angeles	35°12'N	118°02'W
Montreal	45°30'N	73°35'W
London	51°30'N	0°07'W
Rio de Janeiro	22°50'S	43°20'W
Melbourne	35°52'S	145°08'E
Vladivostok	43°06'N	131°47'E
Johannesburg	26°08'S	27°54'E

Write a main program that will read this file and compute and print the surface distances between Los Angeles and all the remaining cities on the list. Alternatively, look up the coordinates of your home town and compute the surface distances to the cities on the list. (*Note:* The maximum separation between any two points on the earth is $\pi R_e = 12{,}437$ miles. You should find that the distance between Rio de Janeiro and Vladivostok is almost that far. Also, you will find that the Los Angeles to London distance is almost the same as Los Angeles to Vladivostok.)

5.18 Indicate whether the following statements are true or false. Explain your answers.
  a. The name of a common block must not be the same as that of any variable in the list.
  b. To use a common block in a subroutine, the block must also appear in the main program.
  c. Two common blocks can appear on the same line, for example,

```
COMMON/AA/X,Y,Z/GG/D,E,F
```

  d. All variables in a common block must be of the same type.
  e. The variables A and S in the following two COMMON statements have the same value.

```
COMMON/LIST/E1,E2,F,W,S,Q,A,X
COMMON/LIST/F,W,Q,X,Z,A,T,S
```

5.19 Identify any compilation errors in the following expressions:
  a. COMMON A,B/O.,1./
  b. REAL A
      A = 2.
      COMMON/LIST/A,B
  c. COMMON/W/X,Y,Z
      DATA X,Y,Z/3*0./
  d. CHARACTER*8 NAME,STREET
      INTEGER ZIP
      COMMON /ADDRES/NAME,STREET,ZIP
  e. FUNCTION F(X)
      COMMON/PARAM/A,B,C,X
  f. COMMON/Q/Q,Q
  g. COMMON/Q/Q/W/W
  h. COMMON/COMMON/COMMON
  i. COMMON/REAL/INTEGER

5.20 You have two function subroutines at your disposal: ROOT(A, F) will find a root of a function $f(x)$ of a single variable when an initial guess (A) is given for the root; DINTGL (A, B, G) will compute the definite integral of $g(t)$ from $t = a$ to $t = b$, that is,

$$\text{DINTGL}(A,B,G) = \int_a^b g(x)\,dx$$

(Do not panic—You do not need to understand integration to do this problem.) Write a program that will find the root of the equation

$$h(x) = 5e^{-2x^2} - \sin\left(\frac{\pi x}{2}\right) + \int_0^x (4t^2 - 5)e^{-t^2}\,dt$$

starting with an initial guess of $x_1 = 1.0$. (Notice that the variable is x and that it appears in the limits of the integral.)

5.21 You have at your disposal a subroutine PLOT(A, B, F) that will produce a graph on the terminal screen of a function $f(x)$ of a single variable from $x = a$ to $x = b$.
  a. Write a program that will graph $\sin(x)$ from 0 to 2π.
  b. Write a program that will read the coefficients of a quadratic and graph the quadratic from $x = -10$ to $x = +10$ where
  (1) The quadratic is coded as a statement function.
  (2) The quadratic is coded as a function subprogram.

5.22 Without executing the program below, determine the values of the printed output. Next, execute the program to verify your answers.

```
PROGRAM XXX
COMMON/B/A,B,C,D
A = 0.
B = 1.
C = 2.
D = 3.
B = G(C)
D = A + C
WRITE(*,*)A,B,C,D
STOP
END
*====================================
FUNCTION G(X)
COMMON/B/D,C,B,A
D = 3.
A = 7.
X = C
G = B + C
RETURN
END
```

5.23 Without executing the program below, determine the value that will be printed for B. Next, execute the program to verify your answers. If the computer results differ from your prediction, determine the source of the error in your prediction.

```
PROGRAM PUZZL
COMMON A
   A = 3.
   C = F(A)
END
*============================
FUNCTION F(X)
COMMON B
   X = 2.
   PRINT *,B
   F = 0.
RETURN
END
```

B
Programming Assignment

Sample Program

Engineering Career Choices: Chemical Engineering

Chemical engineering is the application of the knowledge or techniques of science, particularly chemistry, to industry. Chemical engineers are responsible for the design and operation of large-scale manufacturing plants for all those materials that undergo chemical changes in their production. These materials include all the new and improved products that have so profoundly affected society, such as petrochemicals, rubbers and polymers, new metal alloys, industrial and fine chemicals, foods, paints, detergents, cements, pesticides, industrial gases, and medicines. Chemical engineers also play an important role in pollution abatement and the management of existing energy resources.

Because the field of chemical engineering has grown to be so broad, it is difficult to classify the activities of chemical engineers. A rough subdivision is into large-scale production systems, or chemical processing, and smaller-scale, or molecular, systems.

Chemical Processing

Chemical processing concerns all aspects of the design and operation of large chemical-processing plants. It includes the following areas:

Petrochemicals. The distillation and refinement of fuels such as gasoline, synthetic natural gas, coal liquefaction and gasification, and the production of an infinite variety of products made from petroleum, from cosmetics to pharmaceuticals.

Synthetic materials. The process of polymerization, a joining of simpler molecules into large complex molecules, is responsible for many modern materials such as nylon, synthetic rubbers, polystyrene, and a great variety of plastics and synthetic fibers.

Food and biochemical engineering. The manufacture of packaged food, improved food additives, sterilization, and the utilization of industrial bacteria, fungi, and yeasts in processes like fermentation.

Unit operations. The analysis of the transport of heat or fluid, such as the pumping of chemicals through a pipeline or the transfer of heat between substances. This area also includes the effect of heat transfer on chemical reactions such as oxidation, chlorination, and so on.

Cryogenic engineering. The design of plants operating at temperatures near absolute zero.

Electrochemical engineering. The use of electricity to alter chemical reactions, such as electroplating, or the design of batteries or energy cells.

Pollution control. A rapidly growing field that seeks to monitor and reduce the harmful effects of chemical processing on the environment. Topics of concern are waste-water control, air pollution abatement, and the economics of pollution control.

Molecular Systems

This field involves the application of laboratory techniques to large-scale processes. It includes the following areas:

Biochemical engineering. Application of enzymes, bacteria, and so on to improve large-scale chemical processes.

Polymer synthesis. Molecular basis for polymer properties and the chemical synthesis of new polymers adapted for large-scale production.

Research and development. In all areas of chemical processing.

Preparation for a career in chemical engineering requires a thorough background in physics, chemistry, and mathematics and a knowledge of thermodynamics and physical, analytic, and organic chemistry. Although extensively trained in chemistry, chemical engineers differ from chemists in that their main concern is the adaptation of laboratory techniques to large-scale manufacturing plants.

B.2   Sample Programming Problem

Chemical Engineering: Separation of Two Liquids by Differential Distillation

A common procedure for separating a two-liquid mixture into its components relies on the different volatilities of the constituents. For example, if a liquid mixture of benzene and toluene is heated, the greater volatility of benzene will cause the vapor that is given off to have a higher relative concentration of benzene, while the remaining liquid will be correspondingly depleted. The process occurs at atmospheric pressure and a temperature of 100° C; the rate of drawing off the evaporated vapor is approximately constant. If it is assumed that the vapor and liquid are always in equilibrium, the relative volatility of benzene to toluene is given by the ratio of their vapor pressures,

$$\alpha = \text{relative volatility} = (P_v)_{\text{benzene}}/(P_v)_{\text{toluene}}$$

$$= \frac{(1.536 \times 10^5 \text{ N/m}^2)}{(6.575 \times 10^4 \text{ N/m}^2)}$$

$$= 2.336$$

Next, if the mole fraction (i.e., the ratio of the number of moles of benzene to the total number of moles of benzene and toluene) in the liquid is x and that in the vapor is y, then x and y are related by an equation known as Raoult's law:

$$y = \frac{\alpha x}{1 + (\alpha - 1)x} \qquad \text{Raoult's law} \qquad (B.1)$$

The amount of liquid mixture that is lost to evaporation $(-dL)$ in a time dt is equal to the increase in the amount of vapor $(+dV)$:

$$dV = -dL \qquad (B.2)$$

The amount of benzene in this amount of vapor is ydV, which originated from the evaporation of an amount of $d(xL)$ liquid. Or,

$$y\,dV = -d(xL)$$

$$= -L\,dx - x\,dL \qquad (B.3)$$

That is, the increase in the concentration of the benzene in the vapor comes from the evaporation of an amount $x\,dL$ of the liquid plus a decrease in the relative concentration of benzene in the liquid of an amount $-L\,dx$.

Combining Equations (B.2) and (B.3) yields

$$\frac{dL}{L} = \frac{dx}{y - x} \qquad (B.4)$$

The amount of liquid (dL) that evaporates in each time step (dt) is proportional to the amount of liquid currently present (L). Thus, the rate of evaporation is defined as

$$\frac{dL}{L} = -r\,dt \qquad (B.5)$$

Finally, Raoult's law is used to express y as a function of x, and both sides are integrated from $t = 0$ to a final time T. If the concentration of benzene at $t = 0$ is x_0 and that at $t = T$ is $x(T)$, the result, after some algebra, is

$$x(T)[1 - x(T)]^{-\alpha} = x_0[1 - x_0]^{-\alpha} e^{-(\alpha-1)rT} \qquad (B.6)$$

The computer problem is to solve this equation for the concentration of the benzene remaining in the liquid, $x(T)$, for a variety of times T. If we rearrange Equation (B.5) and define a function $f(x,T)$ as

$$f(x,T) = x(1 - x)^{-\alpha} - x_0(1 - x_0)^{-\alpha}e^{-(\alpha-1)rT} \qquad (B.7)$$

we are looking for the roots of $f(x,T)$.

Details. Using the following values for the constant parameters

$$\begin{aligned}
\alpha &= \text{Relative volatility} &&= 2.336 \\
x_0 &= \text{Initial benzene concentration} &&= 0.44 \\
r &= \text{Evaporation rate of mix} &&= 0.051/\text{hr}
\end{aligned}$$

for each value of the time from $T = 0.5$ hour to 10 hours in steps of one-half hour, use the bisection algorithm to solve for the root of Equation (B.7) and print the results in the form of a table.

The bisection parameters should be EPS = 1.E-4 and IMAX = 30. Because the concentration will be decreasing from x_0, use the interval $\frac{1}{2}x_0 < x < x_0$ for all calculations. A pseudocode outline of the program would be

PROGRAM TWO
Statement Function for F(X,T) = Equation (B.7)
DATA statement for parameters $\alpha, x_0, r, \epsilon, I_{max}$
Print parameters and table heading
For T = 0.5 to 10. in steps of 0.5
    define interval $x_1 = a = \frac{1}{2}x_0$, $x_3 = b = x_0$
    and function values $f_1 = f(x_1,T)$, $f_3 = f(x_3,T)$

> Include bisection code adapted from Figure 4-10.

Once root is obtained, print time and root as one line of the table.
Print *,T,x_2
End of T loop

The FORTRAN code for the program is shown in Figure B-1.

B.3 **Programming Problems**

Engineering Career Choices: Materials Science and Metallurgical Engineering

To a large extent, advances in many areas of engineering in the twentieth century have been made possible by discoveries of new materials and a better understanding of the properties of existing materials. Knowledge of

Figure B-1 _____
Sample program
solution

```
            PROGRAM TWO
*
*-- Differential Distillation.  Because benzene is more volatile than
*-- toluene, the mole fraction (or concentration) of benzene in a
*-- benzene-toluene mixture decreases as the mixture evaporates. For a
*-- given value of time, Equation (B.7), may be solved for the benzene
*-- molar fraction, x.  This is repeated for a range of time values and
*-- a table is printed.
*--
*-- A statement function is used for Equation (B.7) and the bisection
*-- algorithm of Figure 4-10 is adapted for the determination of the
*-- roots.
*------------------------------------------------------------------------
* Variables
*--
*--    Physical Parameters
*--
       REAL F,X0,T,ALPHA,R
*--
*--    X0    --  Initial concentration of benzene in the liquid
*--    ALPHA --  Relative volatility
*--    R     --  Evaporation rate constant
*--    F()   --  Statement function for Equation (B.7)
*--
*--    Bisection Parameters
*--
       REAL X1,X2,X3,F1,F2,F3,A,B,EPS,D,D0
*--
*--    X1,X3,X2  --  Left, right, and midpoint of the
*--                      current interval
*--    F1,F3,F2  --  Function evaluated at these points
*--    A,B, D0   --  Left and right ends of the original
*--                      interval and its width (b-a)
*--     EPS      --  Convergence criterion based on the size of
*--                      the current interval
*--     D        --  Fractional width of the current interval,
*--                      that is,  (x3-x1)/d0
*--     IMAX     --  Maximum number of iterations
*--     I        --  Current iteration counter
*------------------------------------------------------------------------
* Statement function for the function f(x,T)
*--
       F(X,T) = X/(1.-X)**ALPHA - X0/(1.-X0)**ALPHA *EXP((1.-ALPHA)
      +          *R*T)
*--
*------------------------------------------------------------------------
* Initialization
*--
       DATA X0,L0,R,ALPHA,EPS,IMAX/.4,50.,.051,2.37,1.E-4,30/
*--
*--
*--    Open a file for the results
*--
       OPEN(26,FILE='RSLTS2')
*--
```

Figure B-1 _____
(continued)

```
          A = .5*X0
          B = X0
          WRITE(26,*)'The original search interval is from ',A,' to ',B
          WRITE(26,*)'The convergence criterion is (interval) < ',EPS
          WRITE(26,*)'The maximum number of iterations allowed is ',IMAX
          WRITE(26,*)
          WRITE(26,*)'A table of relative benzene concentration in a'
          WRITE(26,*)'benzene-toluene mixture as the mixture evaporates'
          WRITE(26,*)
          WRITE(26,*)'  Time          Benzene           Iterations'
          WRITE(26,*)'  (hrs)      concentration(%)  required '
          WRITE(26,*)'  ------     ---------------      ----   '
          WRITE(26,*)' ',0.,'      ',X0
    *--

          A = .5*X0
          B = X0
          DO 5 T = 0.5,10.,.5
             X1 = A
             X3 = B
             F1 = F(X1,T)
             F3 = F(X3,T)
             D0 = (X3 - X1)

    *--
    *--      +-----------------------------------------+
    *--      | Adapt and copy bisection code for root of |
    *--      | F(X,T).  Note that here the function has  |
    *--      | two variables in the argument list.      |
    *--      +-----------------------------------------+

             WRITE(26,*)' ',T,'     ',ROOT,'   ',I
        5 CONTINUE
    *--
          STOP
          END
```

[Positioning of output numbers was altered by using a text editor.]

```
The original search interval is from   0.200  to  0.400
The convergence criterion is (interval) <  1.000E-04
The maximum number of iterations allowed is    30
```

the physical and chemical principles determining the electrical properties of exotic materials called semiconductors have resulted in the fantastic progress in the field of solid-state devices, from transistors to integrated-circuit chips to large computers. Better understanding of the origins of metallic properties such as hardness, strength, ductility, corrosiveness, and others have led to improved design of automobiles, aircraft, space-craft, and all types of machinery. The field is basically subdivided into metals and nonmetals, although there is often considerable overlap of interests and activities.

Figure B-1
(concluded)

A table of relative benzene concentration in a
benzene-toluene mixture as the mixture evaporates

Time (hrs)	Benzene concentration(%)	Iterations required
0.00	0.4000000	
0.50	0.3946045	13
1.00	0.3891846	13
1.50	0.3837647	13
2.00	0.3783448	13
2.50	0.3729249	13
3.00	0.3675050	13
3.50	0.3621339	13
4.00	0.3567140	13
4.50	0.3513428	13
5.00	0.3459718	13
5.50	0.3406495	13
6.00	0.3352784	13
6.50	0.3299561	13
7.00	0.3246338	13
7.50	0.3193604	13
8.00	0.3140870	13
8.50	0.3088136	13
9.00	0.3035889	13
9.50	0.2984131	13
10.00	0.2932374	13

Materials Science

Materials science concerns the behavior and properties of materials, both metals and nonmetals, from both microscopic and macroscopic perspectives. It includes the following areas:

1. *Ceramics.* Noncrystalline materials, such as glass, that are nonmetallic and that require high temperatures in their processing. Ceramics can be made brittle or flexible, hard or soft, or stronger than steel. They can be made to have a variety of chemical properties.
2. *Polymers.* Structural and physical properties of organic, inorganic, and natural polymers that are useful in engineering applications.
3. *Materials fabrication, processing, and treatment.* All aspects of the manufacture of ceramics, metals, and polymer synthesis, from the growth of crystals and fibers to metal forming.
4. *Corrosion.* Reaction mechanism and thermodynamics of corrosion of metals in the atmosphere or submerged under water or chemicals, whether standing or under stress.

5. *Stress-strain, fatigue-fracture of engineering materials.* Physical properties governing the deformation and fracture of materials and their improvement and use in construction and design.

Metallurgical Engineering

Metallurgical engineering is the branch engineering responsible for the production of metals and metal alloys, from the discovery of ore deposits to the fabrication of the refined metal into useful products. Metallurgical engineers are important in every step in the production of metal from metal ore. Metallurgical engineering includes the following areas:

1. *Mining engineering.* Usually a separate branch of engineering. However, the concerns of mining engineers and metallurgists frequently overlap in the processes of extraction of metals from metal ores and the refinement into usable products. Extraction metallurgy makes use of physical and chemical reactions to optimize metal production.
2. *Metals fabrication.* Metal forming into products such as cans, wires, and tubes; casting and joining of metals—for example, by welding.
3. *Physical metallurgy.* Analysis of stress-strain, fatigue-fracture characteristics of metals and metal alloys to prevent engineering component failures.

Programming Problem B-A: Metallurgical Engineering: Carburization

To improve the hardness characteristics of steel, carbon is added to the steel in a controlled manner by a process called carburizing, which involves the gradual diffusing into the steel of atoms of carbon applied at the metal surface. For example, if a rod of pure iron is welded to a similar rod containing 1% carbon, the carbon content of the pure end is found to vary with time and position down the rod in a manner indicated in Figure B-2. At $t = 0$ the concentration of carbon in the right half is zero; at some later time it is found that the concentration in the enriched half has been depleted near the boundary and carbon atoms have migrated into the pure end. After an infinite amount of time, the distribution of carbon will be uniform throughout. The rate of the transport of the carbon atoms at a point x in the bar is found to be proportional to the negative of the slope of the concentration curve at that point, zero at the extreme ends, and large positive near the middle.

$$F = -D\frac{dC(x,t)}{dx} \tag{B.8}$$

where F is the volume concentration of atoms migrating per second, $C(x,t)$ is the concentration of carbon atoms at position x and time t, and the pro-

Figure B-2
Diffusion of carbon
between rods of
differing
composition

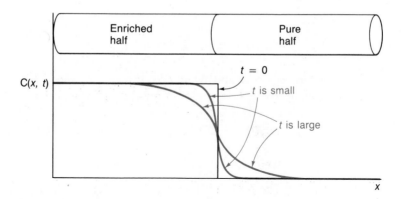

portionality constant D is called the diffusion constant. Combining this equation with the constraint that the total number of carbon atoms remain constant leads to an important equation of engineering and science: the diffusion equation. The diffusion equation is a partial differential equation that you will encounter in later courses in mathematics. The solution of this equation yields the following expression for the concentration of carbon atoms as a function of both position and time:

$$C(x,t) = \tfrac{1}{2}C_0\left[1 - \text{Erf}\left(\frac{x}{2Dt}\right)\right] \tag{B.9}$$

where $\text{Erf}(z)$ is the error function and is tabulated in most books of mathematical tables. If the argument, z, is less than 1.5, a good approximation to the error function is the series expression

$$\text{Erf}(z) \approx \frac{2z}{\sqrt{\pi}}\left[1 - \frac{z^2}{3} + \frac{z^4}{10} - \frac{z^6}{42} + \frac{z^8}{216} - \frac{z^{10}}{1,320}\right] \tag{B.10}$$

The diffusion process is found to be extremely temperature dependent. This can be taken into account in the diffusion constant by expressing it as

$$D = D(T) = D_0 e^{-(q/RT)} \tag{B.11}$$

where D_0 is a constant, q is called the activation energy and is constant, and R is the ideal gas constant (8.314 J/mol-K). The units of D are m^2/sec. Thus, once the constants D_0, R, q, C_0, and the temperature T have been specified, the concentration $C(x,t)$ can be determined for any value of x and t.

Problem Specifics. It is desired to allow the diffusion to take place until the average concentration in the right half reaches C_r, then disconnect the two halves and heat the right half until the concentration smooths out to a uniform concentration that would equal C_r.

The average concentration across the right half could be expressed as

$$C_{avg}(t) = \frac{1}{n+1} \sum_{i=0}^{n} C(x_i, t) \tag{B.12}$$

where $x_i = i\Delta x$ and $\Delta x = L/n$. In this problem we will use $n = 4$ so that the approximate expression for the average is

$$C_{avg}(t) \approx \frac{1}{5}[C(0,t) + C(\Delta x, t) + C(2\Delta x, t) + C(3\Delta x, t) + C(L, t)]$$

$$\Delta x = L/4 \tag{B.13}$$

The problem then is to construct a function $F(t) = C_{avg}(t) - C_r$ and find the root of this function. At this value of time, the average concentration will equal C_r. Thus, a pseudocode outline of the program would be

```
PROGRAM TWOA
Type declarations for
       physical parameters C₀, D₀, q, TEMP, Length, Cᵣ
       bisection parameters a, b, ε, Iₘₐₓ
Data statement or read data file for physical parameters
Data statement or read data file for bisection parameters
Statement functions for
  D(TEMP) = Equation (B.11)
  ERF(Z)  = Equation (B.10)
  C(X,T)  = Equation (B.9)
  CAVG(T) = Equation (B.13)
  F(T) = CAVG(T) − CR
Print all parameters with labels
```

> Adapt bisection code of Figure 4-10 to find root of F(T) and insert here.

Print root in seconds and converted to days.

Use the parameters listed in Table B-1.

Engineering Career Choices: Electrical Engineering

Electrical engineering deals with the application of the principles of electricity and electromagnetism to the manufacture of all forms of machines and devices that either use electricity or produce electrical energy. The field is the largest of all engineering fields. In its beginning in the mid-1800s it was concerned solely with generating electrical energy. It has evolved into a field with broad boundaries, encompassing solid-state devices such as transistors, communication, and computers, and robotics.

Table B-1
Input parameters
for the carburizing
problem

Parameter	Description	Value
C_0	Initial concentration	0.25 (%)
D_0	Diffusion parameter	2.00×10^{-6} m/sec
q	Activation energy	0.34×10^5 J
T	Temperature	1200.0 K
L	Length of bar	0.07 m
C_r	Desired average concentration	0.075 (%)
I_{max}	Iterations limit	30
EPS	Convergence criterion	10^{-4}
a, b	Original bisection interval (must first be converted to seconds)	5.0, 10.0 days

Power

This area involves generation of electrical energy in large fossil-fuel, nuclear, solar, or hydroelectric plants or the efficient utilization of electrical energy by means of motors or illumination devices. Also important are the transmission and distribution of electrical energy through overhead lines, microwaves, light pipes, and superconducting lines.

Solid-State Electronics

In conjunction with modern physics and materials science, exotic semiconducting materials are being developed and used to construct microcircuitry that is used in monitoring and controlling the operations of all kinds of devices, from video games to assembly-line robots. The improved reliability, rapidly shrinking size, and reduced power requirements of modern miniaturized electrical components have created limitless opportunities for applications.

Communications

Communications involves the design and construction of equipment used in the transmission of information via electricity or electromagnetic waves (radio, light, microwaves, etc.). The use of the laser for communication is a topic of modern concern, whereas antenna characteristics and radar are somewhat older.

Computers and Robotics

While electronics deals with the principles associated with the functions of miniaturized components, computer engineers are concerned with designing the complex circuitry that interweaves the components into a computer. Microprocessors, or small computers, are designed to constantly monitor and control the operations of a particular piece of equipment such as a lathe or an autopilot.

Programming Problem B-B: Electrical Engineering:
Comparative Impedance of Two Transmission Lines

Conducting wires are used to carry electrical current I between points that differ in voltage by an amount V. For direct current the relationship between the resultant current and the applied voltage is given by Ohm's law, $V = IR$, where R is the wire resistance, which depends on the material and size of the wire. For alternating current a similar relationship exists between the maximum of the applied alternating voltage and the maximum of the resultant current, $V_{max} = I_{max}Z$, where Z is called the impedance and plays a role similar to the resistance for direct current. The impedance, like the resistance, depends on the size and the material of the conductor; but it is also a function of other factors such as the geometry of the conductor. For example, a double coaxial balanced transmission line consists of two wires, each surrounded by insulating material and encased in a conducting sheath that is grounded. (See Figure B-3). The impedance for this arrangement is

$$Z_D = Z_0 \ln(r/a) \tag{B.14}$$

where r/a is the ratio of the radius of the single coaxial line to the wire radius, and Z_0 is a constant. This arrangement is snaked through a conduit tube of radius $2R$ (the large circle in Figure B-3). An alternative transmission line is a shielded balanced pair, shown in Figure B-4. For this arrangement the expression for the impedance is much more complicated:

$$Z_s = Z_0 \left[\ln\left(2\tau x \frac{1 - x^2}{1 + x^2} \right) - \frac{(1 + 4\tau^2 x^2)(1 - 4x^2)}{16\tau^4 x^2} \right] \tag{B.15}$$

where $\tau = R/a$ is the ratio of the radius of the outside cylinder to the wire radius of the wire, and $x = d/R$ is the ratio of the distance of each wire to the center of the arrangement to the radius of the cylinder.

Figure B-3
Double coaxial
balanced
transmission line

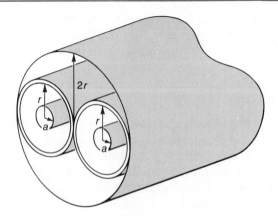

Figure B-4
Shielded balanced
pair transmission
line

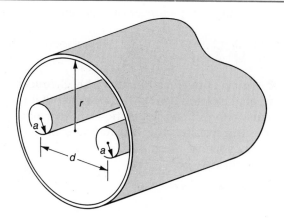

Problem. It is proposed to replace a double coaxial line with a shielded pair line in the same conduit. Additionally, it is important that the replacement have the same impedance as the line it replaces. If the wire radii are the same, and noting that $r \approx \frac{1}{2}R$, we see that we have only one variable to adjust, namely x, the positioning of the wire pair. The geometrical limits on x are seen to be $1 < \tau x < \tau - 1$. To solve for the appropriate value of x, we construct the function

$$f(x) = Z_0 \ln\left(\frac{1}{2}\tau\right) - Z_0\left[\ln\left(2\tau x\frac{1 - x^2}{1 + x^2}\right) - \frac{(1 + 4\tau^2 x^2)(1 - 4x^2)}{16\tau^4 x^2}\right] \qquad \text{(B.16)}$$

and for given values of Z_0 and τ determine the root of $f(x)$.

Details. Use the following values for the parameters in this problem:

$$
\begin{aligned}
a &= \text{Wire radius} & &= 0.0015 \text{ m} \\
R &= \text{Inner conduit radius} & &= 0.0120 \text{ m} \\
\tau &= R/a = 8 \\
Z_0 &= \text{Impedance constant} & &= 1.0 \text{ ohms} \\
x_1, x_3 &= \text{Initial search interval} & &= 0.2, 0.6 \\
\epsilon &= \text{Convergence criterion} & &= 10^{-4} \\
I_{max} &= \text{Iterations limit} & &= 30
\end{aligned}
$$

Use a DATA statement to initialize the parameters and write a statement function for Equation (B.16). Then adapt the bisection code of Figure 4-10 to solve for the root of this function. In addition, to test the sensitivity of the arrangement to the precise placement of the wires, compute the fractional change in the impedance [Equation (B.15)] for a 5% change in the positioning of the wires; that is, if x_r is the root of Equation (B.16), compute

$$[Z_S(1.05x_r) - Z_S(0.95x_r)]/Z_S(x_r)$$

Neatly print the parameters along with the root and the sensitivity. Include in your output the number of iterations that were required.

Programming Problem B-C: Chemical Engineering/Chemistry: Coexistence of Liquids and Gases

Chemical engineers deal continually with chemical and physical interactions between gases and liquids. It is essential that they have some form of approximate mathematical description of the properties of a substance as it undergoes a transition from gas to liquid phases and back. In elementary chemistry you are introduced to the ideal gas equation of state, which for 1 mole of gas may be written

$$P = \frac{RT}{V} \tag{B.17}$$

where
P = Pressure (N/m²)
V = Volume of one mole (m³)
T = Temperature (K)
R = Ideal gas constant = 8.314 J/mol-K

This equation is adequate for low pressures and high temperatures where the liquid state is not present. In fact, the ideal gas law assumes that the substance remains a gas even down to a temperature of absolute zero. Over the years there have been hundreds of suggestions as to how to modify the ideal gas equation to incorporate the possibility of a gas condensing into a liquid. One of the earliest and still one of the best is the Van derWaal's equation of state for an imperfect gas, which may be written in a simplified form as

$$p = \frac{\frac{8}{3}t}{\left(v - \frac{1}{3}\right)} - \frac{3}{v^2} \tag{B.18}$$

where p, v, and t are scaled pressure, volume, and temperature, respectively; that is,

$$p = P/P_c \qquad v = V/V_c \qquad t = T/T_c$$

and P_c, V_c, and T_c are the values of the pressure, volume, and temperature at the critical point—that is, the unique value of P, V, and T at which equal masses of the vapor phase and the liquid phase have the same density. The critical point values are extensively tabulated for most substances. The Van der Waal's equation of state is sketched for three temperatures in Figure B-5. As the temperature is reduced below the critical point temperature ($t = T/T_c < 1$), the gradual development of a hill and a valley in the p-v curve will be interpreted as a transition from gas to liquid. There is,

Figure B-5
Plot of Van der
Waal's equation of
state

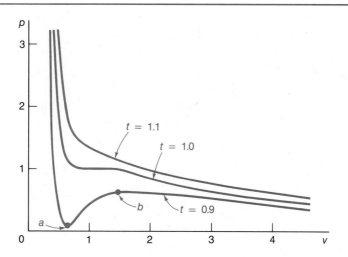

however, a difficulty: the slope of the curve from point a to point b on the graph is positive.

$$\frac{\Delta p}{\Delta v} > 0 \quad \text{Between points } a \text{ and } b$$

This suggests that if the pressure is increased, $p \rightarrow p + \Delta p$, the volume is predicted to increase, $v \rightarrow v + \Delta v$. This is clearly unphysical and must be corrected. If p_a and p_b are the pressures at the points a and b, respectively, the procedure is to replace the unphysical part of the curve (where the slope is positive) with a horizontal straight line as shown in Figure B-6. Along this line the substance can change its volume with the pressure and temperature remaining constant by changing from gas to liquid or liquid to gas. There are a variety of ways to choose the straight line that is to re-place the unphysical segment of the curve. The most straightforward is to determine the points labeled a and b on the curve and the volumes, v_a and v_b associated with these points. A point c on the curve is then defined by the midpoint of the interval $v_a \leftrightarrow v_b$; $v_c = \frac{1}{2}(v_a + v_b)$ and a horizontal line is drawn through point c. The interpretation is then that for a given tempera-ture t, the substance, as a liquid, will follow the curve as pressure is de-creased until $p = p_c$. The volume then will increase at constant pressure as the liquid changes phase into a gas, thus following the line segment. When all the liquid has changed into vapor, the substance once again fol-lows the curve in the gas segment of the plot. Note that in the portion of the curve we are interpreting as liquid, a very large increase in pressure is accompanied by only a modest change in volume, characteristic of a liq-uid; the opposite is true in the vapor segment.

Figure B-6
Coexistence of
liquid-gas phases
on a Van der Waal's
plot

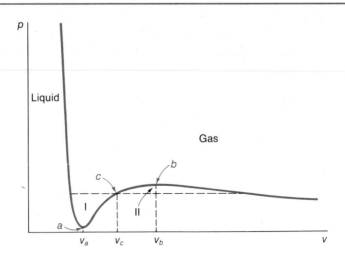

Problem. At the points a and b the tangent to the pressure versus volume curve is horizontal. Thus, the location of the points is the requirement that the derivative dp/dv be zero at these points

$$\frac{dp(v)}{dv} = 0$$

$$= -\frac{\frac{8}{3}t}{\left(v - \frac{1}{3}\right)^2} + \frac{6}{v^3} \qquad \text{(B.19)}$$

which may be written as

$$f(v) = v^3 - C_2 v^2 + C_1 v - C_0 = 0 \qquad \text{(B.20)}$$

where

$$C_2 = \frac{9}{4t} \qquad C_1 = \frac{3}{2t} \qquad C_0 = \frac{1}{4t}$$

Equation (B.20) has three positive real roots, $v = r_1, r_2, r_3$. The smallest, say r_1, will turn out to have a value less than $\frac{1}{3}$ and thus corresponds to a nonphysical region. [From Equation (B.18) we see that if $v < \frac{1}{3}$, the pressure is negative.] Discarding this root, the points a and b in Figure B-5 then correspond to the roots $v_a = r_2$ and $v_b = r_3$. To use the bisection algorithm to find these roots, all that remains is to specify the initial search interval for each of the roots.

To set up the initial search intervals, proceed as follows: Start with $x_{a1} = 0.4$ (i.e., just to the right of $v = \frac{1}{3}$) and evaluate the function $f_{a1} = f(x_{a1})$. Next step along the v axis in steps of size 0.1, and at each step check to see if the function has changed sign. When it does, define the current value of v to be both $x_{a3} = x_{b1} = v$. Continue to step along the axis until the function changes sign again, at which time define the current value of $v = x_{b3}$. The initial search intervals for the two roots are

Root at point a is in the interval $x_{a1} \leftrightarrow x_{a3}$

Root at point b is in the interval $x_{b1} \leftrightarrow x_{b3}$

Make sure your program has a diagnostic check for the case where no root, or only one root, is found.

The bisection algorithm is then used twice to find the two roots, point c is determined by $v_c = \frac{1}{2}(v_a + v_b)$, and the pressure required for condensing the gas into a liquid is determined from $p(v_c)$.

The variables in the problem are all scaled (i.e., divided by the critical point values). Your printed results should not be scaled but rather values with the appropriate units. The units of pressure in SI are called Pascals (Pa) (1 Pa = 1 N/m^2). These can be related to the more familiar units of atmospheres by 1 N/m^2 = 9.87×10^{-6} atm. The parameters for this problem are given in Table B-2.

A short pseudocode outline of the program is given below:

```
Type-declare all parameters
Statement function for p(v) = Equation (B.18)
Statement function for f(v) = Equation (B.20)
For RUN = 1, 4
    READ a data file for the substance name, Tc, Pc, Vc, and T
    Compute the constants C2, C1, C0 to be used in f(v)
    Xa1 = 0.4
    Xa3 = 0.4
    f1 = f(xa1)
    For v = xa1 to 6.0 in steps of 0.1
        IF(f(v) × f1 is negative and xa3 = 0.4)THEN
            Xa3 = v
            Xb1 = v
            f1 = f(v)
```

Table B-2

Input parameters for liquid-gas coexistence problem

Substance	T_c (K)	P_c (Pa)	V_c (m^3/mol)	T (K)
Carbon dioxide (CO_2)	304.26	7.40×10^6	2.02×10^{-5}	280.00
Benzene (C_6H_6)	561.66	4.83×10^6	2.37×10^{-5}	500.00
Nitrogen (N)	126.06	3.39×10^6	4.36×10^{-6}	108.00
Water (H_2O)	647.56	22.0×10^6	7.21×10^{-6}	550.00

ELSE IF($f(v)f_1$ is negative (again))THEN

$x_{b3} = v$

and jump out of the v-loop

END IF

End-of-v-loop

⟨diagnostic for "stepping too far"⟩

FOR ROOT = 1, 2

IF(ROOT = 1)THEN

$x_1 = x_{a1}$

$x_3 = x_{a3}$

ELSE

$x_1 = x_{b1}$

$x_3 = x_{b3}$

ENDIF

Adapt bisection code of Figure 4-10 and insert here.

IF(ROOT = 1)

$v_a = x_2$

ELSE

$v_b = x_2$

ENDIF

End-of-ROOT loop

$v_c = \frac{1}{2}(v_a + v_b)$

p-condense = $p(v_c)$

Print results for this substance

End-of-RUN loop

Elementary Formatted Input–Output

Introduction

Up to this point only a limited number of methods for getting numbers into and out of the computer have been presented, and all of them use list-directed input/output. In almost all cases the output that results is positioned incorrectly, cluttered, or otherwise unsatisfactory. As a temporary remedy it was suggested that you use your text editor to tidy up the output after it has been written to an output file by your FORTRAN program. In many cases this will remain the easiest procedure. But when the program will generate a large amount of numerical output, editing the output can be tedious and time-consuming. This chapter describes the features available in FORTRAN for editing input and output. Editing involves the positioning of numbers and text and the form of the numerical data to be printed or read. Thus, before the results are printed or the data file read, the following questions must be addressed:

> In what form are the numbers?
>> Integers?
>> Real numbers without exponents?
>> Real numbers with exponents?
>> How many significant figures are to be printed?
>
> Where will the numbers appear on the page?
>
> What text is to appear with the numbers?
>
> How should the table headings align with the numbers?

All of these decisions are made in the form of FORMAT statements. Clearly, all this arranging of output (and input) can take considerable

221

time. Formatting the input and output is the most tedious aspect of programming, but it is not terribly difficult to understand. And if you have spent a lot of time and effort getting some intricate code to execute efficiently and correctly, it is certainly worth taking some additional time to arrange the output in a neat, clear, and pleasing form.

The next section describes the changes that need to be made in the familiar READ and WRITE statements in order to use the editing features available in FORTRAN. The actual editing of I/O is done with FORMAT statements that are discussed next. The format specifications that are included in a FORMAT statement depend on the type of information that is being printed or read. The first category of specifications is for numerical quantities, either integers or real numbers, and enables the user to specify the number of digits and the position of the decimal point of each numerical value in either input or output. This is followed by a summary of the FORTRAN positional specifications, commands to skip spaces or lines or to tab to a particular column. Although the primary use of formatting instructions will be to edit the output of a program, FORMAT statements can be used for reading data as well, and the special features associated with formatted READ statements are outlined.

Printing and reading non-numerical quantities—that is, character strings—are particularly useful operations when constructing a table or reading data that includes a list of names, and the I/O of character strings is described in Section 6.5. Finally, several additional input/output options are summarized in Section 6.6. These include features such as skipping to the next page when printing or detecting the end of a file when reading data, among others.

6.2 Formatted I/O Statements

The following list summarizes the list-directed I/O statements that have been used to this point. Recall that an asterisk, *, is used to indicate that a default value will be used in this position.

Input Statement	Meaning
READ (* , *) ⟨input list⟩	The first asterisk designates the input file (default = keyboard). The second designates the format of the input (default = list-directed).
READ (12 , *) ⟨input list⟩	The input is from file number 12, which must be opened and rewound in the FORTRAN program. The format is again default = list-directed.

READ *, ⟨input list⟩	This statement is a shortened form of the preceding statement. The asterisk designates the default format.

Output Statement	Meaning
WRITE(*,*) ⟨output list⟩	The first asterisk designates the output file (default = screen.) The second designates the format of the output (default = list-directed).
WRITE(12,*) ⟨output list⟩	The output is to file number 12, which must be opened in the FORTRAN program. The format is again default = list-directed.
PRINT *, ⟨output list⟩	This statement is a shortened form of the preceding statement. The output file is the screen, and the asterisk designates the default format.

In each of the above statements, the default format designation will be replaced by a statement number of a FORMAT statement, as shown in the list below. (FORMAT statements are described in Section 6.3.)

I/O Statement	Meaning
READ 88, ⟨input list⟩	Read from the keyboard according to format number 88 the values for ...
WRITE(2,12) ⟨output list⟩	Write to file number 2, according to format number 12, the values...

6.3 FORMAT Statements

The form of a FORMAT statement is:

j FORMAT(spec$_1$, spec$_2$, spec$_3$,...)

The integer j is a unique statement number, and, as with all other FORTRAN statements, the word FORMAT begins in column 7 or later. Inside the parentheses is a list of formatting specifications separated by commas (or slashes, /, which are discussed later in this section) relating to the numbers, variables, or characters that are to be read in or printed out by the relevant READ or WRITE statements. The FORMAT statement is a nonexecutable statement, and it may appear anywhere in the program, either before or after the associated READ/WRITE statement.

Because formatted input is more complicated and not as essential as formatted output, FORMAT statements to control output are described first.

Format Specifications: Numerical Descriptors

F Format (Floating-Point or Real Numbers without Exponents)

The form of the F format specification is

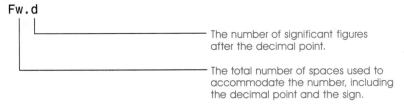

Thus, if the numbers $x = 271.736$, $y = 3.10$ are printed to file number 6 using the statements

```
        WRITE(5,66)X,Y
 66     FORMAT(F10.3,F5.1)
```

the numbers will be positioned as

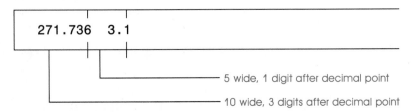

The same numbers printed with

```
        WRITE(6,13)
 13     FORMAT(F7.2,F6.2)
```

would result in

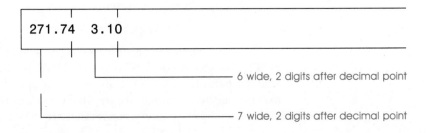

Some Technical Points about Formatted Output

When formatting output, keep in mind two important points:

1. *Avoid column 1.* When writing either to a printer or to the terminal screen, the first column of each line may not be displayed. Many computer systems use the first column of an output line for vertically positioning the output (carriage control). This feature is described in Section 6.6. For now, each line of output should skip column 1.
2. *Output is rounded.* When real numbers are printed, the values displayed are rounded, not truncated. In the example above, the value printed for X is 271.74. The number stored in memory for X, however, is still 271.736.

I Format (Integers)

The form of the I format specification is

For example, if the integer $n = 23$ is printed to the terminal screen by the statements

```
        WRITE(*,21)N
21   FORMAT(I9)
```

the result would be

The number is always positioned to the extreme right of the field. Attempts to print or read numbers using a format that conflicts with the type of the number will result in execution-time errors.

When printing either real or integer values, you must be sure that the field width (w) is large enough to accommodate the anticipated size of the numbers printed. If the field width is too small, the computer will instead fill the entire field with asterisks. For example, an attempt to print X = 123.456 and K = 1234 with formats F5.3 and I3, respectively, will result in output that resembles

```
    *****
    ***         An * indicates field-width overflow.
```

This is not, however, a fatal execution error, and the program will continue.

E Format (Floating-Point or Real Numbers with Exponents)

The form of the E format specification is

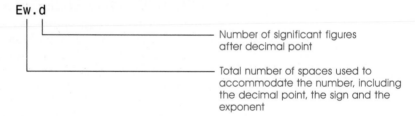

Ew.d

Number of significant figures after decimal point

Total number of spaces used to accommodate the number, including the decimal point, the sign and the exponent

A typical real number with exponent is

-0.12345E-05

which occupies 12 spaces (w) and has five digits (d) following the decimal point. In addition to the mantissa digits (1 2 3 4 5), seven spaces in total are required for the leading sign, leading zero, decimal point, the letter E, and the integer exponent. Thus, when using E formats, w ≥ d + 7. For example, printing the variables $x = 2.71736 \times 10^2$ and $y = 31.0 \times 10^{-11}$ using the statements

```
      WRITE(*,22)X,Y
  22  FORMAT(E14.5,E10.2)
```

would result in

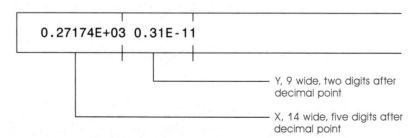

0.27174E+03 0.31E-11

Y, 9 wide, two digits after decimal point

X, 14 wide, five digits after decimal point

Most installations of FORTRAN always print an E format number with a zero to the left of the decimal point. The zero, as well as the plus sign, will be deleted if the number will not otherwise fit in the field.

Format Specifications: Position Descriptors

X Format (Skip a Space)

The form of the X format specification is

nX

Number of spaces to be skipped

For example,

```
        I = 12
        J = 34
        K = 56
        WRITE(*,6)I,J,K
    6   FORMAT(3X,I2,10X,I3,5X,I4)
```

would result in

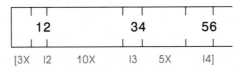

[3X   I2   10X   I3   5X   I4]

(Recall that for the moment we are avoiding printing numbers in column 1.)

Slash (/) Format (Skip to Next Line)

An example of the slash format using the numbers above is

```
        WRITE(*,5)I,J,K
    5   FORMAT(3X,I2/5X,I3///7X,I4)
```

which would result in the output

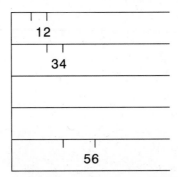

Keep in mind the following points when using the slash format:

- Multiple line skips cannot be specified as n/. To skip two lines and begin on the third, you could use ///, as above. An alternative is the T format, discussed in the next section.
- The line-skip specification need not be separated from other format specifications by commas. However, you may find it easier to read the FORMAT statement by explicitly separating the slashes by commas. Thus, format 5 above could also be written as

```
    5   FORMAT(3X,I2/5X,I3,///,7X,I4)
```

• Immediately following a slash, the next printing position is in column 1.

T Format (Tab)

By using the T format, you can have the printed output (or input) skip to a particular position on the line in much the same way you use a tab key on a typewriter. This format has the following forms:

Tn   Tab to column number *n* moving either right or left.

TRn   Skip forward (tab right) by *n* positions, measured from the current position.

TLn   Skip backward (tab left) by *n* positions, measured from the current position. If *n* is greater than the current column number, the printer will be positioned in column 1.

These forms are particularly useful in constructing tables. For example, if the variables *x, y,* and *z* have the values 1.0, 2.0, and 3.0, respectively, the statements

```
      WRITE(*,*)'     Output Table'
      WRITE(*,*)'     ------------'
      WRITE(*,*)'        |  x  |   '
      WRITE(*,*)'  |  z   |  y   |'
      WRITE(*,11)X,Y,Z
   11 FORMAT(/,T20,F3.1,/,
     +        T26,F3.1,TL15,F3.1)
```

would result in the following output:

```
   Output Table
   ------------
      |  x  |
  |  z   |  y   |
        1.0
   3.0        2.0
```

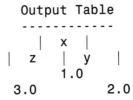

Repeatable Format Specifications

With the exception of the slash and T formats, each format discussed so far may be repeated by preceding the format specification with a multiple integer factor; that is,

```
   3F5.2
```

is the same as

```
   F5.2,F5.2,F5.2
```

It is also possible to have multiples of combinations of format specifications by enclosing groups in parentheses and preceding the parentheses with a multiplicative factor. For example,

```
     WRITE(*,33)X,IA,IB, B,IC,C
33   FORMAT(5(/),T5,F10.5,3(/,T5,I2,2X,F5.2))
```

will print a total of nine lines.

6.4 Using FORMAT Statements for Reading Data

Unquestionably, the safest and most convenient method for reading large amounts of data is to create a data file with the entries separated by commas or blanks and then to read the file by means of a list-directed READ statement such as READ* or READ(*,*). For reasons that will become clear in this section, you should avoid using FORMAT statements entirely when reading numerical data. There are, however, rare instances when this is not possible, such as when the data file was created by someone else or when only pieces of each line are to be read. Understanding the use of FORMAT statements for reading data is not nearly as important as understanding their use in printing output. But because you will probably encounter formatted READ statements used for reading numerical data at some point in your work, they are described here. In this text, however, formatted READ statements are never used to read numerical data.

READ Statements and Blanks

READ statements may interpret blanks as zero. Ordinarily, when reading data the computer will read a blank space as a blank, that is, ignore it. Recall that this is the default situation whenever a data file is opened. (See Section 4.6.) However, if the option BLANK = 'ZERO' were included in the statement that opens the data file, all blanks in the data file would then be interpreted as zeros. This situation can cause considerable confusion regarding the assignment of values. For example, in this case the input line

```
271.736   3.1
```

would actually be read as

```
000271.736003.10000
```

Depending upon the precise fields defined in a FORMAT statement, a wide variety of numbers different from those intended could be read from this line. For example, reading this line using a format

```
10   FORMAT(F8.1,1X,F5.0)
```

would read the values 271.7 and 6003.0. Thus, this option should be avoided when opening a data file. Reading this line with the same FORMAT statement in the normal situation, that is, with blanks ignored, would result in the assignments 271.7 and 63.0, which are still different from what was intended. This example again illustrates the importance of the axiom that all numbers read in must be echo printed to verify correct assignments.

Input Data Consisting of Real Numbers Having an Explicit Decimal Point

If the number appearing in an F or an E field fits in the prescribed width (w) *and* the number has a decimal point, then the placement of the decimal point overrides the d specification in the FORMAT statement. Thus, the first number in

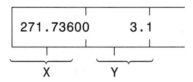

is entered with an F10.5 format, and if it is read with an F10.3 format or an E10.3 format, the assignment to X would again be 271.736.

Input Data Consisting of Real Numbers without an Explicit Decimal Point

If the numerical value being read does not contain a decimal point, the d specification in the F format will act as a negative power-of-10 scaling factor. Thus, if the number 1234 were entered with an F5.2 format, the value stored would be

$$1234 \times 10^{-2} = 12.34 \quad [d = 2]$$

The d specification in the E format works in a similar fashion if the decimal point is not explicitly present. Thus, reading the number 1234E + 4 with a format E9.2 would result in the value

$$(1234E+4) \times 10^{-2} = 0.1234E+6$$

being assigned. When using an E format, numbers without an explicit E field are read as if the E field were E + 00. Thus, if a number such as 1234 were read using an E9.2 format, the assignment would be

$$1234 \rightarrow 1234E+00 \text{ read as } (1234E+00) \times 10^{-2} = 0.1234E+2$$

Of course, a decimal point may never appear in an exponent field. To reduce the potential for incorrect assignments, it is suggested that all numerical data read with F or E formats should contain explicit decimal points.

Finally, the X, /, and T formats may also be included in FORMAT statements that are used to read data. But character strings such as table headings or other text are not permitted in any FORMAT statement that is used for input. It is, however, possible to use FORMAT statements both to read character strings as part of a data line or to print character strings along with numerical values. The reading and printing of non-numerical data are discussed in detail in the next section.

6.5 Elementary Input and Output of Text

The output of most programs will consist of more than just numbers. Tables will have labels and most computed results will require some identification and explanation. The printing of text, called *character strings*, is simple in FORTRAN. More elaborate procedures for handling character strings are addressed in Chapter 8. But for now the elementary methods outlined below will be sufficient for most applications.

The Apostrophe as a String Delimiter

Up to this point, textual material and character strings have been printed using the list-directed output statements

`PRINT *,`	Output list containing character strings and/or numerical values
`WRITE(*,*)`	Output list containing character strings and/or numerical values

in which the character strings are enclosed in apostrophes. A character-string constant can also be included in a FORMAT statement, and the procedure is similar to list-directed output: the string is simply enclosed in apostrophes and separated from other format specifications by commas or slashes. The string may contain any valid symbols available in FORTRAN (see page 23) as well as any of the symbols appearing on the keyboard. The string will be printed exactly as it appears, including blanks. For example,

```
      IDAY  = 11
      IYEAR = 92
      WRITE(*,11)IDAY,IYEAR
   11 FORMAT(T5,'Today is Sept. ',I2,', 19',I2)
```

String of
15 characters

String of 4 characters
including the comma and
blank space

will produce the output

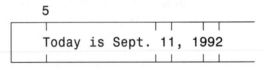

Also, the statements

```
      WRITE(*,12)
 12   FORMAT(T10,60('*'))
```

will result in a line of 60 asterisks.

As a somewhat more complicated example, the statements below indicate how a table can be constructed using FORMAT statements.

```
      WRITE(*,13)
      WRITE(*,14)T1,R1,T2,R2,T3,R3
 13   FORMAT(T5,'Electrical Resistance vs. Temperature',/,
      T10,'Temperature', T25,'Resistance',/,
      T10,' (Deg.-C)',    T25,'  (Ohms)',/,
      T10,'-----------', T25,'----------')
 14   FORMAT(3(T12,F7.3,T26,F7.1,/))
```

Assuming that the variables have been assigned values, these statements would produce the following output:

```
    Electrical Resistance vs. Temperature
         Temperature      Resistance
          (Deg.-C)          (Ohms)
         -----------       ----------
           124.300          10344.3
            93.200          10113.7
            21.700           9958.4
```

If the string itself contains an apostrophe, it can be printed by typing two consecutive apostrophes.

```
      PRINT 12
 12   FORMAT(2X,'Don''t forget today''s assignment')
```

results in

```
  Don't forget today's assignment
```

Replacing the * with Format Specifications

It is often suggested that all the FORMAT statements used in a program or subprogram be grouped together at the end of the FORTRAN code for that program module to avoid interrupting the logical flow of the program. This positioning is especially important for complicated FORMAT statements used in constructing table headings. However, it may be equally distracting to insert a new FORMAT statement every time you wish to print merely one or two numbers. A useful feature in FORTRAN permits the replacement of the default format specification (*), or the number of the FORMAT statement, by the actual format specifications used for output. The procedure is simply to enclose the complete format specification first in parentheses and then in apostrophes; that is,

```
      PRINT 11,A,IA
      WRITE(*,11)A,IA
   11 FORMAT(T5,F5.2,/,T5,I2)
```

could be replaced by

```
      PRINT 11,'(T5,F5.2,/,T5,I2)',A,IA
      WRITE(*,'(T5,F5.2,/,T5,I2)')A,IA
```

Complete format specification
included as character string
in WRITE statement

This method of using simple formatting specifications for output has the distinct advantage of eliminating the need for separate FORMAT statements. Indeed, modern programming style avoids the use of statement numbers. The only unavoidable need for statement numbers is now to mark the terminator of DO loops. We will see in Section 9.4 that this usage may be changed in future versions of FORTRAN.

When using explicit format specifications in a WRITE or a PRINT statement, they must be enclosed in parentheses and delimited before and after by apostrophes. Thus, if the format specifications themselves contain an apostrophe, an error may result. This will happen if the format specifications contain a character string. The remedy is to use a double apostrophe to delimit the string (as when a single apostrophe appears in the middle of a string). To rewrite the output segment

```
      WRITE(*,34)A
   34 FORMAT(T5,'a = ',F5.3)
```

without an explicit FORMAT statement, the format specification would be written as

```
      WRITE(*,'(T5,''a = '',F5.3)')A
```

The A Format for Printing Character Strings

A variable that is of type CHARACTER is printed by means of the alphanumeric format specification Aw, where w is the width of the character expression to be printed. For example, to print a character variable of length 24, the format specification would be

```
          CHARACTER PHRASE*24
          PHRASE = 'Character variable of length 24'
          WRITE(*,77)PHRASE
       77 FORMAT(T5,A24)
```

or

```
       WRITE(*,'(T5,A24)')PHRASE
```

FORTRAN also permits a convenient variation of the above A format specification. In place of "A24" in the format specification, we could simply use "A" and the computer will count the length of the variable and allot the proper number of spaces. For example,

```
    CHARACTER NAME*9, STATE*2
    NAME  = 'Anderson'
    STATE = 'PA'
    WRITE(*,'(T2,A,A,A,A)')'Mr. ',NAME,' lives in ',STATE
                              A4    A9      A10       A2
```

Variations on this form are easy to construct and can make the chore of obtaining intermediate results from a program quite painless.

Input of Character Strings

If a variable has been designated as type CHARACTER, it may be assigned a value by means of assignment statements, as in the previous example, or by reading input data. There are two ways of reading character strings as input data: using a list-directed READ or using the A format.

List-Directed READ	**READ Using an A Format**
CHARACTER NAME*9	CHARACTER NAME*9
READ(*,*)NAME	READ(*,'(A)')NAME

The form of the input for each of these examples is

```
'Anderson'          Anderson
```

That is, when reading a character string with a list-directed READ, the string must be enclosed in apostrophes; with an A format it is not.

From the discussion so far it should be apparent that facility in using character variables for manipulating text is an important and useful part of overall FORTRAN fluency. It is not a skill that comes easily, however, but requires considerable practice. Character-string manipulation is a feature that was added to FORTRAN to broaden the usefulness of the language to applications in fields outside its historical base of science and engineering. Alphabetizing a list or searching through an inventory file are common examples of the use of character variables. As important as these uses may be, our primary concern as engineers is classical "number crunching." More detailed explanations of character-variable features in FORTRAN will be postponed to Chapter 8.

6.6 Additional Input/Output Features

Carriage Control

All the programs and examples thus far have avoided printing in column 1. The reason for this is that many FORTRAN systems have been set up to use the character printed in column 1 of each line as a vertical spacing or carriage-control command. On these systems the character in column 1 is not printed. You should first determine whether or not carriage-control characters are operative on your system.[1] (If this feature is not available on your system, skip this section.) Carriage-control commands are occasionally useful when applied to printed output; they are rarely useful for output viewed at a terminal screen. The four characters that are used for vertical spacing are listed in Table 6-1.

Table 6-1
Vertical spacing control characters

Character	Effect
Blank	Space down one line, then print
0	(Zero) Space down two lines, then print
1	Advance to first line of next page
+	No advance before printing; allows overprinting

---

[1] You can determine whether carriage-control is operative on your system by running the following short program on your computer:

```
PROGRAM CARIAG
    PRINT '(T30,A)' ,        'This is line No. 1'
    PRINT '(A1,T2,A),   '+','This should overwrite line 1'
    PRINT '(A1,T2,A),   '0','This should space down 2 lines'
    PRINT '(A1,T2,A),   '1','This should space to new page'
    PRINT '(T2,A)'  ,        'This is line two, second page'
    PRINT '(A1,T30,A), '+','An overwrite will'
    PRINT '(T30,A)'  ,        'erase earlier line'
    STOP
END
```

The output should then be:

IF Carriage Control Operative	IF Carriage Control Inoperative
This should overwrite line 1This is line 1	This is line No. 1
	+This should overwrite line 1
This should space down 2 lines	0This should space down 2 lines
———— new page ————	1This should space to new page
An overwrite will	+ An overwrite will
erase earlier line	erase earlier line

■ What If the Computer Runs Out of Format?

If the number of elements to be printed or read by a READ/WRITE/PRINT statement exceeds the number allotted in the associated FORMAT statement, the computer will always complete the entire command by reusing the same FORMAT statement, each time starting a new line. Thus,

```
      WRITE(33,17)A,B,C,D,E,F,G
17    FORMAT(T2,2F5.1)
```

will result in three lines with two numbers and a fourth with the single value associated with G. After printing A and B, the WRITE statement runs out of format and continues to print the elements in the list until the list is exhausted. Notice in the final line that the entire format is only partially used. The situation for READ statements is similar. For example, suppose the following input data file is stored on a disk and named DATA3.

Input File DATA3

```
1.0 2.0 3.0 4.0
5.0 6.0 7.0 8.0
9.0 10. 11. 12.
-1.0
```

This input data file is read and printed by the following code:

```
      OPEN(37,FILE = 'DATA3')
      REWIND (37)
      DO 1 LINE = 1,50
         READ(37,'(3F4.0)')A,B,C,D
         IF(A .GT. 0.)THEN
            PRINT *,A,B,C,D
         ELSE
            STOP
         END
1     CONTINUE
```

The result will be

```
1.000    2.000    3.000    5.0000
9.000   10.000   11.000   -1.0000
*****INPUT ERROR -- ATTEMPT TO READ EOF
```

and the program will fatally terminate by reading the end-of-file mark on the data file. The clever use of −1.0 as a flag for the end of the data was missed by the computer by assigning it to D rather than A. Apparently the read format was intended to be '(4F4.0)'.

If the format specifications themselves contain parentheses, the situation is more complicated. The following rule applies.

> If the computer runs out of format, it scans the format specifications right to left and reuses the format starting with the first paired set of parentheses it encounters, or its multiple.

Thus, assuming the real variables A to K have been assigned the values 1.0 to 11.0, respectively,

```
     REAL A,B,C,D,E,F,G,H,I,J,K
     WRITE(*11)A,B,C,D,E,F,G,H,I,J,K
11   FORMAT(T2,'The results are ',/,
   +          T2,'----------------',/,
   +          T2,2(4X,F4.1,'-a'),2(4X,F4.1,'-b'))
```

results in

```
The results are
----------------
      1.0-a      2.0-a    3.0-b    4.0-b
      5.0-b      6.0-b
      7.0-b      8.0-b
      9.0-b     10.0-b
     11.0-b
```

The re-cycled specification was

```
2(4X,F4.1,'-b')
```

Notice that it was only partially used in the last cycle.

Additional Options Available in READ/WRITE Statements

Often a data file will consist of an unknown number of lines, and the program will read some data, compute results, return to the READ statement, and repeat the calculation until the data file is exhausted. However, if the READ statement is used beyond the last data line, an execution-time error is generated. This error can be avoided by placing a trailer data line at the end of the file and after each READ, checking for a known flag.

As illustrated in the example program to read data file DATA3 of the previous section, this procedure is not always successful. A preferred option is available in the READ statement.

READ(unit #, format, ERR = sl_1, END = sl_2)

The option ERR = sl_1 directs the computer to statement number sl_1 if an error was encountered during the read (e.g., a real number with an integer format). The option END = sl_2 causes a transfer to statement number sl_2 only if an END-OF-FILE is encountered. An example follows:

```
        READ(16,11,ERR=100,END=99)X,Y
        READ( *,11,END=99)A,B
        READ( *, *,END=99)I,J
   11   FORMAT(T2,2F5.0)
        WRITE(*,*)'x = ',X,' y = ',Y
        WRITE(*,*)'a = ',A,' b = ',B
        WRITE(*,*)'i = ',I,' j = ',J
        STOP
   99   PRINT *,'End of data file'
        STOP
  100   PRINT *,'Input error'
        STOP
        END
```

One interesting use of the ERR = sl option in the READ statement is to make use of the BACKSPACE command and to reread the entire line as a single character string. The character string can then be printed, and perhaps the read error identified.

```
      CHARACTER LINE*80
          ...        ...
          ...        ...
100   PRINT *,'Input error'
      BACKSPACE (16)
      READ(16,'(A80)')LINE
      WRITE(*,'(A/A80)')'The line in question was',LINE
```

The ERR = sl option may also be included in WRITE statements.

Summary

FORTRAN has available very elaborate means of editing the input and output of a program. A minimum subset of the complete FORTRAN editing commands is described in this chapter. Additional features can be found in the user's guide that accompanies your FORTRAN compiler or in several of the FORTRAN references given in the appendix. The editing features described here will enable the programmer to substantially improve the appearance of a program's output in comparison with earlier results obtained using list-directed output. Editing the input and output of a program is accomplished in FORTRAN by means of FORMAT statements of the form

$\quad$ j $\quad$ FORMAT(spec$_1$, spec$_2$, spec$_3$, ...)

where (j) is a statement number and $spec_1, spec_2, spec_3, \ldots$ are format specifications separated by commas. A FORMAT statement is nonexecutable and may appear anywhere within a program or subprogram. This user-written format will be used in place of the default list-directed format by replacing the second asterisk in READ(*,*) or WRITE(*,*) by the statement-number label of the FORMAT statement. Format specifications can be numerical descriptors:

1. The F format has the form

   Fw.d.

   It is used for the input or output of real numbers without exponents. The w is an integer specifying the total width of the number field, including sign and decimal point, and d is the number of digits to appear after the decimal point. Values of real numbers are rounded when printed.

2. The I format has the form

   Iw

   It is used for the input or output of integers. The w is an integer specifying the total width of the number field. The integer will be printed right-adjusted in the field.

3. The E format has the form

   Ew.d

   The E format is similar to the F format except that the number will be written in scientific notation, as, for example, 3.456E-04.

Format specifications can also be positional descriptors:

1. The X format has the form

   nX

   It will cause the next n spaces to be skipped on the input/output line.

2. The slash (/) format causes the output (or input) to skip to the first column of the next line.

3. The T format acts as a tab key on a typewriter and has three forms: Tn will cause the output (or input) to skip to column number n (moving either right or left); TRn will tab to the right by n columns; and TLn will tab to the left by n columns.

All of the format specifications except T and / may be preceded by an unsigned integer constant, which acts as a repetition factor. Thus, 3F4.1 is identical to F4.1, F4.1, F4.1. Additionally, any group of format specifications may be enclosed in parentheses and the parentheses preceded by a repetition factor.

FORMAT statements may be used to read data as well as arrange the form of the output. However, since a formatted read will require that the data be precisely positioned on the data line, errors are more likely than if a list-directed form of the READ statement is used. In some situations, such as reading only a few numbers located in the middle of a data line, the use of FORMAT statements for input can be justified. Also, formatted reads are commonly used when the data includes character strings.

Character constants may be included in a format list used for output, provided the character constant is enclosed in apostrophes. In fact, the complete format specification list can be stored in a character variable or constant by first enclosing it in apostrophes and parentheses and then replacing the second asterisk in READ(*,*) or WRITE(*,*) by the character constant or variable.

Character variables and constants are usually printed or read using the A format specification Aw, or simply A, where w is the total width of the character input/output fields. If w is omitted, the field is equal to the length of the listed variable or constant. Character strings read with an A format are not enclosed in quotes; strings read using list-directed input must be enclosed in quotes.

Finally, there are several additional features of formatted I/O that can be useful to the programmer:

- The first character on the output line may have been reserved on your computer for controlling the vertical spacing of the output.
- If a READ/WRITE statement "runs out" of format before it runs out of items in the I/O list, the format statement is reused beginning on the next line. The reused format will be the set of specifications contained within the first set of completed parentheses read from the right.
- Including the END = sl option in a READ statement will cause the program to branch to the statement labeled by the specified statement number (sl). This feature is especially useful when reading a file of unknown length.

Problems

6.1 This problem illustrates the use of formatted READ and WRITE statements.
   a. Give two methods of specifying the input device as the keyboard in READ statements.
   b. Give two methods of testing for the end of a data file.
   c. Using only one line of FORTRAN, print e^{π} with an F9.6 format.
   d. If your program has a FORMAT statement that is never used, will the computer detect this and inform you of a possible error? (Try it and see.)

e. Which of the following format specifications can be repeated by preceding them with a multiplying integer? (F,T,E,/,I,X,A)

f. Give an example of when replacing the word READ by WRITE in a correct FORTRAN statement will result in a compilation-time error.

g. Can you GO TO a FORMAT statement? Why or why not?

6.2 Identify the errors, if any, in the following statements:

a. `READ(*)X,Y`   **e.** `READ *,X+Y`

b. `PRINT *,X,YZ`   **f.** `READ(5,6),X,Y`

c. `WRITE(*,*)X+Y`   **g.** `IF(I.GT.0)READ *,I`

d. `READ(5,5)FIVE`

6.3 Locate any execution or compilation errors in the following formatted READ statements. If there are no errors, write OK. (Assume that default typing is used.)

a.   `READ(*,1)X,IX,Y,IY`

    `1 FORMAT(F6.6,I5,2F4.1)`

b.   `READ(*,2)S,Y,IX,IY`

    `2 FORMAT(T2,2(F5.1,I5))`

c.   `READ(*,3)X,Y,Z,W`

    `3 FORMAT(2X,3F7.1)`

d.   `READ(*,4)X,Y,IX,IY`

    `4 FORMAT(150X,2F9.1,2I2)`

e.   `READ(*,5)X,Y,Z,W`

    `5 FORMAT(F4.1,4(1X,F7.2))`

f.   `READ(*,6)X,Y,IX,IY`

    `6 FORMAT(2E9.6,2I9)`

6.4 Identify the errors, if any, in the following WRITE statements and their associated FORMAT statements. If there are no compilation errors, describe the appearance of the output.

a.   `WRITE(*,1)X,Y,X+Y`

    `1 FORMAT(F5.0)`

b.   `WRITE(*,2)X,X**2,EXP(X)`

    `2 FORMAT(4E9.1)`

c.   `WRITE(*,3)X,I,Y,J`

    `3 FORMAT(2('r=',E8.1,'k=',I5))`

d.   `WRITE(*,4)A,B,C,D,E`

    `4 FORMAT(5X,F5.1,TL5,F5.1)`

e.   `WRITE(*,5)'a=',A,'b=',B`

    `5 FORMAT(T5,A2,F3.1)`

f.   `WRITE(*,6)'a=',A,'b=',B`

    `6 FORMAT(T5,A4,F3.1)`

g.   `WRITE(*,7)A,'B=',B`

    `7 FORMAT(T5,'A=',A,2F5.2)`

h.   `WRITE(*,8)A,'B=',B`

    `8 FORMAT(T5,'A=',2(F4.1,A))`

i.   `WRITE(*,9)A`

    `9 FORMAT(T5,'a=',F4.1,'b=',F4.1)`

6.5 Identify the errors, if any, in the following FORMAT statements, assuming an appropriate READ statement of the form

    `READ(*,4)`   ⟨list of variables⟩

a. `4 FORMAT(I1,F3.0,I1,F3.0)`

b. `4 FORMAT(2X,I1,2X,F3.0,2X,2X,I3)`

c. `4 FORMAT(1X,2(I2,F3.1,I2))`

d. `4 FORMAT(T2,I6,F6.7,I2,F3.2)`

```
e. 4 FORMAT(T5,I10,F7.2,2E+02,I4)
f. 4 FORMAT(1X,'i=',I2,'x=',F5.1)
g. 4 FORMAT(T2,I5,TR10,I5,TL10,F5.1,TR10,F6.2)
h. 4 FORMAT(//,2(I5,2/,F4.2))
i. 4 FORMAT(1X,(I1,F3.1,I1))
```

6.6 Using the assignments X = 2., Y = 3., Z = 1./3., I = 2, J = 3, K = 4, determine the ouput of the following WRITE statements. Make sure the output is properly positioned.

```
a.   WRITE(*,1)X,Y,Z
     1 FORMAT(2X,F3.1,2X,F2.0,2X,F7.4)
b.   WRITE(*,2)X,Y,Z
     2 FORMAT(/,2X,F7.5,2(/T2,F6.3,/))
c.   WRITE(*,3)X,I,K,J,Y,Z
     3 FORMAT(5X,F2.0,'*',I2,'=',I2,/,5X,I1,
              '/',F3.1,'=',F7.6)
d.   WRITE(*,4)Y*Z,Y,J,J,J,J
     4 FORMAT(/,4X,F9.6,'/',F2.0,'= ',5I1)
e.   WRITE(*,5)K,J,I
     5 FORMAT(T12,I1,TL2,I1,TL3,I1)
f.   WRITE(*,6)I,J,K
     6 FORMAT(T2,I1,T5,I1,T7,I1)
g.   WRITE(*,7)I,J,K
     7 FORMAT(T2,I1,TR5,I1,TR7,I1)
h.   WRITE(*,8)I,J,K
     8 FORMAT(I2)
i.   WRITE(*,9)X,Y,Z
     9 FORMAT(T2,E7.1,1X,E9.2,1X,E12.5)
```

6.7 Assuming the assignments X = 1.0, Y = 2.0, Z = 1./3., I = 2, J = 3, determine the output from the following statements.

```
a.   PRINT '(2(F4.0,2X),F2.1,2I5)',X,Y,Z,I,J
b.   WRITE(*,1)X,Y,I,J
     1 FORMAT(T5,2E9.1,/,2I2)
c.   WRITE(*,2)X,I,Y,J,Z
     2 FORMAT(2X,E9.1,I5)
d.   WRITE(*,'(F5.1,A4)')X,'  =x'
e.   WRITE(*,3)X,Y,Z
     3 FORMAT(/,F5.0)
f.   WRITE(*,4)I,X
     4 FORMAT(1X,F5.0,I5)
g.   WRITE(*,'(F4.1,A3,I4)')X,'***',I,Y,'---',J,Z
h.   WRITE(*,5)Z,1./Z,1./Z*Z-1.
     5 FORMAT(5X,3E10.3)
```

6.8 Determine the output from the following statements. Use the assignments I = 2, J = 3, K = 4, X = 4., Y = 5., Z = 1./6.

```
a.   WRITE(*,1)
     1 FORMAT(T5,3(4('-'),2X))
b.   WRITE(*,2)I,J,K
     2 FORMAT(2X,'i=',I1,/,2X,'and j=',I1,/,2X,'and k=')
```

```
   c.   WRITE(*,3)I,J,Z
      3 FORMAT(/,2X,'1/(',I1, '*' ,I1,') =',F9.6)
   d.   WRITE(*,4)X,Y,X+Y,1./Z
      4 FORMAT(1X,'x=',F4.1,'y=',F4.1,/,1X,'x+y=',F4.1,
             '1/z=',F4.1)
   e.   WRITE(*,'(1X,3F3.0,3I2)')X,Y,Z,I,J,K
   f.   WRITE(*,'(1X,F5.1,/,1X,I2)')X,I,Y,J,Z,K
   g.   WRITE(*,'(1X,A,I1,A,I1)')'i = ',I,' and k = ',K
   h.   WRITE(*,'(A)')'Candy is dandy, but liquor is ...'
   i.   WRITE(*,5)X,Y,K,X*Y,X*Y*K
      5 FORMAT(//,T5,'Dimensions of room',/,
      +      T5,'Length = ',F5.1,T20,'Width = ',F5.1,T35,
      +                       'Height = ',I5,//,
      +      T10,'Surface Area = ',F12.7,/,
      +      T10,'Volume       = ',E10.2)
   j.   WRITE(*,6)
      6   FORMAT(6(1X,'*',2X),T25,56('X')  ,/,
      +                       T25,56('X')  ,/,
      +      T3,5(1X,'*',2X),T25,56('X')  ,//,
      +         6(1X,'*',2X)               ,//,
      +      T3,5(1X,'*',2X),T25,56('X')  ,/,
      +                       T25,56('X')
      +         6(1X,'*',2X),T25,56('X')  ,//,
      +      T3,5(1X,'*',2X)               ,//,
      +         6(1X,'*',2X),T25,56('X')  ,/,
      +                       T25,56('X')  ,/,
      +      T3,5(1X,'*',2X),T25,56('X')  ,//,
      +         6(1X,'*',2X)               ,//,
      +         3(3(80('X')/)//),3(80('X')/)/)
```

This format will produce an easily recognizable display.

6.9 Write a single line of FORTRAN that will
   a. Print the variables X, Y, and X + Y on separate lines.
   b. Print 'x = ',X and 'y = ',Y on separate lines.

6.10 Write a program to compute the height, $y(t)$, and the velocity, $v(t)$, for a falling object for times $t = 0$ to $t = 10$ sec in steps of 0.2 sec. Use the equations

$$y(t) = -4.9t^2 + 50t \quad \text{(m)} \quad \text{and} \quad v(t) = -9.8t + 50 \quad \text{(m/sec)}$$

and display the results in a neat table with column headings, including units. The numerical results should be centered in the columns and a counter printed for each time value.

6.11 Write a program to read and print the name of a metal and its melting temperature in the form of a table with column headings, including units. In addition, if the melting temperature is greater than 1400° C, print "Too High" on the same line; if less than 600° C, print "Too Low" on the same line. Use carriage-control characters.

6.12 Write a program to read a data file stored on disk and named CLASS, which has a student's last name (A10), gender (M or F, A1), hometown (A10), and class (I1) on each line. The program is to count the number of

a. Male juniors or seniors from Boston
b. All females from Chicago
c. Freshmen from Chicago
In addition, the program should print the names of all students from Detroit, with their name preceded by either Mr. or Ms.

6.13 Write a program to print, with appropriate headings, the integers from 1 to 100. If the number is a perfect cube, print on the same line a statement like

27 is the cube of 3

6.14 Write a program to read and print a FORTRAN program eliminating all comment lines.

6.15 Design FORMAT statements to handle the following:
a. Print a "block" letter, for example,

```
   MM          MM
   MMM         MMM
   MM M      M MM
   MM   M    M   MM
   MM     M M    MM
   MMMM     M    MMMM
```

b. With one format, print a table heading for (i, x_i, y_i) plus positions for five entries in the table.
c. Ask the terminal user if he or she wishes to compute the SUM. If the answer is Yes or YES or yes, instruct the user to enter ten values, one at a time. The program should add the numbers, compute the sum, and display the result in the form

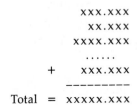

```
        XXX.XXX
         XX.XXX
       XXXX.XXX
        ......
  +      XXX.XXX
       ---------
Total = XXXXX.XXX
```

d. Read the current time of day entered as hh:mmAM (or PM) and compute the number of minutes elapsed in this day thus far.

Arrays and Subscripted Variables

7.1 ## Introduction

The FORTRAN described so far can be used to solve many types of problems. However, there is an entire class of problems that is not easily handled without introducing some new FORTRAN features. Recall the program in Section 4.4 that computed the average of a list of exam scores. Altering that program so it also calculates the deviations from the average presents a problem. The data set will have to be scanned twice: once to obtain the average score and then again to compute the deviations of each score from this average. However, the individual scores were never stored. A single variable was used for the current value of the exam score and was repeatedly updated with each READ statement. If the data were read from a data file, the file could be rewound and the scores read once again. But if the data were entered one item at a time from the keyboard, they would be lost. Each score could be associated with a different variable name as it is read, and these variable names could then be reused. If 400 students took the examination, the READ statement might then appear as

```
READ(*,*)STU1,STU2,STU3, ... ,STU400
```

It will probably take longer to type this single READ statement than it took to enter the entire previous program.

The algebraic notation for this problem suggests a remedy.

$$\text{avg} = \frac{1}{n} \sum_{i=1}^{n} g_i$$

The set of exam scores is represented by the variable g, and individual scores of each student are distinguished from each other by the subscript i.

Subscripted variables in FORTRAN are called *arrays* and are introduced into a program by means of an array-declaration statement, which is described in the next section. Arrays represent a block of computer memory locations all bearing the same name and distinguished by different values for the array subscripts. Using arrays in a program then requires some understanding of the order in which the array elements are internally stored in the computer, which is explained in Section 7.3.

The I/O of arrays is a major concern in most programs and is facilitated in FORTRAN by means of a special form of the DO loop, the *implied DO loop*, which is described next. This is followed by a section detailing the procedures for transferring all or part of an array to a subprogram, an important item in any modular program.

Section 7.6 is devoted to three important and common applications of arrays that form the basis for many more advanced programs: (1) finding the minimum or maximum of an array, (2) sorting an array in ascending or decending order, and (3) plotting a graph on the terminal screen or on the printer.

7.2 Array-Declaration Statements

As we saw in Chapter 1, the feature most responsible for the success of FORTRAN and other higher-level computer languages is the method of automatically assigning an address to variable names. Whenever the compiler encounters a new variable name, it associates the name with a location in memory. The contents of that memory location are then accessible simply by using the variable name. Each variable is allotted one address in memory.

It is also possible to instruct the compiler to reserve more than one memory address, say an entire block of memory, for a single variable name. Each memory location in this block would have the same variable name, but the address of each word would be different—analogous to a subscripted variable. The FORTRAN instructions to accomplish this type of memory allocation are called array-declaration statements. Array-declaration statements specify the particulars of an array (array name, subscript bounds) and come in three distinct forms.

Information Required in Array Declarations

To declare that a variable name will be associated with an array of values, the following information must be supplied by the programmer:

- The name of the array, which must satisfy the rules pertaining to any FORTRAN variable name: must have six or fewer characters; must start with a letter; must use only letters and numerals.
- The type of the array. All elements of the array will be of the same type, which may be real, integer, or character (or complex, double precision, or logical, which are described in Chapter 9).

- The number of subscripts, also called the dimension, in the array. The maximum number of subscripts permitted in FORTRAN is seven.
- The size of the array. The number of elements in an array is determined by the limits on the array subscripts. The subscripts must be integers.

For example, variables named R and M could be default typed and declared as arrays, each with a single subscript that has a lower limit of 1 and an upper limit of 10. Each variable can then accommodate 10 computer words. In a FORTRAN program, once the variable has been declared as an array, these elements are accessed by enclosing the subscript in parentheses following the variable name.

```
R(6) = 13.4 + SIN(2.*X)
M(9) = I + 44
C    = R(6)/3. + COS(2.*X)
R(K+4) = 0.0
```

When referencing an array element, the subscript index may be any integer expression, provided that the value of the index is not outside the prescribed limits (here, 1 to 10). Thus, in the last line of the code above, if $K < -3$ or $K > 6$, an execution error would result.

The limits on the subscripts in an array are specified in an array-declaration statement by indicating the lower and upper limits of the subscript within parentheses following the array name. The form of the specification for an array with one subscript is

$$\langle \text{name} \rangle \, (I_{\text{lower}} : I_{\text{upper}})$$

where "name" is the FORTRAN name of the array, and I_{lower} and I_{upper} are integer constants (not variables) with $I_{\text{lower}} \leq I_{\text{upper}}$. For example,

X(0:5)	Array X contains 6 elements, and its subscript ranges from 0 to 5.
K(-5:5)	Array K contains 11 elements, and its subscript ranges from −5 to 5.
R(1:10)	Array R contains 10 elements.

If the lower bound is omitted, a default value of 1 is assumed. Thus, the array R could also be specified as R(10). In this case the number appearing in the parentheses must be a positive integer. If the array has more than one subscript, the individual subscript limits are separated by commas. The following are two-dimensional arrays.

Y(0:5,-5:5)	Array Y contains 66 elements of the form $y_{i,j}$ with subscript ranges $0 \leq i \leq 5$ and $-5 \leq j \leq 5$.
M(3,3)	Array M contains 9 elements $m_{i,j}$ with $1 \leq i,j \leq 3$.

In FORTRAN the compiler must know precisely how much space to reserve for each variable before the program can begin execution. Thus, the size allotted to an array may not be changed once the program has begun execution. Of course, not all elements of an array need to be used in each run of a program.

Forms of Array-Declaration Statements

Variable names may be associated with arrays in three ways: via type statements, DIMENSION statements, or COMMON statements.

Array Declarations as Part of Type Statements

The standard type-declaration statements may include the specifications for an array, as illustrated below:

```
REAL      X,Y,C(0:5,0:5),G
INTEGER   L(10)
CHARACTER NAME(10)*5
```

Thus, C is an array of 36 elements containing real values; L an array of 10 integers; and NAME an array of 10 character strings, each 5 characters long. The last declaration could also be written as

```
CHARACTER*5 NAME(10)   or   CHARACTER*5 NAME(1:10)
```

Since the preferred practice is to type declare all variable names, including array names, using type statements to declare variables as arrays is the recommended method in FORTRAN.

DIMENSION Statements

An alternative to declaring arrays using only type statements is to use the DIMENSION statement, which is of the following form:

```
DIMENSION  name₁(subscript limits), name₂(subscript limits),...
```

This statement is usually used in conjunction with type statements. For example,

```
REAL      X,Y,C,G
INTEGER   L
CHARACTER NAME*5
DIMENSION C(0:5,0:5),L(10),NAME(10)
```

has exactly the same effect as the type statements above. But in this instance, the two operations of typing the variable names and declaring the arrays are done in separate statements.

Common Statements

Array declarations may also appear in COMMON statements (see Section 5.7). The following three FORTRAN segments have identical effects:

(1)
```
REAL          Y
INTEGER       M,N
CHARACTER*5   NAME
DIMENSION     Y(-1:5),
+             M(4),N(5),
+             NAME(20)
 COMMON/ABLK/Y,M,N
 COMMON/NAME/NAME
```

(3)
```
REAL          Y
INTEGER       M,N
CHARACTER*5   NAME
COMMON/ABLK/Y(-1:5),
+          M(4),N(5)
COMMON/NAME/NAME(20)
```

(2)
```
REAL          Y(-1:5)
INTEGER       M(4),N(5)
CHARACTER*5   NAME(20)
COMMON/ABLK/Y,M,N
COMMON/NAME/NAME
```

Since similar statements defining the COMMON block will appear in both program units that share the variables, and since both of these statements must be of exactly the same length, it is recommended that those arrays in a COMMON block be declared as part of the COMMON statement. Also, since it is important to maintain the same length of a common block each time it is referenced in a COMMON statement, it is usually preferable to declare arrays in common by means of a COMMON statement [example (3) above].

Since modern programming style avoids default typing, instead suggesting that all variables that appear in a program be explicitly type declared, array declarations should be effected by means of either type statements or COMMON statements. The DIMENSION statement is a remnant of earlier versions of FORTRAN. Your programs should never need to include the DIMENSION statement.

Sample Program for the All-University GPA

Assume that a data file contains the grade point average (GPA) of all 8,000 students in a university and that each line of the file contains the following information:

Student's name (character string of length 15 enclosed in apostrophes)

Social Security number as ID (nine-digit integer)

College (single digit designating the various colleges in the university, e.g., Arts and Sciences, Engineering, Business, etc.)

Class (single digit designating freshman, sophomore, etc.)

Gender (either 'M' or 'F')

Credits earned thus far

Credits attempted this semester

GPA for this semester

Overall GPA

A single line of the file might appear as

```
'Williamson  ,D.',234517223,2,2,'F',29,16,3.22,2.84
```

A program to read this file and compute the average overall GPA is shown in Figure 7-1.

Figure 7-1
A program to compute the average GPA of all students

```
      PROGRAM AVGGPA
*
*  The program will read a single, current-semester GPA for
*  each student and store it in the array GPA(). The program
*  assumes that there are fewer than 8000 students. Also,
*  since the data file contains much more information than
*  is required, the list-directed READ must read over
*  several variables until it reaches the desired value for
*  the GPA. If we knew the precise placement of numbers on
*  each line, this READ could be replaced with a formatted
*  READ using a format like FORMAT(T48,F4.2).
*
      REAL SUM,X,GPA(8000)
      INTEGER I,J,K,L,M,N
      CHARACTER NAME*15,SEX*1
      OPEN(8,FILE='GRADES')
      REWIND(8)
      SUM = 0.0
      DO 1 I = 1,8000
*
         READ(8,*,END=99)NAME,J,K,L,SEX,M,N,X,GPA(I)
*
*         Read over all the information on the line out
*         to the value of the student's overall GPA.
*         When the end of the file is reached, branch
*         to statement 99.
*
         SUM = SUM + GPA(I)
    1 CONTINUE
   99 WRITE(*,*)'The end of the data file was reached'
      WRITE(*,*)'It contained a total of ',I-1,' lines'
      AVG = SUM/(I-1.)
      WRITE(*,*)'The all-university average is ',AVG
      STOP
      END
```

To compute the standard deviation, given by the expression

$$\sigma^2 = \frac{1}{n} \sum_{i=1}^{n} |gpa_i - gpa_{avg}|^2$$

a second pass through the list of students will be required. Since all the individual scores were stored in the array GPA( ), these values could be used again in the second summation to compute the standard deviation. This could be accomplished by inserting the following code in the program in Figure 7-1 just before the STOP:

```
      N = I-1
      DEV = 0.0
      DO 2 I = 1,N
          DEV = DEV + (GPA(I) - AVG)**2
    2 CONTINUE
      DEV = SQRT(DEV/N)
      WRITE(*,*)'and the standard deviation is ',DEV
```

The index for the array GPA must not be outside the prescribed limits; that is, it must be a positive integer less than 8,001. If the index is outside this range, all modern compilers will display an execution-time error message. If this were not the case, referencing, for example, GPA(8007) may simply use an element stored in memory seven computer words past the block allocated to the array GPA. This location might contain a number, a format, or some executable instruction, and the result would be unpredictable. This type of error, since it is often extremely difficult to track down, is one of the most serious a programmer can make. Thus, you should determine whether or not your compiler always checks that the subscript is within the limits prescribed in the array declaration, and if it does not, you must always do so yourself.

The program in Figure 7-1 could easily be adapted to compute the individual averages and deviations for each class, for each college, and so on. To do this we could separately dimension four arrays to hold the grades for freshmen, sophomores, juniors, and seniors:

```
REAL FRSH(2000),SOPH(2000),JUNR(2000),SENR(2000)
```

Or we could accommodate all four classes in a single variable GPA(2000, 4), where $gpa_{i,k}$ would contain the overall GPA score for the ith student (from 1 to 2,000) in class k (from 1 to 4). There will now be four separate averages and four counts of the total number in a class. Thus, two additional arrays, AVG(4) and N(4), are needed. The algebraic statement of the problem is

$$c_k = \frac{1}{n_k} \sum_{i=1}^{n_k} gpa_{ik} \qquad \text{Class averages for each } k = 1 \text{ to } 4$$

$$t = \frac{1}{4} \sum_{k=1}^{4} c_k \qquad \text{Average of the four class averages}$$

The program to compute the average GPA by individual classes is shown in Figure 7-2.

This program could be adapted further to calculate the averages classified not only by class but by gender as well (e.g., the average of junior women). In this case the array GPA would be dimensioned as GPA(1000, 4, 2), the last index designating male or female. You should have no trouble constructing code to handle this case.

Figure 7-2

Program for average GPA by individual classes

```
       PROGRAM ALLGPA
*--
*-- This program reads the data file GRADES, reading all
*-- information on each line except for the student's
*-- class and overall GPA.  The average and standard
*-- deviation for each class are then computed.
*------------------------------------------------------------
* Variables
*
       REAL GPA(2000,4),AVG(4),DEV(4),AVGGPA,TGPA,X,SUM
       INTEGER N(4),J1,J2,J3,J4
       CHARACTER*9 CLASS(4),NAME*9,SEX*1
*--
*--    GPA(i,k)  --  Overall GPA for student i in class k
*--    TGPA      --  A temporary storage of the current GPA
*--                  until the student's number is established
*--    AVG(k)    --  Average GPAs for each of four classes
*--    DEV(k)    --  Standard deviations for each class
*--    AVGGPA    --  Overall average GPA
*--    N(k)      --  Number of students in class k
*--    CLASS     --  Names of the four classes
*--    J1-J4     --  Integers read but not needed in the
*--                  calculation
*--    X            A real value read but not needed
*--    NAME,SEX  --  Character values read but not needed
*--    SUM       --  A temporary storage for a summation
*------------------------------------------------------------
* Initialization
*
       DATA AVG,AVGGPA,N/5*0.0, 4*0/
       DATA CLASS /'Freshman ','Sophomore','Junior   ',
      +            'Senior   '/
       OPEN(8,FILE='GRADES')
       REWIND (8)
*--
*--    Read over each value in the data file except for the
*--    student's class (K) and overall GPA.  Keep a running
*--    count of the number in each class in N(K)
*--
       DO 1 I = 1,8000
          READ(8,*,END=99)NAME,J1,K,J2,SEX,J3,J4,X,TGPA
          N(K)       = N(K) + 1
          GPA(N(K),K) = TGPA
          AVG(K)     = AVG(K) + TGPA
     1 CONTINUE
*------------------------------------------------------------
```

7.3 Internal Storage of Arrays

After a program has been compiled, the entire program is stored sequentially in memory; that is, variables, FORMAT statements, arithmetic instructions, and so on are assigned addresses in a string. Thus, we can imagine an array B(5) to be stored as

Figure 7-2
(concluded)

```
* Computation of averages and standard deviations for
* each class
*--
   99  WRITE(*,*)'The end of the data file was reached'
       WRITE(*,*)'It contained a total of ',I-1,' lines'
*--
*--

       WRITE(*,10)
       DO 3 K = 1,4
          AVG(K) = AVG(K)/N(K)
          AVGGPA = AVGGPA + AVG(K)
*--
          SUM = 0.0
          DO 2 I = 1,N(K)
             SUM = SUM + (GPA(I,K) - AVG(K))**2
   2      CONTINUE
          DEV(K) = SQRT(SUM/N(K))
          WRITE(*,11)CLASS(K),N(K),AVG(K),DEV(K)
   3   CONTINUE
       AVGGPA = AVGGPA/4.
       WRITE(*,*)'The all-university average GPA is',AVGGPA
       STOP
*--------------------------------------------------------------
* Formats
*--
   10  FORMAT(//,
  +        T10,'The average grade point averages by class',/,
  +        T10,'          No. of   Average  Stnd. ',/,
  +        T10,'Class     Students   GPA     Dev. ',/,
  +        T10,'--------- --------  -------  -------',/)

   11  FORMAT(T10,A9,T23,I4,T33,F4.2,T42,F4.2)
       END
```

```
          The average grade point averages by class
                     No. of   Average  Stnd.
          Class     Students    GPA    Dev.
          --------- --------  -------  -------
          Freshman    1954     2.52     0.47
          Sophomore   1771     2.61     0.40
          Junior      1862     2.66     0.38
          Senior      1802     2.73     0.36

       The all-university average GPA is    2.628073
```

B(1)
B(2)
B(3)
B(4)
B(5)

An array with two subscripts is usually visualized as a two-dimensional rectangular block; that is, B(2, 4) would be pictured as

$$b_{11} \quad b_{12} \quad b_{13} \quad b_{14}$$
$$b_{21} \quad b_{22} \quad b_{23} \quad b_{24}$$

where the first index characterizes the row and the second the column in the block. But since the computer must store all arrays in a string, the array is actually stored as

$$b_{11}$$
$$b_{21}$$
$$b_{12}$$
$$b_{22}$$
$$b_{13}$$
$$b_{23}$$
$$b_{14}$$
$$b_{24}$$

That is, the first index increments first.

If an array is dimensioned as $A(k_1, k_2)$, then an element of that array referenced as $A(i_1, i_2)$ with $i_1 \leq k_1$, $i_1 \leq k_1$, is the nth element in the block, where

$$n = i_1 + (i_2 - 1)k_2$$

Thus, if two arrays are declared as X(10, 10) and Y(9, 11), then X(3, 7) is the 63rd element of X, and Y(3, 7) is the 69th element of Y. This has important consequences in connection with the input and output of arrays.

The FORTRAN statement

WRITE(*,*)B   B was declared an array as B(2, 4).

will print *all* of the variables with the name B, a total of eight elements. The order in which the elements are printed is the same sequence of elements b_{ij}, as illustrated above. Similarly, a statement like

READ(*,*)B

will read eight elements and store them in the sequence given. The program will not continue until the READ statement has been completed. On the other hand, a FORTRAN statement like

$$B = 25.$$ *Error:* Using array name without specifying subscript

will result in a compilation-time error. Since a unique memory location has not been specified to the left of the assignment operator, this statement cannot be executed. Similarly, the arithmetic operations in the statement

$$z = 2.*B + 1.$$ *Error:* Using array name without specifying subscript

will result in a compilation-time error. No unique value has been specified to be used in place of the symbol B.

In short, in all input/output operations, the appearance of an array name only, without the indices specified, causes the entire contents of the array to be used. In other FORTRAN statements the use of only the variable name will cause a compilation-time error.

7.4 Implied DO Loops

Form of the Implied DO Loop

A special form of DO loop is available exclusively for input/output and is especially useful for printing and reading arrays. The implied DO loop consists of a single-line phrase that includes a list of variables and the loop index limits. The form of the implied DO loop is

(variable list, $I = I_{lower}, I_{upper}, I_{step}$)

The set of variables (each separated by commas) to be printed or read is separated from the normal loop index specifications by a comma, and the entire construction is enclosed in parentheses. Examples of valid implied DO-loop structures are given below:

```
( X(I)  ,  I=1,10)
( X(I),Y(I),Z(I)  ,  I=3,15,3 )
```

Implied DO Loops in Input/Output Statements

The implied DO loop, considered as a unit, can appear in any valid I/O statement along with other variables and arrays and even other implied DO loops. Thus,

```
WRITE(*,*)  (X(I),I=4,8)
```

has the same effect as

```
WRITE(*,*)X(4),X(5),X(6),X(7),X(8)
```

which is distinctly different from

```
    DO 1 I = 4,8
        WRITE(*,*)X(I)
  1   CONTINUE
```

The first two examples print all five numbers on a single line, whereas the last will result in five lines of output from five separate WRITE statements. The difference is that a WRITE statement that includes an implied DO loop is a single execution of a WRITE statement, whereas a WRITE statement within a normal DO loop would require multiple WRITE executions. Similarly, an implied DO loop in a READ statement is interpreted as a single read of a repeated list of variables rather than a repeated read. Thus,

```
    REAL X(0:25)
    WRITE(*,*)(X(I),I=0,25)
```

is the same as

```
    REAL X(0:25)
    WRITE(*,*)X
```

More than one variable may be included in the I/O list of the implied DO loop:

FORTRAN Code

```
    REAL X(0:5)
    DATA X/0.,1.,2.,3.,4.,5./
    WRITE(*,*)('I=',I,X(I)**2,I=3,5)
    WRITE(*,*)(X(I),X(I+1),I=1,3,2)
    WRITE(*,*)(X(3), I=2,5)
    WRITE(*,11)(I,X(I),I=0,3)
 11 FORMAT(T3,'i',T7,'x(i)',/,
  +       (T3,I1,T7,F4.2,/))
```

Output

```
I=3 9.0   I=4 16.0   I=5   25.0
  1.0  2.0  3.0  4.0
  3.0  3.0  3.0  3.0
  i    x(i)
  0    0.00
  1    1.00
  2    2.00
  3    3.00
```

Implied DO loops are useful for reading large data sets, as illustrated in the following example:

```
        REAL X(50),Y(50)
   10   FORMAT(10F5.1)
   11   FORMAT( 2F5.1)

        READ(*,11)(X(I),Y(I),I=1,50)
        READ(*,10)(X(I),Y(I),I=1,50)
```

Structure of Required Data

Number of Lines	Numbers per Line
50	2
10	5 pairs x_i, y_i

Structure of Required Data

	Number of Lines	Numbers per Line

```
     DO 1 I = 1,50
         READ(*,10)X(I),Y(I)
 1   CONTINUE
     READ(*,10)X,Y
```

	Number of Lines	Numbers per Line
(DO loop)	50	2
(READ X,Y)	10	10

First 5 lines for x–s, last 5 for y–s

Implied DO loops may also be nested:

```
         REAL A(4,5)
 10      FORMAT(5F6.2)
         WRITE(*,10)((A(I,J),J=1,5),I=1,4)
```

Inner loop

Outer loop

These nested DO loops will print the elements of A in the following arrangement:

i \\ j	1	2	3	4	5
1	a_{11}	a_{12}	a_{13}	a_{14}	a_{15}
2	a_{21}	a_{22}	a_{23}	a_{24}	a_{25}
3	a_{31}	a_{32}	a_{33}	a_{34}	a_{35}
4	a_{41}	a_{42}	a_{43}	a_{44}	a_{45}

Implied DO Loops in DATA Statements

In addition to I/O statements, implied DO loops may also appear in the variable list of a DATA statement. This is especially useful when there is a need to "zero" an array, that is, initialize all of the elements of the array to zero.

```
         REAL A(10,10)
         DATA (A(I,J),J=1,10),I=1,10)/100*0.0/
```

is equivalent to

```
         REAL A(10,10)
         DATA A/100*0.0/
```

Because a DATA statement is nonexecutable, the implied DO loop index parameter will have no meaning outside the DO loop. Thus,

```
DATA (X(I),I=1,5)/1.,2.,3.,4.,5./
WRITE(*,*)I                              Error: I has no value.
```

The following examples show implied DO loops used within DATA statements.

```
REAL A(5),X,Z(4,4),W(5,5)
INTEGER M(4)
CHARACTER*1 VOWELS(5)
DATA X,(A(J),J=2,4)/3.14,5*1.0/        x = 3.14, a₂ = a₃ = a₄ = 1.0
DATA (VOWELS(K),K=1,5),M/'a','e','i','o','u',4*0/
DATA((Z(I,J),J=1,I),I=1,4)/10*1.0/     Will initialize only the
                                       elements
```

$$z_{11}$$
$$z_{21} \quad z_{22}$$
$$z_{31} \quad z_{32} \quad z_{33}$$
$$z_{41} \quad z_{42} \quad z_{43} \quad z_{44}$$

```
DATA (W(I,I),I=1,5)/5*1.0/             Will initialize the square
DATA((W(I,J),J=I+1,5),I=1,4),          array w as
+    ((W(I,J),I=J+1,5),J=1,4)/20*0.0/
```

$$\begin{bmatrix} 1 & 0 & 0 & 0 & 0 \\ 0 & 1 & 0 & 0 & 0 \\ 0 & 0 & 1 & 0 & 0 \\ 0 & 0 & 0 & 1 & 0 \\ 0 & 0 & 0 & 0 & 1 \end{bmatrix}$$

▮ 7.5 Arrays as Elements of an Argument List

An entire array can be transferred to or from a function or subroutine subprogram simply by including the name of the array in the argument list of the calling statement and in the subroutine/function definition line. Of course, the array must be previously declared and dimensioned in the main (or calling) program. The array must likewise be declared in the subprogram. The purpose of this secondary array declaration is not to allot memory space to the array but merely to inform the subprogram that this variable is an array, already dimensioned elsewhere. For this reason the size of the array as dimensioned in the subprogram may be any value that is less than or equal to the actual declared size in the main program, or it may even be variable. The following examples illustrate this feature.

Main Program   **Subprograms**

```
PROGRAM XXX
REAL A(11),X(10,10)

CALL SUB1(A)          {a₁ ↔ r₁ }      SUBROUTINE SUB1(R)
                      {a₁₀ ↔ r₁₀}     REAL R(10)
                                        ...
                                      END
```

Main Program		**Subprograms**

Main Program

CALL SUB2(A)

$\left\{ \begin{array}{l} a_1 \leftrightarrow s_{-5} \\ a_{11} \leftrightarrow s_5 \end{array} \right\}$

Subprograms

```
SUBROUTINE SUB2(S)
REAL S(-5:5)
   . . .
END
```

N = 3
CALL SUB3(X,N)

$\left\{ \begin{array}{l} x_{11} \leftrightarrow t_{11} \\ x_{91} \leftrightarrow t_{33} \end{array} \right\}$

```
SUBROUTINE SUB3(T,M)
REAL T(M,M)
   . . .
END
```

CALL SUB4(X)

$\left\{ \begin{array}{l} x_{1,1} \leftrightarrow v_1 \\ x_{3,7} \leftrightarrow v_{63} \end{array} \right\}$

```
SUBROUTINE SUB4(V)
REAL V(1)
   . . .
V(7) = . . .
END
```

```
END
```

Any dummy variables in the defining argument list that refer to the dimension size of an array must be integers.

As you can see in the use of subroutines in SUB3 and SUB4 in the example above, when the array being transferred has two or more subscripts, special care must be exercised in the secondary dimensioning. For example, if the array A were declared in the main program as

```
PROGRAM MANE
REAL A(3,3)
CALL ALPHA(A,2)
```

where subroutine ALPHA is defined as

```
SUBROUTINE ALPHA(X,N)
REAL X(N,N)
```

then the execution of the CALL statement will cause a transfer of only four of the nine elements of the array A to the subroutine ALPHA. The four elements transferred will be the first four elements of the array A as they are stored in memory as illustrated at the top of page 260. As a result there would be a very confusing mismatch between the sets of subscripts on the two arrays A and X in the main program and the subroutine, respectively. The easiest way to correct this situation is to transfer the entire array as it was declared in the main program into the subprogram. Then if the subprogram needs to use only part of the array, the size of that smaller block is passed as an additional parameter. Thus, if the array A were declared in the main program to be a 3 by 3 block of numbers, the actual size of the array is NA = 3; in the subroutine, only a 2 by 2 subblock is needed. So, the local size requirements of the array

Identification of Array Elements

Main Program   *Subroutine*

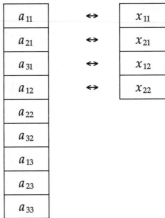

within the subroutine are for a block of size NL = 2. The subroutine AL-PHA could then be rewritten as

```
SUBROUTINE ALPHA(X,NA,NL)
REAL X(NA,NA)
  DO 2 I = 1,NL
  DO 2 J = 1,NL
     X(I,J) = ....
     ....

2   CONTINUE
    RETURN
    END
```

The subroutine uses only an NL by NL subblock of the full array, transferred in as an NA by NA block.

and the reference to the subroutine in the main program would be

```
CALL ALPHA(A,3,2)
```

Finally, since individual elements of an array can be referenced as A(2,1), a statement like

```
CALL BETA(X,Y,A(2,1))
```

would cause a transfer to the subroutine BETA, the numerical value associated with only the one element of the array A. The entire array would not be transferred. Because no parentheses are permitted within the argument list of the definition line of a function or subroutine, a statement like

```
SUBROUTINE GAMMA(X,I,A(I))    Compilation error
```

would not be permitted.

7.6 **Programming Techniques Using Arrays**

Finding the Minimum or Maximum of an Array

In Section 4.3 a simple method for finding the largest or smallest element of a list of numbers was described. This procedure can easily be adapted to finding the minimum and/or maximum of an array. However, we are frequently interested in finding not only *what* the maximum (or minimum) element is but also *where* it is—that is, which element in the array is the largest (or smallest). The value and position of the minimum or maximum element in an array can be found by using a *pointer*, as illustrated in Figure 7-3. A pointer is a separate secondary array that contains the sequencing information for the subscript in the primary array or arrays. Thus, if the sixth element in the array VALUES is found to be the maximum, this fact could be contained in a pointer array called INDEX, where INDEX(1) would have a value of 6 and VALUE (INDEX(1)) would be the maximum

Figure 7-3
Subroutine to
find the value
and position of
the maximum
element of a
one-dimensional
array

```
      SUBROUTINE MINMAX(X,N,XMAX,IMAX,XMIN,IMIN)
      REAL X(N)
*
*     Start by defining the maximum/minimum element
*     to be the first element and the location of
*     each element to be position 1.
*
      XMAX = X(1)
      XMIN = X(1)
      IMAX = 1
      IMIN = 1
      DO 1 I = 2,N
         IF(X(I) .GT. XMAX)THEN
*
*            The current x(i) is larger than the
*            assumed maximum, so redefine the
*            maximum and the position of the maximum.
*
             XMAX = X(I)
             IMAX = I
*
*            These two values are returned
*            by the subroutine.
*
         ENDIF
*
*        Use a similar step for the minimum.
*
         IF(X(I) .LT. XMIN)THEN
             XMIN = X(I)
             IMIN = I
         ENDIF
    1 CONTINUE
      RETURN
      END
```

element. The position of the largest or smallest element of an array with more than one subscript is found in a similar manner.

Sorting Algorithms

Arranging the elements of a list or set into some sort of ordered sequence is called *sorting*. The most common example of sorting is the alphabetizing of a list of names. (This particular problem will be addressed in Chapter 8.) The basic ideas involved in sorting a list of either names or numbers are the same and quite simple. However, the difficulty of sorting a list increases dramatically with the size of the list being sorted, roughly increasing by the square of the size of the list. So while one algorithm may be suitable to sort the records of the students in a university ($\approx 10{,}000$ names), it might be next to useless in sorting the names in the New York City phone book (about 3 million names, or $300^2 = 90$ thousand times more difficult). To a professional programmer, who writes program code that will be used perhaps thousands of times, the efficiency of code is extremely important. The programmer will spend many hours or days rewriting a valid code to optimize the speed and minimize the memory requirements of the program. For most of the rest of us, however, such meticulous care would not be cost-effective. For programs that will be executed only a few times and from which we want an answer quickly, it would be foolish to spend an extra week reducing the run time from 73 seconds to 47 seconds. (Of course, a reduction of run time from 73 hours to 47 hours would be a different matter.) For this reason, only the two simplest sorting algorithms, the selection sort and the bubble sort, are discussed here. Neither of these algorithms would be suitable for excessively long lists, for which extremely sophisticated procedures have been devised.

Selection Sort

The selection sort algorithm (also called the exchange sort) is the most obvious method of arranging a list. It proceeds as follows:

1. Scan the list and find the minimum of the list of n elements.
2. Place this element at the top of the list.
3. Scan the remaining list of $n - 1$ numbers and find the minimum of that set.
4. Place this element next in the list.
5. Continue until the remaining list contains only one number.

The FORTRAN code to accomplish this operation on an array of numbers is given in Figure 7-4. Several features of this code are worth mentioning:

- Notice that the array size is a dummy variable N. Since the array was presumed declared in the calling program, N must be less than or equal to that actual declared size. Also, N is typed as integer and then appears in the next line as the subscript of

Figure 7-4 _____

Subroutine to order
an array of
numbers by the
selection sort
method

```
      SUBROUTINE SORT(X,N)
      INTEGER N,TOP
      REAL X(N),XMIN,TEMP
*
*  TOP is the location (subscript) of the first element
*  in the remaining list.  Thus, for the first pass it
*  has the value of 1.
*
      DO 2 TOP = 1,N
*
*     Scan the list from TOP to N and find the minimum.
*
          XMIN = X(TOP)
          DO 1 I = TOP+1, N
             IF(X(I) .LT. XMIN)THEN
*
*                This value is the new minimum.
*                Swap positions of these two elements.
*                Notice, the interchange requires three
*                lines, not two.
*
                 TEMP = X(I)
                 X(I) = XMIN
                 XMIN = TEMP
             ENDIF
  1       CONTINUE
*
*         Place the minimum at the top of the
*         remaining list.
*
          X(TOP) = XMIN
  2   CONTINUE
      RETURN
      END
```

the array X. Thus, in this case the order of the INTEGER and REAL statements is significant; that is, N could not be used as a subscript index before it is typed as INTEGER.

- Read through the code and follow the development of the re-ordering of the list. After the first pass, X(1) will equal the overall minimum in the list; after the second pass, X(2) will be the second smallest value; and so on.
- During each pass, when a smaller value is found its position is exchanged with the position of the current minimum. When the two values X(I) and XMIN are exchanged, three lines of code are required and a temporary variable, TEMP, is used. If simply

```
      X(I) = XMIN
      XMIN = X(I)
```

had been used, both variables would have been assigned the same value, namely, XMIN.

• After execution of the subroutine SORT, the original list is destroyed and the reordered list is in its place. If you need the original list as well, a copy should be made before the call to SORT.

During the execution of subroutine SORT, a total of

$$(n - 1) + (n - 2) + (n - 3) + \cdots + 2 + 1 = \tfrac{1}{2}n(n - 1)$$

comparisons are made, and, assuming a random initial ordering, the number of interchanges should be somewhat less than half the number of comparisons.

Keep in mind two limitations when using the selection sort algorithm:

1. Even if the original list is already in order, the same number of comparison tests would have to be made, although there would be no replacements.
2. If the original, unsorted list consisted of not just individual numbers, but each number identified additional information as well, such as addresses, bank balances, grades, names, and so on, during each exchange all of these items would also have to be interchanged. These added exchanges could seriously affect the efficiency of the algorithm.

These shortcomings of the selection sort will be corrected shortly with the use of a pointer array. But first consider an alternative algorithm for sorting a list.

Bubble Sort

Another simple sorting algorithm, the bubble sort, is especially useful when the original list is partially sorted to begin with. The idea in the bubble sort algorithm is illustrated in the sequence below.

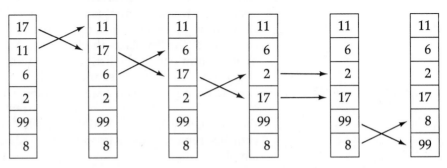

The bubble sort proceeds as follows:

1. Compare the first two elements (17 and 11) and if out of order, exchange.
2. Compare the next pair (now 17 and 6) and if out of order, exchange.

3. Continue this process through the entire list. Notice that after the first pass the largest element in the list (99) has "bubbled" down to the bottom.
4. In the second pass through the list, compare only the remaining elements since the largest element is already in the proper position. The arrangement of the numbers after the second pass will be

6
2
11
8
17
99

The FORTRAN code to accomplish a bubble sort is given in Figure 7-5. The purpose of the variable FLAG is to signal when the entire

Figure 7-5
FORTRAN code
for a subroutine
to execute a
bubble sort

```
      SUBROUTINE BUBBLE(X,N)
      INTEGER N,PASS,FLAG
      REAL X(N)

      DO 2 PASS = N,2,-1
*
*        Start from the bottom element and move up.
*        While FLAG has the value 1, continue sorting.
*
         FLAG = 0
         DO 1  I = 1, PASS-1
*
*           For this pass, compare successive pairs of
*           elements in the remaining set and if out
*           of order, exchange values.
*
            IF(X(I) .GT. X(I+1))THEN
               TEMP     = X(I)
               X(I)     = X(I+1)
               X(I+1) = TEMP
               FLAG     = 1
            ENDIF
    1    CONTINUE
*
*        If there are no exchanges in this pass, the
*        list is sorted and the procedure is terminated.
*
         IF(FLAG .EQ. 0)RETURN
    2 CONTINUE
      RETURN
      END
```

list has been compared and no exchanges have been required. When this happens, the list is in order and the sorting can stop.

Sorting with a Pointer

As mentioned above, a sorting problem is frequently complicated by the fact that many other additional items are associated with each element in the list. Each time the position of two numbers in the list is switched, all the corresponding data must be exchanged as well. In such cases it is much more convenient simply to keep track of the rearrangements by using a pointer. The idea is to leave the original list, X(I), intact while the numerical order of the elements of X are determined and stored in an array INDEX. Thus, the smallest element in the entire list is, say, 0.1, and it is the 12th element of X. The second smallest element is, say, 0.3, and it is the 7th element of the list. The result of the sorting would then result in

```
INDEX(1) = 12
INDEX(2) =  7
```

so that the smallest elements of X( ) would be referenced as

```
X(INDEX(1))    Smallest element, that is, X(12) = 0.1
X(INDEX(2))    Next smallest element, X(7) = 0.3
```

Either the selection sort or the bubble sort can be rewritten using a pointer indexing array. The code for the selection sort with a pointer is given in Figure 7-6. If this subroutine is used to sort an array X that contains the ten numbers 5., 4., 3., 2., 1., 0., 9., 8., 7., and 6., the result is

I	Original Sequence X(I)	Sorted Sequence X(INDEX(I))	Original Position INDEX(I)
1	5.0	0.0	6
2	4.0	1.0	5
3	3.0	2.0	4
4	2.0	3.0	3
5	1.0	4.0	2
6	0.0	5.0	1
7	9.0	6.0	10
8	8.0	7.0	9
9	7.0	8.0	8
10	6.0	9.0	7

Thus, a reference to the name associated with the smallest element in the array X would be

```
NAME(INDEX(1))
```

Figure 7-6
Subroutine that
executes a
selection sort
using a pointer

```
      SUBROUTINE XCHNG(X,INDEX,N)
*
* The array X is sorted, smallest to largest, and is
* not destroyed.  The proper sequence of elements
* will be contained in the array INDEX().  Thus,
* X(Index(1)), X(Index(n)) will be the smallest and
* largest elements of the array.  The array Index
* must be declared in the calling program, but it
* will be assigned values in this subroutine.
*
      INTEGER N,INDEX(N),TOP,TEMP
      REAL X(N)
*
* First initialize the array INDEX to the sequence 1
* to N.
*
      DO 1 I = 1,N
         INDEX(I) = I
    1 CONTINUE
*
      DO 3 TOP = 1, N-1
*
*        The value INDEX(TOP) refers to the element of
*        X that is at the top of the remaining unsorted
*        list.  Initialize XMIN to be the top value.
*
         XMIN = X(INDEX(TOP))

         DO 2 I = TOP,N
*
            IF(X(INDEX(I)) .LT. XMIN)THEN
*
*              If a smaller value is found, redefine the
*              pointers; that is, exchange Index(i) and
*              Index(top) and redefine Xmin.
*
               TEMP       = INDEX(I)
               INDEX(I)   = INDEX(TOP)
               INDEX(TOP) = TEMP
               XMIN       = X(INDEX(TOP))
            ENDIF
    2    CONTINUE
    3 CONTINUE
      RETURN
      END
```

▬ Plotting a Graph on the Line Printer or Terminal Screen

Unlike some other languages, FORTRAN does not have built-in graphics capabilities for easily plotting functions. The simplest alternative is to have your FORTRAN program create a data file containing the numbers to be printed and then use a different software package to read and plot the data. However, you can create your own programs to obtain a rough graph of a function. To do so, you would carefully analyze the steps involved in plotting a graph on ordinary graph paper and attempt to construct an algorithm to mimic these steps on the computer.

Four steps are involved in plotting a graph on a printer:

1. First generate a table of number pairs (x_i, y_i) for $i = 1, n$. These numbers may represent experimental data, such as position versus time for a falling object, or they may be generated from a particular functional relationship between x and y, such as $y(x) = 8x^2$. Once the data set is complete, you can begin to represent the set by points on a graph.

2. Determine the range of both x_i and y_i. This will require a determination of both the minimum and maximum values of x and y in the data set. Then,

$$(\text{Range})_x = (x_{max} - x_{min})$$

$$(\text{Range})_y = (y_{max} - y_{min})$$

These values can then be used for scaling the x and y axes; that is, adjusting the scales of the axes so that the graph fits neatly on the graph paper.

3. Step through the points and graph them one by one. You might not think such a trivial step is worth mentioning. However, graphing a function in this way is one of the surest ways to appreciate the meaning of the term *function*. Since this is so critical to your further understanding of mathematics, it warrants possibly insulting your intelligence. Thus, for each value of x_i (the independent variable) there is a corresponding y_i (the dependent variable). Or, for each value of i there is a pair (x_i, y_i). Since a printer executes one horizontal line at a time and then proceeds to the next line, stepping along the x axis and graphing y values will mean that the graph will have to be constructed moving down the page, not across. (See Figure 7-7.)

4. When one line is displayed, 80 or so characters will be printed (depending on the length of the y axis) for a particular value of x. All of these characters will be blanks except one, which will be an asterisk positioned along the line to correspond to the value of y for this value of x. For example, suppose you have a function $y = f(x)$ that you wish to graph for $0 \le x \le 5$. Thus $(\text{Range})_x = 5$. You also need the range in y values and might determine that

$$y_{max} = 16.38$$

$$y_{min} = -7.21$$

so

$$(\text{Range})_y = 23.59$$

Figure 7-7
On a printer, a graph is executed with *x*-values moving down the page

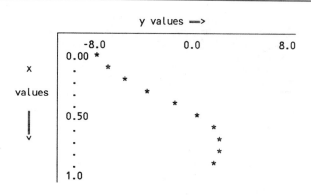

Next, if at $x = 0.3$, $y(0.3) = -3.8$, you need to compute the appropriate position along the horizontal line between y_{min} and y_{max} to place the asterisk. If the *y* axis is to be 51 columns wide, we could first define

$$\text{Ratio} = \frac{y(0.3) - y_{min}}{y_{max} - y_{min}}$$

which is between 0.0 and 1.0 and represents the fraction of the distance along the axis to place the asterisk. The appropriate column position would then be

```
IC = 50.*RATIO
```

The FORTRAN code in Figure 7-8 will produce a rough sketch of the dummy function $f(x)$ for $a \le x \le b$ by following the above steps. A program to plot the function $f(x) = \sin^2(\pi x/10)$ would simply be

```
PROGRAM XXX
EXTERNAL F
CALL PLOT(0.,10.,F)
STOP
END
*===================================
FUNCTION F(X)
  F = SIN(0.31415926*X)**2
  RETURN
END
*===================================
```

The result is shown in Figure 7-9.

Figure 7-8

Subroutine to graph
a function at the
terminal

```
      SUBROUTINE PLOT(A,B,F)
      CHARACTER*1 LINE(0:50),BLANK,STAR
      REAL X(0:40),Y(0:40),XSTEP,YMIN,YMAX,RATIO
      INTEGER IC
      DATA BLANK,STAR,LINE/' ','*',51*' '/
*
*  First generate the table of data pairs x(i),y(i).
*
      XSTEP = (B-A)/40.
      X(0)  = A
      Y(0)  = F(A)
      DO 1 I = 1,40
         X(I) = X(I-1) + XSTEP
         Y(I) = F(X(I))
    1 CONTINUE
*
*  Use the subroutine MINMAX to determine the range.
*  (Be careful with the size!)
*
      CALL MINMAX(Y,41,YMAX,IMAX,YMIN,IMIN)
*
*  Print the overall headings for the y axis.
*
      WRITE(*,10)YMIN,YMAX
*
*  Step through the data pairs; position the asterisk
*  and print line by line.
*
      DO 2 I = 0,40
         RATIO    = (Y(I) - YMIN)/(YMAX - YMIN)
         IC       = 50.*RATIO
         LINE(IC) = STAR
         WRITE(*,11)X(I),(LINE(J),J=0,50)
*
*        Remember to blank out the star to
*        set up for the next line.
*
         LINE(IC) = BLANK
    2    CONTINUE
         RETURN
*-----------------------------------------------------
*  Formats
*
   10 FORMAT(//,T10,'A plot of the function ',/,
     +    T8,'Ymin',T58,'Ymax',/,
     +    T8,F5.2,T58,F5.2,/,
     +    T5,'X',T10,'+',T35,'+',T60,'+',/,
     +    T9,'|',51('-'),'|')
*
   11 FORMAT(T2,F5.2,T9,'|',51A1,'|')
*
      END
```

Contour Plots

A contour plot is often used to represent a function of two variables on a
graph. You have probably seen contour maps that give the elevation of the
land above sea level as closed paths drawn on a normal map. If x repre-

sents the east-west position on the map and y represents the north-south position, then the elevation of any point of land can be written as a function of x and y: elevation $= E(x, y)$. If all those points with an elevation of 100 feet are connected, we would get a curve of constant (100 feet) elevation. Elevations of 200 feet, 300 feet, and so on, are similarly connected, resulting in a set of closed curves for a selection of elevation values, as is illustrated in Figure 7-10. The idea can be applied to any function of two variables.

Figure 7-9
Printer plot of the
function $\sin^2(\pi x/10)$

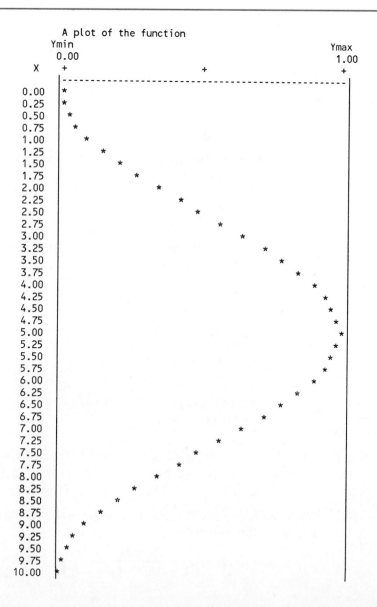

Figure 7-10
Contour map

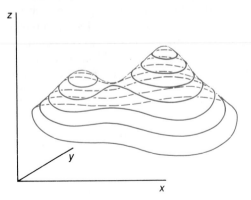

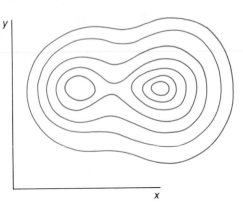

Three-dimensional representation
of a function $z = f(x, y)$. The
curves are contours of equal
height.

Two-dimensional contour
graph of the same function.

The detailed steps would be as follows:

1. Given a function of two variables, $z = f(x, y)$, with known limits on x and y such that $a \le x \le b, c \le y \le d$, compute a two-dimensional table of z values for all combinations of x_i, $i = 0, n_x$ and $y_j, j = 0, n_y$; that is,

   ```
   Z(0:NX,0:NY)
   ```

2. Compute the overall maximum and minimum values of $Z(I, J)$ and thus determine the range of z values.

3. Print out a square array of symbols corresponding to the values of $Z(I, J)$ defined in the following manner:

   a. Let $(Range)_z = z_{max} - z_{min}$.

   b. Replace $z_{ij} \rightarrow 50(z_{ij} - z_{min})/Range_z$. All the z values are now between 0.0 and 50.0.

   c. Construct an integer array

   ```
   IZ(I,J) = Z(I,J)
   ```

   d. For those points z_{ij} that have an $IZ(I, J)$—that is, are divisible by 5—assign a symbol from '0', '1',...,'9', by the relation

   ```
   CONTUR(I,J) = DIGIT(IZ(I,J)/5)
   ```

   where DIGIT(0) = '0', DIGIT(1) = '1', and so on.

   e. If $IZ(I, J)$ is not evenly divisible by 5, assign a blank.

The FORTRAN code for such a program is illustrated in Figure 7-11. The output for the function

$$z = f(x, y) = \frac{8 - 3x + y}{[(x + 0.3)^4 + (y + 0.3)^2]^{1/4}}$$

Figure 7-11

Subroutine to
produce a contour
plot of a function of
two variables

```
          SUBROUTINE SQUARE(A,B,C,D,F)
*
*  will produce a 20 by 20 contour plot of the dummy
*  function f(x,y) for a<x<b, c<y<d.  The minimum/maximum
*  values of the function are determined by adapting sub-
*  routine MINMAX of Figure 7-3.  The contours are repre-
*  sented by integers, 0 for minimum, 9 for maximum.
*------------------------------------------------------------
* Variables
*
          CHARACTER*1 DIGIT(0:9),CONTUR(0:20,0:20)
          REAL A,B,C,D,ZMIN,ZMAX,Z(0:20,0:20)
          INTEGER IZ(0:20,0:20)
*
          DATA DIGIT/'0','1','2','3','4','5','6','7','8','9'/
          DATA CONTUR/441*' '/
          OPEN(1,FILE='SQUARE.OUT')
*------------------------------------------------------------
* Computation
*
*  Fill the z array
*  (left to right in x, top to bottom in y).
*
          DX = (B-A)/20.
          DY = (D-C)/20.
          DO 1 IX = 0,20
          DO 1 IY = 20,0,-1
             X = IX*DX + A
             Y = IY*DY + C
             Z(IX,IY) = F(X,Y)
    1     CONTINUE
*
*  Determine the overall min/max values of the z array.
*
          CALL MINMX2(Z,21,21,ZMIN,ZMAX)
*
*  Scale the z-s and make an integer copy.  If the
*  integer is divisible by 5, assign that point a
*  digit.
*
          DO 2 IX = 0,20
          DO 2 IY = 20,0,-1
             Z(IX,IY) = 49.99*(Z(IX,IY)-ZMIN)/(ZMAX-ZMIN)
             IZ(IX,IY)= Z(IX,IY)
             IF(IZ(IX,IY)/5*5 .EQ. IZ(IX,IY))THEN
                 CONTUR(IX,IY) = DIGIT(IZ(IX,IY)/5)
             ENDIF
    2     CONTINUE
*------------------------------------------------------------
* Print the contour plot.
*
          WRITE(1,10)A,B
          DO 3 IY = 20,0,-1
             Y = IY*(D-C)/20. + C
             WRITE(1,13)Y,(CONTUR(IX,IY),IX=0,20)
    3     CONTINUE
          WRITE(1,12)
          STOP
*------------------------------------------------------------
```

Figure 7-11
(concluded)

```
* Formats
*
   10 FORMAT(//,T10,'a',T71,'b',/,
  +    T8,F5.2,T40,'X',T68,F5.2,/,
  +    T9,'|',61('-'),'|')
*
   12 FORMAT(         T9,'|',61('-'),'|')
   13 FORMAT(T2,F5.2,T9,'|',20(1X,A1,1X),A1,'|')
      END
```

is shown in Figure 7-12. Notice that from the contour plot we can determine that the function appears to have a rather steep maximum at $(x, y) \approx (0.3, 0.3)$ and a more gentle local minimum near $(x, y) \approx (-2, 2)$.

Summary

In FORTRAN an array associates several memory locations to the same variable name. The address within the array is then specified by one or more subscripts (up to a maximum of seven). The types of all elements of the array are determined by the array name.

Figure 7-12
Contour plot of the function $f(x, y) = (8 - 3x + y)/((x+.3)^4 + (y+.3)^2)^{1/4}$

```
         a                                                            b
       -2.00                       X                           2.00
        |-------------------------------------------------------------|
  2.00  | 0  0                1                 2  2  2  2  2  2  2 2|
  1.80  | 0  0             1                 2  2              2  2 2|
  1.60  | 0                1              2                      2 2|
  1.40  | 0             1           2                             2|
  1.20  | 0                        2                               |
  1.00  |             1         2                                  |
  0.80  |                     2              3  3  3                |
  0.60  |          1       2          3              3             |
  0.40  |          1     2       3                   3             |
  0.20  |                           4                   3          |
  0.00  |                        5                      3          |
 -0.20  |       1     2        7        9               3          |
 -0.40  |       1     2  3                 7               3       |
 -0.60  |       1     2  3  4                     4        3       |
 -0.80  |             2                 5  5               3       |
 -1.00  |             2     3        4                     3       |
 -1.20  |             2        3           4  4  4         3       |
 -1.40  |    1        2           3                        3       |
 -1.60  |    1                                             3       |
 -1.80  |    1           2           3                     3  3    |
 -2.00  |    1           2              3                  3  3    |
        |-------------------------------------------------------------|
```

The actual size of an array must be specified at the beginning of a program or subprogram by an array-declaration statement, which may be a standard type statement, a COMMON statement, or a DIMENSION statement. Since all variable names including array names should be type-declared as well, the preferred method of array declaration is to use type statements for those variables not in a COMMON block and COMMON statements for those that are and to avoid the use of DIMENSION statements altogether. The declaration of the size of an array in any of these statements takes the form

$$\langle \text{array name} \rangle (d_1, d_2, \ldots)$$

where d_i specifies the limits of the ith subscript for an array with from one to seven subscripts. The individual subscript specifications are of the form $I_{lower}{:}I_{upper}$ where I_{lower} and I_{upper} may be any integer values provided $I_{lower} \leq I_{upper}$. If the lower limit of the subscript is omitted, a value of 1 is assumed and the colon is not required. Thus, A$(-2{:}3, 4)$ specifies that the array A has two subscripts i_1, i_2, with the limits on the first being $-2 \leq i_1 \leq 3$ and on the second $1 \leq i_2 \leq 4$. This array, along with arrays B and C, could then for example be declared as

```
REAL A(-2:3,4),B
CHARACTER*3 C(-7:2,5)
COMMON/PARAM/B(6)
```

An array with one subscript is stored in memory sequentially by its subscript. An array with two subscripts is usually viewed as a block, with subscripts labeling rows and columns, but is actually stored in memory as a sequential list with the order defined by incrementing the leftmost index first. Arrays with more than two indices are stored similarly.

To reference a single element of an array, the name of the array is given followed by a pair of parentheses containing specific values for each of the array subscripts. The subscript values in the array reference must be within the limits specified in the array declaration. Array elements may then be used in all situations that ordinary FORTRAN variables are used, except that they may not be dummy arguments of functions or subroutines. An entire array is referenced by using the name alone. An entire array may be used only in input/output statements, DATA statements, or in the argument list of a function or subroutine. An array name without subscripts may never be used in arithmetic expressions. Referencing an entire array in I/O or DATA statements is equivalent to listing each and every element of the array in the order in which they are stored in memory.

An implied DO loop may be used only in I/O statements and DATA statements. It is a DO loop that is enclosed in parentheses, written in a single line, and forms a single unit in an I/O or DATA list. The form is

$$(\text{variable list}, I = I_{lower}, I_{upper}, I_{step})$$

Implied DO loops may be nested.

If an entire array is transferred to a subroutine or function, the array must also be declared in the subprogram. Since the actual size of the array has already been declared, the purpose of the secondary declaration is merely to inform the compiler that the name is that of an entire array. Thus, the size declared in the subprogram may be any value that is less than or equal to that in the primary declaration, or may even be variable. To avoid a mismatch of subscripts, it is essential that the secondary size declaration of arrays with more than one subscript be identical to the primary declaration.

Manipulation of large data sets is a common feature of most programs. These data sets, represented by FORTRAN arrays, are then processed in a variety of ways. The values can be scanned to determine the minimum (maximum) of the set, rearranged in ascending/descending order or plotted. The techniques for these particular operations are described in this chapter and are the basis for many advanced programming techniques. The procedure for finding the minimum (maximum) of a list is developed from the simple procedure of scanning the list and keeping track of the current minimum/maximum element and replacing that value when a smaller (larger) element is found. This algorithm is often augmented by including a pointer array to keep track of the position of the minimum (maximum) element in the list. The algorithm to find the minimum (maximum) of a list is used repeatedly in the sorting of an array. First the smallest (largest) element of the array is found and placed at the top; then the operation is repeated for the remainder of the array until the array is exhausted. This operation, which may or may not include a pointer array, forms the basis of the selection sort algorithm. An alternative sorting procedure, called the bubble sort, compares successive pairs in the array and, if out of order, switches the two elements, repeating the process until all elements are in ascending or descending order.

The final programming technique described in this chapter illustrates how the procedures used in drawing a graph of a function, $y(x)$, or of data values, (x_i, y_i), can be translated into a FORTRAN code for plotting a graph on the printer or terminal screen. The steps involved include using a minimum/maximum algorithm to determine the range of values, which then set the scale of the graph, and then, one by one, stepping through the independent variable, for example, x, and printing one line of all blanks with a single asterisk positioned along the line to represent the value of y. This technique is then extended to include graphs of functions of two variables by means of contour plots.

Problems

7.1 Identify and correct any compilation errors in the following declaration statements for numerical arrays. If there are no errors, write OK.

a. REAL M(1)
b. INTEGER REAL(2:1)
c. REAL X(1,2,3,4,5,6,7)
d. DIMENSION INTEGER M(2)
e. DIMENSION REAL X(2)
f. REAL C(2,2.2,2)
g. INTEGER INDEX(N)
   N = 5

h. N = 5
   REAL X(N)
i. REAL X(-3,-9)
j. REAL X(2,2,0:1)
k. DIMENSION R(0:10)
   REAL R
l. REAL R(10)
   DIMENSION R(10)

7.2 Identify and correct any compilation errors in the following declaration statements for character arrays. If there are no errors, write OK.
a. CHARACTER*4 REAL X
b. CHARACTER*4 FOUR(-4:4)
c. CHARACTER*2 TWO(2)*2
d. CHARACTER B2(2:2)*2

7.3 Write the FORTRAN code for a subroutine that will return which element of a square two-dimensional array A of arbitrary size is the smallest; that is, the subroutine should return values for (I1,I2) such that A(I1,I2) is the smallest element of A.

7.4 To determine whether an integer N is a prime number, you must test whether N is divisible by all primes less than $\sqrt{N}$. To do so you must have a table of primes. Write a program to determine the first 100 prime numbers. A pseudocode outline of the program is given below.

```
INTEGER pᵢ, i = 1, 100
p₁ = 2, p₂ = 3
For m = 2, 100
    let k = pₘ + 2
    For i = 1, m
        test whether k is divisible by pᵢ
        IF yes, k not prime,
            let k → k + 2, abort i-loop
            and restart at i = 1
    End i-loop
    If k not divisible by any pᵢ, then
        pₘ₊₁ = k
End m-loop
```

7.5 Write the FORTRAN code for the following two subroutines:
a. SWITCH(A, N) will switch the rows and columns of the square array A(N, N).
b. PIVOT(A, N, K) will scan column K of the square N by N array A and will find which row contains the maximum element. The subroutine will then interchange this entire row with the first row of the matrix.

7.6 Determine the output from the following implied DO-loop structures.

```
      INTEGER K(0:4, 0:4)
      DO 1 I = 0,4
      DO 1 J = 0,4
         K(I,J) = 10*I + J    Thus, K(23) = 23, and so on.
    1 CONTINUE
```

```
a.   WRITE(*,'(10I2)')(K(0,J),J=1,4)
b.   WRITE(*,'(5I3)')((K(I,J),J=1,4),I=1,4)
c.   WRITE(*,2)(I,I=0,4),(M,(K(M,J),J=0,4),M=0,4)
   2 FORMAT(T8,5(I1,TR5),//,
     +         (I1,TR5,5(I2,TR4),/))
d.   WRITE(*,'(5I3)')((K(I,J),J=I,4),I=0,4)
e.   WRITE(*,'(5I3)')((K(I,J),I=4,0,-1),J=0,4)
f.   DO 3 I = 0,4
         WRITE(*,'(5I4)')(K(I,J),J=1,4)
   3 CONTINUE
g.   DO 4 I = 0,4
         WRITE(*,5)(K(I,J),J=4,I,-1)
   4 CONTINUE
   5 FORMAT(T20,5(I3,TL8))
```

7.7 Rewrite the selection sort program in Figure 7-4 to arrange the set in decreasing order.

7.8 Rewrite the selection sort program in Figure 7-4 to also count the number of duplicate values in the set.

7.9 In the bubble sort algorithm in Section 7.6, the largest element of the array "bubbles" down to the bottom of the array after one pass. Rewrite the algorithm so that the smallest element of the set will instead bubble up to the top of the list.

7.10 Rewrite the bubble sort subroutine in Figure 7-5 to include a pointer array. The original list should be left intact. Test your subroutine on a sample list.

7.11 Alter the subroutine PLOT in Figure 7-8 to graph two functions $f(x)$ and $g(x)$ simultaneously over the same range of x values. Print different symbols for each function, and determine an overall minimum/maximum.

7.12 Alter the subroutine PLOT in Figure 7-8 to produce a labeled y axis with four equally spaced tic marks along with the corresponding values of y. For example,

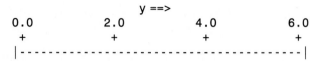

7.13 When plotting a function it is desirable to have the numbers along the x and y axes start and end with whole numbers.
  a. Rewrite the subroutine PLOT in Figure 7-8 to use the function ROUNDR of Figure 5-6 to replace y_{min} and y_{max} by rounded values. Assume that y_{min} is negative and y_{max} is positive so that you want both numbers to be rounded up in magnitude.
  b. This time rewrite the subroutine PLOT in Figure 7-8 to use rounded values for y_{min} and y_{max} but account for the possibility that either one can be positive or negative; that is, if $y_{min} > 0$ then you would want to round y_{min} down and y_{max} up.

7.14 To produce a graph with the x axis horizontal and the y axis vertical, a different procedure must be employed. Once again a table of (x_i, y_i) is first obtained and the range of the x and y values determined. This time the entire plot will be stored in the character array that will represent a page. The page is first initialized to all blanks.

```
CHARACTER PAGE(0:60,0:50)*1
DATA PAGE/3111*' '/
```

Next, step through the tabulated values (left to right in x and from top to bottom in y) and determine the positioning of the points on the page by

$$I_x = 60(x_i - x_{min})/(\text{Range})_x \qquad I_y = 50(y_i - y_{min})/(\text{Range})_y$$

and assign a symbol, say *, to this point, $PAGE(IX, IY) = $ '*'. The array PAGE is then printed with appropriate labels. Use this procedure to produce a graph of the function

$$y(x) = e^{-x} \sin(\pi x) \qquad 0 \le x \le 10$$

7.15 Use the subroutine SQUARE in Figure 7-11 to produce contour plots of the following functions, and from the graphs estimate the region of any minima or maxima of the function.

a. $f(x, y) = \sin(x^2 + y^2)$ $\qquad -1 \le x \le 1$
$\qquad\qquad\qquad\qquad\qquad\qquad -1 \le y \le 1$
b. $g(x, y) = \exp(-x^2 - y^2)$ $\qquad -1 \le x \le 1$
$\qquad\qquad\qquad\qquad\qquad\qquad -1 \le y \le 1$
c. $h(x, y) = (x - 1)^2 + (y - 1)^2$ $\qquad 0 \le x \le 2$
$\qquad\qquad\qquad\qquad\qquad\qquad\qquad 0 \le y \le 2$

7.16 a. Write a function subprogram POLY(X, N, C) that will evaluate a polynomial of degree N in the variable x. The coefficients of the terms in the polynomial are contained in the one-dimensional array c_n. Thus,

$$\text{Poly}(x) = c_n x^n + c_{n-1} x^{n-1} + \cdots + c_2 x^2 + c_1 x + c_0$$

$$= \sum c_i x^i$$

b. Rewrite the function POLY so that no exponentiation is employed. For example,

$$c_3 x^3 + c_2 x^2 + c_1 x + c_0 = (((c_3 x + c_2)x + c_1)x + c_0)$$

c. Rewrite the function POLY so that only x appears in the argument list.

7.17 Use a DATA statement employing implied DO loops to initialize a square 10 by 10 array A(I, J) in the following manner:

$\qquad\qquad a_{ij} = 1$ $\qquad$ for $i = j$ $\qquad$ Along the main diagonal
$\qquad\qquad a_{ij} = 2$ $\qquad$ for $i > j$ $\qquad$ Below the main diagonal
$\qquad\qquad a_{ij} = 0$ $\qquad$ for $i < j$ $\qquad$ Above the main diagonal

7.18 Find any compilation errors in the following expressions:
a. `G = F(X,N(2),C)`
b. `FUNCTION Z(C,N(2),A)`
c. `FUNCTION BISEC(A,B,COS)`

d. SUBROUTINE PRINT(PAGE)
   CHARACTER*1 PAGE(NX,NY)
e. PROGRAM MANE
   REAL X(3,3)
   COMMON/ABLK/Y(2,2)
   CALL Z(X,3)
   END
   SUBROUTINE Z(Y,N)
   REAL Y(N,N)
   COMMON/ABLK/X(2,2)
        ...
   END

f. PROGRAM MANE
   REAL X(3,3)
   COMMON/ABLK/Y(2,2)
   CALL Z(Y,3)
   END
   SUBROUTINE Z(Y,N)
   REAL X(N,N)
   COMMON/ABLK/Y(2,2)
        ...
   END

C

Programming Assignment

The programming problems in this section illustrate the material covered to this point in the text, particularly Chapters 6 and 7. These problems are demanding and will require a considerable amount of time. You should start early and allow ample time for debugging the programs. You should also attempt to structure the programs in modular form, as described in Section 5.6. The programs should contain safeguards with diagnostic PRINT statements to handle any potential problems. A carefully constructed, neat code may take longer to design, but it pays dividends when problems arise. And as your programs grow longer and more complex, the role of the flowchart or pseudocode outline becomes more critical. Again, you will find that the effort you put into a clear outline of the workings of a proposed program will be time well spent.

C.1 Sample Problem

Industrial Engineering: Minimizing Repair Costs

A large manufacturing plant has many identical machines, all of which are subject to failure at random times. Technicians are hired to patrol and service the machines. Determining the appropriate number of technicians to hire depends on the following considerations:

- Good technicians are expensive. We will consider two cases, one using good, experienced, but expensive technicians and the other using cheaper but less-qualified workers. The number of technicians will be designated by R and their hourly wage as W.
- A technician can work on only one machine at a time, so several down machines may have to wait for repair, which will result in a productivity loss to the company. We will assume the loss per machine while it is inoperative is L ($/hr).
- Too many technicians will reduce the number of malfunctioning machines but may result in excessive idle time for these workers.

In addition, the following assumptions regarding the servicing of these machines will be made:

- The failure rate is known and is characterized by the average time between failures for an individual machine:

$$\Phi = \text{Failures per machine per unit time (no./hr)}$$
$$1/\Phi = \text{Time between failures per machine (hr)}$$

- The average repair time is known and is characterized by μ, the repairs per hour for each technician. Thus, $1/\mu$ is the average length of time in hours per machine repair.
- The quantity $\tau = \Phi/\mu$ is called the traffic intensity, and $1/\tau$ represents roughly the number of machines that one technician can handle [(time between machine failures)/(repair time per machine)].

The basic problem is to minimize the cost of the wages to the technicians plus the downtime costs of inoperative machines, that is,

$$\text{Cost}(R) = WR + \langle N_d \rangle L \tag{C.1}$$

where $\langle N_d \rangle$ is the average number of inoperative machines at any one time, which will itself depend on how many technicians (R) are hired. The main complexity of this problem is in calculating $\langle N_d \rangle$.

Let us assume that the likelihood that all machines are working can be represented by a number P_0 between 0 and 1, with $P_0 \approx 0$ representing a very small possibility that all are working and $P_0 \approx 1$ representing near certainty that all are working. Thus, P_0 is the probability that zero machines are down. Similarly, P_1 is the probability that only one machine is down, and P_n is the probability that n machines are down. The following result may then be obtained from queuing theory to relate these probabilities.

If $n < R$,

$$P_{n+1} = \tau \left(\frac{N - n}{n + 1} \right) P_n$$

If $R \leq n < N$, $\tag{C.2}$

$$P_{n+1} = \tau \left(\frac{N - n}{R} \right) P_n$$

where N is the total number of machines. For example, if $N = 50$, $R = 5$, and $\tau = 0.05$, then

$$P_1 = \tau N P_0 \qquad\qquad = 2.50 P_0$$

$$P_2 = \tfrac{1}{2}\tau(N - 1)P_1 = 1.225 P_1 = 3.063 P_0$$

$$P_3 = \tfrac{1}{3}\tau(N - 2)P_2 = 0.800 P_2 = 2.450 P_0$$

$$\vdots$$

$$P_6 = \tau \frac{N - 5}{R} P_5 \qquad = 0.298 P_0$$

$$\vdots$$

Thus, each P_n is proportional to P_0.

Finally, since the probabilities must satisfy the condition

$$\sum_{n=0}^{N} P_n = 1 \tag{C.3}$$

The remaining parameter, P_0, can be determined as follows:

1. Set $P_0 = 1$.
2. Compute all the P_n on this basis.
3. Evaluate the sum in Equation (C.3).
4. Rescale each of the P_n by replacing P_n by P_n/sum.

The average number of down machines may then be expressed as

$$\langle N_d \rangle = \sum_{n=0}^{N} n P_n \tag{C.4}$$

That is, the number of machines down multiplied by the likelihood of that many down, summed over all possibilities.

Once this expression is computed, Equation (C.1) may be evaluated for a variety of values of R and the value that results in a minimum cost determined.

Problem Specifics. Determine the optimum number of technicians to be hired for a variety of situations by constructing a FORTRAN program along the following lines:

1. Write a subroutine FACTR(TAU,R,N,P) that will evaluate all the probability factors P_k using Equation (C.2).
2. The main program should read the input parameters listed in Table C-1 and store them in appropriately named arrays or variables. Two types of machines (good and poor) and two types of technicians (fast and slow) will be considered. Thus, the arrays should be created accordingly: for example, FAIL(2), WAGES(2), and so on.

Table C-1
Input parameters for repair costs problem

Variable Name	Description	Values
N	Number of machines	70
LOSS	Downtime loss per machine ($/hr)	250
RMAX	Maximum number of technicians	15
MACHIN	Machine quality	"good" or "poor"
FAIL	Failure rate of the two types of machines	0.033 or 0.038
WORKER	Type of technician	"fast" or "slow"
WAGE	Hourly wages of the two types of technicians	17.95 or 14.00
FIXR	Repair rate of the two types of technicians	0.40 or 0.34

3. For CASE = 1, the program should
   a. Compute the traffic intensity, τ, and the approximate number of technicians required ($N_{approx} = N\tau$).
   b. For the number of technicians from 3 to 15,

      Call FACTR to compute the probability factors.

      Use Equation (C.4) to compute the average number of down machines.

      Compute and store in COST(R) the downtime cost from Equation (C.1).

   c. Use a subroutine to find the number of technicians that minimizes the downtime cost. Store this result in CBEST (CASE).
4. Determine the overall optimum situation and print with neat and appropriate labels.

The complete FORTRAN program to solve this problem, along with the computed results, is given in Figure C-1.

Figure C-1

FORTRAN code for the minimum repair cost problem

```
      PROGRAM THREE
*
*  This program computes the optimum number of technicians to hire in
*  order to minimize the machine downtime cost.  The program considers
*  four separate cases and for each case runs through the number of
*  technicians (from 3 to 15) and computes the set of probabilities of
*  the number of down machines.  It then computes an average number of
*  down machines and the downtime cost for this case.
*-------------------------------------------------------------------
*  Variables
*
      REAL P(0:70),LOSS,FIXR(2),WAGE(2),COST(3:15),FAIL(2),TAU,
     +     ESTIM,AVG
      INTEGER N,R,WRKR,MCHN
      CHARACTER*4 WORKER(2),MACHIN(2)
*
*      P(k)   --  The unnormalized probabilities of k machines being
*                 down; computed in subroutine FACTR
*      WORKER --  Type of technician (either fast or slow)
*      WAGE   --  Corresponding wages of the two technician types
*      FIXT   --  Repair rate for each of the two technician types
*      MACHIN --  Quality of machines (either good or poor)
*      FAIL   --  Known failure rate of the two machine types
*      LOSS   --  Downtime cost per machine ($/hr)
*      N      --  Total number of machines to service
*      R      --  Current number down
*      WRKR   --  Worker class (either 1 or 2)
*      MCHN   --  Machine class (either 1 or 2)
*      TAU    --  (failure rate)/(repair rate) = traffic intensity
*      ESTIM  --  N*TAU is approximately the number of technicians.
*      AVG    --  Average number of machines down for each case
*      COST(R)--  Downtime cost for this case and for R down machines
*-------------------------------------------------------------------
*  Initialization
*
```

Figure C-1 _____
(continued)

```
                  DATA WORKER,MACHIN/'fast','slow','good','poor'/
                  DATA RMAX,LOSS,FIXR,WAGE/15,250.,0.40,0.35,17.95,14.00/
                  DATA FAIL /0.033,0.038/
                  N = 70
      *-------------------------------------------------------------------
      * Write table headings and parameter values.
      *
                  WRITE(*,11)LOSS,N,WORKER,WAGE,FIXR,MACHIN,FAIL
                  WRITE(*,12)
      *
      * Step through the four combinations of workers and machines.
      *
                  DO 4 WRKR = 1,2
                  DO 4 MCHN = 1,2
                     TAU = FAIL(WRKR)/FIXR(MCHN)
                     ESTIM = N*TAU
      *
      *             For this case compute the average number of down machines
      *             using Equations (C.3) and (C.4) for each possible number of
      *             technicians, r = 3 to 15.
      *
                     DO 3 R = 3,15
                        CALL FACTR(TAU,R,N,P)
                        TOP = 0.0
                        BOT = 0.0
                        DO 2 I = 1,N
                           TOP = TOP + I*P(I)
                           BOT = BOT +   P(I)
            2           CONTINUE
                        AVG = TOP/BOT
                        COST(R) = WAGE(WRKR)*R + AVG*LOSS
            3        CONTINUE
      *
      *             Determine which value of r corresponds to a minimum
      *             downtime cost.
      *
                     CALL MIN(COST,15,CMIN,IMIN)
      *-------------------------------------------------------------------
      * Output
      *
                  WRITE(*,10)WORKER(WRKR),MACHIN(MCHN),TAU,ESTIM,IMIN,CMIN
            4 CONTINUE
      *-------------------------------------------------------------------
      * Formats
      *
         10 FORMAT(T13,A4,T21,A4,T29,F5.3,T40,F3.1,T50,I3,T59,'$',F7.2)
      *
         11 FORMAT(T5,'A cost comparison of several combinations of',/,
            + T5,'technicians and machines',//,
            + T5,'Basic Parameters',/,
            +T10,'Downtime loss per machine    = $',F7.2,/,
            +T10,'Total number of machines     = ',I4,/,
            +T10,'Types of technicians:   ',A4,'      or       ',A4,/,
            +T10,'                         ----              ----',/,
            +T10,'   Corresponding wages ',F5.2,'/hr       ',F5.2,'/hr',/,
            +T10,'   and repair rates    ',F5.3,'/hr       ',F5.2,'/hr',//,
            +T10,'Types of machines:       ',A4,'     or     ',A4,/,
            +T10,'                         ----              ----',/
            +T10,'   Fail rates           ',F5.3,'/hr       ',F5.2,'/hr',/)
      *
```

Figure C-1
(concluded)

```
      12 FORMAT(//,T5,'The various cases considered:',/,
        +/,T10,'   Type     Type              Estimate   Optimum    Total  ',
        +/,T10,'    of       of     Traffic  of No. of    Number   Downtime',
        +/,T10,'  Worker  Machine Intensty Technicians Required    Cost  ',
        +/,T10,'  ------  ------- -------- ----------   --------   -------')
         STOP
         END
*======================================================================
         SUBROUTINE MIN(A,N,AMIN,IMIN)
         REAL A(3:N)
*
*  Finds the minimum element of the array A() starting from A(3).
*
         IMIN = 3
         AMIN = A(3)
         DO 1 I = 4,15
            IF(A(I) .LT. AMIN)THEN
               AMIN = A(I)
               IMIN = I
            ENDIF
       1 CONTINUE
         RETURN
         END
*======================================================================
         SUBROUTINE FACTR(TAU,R,N,P)
*
*  Uses Equation (C.2) to compute the probabilities of R down machines.
*
         INTEGER R
         REAL P(0:N)
*
         P(0) = 1.
         DO 1 I = 0,R-1
            P(I+1) = TAU*(N-I)/(I+1.)*P(I)
       1 CONTINUE
         DO 2 I = R,N-1
            P(I+1) = TAU*(N-I)/R*P(I)
       2 CONTINUE
         RETURN
         END
```

A cost comparison of several combinations of
repairmen and machines

Basic Parameters
    Downtime loss per machine   = $ 250.00
    Total number of machines   =   70

Types of technicians:	fast	or	slow
	----		----
Corresponding wages	17.95/hr		14.00/hr
and repair rates	0.400/hr		0.35/hr
Types of machines:	good	or	poor
	----		----
Fail rates	0.033/hr		0.04/hr

The various cases considered:

Type of Worker	Type of Machine	Traffic Intensty	Estimate of No. of Technicians	Optimum Number Required	Total Downtime Cost
fast	good	0.082	5.8	9	$1526.84
fast	poor	0.094	6.6	10	$1714.34
slow	good	0.095	6.7	11	$1684.42
slow	poor	0.109	7.6	12	$1893.17

Programming Problem C-A: Chemical Engineering:
Compressibility Factors for Real Gases

In this problem a series of data tables will be generated and then graphed
on the computer. In one application a simple table of numbers will be plotted using an adaptation of the printer plot subroutine of Figure 7-8. In a
more complicated application, you will need to use additional library software to plot the tables on either a plotter or your printer.

As mentioned in Programming Problem B-C, it is important for
chemical engineers to understand the properties of real gases in contrast
to ideal gases. There have been numerous attempts to formulate equations
of state for a substance that would accurately represent the properties of
the gas over a broad range. The Beattie–Bridgeman equation is a complicated empirical fit to the data and is accurate as long as the gas is far from
the liquid state. This equation is

$$p = \frac{Z_0^{-1}t}{v}(1 - \epsilon)\left(1 + \frac{B}{v}\right) - \frac{AZ_0^{-2}}{v^2} \tag{C.5}$$

where p, v, and t are the so-called reduced pressure, volume, and temperature; that is, the actual pressure, volume, and temperature are related to p,
v, and t by

$$p = \frac{P}{P_c} \qquad v = \frac{V}{V_c} \qquad t = \frac{T}{T_c}$$

and P_c, V_c, and T_c are the critical point values that are tabulated for each
gas. (See also Programming Problem B-C.) Also,

$$Z_0 = \frac{P_c V_c}{RT_c}$$

P = Pressure (Pa)

T = Temperature (K)

v = Molar volume (m^3/mol)

R = Ideal gas constant = 8.314 J/mol-K

$A = A_0(1 - a/v)$

$B = B_0(1 - b/v)$

$\epsilon = c/vt^3$

and A_0, B_0, a, b, and c are the five experimental parameters in the equation
that depend upon the specific gas in question.

A quantity frequently used in chemical engineering problems is the compressibility of a gas defined as

$$Z = \frac{pv}{t} Z_0 \qquad\qquad (C.6)$$

which for an ideal gas would be constant and equal to 1. For a real gas this quantity is then a measure of the deviation of the real gas from the ideal and is useful in isolating thermodynamic regions where the ideal gas equation may or may not be used; that is, when $Z \approx 1$ we would expect the real gas to mimic the ideal gas in all of its features and that the simpler ideal gas equation may be used in place of the more complicated Beattie–Bridgeman equation. The purpose of this problem is to generate a table of Z versus P, which can then be used in this manner.

Problem Specifics. Your program should do the following:

1. Ask the user which of the five gases is to be used and then read the Beattie–Bridgeman parameters for that particular gas from a previously created data file. Use character variables for the names of the gases. The parameters are listed in Table C-2.
2. For the first calculation use a temperature of $T = 1.1T_c$.
3. For 61 values of the volume from $v = v_{lo}$ to $v = v_{hi}$ in equally spaced steps, compute the pressure P and compressibility Z and store in arrays P(5,0:60), Z(5,0:60) for each of the five gases in Table C-2.
4. Repeat step 3 for $T = 1.2T_c$, $1.5T_c$, $2.0T_c$, and $5.0T_c$.
5. For one of the two applications below, plot the results:

   Application I: Adapt the subroutine PLOT of Figure 7-8 to plot the contents of the array P(5,I) $i = 0,60$ by producing five simultaneous graphs versus the volume. Use different symbols for each of the five curves. Also, use this subroutine to plot a second graph of Z versus volume.

   Application II: What the engineer is actually interested in is a plot of Z versus P, not Z versus V. What we have at the moment are five sets of Z and P values—we do not have a direct

Table C-2

Input parameters for use in the problem to compute the compressibility factors of real gases

Gas	Critical Point Values			Beattie–Bridgeman Parameters						Volume Limits	
	T_c	P_c	V_c	A_0	a	B_0	b	c	Z_0	V_{lo}	V_{hi}
Air	132.78	37.7E5	8.30E-5	0.408	0.232	0.555	−0.132	0.223	0.283	1.00	25.0
Carbon dioxide (CO_2)	304.44	73.9E5	9.43E-5	0.585	0.757	1.111	0.768	0.248	0.275	1.00	25.0
Oxygen (O_2)	154.44	50.8E5	7.43E-5	0.465	0.345	0.623	0.057	0.175	0.294	1.00	25.0
Hydrogen (H_2)	33.22	13.0E5	6.49E-5	0.340	−0.078	0.323	−0.671	0.212	0.305	1.00	25.0
Ammonia (NH_3)	405.56	112.8E5	7.24E-5	0.240	2.353	0.472	2.640	0.987	0.242	1.00	25.0

relationship between the two. And since the pressure values are not equally spaced, it is not easy to have a subroutine like PLOT produce a graph. However, given two sets of numbers, many software packages that will automatically plot one versus the other are available. These packages come in two types: (1) a FORTRAN subroutine that is called in the main program to automatically plot an array y_i versus x_i on special paper; and (2) special non-FORTRAN software packages that will read a data file created by your program that contains the sets of numbers to be plotted and then produce a graph. Thus, you will have to determine the local procedures for plotting a graph in your computing environment and adapt them to produce five simultaneous plots of Z versus P.

Programming Problem C-B: Minimum of a Multidimensional Array or Function

The procedures given in Section 4.3 for finding the minimum of a function $f(x)$ or a list of numbers is easily implemented provided the search is only in one direction (e.g., along the x direction or down the list). The problem is considerably more complicated, however, if several independent variables are involved. A moderately simple, though somewhat inefficient, procedure is to construct an algorithm along the following lines: Consider a set of numbers that are a function of two variables or indices. The set can be thought of as a rectangular array, a_{ij}. Pick a starting point anywhere within the array and examine a_{ij} and the neighboring points in the array. If the minimum of these nine values is a_{ij}, we have found a local minimum. If not, replace a_{ij} by the minimum of the set and repeat the procedure for this new point in the array. This process is continued until a minimum is found or until an edge of the array is reached. The idea is illustrated on the rectangular set of numbers in Figure C-2.

Figure C-2
Illustration of a stepping procedure that can be used to find the minimum of a two-dimensional array of numbers

9	9	8	7	6	5	4	4	5	7	8	9
8	8	7	6	5	4	3	3	5	7	8	7
7	7	6	5	4	3	2	3	4	5	7	6
7	6	5	4	4	3	2	1	2	4	6	7
8	7	6	5	4	4	2	1	0	2	5	6
9	8	7	6	5	4	2	1	1	2	4	5
9	9	8	7	6	5	3	2	1	1	2	4
9	8	7	7	6	6	5	4	2	2	3	5

The algorithm to find the maximum of a function of two (or more) variables proceeds in a similar manner:

Define a starting point (x_0, y_0)
Initialize the minimum
    $(x_{min}, y_{min}) = (x_0, y_0)$
    $f_{min} = f(x_{min}, y_{min})$
    and step sizes dx, dy
    For Step = 1,MAX
        For i_x = −1,0,+1 and
        For i_y = −1,0,+1, but not both zero
            $x = x_{min} + i_x dx$
            $y = y_{min} + i_y dy$
            IF(x is outside bounds)THEN
                $x = x_{min}$
            IF(y is outside bounds)THEN
                $y = y_{min}$
            ENDIF
            IF($f(x,y) < f_{min}$)THEN
                redefine the minimum
                    $(x_{min}, y_{min}) = (x,y)$
                    $f_{min} = f(x_{min}, y_{min})$
          ENDIF
        End i_x, i_y loop
        IF $[(x_{min}, y_{min}) = (x_0, y_0)$, i.e., no change]THEN
            The point is a local minimum, so reduce
            the step size, dx = dx/5, dy = dy/5
        ELSE
            Test for convergence $[(x_{min}-x_0)^2 + (y_{min}-y_0)^2] < \epsilon$
        ENDIF
    End step loop

Problem Specifics. Use the outline above to construct a subroutine to find the minimum value of a function of two variables. Then write a program to use this subroutine to find the optimum design of a water-carrying trough. The trough is to be made from a strip of sheet metal of width $d = 30$ cm. The edges will be bent up to angles θ to form sides of length t. Both sides are identical. (See Figure C-3.)

To maximize the capacity of the trough, we wish to find the value of both t and θ that will maximize the cross-sectional area, $A(t,\theta)$, which is given by

$$A(t,\theta) = (d - 2t)t \sin \theta + t^2 \sin \theta \cos \theta \qquad (C.7)$$

Your program should use the starting values $(t_0, \theta_0) = (d/5, \pi/4)$. The program should be limited to 5,000 steps and stop when the distance between two successive points is $\leq \epsilon = 10^{-5}$. Also, a warning diagnostic

Figure C-3
Water-carrying
trough formed from
sheet metal

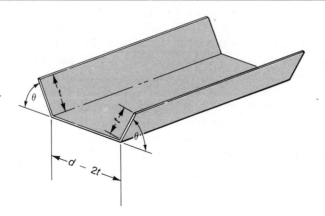

should be printed if the edge of the physical region is reached; that is, $0 \le t \le d/2$ and $0 \le \theta \le \pi/2$. If successful, the program should print the optimum values of t and θ and the current step sizes along with the optimum area.

By the way, the analytical solution, easily obtained by methods of advanced calculus, is $(t_{min}, \theta_{min}) = (d/3, \pi/3)$.

Programming Problem C-C: Mechanical Engineering:
Cooling Fins on a Steam Pipe

The heat from a steam pipe is more effectively transferred to its surroundings by the addition of metal radiator fins. The fins are heated by the pipe, and because of their large surface area can efficiently transfer heat by radiation and convection to the surrounding air. To simplify the analysis, we will assume that the steam pipe is square and that the fin is rectangular, as shown in Figure C-4.

Figure C-4
Steam pipe
surrounded by a
radiator fin
(distances are in
meters)

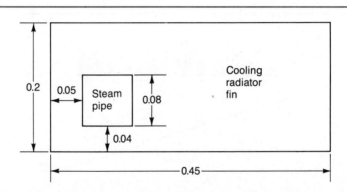

The first step in determining the heat transfer is to compute the temperature distribution $T(x, y)$ across the area of the fin. This computation is ordinarily a complex mathematical problem requiring sophisticated techniques. However, the algorithm for a numerical solution is quite transparent and is based on some simple ideas concerning temperature and heat flow.

A fundamental property of heat flow is that of diffusion. A hot or cold spot will smooth or average out in time, and the final temperature distribution will be the smoothest possible distribution consistent with the constraints of the problem. For example, if a metal bar has one end in ice water (0° C) and the other end in boiling water (100° C) and the rest of the bar is insulated, the final temperature distribution in the bar will be simple linear decrease across the length of the bar. (See Figure C-5.)

Notice that the final temperature at any point x_0 in the bar is the average of points equally spaced to the left and the right. This idea of the final temperature being the average of neighboring points is the hallmark of a diffusion process and can easily be extended to more than one dimension. It is simple to adapt the principle to our radiator fin problem. First, superimpose a two-dimensional grid (called the mesh) over the fin and pipe (Figure C-6) and assign an initial guess for the temperature at each point in the grid, T_{i_x, i_y} for $i_x = 0$ to 45 and $i_y = 0$ to 20. Then using these values, for every point on the fin, compute the average of the temperatures of its four nearest neighboring points.

$$T_{i_x, i_y}^{\text{new}} = (T_{i_x+1, i_y} + T_{i_x-1, i_y} + T_{i_x, i_y+1} + T_{i_x, i_y-1})/4 \tag{C.8}$$

These values are compared with the original set, and if convergence has not been achieved the procedure is repeated. The same algorithm can be used to find the temperature distribution on an airplane wing or on a thin semiconductor wafer.

Problem Specifics. Write a program to solve for the temperature distribution on the radiator fin and to execute a contour printer plot of the results (see Section 7.6). The principal elements of such a program are as follows:

Figure C-5
Equilibrium
temperature
distribution in a bar

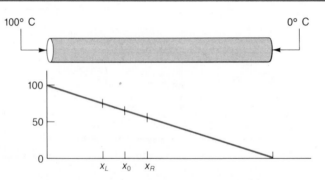

Figure C-6
Mesh used for the
radiator fin problem

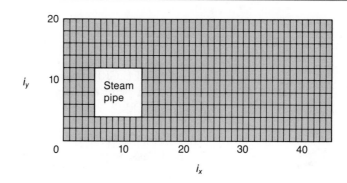

- The value of the temperature at the edges of the fin and inside the pipe should be initialized via a DATA statement using implied DO loops. (Use $T_{steam} = 180°$ C, $T_{air} = 20°$ C.)
- For all interior grid points, start with an initial guess of $T_{ij}^{old} = 50$.
- Write a subroutine AVG(NX,NY,TOLD,TNEW,DELTA) to compute a new set of interior temperatures, T_{ij}^{new}, using Equation (C.8). The subroutine should also compute

$$\Delta = \frac{1}{N} \sum_{i=0}^{45} \sum_{j=0}^{20} |T_{ij}^{new} - T_{ij}^{old}| \tag{C.9}$$

where N is the total number of interior points.
- Write a subroutine GRID that will produce a contour plot of the final temperatures on the radiator fin. An outline of this subroutine would be:

```
SUBROUTINE GRID(T,NX,NY)
REAL T(0:NX,0:NY)
CHARACTER*1 FIN(0:45,0:20),DIGIT(0:9),BLANK
DATA DIGIT,BLANK/'0','1','2','3','4','5','6',
+     '7','8','9',' '
Call a Subroutine MINMAX to find and print the
      minimum/maximum elements of T.
    For all interior points
      let k = 50(Tij − Tmin)/(Tmax − Tmin)
      IF(k is divisible by 5; [K/5*5 .eq. K])THEN
          FINij = DIGIT(k)
      ELSE
          FINij = BLANK
      ENDIF
    For outside boundary FINij = '*'
    For inside boundary and inside pipe FINij = 'X'
RETURN
```

- In the main program:

  For Pass = 1, 50
   CALL AVG to compute δ
   IF ($\delta < \epsilon = 10^{-2}$) THEN
    CALL GRID
    and print δ, and Pass
    STOP
   ENDIF
   Print "Excessive iterations Diagnostic"
  End Pass loop

- Repeat the entire calculation with the bottom edge of the radiator fin in ice water.

Programming Problem C-D: Nim

At this point we will take some time out from engineering programs to write a program strictly for fun—well, maybe not exclusively for fun. In the event you decide to leave engineering, you could possibly make your fortune writing computer games. As a first step along such a path, you are invited to write an interactive program to play (and win!) the game of nim (Problem 1.5).[1]

The game consists of placing any number of counters (say, less than 10) in any number of rows (say, less than 6). Each player then alternately removes any nonzero number of counters from any one row. The player removing the last counter is the winner. The winning strategy can be found in Chapter 1. A sketch of the program, which will consist of numerous calls to subroutines, is given in Figure C-7. The output from your program should consist of the complete dialogue between the computer and the player for one play of the game.

One conclusion you will reach from this problem is that the actual algorithm in a computer game is almost always a minor part of the complete code. The dominant part of the code is concerned with input and output.

---

[1]Professor E.U. Condon, then a scientist at Westinghouse Research Labs., designed and constructed a rudimentary computer that would play the game of nim for display at the 1939 World's Fair in New York City. This device was one of the many technological highlights of the fair.

Figure C-7 _____

Outline of the nim program

```
PROGRAM NIM
    CALL INTRO  ─⎡Displays instructions to the player, asks for how many rows and how many
               ⎢counters in each row; checks for zeros and negatives, and asks "Who goes
               ⎣first?" Assign PLAYER = 1 for player's move, 0 for computer's move.

    CALL DISPLA─⎡Prints the current arrangement of "X"-s by rows.
    MOVEP = 0
    MOVEC = 0
    For Pass = 1,20
        IF(Player = 1)THEN
            Ask player for move
            CALL ALTER─⎡Rearranges the number of X-s in each row accordingly.

            CALL CHECK─⎡Checks the current arrangement to see if it is
                       ⎢a winning combination. If it is, let SETUP = 1;
                       ⎣if not, SETUP = 0.

            IF (Setup = 1)THEN
                    Print congratulatory message
            ELSE
                    Print derogatory message No. MOVEP. (i.e.,
                        a different message every time this occurs).
            ENDIF
            MOVEP  = MOVEP + 1
            PLAYER = 0
        ELSE
            IF(MOVEP = 0)Print derogatory message indicating bad choice

            CALL MYMOVE─⎡Computes the optimum move according to the winning
                        ⎢strategy. If a winning move is not possible, execute
                        ⎣a stalling move.

            CALL ALTER
            MOVEC  = MOVEC + 1
            PLAYER = 1
        ENDIF
        CALL DISPLAY

        CALL ENDGAM ─⎡Determines whether the game has ended
                     ⎢(FINIS = 1) and who has won (WINNER = 1
                     ⎣for player, 0 for the computer).

        IF(FINIS = 1)THEN
            IF(WINNER = 1)Print incredulous remark and stop.
            IF(WINNER = 0)Print nasty comment and stop.
        ENDIF
        Print "Excessive number of steps" Diagnostic
    End - Pass loop
```

Nonnumerical Applications: Character Variables

8.1 Introduction

Nonnumerical applications of computers, such as graphics and word processing, are the areas of computer science growing most rapidly. Even though engineers use computers primarily to solve mathematical problems or to analyze numerical data, they are increasingly finding the character manipulation abilities of the computer to be of significant value in their work. This chapter deals with applications of character variables in a variety of situations, such as sorting a list of names or plotting a graph on the printer or terminal screen.

The basic properties of character-type variables, originally introduced in Section 2.2, are reviewed in the first section and are followed by a description of the procedures for characterizing substring elements of a larger character string, for scanning a character string for the occurrence of a particular substring, and for combining two or more character strings into a single character string.

The principal operation involving character variables is that of comparison: two character strings are compared using an IF test to determine whether the strings are the same or whether one string has a *value* greater than or less than the other. In Section 8.6 it is explained how, for example, the binary value for the symbol 'A' is less than that of the symbol 'B' and how this property of character constants can be used to rearrange or to alphabetize a list of names.

8.2 Review of Character Variables

A variable is defined to be of type CHARACTER with a length of (integer) characters by a statement

CHARACTER name$_1$*⟨sl$_1$⟩, name$_2$*⟨sl$_2$⟩, ...

or

$$\text{CHARACTER} * \langle sl \rangle \quad name_1, name_2, name_3, \ldots$$

where $\langle sl_1 \rangle$, $\langle sl_2 \rangle$, ... are the lengths of the character strings to be stored in the variables $name_1$, $name_2$, $name_3$, ... In the second statement, all the variable names have a common string length of $\langle sl \rangle$. For example,

```
CHARACTER*5 METAL, OXIDE, ACID(6)     All are of length five.
CHARACTER GAS(5)*6, SYMBOL(8)*1       Each of the five
                                      elements of GAS
                                      is of length six.
```

These variables may then be assigned *values*, which must be a sequence of characters.

Assignment Statement	Value Stored
METAL = 'Steel'	S t e e l
OXIDE = 'Al3O2'	A l 3 O 2
ACID(1) = 'H2CO3'	H 2 C O 3
GAS(1) = 'Neon'	N e o n ☐ ☐

If the value assigned is shorter than the declared length of the variable, the remaining space is filled with blanks.

ACID(2) = 'H2S'	H 2 S ☐ ☐

If the value assigned is longer than the declared length of the variable, the value is truncated from the right until it fits the length of the variable.

SYMBOL(1) = 'Cl'	C
SYMBOL(2) = GAS(1)	N
GAS(2) = SYMBOL(2)	N ☐ ☐ ☐ ☐ ☐

These values may be compared in IF tests, as shown in Table 8-1. Character variables are input and output with the A format.

```
WRITE(*,'(T5,A5)')METAL
```

or

```
WRITE(*,'(T5,A)')METAL
```

Remember that character variables contain coded values for symbols and can never be used in any arithmetic expressions.

```
CHARACTER M*5
INTEGER N
N =  3 + 4       N contains the numerical value 7.
M = '3 + 4'      M contains the symbols '3 + 4'.
```

8.3 Character Substrings

The result of an assignment statement involving a character variable is to store in the variable a set of symbols in a so-called string. A character string may be any length from one to several thousand characters. It is often necessary to access parts of a long string. The parts of a complete string are called *substrings*. The form of a reference to a character substring is shown in Figure 8-1.

For example, if a character variable ABCS is defined as

```
CHARACTER ABCS*26
ABCS = 'abcdefghijklmnopqrstuvwxyz'
```

Table 8-1

Testing for equality of character strings

Comparison	Value of Comparison	Comments
IF(METAL .EQ. 'Steel')	(true)	
IF(METAL .EQ. 'STEEL')	(false)	Lower- and uppercase different characters.
IF('Neon'.EQ. GAS(1))	(true)	The shorter string 'Neon' is extended with blanks to match the length of the longer string GAS(1) before the comparison.
IF(SYMBOL(1).EQ. 'Cl')	(false)	Compares C with C l

Figure 8-1 _____
Character substring
reference

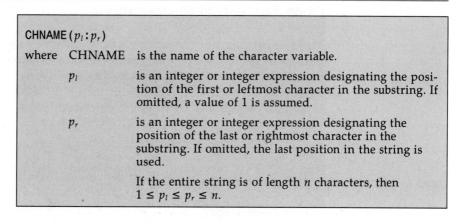

CHNAME$(p_l:p_r)$

where   CHNAME   is the name of the character variable.

p_l is an integer or integer expression designating the position of the first or leftmost character in the substring. If omitted, a value of 1 is assumed.

p_r is an integer or integer expression designating the position of the last or rightmost character in the substring. If omitted, the last position in the string is used.

If the entire string is of length n characters, then $1 \leq p_l \leq p_r \leq n$.

then the references to a substring might be

Substring Reference	Value
ABCS(1:2)	'ab'
ABCS(3:6)	'cdef'
ABCS(:4)	'abcd'
ABCS(20:)	'tuvwxyz'
ABCS(4:4)	'd'
ABCS(:)	Same as ABCS—that is, the entire string

If the character variable itself is a dimensioned array, then substrings of each array element may be referenced in a similar manner. A particular element in the array is given first, followed by the specification of the substring in that element. For example, if character arrays are declared and assigned values as

```
CHARACTER NAME(6)*8, ADDRESS(0:5)*26, A*2
NAME(2) = 'Jones'
ADDRESS(0) = '1442 State St., Boston, MA'
```

then the statement

```
A = NAME(2)(2:3)
```

would assign to A the value of the second and third characters in the second element of the array NAME, that is, the value 'on'. And the statement

```
ADDRESS(0)(6:10) = 'Main'
```

would replace the substring 'State' by 'Main'. Notice that 'Main' is first extended to length 5 before the assignment.

Just as with an array, you must make sure that the substring specifications are within the bounds of the complete character string. If p_l is less than 1 or p_r is greater than the length of the string, an execution error will result.

8.4 Intrinsic Functions Used in Character Substring Operations

Many applications of character variables involve searching a string for a particular substring and then performing a replacement. Two intrinsic functions designed for use in such situations, LEN, which determines the length of a string, and INDEX, which scans a longer string for the occurrence of a particular substring, are described below.

Length of a String: Function LEN

The FORTRAN function LEN simply returns the length of the character string that is the argument of the function.

```
LEN(string)
```

Some examples are

```
CHARACTER A*4,B*5
INTEGER I,K,M,N
A = '1234'
B = 'Name'
I = LEN(A)
K = LEN(B)

M = LEN(A(2:4))

N = LEN(A)/LEN('abc')
```

Value assigned to I is 4.

Value assigned to K is 5. The value stored in B is | N | a | m | e | | .

Value assigned to M is 3. The length of the substring is (4 − 2) + 1.

LEN('abc') is 3, so N is assigned the value 1.

Location of a Substring: Function INDEX

The FORTRAN function

```
INDEX(string,substring)
```

will return the position of the substring within the string. Both entries in the argument list must be of type CHARACTER. If the second character string in the argument list occurs as a substring in the first, the result is an integer corresponding to the starting position of the substring within the first named string. If a match is not found, including the case where the substring is larger than the string, the value returned is zero. If there is more than one match within the string, only the starting position of the first occurrence is given. For example,

```
CHARACTER ABCS*26,A*1,B*2
ABCS = 'abcdefghijklmnopqrstuvwxyz'
A    = 'a'
B    ='b'
I = INDEX(ABCS,A)
```

Note, stored in B, is | b | | .

Value assigned to I is 1.

```
J = INDEX(ABCS,'c')        Value assigned to J is 3.
K = INDEX(ABCS,'def')      Value assigned to K is 4.
L = INDEX(ABCS,B)          Value assigned to L is 0; the substring b
                           is not contained in ABCS.
ABCS(INDEX(ABCS,'p'):INDEX(ABCS,'r') = '**********'
                           The positions p through r are replaced
                           with asterisks. Notice the string on
                           the right is truncated.
```

8.5 Character Expressions: Concatenation

The only character-string operation provided in FORTRAN is called *concatenation*, which means joining together. If S_1 and S_2 are two character strings of length n_1 and n_2, respectively, then the concatenation of S_1 and S_2 is effected by the operator // (two slashes, interpreted as a single symbol). Thus,

$$S_1//S_2$$

has a value of a string of length $n_1 + n_2$, consisting of the two individual strings joined into one. For example,

```
CHARACTER*10 NAME1,NAME2
NAME1 = 'John Smith'
NAME2 = NAME1(6:)//','//NAME1( :4)
```

Successive concatenations proceed from left to right, so

```
NAME →  S m i t h , J o h n
```

The code to read a list of names in the form first name, middle initial, last name and to store them last name first would then be

```
        CHARACTER*30, XX, NAME(100)
        INTEGER DOT,LAST,I
        I = 1
        DO 1 I = 1,100
            READ(*,'(A)',END=99)XX
*
*           Scan the name and find the location of
*           the period after the middle initial
*
        DOT  = INDEX(XX,'.')
*
*           While the end of the name is the
*           occurrence of two successive blanks
        LAST = INDEX(XX,'  ') - 1
        NAME(I) = XX(DOT+2:LAST)//',
                  '//XX( :DOT)
     1  CONTINUE
```

8.6 Comparing Character Strings

Relative Sequencing of Character Values

Associated with each character on your computer is a binary code. Because this binary code has a numerical value, the "values" associated with individual characters can be compared. This feature has already been used in comparisons that determine whether or not two strings are identical:

$$\text{IF}\,(\text{string}_1\ \text{.EQ.}\ \text{string}_2)\,\text{THEN}$$

Additionally, the binary code for symbols 'A', 'B', ..., 'Z' has been set up so that the value of 'A' is less than the value of 'B', is less than the value of 'C', and so on. The same relative arrangement exists among the lowercase letters; and the value of any uppercase letter is less than the value of any lowercase letter. Furthermore, the value of a blank is less than the value of any letter.[1] This hierarchy permits a variety of comparisons of character strings that can then be used to rearrange or to alphabetize a list of names. A few examples of such comparisons are shown in Table 8-2. Once again, if the character variables being compared are of unequal length, the shorter variable is extended by adding blanks to the right before the comparison.

You may occasionally need to compare digits with letters, as in ('A1' .GT. 'Aa'). Since the relative ordering of digits and letters has not been standardized in FORTRAN, the result of such a comparison is unpredictable. However, there is a FORTRAN intrinsic function that will tell you what ordering of characters is used at your computer center: the function CHAR(I). The range of I values is also system-dependent and may take some experimenting to determine. On my computer the allowed range of I is from 0 to 255 and the function CHAR(I) returns a single character for each value of I in this range. Thus CHAR(0) returns the character ⟨blank space⟩, meaning that this character has the smallest binary value of

Table 8-2
Comparing the values of character strings

Comparison Expression	Value	Comments
('A' .LE. 'G')	⟨true⟩	
('AA' .LE. 'A ')	⟨false⟩	Blank < 'A' so A A > A
('Aa' .LE. 'AA')	⟨false⟩	'a' > 'A' so A a > A A
('Jones'.LE.'Jonez')	⟨true⟩	

[1] Unfortunately, the relative order of the digits is *not* standard in FORTRAN. Depending on the local system, the values associated with the symbols representing the digits may be greater or less than the values associated with the alphabet.

all the allowed symbols. Printing out all the remaining 255 defined symbols by means of the function CHAR will then establish their relative ordering.

```
        DO 1 I = 0,255
            WRITE(*,'(T5,I3,T10,A1)')I,CHAR(I)
    1   CONTINUE
```

If you try this on your computer, you may have to alter the limits of the DO loop to find the location of the commonly used symbols.

The inverse of the function CHAR is the intrinsic function ICHAR( ). The argument of this function is a single character, and the function returns the local sequencing number associated with that character on your computer. Thus, on all computers the value of ICHAR('') will be zero. On my computer the value of ICHAR('A') is 65, whereas ICHAR('Z') is 90 and ICHAR('a') is 97.

Using Sorting Algorithms to Alphabetize a List

In Section 7.6 several procedures for sequencing a list of numbers were discussed. Since we now have the ability to compare character strings, we can use these same procedures to alphabetize a list of names. Thus, scanning a list of names to find the minimum might determine the minimum "value" to be 'Aardvark,' and this name would be put at the top of the list.

Then, to use the subroutines of Chapter 7 to collate a list of names, two steps need to be addressed:

1. The dummy array name that contains the information that is to be sorted must be changed from type REAL to type CHARACTER.
2. The string length of the data items in the dummy array in the subroutine must be made to match the length of the names in the actual data set.

Character Variables as Dummy Variables in an Argument List

When transferring a character variable to a subroutine, two rules that relate to the length of the character string must also be considered:

1. The length of the dummy character variable in the subroutine argument list must not be greater than the length of the actual variable being transferred into the subroutine. For example,

```
        PROGRAM MANE
        CHARACTER*8 NAMES(10)
        CALL SORT(NAMES,10)
            .
            .
            .
        END
```

```
        SUBROUTINE SORT(A,N)
        CHARACTER A(N)*10
                  .
                  .
                  .
        RETURN
        END
```

would effect a valid and complete transfer of the array NAMES. If the secondary type statement were instead CHARACTER A (N)*9, only the first nine characters of the elements of the array NAMES would be transferred. However, if it were CHARACTER A(N)*11, a compilation error would be generated. The length of the dummy array cannot itself be specified as a dummy variable, as

```
        SUBROUTINE SORT(A,N,L)
        CHARACTER A(N)*L            Error: String length cannot be
                                    specified by a variable.
```

However, there is an alternative in FORTRAN that accomplishes the same thing.

2. The length specification of a dummy character variable may be made adjustable in the following manner:

```
        SUBROUTINE BBB(A,B,N)
        CHARACTER A(N)*(*), B*(*)
```

In this situation the string length of the dummy variable B and all the elements of the dummy array A are set equal to the declared length of the actual arguments that appear in the CALL statement. [The specification (*) once again refers to a default value.] Thus,

```
        SUBROUTINE SORT(A,N)
        CHARACTER A(N)*(*)
```

will accommodate an input array of any previously declared length.

Subroutine Using a Pointer to Alphabetize a List

In the most common situation, numerous other data items, such as ADDRESS( ), PHONE( ), GRADES( ), and so on, will be associated with each name. To avoid rearranging each of these arrays as well, an algorithm employing a pointer can be used. The subroutine of Figure 7-6 may be rewritten for this purpose. The result is shown in Figure 8-2. In this subroutine the dummy character array NAME is declared to be of adjustable string length. However, the local variable MIN, which is used to tempo-

Figure 8-2
Subroutine to
alphabetize a list of
names using a
pointer

```
      SUBROUTINE COLLAT(NAME,INDEX,N)
*
*  The array NAMES is sorted in alphabetic order and is
*  not destroyed.  The proper sequence of elements will
*  be contained in the array INDEX. Thus, NAME(Index(1))
*  NAME(Index(n)) will be the first and last elements
*  of the reordered array.  The array INDEX must be
*  declared in the calling program, but it will be
*  assigned values in this subroutine.  The dummy array
*  containing the names is type declared to be of
*  adjustable string length.
*
      INTEGER N,INDEX(N),TOP,TEMP
      CHARACTER NAME(N)*(*),MIN*20
*
*  First initialize the array INDEX to the sequence 1
*  to N.
*
      DO 1 I = 1,N
         INDEX(I) = I
 1    CONTINUE
*
      DO 3 TOP = 1, N-1
*
*         The value INDEX(TOP) refers to the element of
*         X that is at the top of the remaining unsorted
*         list.  Initialize MIN to be the top name.
*
         MIN = NAME(INDEX(TOP))

         DO 2 I = TOP,N
*
            IF(X(INDEX(I)) .LT. MIN)THEN
*
*            If a smaller value is found, redefine the
*            pointers; that is, exchange Index-i and
*            Index-top and redefine MIN.
*
               TEMP       = INDEX(I)
               INDEX(I)   = INDEX(TOP)
               INDEX(TOP) = TEMP
               MIN        = NAME(INDEX(TOP))
            ENDIF
 2       CONTINUE
 3    CONTINUE
      RETURN
      END
```

rarily store the minimum name in the remaining list, does not appear
in the argument list of the subroutine and therefore cannot be of adjustable length.

Sample Program That Employs Alphabetic Reordering

In Section 4.6 a program to read a data file containing student exam and
homework scores, compute a final grade, and print the results separately for the students in each of the several colleges in the university was

described. We now return to that project and rewrite the program using some of the FORTRAN techniques developed since then. The addition of FORMAT statements, arrays, subroutines, and, in particular, the ability to alphabetize a list, will substantially improve the original program, which is listed in Figure 4-10. The new program and output are shown in Figure 8-3. The output is the same as it was for the earlier program except that the names are now in alphabetic order and the output was not rearranged by using an editor program.

Figure 8-3 _____

Program ASSIGN for determining grades is rewritten using arrays, formats, and the subroutine COLLAT to alphabetize the names

```
      PROGRAM ASSIGN
*
*     See Figure 4-11 for earlier version and for the data file.
*
      CHARACTER GRADE(30)*1, NAME(30)*10,KOLEGE(3)*15
      INTEGER CLASS(30),COLEGE(30),Q1(30),Q2(30),Q3(30),
     +        HW(30),EXAM(30),TOTAL(30),INDEX(30)
      REAL PERCNT(30)
      DATA KOLEGE/'Arts & Sciences','Engineering','Business '/
*
      OPEN(22,FILE='GRADES')
      REWIND (22)
      OPEN(33,FILE='RESULTS')
*
      DO 1 I = 1,30
         READ(22,*,END=2)NAME(I),CLASS(I),COLEGE(I),Q1(I),
     +                   Q2(I),Q3(I),HW(I),EXAM(I)
         TOTAL(I) = Q1(I)+Q2(I)+Q3(I)+HW(I)+3*EXAM(I)
    1 CONTINUE
    2 N = I - 1
*
      CALL GRADER(TOTAL,GRADE,PERCNT,N)
      CALL COLLAT(NAME,INDEX,N)
*
      DO 4 K = 1,3
         WRITE(33,10)KOLEGE(K)
         DO 3 I = 1,N
            M = INDEX(I)
            IF(COLEGE(M) .EQ. K)THEN
               WRITE(33,11)NAME(M),Q1(M),Q2(M),Q3(M),HW(M),
     +                     EXAM(M),PERCNT(M),GRADE(M)
            ENDIF
    3    CONTINUE
    4 CONTINUE
      STOP
*------------------------------------------------------------
* Formats
   10 FORMAT(/,T5,50('-'),/,
     +    T5,'For students in the college of ',A,/,
     +    T5,'          Hour quizzes Home Final Tot.      '/,
     +    T5,'Name         1  2  3  work exam pct. Grade'/,
     +    T5,'---------    -- -- -- ---- ---- ---- -----')
   11 FORMAT(T5,A,T15,3I4,T29,I3,2X,I3,3X,F4.1,T47,A1)
      END
*============================================================
      SUBROUTINE GRADER(TOT,GRADE,PCT,N)
```

Figure 8-3
(concluded)

```
*
*  This subroutine computes the percent score for
*  each student and from it a letter grade.
*
       REAL PCT(N)
       INTEGER TOT(N)
       CHARACTER GRADE(N)*1,LETTR(5)*1
       DATA LETTR/'A','B','C','D','F'/
          DO 2 I = 1,N
               PCT(I) = 100.*TOT(I)/700.
               GRADE(I) = 'F'
               DO 1 L = 4,1,-1
                   CUT = 100. - L*10.
                   IF(PCT(I) .GT. CUT)THEN
                       GRADE(I) = LETTR(L)
                   ENDIF
1              CONTINUE
2          CONTINUE
       RETURN
       END
*============================================================
       SUBROUTINE COLLAT(NAME,INDEX,N)
*    ......
       END
```

For students in the college of Arts & Sciences

Name	Hour quizzes 1	2	3	Home work	Final exam	Tot. pct.	Grade
Greeley	95	92	91	30	85	80.4	B
McDermitt	71	65	66	61	69	67.1	D
Novak	66	50	59	66	62	61.0	D
Strauss	91	96	93	88	94	92.9	A

For students in the college of Engineering

Name	Hour quizzes 1	2	3	Home work	Final exam	Tot. pct.	Grade
Reeves	71	65	80	80	72	73.1	C
Taylor	66	75	77	67	82	75.9	C

For students in the college of Business

Name	Hour quizzes 1	2	3	Home work	Final exam	Tot. pct.	Grade
Brown	71	80	77	65	73	73.1	C
Cassidy	82	71	88	56	71	72.9	C
Chen	77	75	80	86	83	81.0	B
Hunsicher	82	89	91	75	84	84.1	B
Levy	61	68	60	42	57	57.4	F
Nelson	91	86	94	92	91	90.9	A
Stephenson	45	60	62	21	51	48.7	F
Wilson	71	65	82	80	77	75.6	C

Summary

Techniques for manipulating character strings are rapidly becoming one of the basic skills expected of a FORTRAN programmer. Since character strings cannot be part of an arithmetic expression, most applications are built around either the comparison of strings or the combination of two strings into one.

Character strings can be compared using IF statements. Each character available to the input/output devices connected to a FORTRAN program is associated with an integer code that is constructed so that the code for 'A' has a value less than that for 'B', and so on. Additionally, '0' is less than '1', and 'A' is less than 'a'. Thus, in addition to tests for equality, character strings, like ordinary numbers, may be compared for relative ordering. Using this property, a list of names can be alphabetized by making minor changes to a variety of sorting algorithms. When comparing two character strings, remember that the strings are first adjusted to be of the same length by padding the shorter with blanks to the right. Also, most compilers will use only the first few (6 to 10) characters when comparing long character strings.

A segment of a character string (a character substring) stored in a character variable may be referenced by using the variable name followed by parentheses containing integers designating the position of the beginning and end of the substring within the larger string. The integers are separated by a colon. For example, if A = 'name', then A(2:3) has the value 'am'.

Several intrinsic functions related to character variables are available in FORTRAN:

LEN (string)	Simply returns an integer value representing the length of the character string in the parentheses.
INDEX (string$_1$, string$_2$)	Searches the longer string ⟨string$_1$⟩ for the presence of the shorter string ⟨string$_2$⟩ and if present returns the position of the first character of the shorter string. If not present, a value of zero is returned.
CHAR(I)	Returns the ith character in the system-defined collating sequence.
ICHAR(CH)	Returns the position of the single character ⟨CH⟩ in system collating sequence.

Two character strings are combined into one by means of the concatenation operator // (two slashes, interpreted as a single symbol).

If a character variable of a specified length appears in the argument list of a function or subroutine, it must likewise be typed as a character variable in the referenced subprogram. However, in the secondary typing a default symbol, (*), may be used to indicate the string length. The string within the subprogram then assumes the length specified in the calling program unit. A dummy integer variable may not be used to indicate the length of a string. For example,

```
SUBROUTINE SORT(A,N,L)
CHARACTER A(N)*(*)     The elements of A assume the length
                       specified in calling program.
```

but

```
CHARACTER A(N)*L     Error: String length cannot be specified by
                     a variable.
```

Problems

8.1 Starting with the character-variable declaration and initialization statements

```
CHARACTER*5 B,C,D(0:3)
CHARACTER  A*1,E*1,F*2
DATA A,B/'A','12345'/
```

determine the value assigned to variables by means of the assignment statements below:

a. C = A
   E = C
b. F = B(:4)
c. D(0)(3:4) = B(2:3)
d. D(1)(:) = B(:)
e. D(2) = A//F//B(:2)
f. D(3) = B(5:5)//B(4:4)//B(3:3)//B(2:2)//B(1:1)
g. C = A//B

8.2 Write a program to read a character string ending with a period and print the string in reverse order. Assume the length of the string is less than 80 characters.

8.3 Write a program that will read a paragraph consisting of less than 25 lines and count the number of words. Assume that each line is 70 characters long, each line ends with at least two blank spaces, each sentence ends with a period followed by a single blank space, and no words are hyphenated. Also, the paragraph has fewer than 25 sentences and the first line is not indented.

8.4 Write a program to read a document of unknown length and everywhere replace the word "under" by "below." Watch out for compound words.

8.5 Write the code to read the phone book for the name 'Jones, James J.' who lives on 'Jennings St.' and to print the phone number. The phone number in the listing is always in the form XXX-XXXX. (Use the intrinsic function INDEX to locate the various substrings in each line of the phone book.)

8.6 a. Use the function CHAR to determine the collating sequence of all the symbols available on your computer.

    b. Use the function ICHAR to determine the sequencing number associated with 'A', 'Z', 'a', and 'z'.

    c. Use the results of parts a and b and the functions CHAR and ICHAR to write a subroutine that will take a character array LINE(80)*1 representing a line of text and replace all uppercase letters by their corresponding lowercase letters in that line.

8.7 Let each digit of a huge integer (less than 200 digits) be stored, right-adjusted, in the integer array L(200). Write the FORTRAN code to accomplish the following:

    a. If all of the digits of L are multiplied by an integer k, it would be useful to incorporate the normal arithmetic concept of carrying in the multiplication. Thus, if the number 6,715 is stored in L as

L_5	L_4	L_3	L_2	L_1
0	6	7	1	5

and multiplied by 7, the elements of L become

L_5	L_4	L_3	L_2	L_1
0	42	49	7	35

which we would prefer to write as

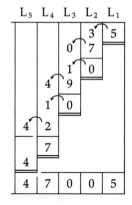

L_5 L_4 L_3 L_2 L_1

4	7	0	0	5

Using the values originally stored in L, determine the output of the following FORTRAN segment for $k = 7$ and $k = 77$ and demonstrate that it accomplishes the task of carrying.

```
      NTERMS = 200
      ICARRY = 0
      DO 1 I = 1,NTERMS
         L(I)   = L(I)*K + ICARRY
         ICARRY = L(I)/10
         L(I)   = L(I) - 10*ICARRY
    1 CONTINUE
```

    b. Write a subroutine that will compute $n!$ exactly for any n less than 100. Note that 99! has 156 digits.

c. Write a subroutine that will take the huge integer stored in L and form a copy of it in the character array DIGIT(200)*1, wherein each element of DIGIT is a numerical symbol from '0' to '9' in place of the numerical values 0 to 9 stored in L. Next, the subroutine should replace all the leading zeros (and only the leading zeros) in DIGIT by blanks and print the final result.

8.8 The following FORTRAN code was used to read a line of text and to produce an encrypted message. Write a similar program to in turn read the encrypted message and reproduce the original message.

```
      PROGRAM CYPHER
      CHARACTER LINE(60)*1
      WRITE(*,*)'Enter line to be scrambled'
      READ(*,'(60A1)')LINE
      ICAP = ICHAR('A')
      ILC  = ICHAR('a')
      DO 1 I = 1,60
         K = ICHAR(LINE(I))
         KK = K
         IF(K .GE. ICAP .AND. K .LE. ICAP+26)THEN
              IF(K-ICAP+5 .LT. 26)THEN
                  KK = K - ICAP + 5   + ILC
              ELSE
                  KK = K - ICAP + 5 - 26 + ILC
              ENDIF
         ELSEIF(K.GE.ILC .AND. K.LE.ILC+26)THEN
              IF(K-ILC+9 .LT. 26)THEN
                  KK = K - ILC + 9  + ICAP
              ELSE
                  KK = K - ILC + 9 -26 + ICAP
              ENDIF
         ENDIF
         LINE(I) = CHAR(KK)
    1    CONTINUE
      WRITE(*,'(T2,50A1)')LINE
      END
```

If the encrypted message is

> ktwywfs JWM rJCQNVJCRLB JAN NJBH, CNGC NMRCRWP RB WXC

determine the original message.

Additional FORTRAN Features

9.1 Introduction

FORTRAN, like any language, contains, in addition to the basic vocabulary and grammar, an extensive collection of features of a more subtle nature that can frequently be useful to the more advanced student. Several of the most commonly used of these specialized FORTRAN topics are described in this chapter; a short description of the remaining FORTRAN features can be found in the extensive list of FORTRAN rules and regulations given in the appendix.

There are, in addition to the familiar data types used to this point (CHARACTER, INTEGER, and REAL), three other possible classifications of variable names. These are DOUBLE PRECISION, COMPLEX, and LOGICAL type variables and constants, which are described in the next section. Included in this discussion is a description of the IMPLICIT statement, which allows you to alter the standard default typing of variable names. Then follows a brief account of two additional mechanisms for assigning values to variables: the PARAMETER statement and the BLOCK DATA subprogram module, along with a summary of the proper sequencing of all of the different types of FORTRAN statements introduced in this text. Next, the DoWhile structure, which is available to students using an *extended* version of FORTRAN, is described. Finally, the properties of commonly used FORTRAN intrinsic functions, including several functions not used to this point, are, for convenience, collectively listed in two tables.

9.2 Additional Data Types Available in FORTRAN

Most programs require only the three data types presented so far: integer, real, and character. But in special situations such as a program plagued by round-off error or a problem involving functions of a complex variable, the types may not be suitable or sufficient. Three additional data types are

312

available in FORTRAN for use in more advanced programming problems: double precision, complex, and logical.

▇▇ Type Double Precision

As you know, because of the finite length of a computer word, the real-number computations done by a computer are only approximate arithmetic. A computer will carry anywhere from 8 to 14 significant digits for each real variable; therefore, every arithmetic operation involves some round-off error, a loss of significant digits. Most of the time the effects of round-off error are relatively harmless, causing inaccuracies in only the last one or two digits of a number. But in some situations round-off error can invalidate a calculation. For example, when subtracting two nearly equal numbers, most of the significant digits will be lost and the accuracy of the result substantially reduced. If the two numbers were A = 1.0000032 and B = 1.0000031, each with eight significant digits, then the difference, C = A − B = 0.0000001 would contain only *one* significant digit. One remedy to a problem such as this would be to declare the variables in question to be of type double precision. In FORTRAN, variables or constants of type double precision contain twice the number of digits as an ordinary real type value. This is accomplished by allotting two internal computer words to each double-precision value. The form of the type statement for these variables is

DOUBLE PRECISION name$_1$, name$_2$, ...

which, like other type statements, is nonexecutable and must appear before the first executable statement.

Double-precision constants with an exponent use the letter D to designate the exponent part of the number instead of the letter E, which is used when writing real numbers; that is, the number 3.51D+06 is type double precision, whereas 3.51E+06 is type real, or single precision.

Similarly, when printing or reading double-precision numbers, the E format should be replaced by a D format (i.e., E9.2 → D9.2). In almost all respects the D format is identical to the E format; the single exception is that when a number is printed with a D format a D will appear in the exponent, indicating the number is double precision. Double-precision numbers may be read or written using F or E formats without loss of accuracy.

Arithmetic expressions involving real numbers and double-precision numbers or integers and double-precision numbers are a new form of mixed-mode arithmetic and must be treated carefully. Double-precision variables are defined to have "dominance" over reals, which in turn have dominance over integers (see Section 2.5). Consider the results of the following mixed-mode operations.

```
INTEGER I
REAL    R
DOUBLE PRECISION DP1, DP2, DP3
DATA I,R/5, 4.2/
```

DP1	= 6.3	The real constant 6.3 is converted to double precision before being assigned to the variable DP1.
DP2	= 6.3D0	This is the correct way to specify that the constant 6.3 is double precision. Thus, no mode conversion is needed.
DP3	= DP1/R	R is first converted to double precision before dividing. The result is DP3 = 1.5D0.
I	= DP1/R	As in the preceding line, the result on the right is double precision, 1.5D0, and is truncated to 1 when assigned to the integer I.

A Warning about Mode Conversion

The binary representation of decimal numbers results in most ordinary decimal numbers being represented by a nonterminating binary sequence, which is truncated when the number is stored. Precisely how many bits are retained depends on whether or not the number being stored is real or double precision. Thus, 1.10 and 1.10D0 probably represent different values. As a result, even though the result of 2.2D0 − 1.1 is double precision, it may not be more accurate than 2.2 − 1.1.

Because the computer executes double-precision arithmetic at a much slower rate (more than a factor of 2 slower) than ordinary arithmetic, double-precision variables should be invoked only when absolutely necessary.

Function subprograms may also be typed as double precision:

```
DOUBLE PRECISION FUNCTION A(X)
```

has the same effect as

```
FUNCTION A(X)
DOUBLE PRECISION A
```

In addition, all of the commonly used library functions, such as SIN(X), EXP(X), and LOG(X), that accept real values for input will accept double-precision values as input. The value returned by these functions will then automatically be double precision. This is not the case with a user-written subprogram.

If a double-precision value is used in the argument list of a referenced subprogram, the corresponding dummy variable in the subprogram definition must also have been declared double precision. In other words, when passing variables back and forth between program modules, make sure that the types of the variables match in both locations.

Type Complex

In algebra you learned that a generalization of the ordinary set of real numbers is the set of complex numbers written in the form

$$a + ib$$

where i is used to designate the square root of −1 ($i = \sqrt{-1}$), and a is called the real part and b the imaginary part of the number. Both a and b are themselves ordinary real numbers. Complex numbers occur frequently in scientific and engineering applications, and the common arithmetic operations of addition, subtraction, and multiplication can be generalized to include complex numbers.

$$(a_1 + ib_1) + (a_2 + ib_2) = (a_1 + a_2) + i(b_1 + b_2)$$
$$(a_1 + ib_1) - (a_2 + ib_2) = (a_1 - a_2) + i(b_1 - b_2)$$
$$(a_1 + ib_1)(a_2 + ib_2) = (a_1a_2 + i^2b_1b_2) + i(a_1b_2 + a_2b_1)$$
$$= (a_1a_2 - b_1b_2) + i(a_1b_2 + a_2b_1)$$

Dividing complex numbers is more complicated. If we designate the multiplicative inverse of the complex number $c = a + ib$ as c^{-1}, we can easily show (see Problem 9.6) that

$$c^{-1} = \frac{a - ib}{a^2 + b^2}$$

Furthermore, the complex conjugate of a complex number c is defined as

$$c^* = a - ib \qquad \text{Complex conjugate of } c = a + ib$$

and the magnitude of a complex number is defined as

$$|c| = (a^2 + b^2)^{1/2} \qquad \text{Magnitude of } c = a + ib$$

Thus, the inverse of c is $c^*/|c|^2$ and the division of two complex numbers c_1/c_2 would be computed as $c_1c_2^*/|c_2|^2$.

One of the most attractive features of FORTRAN is the ease with which complex arithmetic can be effected in the language. The first step is to declare variables that will contain complex values as type complex by means of the type-declaration statement

COMPLEX name$_1$, name$_2$, ...

Next, complex constants are written in FORTRAN in terms of two real numbers corresponding to the real and imaginary parts enclosed in parentheses and separated by a comma. Once again, mixing the mode of the elements of an arithmetic expression can cause some confusion.[1] Some examples of statements involving complex numbers follow:

```
COMPLEX Z,S,T,U, ROOT
Z = (3.,4.)               That is, z = 3 + 4i
S = (0.,2.)               s = 2i
T = (2.,0.)               t = 2 (same effect as t = 2.)
U = S*Z                   u = 2i(3 + 4i) = -8 + 6i = (-8.,6.)
ROOT = SQRT((-4.,0.))     If the argument of SQRT is complex, the
                          result is also complex; that is, root = 2i.
                          SQRT(-4.) would result in an error.[2]
```

---

[1] Although mixed-mode replacement between complex and double precision is permissible, *all* mixed-mode arithmetic expressions involving complex and double-precision values are forbidden. Thus, COMPLX = DBLPRN and DBLPRN = COMPLX are permitted, whereas COMPLX*DBLPRN is not.

[2] As with double precision, if the argument of an intrinsic function is complex, the value returned is also automatically returned as complex. This is true of all the common intrinsic functions: SIN, COS, EXP, LOG, LOG10, SQRT, and ABS. However, the functions TAN, ASIN, ACOS, ATAN, SINH, and COSH will accept double-precision values but will not accept complex values as input.

When a complex number is read using a list-directed READ statement, the form entered must include the enclosing parentheses and the comma separating the real and imaginary parts. Similarly, when a complex number is printed using a list-directed output statement, the form displayed will include parentheses and a separating comma.

```
COMPLEX A,B
READ *, A,B          Enter (4.,5.),(1.,0.)
PRINT*, 'a*a = ',A*A   Output is a*a = (-9.00,40.0)
```

Formatted READ and WRITE statements may also be used to input and output complex numbers provided that two real-number fields are given for each complex number.

Table 9-1 shows several FORTRAN intrinsic functions that are used when dealing with complex numbers (see also Table 9-2 on page 326).

Many of the common numerical techniques developed with real-number arithmetic in mind remain valid when the number set is generalized to include complex numbers. For example, if the magnitude of a complex number c, $|c| = (a^2 + b^2)^{1/2}$, is used when comparing the size of two complex numbers, the procedures used to find the minimum and maximum and the sorting algorithms for real numbers can easily be converted to handle complex numbers. Many of the numerical methods that will be developed in the next several chapters can also be easily adapted to problems involving complex numbers.

Type Logical

The result of a logical relation of the form (2.**2 .EQ. 4.) must be a value of either ⟨true⟩ or ⟨false⟩. The FORTRAN data type that is used to store these values is type logical. A variable name may be declared to be of type logical with a type statement of the form

LOGICAL name₁, name₂, ...

Variable names declared in this manner are permitted to contain only logical constants. There are only two logical constants:

Table 9-1

FORTRAN intrinsic functions associated with complex numbers

Intrinsic Function Name	Definition	Type of Result	Example
ABS(C)	$|c| = (a^2 + b^2)^{1/2}$	Real	ABS((2.,3.)) → 5.
REAL(C)	Real part of $c = a + ib$	Real	REAL((2.,3.)) → 2.
AIMAG(C)	Complex part of c	Real	AIMAG((2.,3.)) → 3.
CONJG(C)	$|c| = (a^2 + b^2)^{1/2}$	Complex	CONJG((2.,3.) → (2.,-3.)

```
.TRUE.   .FALSE.
```

The periods at the beginning and end of the word are part of the constant.

```
LOGICAL TEST
TEST = .TRUE.
IF((2**2 .EQ. 4) .AND. TEST)THEN
```
[That is, ⟨true⟩ and ⟨true⟩ → ⟨true⟩]

In addition to the logical combinatorial operators .AND. and .OR., two more operators may prove useful:

```
.EQV.    Equivalent
.NEQV.   Not equivalent
```

may be used to compare two logical variables, constants, or expressions to determine whether or not they have the same value. Thus, if both sides of .EQV. are the same, either ⟨true⟩ or ⟨false⟩, the entire expression is ⟨true⟩; otherwise it is ⟨false⟩. Thus,

```
((4.LT.0) .EQV. (1.EQ.0))
```
→ ⟨true⟩

whereas

```
((4.LT.0) .AND. (1.EQ.0))
```
→ ⟨false⟩

Using logical variables and constants is rather artificial and unnecessary in most programs, and unless they are an essential part of the computational algorithm, they should be avoided.

IMPLICIT Type Statements

Explicit typing of variable names is achieved by means of the six type statements: REAL, INTEGER, CHARACTER, DOUBLE PRECISION, COMPLEX, and LOGICAL statements placed in any order at the top of the program module. FORTRAN will automatically default type variable names, unless instructed otherwise, as

| type integer | Names that begin with the letters I through N |
| type real | All others |

The FORTRAN IMPLICIT statement allows you to alter the manner in which variable names are default typed. The form of the statement is

```
IMPLICIT ⟨type⟩ (L₁ - L₂)
```

where L_1 and L_2 are single letters, and ⟨type⟩ may be any of the six FORTRAN number types. This statement then forces all variable names that begin with the letters L_1 through L_2 to be of the specified type. Thus,

```
IMPLICIT REAL (A-Z)
```

will cause all variables, unless otherwise explicitly typed, to be real. Like other type statements, the IMPLICIT statement is nonexecutable and must precede all executable statements. More significantly, it affects only those statements that follow it and so should be the first line after the PRO-GRAM/SUBROUTINE/FUNCTION line.

A common programming error is misspelling or mistyping a variable name. Usually, the misspelled variable will not have been assigned a value, and when it is used in an arithmetic expression an execution-time error will result. These errors are sometimes difficult to trace. Using the IMPLICIT statement you can construct a "trick" to detect misspellings immediately at compilation time. The idea is to implicitly type all variables as CHARACTER*1 at the start of the code, and explicitly type all variables that appear later. If any variables that have not been explicitly typed (i.e., misspellings) are found in the program, they will be of type character; therefore, arithmetic expressions involving these variables will be illegal.

```
      PROGRAM SPEL
      IMPLICIT CHARACTER*1 (A-Z)
      REAL X(0:50), Y(0:50)
      INTEGER LOW,HI,I
      DATA LOW HI/20, 70/
      DO 1 I = 0,50
         X(I) = I*(HI - LO)/50.
         Y(I) = F(X(I))
   1  CONTINUE
```

The variable LOW is misspelled as LO in the DO loop. Because LO is implicitly typed as character, this statement will result in a compilation error.

A more common application of the IMPLICIT statement is as a "quick fix" to a numerical algorithm that has failed because of round-off error. If you find that the procedure you are using is not accurate enough, you may decide that the easiest (but not always the best) next step is to convert the calculation to double precision. The quickest way to do this conversion with an already working code is to implicitly type all variables as double precision at the beginning. Additionally, you should also change all constants in the code to double precision; that is, numbers like 2. should be replaced by 2.D0.[3] All subprograms referenced by the program must be likewise altered. This procedure will frequently result in a very inefficient program. Once you get the program to execute correctly, you should rewrite the code to avoid double precision where it is not critical to the calculation.

9.3 Initializing Variables at Compilation Time

Values are assigned to variable names and stored in memory locations during the execution of a program either through an assignment statement or by means of a READ statement, both of which are executable

---

[3] See the warning on page 314.

statements. An alternate means, the DATA statement, has frequently been employed when it would be wasteful or distracting to create a separate data file. (The DATA statement was discussed in Section 4.6.) Two additional methods of assigning values to parameters prior to execution are available: the PARAMETER statement and the BLOCK DATA subprogram.

PARAMETER Statements

Most programs require the initialization of numerous constants before the computation can commence. These assignments differ from the initialization of the variables of the problem, which will be changed from one run to the next by reading input data. Each FORTRAN assignment statement, since it is an executable statement, adds to the execution time of the program. If the assignments occur in a subprogram that is referenced hundreds of times, the resulting costs both in time and money can be significant. The PARAMETER statement is meant to be used in those situations where a FORTRAN variable is to be assigned a value (during compilation) and it is intended that this value never be altered. An example is PI = 3.1415926. All variables defined in a program, whether they are initialized by an assignment statement, a READ statement, or a DATA statement can be reassigned a different value later in the code—all, that is, except variables initialized by means of the PARAMETER statement. The PARAMETER statement, though it assigns values during compilation like a DATA statement, differs from the DATA statement in two important respects:

1. Once a variable name has been assigned a value in a PARAMETER statement, the compiler will not permit the value of that variable to be altered thereafter in the program.
2. Variable names initialized in a PARAMETER statement are formally called *named constants,* meaning that they may then be used in place of ordinary numerical constants in all subsequent FORTRAN statements except format edit specifications or as designations for statement numbers.

The form of the parameter statement is

PARAMETER (name$_1$ = value$_1$, name$_2$ = value$_2$, . . .)

where name$_1$, name$_2$, . . . are FORTRAN variable names, and value$_1$, value$_2$, . . . are the numerical values they are to be permanently assigned. These values may be constants, constant expressions, or character strings similar to normal assignment statements. There are a few limitations on the constant expressions to the right of the assignment operator in a PARAMETER statement that differ from normal assignment statements:

- References to function subprograms or statement functions are not permitted.

- When a variable name appears on the right, it must have been defined earlier in the same or a prior PARAMETER statement in the same program module.
- Default typing of variables will be used unless an explicit type statement precedes the PARAMETER statement.
- Exponentiation is permitted only if the exponents are integers.

For example,

```
PROGRAM MANE
REAL PI, TWOPI
INTEGER EXIT,INPUT,SIZE,SIZE2
COMPLEX C
CHARACTER*8 DATFIL, FORMT
PARAMETER (PI = 3.1415926)      But PI = ACOS(−1.) would not
PARAMETER (TWOPI = 2.*PI)       be permitted.
PARAMETER (EXIT = 99, INPUT = 22, SIZE=15, SIZE2=
+ SIZE*SIZE)
PARAMETER (DATFIL = 'PROG2.DAT')
PARAMETER (FORMT = '(15F5.2)')
REAL A(SIZE,SIZE)               Note the important distinction:
                                SIZE is not a dummy variable.
                                Identical to REAL A(15,15).

DATA A/SIZE2*0.0/               Identical to DATA A/225*0.0/
OPEN(INPUT,FILE = DATFIL)       Identical to OPEN (22,FILE =
                                'PROG.DAT')
READ (INPUT,FORMT) A            Identical to READ(22,'(15F5.2)')A
READ (22,FORMT,END=EXIT)        Error: Values assigned in a
                                PARAMETER statement may not
                                be used in place of statement
                                numbers.

READ(22,'(SIZE(F5.2))')A        Error: Values assigned in a
                                PARAMETER statement may not
                                be used within a format
                                specification.
```

By far, the most common use of a PARAMETER statement is to define the size of numerous common-size arrays that appear in a main program. Thus

```
PROGRAM MANE
REAL A(12,12), B(12,12), C(12)
CHARACTER NAME(12)*8
DATA A/144*0.0/
```

is identical to

```
PROGRAM MANE
PARAMETER (N = 12, N2 = 144)
REAL A(N,N), B(N,N), C(N)
CHARACTER NAME(N)*8
DATA A/N2*0.0/
```

In the latter case, to rerun the program with a different size for all the arrays, only changes to one line of the program are required.

As a final example of the use of PARAMETER statements, consider the problem of assigning −1 to all the elements of an array by using a DATA statement. Since parentheses are not permitted in the value list of a DATA statement, the following solution would be incorrect:

```
INTEGER M(50)
DATA M/50*(-1)/     Error: Parentheses are not permitted.
```

The remedy would be

```
PARAMETER (K = -1)
INTEGER M(50)
DATA M/50*K/
```

The imaginative use of PARAMETER and DATA statements is a distinctive feature of modern programming style.

BLOCK DATA Subprogram Modules

The DATA statement was introduced in Section 4.6, the COMMON statement in Section 5.7. Both have been used extensively since then. One serious limitation involving the simultaneous use of these statements in the same program remains. As indicated in Section 5.7, variables in a labeled common block may not be initialized by means of a DATA statement. FORTRAN does, however, provide a remedy, albeit a rather awkward one, in the form of the BLOCK DATA subprogram module.

A BLOCK DATA subprogram is used exclusively for assigning values to variables in labeled common blocks. As with any program module, it begins with a definition line, which is of the form

```
BLOCK DATA ⟨name⟩
```

and terminates with an END statement. The name is optional. If included it must not be the same as any other program module or any named common block. The BLOCK DATA subprogram may not contain any executable statements. An example of a BLOCK DATA subprogram is given below:

```
BLOCK DATA CLASS
PARAMETER (N = 8)
INTEGER QUIZ1,HW
REAL    GPA
CHARACTER*12 NAME
COMMON/KLASS/QUIZ1(N), HW(N), GPA(N)
COMMON/NAMES/NAME(N)
DATA QUIZ1/ 78,  86,  89,  46,  77,  69,  96,  83/
DATA    HW/ 45,  33,  45,  18,  39,  42,  45,  37/
DATA   GPA/2.33,3.46,3.32,1.74,2.84,2.21,3.92,3.01/
DATA NAME/'Anderson  ,P','Buchanan  ,A','Cassidy   ,H',
+         'Foley     ,D','Gerhard   ,M','Moore     ,T',
+         'Smith     ,K','Wagner    ,J'/
END
```

9.4 Order of FORTRAN Statements

Numerous new FORTRAN statements have been introduced in this chapter, and you may be uncertain about the relative ordering of the various types of executable and nonexecutable statements. The correct arrangement is indicated in Figure 9-1. Within each group, the various statements of the same classification may appear in any order, but the groups must be arranged as shown. Statements that can appear anywhere within more than one group are indicated in vertical columns that overlap two or more groups. For example, DATA statements may appear anywhere after the

Figure 9-1

Ordering of the various types of FORTRAN statements. Each group of statements must be positioned as shown; however, statements within a group may be rearranged. Statements that appear in vertical columns that overlap two or more groups may be placed anywhere in that vertical arrangement.

PROGRAM/SUBROUTINE/FUNCTION				Comments
IMPLICIT			FORMAT	
INTEGER Type REAL declarations CHARACTER DOUBLE PRECISION LOGICAL	PARAMETER			
DIMENSION COMMON Specification EXTERNAL statements INTRINSIC				
STATEMENT FUNCTIONS				

Assignment statements
DO
CONTINUE
IF
ELSE
ELSEIF
ENDIF
GO TO
CALL
RETURN
STOP
PAUSE
OPEN
CLOSE
REWIND
READ
WRITE
PRINT
	DATA			

END				

various nonexecutable statements, either before or after statement-function definitions.

The following points about statement ordering are worth repeating:

- Comment lines may appear anywhere in a program. Those that are placed after an END statement will be listed with the next program unit.
- FORMAT statements may appear anywhere within a program or subprogram. The preferred style is to group them at the end.
- The END statement must be the last statement of each program module.
- Specification statements generally precede executable statements. The arrangement of statements within the specification grouping is: PARAMETER statements can appear anywhere in the group but must be placed before any reference to the values being assigned; IMPLICIT statements must precede all other specification statements (except PARAMETER statements).
- DATA statements may be placed anywhere after the specification statements and before, after, or among the statement functions. The recommended placement is after the specifications and before all statement functions.
- Statement functions must appear after the specification statements and before the first executable statement. When there is more than one statement function, the ordering must be such that each function references only those placed above it.

9.5 DoWhile Structure in Extended FORTRAN

In Section 3.4 the construction of FORTRAN loops was described in terms of a DoWhile–EndDo structure. At that time you were advised that present versions of standard FORTRAN 77 do not support explicit DO WHILE and END DO statements. However, many local installations of FORTRAN 77 do permit these statements, and you should determine whether this is the case in your computing environment. A version of FORTRAN 77 that allows for DO WHILE statements is usually called *extended* FORTRAN. Any program that employs one or more loops will benefit from a rewrite using the new loop-control statements.

The form of the extended FORTRAN DO WHILE statement is

DO [statement number] WHILE (logical expression)

The statement number is enclosed in brackets to indicate that it is optional. The brackets do not appear in the actual FORTRAN statement. If a statement number is included, it specifies the loop-terminating statement, which may be any of the allowed executable statements normally used to terminate a DO loop, or it may be an END DO statement (see below). The logical expression within the parentheses is tested at the beginning of each cycle of the loop, including the first. If the expression is evaluated as ⟨true⟩, the body of the loop is executed; otherwise, control is transferred to the statement following the loop terminator.

The preferred terminus of a DoWhile structure is the END DO statement, which has the form

```
END DO
```

An END DO statement must be used to terminate a DO or a DO WHILE if the optional terminal statement number has been omitted. An END DO may have a statement number. Two examples follow:

$$I_{sum} = \sum_{i=0}^{100} i$$

```
I    = 0
ISUM = 0
DO WHILE (I .LT. 100)
     ISUM = ISUM + I
     I    = I + 1
END DO
```

$$e^x = \sum_{n=0}^{\infty} \frac{x^n}{n!}$$

```
READ(*,*)X
N    = 1
SUM  = 0.0
TERM = X
DOWHILE (ABS(TERM) .LT. 1.E-6)
     SUM  = SUM + TERM
     TERM = TERM*X/(N+1.)
     N    = N + 1
     IF(N .GT. 100)THEN
          WRITE(*,*)'Series not converging'
          STOP
     ENDIF
ENDDO
```

The DoWhile structure can be used with or without an END DO statement. The following code executes Newton's algorithm for the square root.

```
READ(*,*)C
X = 0.5*(C + 1.)
I = 0
```

```
      DO 99 WHILE (ABS(X*X - C) .GT. 1.E-6)
         X = 0.5*(X + C/X)
         I = I + 1
         IF(I .GE. 50)THEN
             WRITE(*,*)'Method not converging'
             STOP
         ENDIF
   99 CONTINUE
```

Most of the structured features of FORTRAN 77 reduce the need for statement-number labels. As a result it is possible to write code that is to a large extent readable in a continuous path from beginning to end. Generally, statement numbers are associated with FORTRAN statements to provide alternative paths through the program, which in turn can make the program difficult to decipher. With the introduction of the DO WHILE and END DO statements into the language, there remains, except for FORMAT statements, no compelling reason for using statement numbers at all.

9.6   Additional FORTRAN Intrinsic Functions

The most commonly used intrinsic functions in scientific and engineering applications were introduced in Section 2.7. Numerous other intrinsic functions are available in FORTRAN; several of these are listed in Tables 9-2 and 9-3.

Most FORTRAN mathematical intrinsic functions come in a variety of forms depending on the data type of the argument. For example, DSQRT(D) can be used if the argument is double precision, and the computed result will then also be double precision. Similarly, CSQRT(C) can be used if the argument is a complex number, and the result will be of type complex. A convenient alternative to choosing the function to fit the type of its argument is to use the generic function names that are provided in FORTRAN. For example, the generic name for computing a square root is SQRT( ). If the argument is real, the result returned is likewise real; if the argument is double precision, the result returned is double precision; and so on. The specific names (DSQRT, CSQRT, etc.) have been retained in FORTRAN to provide compatibility with earlier versions. Your programs should employ generic function names exclusively, whenever possible.

9.7   Conclusion

We have now covered all of the elements of FORTRAN grammar necessary to construct programs to solve almost any problem that can be solved by a computer. A few additional FORTRAN statements that were not discussed in the chapter are described in the appendix.

Table 9-2
FORTRAN mathematical intrinsic functions

Generic Function Name	Description	Permissible Arguments			
		Real	Integer	Double Precision	Complex
SQRT(X)	$\sqrt{x}$	Yes	No	Yes	Yes
EXP(X)	e^x, exponential	Yes	No	Yes	Yes
LOG(X)	$\ln(x)$, natural logarithm	Yes	No	Yes	Yes
LOG10(X)	$\log(x)$ base-10 logarithm	Yes	No	Yes	No
ABS(X)	$\lvert x \rvert$ absolute value, for complex argument returns $(a^2 + b^2)^{1/2}$	Yes	Yes	Yes	Yes
SIN(X)	Trigonometric sine, argument is in radians	Yes	No	Yes	Yes
COS(X)	Trigonometric cosine, argument is in radians	Yes	No	Yes	Yes
TAN(X)	Trigonometric tangent, argument is in radians	Yes	No	Yes	No
ASIN(X) ACOS(X) ATAN(X)	Inverse trigonometric functions, result is in radians; if $x = \tan(\theta)$, then $\theta = \text{ATAN}(X)$	Yes Yes Yes	No No No	Yes Yes Yes	No No No
SINH(X) COSH(X) TANH(X)	Hyperbolic functions $\sinh(x) = \frac{1}{2}(e^x - e^{-x})$ $\cosh(x) = \frac{1}{2}(e^x + e^{-x})$ $\tanh(x) = \sinh(x)/\cosh(x)$	Yes Yes Yes	No No No	Yes Yes Yes	No No No
MOD(X,Y)	Remainder of division of x by y	Yes	Yes	Yes	No
MAX(X1,X2, . . .)	Maximum element in list	Yes	Yes	Yes	No
MIN(X1,X2, . . .)	Minimum element in list	Yes	Yes	Yes	No

Thousands of subtle points have been glossed over or even purposely ignored. You do not learn programming or anything else by first memorizing a myriad of details. These will come naturally with time and experience. You must first develop confidence in your ability to solve complicated problems with the tools you already have. The analogy with foreign languages is apt. The best way to become fluent in a language is not to expend great effort learning a vocabulary by memorization but rather to begin communicating as soon as you can with the vocabulary you currently have.

An important responsibility of an introductory programming text is to see to it that the student does not fall into a variety of bad habits that

Table 9-3
FORTRAN intrinsic functions for converting data types

Function Name	Description	Real	Integer	Double Precision	Complex	Type of Result
				Permissible Arguments		
REAL(X)	Converts argument to real	Y	Y	Y	Y	Real
INT(X)	Truncates argument to integer	Y	Y	Y	Y	Integer
CMPLX(X) or	Converts argument to complex (X,0)	Y	Y	Y	Y	Complex
CMPLX(X1,X2)	Converts argument to complex (X1,X2)					
NINT(X)	Rounds argument to nearest integer	N	Y	Y	N	Same as argument
LEN(CH)	Returns length of character string	Single character string				Integer
INDEX(CH1,CH2)	Returns position of string CH2 within string CH1	Two character strings				Integer
CHAR(I)	Returns *i*th character in system-defined collating sequence	N	Y	N	N	A single character
ICHAR(CH)	Returns the position of the single character CH in system-collating sequence	A character string of length 1				Integer

may not appear serious now but will be difficult to break later. It was for this reason that the many programming style suggestions associated with structured programming were repeatedly stressed in even the simplest of programs. Structured programming was devised to aid in the logical construction of programs, and you should try to segment and "layer" even the simplest codes. In addition, your programs should contain every kind of internal check for potential errors that you can devise. By now you are well aware that some execution-time errors are extremely difficult to track down; in such cases helpful clues supplied by the programmer are greatly appreciated.

The challenge now is to use the FORTRAN developed to this point and to attempt to dovetail it with the mathematics, science, and engineering that you already know or will soon encounter. Once that is accomplished, you will be quite fluent in the mathematical analysis of engineering and science problems.

Problems

9.1 Are the following statements true or false? Explain your answers.
  a. Any PARAMETER statement must precede all type statements.
  b. Variables typed as real may also be typed as double precision in the same program unit.
  c. Variables implicitly typed as integer may also be typed as real in the same program unit.
  d. Variables initialized in a DATA statement may not be altered in the same program unit.
  e. Character variables may not be initialized via a DATA statement; a PARAMETER statement must be used instead.
  f. Complex variables may not appear in a DATA statement.

9.2 Use a DATA statement to initialize a square 10 by 10 array, A(I, J), in the following manner:

$$a_{ij} = +1 \quad \text{for } j > i \quad \text{above the main diagonal}$$

$$a_{ii} = 0 \quad \text{along the main diagonal}$$

$$a_{ij} = -1 \quad \text{for } j < i \quad \text{below the main diagonal}$$

You will also need a PARAMETER statement (for the -1's) and several nested implied DO loops in the DATA statement.

9.3 Rewrite the FORTRAN code in Section 3.4 for Newton's method for finding the square roots of numbers to find the square root of a complex number. Test the program by evaluating the square roots of a negative real number and of an arbitrary complex number. Verify your answer by comparing the square of the result with the test number. (*Note:* For a test for "smallness" of a complex number c, use

```
IF((ABS(C)) .LT. 1.E-G)THEN
```

That is, the sum of the squares of the real plus imaginary parts determines the "size" of the complex number.)

9.4 Write a FORTRAN program to use the method of successive substitutions (see Problem 3.12) to find a complex root of a function. Test the program by finding a root of

$$f(x) = x^3 - 4x^2 + 6x - 4 = 0 \quad \text{Exact roots} = 1 + i, 1 - i, 2$$

[*Hint:* Write the equation as $x = \frac{1}{2}[x^3 + 6x - 4]^{1/2}$ and start with $x_0 = (1.0, 0.5)$.]

9.5 Determine the output of the following program.

```
PROGRAM ANDOR
LOGICAL A,B,C,D,E
DATA A, C/.FALSE.,.TRUE./
DO 1 I = -1,1
    B = (I.GT.0)
    D = B .AND. (A.OR.C)
    E = B .AND. A .OR. C
```

```
           IF(D .NEQV. E)THEN
              WRITE(*,*)'The order of AND/OR makes'
              WRITE(*,*)'a difference for '
              WRITE(*,*) B, ' .AND. ', A , ' .OR. ', C
           ENDIF
         1 CONTINUE
           END
```

9.6 Division of complex numbers can be defined in terms of the multiplicative inverse of the number, which can be obtained in the following manner:

$$c = a + ib \qquad a \text{ and } b \text{ are known}$$

$$c^{-1} = \alpha + i\beta \qquad \alpha \text{ and } \beta \text{ are to be determined}$$

$$c(c^{-1}) = 1 = (a + ib)(\alpha + i\beta)$$

$$= (a\alpha - b\beta) + i(a\beta + b\alpha) = 1 + 0i$$

So

$$b\alpha + a\beta = 0$$

$$a\alpha - b\beta = 1$$

a. Solve these equations for (α, β) in terms of (a, b) to obtain

$$\alpha = \frac{a}{a^2 + b^2} \qquad \beta = \frac{-b}{a^2 + b^2}$$

b. Test these equations directly on the computer by executing a program to read two complex numbers, X, Y, and evaluate and print X/X, X/Y, Y/X, (X/Y)*(Y/X).

9.7 Determine any compilation errors in the following expressions. If there are no errors, write OK.
a. `PARAMETER (PI = ACOS(-1.))`
b. `PARAMETER (K = 2)`
`   OPEN(K,FILE = 'DATA')`
c. `PARAMETER (N = 44)`
`   GO TO N`
d. `PARAMETER (N = 4)`
`   REAL A(N)`
`   DATA (A(I), I = 1,N)/N*3.0/`
e. `PARAMETER (N = 4)`
`   INTEGER A(N)`
`   DATA (A(I), I = 1,N)/N*N/`
f. `CHARACTER NAME*3,STUDENT*12`
`   PARAMETER (NAME = '(A)')`
`   READNAME,STUDENT`

D
Programming
Assignment

In this programming assignment you will construct moderately complicated programs in modular form, employing numerous subprograms and using the FORTRAN statements introduced in Chapters 8 and 9.

■ Engineering Career Choices: Aeronautical/Aerospace Engineering

Among the youngest of the engineering disciplines, aeronautical/aerospace engineering is concerned with all aspects of the design, production, testing, and utilizing of vehicles or devices that fly in air (aeronautical) or in space (aerospace), from hang gliders to space shuttles. Since the science and engineering principles involved are so broad-based, aeroengineers usually specialize in a subarea that may overlap with other engineering fields such as mechanical, metallurgical/materials, chemical, civil, or electrical engineering. Such subareas include the following:

1. *Aerodynamics.* The study of the flight characteristics of various structures or configurations. Typical considerations are the drag and lift associated with airplane design, or the onset of turbulent flow. A knowledge of fluid dynamics is essential. The modeling and testing of all forms of aircraft is part of this discipline.

2. *Structural design.* The design, production, and testing of aircraft and spacecraft to withstand the wide range of in-flight demands on these vehicles. Similar problems involving other types of vehicles, such as underwater vessels, are in the province of the structural engineer.

3. *Propulsion systems.* The design of internal combustion, jet, and liquid- and solid-fuel rocket engines and their coordination in the overall design of the vehicle. Rocket engines, especially, require innovative engineering to accommodate the extreme temperatures of storing, mixing, and burning fuels such as liquid oxygen.

4. *Instrumentation and guidance.* The aerospace industry has been a leader in developing and utilizing solid-state electronics in the form of microprocessors to monitor and adjust the operations of hundreds of air- and spacecraft functions. This field uses the expertise of both electrical engineers and aeroengineers.

5. *Navigation.* The computation of orbits within and outside the atmosphere, and the determination of the orientation of a vehicle with respect to points on the earth or in space.

Sample Problem: Range of a Constant Thrust Rocket

The most important characteristic of a rocket's trajectory is the final point of impact. Calculating the complete trajectory, including the point of impact, is a complicated task that depends on the detailed parameters describing the rocket engine, an understanding of air drag, and the characteristics of trajectories on a spherical earth. As a first approximation, we will neglect the latter two complications and concentrate on the trajectories of a particular type of rocket engine on a flat earth and with no air resistance.

A common type of rocket engine is called a constant thrust engine. This type of engine produces a constant force of propulsion during the entire time the engine is running or until the engine runs out of fuel. Since the force is constant and the mass of the rocket is continually decreasing as it burns fuel, the acceleration of the rocket is likewise continually increasing as long as the engine is on. Once the engine is shut off, the rocket follows a so-called ballistic trajectory.

The force diagram for the rocket in flight is shown in Figure D-1. Notice in this diagram that the orientation of the rocket and its actual direction of velocity are not the same. To maximize the range of the trajectory, it is found that the direction of thrust should be held constant at a particular angle θ during the entire period of engine burning. In the figure,

T = Thrust of the rocket engine (N)
θ = Fixed angle of inclination of T with respect to the horizontal
m = Current mass of the rocket (payload plus current fuel) (kg)
g = Gravitational acceleration (m/sec²), assumed constant

Figure D-1
Force diagram for a
rocket in flight

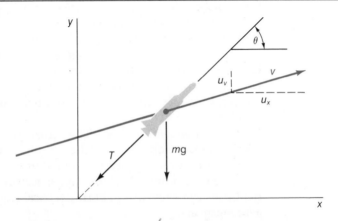

$\mathbf{v}$ = The instantaneous velocity of the center of mass of the rocket; the velocity vector has components $\mathbf{v}_x, \mathbf{v}_y$

Newton's second law ($\mathbf{F} = \mathbf{ma}$) can be used to solve this problem for the rocket's trajectory. For strictly vertical flight ($\theta = \pi/2$), this problem is often analyzed in introductory physics. For motion in both the x and y directions, the analysis is more complicated but straightforward.[1]

The results depend on the following characteristics of the rocket engine:

M_0 = Original mass of the rocket plus fuel

v_e = Exhaust velocity of the propellant relative to the rocket engine

Ω_0 = Ratio of the original fuel to the total mass

β = Burn rate of the rocket engine

t_{max} = Maximum burning time of the engine ($= \Omega_0 M_0/\beta$)

t_c = Cutoff time, the time the engine is switched off (must be less than t_{max})

θ = Optimum thrust inclination angle

The angle θ is a solution of the equation

$$Q\sigma^3 = \sigma^2 - \tfrac{1}{2} \tag{D.1}$$

where $\sigma = \sin\theta$, and

$$Q = -\frac{[\Omega_0 + \ln(1 - \Omega_0)]}{[\ln(1 - \Omega_0)]^2} \times \frac{gt_c}{v_e\Omega_0} \tag{D.2}$$

Newton's equations are then solved assuming constant thrust up to the time of cutoff ($t \le t_c$). After cutoff the force on the rocket is simply gravity. The result is that the position and velocity of the rocket at the time the rocket is turned off are

$$x_c = (v_e \cos\theta)t_c f(t_c)$$

$$y_c = (v_e \sin\theta)t_c f(t_c) - \tfrac{1}{2}gt_c^2$$

$$(v_c)_x = -(v_e \cos\theta) \ln(1 - \Omega_0 t/t_{max})$$

$$(v_c)_y = -(v_e \sin\theta) \ln(1 - \Omega_0 t/t_{max}) - gt_c \tag{D.3}$$

where

$$f(t) = 1 + \ln(1 - \Omega_0 t/t_{max})[(t_{max} - \Omega_0 t)/(\Omega_0 t)] \tag{D.4}$$

Thereafter, the rocket follows a ballistic trajectory given by

$$x(t) = x_c + (v_c)_x(t - t_c) \tag{D.5}$$

$$y(t) = y_c + (v_c)_y(t - t_c) - \tfrac{1}{2}g(t - t_c)^2 \tag{D.6}$$

---

[1] See Angelo Miele, *Flight Mechanics*, vol. 1 (Reading, Mass.: Addison-Wesley, 1962).

The rocket hits the ground at a time t_{hit} defined by $y(t - t_{hit}) = 0$, that is, the positive root of Equation (D.5). The x position at the time of hit is the range of the trajectory.

$$\text{Range} = x(t - t_{hit}) \qquad (D.7)$$

Thus, given the rocket characteristics, v_e, Ω_0, and t_{max}, and the time of cutoff, t_c, the range of the rocket's trajectory may be computed as follows:

1. Use Equation (D.2) to compute the factor Q.
2. Solve for the root of Equation (D.1) and thereby determine the optimum inclination angle $\theta = \sin^{-1}(\sigma)$.
3. Compute the positions and velocities at cutoff using Equations (D.3).
4. Solve for the positive root of Equation (D.6) to determine t_{hit}.
5. Compute the range of the trajectory via Equation (D.5).

Problem Specifics. The characteristics of our rocket engine are

$$v_e = 5{,}000 \text{ (m/sec)}$$
$$M_0 = 30{,}000 \text{ (kg)}$$
$$\Omega_0 = 0.80$$
$$\beta = 260 \text{ (kg/sec)}$$
$$t_{max} = \frac{\Omega_0 M_0}{\beta} = 92.307 \text{ (sec)}$$

Determine the range of the trajectories for cutoff times from $t_c = \frac{1}{2} t_{max}$ to $t_c = t_{max}$ in steps of 1 second.

The program will have subprogram modules

FUNCTION Q	Determines Q from Equation (D.2).
FUNCTION CUBRT(Q,X)	Solves for the root of the cubic Equation (D.1) by successive substitutions; that is, start with an initial guess for σ ($\frac{1}{2} \le \sigma \le 1$) and write the equation as $\sigma = (Q\sigma^3 - \frac{1}{2})^{1/2}$.
FUNCTION F(T)	The function of Equation (D.4)
FUNCTION QUADR(A,B,C)	Returns the positive root of the quadratic $at^2 + bt + c$
FUNCTION RANGE(THIT)	Equation (D.7)

The program should use common blocks where appropriate. Neatly print the input parameters and a table of the range versus cutoff time. Finally, graph the range versus cutoff time.

Sample Problem Solution. The complete FORTRAN program to solve this problem, along with a sample of the computed results, is given in Figure D-2. A graph of the rocket's range versus cutoff time is given in Figure D-3.

Figure D-2
FORTRAN code for
the rocket trajectory
problem

```
      PROGRAM ROCKET
*--
*-- This program will compute the features of the trajectory of a
*-- rocket with an engine that develops a constant thrust until
*-- cutoff.  The rocket cutoff time and position are computed and
*-- the overall range of the rocket is determined.  Additionally,
*-- the complete trajectory is determined and written to a data
*-- file.  These data are then plotted on a plotter.  The major
*-- assumptions are that the inclination angle of the rocket to the
*-- horizontal is fixed and that air resistance is negligible.
*------------------------------------------------------------------
* Variables
*
      REAL VE,MO,BURN,TMAX,DT,TCUT,XCUT,YCUT,VXCUT,VYCUT,THIT,
     +     Q,THEAT,OMEGA,G
      COMMON/PARAM/OMEGA,TMAX
*
*   --Input Parameters---
*
*      VE      --  Velocity of exhaust relative to the rocket
*      MO      --  Original rocket mass including fuel
*      BURN    --  Rate of burning fuel
*      G       --  Gravitational acceleration
*      OMEGA   --  Ratio of fuel mass to total mass
*      TMAX    --  Maximum burn time (when fuel is exhausted)
*
*   --Intermediate Computed Quantities--
*
*      QUE     --  Parameter in equation for optimum angle
*      THETA   --  Optimum thrust inclination angle
*      TCUT    --  Cutoff time
*      ILO,IHI--  Integer limits of time steps (in seconds)
*
*   --Computed Results--
*
*      VXCUT   --  Positions and velocities at cutoff
*      VYCUT
*      VCUT
*      XCUT
*      THIT    --  The time the rocket strikes the ground
*      RANGE   --  The range of the trajectory
*------------------------------------------------------------------
* Initialization
*
      DATA G, VE, MO, BURN, OMEGA/9.8, 5.E3, 3.E4, 260., 0.8/
      TMAX  = OMEGA*MO/BURN
      DT    = TMAX/20.
*
* The limits of the cutoff time loop are integers.  The time
* step will be 1 second.
*
      ILO   = TMAX/2.
      IHI   = TMAX
      WRITE(*,11)VE,MO,OMEGA,BURN
*------------------------------------------------------------------
```

Figure D-2 _____
(continued)

```
                        WRITE(*,13)
                        DO 2 I = 1,IHI-ILO
                           TCUT  = ILO + I
                           QUE   = Q(OMEGA,TCUT,VE,G)
                           THETA = ASIN(CUBRT(QUE,.6))
*
*    The position and velocity at cutoff
*
                           XCUT  = VE*COS(THETA)*TCUT*F(TCUT)
                           YCUT  = VE*SIN(THETA)*TCUT*F(TCUT) - .5*G*TCUT**2
                           VXCUT = -VE*COS(THETA)*LOG(1.-OMEGA*TCUT/TMAX)
                           VYCUT = -VE*SIN(THETA)*LOG(1.-OMEGA*TCUT/TMAX) - G*TCUT
                           VCUT  =  SQRT(VXCUT**2 + VYCUT**2)
*
*    The time of impact is a solution of a quadratic
*
                           THIT  = TCUT + QUADR(-.5*G,VYCUT,YCUT)
                           R     = RANGE(XCUT,VXCUT,THIT)
                           WRITE(*,14)THETA,TCUT,XCUT/1000.,YCUT/1000.,VCUT/1000.
                        +        ,THIT/60.,R/1000.
                     2  CONTINUE
                        WRITE(*,15)
                        STOP
*----------------------------------------------------------------------
* Formats
*
     11    FORMAT(T10,'A computation of a rocket trajectory',/,
           +    T5,'Input Parameters',//,
           +    T10,'Exhaust    Original     Ratio of      Burn  ',/
           +    T10,'Velocity   Total Mass   Fuel to       Rate  ',/
           +    T10,'(m/sec)     (kg)        Total Mass   (kg/s) ',/
           +    T10,'--------    --------    ----------   -------',//,
           +    T10,F8.2,T21,F8.2,T36,F4.1,T44,F8.2)
*
     13    FORMAT(//,T2,'Results of the calculation',/,
           +T5,'------------------------------------------------------',/
           +T5,'|Optimum|Time  |   Position, Velocity   | Time |Range |',/
           +T5,'|Thrust |of    |     at Cutoff          | of   |of    |',/
           +T5,'|Angle  |Cutoff| x      y    Velocity|Flight|Flight|',/
           +T5,'|(deg.) |(sec) |(km)   (km)  (km/sec)|(min) |(km)  |',/
           +T5,'|------ |------|-------|-------|-------|------|-----|')
*
     14    FORMAT(T5,'|',F7.2,T13,'|',F5.0,T20,'|',F6.2,T28,'|',F6.2,T36,
           +    '|',F6.1,T44,'|',F6.2,T52,'|', F6.1,'|')
*
     15    FORMAT(T5,55('-'))
           END
*======================================================================
           FUNCTION RANGE(XO,VO,THIT)
           REAL  XO,VO,THIT,RANGE
*
*   The range of the trajectory is the x position when t = thit.
*
           RANGE = XO + VO*THIT
           RETURN
           END
*======================================================================
```

Figure D-2
(continued)

```
         FUNCTION QUADR(A,B,C)
         REAL DISC, QUADR, A,B,C
*
*  The root of the quadratic at^2 + b^t + c is returned as QUAD.
*
         DISC = B**2 - 4*A*C
         QUADR= (-B + SQRT(DISC))/2./A
         RETURN
      END
*==================================================================
         FUNCTION F(T)
         REAL TMAX,T,OMEGA,F
         COMMON/PARAM/OMEGA,TMAX
*
*  The function of Equation (D.4)
*
         F = 1. + (TMAX - T*OMEGA)*LOG(1-OMEGA*T/TMAX)/(OMEGA*T)
         RETURN
      END
*==================================================================
         FUNCTION Q(OMEGA,TC,VE,G)
         REAL OMEGA,TC,VE,G,Q
*
*  The function of Equation (D.2)
*
         Q = -(OMEGA + LOG(1.- OMEGA))/(LOG(1.-OMEGA))**2
     +        *(G*TC)/(VE*OMEGA)
         RETURN
      END
*==================================================================
         FUNCTION CUBRT(Q,X)
         REAL Q,X,CUBRT,TEST
*
* Solves for the root of the cubic equation (D.1) by
* successive substitutions.  (If no root in 50 steps, STOPs.)
*
         DO 1 I = 1,50
            TEST = SQRT(Q*X**3 + .5)
            IF(ABS(TEST - X) .LT. 1.E-5)THEN
               CUBRT = TEST
               RETURN
            ELSE
               X = TEST
            ENDIF
    1    CONTINUE
         WRITE(*,*)'Excessive iterations in CUBRT'
      END
```

```
         A computation of a rocket trajectory
      Input Parameters
```

Exhaust Velocity (m/sec)	Original Total Mass (kg)	Ratio of Fuel to Total Mass	Burn Rate (kg/s)
5000.00	30000.00	0.8	260.00

Figure D-2
(concluded)

Results of the calculation

Optimum Thrust Angle (deg)	Time of Cutoff (sec)	Position, Velocity at Cutoff			Time of Flight (min)	Range of Flight (km)
		x (km)	y (km)	Velocity (km/sec)		
45.76	47.	39.16	29.39	2.3	0.46	89.4
45.77	48.	41.00	30.84	2.4	0.47	93.8
45.79	49.	42.89	32.33	2.4	0.48	98.4
45.81	50.	44.83	33.86	2.5	0.49	103.1
...	...	...	...	...	...	
46.42	85.	153.24	125.62	6.1	0.91	404.9
46.44	86.	157.85	129.72	6.3	0.93	419.7
46.45	87.	162.56	133.94	6.4	0.94	435.1
46.47	88.	167.40	138.29	6.6	0.95	451.1
46.49	89.	172.36	142.75	6.8	0.97	467.8
46.51	90.	177.45	147.35	7.0	0.98	485.2
46.53	91.	182.67	152.09	7.2	1.00	503.3
46.54	92.	188.02	156.97	7.4	1.01	522.2

Figure D-3
Range of the rocket
trajectory as a
function of the time
of cutoff

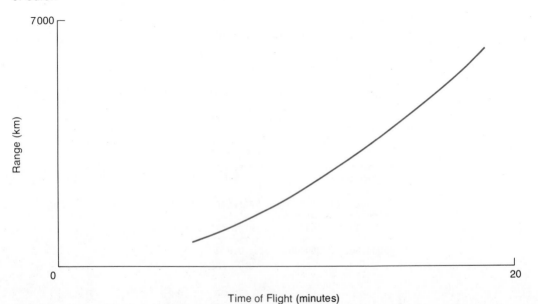

Range (km)

7000

0

20

Time of Flight (minutes)

Variations. Add statements to the rocket problem to compute and print the following:

- The actual miles-per-gallon ratio for the rocket for each value of t_{cut}. Use 1 km = 0.6214 mile, and assume that 1 gallon of fuel has a mass of 3.5 kg.
- The cost per kilometer for each kilogram of payload assuming the cost of fuel is $14 per gallon. (Assume that the mass of the payload is M_0 less the mass of burned fuel.)

As a second variation, rewrite the entire program to read a desired range R_0 and to compute the corresponding cutoff time. This problem is much more difficult. You will have to construct a function FNC(t) = RANGE(t) − R_0 and find the root of this function by the bisection method.

D.2 Programming Problems

Programming Problem D-A: Chemical Engineering: Optimum Depth of a Fluidized-Bed Reactor

A fluidized-bed chemical reactor is a structure that is used extensively in chemical engineering to provide more uniform contact for chemical reactions such as catalytic cracking in petroleum processing or heat transfer in combustion operations. A fluidized reactor contains a bed of granular material through which a fluid is flowing at a rate sufficiently high to suspend the material (akin to "quicksand" conditions). An important design concern is to make the reactor high enough to prevent the loss of the bed particles. In addition, an operating constraint is to keep the rate of fluid flow through the reactor sufficient to suspend the material but not enough to "flush" the material out of the reactor. The reactor is sketched in Figure D-4.

Figure D-4
Fluidized-bed
chemical reactor

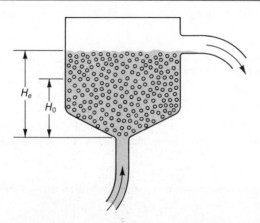

Once the fluid is flowing in the reactor, the total height of the fluid plus material increases to the expanded height H_e, which is given by the expression

$$H_e = H_0(1 + f) \sum_{i=1}^{n} \left[\frac{p_i}{(1 - \varepsilon_i)} \right] \tag{D.8}$$

where H_0 = Static (unexpanded) bed height (m)
f = Void fraction of the unexpanded bed
p_i = Fraction of bed particles with diameter d_i (m)
ε_i = Porosity or void fraction of the expanded bed part that is made up of particles of size d_i

The individual void fractions ε_i for the expanded bed for particles of size d_i can be found from

$$\frac{\varepsilon_i^3}{(1 - \varepsilon_i)} = F(q, d_i) \tag{D.9}$$

where $F(q, d_i)$ is a function that depends on the flow rate q and the particle size d_i and is given by

$$F(q, d_i) = \frac{180}{g} \frac{\mu}{(\rho_s - \rho)} \frac{q}{d_i^2} \tag{D.10}$$

where g = Gravitational acceleration, 9.8 m/sec^2
μ = Fluid viscosity (N − sec/m^2)
ρ_s = Particle density (kg/m^3)
ρ = Fluid density (kg/m^3)
q = Reactor-bed flow rate (m/sec)

The cubic equation for the void fractions can be written as

$$\varepsilon = F^{1/3}(1 - \varepsilon)^{1/3} \tag{D.11}$$

This equation is solved for a particular value of q and d_i by guessing a value for ε_i, inserting it into the expression on the right, and computing a new value for ε_i. If the new value is sufficiently close to the guess, a solution has been found; if not, the new value is inserted into the right and the process continued until successive values differ less than some small quantity. This process is known as successive substitutions.[2] For a given flow

---

[2] The method of successive substitutions does not always work. If we are attempting to find the root of an equation written in the form

$$x = f(x)$$

in an iterative manner—that is,

$$x_{k+1} = f(x_k)$$

and if the unknown root is designated by α [i.e., $\alpha = f(\alpha)$], we begin by assuming that x_k is near α,

$$x_k = \alpha + \delta_k$$

and that each successive iteration is an improvement ($|\delta_{k+1}| < |\delta_k|$).

Table D-1
Static-bed reactor
parameters

Static Height H_0	Static Void Fraction f	Particle Density ρ_s	Size Distribution $(i = 1, 4)$ p_i	Particle Size $(i = 1, 4)$ $d_i(10^{-3}\,\text{m})$
4.5	0.45	2666.0	0.256	2.0
			0.350	8.4
			0.295	4.0
			0.099	1.3

rate q, the void fractions ε_i for each of the constituent particles in the bed can be obtained by this means. Once all the ε_i's have been computed, the sum in Equation (D.8) can be evaluated and the bed height H_e determined.

Problem Specifics. There are particles of identical material but of four different sizes in the static bed. The static-bed reactor characteristics are given in Table D-1. The properties of the fluid flowing through the reactor are

$$\mu = \text{Viscosity} = 8.13 \times 10^{-3}$$
$$\rho = \text{Density} = 1{,}000$$

The FORTRAN program should contain the following subprogram modules:

- A function subprogram F(Q, D, N) for Equation (D.10), where D is an array of size N. The values of μ, g, and ρ should be passed to the function via a COMMON statement.

But if δ_k is small, then the derivative of $f(x)$ is approximately

$$f'(\alpha) = \frac{f(\alpha + \delta_k) - f(\alpha)}{\delta_k} = \frac{f(\alpha + \delta_k)}{\delta_k} - \frac{\alpha}{\delta_k}$$

or

$$\alpha + \delta_{k+1} = f(\alpha + \delta_k) = \alpha + f'(\alpha)\delta_k$$

Thus, for the procedure to converge ($|\delta_{k+1}| < |\delta_k|$), the magnitude of the derivative of $f(x)$ near the root *must* be less than 1. For this reason, successive substitutions applied to the equation,

$$x^3 - \frac{1 - x}{8} = 0$$

written in the form

$$x = \frac{1}{2}(1 - x)^{1/3}$$

will work, whereas

$$x = 1 - 8x^3$$

will not. (The root is near 0.418.)

- A function subprogram CUBRT to solve for the root of Equation (D.11) by successive substitutions. The function should print a diagnostic if no root is found within 50 iterations. The convergence criterion should be $|\varepsilon_{new} - \varepsilon_{old}| < 1.\text{E-}4$.
- A function subprogram HEX(H0, F, P, EPS, N) for Equation (D.8). The variables P and EPS are arrays of size N.

The main program then performs the following functions:

- Initialize the parameters in Table D-1. Use DATA statements for the arrays P, EPS. Recall that the variables μ, g, and ρ are to be in a common block. The input parameters should be neatly printed.
- For flow rates q = 0.004 to 0.012 m³/sec, first compute the individual particle void fractions (ε_i) using Equations (D.10) and (D.11) and the functions F and CUBRT; and then determine the expanded height using function HEX and print the results as one line of a table.

Finally, if you have a plotter available, graph H_e versus q.

Programming Problem D-B: Electrical Engineering:
A Double-Precision Root Solver

A common operation in computational algorithms is the addition of a small correction term to a not-so-small base term. Often a great deal of effort has gone into the evaluation of the correction term, yet when it is added to the base term most of the significant figures in it are lost. As discussed earlier, this loss of significant figures is a consequence of the finite word length of the computer. For example, on a machine with an eight-digit word length, if the base term is x_0 = 1.0000000 and the correction term is evaluated as δx = 1.2345678E-6, then the sum $x_0 + \delta x$ becomes

$$
\begin{array}{r}
1.0000000 \\
+ \ 0.0000012345678 \\
\hline
= \ 1.0000012
\end{array}
$$

and six of the eight significant figures of δx have been lost. If extreme accuracy is important, all parameters in the calculation could be declared double precision; however, a price is paid in significantly increased execution times. For algorithms of this type there is a better way. Since extreme accuracy is desired in only the base and the sum but is not needed in δx, the trick is to declare x_0 and SUM as double precision and δx as single precision (i.e., real). Returning to our eight-digit machine, this means the code

```
    DOUBLE PRECISION ONE,SUM
    REAL              DX
    ONE = 1.D0
    DX  = .12345678E-6
    SUM = ONE + DX    This is mixed-mode arithmetic.
                      The result is double precision.
```

is numerically equivalent to

$$
\begin{array}{r}
1.000000000000000 \\
+\ 0.0000012345678 \\
\hline
=\ 1.000001234567800
\end{array}
$$

Thus, this simple alteration to the program, which does not measurably increase execution times, nonetheless retains all the significant figures of the correction term.

Problem: Radar Speed Traps. A common highway-patrol radar speed-detection apparatus emits a beam of microwaves at frequency f_0. The beam is reflected off an approaching car, and the reflected beam is picked up and analyzed by the apparatus. The frequency of the reflected beam is slightly shifted from f_0 to f due to the motion of the car. The relationship between the speed of the car and the two microwave frequencies is

$$
v = \frac{c}{n}\frac{f - f_0}{f + f_0}
\tag{D.12}
$$

where c is the speed of light (and microwaves) and n is the index of refraction of microwaves in air. The emitted waves have a frequency of $f_0 = 2 \times 10^{10}$ sec^{-1}, and the other constants have values

$$
c = 2.99792458 \times 10^8 \text{ m/sec}
$$
$$
n = 1.00031
$$

A zealous officer has been ticketing motorists whose speeds are measured as $v \geq 55.01$ mph. The problem is to convince a judge that the apparatus is not sufficiently accurate to discriminate between 55.00 and 55.01 mph. The argument will hinge on the selectivity of the electronic equipment. The radar device actually measures the difference δf between the received frequency f and the emitted frequency f_0 to an accuracy of one part in 10^4 (i.e., 0.01%).

Problem Specifics. After converting the speeds $v_1 = 55.00$ mph and $v_2 = 55.01$ mph to m/sec, the major task of the program is to solve Equation (D.12) for the received frequencies, f_1 and f_2, associated with these speeds. Although this problem can be solved algebraically without much effort, here we will use the computer. Once these frequencies are obtained, the corresponding frequency shifts $\delta f_1 = |f_1 - f_0|$, $\delta f_2 = |f_2 - f_0|$

are computed. If they are the same to four significant figures, the judge will be convinced; otherwise, you pay the fine.

Your program should contain the following subprogram modules:

- A function VEL(F) representing Equation (D.12). The function will be single precision but the variables F and F0 will be double precision. The parameters f_0, c, and n should be passed through a common block.
- An adapted double-precision version of the bisection subroutine of Figure 5-4.

SUBROUTINE BISEC(A,B,EPS,IMAX,I,ROOT)

This subroutine will be used to find a root of VEL(F) − V, where V corresponds to either 55.00 or 55.01 mph. Note that A, B, F, and several other variables in the subroutine will have to be declared double precision. Use A = .99D0*F0, B = 1.01D0*F0, and use a convergence criterion of the form $|f - f_0|/f_0 < 1.E-4$.

The main program will find the frequencies corresponding to the two speeds, compute the two frequency shifts, and compare them. Print a statement depending on whether the two shifts are the same or different to four significant figures.

Programming Problem D-C: Electrical Engineering: Complex Numbers and AC Circuits

The fundamental equations governing the effects of the basic elements of electric circuits relate the voltage drop across the element to the current flowing through it. These relations are

Resistors $\qquad$ $V_R = RI$

Inductors (coils) $\qquad$ $V_L = L\dfrac{dI}{dt}$ (D.13)

Capacitors $\qquad$ $\dfrac{dV}{dt} = \dfrac{1}{C}I$

where V = Voltage drop (volts)
I = Current (amperes)
R = Resistance (ohms)
L = Inductance (henries)
C = Capacitance (farads)

If each of these elements is connected in series to an oscillating voltage supply,

AC
voltage
supply
of frequency
$\omega/2\pi$

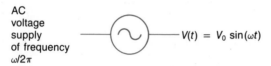

$V(t) = V_0 \sin(\omega t)$

as illustrated in the following figure,

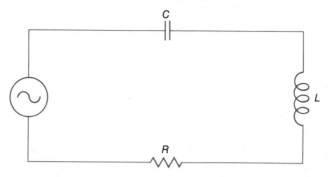

the equation for the circuit simply states that the voltage from the voltage supply must equal the sum of the voltage drops across the three elements.

$$V(t) = V_C + V_L + V_R \tag{D.14}$$

This equation is then solved for the current I as a function of time, which is not as trivial as it seems, since the three equations in Equation (D.13) are actually differential equations. However, the solution can be made to appear trivial by using complex numbers.

First, recall an important identity from algebra (DeMoivre's theorem)

$$e^{i\theta} = \cos \theta + i \sin \theta$$

Next, since the current is alternating, we expect a solution of the form

$$I(t) = I_0 \cos(\omega t)$$

But if, instead, we make the replacement

$$I(t) \rightarrow I_0 e^{i\omega t} \qquad \langle = I_0 \cos(\omega t) + i I_0 \sin(\omega t) \rangle$$

the *actual* current is simply the *real* part of this expression. Inserting this expression into Equation (D.13), we obtain

$$V_R = RI_0 e^{i\omega t} = RI(t)$$

$$V_L = LI_0 e^{i\omega t}(i\omega) = i\omega LI(t)$$

$$V_C = \frac{1}{C}I_0 \frac{e^{i\omega t}}{i\omega} = \frac{1}{i\omega}\left[\frac{1}{C}I(t)\right] \tag{D.15}$$

where the following calculus relations were used:

$$\frac{d}{dt}(e^{i\omega t}) = i\omega e^{i\omega t}$$

$$\int e^{i\omega t}\, dt = \frac{1}{i\omega}e^{i\omega t} + C$$

Inserting these results into Equation (D.15) results in

$$V(t) = V_0 \sin(\omega t) = V_R + V_L + V_C$$

$$= \left[R + i\left(\omega L - \frac{1}{\omega C}\right)\right]I(t)$$

$$= ZI(t) \tag{D.16}$$

where Z is called the complex impedance of the AC circuit. It is analogous to ordinary resistance in DC circuits. The actual current is then

$$I_{\text{actual}}(t) = \text{Real part}\left[\frac{V(t)}{Z}\right]$$

$$= V_0 \sin(\omega t)\left[\text{Real part}\left(\frac{1}{Z}\right)\right] \tag{D.17}$$

The measured AC current is an average of $|I_{\text{actual}}(t)|$ over one cycle. The average of the $|\text{sine}|$ is $1/\sqrt{2}$, so that

$$\langle I_{\text{actual}}\rangle = \frac{1}{\sqrt{2}}V_0 \,\text{Re}\left(\frac{1}{Z}\right) \tag{D.18}$$

where Re( ) means "real part of ( )" and the angle brackets designate an average over one cycle.[3] The measured AC voltage, say, across the resistor is then

$$\langle V_r \rangle = R\langle I_{\text{actual}}\rangle \tag{D.19}$$

Problem. Use the values

$$V_0 = 10.0 \text{ volts}$$
$$C = 3.35 \times 10^{-7} \text{ farads}$$
$$L = 1.5 \times 10^{-7} \text{ henries}$$

for the supply voltage, capacitance, and the inductance. Then, for each of the values of resistance

$$R = 0.167,\ 0.066,\ 0.250 \text{ ohms}$$

---

[3] More precisely, $\langle \sin^2(\omega t)\rangle_{\text{one cycle}} = 1/2$.

compute 51 values of the complex impedance Z defined in Equation (D.13) for values of ω from $\omega = 2\pi \times 5 \times 10^5$ to $2\pi \times 10 \times 10^5$ in steps of $2\pi \times 1 \times 10^4$. For each complex value of Z, compute the voltage across the resistor using Equation (D.16). Plot separate curves for each of the three values of the resistance.

Details. Your program should have the following subprogram modules:

- A COMPLEX function IMPEDC($R, L, C, OMEGA$) that uses Equation (D.16) to compute the complex impedance. The parameters R, L, C, and OMEGA are real.
- A real function CURRNT($V0, Z$) that uses Equation (D.18) to compute the actual current averaged over one cycle. (Z is complex.)

The main program should contain the following loops:

For R = 0.006, 0.167, 0.250 ohms

For $\omega = \frac{1}{2}\omega_0$ to $2\omega_0$ in steps of $\dfrac{\omega_0}{20}$.

Compute the impedance and the voltage across the resistor using the function IMPEDC, CURRNT, and Equation (D.19). The results should be stored in arrays W(0:30), V(3,0:30).

End-ω loop

End-R loop

Produce simultaneous plots of the three voltages versus frequency ω.

If the real part of a complex number $z = a + ib$ is A and the imaginary part is B (both real), then the FORTRAN assignment statement for Z is

```
Z = CMPLX(A,B)
```

Similarly, the real part of a complex number is obtained in FORTRAN by using the intrinsic function REAL( ), as

```
A = REAL(Z)
```

and the imaginary part by using the intrinsic function AIMAG( ),

```
B = AIMAG(Z)
```

Taylor Series and Numerical Differentiation

Introduction

In the mathematics courses you have taken, almost all of the problems you have faced had solutions that could be expressed in terms of relatively simple algebraic expressions. These so-called closed-form solutions may have involved combinations of trigonometric functions, radicals, exponentials, or logarithms. But regardless of how complicated the answer, you probably felt more comfortable with them than with a numerical result expressed, for example, as

$$\int_0^5 e^{-x^2} dx$$

This integral cannot be expressed in terms of simpler functions, and we somehow have the feeling that this result is less satisfactory than, say, $\sqrt{7}$. Both expressions represent well-defined numbers. But to compare them to other numbers we still have some numerical operations to carry out (push the $\sqrt{}$ key on a calculator, or numerically estimate the area under the curve e^{-x^2} from $x = 0$ to $x = 5$). Numerical analysis is the study of procedures whereby approximate answers are obtained for problems that do not have a closed-form solution or whose closed-form solution is too complicated to be useful. Most real problems fall into this category.

In calculus it is important to develop a facility to reason abstractly, so expressions involving symbolic variables are preferred over numerical results. Yet in actual engineering and scientific applications, a numerical answer is almost always the best you can hope for. Real problems rarely have neat and tidy answers in terms of simple functions.

Numerical analysis is an essential tool for all engineers, as important as any other skill. Even engineers who rely on code written by someone else to solve problems must be well versed in numerical methods to appreciate the limitations and range of the "canned" routines. The most important quality of a result, more important than the result itself, is the estimate of its validity.

A course in numerical methods has traditionally been a junior- or senior-level mathematics course for scientists and engineers. The reasons for this are not at all compelling. The primary reason is that physics needs calculus, so calculus must come first in the mathematics curriculum. Ordinarily, beginning students take only one mathematics course at a time and so other noncalculus topics must be postponed. The impression is then given that since topics like linear algebra, matrices, or series expansions appear in junior and senior courses, they are "advanced" topics and thus more difficult than calculus, when just the opposite is true. Of course, since these topics are presented to an audience of advanced students, they are presented in a more sophisticated manner than is necessary. The treatment presented here is designed for students who have had one semester of calculus or who are now taking a first calculus course. However, most of these topics will be discussed in this and the following chapters.

As was mentioned in the introduction to Chapter 1, modern computers have revolutionized the way we do mathematics, and it is important that the beginning mathematics curriculum both recognize this and adjust to it. Some topics in mathematics are well suited to learning through machine computation. In fact, topics like elementary differential equations, definite integrals, series, matrices, curve fitting, and interpolation are perhaps best learned by the process of meticulously coding the appropriate algorithms and discovering the limitations of a particular numerical method. Translating an algorithm into a working program is, as you are well aware, a stringent test of the depth of your understanding of the algorithm.

It is hoped that you will use this text to learn mathematics via computers to supplement what you learn in calculus and science. You should try to incorporate the FORTRAN and the mathematics. We will insist that the mathematics is not understood unless you are able to code it for the computer.

Many of the numerical methods discussed in this chapter are but variations on a single theme:

> It is frequently desired to effect a complicated mathematical operation on a complicated function. The problem is rendered tractable by approximating it by a somewhat simpler operation on a decidedly simpler function over a limited range. Typically a function will be replaced by a straight line or a parabola for points in the region of interest.

In this chapter we first describe the procedures for replacing an arbitrary function over a limited region by a series expansion, called the Taylor series. Retaining just the first few terms in such a series will then provide a mechanism for successively approximating the function by simpler expressions such as a straight line, a parabola, or a polynomial of arbitrary degree. This is followed by an introduction to the inverse problem, that of constructing a function to approximate a set of data points. A variety of difference equations are presented that can be used to obtain estimates of the derivatives of a function known only at a discrete set of points. These derivatives may then be used to build a series approximation to the function. Finally, for comparison, the Lagrange Interpolation Polynomial, a single function that will precisely match the data points over the entire range, is briefly described.

10.2 Taylor Series

Meaning of a Taylor Series

You are familiar with the notation for trigonometric functions

$\sin(x)$, $\cos(\theta)$, $\tan(\beta)$, and so on

or with logarithms and exponentials,

$\log(x)$, $\ln(y)$, e^z

If you had to tell the computer what these things mean, could you do it? You might start off by recognizing that each is a *function* or mapping; that is, given any x you can determine something called $\sin(x)$ or $\ln(x)$. The "meaning" then of $\sin(x)$ is contained in the algorithm for its computation. Which is? Well, one way of computing $\sin(x)$ is based on its series expansion, which we saw in Section 4.4. Namely,

$$\sin(x) = x - \frac{x^3}{3!} + \frac{x^5}{5!} - \frac{x^7}{7!} + \cdots \qquad (10.1)$$

Notice that since this is an *identity* (true for all x), the expression on the right is more than just equal to $\sin(x)$—it *is* $\sin(x)$. Any other method of calculating $\sin(x)$ must be equivalent to this series. Now we will answer the difficult question of where this series came from. We begin with the derivative of a power of x

$$\frac{d(x^n)}{dx} = nx^{n-1}$$

Furthermore, we will use the notation

$$\frac{df(x)}{dx}\bigg|_0$$

to mean the value of the derivative at $x = 0$ (i.e., first differentiate, then set $x = 0$). Next we differentiate the entire series for $\sin(x)$ with respect to x once and set $x = 0$. We obtain

$$\frac{d[\sin(x)]}{dx}\bigg|_0 = 1 - \frac{3x^2}{3!}\bigg|_0 + \frac{5x^4}{5!}\bigg|_0 - \cdots = 1 \tag{10.2}$$

Continuing, we can further differentiate the entire series again and set $x = 0$ to obtain

$$\frac{d^2 \sin(x)}{dx^2}\bigg|_0 = 0 - \frac{6x}{3!}\bigg|_0 + \frac{20x^3}{5!}\bigg|_0 - \frac{42x^5}{7!}\bigg|_0 + \cdots = 0 \tag{10.3}$$

Since $6/3! = 1$, it is clear that the third derivative evaluated at $x = 0$ will be -1. We could keep this up forever, or at least until we found a pattern. The result would be

$$\frac{d^n[\sin(x)]}{dx^n}\bigg|_0 = 0 \qquad \text{if } n \text{ is even}$$

$$= (-1)^{(n-1)/2} \qquad \text{if } n \text{ is odd} \tag{10.4}$$

Assuming that differentiating an infinite number of terms is an allowed operation (since the series is valid for all x, it is), we obtain the interesting result that we now know *all* the derivatives of $\sin(x)$ at $x = 0$. A much more startling result is the converse: if we know *all* the derivatives of a function at a particular point, we know the function *everywhere* and we know it uniquely.[1] This statement is the essence of Taylor series, which can be proved in a flagrantly nonrigorous manner, that is, graphically.

Suppose we know the value of a function of x at a particular value of x, say, $y_a = f(x = a)$. (See Figure 10-1.) And we wish to have an approximate value of the function *near $x = a$*. The simplest approximation is to assume that the value of the function remains about the same—that is, the 0th-order approximation

$$f(x) \simeq f(a) \qquad \text{if } |x - a| \text{ is small}$$

That is, if we are very close to the point $x = a$, this may not be a bad approximation.

With a bit of thought we can easily improve on this approximation. For the next level of approximation we might assume that the function between a and x is smooth enough to be approximated by a straight line. The slope of the line we pick for this approximation would be the same as that of the tangent line at $x = a$. Thus, the first-order approximation would be

$$f(x) \simeq f(a) + \Delta \qquad \text{if } |x - a| \text{ is small} \tag{10.5}$$

---

[1] As with all mathematical statements of this kind, there are some limitations on "everywhere" and "uniquely", as we shall see shortly.

Figure 10-1
Tangent line at the
point $x = a$

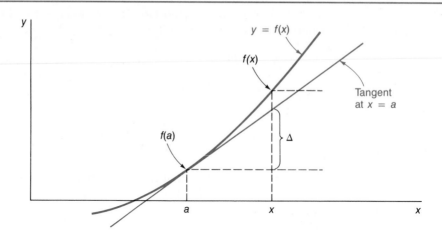

where Δ is defined in Figure 10-1. However, recall that the slope of a tangent line at a point is defined to be equal to the derivative at that point, so

$$\text{Slope of tangent at } x = a = \frac{\text{Opposite}}{\text{Adjacent}} = \frac{\Delta}{x - a} = \left(\frac{df}{dx}\right)\bigg|_{x=a} \qquad (10.6)$$

or

$$\Delta = \left(\frac{df}{dx}\right)\bigg|_{x=a} (x - a) \qquad (10.7)$$

and thus Equation (10.5) becomes

$$f(x) \simeq f(a) + \left(\frac{df}{dx}\right)\bigg|_{x=a} (x - a) \qquad (10.8)$$

The next level of approximation would be to improve on the straight line and assume that the function $f(x)$ between a and x can be approximated by a parabola. Since we have already determined the straight-line approximation to $f(x)$, we could use this information in our selection of the quadratic fit.

$$f(x) \approx \text{parabola}(x) = f(a) + \left(\frac{df}{dx}\right)\bigg|_{x=a} (x - a) + c_2(x - a)^2 \qquad (10.9)$$

And to determine the parameter c_2 we would require that the parabola approximate the function $f(x)$ as closely as possible by matching the value of both expressions, along with their first and second derivatives, at the point $x = a$.

$$f(x)|_{x=a} = \text{parabola}(x)|_{x=a}$$

$$= \left[f(a) + \left(\frac{df}{dx} \right) \bigg|_{x=a} (x - a) + c_2(x - a)^2 \right] \bigg|_{x=a}$$

$$= f(a)$$

$$\left(\frac{df}{dx} \right) \bigg|_{x=a} = \frac{d[\text{parabola}(x)]}{dx} \bigg|_{x=a}$$

$$= \left[0 + \left(\frac{df}{dx} \right) \bigg|_{x=a} \times 1 + 2c_2(x - a) \right] \bigg|_{x=a}$$

$$= \left(\frac{df}{dx} \right) \bigg|_{x=a}$$

and

$$\left(\frac{d^2f}{dx^2} \right) \bigg|_{x=a} = \frac{d^2[\text{parabola}(x)]}{dx^2} \bigg|_{x=a}$$

$$= [0 + 0 + 2c_2]|_{x=a}$$

$$= 2c_2$$

Thus,

$$c_2 = \frac{1}{2} \left(\frac{d^2f}{dx^2} \right) \bigg|_{x=a}$$

and the second-order approximation would be

$$f(x) \approx f(a) + \left(\frac{df}{dx} \right) \bigg|_{x=a} (x - a) + \frac{1}{2} \left(\frac{d^2f}{dx^2} \right) \bigg|_{x=a} (x - a)^2 \tag{10.10}$$

We could continue the procedure of replacing the function $f(x)$ by polynomials of higher and higher order indefinitely, or until we see a pattern emerging. The result would be the Taylor series[2]

$$f(x) = f(a) + f'(a)(x - a) + f''(a)\frac{1}{2!}(x - a)^2 + \cdots$$

$$+ f^{[n]}(a)\frac{1}{n!}(x - a)^n + \cdots \tag{10.11}$$

The main point to emphasize in Equation (10.11) is that this equation is no longer an approximation, but if expressed as an infinite series the relation is exact and an identity, valid for all x for which the series converges. The proof of this statement can be found in most calculus texts.

---

[2] This equation was introduced by Brook Taylor in 1715.

However, from the graphical interpretation of the first few items in the series, it does appear plausible. The conclusion is then, *if* we know *all* of the derivatives of a function at a single point, we know the function everywhere. (Again, there are technical qualifications on "everywhere" that will be discussed later in this chapter.) Since the Taylor series expansion defines an algorithm for computing the function, it in turn encompasses the complete meaning of the function.

In general, the smaller the quantity $|(x - a)|$ the fewer the number of terms required to obtain a sufficiently accurate value for $f(x)$. For example, if $(x - a) = h$ and $|h| \ll 1$, then

$$f(x) = f(a + h) \simeq f(a) + f'(a)h \tag{10.12}$$

or solving this equation for $f'(a)$ we obtain

$$f'(a) = \left(\frac{df}{dx} \right)\bigg|_{x=a} \simeq \frac{f(a + h) - f(a)}{h} \tag{10.13}$$

which is just what you would expect.

The special case of Equation (10.11) in which $a = 0$ is called the *Maclaurin series*.

$$f(x) = f(0) + f'(0)x + f''(0)\frac{x^2}{2!} + f'''(0)\frac{x^3}{3!} + \cdots + f^{[n]}(0)\frac{x^n}{n!} + \cdots$$

$$\tag{10.14}$$

To illustrate the use of Equations (10.11) and (10.14), a number of examples are given in the next section.

▬ Examples of Taylor and Maclaurin Series

To obtain either the Taylor or Maclaurin series expansion for a function, we must first compute *all* the derivatives of the function at a point. In many situations this formidable-sounding task is actually quite easy. If the function is a polynomial with positive integer powers of x, then eventually the higher derivatives of the polynomial will all be zero. Consider the following two examples:

1. Find the Maclaurin series for $f(x) = x^4 - 8x^3 + 24x^2 - 32x + 16$.

$$f(0) = (x^4 - 8x^3 + 24x^2 - 32x + 16)|_0 = 16$$
$$f'(0) = (4x^3 - 24x^2 + 48x - 32)|_0 \qquad = -32$$
$$f''(0) = (12x^2 + 48x + 48)|_0 \qquad = 48$$
$$f'''(0) = (24x - 48)|_0 \qquad = -48$$
$$f^{[iv]}(0) = 24 \qquad = 24$$

All higher derivatives are zero, and thus after inserting these terms into Equation (10.14) we obtain

$$f(x) = x^4 - 8x^3 + 24x^2 - 32x + 16$$

which is exactly what we started with. Notice that since *all* the higher derivatives are zero, the infinite series has collapsed into a finite expression, a polynomial. The original series is said to terminate after the fourth-order term. Since we started with a polynomial, the result must also be a polynomial and it must be the same polynomial.

2. Find the Taylor series for the same function with $a = 2$. Proceeding in the same manner as in the example above except that all the terms are evaluated at $x = 2$ instead of zero, we obtain the following result:

$$f(2) = 0 \qquad \text{0th order} = 0$$

$$f'(2) = 0 \qquad \text{1st order} = 0$$

$$f''(2) = 0 \qquad \text{2nd order} = 0$$

$$f'''(2) = 0 \qquad \text{3rd order} = 0$$

$$f^{[iv]}(2) = 24 \qquad \text{4th order} = \frac{24}{4!}(x - 2)^4$$

All higher derivatives are zero. In this case the Taylor series expansion for the polynomial gives the result

$$f(x) = (x - 2)^4$$

which, when multiplied out, is seen to be identical to the original polynomial.

More interesting situations are those that result in nonterminating infinite series. The following three examples are the series expansions for some transcendental functions. A *transcendental function* is one whose evaluation cannot be reduced to a finite number of arithmetic operations; that is, its simplest representation must be an infinite series.

Keep in mind that the key to obtaining a series expansion for any function is the ability to evaluate *all* the derivatives of the function at a single point.

1. Maclaurin series expansion for e^x. The symbol e^x is defined by the relation

$$\frac{d}{dx}e^x = e^x \qquad\qquad (10.15)$$

It should be obvious to you that this single equation defines *all* the derivatives of e^x; thus,

$$\frac{d^2}{dx^2}(e^x) = \frac{d}{dx}\left(\frac{de^x}{dx}\right) = \frac{d}{dx}(e^x) = e^x$$

and so on, and so all the derivatives of e^x are simply e^x. Furthermore, in the Maclaurin series all the derivatives are evaluated at $x = 0$, where $e^0 = 1$. The Maclaurin series for e^x is then

$$f(x) = f(0) + f'(0)x + f''(0)\frac{x^2}{2!} + f'''(0)\frac{x^3}{3!} + \cdots$$

$$e^x = e^0 + e^0 x + e^0\frac{x^2}{2!} + e^0\frac{x^3}{3!} + \cdots \tag{10.16}$$

$$e^x = 1 + x + \frac{x^2}{2!} + \frac{x^3}{3!} + \cdots + \frac{x^n}{n!} + \cdots$$

2. Maclaurin series for hyperbolic functions. We define two functions by the relations

$$\frac{d[\text{sink}(x)]}{dx} = \text{swim}(x)$$

and

$$\frac{d[\text{swim}(x)]}{dx} = \text{sink}(x)$$

$$\text{sink}(0) = 0$$

$$\text{swim}(0) = 1$$

To obtain the Maclaurin expansion for the function $\text{sink}(x)$, we must first evaluate the derivatives at $x = 0$.

$$\text{sink}(0) = 0$$

$$\text{sink}'(0) = \text{swim}(0) = 1$$

$$\text{sink}''(0) = \text{swim}'(0) = \text{sink}(0) = 0$$

$$\vdots$$

And thus the Maclaurin series for the function is easily seen to be

$$\text{sink}(x) = x + \frac{x^3}{3!} + \frac{x^5}{5!} + \frac{x^7}{7!} + \cdots \tag{10.17}$$

Similarly, the series for the companion function $\text{swim}(x)$ is found to be

$$\text{swim}(x) = 1 + \frac{x^2}{2!} + \frac{x^4}{4!} + \frac{x^6}{6!} + \cdots \tag{10.18}$$

The functions sink(x) and swim(x) are actually the same as the hyperbolic functions sinh(x) and cosh(x), respectively. The mathematically meaningless symbols "sink" and "swim" become well-defined functions once we specify their derivatives at a point. It will be shown that the two series expressions are valid for all values of x, and as a consequence we can manipulate the series just as we would ordinary functions. For example, by adding the two series you can show that

$$e^x = \sinh(x) + \cosh(x)$$

3. The Maclaurin series for sin(x). The determination of the series expansion for the sin(x) once again hinges on the evaluation of the derivatives at $x = 0$. These are defined by

$$\frac{d[\sin(x)]}{dx} = \cos(x) \tag{10.19}$$

$$\frac{d[\cos(x)]}{dx} = -\sin(x) \tag{10.20}$$

and

$$\sin(0) = 0 \qquad \cos(0) = 1$$

Using these relations you should have no difficulty verifying the results for the derivatives of the sin(x) [see Equation (10.4)] and then obtaining the result

$$\sin(x) = x - \frac{x^3}{3!} + \frac{x^5}{5!} - \frac{x^7}{7!} + \cdots \tag{10.21}$$

4. The Taylor series for $f(x) = (x)^{1/3}$ with $a = 1$. Evaluating the derivatives at $x = 1$, we obtain the following:

$$f(1) = x^{1/3}\big|_1 \qquad\qquad \text{0th order} = 1$$

$$f'(1) = \left(\frac{1}{3}x^{-2/3}\right)\bigg|_1 \qquad \text{1st order} = \frac{1}{3}(x-1)$$

$$f''(1) = \left(-\frac{2}{9}x^{-5/3}\right)\bigg|_1 \qquad \text{2nd order} = -\frac{1}{9}(x-1)^2$$

$$f'''(1) = \left(\frac{10}{27}x^{-8/3}\right)\bigg|_1 \qquad \text{3rd order} = \frac{5}{81}(x-1)^3$$

And so the expansion for $x^{1/3}$ to third order about the point $x = 1$ is

$$f(x) = x^{1/3} \simeq 1 + \frac{1}{3}(x-1) - \frac{1}{9}(x-1)^2 + \frac{5}{81}(x-1)^3 + \cdots \tag{10.22}$$

Finally, listed below are several Maclaurin series expansions of common mathematical functions. Each of these series can be derived by the methods of this section.

$$e^x = 1 + x + \frac{1}{2}x^2 + \frac{1}{6}x^3 + \frac{1}{24}x^4 + \cdots + \frac{x^n}{n!} + \cdots$$

$$\sin x = x - \frac{1}{6}x^3 + \cdots + (-1)^{n+1}\frac{1}{(2n-1)!}x^{2n-1} + \cdots$$

$$\cos x = 1 - \frac{1}{2}x^2 + \cdots + (-1)^n\frac{1}{(2n)!}x^{2n} + \cdots$$

$$\sinh(x) = x + \frac{1}{6}x^3 + \cdots + \frac{1}{(2n+1)!}x^{2n+1} + \cdots$$

$$\cosh(x) = 1 + \frac{1}{2}x^2 + \cdots + \frac{1}{(2n)!}x^{2n} + \cdots$$

$$\ln(1+x) = x - \frac{x^2}{2} + \frac{x^3}{3} - \frac{x^4}{4} + \cdots + (-1)^{n+1}\frac{x^n}{n} + \cdots$$

$$(\text{for } -1 < x \le 1)$$

■■■ Convergence of an Infinite Series

The Maclaurin series, Equation (10.14), could also be written in a shorter form as

$$f(x) = \sum_{p=0}^{\infty} a_p x^p = a_0 + a_1 x + a_2 x^2 + \cdots \tag{10.23}$$

where

$$a_p = \frac{1}{p!}\left(\frac{d^p f}{dx^p}\right)\Bigg|_0$$

If the series terminates, that is, contains only a finite number of terms,

$$\sum_{p=0}^{n} a_p x^p = a_0 + a_1 x + a_2 x^2 + \cdots + a_n x^n$$

it simply represents a polynomial and is thus obviously a well-defined function for all values of x. An infinite series is a different matter. Since it is clearly not possible to add up an infinite number of terms, if the series is to make any sense whatever, somewhere in the series the terms are going to have to become smaller and eventually approach zero. It may be possible to then approximate the exact value represented by the series to an *arbitrary* degree of accuracy by terminating the summation somewhere in the series. If so, the series is said to converge. If not, the series cannot be used to represent any number. We will see that the above series will in some cases converge to a number for any value of x, whereas in other cases convergence is possible only for a limited range of x. A necessary condition then for a series to converge (i.e., to represent a well-defined number) is that the nth term approach zero as n approaches infinity.

Necessary Condition for Convergence

$$\lim_{n \to \infty}(a_n x^n) \to 0 \qquad (10.24)$$

Unfortunately, in some circumstances even if this condition is satisfied the series may still not converge. The sufficient condition for the convergence of a series is usually expressed in terms of the ratio test. The *ratio test* examines the ratio of successive terms in the series and requires that eventually each term be smaller in absolute magnitude than the term that preceded it.

Sufficient Condition for Convergence—The Ratio Test

$$\lim_{n \to \infty}\left|\frac{(\text{term})_{n+1}}{(\text{term})_n}\right| < 1 \qquad (10.25)$$

Even though the terms in a series approach zero, the series may still diverge. The so-called harmonic series

$$1 + \frac{1}{2} + \frac{1}{3} + \frac{1}{4} + \cdots + \frac{1}{n} + \cdots \qquad (10.26)$$

is the classic example. Obviously the terms will approach zero as $n \to \infty$, yet if you attempt to sum this series you will find that the accumulated sum will slowly grow without limit.

n	Sum of the First n Terms of the Harmonic Series
10	2.928968
100	5.187378
1000	7.485471
10000	9.787606
100000	12.090146

The series fails the ratio test since

$$\text{Ratio} = \left|\frac{n}{(n + 1)}\right| \to 1 \qquad \text{as } n \to \infty$$

The terms, though approaching zero, are not decreasing fast enough to result in their accumulation being finite.

Another example is the series

$$1 - 1 + 1 - 1 + 1 - 1 + \cdots$$

This series has a sum that is either 0 or 1 depending on where you stop in the addition. The series clearly does not diverge, but it does not converge either. It fails both tests for convergence and thus cannot represent a well-defined number.

The ratio test was used in constructing algorithms for numerically summing an infinite series in Section 4.4. For example, the ratio of successive terms in the expansion for e^x is given by [see Equation (10.16)]:

$$R = \left(\frac{x^{n+1}}{(n+1)!} \right) \left(\frac{n!}{x^n} \right) = \frac{x}{n+1}$$

We see that R approaches 0 as n approaches ∞ regardless of the value of x, so that the expansion is valid and converges for *all* values of x.[3]

The Maclaurin series for the logarithm is found to be (see Problem 10.1)

$$\ln(1 + x) = x - \frac{x^2}{2} + \frac{x^3}{3} - \frac{x^4}{4} + \cdots \pm \frac{x^n}{n} + \cdots \qquad (10.27)$$

so that the ratio of the successive terms is

$$R = \left(\frac{n}{n+1} \right) x$$

and as $n \to \infty$, this ratio will approach $1x$. The ratio test then guarantees that the series will converge for values of $|x| < 1$. For positive values of x, the terms in Equation (10.27) alternate in sign and a significant amount of cancellation will occur in the summation, which may in turn result in the convergence of an otherwise divergent series. For the special case of an alternating series, the condition for convergence is simply that the terms approach zero as $n \to \infty$. Thus, the series

$$1 - \frac{1}{2} + \frac{1}{3} - \frac{1}{4} + \frac{1}{5} - \cdots$$

has a sum that is finite and equal to the $\ln(2)$. Notice that if $x = -1$ is inserted in Equation (10.27) the result is then the negative of the harmonic series. This confirms that $\ln(0) \to -\infty$.

Mathematical convergence of the Taylor or Maclaurin series is essential for the series expansion to be valid. A guarantee of convergence, however, is not always enough to someone who wishes to use the series to

---

[3] An interesting question is whether the individual terms then satisfy the necessary condition of approaching zero; that is, does $x^n/n! \to 0$ regardless of the value of x? The answer is yes. We have just shown that the series converges for all x, so the individual terms must approach zero.

compute a value for the function. Rapid convergence is most desired for computational purposes. For example, if we use the series for e^x given in Equation (10.16) to calculate e^{15}, the first several terms will be found to progressively increase in size. In fact, since the ratio of successive terms is $x/(n + 1)$, the terms will not even begin to diminish until the 15th term. The value of the 15th term is 334,864.6. If we continue to add terms until the size of the term is small, say, 10^{-3} or less, the expansion will include 45 terms. This will thus require a great deal of computation and will likely result in considerable round-off error. A more economical procedure would be to evaluate $e^{0.1}$ and then raise this to the 150th power.

There are numerous tricks for accelerating the convergence of a series by grouping terms or replacing the series by an equivalent series that converges faster. These procedures are rather clever and interesting and can be quite useful. However, their discussion here would take us too far afield. The interested student should see *Modern Computing Methods* 2nd ed., by van Wijngaarden and published by Philosophical Library, London, 1961.

Remainder Term

In calculus texts it is shown that the Taylor formula may be written as

$$f(x) = f(a) + f'(a)(x - a) + f''(a)\frac{(x - a)^2}{2!} + \cdots$$

$$+ f^{[n]}(a)\frac{(x - a)^n}{n!} + R_{n+1}(x) \qquad (10.28)$$

where

$$R_{n+1}(x) = f^{[n+1]}(\xi)\frac{(x - a)^{n+1}}{(n + 1)!} \qquad (10.29)$$

and ξ is some (unspecified) value between x and a. This term is called the remainder in Taylor's formula and represents the error incurred when the series is terminated after n terms. Since ξ is unspecified, we cannot determine the value of the remainder precisely, but it is often possible to calculate its maximum value and use this as the truncation error.

For example, suppose that you need a fast algorithm for the cube root of numbers that are close to 1. The function $f(x) = x^{1/3}$ could be Taylor-expanded about the point $a = 1$. The result through terms of order 3 was given in Equation (10.22). The truncation error is then the maximum value of the expression

$$\epsilon = \left|\frac{d^4(x^{1/3})}{dx^4}\right|_{\text{max}} \frac{(x - 1)^4}{4!} = -\frac{80}{81}\xi^{-11/3}\frac{(x - 1)^4}{24}$$

Notice that for a specific value of x, Equation (10.28) is valid only for some particular (unknown) value of ξ. In order to determine what value of ξ to use in $R_4(x)$ we must already know the exact value of $x^{1/3}$, which if known would render the series expansion superfluous. So, in those cases where a knowledge of the truncation error is important, it can be estimated by using the value of ξ that causes the expression to be a maximum. In the present case that would correspond to using the value of ξ in the range x to 1. These expressions are computed for a variety of x values and presented in Table 10-1.

Error Estimates by Order

If the function $f(x)$ is moderately complicated, it can often be extremely difficult to use the remainder expression to estimate the size of the truncation error. A less accurate but more convenient procedure is simply to make use of the fact that no matter how complicated the remainder term may be, we at least know that it is proportional to $(x - a)^{n+1}$ and that successive terms must diminish in size.

The notation $\mathcal{O}(x - a)^n$ is used to indicate that an expression *is of order* $(x - a)^n$, meaning that the term "varies as" $(x - a)^n$ or "is proportional to" $(x - a)^n$. Thus, if a Taylor series is truncated after five terms, we say that the series expression for $f(x)$ "is accurate to $\mathcal{O}(x - a)^6$." The notation when applied to a Taylor series means a bit more than that the remainder term is proportional to $(x - a)^6$, it implies that since the series converges,

$$\mathcal{O}(x - a)^7 < \mathcal{O}(x - a)^6$$

This is of course true if $|x - a| < 1$, but for the terms in the series should also be true even if $|x - a| > 1$.[4]

The expansion for e^x may then be written as

$$e^x = 1 + x + \frac{x^2}{2!} + \mathcal{O}(x^3) \tag{10.30}$$

denoting that the error in truncating after the x^2 term is of order x^3. From the definition of $\mathcal{O}(x^n)$ it is clear that the following relations are valid:

Table 10-1

Comparison of the remainder term and the actual error

	$f(x) = x^{1/3}$			
x	$x^{1/3}$ (from series to 3rd order)	$x^{1/3}$ (exact)	Actual Error	Maximum Value of Remainder $(R_{4,max})$
0.7	0.8883. . .	0.8879. . .	0.0004	0.0012
0.8	0.92840. . .	0.92832. . .	0.00008	0.00015
0.9	0.965494. . .	0.965489. . .	0.000004	0.000006
0.95	0.9830478. . .	0.9830476. . .	0.00000027	0.00000031
1.10	1.032284. . .	1.032280. . .	0.0000038	0.0000041

---

[4] To be precise, this may not be true for the first few terms in an expansion or if some of the terms are accidentally zero.

$$\mathcal{O}(x^3)\mathcal{O}(x^7) = \mathcal{O}(x^{10})$$

$$5x^2\mathcal{O}(x^4) = \mathcal{O}(x^6)$$

$$[\mathcal{O}(x^2)]^3 = \mathcal{O}(x^6)$$

$$\mathcal{O}(x^4) < \mathcal{O}(x^3)$$

The series expansion for $\sin(x)$ could also be written to $\mathcal{O}(x^3)$ as[5]

$$\sin(x) = x + \mathcal{O}(x^3)$$

We can employ both of these series to then obtain the Taylor series for the more complicated function $f(x) = e^{\sin(x)}$:

$$e^{\sin(x)} = 1 + [\sin(x)] + \frac{[\sin(x)]^2}{2} + \mathcal{O}\{[\sin(x)]^3\}$$

$$= 1 + [x + \mathcal{O}(x^3)] + \frac{1}{2}[x + \mathcal{O}(x^3)]^2 + \mathcal{O}\{[x + \mathcal{O}(x^3)]^3\}$$

$$= 1 + x + \frac{1}{2}x^2 + \mathcal{O}(x^3) \tag{10.31}$$

The same expression could also be obtained for $e^{\sin(x)}$ by evaluating the derivatives at $x = 0$ and constructing the Taylor (or Maclaurin) series. Since the Taylor series is a unique representation of a function, a valid series expansion for a function obtained by any means whatsoever must be identical to the Taylor series.

The utility of a series representation for a complex function can be appreciated if you are faced with the task of obtaining a numerical result for the integral

$$\int_{0.0}^{0.2} e^{\sin(x)}\,dx$$

This integral cannot be done analytically, that is, expressed in a closed form. However, using Equation (10.31) a numerical answer is easily obtained.

$$\int_{0.0}^{0.2} e^{\sin(x)}\,dx = \int_{0.0}^{0.2}\left[1 + x + \frac{x^2}{2} + \mathcal{O}(x^3)\right]dx$$

$$= \left[x + \frac{x^2}{2} + \frac{x^3}{6} + \mathcal{O}(x^4)\right]\Bigg|_{0.0}^{0.2}$$

$$= 0.221 \pm \mathcal{O}|0.0016|$$

---

[5] Notice that since there is no x^2 term in the expansion for $\sin(x)$, terminating after the x term will result in a series accurate to $\mathcal{O}(x^3)$.

A very important consideration when combining two approximate expressions is:

The accuracy of a combination of two or more approximations is no more accurate than the *least* accurate piece.

Thus, if the algorithm to compute e^x were very accurate and time consuming, say to $\mathcal{O}(x^{10})$, whereas the procedure to obtain $\sin(x)$ were fast and less accurate, say to $\mathcal{O}(x^3)$, then not only would combining the two to compute $e^{\sin(x)}$ be accurate to only $\mathcal{O}(x^3)$, but the lengthy and accurate algorithm for e^x would be wasted—a very inefficient procedure. No part of an algorithm should be excessively accurate if *any* other part of the algorithm will be less precise.

A final point is that it is extremely important in a calculation to know the accuracy of the numbers at each stage. For example, if an approximation like

$$e^x \simeq 1 + x + \frac{x^2}{2}$$

is used to calculate $e^{0.1112}$ and the computer is then instructed to print the result with an F11.8 format, the machine dutifully complies with

    1.11738272

And if it is not known in advance that the last five digits are meaningless, obvious difficulties could result.

Uses of Taylor Series

The Taylor series formula, Equation (10.11), is useful in the construction of simpler computational algorithms of varying accuracy for much more complicated functions. Just as important, the Taylor series provides a "recipe" for the evaluation of a function, thereby completely specifying the meaning of the function.

The Taylor series is the starting point for much of numerical analysis. For example, frequently a function is known only at a finite number of points. The Taylor formula can be used to fill in the function between points (interpolation) or to predict the value at some subsequent point (extrapolation). Taylor series are also used to construct procedures for numerically differentiating and integrating a function and for solving differential equations.

10.3 Numerical Differentiation

The definition of a derivative in calculus is based on the idea of a *limit* of a function of a *continuous* variable

$$\frac{df(x)}{dx} = \lim_{\Delta x \to 0} \left| \frac{f(x + \Delta x) - f(x)}{\Delta x} \right| \tag{10.32}$$

and for a variety of functions, this operation can be expressed in terms of simple closed-form expressions. Using this definition, equations like

$$\frac{d(x^n)}{dx} = nx^{n-1}$$

$$\frac{d[\sin(x)]}{dx} = \cos(x)$$

$$\frac{d(e^{ax})}{dx} = ae^{ax}$$

are derived. However, the result of a computer operation is a number, not a function. So, we must replace all the algebraic rules learned for differentiating various functions with a numerical procedure that will take an arbitrary function and return the *value* of its derivative at a specified point. The procedure could be based on the definition above, but, computationally, the process of a limit is inherently unstable (division by small numbers, subtraction of two nearly equal numbers) and so more well-behaved algorithms must be developed.

Finite Difference Calculus

The calculus of finite differences employs the fundamental ideas of ordinary calculus up to the point of taking the limit $\Delta x \to 0$. In the finite difference calculus, Δx is treated as a small quantity, but not infinitesimal. Many of the equations we derive will look familiar to you from calculus, the principal distinction being that we must keep track of correction terms proportional to Δx, terms that would vanish in ordinary calculus.

To obtain an approximate expression for the derivative of a function, $f'(x)$, we begin with the Taylor series expansion written as

$$f(x + \Delta x) = f(x) + f'(x)\Delta x + f''(x)\frac{\Delta x^2}{2!} + f'''(x)\frac{\Delta x^3}{3!} + \cdots \tag{10.33}$$

This is a Taylor series expansion of the function about the point x. Formally solving this equation for $f'(x)$, we obtain

$$f'(x) = \frac{1}{\Delta x}\left\{ f(x + \Delta x) - f(x) - f''(x)\frac{\Delta x^2}{2!} - f'''(x)\frac{\Delta x^3}{3!} - \cdots \right\}$$

$$= \left\{ \frac{f(x + \Delta x) - f(x)}{\Delta x} \right\} - \Delta x \left\{ \frac{f''(x)}{2!} + \frac{f'''(x)}{3!}\Delta x + \cdots \right\}$$

$$= \left\{ \frac{f(x + \Delta x) - f(x)}{\Delta x} \right\} + \mathcal{O}(\Delta x) \qquad (10.34)$$

The function is next specified at equally spaced points beginning at $x = a$,

$$
\begin{array}{ll}
x_0 = a & f_0 = f(a) \\
x_1 = a + \Delta x & f_1 = f(a + \Delta x) \\
x_2 = a + 2\,\Delta x & f_2 = f(a + 2\,\Delta x) \\
\quad \cdots & \quad \cdots \\
x_i = a + i\,\Delta x & f_i = f(a + i\,\Delta x)
\end{array}
$$

so that at $x = x_i$

$$f'(x_i) = f'_i = \frac{f_{i+1} - f_i}{\Delta x} + \mathcal{O}(\Delta x)$$

Forward and Backward Difference Equations

First Difference Equations. If we define the *first forward difference* of the function $f(x)$ as

$$\Delta f_i \equiv f_{i+1} - f_i \qquad \text{First forward difference} \qquad (10.35)$$

then the equation for the derivative may be written as

$$f'_i = \frac{\Delta f_i}{\Delta x} + \mathcal{O}(\Delta x) \qquad (10.36)$$

This relation states that the derivative at a point x_i is approximately equal to the slope of the line connecting (x_i, f_i) and the *next* point (x_{i+1}, f_{i+1}).

A similar equation relating f' to the slope between (x_i, f_i) and the *previous* point is easily obtained by replacing Δx by $-\Delta x$ in Equations (10.33) and (10.34) to yield

$$f'(x) = f'_i = \frac{f(x_i) - f(x_{i-1})}{\Delta x} + \mathcal{O}(\Delta x)$$

$$= \frac{f_i - f_{i-1}}{\Delta x} + \mathcal{O}(\Delta x) \qquad (10.37)$$

We then define the *first backward difference* at x_i as

$$\nabla f_i \equiv f_i - f_{i-1} \qquad \text{First backward difference} \qquad (10.38)$$

and write Equation (10.36) as

$$f_i' = \frac{\nabla f_i}{\Delta x} + \mathcal{O}(\Delta x) \tag{10.39}$$

These two approximations to the first derivative are illustrated in Figure 10-2.

Second Difference Equations. The second forward difference at x_i is defined as

$$
\begin{aligned}
\Delta^2 f_i &= \Delta(\Delta f_i) \\
&= \Delta(f_{i+1} - f_i) \\
&= \Delta f_{i+1} - \Delta f_i \\
&= (f_{i+2} - f_{i+1}) - (f_{i+1} - f_i) \\
&= f_{i+2} - 2f_{i+1} + f_i \quad \text{Second forward difference}
\end{aligned}
\tag{10.40}
$$

and it is easily shown (see Problem 10.10) that

$$f_i'' = \frac{\Delta^2 f_i}{\Delta x^2} + \mathcal{O}(\Delta x) \tag{10.41}$$

Repeating the procedure for backward differences, we easily obtain

$$
\begin{aligned}
\nabla^2 f_i &= \nabla(\nabla f_i) \\
&= f_i - 2f_{i-1} + f_{i-2} \quad \text{Second backward difference}
\end{aligned}
\tag{10.42}
$$

Figure 10-2
Graphical interpretation of the forward and backward expressions for the first derivative

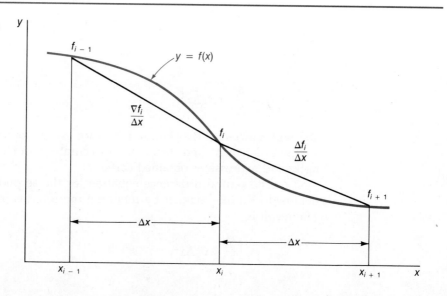

and

$$f_i'' = \frac{\nabla^2 f_i}{\Delta x^2} + \mathcal{O}(\Delta x) \tag{10.43}$$

Central Difference Equations. More symmetrical expressions for numerical derivatives can be derived by combining and averaging the equations for forward and backward differences.

$$\delta f_i \equiv \frac{1}{2}(\Delta f_i + \nabla f_i)$$

$$= \frac{1}{2}[(f_{i+1} - f_i) - (f_i - f_{i-1})]$$

$$= \frac{1}{2}(f_{i+1} - f_{i-1}) \quad \text{First central difference} \tag{10.44}$$

The central difference may be related to the first derivative of $f(x)$ at x_i in a manner similar to that used for forward and backward differences. Rewriting the Taylor series first with Δx and then with $-\Delta x$,

$$f_{i+1} = f(x_i + \Delta x) = f(x_i) + f'(x_i)\Delta x + f''(x_i)\frac{\Delta x^2}{2!} + f'''(x_i)\frac{\Delta x^3}{3!} + \cdots$$

$$f_{i-1} = f(x_i - \Delta x) = f(x_i) - f'(x_i)\Delta x + f''(x_i)\frac{\Delta x^2}{2!} - f'''(x_i)\frac{\Delta x^3}{3!} + \cdots$$

Subtracting the second equation from the first, the even derivatives cancel and we obtain

$$\frac{1}{2}(f_{i+1} - f_{i-1}) = f_i'\Delta x + \Delta x^3 \left(\frac{1}{3!}f_i''' + \frac{\Delta x^2}{5!}f_i^{[v]} + \cdots \right)$$

so that

$$f_i' = \frac{\delta f_i}{\Delta x} + \mathcal{O}(\Delta x^2) \tag{10.45}$$

You will notice that the central difference expression for the derivative is second-order in Δx and thus is more accurate than either the forward or backward expressions obtained earlier.

The central difference equation for the second derivative can be obtained in a like manner by retaining more terms in the Taylor series. The result is

$$f_i'' = \frac{\delta^2 f_i}{\Delta x^2} + \mathcal{O}(\Delta x^2) \tag{10.46}$$

where

$$\delta^2 f_i = \frac{1}{2}[\Delta^2 f_{i-1} + \nabla^2 f_{i+1}]$$

$$= \frac{1}{2}[(f_{i+1} - 2f_i + f_{i-1}) + (f_{i+1} - 2f_i + f_{i-1})]$$

$$= f_{i+1} - 2f_i + f_{i-1} \quad \text{Second central difference} \tag{10.47}$$

■ Example of Data Analysis Using Numerical Derivatives

A standard experiment in introductory physics is to measure the rate of fall of a light spherical object in air. The forces acting on the ball during its fall are gravity and air drag. The functional form of the air-drag force is unknown, except that it is known to depend on the velocity. Newton's second law, $F = ma$, then reads

$$F = ma = m\frac{d^2 y(t)}{dt^2} = mg + f_{\text{drag}}(v) \tag{10.48}$$

where $y(t)$ is the distance of fall at time t, g is the gravitational acceleration, m is the mass of the ball, and $f_{\text{drag}}(v)$ is the unknown air-drag force. The data from the experiment consist of a table of y versus t values, evenly spaced at $\frac{1}{40}$ of a second. By computing the numerical first derivative of this set, we can estimate the velocity v; the second derivatives will yield the acceleration and thus determine the air-drag force as a function of time.

$$\left(\frac{1}{m}\right)f_{\text{drag}}(v) = a - g$$

The data and the numerical derivatives are presented in Table 10-2. In Figure 10-3 the tabulated values of v_i and $-(a_i - g)$ are used to construct a graph of $(1/m)f_{\text{drag}}$ versus v^2 to test the hypothesis that f_{drag} is proportional to v^2.

$$f_{\text{drag}}(v) = -\gamma m v^2 \tag{10.49}$$

where γ is the air-drag coefficient. From the graph we see that the data suggest that an approximate value for γ would equal the slope of the line drawn through the data points; that is, $\gamma \approx 0.12 \text{ m}^{-1}$.

■ Solving Differential Equations Using Difference Expressions

Although we will not study differential equations in detail until Chapter 15, it is instructive to have at least a glimpse of how difference expressions can be used to numerically solve some common equations.

Table 10-2

Numerical first and second derivatives of experimental free-fall data

i	t_i (sec)	y_i (m)	v_i (m/sec)	a_i (m/sec^2)	$(a_i - g)$ (m/sec^2)
1	0.025	0.0075			
2	0.050	0.0185	0.560	9.60	−0.20
3	0.075	0.0355	0.790	8.80	−1.00
4	0.100	0.0581	1.010	8.80	−1.00
5	0.125	0.0860	1.212	7.36	−2.44
6	0.150	0.119	1.200	7.68	−2.12
7	0.175	0.156	1.568	5.76	−4.04
8	0.200	0.197	1.720	6.40	−3.40
9	0.225	0.242	1.880	6.40	−3.40
10	0.250	0.291	2.020	4.80	−5.00
11	0.275	0.343	2.140	4.80	−5.00
12	0.300	0.398	2.240	3.20	−6.60
13	0.325	0.455	2.340	4.80	−5.00
14	0.350	0.515	2.440	3.20	−6.60
15	0.375	0.577	2.520	3.28	−6.60
16	0.400	0.641	2.592	2.56	−7.24
17	0.425	0.707	2.650	2.08	−7.72
18	0.450	0.774	2.700	1.92	−7.88
19	0.475	0.842	2.740	1.28	−8.52
20	0.500	0.910	2.768	0.96	−8.84
21	0.525	0.980	2.790	0.80	−9.00
22	0.550	1.050	2.800	0.00	−9.80
23	0.575	1.120			

Figure 10-3

Plot of air-drag force versus velocity squared

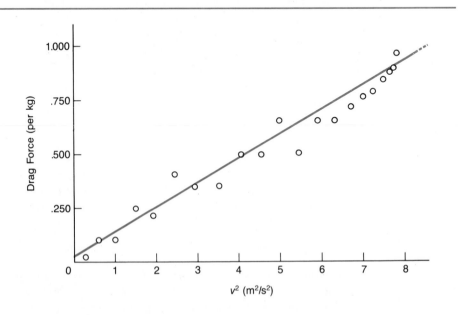

Again consider the equation defining the motion of an object falling in air. Assuming the air drag is given by an expression like Equation (10.49), Newton's second law then reads

$$F = ma = m\frac{dv}{dt} = mg - \gamma m v^2 \tag{10.50}$$

If we next replace the derivative of v with respect to t by the forward difference approximation, we obtain

$$\frac{v_{i+1} - v_i}{\Delta t} = g - \gamma v^2 \tag{10.51}$$

which can be rewritten in a form more suggestive of a numerical solution:

$$v_{i+1} = v_i + (g - \gamma v_i^2)\Delta t \tag{10.52}$$

Thus, if we begin with $v_0 = 0$, $\gamma = 0.12$, and $\Delta t = 1/40$ second, we can determine v_1. From v_1 we can compute v_2, and so on.

The FORTRAN code to numerically solve for the velocity during the first 100 time steps, based on the assumption that f_{drag} is proportional to v^2 would be

```
PROGRAM VELOC
PARAMETER (N = 100)
REAL V(0:N),DT,GAMMA,G
DATA V(0),DT,GAMMA,G /0., 0.025, 0.12, 9.80/
WRITE(*,*)' i       time       velocity'
DO 1 I = 0,N-1
    V(I+1) = V(I) + (G - GAMMA*V(I)**2)*DT
    WRITE(*,'(I4,T9,F6.3,T19,F6.3)')I,I*DT,V(I)
1 CONTINUE
STOP
END
```

The solution obtained by this means is not particularly accurate since the error is proportional to Δt and the error in each step is added to the error from the previous step. Much of the research activity in numerical analysis is concerned with obtaining accurate and reliable solutions of differential equations using efficient algorithms. We shall return to this topic in Chapter 15.

10.4 Interpolation

One purpose of a Taylor series is to replace a complicated function by a simpler approximation to that function. Thus, a straight-line approximation to a function in the vicinity of a point x_0 would retain only the first two terms of the series expanded about x_0. Similarly, a quadratic approximation would retain three terms, and so on.

A different use of the Taylor series would be to draw a smooth curve through evenly spaced data points. For example, if we have a collection of data labeled as (x_i, y_i) for $i = 1, n$ we could use the equations of Section 10.3 to numerically compute the approximate first and second derivatives of the data at a particular point. These derivatives could then be used to construct a Taylor series of the function the data supposedly represent in the vicinity of that point.

For example, consider the data set (x_i, y_i) listed in Table 10-3. [These numbers were generated by evaluating the function $f(x) = \sin(x) - x \cos(x)$ at the 11 points $x_i = 0, 0.1, \ldots, 1.0$.] The values of y_i are then used to compute the first and second central difference approximations to

Table 10-3
Using numerical derivatives and the Taylor series to interpolate data; a comparison of the interpolated values with the actual function

			At Tabulated Points			At Intermediate Points	
i	x_i	y_i	$\dfrac{\delta^2 y_i}{(\Delta x)^2}$	$\dfrac{\delta y_i}{\Delta x}$	Approximate $y(x) \approx$ Taylor Series	Exact $f(x) =$ $\sin(x) - x\cos(x)$
0	0.00	0.000000				
	0.05				−0.000082	0.000042
1	0.10	0.000333	0.01328	0.19900		
	0.15				0.001123	0.001246
2	0.20	0.002656	0.04293	0.39402		
	0.25				0.005175	0.005295
3	0.30	0.008919	0.09169	0.58115		
	0.35				0.014117	0.014230
4	0.40	0.020994	0.15858	0.75656		
	0.45				0.029764	0.029868
5	0.50	0.040634	0.24224	0.91665		
	0.55				0.053799	0.053892
6	0.60	0.069441	0.34097	1.05801		
	0.65				0.087732	0.087812
7	0.70	0.108828	0.45275	1.17756		
	0.75				0.132872	0.132938
8	0.80	0.159991	0.57525	1.27246		
	0.85				0.190295	0.190344
9	0.90	0.223878	0.70589	1.34035		
	0.95				0.260816	0.260848
10	1.00	0.301169				

the derivatives of this function at each of the interior points. Using these values for the derivatives, the Taylor series through quadratic terms is constructed and as an approximation to the actual function represented by the data. Finally, the approximate expression is evaluated at the intermediate points $(x_i + 0.05)$ and compared with the actual function values at these points.

Using this idea we have thus estimated the value of the underlying function at positions between actual data points; that is, we have "interpolated" the data by smoothly fitting a curve through the actual known points. The fitting curve was, in this case, chosen to be the Taylor series approximation based on numerical central difference expressions for the derivatives. There are numerous other procedures for smoothly drawing a curve through discrete points. This topic will be discussed again in Chapter 13.

Lagrange Interpolation Polynomial

The Taylor series approximation is designed to smoothly fit a function over a limited range. A single Taylor series expansion about a point (x_0, y_0) certainly cannot be expected to go exactly through each and every remaining data point (x_i, y_i). In the example above, a different Taylor series was obtained for each of the data points. It is not difficult to construct a polynomial that will go exactly through each and every data point. This polynomial is called the *Lagrange interpolation polynomial*.

Consider the problem of drawing a line $y(x) = ax + b$ through two points (x_0, y_0) and (x_1, y_1). As one procedure for doing this, consider

$$y(x) = y_0 \frac{(x - x_1)}{(x_0 - x_1)} + y_1 \frac{(x - x_0)}{(x_1 - x_0)}$$

Notice that this expression has been constructed so that the conditions $y(x_0) = y_0$ and $y(x_1) = y_1$ are automatically satisfied.

Next try the same procedure to fit a quadratic through three points, (x_0, y_0), (x_1, y_1), and (x_2, y_2):

$$y(x) = y_0 \frac{(x - x_1)(x - x_2)}{(x_0 - x_1)(x_0 - x_2)} + y_1 \frac{(x - x_0)(x - x_2)}{(x_1 - x_0)(x_1 - x_2)} + y_2 \frac{(x - x_0)(x - x_1)}{(x_2 - x_0)(x_2 - x_1)}$$

It is not difficult to see that the generalization to n data points would be

$$y(x) = \sum_{k=0}^{n} y_k \left\{ \prod_{\substack{i=0 \\ i \neq k}}^{n} \frac{(x - x_i)}{(x_k - x_i)} \right\} \tag{10.53}$$

where the notation Π is used to indicate a continued product; that is,

$$\prod_{i=0}^{n} a_i \equiv a_0 \times a_1 \times a_3 \times \cdots \times a_n$$

Notice that in the product the term $i = k$ is excluded. This product is evaluated for each value of k, multiplied by y_k, and summed over k. Additionally, this equation is not limited to equally spaced points.

Equation (10.53) is relatively easy to implement in terms of a FORTRAN function and would appear to be the ultimate answer in fitting a curve to data. After all, it is designed to go precisely through every data point. However, as with all numerical procedures, there are limitations. The Taylor series approximation to a function has the advantage of being a "smooth" fit to the data and the disadvantage of being valid only over a limited range. On the other hand, although the Lagrange interpolation polynomial extends over the entire range of the data, it is very likely that it is "not smooth." For example, if the data consist of 20 points, the Lagrange function will be a polynomial of degree 19 and will exhibit numerous "wiggles" that are unlikely to be an accurate representation of the actual function represented by the data.

This is illustrated in Figure 10-4, where nine data points are fit with a Lagrange interpolation polynomial. This is compared on the same figure with a fit to every other data point and with a fit only to the ends and the midpoint. Notice that the exact fit to relatively smooth data has generated a wildly oscillating function that gets worse as more data points are included. The Lagrange function thus should never be used to fit data. Its utility is strictly as an element of various integration algorithms that will be developed in Chapter 14.

Summary

The standard method of expressing a function in terms of the elementary operations of addition, subtraction, multiplication, and division is the Taylor series:

Figure 10-4
Comparison of Lagrange interpolation polynomial fits through 3, 5, and 9 data points

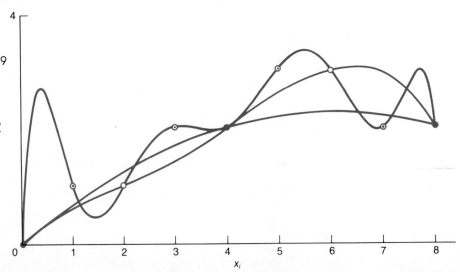

$$f(x) = f(a) + f'(a)(x - a) + \frac{1}{2!}f''(a)(x - a)^2 + \cdots + \frac{1}{n!}f^{[n]}(a)(x - a)^n + \cdots$$

which represents an expansion of the function $f(x)$ about the point $x = a$. The function and all of its derivatives are evaluated at $x = a$. Successive terms in the series correspond to approximating the function by higher-order polynomials in x. For example, retaining only the first two terms results in a linear approximation to the function with a line through the point $[a, f(a)]$ with a slope equal to $f'(a)$. A special case of the Taylor series with $a = 0$ is called the Maclaurin series:

$$f(x) = f_0 + f_0'x + \frac{1}{2!}f_0''x^2 + \cdots + \frac{1}{n!}f_0^{[n]}x^n + \cdots$$

Examples of Maclaurin series for several common mathematical functions are:

$$e^x = 1 + x + \frac{1}{2}x^2 + \frac{1}{6}x^3 + \frac{1}{24}x^4 + \cdots + \frac{x^n}{n!} + \cdots$$

$$\sin x = x - \frac{1}{6}x^3 + \cdots + (-1)^{n+1}\frac{1}{(2n-1)!}x^{2n-1} + \cdots$$

$$\cos x = 1 - \frac{1}{2}x^2 + \cdots + (-1)^n\frac{1}{(2n)!}x^{2n} + \cdots$$

$$\sinh(x) = x + \frac{1}{6}x^3 + \cdots + \frac{1}{(2n+1)!}x^{2n+1} + \cdots$$

$$\cosh(x) = 1 + \frac{1}{2}x^2 + \cdots + \frac{1}{(2n)!}x^{2n} + \cdots$$

$$\ln(1 + x) = x - \frac{x^2}{2} + \frac{x^3}{3} - \frac{x^4}{4} + \cdots + (-1)^{n+1}\frac{x^n}{n} + \cdots$$

$$\text{(for } -1 < x \leq 1)$$

- Convergence Criteria for Infinite Series:
  The Ratio Test:
  If a series is represented by $\sum_{n=1}^{\infty} a_n x^n$, then the series will converge (diverge) if r is less than (greater than) 1, where

$$r \equiv \lim_{n \to \infty} \left| \frac{a_{n+1}x^{n+1}}{a_n x^n} \right|$$

- Truncation of a Series
  An expression obtained from a Taylor series by truncating terms of order n or higher will produce an error that is proportional to x^n.

- Numerical Differentiation

Approximate expressions for the derivative of a function $f(x)$ at a point x_i are:

	Forward Difference	Backward Difference	Central Difference
	$\Delta f_i \equiv f_{i+1} - f_i$	$\nabla f_i \equiv f_i - f_{i-1}$	$\delta f_i \equiv \frac{1}{2}(f_{i+1} + f_{i-1})$
$f_i' =$	$\dfrac{\Delta f_i}{\Delta x} + \mathcal{O}(\Delta x)$	$\dfrac{\nabla f_i}{\Delta x} + \mathcal{O}(\Delta x)$	$\dfrac{\delta f_i}{\Delta x} + \mathcal{O}(\Delta x^2)$
$f_i'' =$	$\dfrac{\Delta^2 f_i}{\Delta x^2} + \mathcal{O}(\Delta x)$	$\dfrac{\nabla^2 f_i}{\Delta x^2} + \mathcal{O}(\Delta x)$	$\dfrac{\delta^2 f_i}{\Delta x^2} + \mathcal{O}(\Delta x^2)$
	$\dfrac{(f_i - 2f_{i+1} + f_{i+2})}{\Delta x^2}$	$\dfrac{(f_i - 2f_{i-1} + f_{i-2})}{\Delta x^2}$	$\dfrac{(f_{i+1} - 2f_i + f_{i-1})}{\Delta x^2}$

Problems

10.1 Determine the Maclaurin series for the following functions; for part e obtain the general expression for the ratio of successive terms.

a. $(2x - 1)^5$

b. e^{2x} Note: $\dfrac{d}{dx}(e^{ax}) = ae^{ax}$

c. $\cos(1 + 2x)$ Note: $\dfrac{d}{dx}\{\cos[f(x)]\} = -\sin[f(x)]\dfrac{df(x)}{dx}$

d. $(1 - x)^{1/2}$

e. $\ln(1 + x)$ Note: $\dfrac{d}{dx}\{\ln[f(x)]\} = \dfrac{1}{f(x)}\dfrac{df}{dx}$

10.2 Determine the maximum value of the remainder term after including six terms in the series for the first three functions of Problem 10.1. Use first $x = 1/2$, then $x = 2$.

10.3 Determine the Taylor series expansions of the following functions:

a. $32x^5 - 80x^4 + 80x^3 - 40x^2 + 10x - 1$ With $a = 1/2$

b. $\cos(1 + 2x)$ With $a = -1/2$

c. $\ln(2 + x)$ With $a = -1$

10.4 For each of the functions in Problem 10.3, evaluate the Taylor series expressions, retaining terms through x^3 at $x = 0$ and $x = 1$, and compare with the exact value of the function.

10.5 Determine the maximum value of the remainder term in the series expansion for e^x after including six terms. Use $x = 0.1$ and then $x = 10.0$. Compare this with the difference between the sum of the first six terms of the series for $x^{0.1}$ and e^{10}, respectively.

10.6 Using the Maclaurin series expansion for $\sin(x)$ and $\cos(x)$, show that

$$e^{ix} = \cos(x) + i\sin(x)$$

where $i = \sqrt{-1}$, $i^2 = -1$, $i^3 = -i$, and so on.

10.7 Use the fact that

$$e^x = 1 + x + \mathcal{O}(x^2)$$

and

$$\ln(z) = (z - 1) + \mathcal{O}[(z - 1)^2]$$

to determine the series expansion for $\ln(e^x)$ valid to $\mathcal{O}(x^2)$. [*Note:* The answer is obviously $\ln(e^x) = x$. But go through the algebra anyway.]

10.8 Use the fact that

$$e^x = 1 + x + \frac{x^2}{2} + \mathcal{O}(x^3)$$

and

$$\ln(z) = (z - 1) - \tfrac{1}{2}(z - 1)^2 + \mathcal{O}[(z - 1)^3]$$

to determine the series expansion for $\ln(e^x)$ valid to $\mathcal{O}(x^3)$.

10.9 The Maclaurin series for $e^{\sin(x)}$ is

$$e^{\sin(x)} = 1 + x + \frac{x^2}{2} - \frac{x^4}{8} + \mathcal{O}(x^5)$$

a. Prove this result by using the equations

$$\frac{d}{dx}(e^{\sin(x)}) = [\cos(x)]e^{\sin(x)}$$

$$\frac{d}{dx}[\cos(x)e^{\sin(x)}] = [\cos^2(x) - \sin(x)]e^{\sin(x)}$$

b. Obtain the same result directly by using the two series

$$e^z = 1 + z + \frac{z^2}{2!} + \frac{z^3}{3!} + \frac{z^4}{4!} + \mathcal{O}(z^5)$$

and

$$\sin(x) = x - \frac{x^3}{3!} + \mathcal{O}(x^5)$$

10.10 Use Equation (10.33) to expand $f(x_i + \Delta x)$ and $f(x_i + 2\Delta x)$ and then use these equations to prove the result quoted in Equation (10.41).

10.11 Use Equation (10.41) to replace f'' in Equation (10.34) and thereby obtain the following forward difference result for f' that is accurate to $(\Delta x)^2$.

$$f_i' = \frac{-f_{i+2} + 4f_{i+1} - 3f_i}{2\,\Delta x} + \mathcal{O}(\Delta x)^2$$

10.12 Using the following data, obtain numerical values for $f_2', f_5', f_0', f_6', f_6'$ that are of order $\mathcal{O}(0.1)^2$. (*Note:* For f_0' you will have to use the results of Problem 10.11.)

i	x_i	$f(x_i)$
0	0.0	2.00
1	0.1	2.04
2	0.2	2.20
3	0.3	2.84
4	0.4	5.40
5	0.5	6.68
6	0.6	7.32
7	0.7	7.64
8	0.8	7.80
9	0.9	7.88
10	1.0	7.92

10.13 Obtain the numerical first and second derivatives using the central difference expressions of $f(x) = e^x$ at $x = 0.0, 1.0, 2.0$ that are correct to $\mathcal{O}(0.1)^2$
and compare with the exact answers.

10.14 Reproduce the first three lines of Table 10-3 using the function
$f(x) = e^x - 1$.

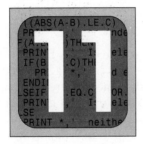

Roots of Equations

11.1   Introduction

One of the most common tasks in science and engineering is finding the roots of equations, that is, given a function $f(x)$, finding values of x such that $f(x) = 0.0$. This type of problem also includes determining the points of intersection of two curves. If the curves are represented by functions $f(x)$ and $g(x)$, the intersection points correspond to the roots of the function $F(x) = f(x) - g(x)$.

Root-solving techniques are important for a number of reasons. They are useful, easy to understand, and usually easy to carry out. Thus, with a minimum of instruction you are able to solve genuine problems in engineering. A vital element in numerical analysis is appreciating what can or cannot be solved and clearly understanding the accuracy of the answers obtained. Since this appreciation and understanding come mostly from experience, you need to begin solving numerical problems immediately. Besides, you will find that root-solving problems are fun.

Some examples of the types of functions that are encountered in root-solving problems are

$$ax^2 + bx + c = 0 \quad (11.1)$$

$$2x^4 - 7x^3 + 4x^2 + 7x - 6 = (x - 1)(x + 1)(x - 2)(2x - 3) = 0 \quad (11.2)$$

$$x^5 - 2x^3 - 5x^2 + 2 = 0 \quad (11.3)$$

$$\sin^5(x) + \sin^3(x) + 5\cos(x) - 7 = 0 \quad (11.4)$$

$$100e^{-x} - \sin(2\pi x) = 0 \quad (11.5)$$

The general quadratic equation, Equation (11.1), can be solved easily and exactly by using the quadratic formula:

$$r_1 = \frac{-b + \sqrt{(b^2 - 4ac)}}{2a} \quad (11.6)$$

$$r_2 = \frac{-b - \sqrt{(b^2 - 4ac)}}{2a}$$

Equation (11.2) can be solved exactly by factoring the polynominal. The roots are then clearly 1, −1, 2, $\frac{3}{2}$. However, most polynomials cannot be factored so easily, and other more general techniques are required. There are formulas for the exact solution of general cubic or quartic equations, but they are cumbersome and thus seldom used. No exact formula is possible for a polynomial like Equation (11.3), in which the highest power of x is greater than 4. For these polynomials numerical means must generally be used to determine the roots.

You will recall from high school algebra that a polynomial of degree n (i.e., the highest power of x is x^n) has precisely n roots, of which some may be complex numbers and others may be multiple roots. Thus, Equation (11.3) has three real roots,

$r_1 = -0.712780744625\ldots$

$r_2 = 0.57909844162\ldots$

$r_3 = 2.0508836199\ldots$

and two complex roots,

$r_4 = 0.757225433526 + i(0.57803468208)$

$r_5 = 0.757225433526 - i(0.57803468208)$

The equation

$$x^2 - 2x + 1 = 0$$

can be factored as

$$(x - 1)^2 = 0$$

and has two real roots, both of which happen to be the same value. In this case the root is said to be a multiple root with multiplicity 2.

Equations (11.4) and (11.5) are called *transcendental equations* and represent an entirely different class of functions. Transcendental equations typically involve trigonometric, exponential, or logarithmic functions and cannot be reduced to any polynomial equation in x. The real roots of a polynomial are usually classified as being either rational numbers (that is, a simple fraction) or irrational (for example, $\sqrt{2}$). The roots of transcendental equations are often transcendental numbers like π or e. Irrational numbers and transcendental numbers are represented by nonrepeating decimal fractions and cannot be expressed as simple fractions. These numbers are important to mathematics since they are responsible for the real number system being dense or continuous. Thus, the classification of equations as polynomials or transcendental and the roots of these equations as rational or irrational is vital to traditional mathematics; however, the distinction is of less consequence to the computer. In fact, not only is the number system available to the computer not continuous, it is a finite set.

At any rate, when finding the roots of equations, the distinction between polynomials and transcendental equations is unnecessary and the same numerical procedures are applied to both. The distinction between the two types of functions is, however, important in other regards. For example, many of the theorems you learned concerning roots of polynomials do not apply to transcendental equations. Thus, both Equations (11.4) and (11.5) have an infinite number of real roots.

All of the root-solving techniques discussed in this chapter are iterative; that is, you specify an interval that is known to contain a root or simply an initial guess for the root and the various recipes will return a more limited interval or a better guess. The first type of procedure begins with an interval containing a root and reduces that interval using methods based on the bisection technique. The second type of procedure, known as Newton's method, approximates the function by straight lines to rapidly narrow-in on a root starting from an initial guess. Each method is repeated using the new interval or the improved estimate of the root until a root of desired accuracy is obtained or until the method encounters difficulties and fails.

Some of the schemes we will discuss will be guaranteed to find a root eventually but may take considerable computer time to arrive at the answer. Others may converge to a root much faster but are more susceptible to problems of divergence; that is, they come with no guarantees. The relative rates of convergence of each of the methods is analyzed in Section 11.4.

The secant method, a particularly popular method possessing the rapid convergence rate of Newton's method and using the finite-difference expressions of Chapter 10 to replace the function by straight-line segments, is described in Section 11.5. Finally, in Section 11.6, methods specifically designed to find roots of polynomials are briefly described.

The common ingredient in all root-solving recipes is that potential computational difficulties of any nature are best avoided by mustering as much intelligence as possible in the initial choice of the method used and the accompanying initial guess. This part of the problem is often the most difficult and time-consuming. The art involved in numerical analysis consists in balancing time spent optimizing the solution of the problem before computation against time spent correcting unforeseen errors during computation. If at all possible, the function should be roughly sketched before root solving is attempted, either by using the plotting routines of Section 7.6 or by generating a table of function values that are then graphed by hand. These graphs are extremely useful to the programmer not only in estimating the first guess for the root but also in anticipating potential difficulties. If a sketch is not feasible, some method of monitoring the function must be utilized to arrive at some understanding of what the function is doing before the actual computation is initiated. The methods of this chapter will illustrate the benefits of a well-thought-out computational algorithm combined with accurate knowledge concerning the behavior of the function in question and are a corollary to the well-known programmer's axiom

$$G\text{-}I/G\text{-}O$$

11.2 Refinement of the Bisection Method

The bisection method was discussed in detail in Chapter 4. There it was used as an example of programming techniques. It is a so-called brute-force method and is rarely used, since for almost any problem an alternative method that is faster, more accurate, and only slightly more complex is available. All of the refinements of the bisection method that might be devised are based on attempts to use as much information as is available about the behavior of the function at each iteration. In the ordinary bisection method, the only feature of the function that is monitored is its sign. Thus, if we were searching for roots of the function

$$f(x) = 2e^{-2x} - \sin(\pi x)$$

we would begin the search, as in Chapter 4, by stepping along the x axis and watching for a change in sign of the function.

i	x_i	$f(x_i)$
0	0.0	2.00
1	0.1	1.33
2	0.2	0.75
3	0.3	0.29
4	0.4	−.05

The next step in the bisection procedure is to reduce the step size by half, that is, try $x_5 = 0.35$. However, from the magnitudes of the numbers above we would expect the root to be closer to 0.4 than to 0.3. Thus, by using information about the size of the function in addition to its sign, we may be able to speed up the convergence. In the present case we might interpolate the root to be approximately

$$\left[\frac{0.29 - 0.0}{0.29 - (-0.05)} \right] = \left(\frac{f_3 - 0}{f_3 - f_4} \right) = 0.853$$

of the distance from $x_3 = 0.3$ to $x_4 = 0.4$, or $x_5 = 0.3853$. Continuing in this manner and interpolating at each step, we would obtain the following results:

i	x_i	$f(x_i)$
3	0.30	0.29
4	0.40	-0.05
5	0.385	-0.0083
6	0.3823	-0.0013
7	0.3819	-0.00019
8	0.38185	-0.000028
9	0.38184	-0.000004

Comparing these results with the bisection method applied to a similar function in Section 4.5, we see that the convergence rate for the present method is significantly faster. The next task is to formalize this procedure into a method suitable for a general function.

Regula Falsi Method

The basic idea in the first refinement of the bisection algorithm is that the new method will be essentially the same as bisection except that in place of using the midpoint of the interval at each step of the calculation, an interpolated value for the root is used. The method is illustrated in Figure 11-1. In the figure a root is known to exist in the interval $(x_1 \leftrightarrow x_3)$, and in the drawing, f_1 is negative whereas f_3 is positive. The interpolated

Figure 11-1
Estimating the root
by interpolation

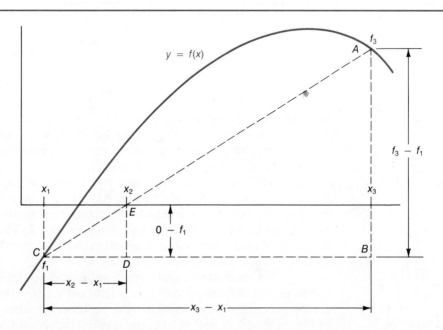

position of the root is x_2. Since the two triangles ABC and CDE are similar, the lengths of the sides are related by

$$\frac{DE}{AB} = \frac{CD}{BC}$$

or

$$\frac{0.0 - f(x_1)}{f(x_3) - f(x_1)} = \frac{x_2 - x_1}{x_3 - x_1}$$

which may be solved for the unknown position x_2 to yield

$$x_2 = x_1 - (x_3 - x_1)\frac{f_1}{f_3 - f_1} \tag{11.7}$$

This value of x_2 then replaces the midpoint used in the bisection algorithm, and the rest of the procedure remains exactly the same. Thus, the next step would be to determine whether the actual root is to the left or to the right of x_2. As before,

> IF $f_1 \times f_2 < 0$ THEN the root is on the left
> IF $f_2 \times f_3 < 0$ THEN the root is on the right

In the figure the root is to the left of x_2, so the interval used for the next iteration would be

```
X3 = X2
F3 = F2
X2 =              Use Equation (11.7).
F2 = FNC(X2)
```

In other words, to employ this slightly faster algorithm, the only change that has to be made to the previous bisection code is to replace statements of the form

```
 •   X2 = (X1 + X3)/2.
```

by a statement based on Equation (11.7).

This method is still guaranteed to obtain a root eventually and will almost always converge faster than the conventional bisection algorithm. We do, however, pay a small price. The values of f_1 and f_3 used in Equation (11.7) may be very nearly equal, and we could be plagued by round-off errors in their difference. Also, in the bisection algorithm we could predict with some precision the number of iterations required to obtain the root to a desired accuracy. (See Section 4.5.) This prediction is no longer possible if we use the interpolated values, and the code *must* now include a check for excessive iterations.

This method illustrates that an almost trivial change in the algorithm, which is based on more intelligent monitoring of the function, can reap considerable rewards in more rapid convergence. The formal name of the method just described is the *regula falsi method* (the method of false position).

Are there any additional improvements in the basic bisection algorithm that can be easily implemented? To answer this question we must examine in more detail the manner in which the regula falsi method arrives at a solution. This is best done graphically. The calculation begun in Figure 11-1 is continued in Figure 11-2. Notice that in this example, in which the function is concave downward near the root, the value of the left limit of the search interval near the root, x_1, never changes. The actual root always remains in the left segment in each iteration. The right segment of the interval, $x_3 - x_2$, shrinks quite rapidly; but the left segment, $x_2 - x_1$, does not. If the function were concave upward, the converse would be true. Thus, a drawback in the regula falsi method is that even though the method converges more rapidly to a value of x that results in a "small" $|f(x)|$, the interval containing the root does *not* diminish significantly.

Modified Regula Falsi Method

Perhaps the procedure can be made to converge more rapidly if the interval can somehow be made to collapse from both directions. One way to accomplish this is demonstrated in Figure 11-3. The idea is as follows:

> IF(the root is determined to lie in the left segment $x_2 - x_1$)THEN
> > The interpolation line is drawn between
> > the points $(x_1, \frac{1}{2}f_1)$ and (x_3, f_3)
> ELSEIF(the root is in the right segment)THEN
> > The interpolation line is drawn between
> > the points (x_1, f_1) and $(x_3, \frac{1}{2}f_3)$
> ENDIF

Thus, the slope of the line is *artificially* reduced. The effect of this reduction is that if the root is in the left of the original interval, it will eventu-

---

Figure 11-2
Graphical illustration of several iterations of the regula falsi algorithm

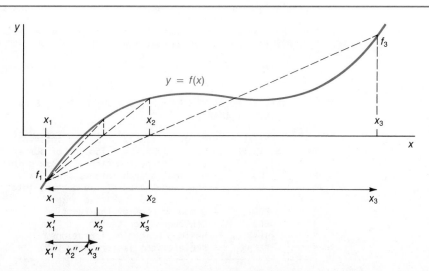

Figure 11-3 _____

Graphical illustration of the modified regula falsi method

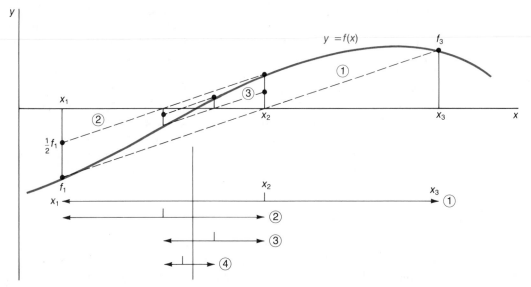

ally turn up in the right segment of a later interval and subsequently will alternate between left and right. This last modification to the bisection method in combination with the regula falsi method is known as the *modified regula falsi method,* a very powerful and popular procedure for finding roots of equations. The alterations to the original bisection code of Chapter 4 (Figure 4-9) are quite trivial and are shown in Figure 11-4. A

Figure 11-4 _____

FORTRAN code for the modified regula falsi method

```
        SUBROUTINE MODRFL(XA,XC,EPS,IMAX,I,ROOT,F)
*
* A root of the function f(x) is determined by the modified
* regula-falsi method. The maximum number of iterations permitted
* is IMAX.  The convergence criterion is when the fractional size
* of the search interval (x3-x1)/(b-a) < eps.  A relaxation factor
* of 0.9 is used and the actual number of iterations is returned
* as I.
*-------------------------------------------------------------------
* Variables
*
        REAL XA,XC,X1,X2,X3,F1,F2,F3,D,D0,EPS,ROOT,RELAX
        INTEGER I,IMAX
*
*        XA,XC    -- Original limits of search interval
*        X1,X3,X2 -- Left, right, and midpoint of current interval
*        F1,F3,F2 -- Value of the function at these points
*           D0    -- Original search interval (x3 - x1)
*           D     -- Fractional size of the current interval,
*                    that is, (x3 - x2)/(xc - xa)
*        ROOT     -- Computed root of the function
*        EPS      -- Convergence criterion
*        IMAX     -- Maximum number of iterations
*        RELAX    -- "Relaxation" factor (here 0.9)
*-------------------------------------------------------------------
```

Figure 11-4
(concluded)

```
* Initialization
*
      RELAX = 0.9
      X1 = XA
      X3 = XC
      F1 = F(X1)
      F3 = F(X3)
      D0 = ABS(X3 - X1)
*-------------------------------------------------------------
* Iterations
*
      DO 1 I = 1,IMAX
          D  = (X3 - X1)/D0
          X2 = X1 - D*D0*F1/(F3 - F1)
          F2 = F(X2)
          WRITE(*,'(I3,F15.12)')I,X2
          IF(ABS(D) .LT. EPS)THEN
              ROOT = X2
              RETURN
          ELSE
*
*             Check for crossing on left or right
*
              IF(F1*F2 .LE. 0.)THEN
                  X3 = X2
                  F3 = F2
                  F1 = RELAX*F1
              ELSEIF(F2*F3 .LT. 0.)THEN
                  X1 = X2
                  F1 = F2
                  F3 = RELAX*F3
              ELSE
*
*                 No crossing, likely error in function
*
                  WRITE(*,11)I
                  PAUSE 'Fatal Error in MODRFL'
                  RETURN
              ENDIF
          ENDIF
    1     CONTINUE
      WRITE(*,10)IMAX,X2,F2,D
      PAUSE 'Excessive iterations in MODRFL'
*-------------------------------------------------------------
   10 FORMAT(//,
     +T5,'=============ERROR IN REGFAL===================',/,
     +T5,'|   The search for a root has failed due to    |',/,
     +T5,'|               Excessive Iterations           |',/,
     +T5,'| After the maximum number of iterations (',I3,') |',/,
     +T5,'| the latest values of the function are        |',/,
     +T5,'| f(',E12.5,'   ) = ',E8.1,' and the fractional|',/,
     +T5,'| size of the interval dx/d0 = ',E9.2 ,'       |',/,
     +T5,'=============Program Terminated================|')
*
   11 FORMAT(//,
     +T5,'=============ERROR IN REGFAL===================',/,
     +T5,'|   The search for a root has failed due to    |',/,
     +T5,'|               No Root in Interval            |',/,
     +T5,'| In step ',I3,' the function does not change  |',/,
     +T5,'| sign in the interval.  It is likely that the |',/,
     +T5,'| function was coded incorrectly.              |',/,
     +T5,'=============Program Terminated================|')
      END
```

comparison of the rate of convergence of the three methods applied to the function

$$f(x) = 2e^{-2e} - \sin(\pi x)$$

is illustrated in Table 11-1.

A slope-reduction factor of one-half was used in constructing the drawing in Figure 11-3 and is an example of what is called a *relaxation factor*, a number used to alter the results of one iteration before inserting them into the next. Determining the optimum relaxation factor is almost always an extremely complex problem in any calculation and is well beyond the scope of this text. However, in this instance a little trial and error shows that a less drastic decrease in the slope will result in improved convergence. Using a reduction factor of 0.9 should be adequate for most problems; this factor was used to generate the values in Table 11-1.

The FORTRAN code in Figure 11-4 requires some explanation:

1. The function F(X) is evaluated only once per cycle. If the function is complicated and therefore costly to compute, this measure of efficiency can be attractive, even decisive, in choosing the appropriate method of solution.
2. The code can terminate in only two ways:
   a. One success path: If the current fractional size of the search interval [i.e., (current interval)/(original interval)] is less than the user-supplied convergence criterion. If so, the original aim of the program, to narrowly bracket a root, has been achieved. There is no guarantee that this criterion will result in a value of $f(x)$ that is "small." The point is, however, that successive iterations have resulted in only small changes in the interval containing the root and so continuing the process is not necessary or productive.

Table 11-1

Bisection, regula falsi, and modified regula falsi methods applied to $f(x) = 2e^{-2x} - \sin(\pi x)$

i	Bisection x_2	Regula Falsi x_2	Modified Regula Falsi x_2
1	0.35	0.385	0.385
2	0.375	0.3823	0.3820
3	0.3875	0.3819	0.38183
4	0.38125	0.38185	0.381843
5	0.38438	0.381844	0.38184267
6	0.38281	0.381843	0.38184276
7	0.38203	0.3818428	0.38184275
8	0.38164	0.38184275	0.38184275

b. Two failure paths:
  (1) IF the number of iterations is greater than I_{max}—STOP. This test allows the programmer to specify the maximum cost he or she will accept for an attempted solution. Since in the regula falsi and modified regula falsi methods the number of iterations is not predictable, this form of safeguard is essential. It is also a prudent precaution against unforeseen errors in the construction of the problem that could cause the program to cycle forever and not obtain a solution. Statements of this type are required in any program in which there is a danger of infinite looping.
  (2) IF the function does not change sign ($f_1 \times f_3 > 0$)—STOP. Since the original interval was known to contain a root, the only way this condition can arise is by error. Usually the error is in the code for the function $f(x)$; that is, you are attempting to find a root of a function different from the one intended.

■ Comparison of the Algorithms Based on Bisection

The characteristic features of the three methods discussed in this section are listed below:

Bisection	Success based on size of interval
	Slow convergence
	Predictable number of iterations
	Interval halved in each iteration
	Guaranteed to bracket a root
Regula falsi	Success based on size of function
	Faster convergence
	Unpredictable number of iterations
	Interval containing root is *not* small
	Monitors size of function as well as its sign
Modified regula falsi	Success based on size of interval
	Faster convergence
	Unpredictable number of iterations

Of the three methods, the modified regula falsi is probably the most efficient for common problems and is the recommended algorithm whenever the only information available is that the function changes sign between x_1 and x_3.

The requirement that the initial search interval be one in which the function changes sign (only once) can occasionally be troublesome.

The problem of finding the root of a function like

$$f(x) = x^2 - 2x + 1 = (x - 1)^2$$

is not suited to any of the algorithms based on bisection since the function never changes sign. This difficulty will occur whenever the root of the function is a multiple root of even multiplicity. The method that overcomes some of these limitations is Newton's method.

11.3   Newton's Method for Root Solving

In Section 11.2 we saw that incorporating more information about the behavior of the function into the root-solving algorithm can produce improvements in both the rate of convergence of the method as well as the accuracy of the final result. Newton's method is a further step in this direction—that is, using as much information as possible in the construction of the method. Not surprisingly, the result is a dramatic improvement in the rate of convergence in most situations. However, as we shall see, Newton's method differs from the earlier procedures in that it does not guarantee that a root will be found in all cases, and unfortunately, it often will diverge. (The problem of divergence will be discussed later in the chapter.)

Derivation of Newton's Method

Newton's method (also called the *Newton–Raphson method*) can be derived by starting with the Taylor series for the function $f(x)$ with x_0 being used in place of a [see Equation (10.11)].

$$f(x) = f(x_0) + \frac{df}{dx}\bigg|_{x=x_0} (x - x_0) + \frac{1}{2!} \frac{d^2f}{dx^2}\bigg|_{x=x_0} (x - x_0)^2 + \cdots \qquad (11.8)$$

Now, if $|x - x_0|$ is small, we need retain only a few terms in the series. To find a root of the function, we seek an x such that $f(x) = 0$ or

$$f(x) = 0 = f(x_0) + \frac{df}{dx}\bigg|_{x_0} (x - x_0) + \frac{1}{2!} \frac{d^2f}{dx^2}\bigg|_{x_0} (x - x_0)^2 + \cdots$$

If we blindly assume that the desired root x is near the value x_0, then

$$f(x) = 0 \approx f(x_0) + \frac{df}{dx}\bigg|_{x_0} (x - x_0) \qquad (11.9)$$

And of course if x is not near x_0, this equation may not even be approximately true.

In Equation (11.9) everything except x (the root) is known, and so we can solve for x. Reintroducing the notation

$$f' = \frac{df}{dx}$$

Equation (11.9) becomes

$$-f(x_0) = f'(x_0)(x - x_0)$$

or

$$x = x_0 - \frac{f(x_0)}{f'(x_0)} \tag{11.10}$$

If our assumption of $|x - x_0|$ being small is valid, then Equation (11.10) will be a good estimate of the actual root of the function. But if $|x - x_0|$ is not small, what have we done? The answer is illustrated in Figure 11-5.

Replacing the function $f(x)$ by the first two terms in its Taylor series is seen to be equivalent to approximating the function by a straight line through the point (x_0, f_0), which has the same slope as the tangent to the curve at that point. Then setting this approximation to $f(x)$ equal to zero, we find the point where the line intersects the axis. Thus, as you can see in Figure 11-5, this procedure will not in general give the actual root of $f(x)$. However, the value generated by Equation (11.10) is closer to the actual root than was the starting point x_0. Newton's method then consists of repeating this process; that is, starting from an initial guess for the root of $f(x)$, say, x_0, calculate an improved guess x_1 from Equation (11.10)

$$x_1 = x_0 - \frac{f(x_0)}{f'(x_0)}$$

Next use the improved value x_1 for the root in the next cycle to calculate the second improvement on the root,

$$x_2 = x_1 - \frac{f(x_1)}{f'(x_1)}$$

and so on.

Figure 11-5
Replacing a function by two terms of a Taylor series

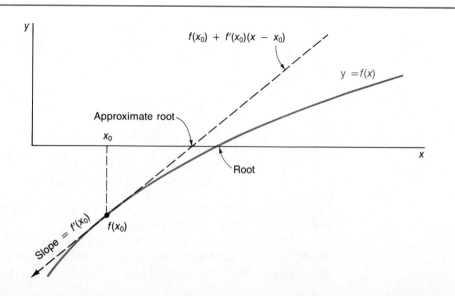

The point to keep in mind is that Newton's method attempts to find a root of a function $f(x)$ by repeatedly approximating the function by straight lines. In each iteration, since we are monitoring not only the value of the function but also its slope, a substantial amount of information about the behavior of the function is used in constructing the next step. In this sense, the information content of Newton's method is quite high.

Numerical Examples

Square Roots

The rate of convergence of Newton's method applied to most equations is quite impressive. For example, the square root of a number can be obtained in the following manner: Given a number C, we wish to determine a value of x such that $x = C^{1/2}$; or to phrase the problem in a different way, we wish to find a root of the equation

$$F(x) = x^2 - C$$

Applying Newton's method to this function, using

$$F'(x) = 2x$$

and an initial guess of x_0 for the square root, we obtain the following expression for the improved estimate of the square root.

$$x_1 = x_0 - \frac{F(x_0)}{F'(x_0)} = x_0 - \frac{x_0^2 - C}{2x_0}$$

$$= \frac{1}{2}\left(x_0 + \frac{C}{x_0}\right) \tag{11.11}$$

This equation was used earlier to construct the FORTRAN code to compute square roots (see Figure 3-16).

To illustrate, we take $C = 111$ with $x_0 = 20$, an obviously poor first guess. Equation (11.11) then generates the following values for $\sqrt{111}$.

Iteration	x	x^2
0	20.0	400.
1	12.78	163.2
2	10.73	115.2
3	10.537	111.04
4	10.53565	111.0000032
5	10.53565375	111.0000000001

Five iterations, beginning with a poor first guess, have resulted in an answer correct to nine significant figures.

This procedure can easily be adapted to finding the nth root of a number. A note of caution: Newton's method does not always converge as quickly as it did in this example.

Intersection of Two Functions

As an example of a more complicated problem utilizing Newton's method, we next solve for the roots of the function

$$f(x) = 100e^{-x} - 5 \sin\left(\frac{\pi}{2}x\right) = 0 \tag{11.12}$$

which can also be written as

$$100e^{-x} = 5 \sin\left(\frac{\pi}{2}x\right) \tag{11.13}$$

Thus, a root of Equation (11.12) will correspond to the points of intersection of the two functions on the left and right sides of Equation (11.13). The two sides of Equation (11.13) are separately plotted in Figure 11-6, and it is clear that there are an infinite number of intersection points. We must therefore be careful in our analysis. The first root appears to be near $x = 4.0$. From what we know about Newton's method, we would anticipate problems if an initial guess of $x > 5.0$ were chosen. Because the basic approximation is to replace functions by straight lines, starting at $x > 5.0$ would very likely cause the procedure to narrow in on one of the many roots beyond the first. With these considerations made, we begin the calculation at $x = 4.0$:

$$f(x) = 100e^{-x} - 5 \sin\left(\frac{\pi}{2}x\right)$$

$$f'(x) = -100e^{-x} - 5\frac{\pi}{2} \cos\left(\frac{\pi}{2}x\right)$$

$$\Delta x_0 = -\frac{f(x_0)}{f(x_0)}$$

$$x_1 = x_0 + \Delta x_0$$

Figure 11-6
Points of intersection of $100e^{-x}$ and $5 \sin\left(\frac{\pi}{2}x\right)$

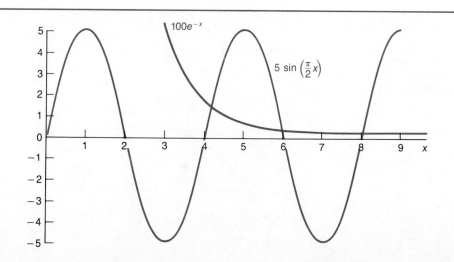

Step	x	$f(x)$	$f'(x)$	Δx
0	4.0	1.83	-9.68	0.189
1	4.189	0.05	-9.03	0.0058
2	4.19492	0.000086	-9.00	0.0000096
3	4.1949316	5×10^{-7}	-9.00	5×10^{-10}
4	4.194931571	$<10^{-12}$	$\vdots$	$\vdots$

Newton's method is used in several of the problems at the end of the chapter. If the function is reasonably simple, it is instructive and good practice to carry out the calculation on a pocket calculator, especially if your calculator has several storage registers for $f(x)$, $f'(x)$, and Δx. For more complicated problems, you can use the FORTRAN subroutine in Figure 11-11 or write your own.

Potential Problems Using Newton's Method

Newton's method is the most popular root-solving technique, and it can usually be relied upon to find a root quickly and accurately. However, in certain situations the method will fail:

1. A poor initial guess may cause the method to fail. If the initial guess x_0 is such that $f'(x_0)$ is small (slope nearly horizontal), the first iteration may be thrown out of the region of interest (see Figure 11-7). Also, if the initial guess is in a region where the function has a local minimum but no root, the method will likely fail (see Figure 11-8).
2. The method will not be able to find a root whenever the derivative at the root is infinite (see Figure 11-9). This situation is rarely encountered and is usually ignored in constructing a FORTRAN code.
3. The method may have difficulties with multiple roots (see Figure 11-10. At the position of a multiple root, both $f(x)$ and

Figure 11-7

Horizontal slope causes Newton's method to fail

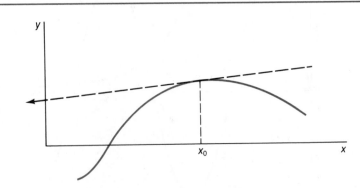

Figure 11-8
Starting Newton's
method near a
local minimum may
cause it to fail

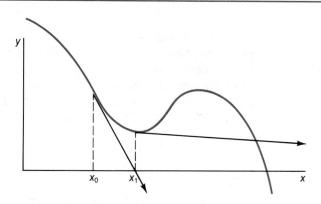

Figure 11-9
Vertical slope at a
root will cause
Newton's method
to fail

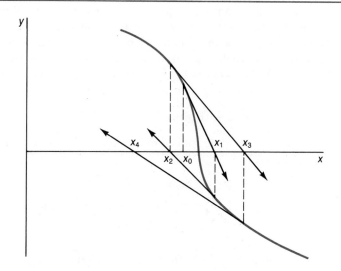

Figure 11-10
Function and its
slope are both zero
at a multiple root

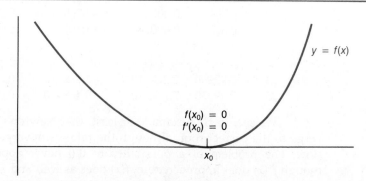

$f'(x)$ are zero and we would anticipate that the algorithm would fail in attempting to compute $\Delta x = -f/f' \to 0/0$.

These problems must be anticipated in writing the FORTRAN code that implements Newton's method, and if encountered the program should print a diagnostic message identifying the problem. The first type of problem is easily corrected by starting over with a better first guess, perhaps suggested by a rough sketch of the function. The problem associated with multiple roots cannot be corrected so easily and requires a special procedure.

Multiple Roots

We have predicted that Newton's method will fail at a multiple root because of the operation of dividing zero by zero. Of course, dividing anything by zero on the computer is forbidden. However, in mathematics the operation 0/0 is not forbidden. It is simply an *undetermined form*; that is, 0/0 is neither zero nor infinity. It has no numerical value until it is defined to be a specific value in a particular problem. So perhaps the anticipated problem is not a problem at all. As always, the best way to determine whether or not a problem exists is to carefully carry out a step-by-step calculation.

Consider the function

$$f(x) = (x - 1)^4 \sin(x) \tag{11.14}$$

which has a multiple root of multiplicity 4 at $x = 1.0$. The derivative of the function is

$$f'(x) = 4(x - 1)^3 \sin(x) + (x - 1)^4 \cos(x) \tag{11.15}$$

which is also zero at $x = 1.0$. Applying Newton's method with an initial guess of $x_0 = 0.5$ results in the following:

Step	x	$f(x)$	$f'(x)$	$\Delta x = -f/f'$
0	0.50	0.02996	$-.1849$	0.1620
1	0.66	0.0080	$-.0850$	0.0947
2	0.757	0.0024	$-.0369$	0.0650
3	0.822	0.00074	$-.0159$	0.0465
$\vdots$	$\vdots$	$\vdots$	$\vdots$	$\vdots$
24	0.99960	2.2×10^{-13}	-2.2×10^{-9}	0.00010
25	0.99970	7.1×10^{-14}	-9.4×10^{-10}	0.00007

We see, in this example at least, that Newton's method will converge to the correct root, although the rate of convergence is torturously slow. The problem of a possibility of 0/0 never appeared, since even though $f'(x)$ does approach zero, $f(x)$ does as well and at a faster rate.

In addition to suffering from a slow convergence rate for multiple roots, Newton's method may yield a result that is invalidated by round-off error caused when both f and f' are extremely small. To amend the procedure we begin by noting that if $f(x)$ has a multiple root of multiplicity m at $x = r$, then $f(x)$ can formally be written as

$$f(x) = (x - r)^m g(x) \tag{11.16}$$

Since we do not yet know the value of r, $g(x)$ is likewise unknown. We can, however, assume that $g(x)$ is *not* zero (or extremely small) at $x = r$. Then applying Newton's method with an initial guess of x_0 near r, we have

$$f(x_0) = (x_0 - r)^m g(x_0)$$

and

$$
\begin{aligned}
f'(x_0) &= m(x_0 - r)^{m-1}g(x_0) + (x_0 - r)^m g'(x_0) \\
&= (x_0 - r)^m g(x_0)\left[\frac{m}{x_0 - r} + \frac{g'(x_0)}{g(x_0)}\right] \\
&= f(x_0)\left[\frac{m}{x_0 - r} + \frac{g'(x_0)}{g(x_0)}\right]
\end{aligned}
\tag{11.17}
$$

The assumptions we have made regarding x_0 and $g(x)$ ensure that the first term in the brackets in Equation (11.17) is much larger than the second. Thus we can approximate this equation as

$$f'(x_0) \simeq f(x_0)\frac{m}{x_0 - r} \tag{11.18}$$

Solving this equation for the root r, we obtain

$$r = x_0 - m\frac{f(x_0)}{f'(x_0)} \tag{11.19}$$

which is almost the same as the original Newton algorithm. The only difference is that for a function with a root of multiplicity m, the replacement $x \to x - f/f'$ becomes $x \to x - mf/f'$.

As a test of this procedure, the root of the earlier function in Equation (11.14) is recomputed below. The multiplicity of the root at $x = 1.0$ is 4.

Step	x	$f(x)$	$f'(x)$	$\Delta x = -4f/f'$
0	0.500	0.02996	-0.1848	0.6483
1	1.1483	0.000442	0.0121	-0.1459
2	1.00243	2.9×10^{-11}	4.9×10^{-8}	-0.002432
3	1.00000094	6.7×10^{-25}	2.8×10^{-18}	-0.000000944
4	1.0000000000	3.5×10^{-52}	9.9×10^{-39}	-1.4×10^{-13}
5	1	9.7×10^{-107}	1.2×10^{-79}	-3.3×10^{-27}

Obviously, the desired convergence rate has been restored with this simple amendment to Newton's method.

■■ FORTRAN Code for a Subroutine Implementing
Newton's Method for Root Solving

The FORTRAN code for a subroutine that implements Newton's method
for finding a root of a dummy function F(X) is given in Figure 11-11. The
subroutine has several important features:

1. Newton's method requires *two* functions, F(X) and DFDX(X),
   to be supplied in addition to the subroutine. If the function

Figure 11-11
FORTRAN code for
a subroutine that
implements
Newton's method
for root solving

```
      SUBROUTINE NEWTON(X,EPS,IMAX,DXMAX,MULT,ROOT,F,DFDX,N)
*
*  Newton's algorithm, Xnew = Xold + dx, where
*
*                   dx = -f(Xold)/dfdx(old)
*
*  is used to find a root of the function f(x). Additionally,
*  the derivative of the function, called dfdx(), is required
*  as a user-coded function.  The initial guess for the root
*  is X, and convergence is attained when |dx| < eps.
*-------------------------------------------------------------
*  Variables
*
      REAL X,EPS,DXMAX,ROOT,F,DFDX,F1,DF,DX
      INTEGER N,IMAX,MULT
*
*     IMAX  -- Maximum number of iterations
*     DXMAX -- Limit on the size of computed dx's
*     N     -- Actual number of iterations
*     MULT  -- Assumed multiplicity of the root
*              (usually mult = 1)
*     ROOT  -- Value computed for the root of f(x)
*-------------------------------------------------------------
*  Iterations
*
      DO 1 I = 1,IMAX
         DF = DFDX(X)
         IF(DF .EQ. 0.)THEN
            WRITE(*,12)I,X,F(X)
            PAUSE 'Fatal Error in NEWTON'
            RETURN
         ENDIF
         DX = -MULT*F(X)/DFDX(X)
         IF(ABS(DX) .LT. EPS)THEN
            ROOT = X + DX
            N    = I
            RETURN
         ELSEIF(ABS(DX) .GT. DXMAX)THEN
            WRITE(*,10)I,DX
            PAUSE 'Fatal Error in NEWTON, method diverging'
            RETURN
         ENDIF
         X = X + DX
    1 CONTINUE
      WRITE(*,11)X,F(X),DX
      PAUSE 'ERROR in NEWTON, method not converging'
*-------------------------------------------------------------
```

Figure 11-11
(concluded)

```
* Formats
*
   10  FORMAT(//,
       +T5,'===============ERROR IN NEWTON==============',/,
       +T5,'|   In iteration No.-',I3,'                |',/,
       +T5,'|   The current value of dx = ',E8.1,'     |',/,
       +T5,'|   is larger than the prescribed limit    |',/,
       +T5,'===============Program Terminated============',/)
*
   11  FORMAT(//,
       +T5,'===============ERROR IN NEWTON==============',/,
       +T5,'|  Newton fails due to excessive iterations |',/,
       +T5,'|  After executing the maximum number of steps|',/,
       +T5,'|     f(',E12.5,'   ) = ',E8.1,'           |',/,
       +T5,'|  and the latest dx = ',E8.1,'            |',/,
       +T5,'===============Program Terminated============',/)
*
   12  FORMAT(//,
       +T5,'===============ERROR IN NEWTON==============',/,
       +T5,'|   In iteration No.-',I3,'                |',/,
       +T5,'|   The current value of df is EXACTLY zero |',/,
       +T5,'|   The problem is likely in the code for df/dx|',/,
       +T5,'===============Program Terminated============',/)
       END
```

F(X) is complicated, its first derivative is most likely much worse, and so using this procedure often requires considerable extra time and effort spent in programming the derivative function. In these cases it is probably more convenient to use the modified regula falsi method (if an interval containing a root is known) or the secant method (if only an initial guess for the root is known). (The secant method is discussed in Section 11.5.)

2. The presumed multiplicity of the root is M. This will usually be 1, but the alteration discussed in the previous section to accommodate multiple roots is so easily incorporated that this extra parameter is included in the argument list.

3. The subroutine has three failure paths:

   a. IF (iteration $> I_{max}$), then STOP. Once again, statements of this type are always required in all iterative programs as a safety check to protect against a variety of programming errors. As with all abnormal exits, a diagnostic message that includes the latest values of the variables is printed.

   b. IF (f' is identically zero), then STOP. As a precaution, before the operation f/f' is attempted, the possibility of $f' = 0$ is checked. If it is zero, the program prints current values and stops. A likely source of the problem is in the coding of the derivative function.

c. If any correction Δx is larger in magnitude than the user-supplied maximum, it is presumed that the algorithm has jumped out of the region of interest and the program is terminated. Either a better first guess or a larger Δx_{max} should be tried next.

4. The subroutine has one success path: If the magnitude of a correction ($\Delta x = -f/f'$) is less than the programmer-supplied convergence criterion (EPS), the subroutine returns a value of the ROOT, the latest value of the increment DX, and the number of iterations required, N. We have already seen that a small value of $|f(x)|$ does not ensure that the root is closely bracketed, so a success path based on the size of the function is not included.

11.4   Rate of Convergence*

In the problems considered so far, Newton's method appears to converge faster than the procedures based on the bisection method, which is not surprising since the information content of the Newton algorithm is greater. This observation can be made more precise: If the root of the function is labeled r, then the actual error in the nth iteration, ε_n, would be

$$x_n = r + \varepsilon_n \tag{11.20}$$

and

$$x_{n+1} = r + \varepsilon_{n+1}$$

where

$$x_{n+1} = x_n + \Delta x_n$$

$$\Delta x_n = -\frac{f(x_n)}{f'(x_n)}$$

and the change in the error in one step would therefore be

$$\varepsilon_{n+1} - \varepsilon_n = (x_{n+1} - x_n) = \Delta x_n = -\frac{f(x_n)}{f'(x_n)} \tag{11.21}$$

Expanding both $f(x_n)$ and $f'(x_n)$ in a Taylor series, we obtain

$$f(x_n) = f(r + \varepsilon_n) = f(r) + \varepsilon_n f'(r) + \frac{1}{2} \varepsilon_n^2 f''(r) + \ldots \tag{11.22}$$

$$f'(x_n) = f'(r + \varepsilon_n) = f'(r) + \varepsilon_n f''(r) + \frac{1}{2} \varepsilon_n^2 f'''(r) + \ldots \tag{11.23}$$

---

*This section contains more advanced material and may be omitted without a loss of continuity.

Since $f(r)$ is zero and ε_n is presumed small, we can approximate Equations (11.22) and (11.23) as

$$f(x_n) \simeq \varepsilon_n f'(r) \left[1 + \frac{1}{2} \varepsilon_n \frac{f''(r)}{f'(r)} \right] \tag{11.24}$$

$$f'(x_n) \simeq f'(r) \left[1 + \varepsilon_n \frac{f''(r)}{f'(r)} \right] \tag{11.25}$$

so that Equation (11.21) becomes

$$\varepsilon_{n+1} - \varepsilon_n \simeq -\varepsilon_n \frac{1 + [\frac{1}{2}\varepsilon_n f''(r)/f'(r)]}{1 + [\varepsilon_n f''(r)/f'(r)]} \tag{11.26}$$

Next, using the expansion $(1 + \alpha)^{-1} = 1 - \alpha + \alpha^2 - \alpha^3 + \cdots \; (\alpha \ll 1)$, this becomes

$$\varepsilon_{n+1} - \varepsilon_n = -\varepsilon_n \left[\left(1 + \frac{1}{2} \varepsilon_n \frac{f''(r)}{f'(r)} \right) \left(1 - \varepsilon_n \frac{f''(r)}{f'(r)} + \left[\varepsilon_n \frac{f''(r)}{f'(r)} \right]^2 - \cdots \right) \right]$$

$$\simeq -\varepsilon_n \left[1 - \frac{1}{2} \varepsilon_n \frac{f''(r)}{f'(r)} \right] \tag{11.27}$$

so that we finally obtain

$$\varepsilon_{n+1} \simeq \frac{1}{2} \varepsilon_n^2 \frac{f''(r)}{f'(r)} \tag{11.28}$$

or

$$\varepsilon_{n+1} = \mathcal{O}(\varepsilon_n^2) \tag{11.29}$$

Thus, if the error in the nth step is 0.3, the error in the next step should be roughly 0.09. The convergence of Newton's method is then said to be of second order. If you scan the numerical results obtained so far in this section, you will see that this is more or less satisfied if the root is not a multiple root.

It can similarly be shown that the bisection-based algorithms are first-order convergent, that is, $\varepsilon_{n+1} \propto \varepsilon_n$. Also, since these methods are known to converge, the proportionality constant must be less than one.[1]

11.5 Secant Method

The principal disadvantage in using Newton's method is that you must supply the code for two functions, $f(x)$ and $f'(x)$. Frequently, the task of finding the root of a function will be only an incidental part of a larger

---

[1] In the ordinary bisection method the interval containing the root is halved in each step, so the error in each iteration is likewise reduced by a factor of $\frac{1}{2}$.

problem, and it may be inconvenient or distracting to take the time to code a separate function. In these cases you may wish to use some root-solving subroutine in your personal library that only requires the function $f(x)$ in its argument list. If an interval containing a root is known, the modified regula falsi method would be suitable. If such an interval is not known or if the faster convergence rate of Newton's method is important, we could still use the basic Newton algorithm but let the computer attempt to compute the derivative numerically. Of course, the computer will only determine approximate values for the derivative, which means that some information about the function is being lost, so this procedure will not be as rapidly convergent as Newton's method.

We can start with the basic ideas of Newton's method

$$x_1 = x_0 + \Delta x_0$$

$$\Delta x_0 = \frac{f(x_0)}{f'(x_0)}$$

and use an approximate expression for the derivative,[2]

$$f'(x) \approx \frac{f(x + \Delta x) - f(x)}{\Delta x}$$

where Δx is a known small quantity, say Δx_0. Thus, we begin the procedure with *two* input quantities: an initial guess x_0, and a guess for the 0th correction, Δx_0. The starting values then correspond to knowing two points on the curve of f versus x; namely, (x_0, f_0) and (x_1, f_1), where

$$x_1 = x_0 + \Delta x_0$$

$$f_1 = f(x_1)$$

We then use the above expressions to compute the next correction

$$\Delta x = -\frac{f(x_0)}{\left(\dfrac{f(x_0 + \Delta x_0) - f(x_0)}{\Delta x_0} \right)} = -\Delta x_0 \frac{f_0}{f_1 - f_0}$$

$$= \Delta x_0 - \Delta x_0 \left(1 + \frac{f_0}{f_1 - f_0} \right)$$

$$= \Delta x_0 + \Delta x_0 \frac{f_1}{f_0 - f_1} \equiv \Delta x_0 + \Delta x_1$$

where Δx_1 is the *improvement* in the estimate of the interval.

The algorithm is

- Start with the guesses $(x_0, x_1 = x_0 + \Delta x_0)$.
- Compute the improvement to the interval,

$$\Delta x_1 = \frac{f_1}{f_0 - f_1} \Delta x_0$$

---

[2] This is the first forward difference expression for the derivative; see Equation (10.36).

- Replace the pair of values $(x_0, \Delta x_0)$ by the pair $(x_1, \Delta x_1)$.
- The next pair of points is $(x_1, x_2 = x_1 + \Delta x_1)$.

Whereas Newton's method is equivalent to repeatedly replacing the function by straight lines that are tangent to the function, the secant method can be shown (see Problem 11.13) to be equivalent to repeatedly replacing the function by straight lines drawn through the points (x_0, f_0) and (x_1, f_1) — that is, *secant* lines. The FORTRAN code for a subroutine implementing the secant method is given in Figure 11-12.

Since the secant method is based on Newton's method it possesses similar divergence problems, and similar checks are built into the FORTRAN code for the subroutine. The secant method is probably the most popular method used to find the root of a function.

Figure 11-12
FORTRAN code for
the secant method

```
      SUBROUTINE SECANT(X,DX,EPS,IMAX,DXMAX,ROOT,F,N)
*--
*-- The secant method consists of using Newton's method to find
*-- the root of the function f(x) by using approximate numerical
*-- values for the derivative of f(x).  The initial guess for
*-- the root is X and an additional estimate for the interval
*-- containing the root (DX) is required.  Convergence is ac-
*-- hieved when ABS(DXnew) < EPS.  The additional parameters
*-- in the call are
*--
*--        IMAX  --  Maximum number of iterations allowed
*--        DXMAX --  Limit on the size of computed DXs
*--        N     --  Actual number of iterations used
*--        ROOT  --  Computed value of the root
*--
      REAL    X,X0,DX,DX0,F0,FTOP,DXMAX,EPS,ROOT
      INTEGER I,IMAX,N
*------------------------------------------------------------
* Initialize variables for the guess for ROOT and interval
*--
      X0  = X
      DX0 = DX
      F0  = F(X0)
      DO 1 I = 1,IMAX
         X1  = X0 + DX0
         F1  = F(X1)
         IF(F1 .EQ. 0.0)THEN
*--
*--          Accidentally found the exact root
*--
            ROOT = X1
            N = I
            RETURN
         END IF
*--
         DX1 = DX0/(F0/F1 - 1.)
         IF(ABS(DX1) .GT. DXMAX)THEN
*--
*--          New dx is too large, probably diverging
*--
```

Figure 11-12
(concluded)

```
                        WRITE(*,12)I,X0,DX1,F0
                        PAUSE 'Fatal Error in SECANT, method diverging'
                        RETURN
                  ELSEIF(ABS(DX1) .LT. EPS)THEN
*--
*--                Success path
*--
                        ROOT = X1 + DX1
                        N    = I
                        RETURN
                  ELSE
                     IF(ABS(DX1) .GT. 2.*ABS(DX0))THEN
*--
*--                      Successive values of dx are not getting
*--                      smaller, print a warning but continue
*--
                           WRITE(*,13)I,X0,F0
                     ENDIF
                     WRITE(*,*)I,X0
                     X0  = X1
                     DX0 = DX1
                     F0  = F1
                  END IF
    1       CONTINUE
            WRITE(*,11)X0,F0
            PAUSE 'ERROR in SECANT, method not converging'
*-------------------------------------------------------------------
* Formats
*--
    11   FORMAT(//,
         +T5,'================ERROR IN SECANT===============',/,
         +T5,'| Secant fails due to excessive iterations    |',/,
         +T5,'| After the maximum number of iterations,      |',/,
         +T5,'| f(',E12.5,   ') = ',E8.1,'                |',/,
         +T5,'==============Program terminated==============',/)
*--
    12   FORMAT(//,
         +T5,'================ERROR IN SECANT===============',/,
         +T5,'| In step ',I3,' dx = ',E8.1,' > dx-max        |',/,
         +T5,'|Current values are f(',E12.5,   ') = ',E8.1,'||',/,
         +T5,'|==============Program Terminated==============',/)
*--
    13   FORMAT(//,
         +T5,'===============WARNING FROM SECANT============',/,
         +T5,'| In step ',I3,' the latest dx is more than twice|',/,
         +T5,'| as large as the previous dx.  Current values|',/,
         +T5,'| are f(',E12.5   ,') = ',E8.1,'               |',/,
         +T5,'===============Program Continues=============',/)
         END
```

▆▆▆▆ 11.6 Root-Solving Procedures for Polynomials*

All the root-solving techniques discussed to this point can be used on any continuous function of a single variable, including polynomials. However,

---

*This section contains more advanced material and may be omitted without a loss of continuity.

polynomial functions are special since the roots of polynomials must satisfy a variety of conditions that do not apply to transcendental or nonpolynomial functions. Many of these conditions are demonstrated in a high school algebra course and are simply quoted below without proof.

Properties of Roots of Polynomials

Number of Roots of a Polynomial

An nth-degree polynomial of the form

$$f(x) = a_n x^n + a_{n-1} x^{n-1} + \cdots + a_1 x + a_0 \qquad (11.30)$$

where $a_n \neq 0$, has precisely n roots, which may be real or complex, single or multiple, and the complex roots always appear in pairs; that is, if

$$x_+ = a + ib \qquad a, b \text{ real}, \; i = \sqrt{-1}$$

is a root, then

$$x_- = a - ib$$

is also a root.

Descartes' Rule of Signs

If the number of sign changes of the coefficients of the polynomial is n, then

Positive real roots	The number of positive real roots is either n or n minus an even integer.
Negative real roots	The number of negative real roots is determined by rewriting the polynomial with $x \to -x$, counting the sign changes in the new polynomial, and applying the rule for positive roots.

For example, the equation

$$f(x) = x^4 - 5x^3 + 5x^2 + 5x - 6 = 0 \qquad (11.31)$$

has three sign changes as we read the coefficients across $(+ \downarrow - \downarrow + \; + \downarrow -)$ and thus will have either 3 or 1 real positive roots. The equation with x replaced by $-x$,

$$f(-x) = x^4 + 5x^3 + 5x^2 - 5x - 6 = 0$$

has only one sign change in the coefficients, and so there must be one negative real root. The roots of this polynomial are 1, 2, 3, and -1.

Newton's Relations

Newton derived a collection of relations between the coefficients of a polynomial and various sums and products of the roots. Two of these relations are

$$\frac{a_{n-1}}{a_n} = -(\text{sum of all roots}) \tag{11.32}$$

$$\frac{a_0}{a_n} = (-1)^n(\text{product of all roots}) \tag{11.33}$$

In Equation (11.31) these relations yield

$$\frac{a_3}{a_4} = -\frac{5}{1} = -(1 + 2 + 3 - 1)$$

and

$$\frac{a_0}{a_4} = -\frac{6}{1} = (-1)^4[(1)(2)(3)(-1)]$$

Numerous root-solving techniques that employ the above properties of polynomial roots have been devised. Every one of these methods is superior to the more general methods discussed so far in terms of rate of convergence, efficiency of computation, and freedom from divergences. However, these methods are usually much more complicated, and so in most instances it is preferable to use the slower but more familiar techniques. Occasionally, though, it may be necessary to find the root of a polynomial thousands of times, with the coefficients slightly altered each time. Clearly, in such cases rapid convergence becomes a critical consideration and more exotic, special techniques are called for. One of the simplest, is the Birge–Vieta method, which is discussed below. For other techniques specially suited to polynomials, see *Mathematical Methods for Digital Computers*, A. Ralston and H. S. Wilf, editors, published by John Wiley, New York, 1967.

Birge–Vieta Method for Roots of Polynomials

The Birge–Vieta method is nothing more than Newton's method using special properties of polynomials to evaluate the function and its first derivative efficiently. The procedure is based on the operation of synthetic division, which, to refresh your memory, is discussed below.

Synthetic Division

To apply Newton's method to a polynomial, both the function and its first derivative must be evaluated at the initial estimate of the root x_0. We can write the polynomial $f(x)$ as

$$f(x) = (x - x_0)g(x) + R_1 \qquad (11.34)$$

where R_1 is the remainder of the division of $f(x)$ by $(x - x_0)$. Note that this remainder is equal to $f(x_0)$. Also, if $f(x)$ is a polynomial of degree n, $g(x)$ is of degree $n - 1$.

Next, Equation (11.34) is differentiated to yield

$$f'(x) = g(x) + (x - x_0)g'(x) \qquad (11.35)$$

So $f'(x_0) = g(x_0)$. To evaluate $g(x_0)$, we write an equation similar to Equation (11.34):

$$g(x) = (x - x_0)h(x) + R_2 \qquad (11.36)$$

That is, R_2 is the remainder of the division of $g(x)$ by $(x - x_0)$. Thus, once the two remainders have been determined,

$$\frac{f(x_0)}{f'(x_0)} = \frac{R_1}{R_2}$$

The remainders will be computed using synthetic division. Writing the two polynomials in terms of their coefficients, we obtain

$$
\begin{aligned}
f(x) &= a_n x^n + a_{n-1} x^{n-1} + \cdots + a_1 x + a_0 \\
&= (x - x_0)(b_{n-1} x^{n-1} + b_{n-2} x^{n-2} + \cdots + b_1 x + b_0) + R_1 \\
&= b_{n-1} x^n + (b_{n-2} - x_0 b_{n-1}) x^{n-1} + (b_{n-3} - x_0 b_{n-2}) x^{n-2} + \cdots \\
&\qquad + (b_0 - x_0 b_1) x + (R_1 - x_0 b_0) \qquad (11.37)
\end{aligned}
$$

Since Equation (11.37) is an identity, true for all x, the coefficients of each power of x may be independently equated; thus,

$$
\begin{aligned}
b_{n-1} &= a_n \\
b_{n-2} &= a_{n-1} + x_0 b_{n-1} \\
b_{n-3} &= a_{n-2} + x_0 b_{n-2} \\
&\ \ \vdots \\
b_1 &= a_2 + x_0 b_2 \\
b_0 &= a_1 + x_0 b_1 \\
R_1 &= a_0 + x_0 b_0
\end{aligned}
$$

For example, to obtain the remainder of dividing Equation (11.31) by $(x - 5)$, these relations would yield

$$f(x) = x^4 - 5x^3 + 5x^2 + 5x - 6 \quad \text{divided by} \quad (x - 5)$$

Long Division   **Synthetic Division**

$$\begin{array}{r} 1x^3 + 0 + 5x + 30 \\ \hline (x - 5)\,|\,x^4 - 5x^3 + 5x^2 + 5x - 6 \end{array} + 144$$

$$b_3 = a_4 = 1$$

$$x^4 - 5x^3$$

$$0 \quad + 5x^2 + 5x - 6$$
$$0 \qquad 0 \qquad\qquad\qquad b_2 = a_3 + x_0 b_3 = -5 + 5 \times 1 = 0$$

$$5x^2 + 5x - 6$$
$$5x^2 - 25x \qquad\qquad b_1 = a_2 + x_0 b_2 = 5 + 5 \times 0 = 5$$

$$30x - 6$$
$$30x - 150 \qquad\qquad b_0 = a_1 + x_0 b_1 = 5 + 5 \times 5 = 30$$
$$144 \qquad\qquad R_1 = a_0 + x_0 b_0 = -6 + 5 \times 30 = 144$$

Thus $f(x) = (x - 5)(x^3 + 5x + 30) + 144$. Since all the coefficients of the polynomial $g(x)$ have been determined, we can divide once more to obtain the second remainder R_2.

$$g(x) = (x - x_0)(c_{n-2}x^{n-2} + c_{n-3}x^{n-3} + \cdots + c_1 x + c_0) + R_2$$
$$c_{n-2} = b_{n-1}$$
$$c_{n-3} = (b_{n-2} + x_0 c_{n-2})$$
$$c_{n-4} = (b_{n-3} + x_0 c_{n-3})$$
$$\vdots$$

Using the values obtained for the b_i's yields

$$c_2 = b_3 = 1$$
$$c_1 = (b_2 + x_0 c_2) = [0 + 5(1)] = 5$$
$$c_0 = (b_1 + x_0 c_1) = [5 + 5(5)] = 30$$
$$R_2 = (b_0 + x_0 c_0) = [30 + 5(30)] = 180$$

Thus, Newton's method would generate the next estimate for the root as

$$x_1 = x_0 - \frac{R_1}{R_2} = 5 - \frac{144}{180} = 4.2$$

FORTRAN Code for the Birge–Vieta Method

The algebraic procedure outlined above may appear a bit awkward, but the FORTRAN code that implements it is amazingly short and efficient. Assuming that the coefficients of the polynomial $f(x)$ have been stored in an array $A(0:N)$, the algorithm would be

$$x_0 = \text{Initial guess}$$
$$b_{n-1} = a_n$$
DO 1 i = n - 2, 0, -1
$$\qquad b_i = a_{i+1} + x_0 b_{i+1}$$

```
1 CONTINUE
  R₁ = a₀ + x₀b₀
  Cₙ₋₂ = bₙ₋₁
  DO 2 i = n - 3, 0, -1
        cᵢ = bᵢ₊₁ + x₀cᵢ₊₁
2 CONTINUE
  R₂ = b₀ + x₀c₀
```

But a little thought reveals that *all* the b_i's are not needed to compute an individual c_i, and so the two loops can be combined:

```
  x₀ = ...
  bₙ₋₁ = aₙ
  cₙ₋₂ = bₙ₋₁
  DO 1 i = n - 2, 1, -1
       bᵢ = aᵢ₊₁ + x₀bᵢ₊₁
       cᵢ₋₁ = bᵢ + x₀cᵢ
1 CONTINUE
  b₀ = a₁ + x₀b₁
  R₁ = a₀ + x₀b₀
  R₂ = b₀ + x₀c₀
```

Furthermore, none of the coefficients b_i, c_i are needed after R_1 and R_2 are obtained, so it is unnecessary to store them in an array. Thus, the final FORTRAN version of the program segment to compute R_1 and R_2 would simply be

```
      XO = ...
      B = A(N)
      C = B
      DO 1 I = N - 2, 1, -1
          B = A(I + 1) + XO*B
          C = B          + XO*C
1     CONTINUE
      B  = A(1) + XO*B
      R1 = A(0) + XO*B
      R2 = B    + XO*C
```

The Birge–Vieta method will require the same number of iterations to converge as would an ordinary Newton's method; the advantage is that in each iteration only elementary arithmetic operations are employed, exponentiation is avoided, and the algorithm will therefore be significantly more efficient in computing each Δx.

11.7 Comparison of Root-Solving Methods

To find a root of a function, the first step is to learn as much as possible about the behavior of the function. A graph, if possible, is recommended. This information is then used to select one of the root-solving techniques.

Basically, there are two classes of algorithms, depending on whether you are starting with an interval containing a root or with an initial estimate of the root. The bisection-based procedures begin with an interval that is known to contain a root and are guaranteed to converge to a prescribed bracketing of the root. Of these methods, the modified regula falsi is the fastest-converging and is recommended.

If only an initial estimate of the root is the starting point, the algorithms based on Newton's method must be used. If the function and its first derivative are not too complicated, the basic Newton method is the most rapidly converging. Of course, the code must contain safeguards for the several sources of divergence possible in Newton's method along with diagnostic PRINT statements. If the root is presumed to be a multiple root, the algorithm can be easily adapted to incorporate this possibility.

If the function and its first derivative are complicated and coding the derivative function would present a potential source of error, the secant method is suggested. The same safeguards that apply to Newton's method should be built into the secant code.

If the function is a polynomial and an efficient code is essential, the Birge–Vieta method is suggested.

A reminder about EXTERNAL statements: If any of the procedures discussed in this chapter are coded in the form of a FORTRAN subroutine, the references within the subroutine to the function should be to a dummy function—for example, F(X) or FNC(X). The subroutine is then called from a main program to compute the root of a specific function—for example, SPEED(T). In the CALL statement, the actual function name (say, SPEED) is used and this name *must* be declared EXTERNAL at the beginning of the program.

```
EXTERNAL SPEED
    . . .
CALL REGFAL(A,B,EPS,IMAX,ANSWER,SPEED)
```

Additionally, the root-solving subroutines will be expecting a function with a single variable in its argument list. Your functions should then be constructed in this form with any additional parameters that the function requires passed through a COMMON statement.

Summary

Each of the root-solving methods described in this chapter is of an iterative nature. In algorithms based on the bisection method, it is assumed that an interval is initially given that is known to contain a single root of the function. This interval is then refined by repeatedly evaluating the function at points within the interval and then, by monitoring the sign of the function, determining in which subinterval the root lies. If the left and right ends of the current interval are x_1 and x_3, respectively, the standard bisection method uses the function evaluated at the midpoint, $x_2 = \frac{1}{2}(x_1 + x_3)$. The sign of the function at x_2 is compared with that at either end of the interval to determine which half of the interval contains the root. The full interval is then replaced by this half and the process repeated. After n iterations, the root will be contained in an interval of size $(x_3 - x_1)/2^n$.

In the regula falsi method, the conditions are the same as for the bisection method. But instead of using the midpoint of the interval, a straight line connecting the points at the ends of the interval is used to interpolate the position of the root. The intersection of this line with the x-axis determines the value of x_2 to be used in the next step. This value of x_2 is given by the equation

$$x_2 = x_1 - (x_3 - x_1)\frac{f_1}{f_3 - f_1}$$

in place of the equation for the midpoint. Convergence is faster than with the bisection method. However, it is likely that the interval will collapse down to the root from one side only.

The modified regula falsi method is the same as the regula falsi method except for the following change: in each iteration, when the full interval is replaced by the subinterval containing the root, a relaxation factor is used to first modify the value of the function at the fixed end of the subinterval. A relaxation factor of approximately 0.9 is suggested. This additional feature will cause the interval to collapse from both ends, and convergence is then based on interval size. This method is the preferred procedure for finding a root of a function that is not too expensive to evaluate and that is known to have a root in a specified interval.

In Newton's method and its variations, the user must supply an initial guess, x_0, for the root of the function $f(x)$. The guess should not be near any local minima or maxima of the function. Newton's method and its variations are second-order procedures (the bisection techniques are first order).

In the most basic form of Newton's method, the function is replaced by the tangent line to the function at the point (x_0, f_0). The root of the tangent line is then computed to be at $x_1 = x_0 + \Delta x_0$, where $\Delta x_0 = -f_0/f_0'$. This value then becomes the improved guess, and the process is repeated until successive changes in x are sufficiently small. Newton's method can fail for a variety of reasons. It requires that both the function $f(x)$ and its first derivative $f'(x)$ be supplied as FORTRAN coded functions. It is not required that the function change sign at the root.

If the root of the function is a multiple root (or thought to be a multiple root), convergence can often be greatly accelerated by replacing the above prescription for Δx_0 by

$$\Delta x = -m \frac{f_0}{f_0'}$$

where m is the presumed multiplicity.

The secant method is similar to Newton's method except that approximate numerical expressions are used for the derivatives of the function. This is equivalent to replacing the function by a secant line through two points and finding the point of intersection of the line with the x-axis. The algorithm thus begins *two* input numbers, x_0 and Δx_0, corresponding to initial guesses for the root and for an interval containing the root. This pair of values is then replaced by the pair $(x_1, \Delta x_1)$ where

$$x_1 = x_0 + \Delta x_0$$

and

$$\Delta x_1 = \frac{f_1}{f_0 - f_1} \Delta x_0$$

and the process is continued until the new interval Δx is sufficiently small. Because the secant method preserves the higher order of Newton's method while dropping the requirement of a separately coded FORTRAN function for the derivative of $f(x)$, it is usually preferred over all others for the initial attempt to find the root of $f(x)$. However, it suffers from the same potentials for failure as the Newton's method.

The Birge–Vieta method is suitable only for finding roots of polynomials. The idea is identical to Newton's method except that instead of evaluating f_0/f_0' by differentiating the function, synthetic division is used to divide the polynomial for $f(x_0)$ by the polynomial $f'(x_0)$. In addition to an initial guess, x_0, the user must supply the order of the polynomial and an array containing the polynomial coefficients.

Root-solving methods are amenable to FORTRAN coding. However, the success of a program to find the root of a function usually depends on the quality of the information supplied by the user; that is, how accurate is the initial guess or search interval, and how well does the method chosen match the circumstances of the problem. Execution-time problems are most frequently traceable to errors in coding the function or to inadequate user-supplied diagnostics for potential problems.

Problems

11.1 Roughly reproduce the sketch in Figure 11-13 and then graphically apply the regula falsi method for three iterations.

Figure 11-13
Function for
Problem 11.1

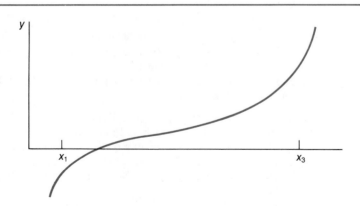

11.2 Using a pocket calculator, apply the regula falsi procedure for three iterations to the following functions:
   a. $f(x) = xe^{-x^2} - \cos(x)$ $\quad a = 0, b = 2$; exact root $= 1.351491185\ldots$
   b. $g(x) = x^2 - 2x - 3$ $\quad a = 0, b = 4$; exact root $= 3.0$
   c. $h(x) = e^x - (1 + x + x^2/2)$ $\quad a = -1, b = 1$; exact root $= 0.0$
   d. $F(x) = x^3 - 2x - 5$ $\quad a = 1, b = 3$; exact root $= 2.0945514815\ldots$
   e. $G(x) = 10 \ln(x) - x$ $\quad a = 1, b = 2$; exact root $= 1.1183255916\ldots$

11.3 Roughly reproduce Figure 11-13 and then graphically apply the modified
regula falsi method for three iterations.

11.4 Write a program that calls the modified regula falsi subroutine MODRFL
of Figure 11-4 to find the root of a function.
   a. Use this program to find the root of one of the functions in Problem 11.2
   to an accuracy of 10^{-5}.

Figure 11-14
Function for
Problem 11.6

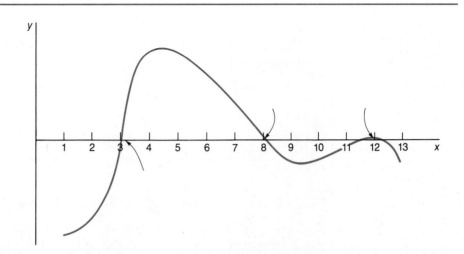

b. Change the relaxation factor from 0.9 to 0.75 and rerun the program. Comment on the difference between the two calculations.

11.5 Write a program that calls the Newton's method subroutine of Figure 11-11 to find the root of a function. Use this program to find the roots of each of the functions of Problem 11.2. You will have to specify a suitable first guess for each of the calculations. Use $\varepsilon = 10^{-5}$. [*Note:* Function $h(x)$ may cause special problems.]

11.6 In the figure sketched in Figure 11-14, the exact roots of the function are located at $x = 3.1, 8.0$, and 12.0. In attempting to find the roots of this function, what are the probable results of the calculation if

a. The initial guess is 5.2 and Newton's method is used.
b. The initial guess is 6.2 and Newton's method with a multiplicity factor $M = 2$ is used.
c. The initial guess is 3.0 and Newton's method is used.
d. The regula falsi method is used with $x_1 = 6.0$ and $x_3 = 12.8$.
e. The secant method is used with an initial guess of $x_0 = 10.0$ and an interval $\Delta x = 1.0$.

11.7 The values of the function

$$f(x) = x^3 - 5.5x^2 + 9.68x - 5.324$$

are tabulated in Table 11-2. The function has one multiple root and one single root.

a. From the tabulated values estimate the vicinity of the multiple root. Which is the best method to use to improve the estimate of this root? Explain your answer.
b. Find the multiple root accurate to six significant figures.

11.8 The polynomial

$$p(x) = 25x^5 - 135x^4 + 256x^3 - 256x^2 + 231x - 121$$

has three real positive roots in the range $0 \le x \le 4$.

Table 11-2
Tabulated values of
the function in
Problem 11.7

x	$f(x)$
0.00	−5.324
0.25	−3.23
0.50	−1.64
0.75	−0.74
1.00	−0.14
1.25	0.14
1.50	0.20
1.75	0.13
2.00	0.04
2.25	0.003
2.50	0.13
2.75	0.50
3.00	1.22
3.25	2.37

a. First make a table of function values in this range to estimate the vicinity of the roots. (*Note:* Some roots may be multiple roots.)
b. Using whatever method is appropriate, determine the exact values of the real roots.
c. Once the three real roots, r_1, r_2, and r_3, are found, use synthetic division to determine the factors of $p(x)$, that is,

$$p(x) = (x - r_1)(x - r_2)(x - r_3)h(x)$$

Once you have found $h(x)$ you will be able to determine the remaining two complex roots.

11.9 Using Newton's method, show that if x_0 is a guess for the value of the nth root of a number C, then an improved guess is

$$x_0 = \frac{1}{n}\left[(n - 1)x + \frac{C}{x_0^{n-1}}\right]$$

[*Hint:* Show that this problem is the same as finding the root of the equation $f(x) = x^n - C$.]

11.10 In the early days of computing, calculators were mechanical, not electronic, and the earliest of these could multiply but not divide. Use Newton's method to devise a scheme that does not employ division to iteratively calculate the inverse of a number C beginning with an initial guess x_0. [The condition on the initial guess is that $(2 - x_0 C)$ be positive.]

11.11 Use the function $f(x) = x^2 - 2xe^{-x} + e^{-2x}$ to answer parts a–c.
a. Starting at $x = 0$, step along the x axis in steps of 0.2 until you have determined the vicinity of the root. Then after establishing an initial guess for the root, apply Newton's method for four iterations.
b. In part a you should have concluded that the root was a multiple root. Redo the calculation, this time including the modification to Newton's method for a root of multiplicity 2. Is the accuracy improved?
c. Write a program that duplicates the calculation in parts a and b; that is, the program should step along the x axis, determine an initial guess for a root, and determine whether the root is likely to be a multiple root. (*Note:* This function will not change sign.) Monitor the function with a test like

```
IF (|f_new| < |f_old|) THEN
     function still decreasing, so...
ELSE
     function has approached possible root, so...
ENDIF
```

11.12 Write a program that calls the secant method subroutine of Figure 11-12 to find the root of a function. Use this program to find the root of the function $f(x) = x^2 - 2x + 0.9$ starting with an initial guess of $x_0 = 0.6$ and an interval $\Delta x_0 = 0.3$. Next alter the subroutine to print a table of values of

$$\begin{array}{|c|c|c|c|c|c|} \hline x_0 & \Delta x_0 & f(x_0) & x_1 = x_0 + \Delta x_0 & f(x_1) & \Delta x_1 \\ \hline \end{array}$$

for each iteration of the calculation.

11.13 The subroutine SECANT of Figure 11-12 was used to find a root of the function $f(x) = x^2 - 2x + 0.9$ starting with an initial guess of $x = 0.6$, $dx = 0.4$ and the values of x and dx were printed for each iteration. The results are:

Step	x	dx
0	0.600	0.300
1	0.900	-0.180
2	0.720	-0.057
3	0.663	0.022
4	0.685	-0.001

Carefully graph the function for $0.5 \le x \le 1.0$ and use the above numbers to graphically demonstrate how the secant method arrives at a root of the function.

11.14 Write a complex version of the secant method subroutine of Figure 11-12. The parameters EPS and DXMAX should remain as real values. Also, the initial guess for x_0 and Δx_0 must have a nonzero imaginary part. Test the program on the functions $f(x) = x^2 + 1$ and $g(x) = e^x + 1$.

11.15 Write a double-precision version of
a. The modified regula falsi subroutine of Figure 11-4
b. The Newton's method subroutine of Figure 11-11
c. The secant method subroutine of Figure 11-12

11.16 Apply the Birge–Vieta method by hand for three iterations to find a root of the polynomials
a. $f(x) = x^4 + 6x^3 + 3x^2 - 10x$ Initial guess $x_0 = 4.0$
b. $g(x) = 8x^3 + 12x^2 + 14x + 9$ Initial guess $x_0 = -\frac{1}{2}$
c. $h(x) = x^4 - 2x^3 + 2x^2 - 2x + 1$ Initial guess $x_0 = \frac{3}{4}$
d. $g(x) = x^4 + 7.7x^3 + 39.1x^2 + 14.4x - 13$ Initial guess $x_0 = \frac{1}{2}$

11.17 In this problem you are to estimate the roots of a polynomial without using a calculator or a computer. You may use Newton's relations, the sign rules of Descartes, and the values of the polynomials at $x = 0$ and ± 1.
a. Determine all four roots of $f(x) = x^4 + 6x^3 + 3x^2 - 10x$.
b. Show that the function $g(x) = 8x^3 + 12x^2 + 14x + 9$ has only one real root and that it is in the interval $-1 \le x \le 0$.
c. Use the value of the derivative of the function

$$h(x) = x^4 - 2x^3 + 2x^2 - 2x + 1$$

at one of the real roots to determine three remaining roots.
d. Show that the function

$$g(x) = x^4 + 7.7x^3 + 39.1x^2 + 14.4x - 13$$

has only one positive real root and one negative real root, and that the positive real root is less than 1. Also show that the real part of the complex roots is greater than 3.3.

11.18 Write a subroutine that implements the Birge–Vieta method to find a root of a polynomial of degree n. Use the subroutine to find the indicated root of each of the polynomials of Problem 11.16 to an accuracy of 10^{-5}.

E

Programming
Assignment

Sample Program

Mechanical Engineering: Cooling Curve for Transfer Ladle Cars

The transfer of molten pig iron from a blast furnace to the steelmaking facilities is a seemingly simple procedure. The molten iron is placed in an elongated tilting ladle railroad car as pictured in Figure E-1. If the distance to be transferred is considerable or if for other reasons the molten iron will remain in the ladle car, it is very important that the cooling rate of the car and its contents be continually monitored. If the molten iron begins to solidify in the transfer car, you can imagine the resulting problems.

The purpose of this problem is to estimate and plot the temperature of the molten iron versus time based on two assumptions:

1. The heat (Q) flowing out from the iron through the car walls (J/sec = watts) is equal to the heat transferred from the car surface to the air by convection and radiation

$$Q_{cond} = Q_{conv} + Q_{rad} \qquad (E.1)$$

The conduction term depends on the geometry of the ladle car. If we approximate the car as a cylinder of length L, outer radius a, and wall thickness δ, and if the car material has a heat conductivity k, the heat flow Q_{cond} can then be expressed approximately as

$$Q_{cond} = k\frac{A_\lambda}{\delta}[T(t) - T_s] \qquad (E.2)$$

where A_λ is the log-mean area involved in the heat conduction, $T(t)$ is the temperature of the molten iron at time t, and T_s is the temperature of the outside surface of the car.

Figure E-1 _____
Sketch of a 150-ton
transfer ladle car

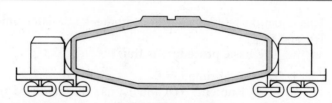

The log-mean area A_λ is expressed in terms of the areas of the outside cylinder surface ($A_o = 2\pi a L$) and the inside surface [$A_i = 2\pi(a - \delta)L$] as

$$A_\lambda = \frac{A_o - A_i}{\ln(A_o/A_i)} \tag{E.3}$$

which can be written as

$$A_\lambda = -\frac{2\pi\delta L}{\ln(1 - \delta/a)}$$

(*Note:* The logarithm is negative, so A_λ is positive.)

2. If the temperature of the surrounding air is T_a, the heat loss from the car to the air is

$$Q_{conv} + Q_{rad} = h_c A_\lambda (T_s - T_a)^{5/4} + \sigma\epsilon A_\lambda(T_s^4 - T_a^4) \tag{E.4}$$

where h_c = Coefficient for convective heat transfer from a cylinder

σ = Coefficient for radiative heat transfer, Stefan–Boltzman constant

ϵ = Emissivity of the car's surface

Thus, Equation (E.2) may be written as

$$T(t) = T_s - \frac{a}{k \ln(1 - \delta/a)}[h_c(T_s - T_a)^{5/4} + \sigma\epsilon(T_s^4 - T_a^4)] \tag{E.5}$$

Knowing the temperature of the iron at a time t, $T(t)$, and the air temperature T_a, we will use this equation to determine the temperature of the car surface, T_s.

The rate of heat loss by the molten iron is related to its temperature through its specific heat C by

$$Q_{cond} = -mC\frac{\Delta T}{\Delta t}$$

$$= -mC\frac{T(t + \Delta t) - T(t)}{\Delta t} \tag{E.6}$$

where m is the mass of the molten iron and C its specific heat. This equation may be written as

$$T(t + \Delta t) = T(t) - \frac{\Delta t Q_{cond}}{mC} \tag{E.7}$$

This equation will be used to compute T at a later time $t + \Delta t$, knowing $T(t)$ and Q_{cond}.

The basic procedure is thus

1. Start at time $t = 0$.
    a. Knowing $T(t)$ and T_a, use the modified regula falsi method to solve Equation (E.5) for the car's surface temperature, T_s.

b. Then use Equation (E.2) to compute the heat loss, Q_{cond}.

c. The temperature at the next time step, $T(t + \Delta t)$, can be calculated using Equation (E.7).

2. Increment $t \rightarrow t + \Delta t$ and repeat.

Problem Specifics. The input parameters for this problem are listed in Table E-1. These parameters should be stored in a data file that will be read by the program. The calculation should proceed as follows:

1. Read all the input data from the data file and echo print.

2. For $t = 0$ to 25 hours in steps of .25 hours,

   a. Determine the initial search interval for the root of Equation (E.6). For the first calculation ($t = 0$) use the interval $T_a < T_s < T_0$; for all subsequent steps use an interval based on the first calculation. For example, if T_s is the latest computed surface temperature, the next computed value should be only slightly lower. Thus, a reasonable interval to use fo the next calculation might be
   $$T_s - (T_s - T_a)/25 \leftrightarrow T_s.$$

   b. Call the modified regula falsi subroutine of Figure 11-4 to find the root of a function based on Equation (E.5). The function will require additional parameters that can be passed to it be means of a COMMON statement.

   c. Use Equations (E.2) and (E.7) to compute the temperature at the next time step.

3. Print a table of the temperatures versus time. If the temperature falls below the iron solidification temperature, print a warning in the tabulated results.

4. Call a subroutine PLOT (see Figure 7-8) to produce a plot of the results.

Table E-1
Input parameters
for the cooling
curve problem

$a =$	1.50	= outer radius of ladle car (m)
$L =$	8.00	= length of ladle car (m)
$\delta =$	0.50	= thickness of car walls (m)
$k =$	4.20	= heat conductivity of walls (watt/K-m)
$h_c =$	1.70	= heat convection coefficient for a cylinder (watt/K-m)
$\epsilon =$	0.80	= emissivity of ladle car surface
$m =$	1.3×10^5	= mass of molten iron (kg)
$C =$	1172.0	= effective specific heat of molten iron (J/kg-K)
$T_a =$	25.0	= air temperature (°C)
$\sigma =$	5.67×10^{-8}	= radiative heat coefficient (watt/K-m^2)
$\delta t =$	0.25	= time step (hrs), convert to seconds
$t_{max} =$	25.0	= maximum time (hrs)
$T_{solid} =$	1157.0	= solidification temperature of molten iron (°C)
EPS $=$	1×10^{-3}	= convergence criterion for the regula falsi method
$I_{max} =$	40.0	= maximum number of iterations permitted
$T(0) =$	1800.0	= initial temperature of molten iron (°C)

[*Note:* All internal values of temperature are in Kelvin, but all the printed values should be in degrees Celsius (K − 273 = °C). Also, the times are in hours, but Δt in Equation (E.7) must be in seconds.]

The FORTRAN code for this problem is given in Figure E-2. The output is shown in Figure E-3.

Figure E-2
FORTRAN code for the cooling curve problem

```
          PROGRAM FIVE
*
* This program will determine the approximate cooling rate of
* molten iron in a transfer ladle railroad car.  The purpose
* is to monitor the temperature to avoid solidification.
*
*  The procedure is as follows:
*    a. Knowing the temperature of the iron at time zero, the sur-
*       face temperature of the car is computed by solving Equation
*       (E.6) by the modified regula falsi method.
*    b. Once the surface temperature is known, the heat lost to
*       the air is obtained by Equation (E.7).
*    c. The temperature of the molten iron at the next time step is
*       then computed by using Equation (E.8) and the time is then
*       incremented.
*
*    The entire calculation is repeated for 25 time steps, and the
* results are printer-plotted.
*------------------------------------------------------------------
* Variables
*
          PARAMETER (N = 25)
          REAL A,L,DELTA,COND,HC,EMIS,MASS,C,TA,SIGMA,DT,TMAX,TSOL,
     +       T(0:N),TIME(0:N),AREA,QCOND,X1,X2,X3,F1,F2,F3
     +       ,COND0
          INTEGER IMAX,TSTEP
          CHARACTER FLAG*3
*
*        A     -- Outer radius of ladle car
*        L     -- Length of ladle car
*        DELTA -- Thickness of car walls
*        COND  -- Heat conductivity of walls
*        HC    -- Convection coefficient of a cylinder
*        EMIS  -- Emissivity of car surface
*        MASS  -- Mass of molten iron
*        C     -- Effective specific heat of molten iron
*        TA    -- Air temperature (K)
*        SIGMA -- Radiative heat coefficient
*        DT    -- Time step (sec)
*        TMAX  -- Maximum time (sec)
*        TSOL  -- Solidification temperature
*        TS    -- Temperature of car surface
*        IMAX  -- Iterations limit (for MODRFL subroutine)
*        EPS   -- Convergence criterion
*        TIME()-- Time values in hours
*        T()   -- Computed iron temperatures as a function of time
*        AREA  -- Area of the car surface
*        QCOND -- Net heat flow from surface
*     X1,X2,X3-- Position values in modified regula falsi method
*     F1,F2,F3-- Function values in modified regula falsi method
*------------------------------------------------------------------
```

Figure E-2
(continued)

```
* The equation to solve for the iron temperature must be EXTERNAL
*
      EXTERNAL TEMP
*
*     And it requires the parameters in the following block
*
      COMMON/PARAM/HC,SIGMA,EMIS,TA,A,COND,DELTA,TT
*-------------------------------------------------------------------
* Initialization
*
*     All the data are read from a data file
*
      OPEN(21,FILE='PROG5.DAT')
      REWIND (21)
      OPEN(37,FILE='PROG5S.OUT')
      READ(21,*)A,L,DELTA,COND,HC,EMIS,MASS,C,TSOL,TA,SIGMA,
     +     DT,TMAX,EPS,IMAX,T(0)
*
      PI = ACOS(-1.)
      AREA = 2.*PI*A*L
*
*     Echo print the data
*
      WRITE(37,10)A,L,DELTA,COND,HC,EMIS,MASS,C,TSOL-273.0,
     +        T(0),TA-273.0,SIGMA,DT,TMAX
      WRITE(37,11)EPS,IMAX
*-------------------------------------------------------------------
* Computation
*
*     Step in time from 0 to TMAX.  The time is in hours, whereas
*     the equation requires time in seconds.
*
      DT    = TMAX/N
      DTSEC = DT*60.*60.
      DO 8 TSTEP = 0,N-1
           TT = T(TSTEP)
           TIME(TSTEP) = TSTEP*DT
*
*         The end points of the search interval for TIME = 0 are
*
           IF(TSTEP.EQ. 0)THEN
               X1 = T(0)
               X3 = TA + 1.
*
*               whereas for later steps we use
*
           ELSE
               X1 = TS - 1./25.*(TS-TA)
               X3 = TS
           END IF
*
*         Next, with these end points, solve for the root of
*         the function by the modified regula falsi method.
*
           CALL MODRFL(X1,X3,EPS,IMAX,I,TS,TEMP)
```

Figure E-2 _____
(continued)

```
*                    Once the root TS is obtained, compute the heat flow
*                    from Equation (E.7)
*
             QCOND = COND*AREA*(T(TSTEP)-TS)/DELTA
*
*                    The next value of the iron temperature can now be com-
*                    puted using Equation (E.8). (Note dt must be in seconds.)
*
             T(TSTEP+1) = T(TSTEP) - DTSEC*QCOND/MASS/C
*
    8    CONTINUE
*         ----------END-OF-TIME-STEP-LOOP----------------------------
         TIME(N) = N*DT
*
*         Print the table of temperatures for this case. (If the
*         iron temperature falls below Tsol, print a warning.)
*
         WRITE(37,12)
         DO 4 I = 0,N
           IF(T(I) .GT. TSOL)THEN
               WRITE(37,13)TIME(I),T(I) - 273.
               FLAG = 'ON'
           ELSEIF(FLAG .EQ. 'ON ')THEN
               WRITE(37,14)TIME(I),T(I) - 273.
               FLAG = 'OFF'
           ELSE
               WRITE(37,13)TIME(I),T(I) - 273.
           END IF
    4    CONTINUE
         WRITE(37,15)
*----------------------------------------------------------------------
* Plotting Section
*
         CALL PLOT(TIME,T,N)
         STOP
*----------------------------------------------------------------------
* Formats
*
    10   FORMAT(///,T3,'Input Parameters for Program Five',//,
        +T5,'Temperature dependence of a railroad ladle car filled ',
        +    /,T5,'with molten iron',//,
        +T5,'Outer radius of the ladle car',T40,'= ',F5.2,' (m)',/,
        +T5,'Length of the ladle car',      T40,'= ',F5.2,' (m)',/,
        +T5,'Thickness of the car walls',   T40,'= ',F5.2,' (m)',/,
        +T5,'Conductivity of car walls',    T40,'= ',F5.2,' watt/m-K',/,
        +T5,'Heat convection coefficient',  T40,'= ',F5.2,' watt/m-K',/,
        +T5,'Emissivity of car surface',    T40,'= ',F5.2,/,
        +T5,'Mass of molten iron',          T40,'= ',E9.3,'(kg)',/,
        +T5,'Specific heat of the iron',    T40,'= ',F5.0,'J/kg-K',/,
        +T5,'Iron solidification temperature',T40,'= ',F5.0,' OC',/,
        +T5,'Initial temperature of the iron',T40,'= ',F5.0,' OC',/,
        +T5,'Temperature of the air',       T40,'= ',F5.1,' OC',/,
        +T5,'Radiative heat coefficient',   T40,'= ',E9.3,//,
        +T5,'The integration is in time steps of ',F5.3,' hours',/,
        +T5,'from zero to a final time of          ',F5.1,' hours')
*
```

Figure E-2
(concluded)

```
 11    FORMAT(//,
      +T5,'The equation is solved by the modified regula falsi',
      +        ' method'/,
      +T5,'using a convergence criterion = ',E8.1,' and',/,
      +T5,'a limit on the number of iterations = ',I2)
 *
 12    FORMAT(//,T5,'Table of temperatures vs time',/,
      +T12,'Time',T25,'Temperature',/,
      +T12,'(hrs)',T25,'  (OC)',/,
      +T12,'----',T25,'-----------')
 *
 13    FORMAT(T11,F5.2,T27,F7.2)

 15    FORMAT(//,T20,'The calculation is completed',/,
      +T20,'Next plot the results')
 *
 14    FORMAT(T11,F5.2,T27,F7.2,2X,'****DANGER'
      +  ,'**** IRON SOLIDIFIED')
 *
       END
 *================================================================
       FUNCTION TEMP(TS)
       REAL COND
       COMMON/PARAM/HC,SIGMA,EMIS,TA,A,COND,DELTA,T

       TEMP = T - TS + (HC*(TS-TA)**1.25 +
      +     SIGMA*EMIS*(TS**4-TA**4))*A/(COND*LOG(1. - DELTA/A))
       RETURN
       END
 *================================================================
       SUBROUTINE MODRFL(XA,XC,EPS,IMAX,I,ROOT,F)

       ┌─────────────────────┐
       │  From Figure 11-4   │
       └─────────────────────┘
 *================================================================
       SUBROUTINE PLOT(X,Y,N)

       ┌─────────────────────┐
       │  From Figure 7-7    │
       └─────────────────────┘
 *================================================================
```

E.2 Programming Problems

Programming Problem E-A: Civil Engineering
and Mechanics: Buckling of a Tall Mast

A standard but complex problem in civil engineering and mechanics is to
determine how tall a mast can be before it will begin to buckle under its
own weight. The solution of this problem, which is usually covered in an
advanced mechanics course, yields the following result.[1]

---

[1] See, for example, S. Timoshenko, *Strength of Materials* (Princeton, N.J.: Van Nostrand, 1955), part I.

Figure E-3 _____

Output from the
cooling curve
program

Input Parameters for Program Five

Temperature dependence of a railroad ladle car filled
with molten iron

Outer radius of the ladle car	= 1.50 (m)
Length of the ladle car	= 8.00 (m)
Thickness of the car walls	= 0.50 (m)
Conductivity of car walls	= 4.20 watt/m-K
Heat convection coefficient	= 1.70 watt/m-K
Emissivity of car surface	= 0.80
Mass of molten iron	= 0.130E+06(kg)
Specific heat of the iron	= 1172.J/kg-K
Iron solidification temperature	= 1157. 0C
Initial temperature of the iron	= 1800. 0C
Temperature of the air	= 25.0 0C
Radiative heat coefficient	= 0.560E-07

The integration is in time steps of 0.250 hours
from zero to a final time of   25.0 hours

The equation is solved by the modified regula falsi method
using a convergence criterion = 0.1E-02 and
a limit on the number of iterations = 40

Table of temperatures vs. time

Time (hrs)	Temperature (0C)	
----	-----------	
0.00	1527.00	
1.00	1506.24	
2.00	1485.76	
3.00	1465.58	
4.00	1445.68	
5.00	1426.06	
6.00	1406.72	
7.00	1387.65	
8.00	1368.85	
9.00	1350.32	
10.00	1332.05	
11.00	1314.03	
12.00	1296.27	
13.00	1278.76	
14.00	1261.49	
15.00	1244.47	
16.00	1227.69	
17.00	1211.14	
18.00	1194.83	
19.00	1178.75	
20.00	1162.89	
21.00	1147.25	****DANGER**** IRON SOLIDIFIED
22.00	1131.84	
23.00	1116.64	
24.00	1101.65	
25.00	1086.88	

The calculation is completed
Next plot the results

Figure E-3 _____
(concluded)

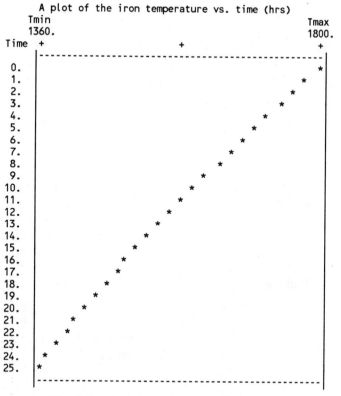

```
           A plot of the iron temperature vs. time (hrs)
           Tmin                                            Tmax
           1360.                                           1800.
    Time    +                         +                      +
            +-----------------------------------------------+
      0.    |                                              *|
      1.    |                                           *   |
      2.    |                                         *     |
      3.    |                                       *       |
      4.    |                                     *         |
      5.    |                                   *           |
      6.    |                                 *             |
      7.    |                               *               |
      8.    |                             *                 |
      9.    |                           *                   |
     10.    |                         *                     |
     11.    |                       *                       |
     12.    |                     *                         |
     13.    |                   *                           |
     14.    |                 *                             |
     15.    |               *                               |
     16.    |             *                                 |
     17.    |           *                                   |
     18.    |         *                                     |
     19.    |       *                                       |
     20.    |     *                                         |
     21.    |   *                                           |
     22.    |  *                                            |
     23.    | *                                             |
     24.    |*                                              |
     25.    |*                                              |
            +-----------------------------------------------+
```

The following quantities are defined:

L = Mast length (m)

Y = Young's modulus of the material (N/m²). Young's modulus is an experimental value of the ratio of the size of a deformation to the applied force.

λ = Mass per unit length of the mast (kg/m)
(*Note:* λ = density × cross-sectional area of the mast)

I_2 = Second area of moment of inertia of the mast given as $\pi r^4/2$, where r is the radius of the round mast

x = Dimensionless parameter that is related to the above quantities by

$$x = \frac{4}{9} g \frac{\lambda L^3}{Y I_2} \qquad g = 9.8 \text{ m/sec}^2 \qquad \text{(E.8)}$$

It is found that the mast will just begin to buckle when x has the value corresponding to the smallest positive root of the function

$$F(x) = \sum_{n=0}^{\infty} a_n x^n \qquad \text{(E.9)}$$

where

$$a_0 = 1$$

$$a_1 = -\frac{3}{4}\left(\frac{1}{2}a_0\right) = -\frac{3}{8}$$

$$a_2 = -\frac{3}{4}\left(\frac{1}{10}a_1\right) = \frac{9}{320}$$

$$\vdots$$

$$a_{n+1} = -\frac{3}{4}\frac{1}{(n+1)(3n+2)}a_n \qquad (E.10)$$

The problem is then to find the first root of Equation (E.9), say x_1, and once this value is determined, to specify the maximum lengths of a mast for a variety of materials. The root-solving technique to be used is the secant method, and the program will have to step in small increments of x starting at zero to first determine the vicinity of the root.

Problem Specifics. The calculations should proceed as follows:

1. Write a FORTRAN function subprogram for the function of Equation (E.9). The summation should be terminated when the absolute value of an individual term $<\epsilon = 10^{-6}$. Successive terms can be determined from

$$\text{Term}_{n+1} = -\text{Term}_n \times \frac{3}{4}\frac{x}{(n+1)(3n+2)}$$

2. Write a data file containing the information in Table E-2.
3. The FORTRAN program should perform the following operations:
   a. Starting at $x = 0$, step along the x axis in steps of size $\Delta x = 0.25$ to find the first time that the function changes

Table E-2
Young's modulus and density values for various materials

Material	Young's Modulus, Y (N/m²) ($\times 10^{10}$)	Density, ρ (kg/m³) ($\times 10^3$)
Aluminum (cast)	5.6–7.7	2.70
Brass	9.02	8.44
Gold	7.85	19.3
Iron (cast)	8.4–9.8	7.86
Lead	1.5–1.67	11.0
Platinum	16.7	21.4
Steel	20.0	7.83
Tin	3.9–5.39	7.29
Tungsten	35.5	18.8

sign. The initial guess for the root is then the latest value of x, and the initial guess for the interval is Δx.

b. Call the secant subroutine of Figure 11-12 to find the root of the function to an accuracy of 10^{-4}.

c. Print the initial guess for x and Δx along with the computed root, the value of the function at the root, and the number of iterations required.

d. Open the data file and for each of the materials listed,

(1) Read a line of material characteristics.

(2) Compute the maximum mast length from Equation (E.9). (Assume that all masts have a radius of $r = 0.10$ m.)

(3) Print the names and characteristics of this material along with the computed value of the mast length. (*Note*: For those materials with a range of Young's moduli, a corresponding range of masts must be printed.)

(4) Use the "END =" option in the READ statement to terminate the program.

Programming Problem E-B: General Engineering: Functions Describing Diffusion

Diffusion is a process encountered in most areas of science and engineering. It describes the movement of neutrons through a nuclear reactor, the transport of heat through materials, the intrusion of one fluid into an adjacent fluid, the propagation of a disturbance in a line of freeway traffic, and numerous other phenomena. The solution for each case depends on the specifics of the problem. But the mathematical function describing diffusion is always a function that decays exponentially in time, and the dependence on the coordinates is a function of the geometry of the problem. A particularly simple geometry is that of a sphere.

Consider the problem of a sphere of radius a, which is at an initial temperature of T_0. If the material is characterized by a diffusivity α^2 and it is placed in 0° C air, the sphere will slowly cool by convection and radiation.[2] If the rate of temperature decrease at the surface is characterized by an experimental constant h, the solution for the temperature at the center of the sphere is

$$T_c = T_0\left(\frac{ah}{\sigma}\right) \sum_{n=1}^{\infty} C_n^{(-\beta_n^2 t)} \tag{E.11}$$

---

[2] The diffusivity of a material is defined as $\alpha^2 = \dfrac{\text{thermal conductivity}}{(\text{specific heat})(\text{density})} = \dfrac{\lambda}{c\rho}$.

where

$$\beta_n^2 = \theta_n \frac{\alpha^2}{a^2} \tag{E.12}$$

$$C_n = \frac{4 \sin(\theta_n)}{2\theta_n - \sin(2\theta_n)} \tag{E.13}$$

and θ_n is the nth root of the equation

$$\tan(\theta_n) = \frac{1}{1 - (ah/\sigma)} \theta_n \tag{E.14}$$

The values of the physical parameters to use in this problem are

$T_0 = 250 \ ^\circ\text{C}$
$\alpha^2 = 1.2 \times 10^{-5} \ \text{m}^2/\text{sec}$
$h = 23.0 \ \text{W/m}^2\text{-}^\circ\text{C}$
$\sigma = 46.0 \ \text{W/m-}^\circ\text{C}$
$a = 0.1 \ \text{m}$

The problem is to determine and tabulate the first 10 roots of Equation (E.14) and then to use Equation (E.11) to compute the temperature at the center of the sphere for values of time $t = 0$ to $t = 3600$ sec (1 hour) in steps of 60 seconds.

Problem Specifics. The calculations should proceed as follows:

1. Write a function subprogram $TC(t)$ based on Equation (E.11) that will return the temperature at the center of the sphere at a time t. The function will require the first 10 roots of Equation (E.14), which will be computed below and stored in an array THETA(N). These roots, along with other parameters, should be passed to the function via a COMMON statement.
2. Write a function subprogram $f(\theta)$ based on Equation (E.14) that will be zero when θ is a solution of Equation (E.14). The function will also require that a, h, and σ be passed to it by means of a COMMON statement.
3. Carefully differentiate the algebraic expression for $f(\theta)$ and write a function subprogram $df/d\theta$. Note that

$$\frac{d[\tan(x)]}{dx} = \frac{1}{\cos^2(x)}$$

4. Write a FORTRAN program that will start at $\theta = 0.1$ and step in values of $d\theta = 0.1$ to find the first time that $f(\theta)$ changes sign. The first root should be found to be near 0.4.
   a. The program then calls subroutine NEWTON of Figure 11-11 to refine this estimate to the first root. Use

EPS $= 10^{-5}$ and IMAX $= 15$. Store the value for the first root in THETA(1).

b. You must be extremely careful in searching for the remaining nine roots. If you continue to step in θ, you will find that the function changes sign as θ crosses $\pi/2$ but does *not* go through zero; that is, $\tan(\pi/2) = \infty$, and the function is not continuous. From a sketch of both sides of Equation (E.14), you can see that the subsequent roots are slightly to the left of multiples of $\pi/2$. For all roots after the first you should begin with the initial guess

$$\theta_n \simeq \left(n - \frac{1}{2}\right)\pi\left[1 - \frac{1}{(n - \frac{1}{2})^2\pi^2k^2}\right] \qquad n = 2,3,\ldots,9$$

where

$$k = 1 - \left(\frac{ah}{\sigma}\right)$$

5. Once the 10 roots have been computed and neatly printed, the function $TC(t)$ can be used to evaluate the temperature of the center of the sphere. For $t = 0$ to 10 hours (36,000 sec) in steps of $\frac{1}{2}$ hour, compute a table of temperature versus time.

6. Use the subroutine PLOT of Figure 7-8 to plot the temperature versus time.

Programming Problem E-C: Chemistry/Chemical Engineering: Determining the Diffusion Constant

The diffusion of one fluid into another is a phenomenon that is of great importance in several areas of engineering, especially chemistry and chemical engineering. The rate at which diffusion takes place is governed by the diffusion constant D, which represents the average rate of unit displacement by a fluid particle. One of the most common methods of measuring the diffusion constant is to fill a small capillary tube with one liquid, immerse the tube in a second liquid, and measure the concentration of molecules of one fluid as it diffuses into the other as a function of time. This may be done by labeling the intruder fluid with radioactive isotopes or simply by observing the color change of, for example, ink diffusing into water.

The relationship between the concentration at a later time, $C(t)$, and the initial concentration at time $t = 0$, C_0 is given by the equation

$$R = \frac{C(t)}{C_0} = 1 + \frac{1}{2}\frac{\Delta C}{C_0}\left(1 - \frac{4}{\pi}\sum_{\substack{n=1 \\ (\text{odd})}}^{\infty}\frac{(-1)^{(n-1)/2}}{n}e^{-n^2\gamma^2Dt}\right) \qquad (E.15)$$

where $\gamma = \pi/L$ (Use $L = 0.1$ m)

$L = $ Thickness of the medium into which the test liquid is diffusing (m)

C_0 = Original concentration of the diffusing substance

$C(t)$ = Concentration of the diffusing substance midway into the solution at a time t

$\Delta C/C_0$ = Fractional increase in concentration of the diffusing substance at the interface between the two liquids

R = Ratio of increased concentration to original concentration measured at time t (in sec)

t = Time in seconds

D = Diffusion constant (units are m^2/sec and a typical value is 1×10^{-5} to 1×10^{-4})

At a specific value of time, the concentrations $C(t)$, C_0 are measured and the ratio of concentrations $R = C(t)/C_0$ is computed. Equation (E.15) is then solved for the diffusion constant D.

We can use the secant method to determine the diffusion constant by first rewriting Equation (E.15) as

$$F(D) = 1 + R_0\left(1 - \frac{4}{\pi} \sum_{\substack{n=1 \\ (\text{odd})}}^{\infty} \frac{(-1)^{(n-1)/2}}{n} e^{-n^2 aD}\right) - R \qquad \text{(E.16)}$$

where

$$R_0 = \frac{1}{2}\frac{\Delta C}{C_0} \qquad \text{and} \qquad a = \gamma^2 t$$

The value of the diffusion constant then corresponds to a root of this equation.

Problem Specifics. The calculations should proceed as follows:

1. Write a FORTRAN function subprogram based on Equation (E.16). The additional parameters should be passed to the function via a COMMON statement. The sum should be terminated when the absolute value of a term $< \epsilon = 10^{-6}$.

2. Write a program that will
   a. Initialize the parameters by means of a DATA statement. Use the following values:

   $$C(t)/C_0 = 1.01$$
   $$t = 120 \text{ sec}$$
   $$\Delta C/C_0 = .30$$
   $$\text{Name of liquid} = \text{Cadmium sulfide}$$

   b. Compute R_0 and a.
   c. Starting with $D = 10^{-6}$ and a step size $\Delta D = 1 \times 10^{-6}$, step in values of D until the function changes sign. Then use the most recent values of D as the initial guess for the secant subroutine of Figure 11-12 to refine the root to an accuracy of 10^{-11}.

Linear Simultaneous Equations: Matrices

From the earliest days of the computer age it was clear that one type of problem, solving numerous simultaneous equations in many unknowns, was particularly well suited to a machine-aided solution. In every real problem there are numerous variables to consider, and changes in any one will affect all the others. If the relationships between all of the variables can be expressed in terms of many equations in which no variable appears with a power higher than 1, the problem is then appropriate for the field of mathematics called *linear algebra*. This branch of mathematics was invented long before the computer to simplify the structure of multivariable problems. Coupled with the computer, unimaginably huge problems involving hundreds of variables have been solved, and the procedures have been extended in some special cases to nonlinear problems or problems involving inequalities in place of equations. The modern advances in this field are important in virtually all areas of engineering and science.

You have already studied the method for solving two linear equations in two unknowns and perhaps three equations in three unknowns. Beyond that, except in very special circumstances, a solution by hand calculation becomes terribly tedious. To develop machine codes for the more complicated situations, we will, as always, carefully step through the simpler calculation and attempt to generalize the procedures.

The keystone in the development of computer codes to solve many simultaneous equations will be the introduction of a new notation to simplify the statement of the problem. This notation is called *matrices*. In the history of science and mathematics there are numerous examples of dramatic progress in a particular field following the introduction of a simplifying notation, one that makes it possible to highlight the major points by suppressing less important details. The notation of vectors or the Leibnitz notation of calculus in use today are two such examples.

A third example, that of matrix notation, described in the next section will permit you to symbolically manipulate an entire set of simultaneous equations written concisely as $[A]\mathbf{x} = \mathbf{b}$, where $\mathbf{x}$ and $\mathbf{b}$ are *vectors* and $[A]$ is a matrix of numbers. The ultimate task of this chapter is to solve this equation for the unknowns contained in the vector $\mathbf{x}$ by symbolically writing the solution as $\mathbf{x} = \mathbf{b}/[A]$. Division of matrices, like division of ordinary numbers, consists of finding the multiplicative inverse, $[A^{-1}]$, so that $\mathbf{x} = [A^{-1}]\mathbf{b}$. However, unlike ordinary numbers, not all matrices have an inverse. The condition for the existence or nonexistence of an inverse of a matrix is expressed in terms of the *determinant* of the matrix, which is described in Section 12.3. The solution of the set of equations may be expressed in terms of determinants by means of Cramer's rule described in Section 12.4. However, a more systematic approach known as the Gauss–Jordan method is better suited to a computer program and is explained in Sections 12.5 and 12.6. Next, an iterative technique for solving simultaneous equations, the Gauss–Siedel method, is described. The Gauss–Siedel method is particularly useful when the matrix is extremely large and contains a great many zeros. Finally, several utility computer programs are developed for printing or multiplying matrices.

12.2 Notation of Matrices

The utility of a new notation for handling simultaneous equations is best illustrated by the following common mathematical ploy. We begin by solving a trivial example. Then in successive stages the example is generalized to accommodate a much broader set of problems. The generalized problem then leads into a variety of new considerations, such as the multiplication of matrices or the definition of the determinant of a matrix.

Square Matrices and Column Vectors

Recall how you would solve two equations in two unknowns. For example,

$$3x - 1y = 7 \tag{12.1}$$

$$2x - 4y = -2 \tag{12.2}$$

One method of attack might involve subtraction of a multiple of one equation from the other with the hope of eliminating one of the variables. Thus, multiplying Equation (12.2) by $\frac{3}{2}$, the pair of equations becomes

$$3x - 1y = 7$$

$$3x - 6y = -3 \tag{12.3}$$

Next, replacing Equation (12.3) by Equation (12.3) minus Equation (12.1) yields

$$3x - 1y = 7$$

$$5y = 10 \qquad (12.4)$$

and the solution for y is $y = 2$. Substituting this value back into the first equation then determines the solution for x.

$$3x - 1(2) = 7$$

$$3x = 9$$

Thus, the solution to the original two equations is the number pair $(x, y) = (3, 2)$.

The reason that such a trivial example has been treated in such detail is that we intend to construct a much more general procedure that is based on the elementary operations just carried out on the simple two equations with two unknowns problem. As a first step in this direction, the original equations are rewritten a bit more formally as

$$a_{11}x_1 + a_{12}x_2 = b_1$$

$$a_{21}x_1 + a_{22}x_2 = b_2 \qquad (12.5)$$

where comparison with the earlier pair of equations leads to the assignments

$$\begin{pmatrix} a_{11} & a_{12} \\ a_{21} & a_{22} \end{pmatrix} = \begin{pmatrix} 3 & -1 \\ 2 & -4 \end{pmatrix} \qquad \begin{pmatrix} b_1 \\ b_2 \end{pmatrix} = \begin{pmatrix} 7 \\ -2 \end{pmatrix} \qquad \begin{pmatrix} x_1 \\ x_2 \end{pmatrix} = \begin{pmatrix} x \\ y \end{pmatrix}$$

Notice that with this notation the two equations can be written

$$\sum_{j=1}^{2} a_{1j}x_j = b_1 \qquad \text{New Equation (12.1)}$$

$$\sum_{j=1}^{2} a_{2j}x_j = b_2 \qquad \text{New Equation (12.2)}$$

Or both equations can even be written simultaneously as

$$\sum_{j=1}^{2} a_{ij}x_j = b_i \qquad (12.6)$$

so that if $i = 1$ is substituted in Equation (12.6), Equation (12.1) is duplicated, and if $i = 2$, Equation (12.2) is duplicated.

For a problem involving only two unknowns this formalism is a waste of time, since the solution was obtained so easily without a new notation. However, for more complicated problems the process of replacing the coefficients in the equations by a single variable name with two subscripts (a_{ij}) and all the variables by a single variable name with a single subscript (x_i) will make a significant difference. Consider a problem involving five equations in five unknowns:

$$7v + 2w + x - y + 5z = 7$$

$$2v - 4x - 2y + z = 2$$

$$-4w + x - 6y - z = 2$$

$$-3v - 2y + 9z = 20$$

$$3v + 3w + 3x + 3y + 3z = 1 \tag{12.7}$$

If we replace the variable names (v, w, x, y, z) with $(x_1, x_2, x_3, x_4, x_5)$ and let the set of coefficients in the problem be collectively called a_{ij} with $i = 1, 5$ and $j = 1, 5$ and the constants on the right-hand side be identified as b_i, $i = 1, 5$, the entire set of equations can be written as

$$\sum_{j=1}^{5} a_{ij}x_j = b_i$$

where the identification of the number sets a_{ij}, b_i are

$$a_{ij}$$

Col #						
j	1	2	3	4	5	
Row #						
i						
1	7	2	1	-1	5	
2	2	0	-4	-2	1	
3	0	-4	1	-6	-1	
4	-3	0	0	-2	9	
5	3	3	3	3	3	

$$b_i$$

Row #	
i	
1	7
2	2
3	2
4	20
5	1

The elements of the square array of numbers a_{ij} are specified by the *row* and *column* of a location in the array; that is, the elements of a_{ij} are labeled $a_{\text{row,col}}$. Thus, a_{45} (fourth row, fifth column) is 9. To duplicate, say, the fourth equation in the set of Equations (12.7) from the array of numbers, we use the fourth rows of both a_{ij} and b_i to get

$$\sum_{j=1}^{5} a_{4j}x_j = -3x_1 + 0x_2 + 0x_3 - 2x_4 + 9x_5 = 20 \tag{12.8}$$

One of the tedious aspects in writing the set of Equations (12.7) is that the variable names are written repeatedly and unnecessarily. Thus, if it is agreed that the first variable in each equation is always v (or x_1), we could eliminate the variable names from the equation, and the set could be written in block form as

$$
\begin{array}{ccccc}
x_1 & x_2 & x_3 & x_4 & x_5 \\
\end{array}
\qquad b_i
$$

$$
\begin{bmatrix}
7 & 2 & 1 & -1 & 5 \\
2 & 0 & -4 & -2 & 1 \\
0 & -4 & 1 & -6 & -1 \\
-3 & 0 & 0 & -2 & 9 \\
3 & 3 & 3 & 3 & 3
\end{bmatrix}
=
\begin{bmatrix}
7 \\
2 \\
2 \\
20 \\
1
\end{bmatrix}
$$

The set of numbers in the square array on the left, that is, a_{ij}, is called a *square matrix*. The numbers on the right, b_i, form a *column matrix*,[1] or a *vector*. The variables x_i could also be grouped as a column matrix. In a drastic simplification of the original set of equations, we could symbolically write Equation (12.7) as

$$[A]\mathbf{x} = \mathbf{b} \tag{12.9}$$

where the symbol $[A]$ is used to represent the entire array a_{ij} and $\mathbf{x}, \mathbf{b}$ are used to represent the column vectors x_i, b_i.

The key to understanding Equation (12.9) as the representation of the entire set of Equations (12.7) is to precisely specify what is meant by the multiplication in Equation (12.9).

Multiplication of Matrices

The multiplication of a square matrix times a column matrix, as in Equation (12.9), is defined as follows: If we take the fourth row of the matrix $[A]$ and multiply each element in turn by a corresponding element of the column matrix $\mathbf{x}$ and successively add the products of elements, then the result is equal to the fourth element (or fourth row) of the column matrix $\mathbf{b}$; that is,

$$
\begin{bmatrix}
7 & 2 & 2 & -1 & 5 \\
2 & 0 & -4 & -2 & 1 \\
0 & 4 & 1 & -6 & -1 \\
-3 & 0 & 0 & -2 & 9 \\
3 & 3 & 3 & 3 & 3
\end{bmatrix}
\begin{bmatrix}
x_1 \\
x_2 \\
x_3 \\
x_4 \\
x_5
\end{bmatrix}
=
\begin{bmatrix}
7 \\
2 \\
2 \\
20 \\
1
\end{bmatrix}
$$

---

[1] In general, a matrix is any rectangular array of numbers. The elements of the array are arranged by rows and columns and are enclosed in brackets.

or

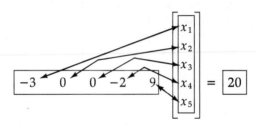

$$-3x_1 + 0x_2 + 0x_3 - 2x_4 + 9x_5 = 20$$

which duplicates the fourth equation of Equations (12.7). The first of Equations (12.7) is duplicated by multiplying element by element and summing the *first* row of $[A]$ by $\mathbf{x}$ and setting the result equal to the *first* element of $\mathbf{b}$. In this way we can reconstruct all of the original equations from the notation $[A]\mathbf{x} = \mathbf{b}$.

This procedure for multiplying a square matrix times a column matrix can easily be generalized to multiplying a square matrix by a square matrix of like size.

$$[A] \qquad \times \qquad [B] \qquad = \qquad [C]$$

$$\begin{bmatrix} a_{11} & a_{12} & a_{13} \\ a_{21} & a_{22} & a_{23} \\ a_{31} & a_{32} & a_{33} \end{bmatrix} \times \begin{bmatrix} b_{11} & b_{12} & b_{13} \\ b_{21} & b_{22} & b_{23} \\ b_{31} & b_{32} & b_{33} \end{bmatrix} = \begin{bmatrix} c_{11} & c_{12} & c_{13} \\ c_{21} & c_{22} & c_{23} \\ c_{31} & c_{32} & c_{33} \end{bmatrix} \qquad (12.10)$$

Now in Equation (12.9) we obtained the (*i*th row, first column) element of $\mathbf{b}$ by multiplying the *i*th row of $[A]$ by the first column of $\mathbf{x}$. Of course, in that case the vectors $\mathbf{x}$ and $\mathbf{b}$ have only one column. The generalized multiplication implied in Equation (12.10) could be defined analogously as

$$c_{ij} = (i\text{th row of } [A])(j\text{th column of } [B])$$

or

$$c_{23} = \begin{bmatrix} a_{11} & a_{12} & a_{13} \\ \boxed{a_{21} \quad a_{22} \quad a_{23}} \\ a_{31} & a_{32} & a_{33} \end{bmatrix} \begin{bmatrix} b_{11} & b_{12} & \boxed{b_{13}} \\ b_{21} & b_{22} & \boxed{b_{23}} \\ b_{31} & b_{32} & \boxed{b_{33}} \end{bmatrix}$$

$$= a_{21}b_{13} + a_{22}b_{23} + a_{23}b_{33} = \sum_{j=1}^{3} a_{2j}b_{j3}$$

Each of the nine elements of the matrix $[C]$ is defined in a similar fashion. All nine equations defining the elements of $[C]$ can be succinctly written as

$$c_{ij} = \sum_{k=1}^{3} a_{ik}b_{kj} \qquad (12.11)$$

Matrix multiplication defined in this manner can be generalized to square matrices of any size.

The following example illustrates the rather surprising fact that matrix multiplication in general is not commutative. Consider the four-square 3 by 3 matrices.

$$[A] = \begin{bmatrix} 0 & 0 & 0 \\ 0 & 0 & 1 \\ 0 & -1 & 0 \end{bmatrix} \quad [B] = \begin{bmatrix} 0 & 0 & -1 \\ 0 & 0 & 0 \\ 1 & 0 & 0 \end{bmatrix}$$

$$[C] = \begin{bmatrix} 0 & -1 & 0 \\ 1 & 0 & 0 \\ 0 & 0 & 0 \end{bmatrix} \quad [I_3] = \begin{bmatrix} 1 & 0 & 0 \\ 0 & 1 & 0 \\ 0 & 0 & 1 \end{bmatrix}$$

The matrix $[I_3]$ is called the 3 by 3 *identity* matrix. It is easily shown that for any 3 by 3 matrix $[M]$,

$$[I_3][M] = [M][I_3] = [M]$$

Identity matrices of arbitrary size are defined in a like manner, and all have the feature that there are 1's on their main diagonal (the elements I_{ij} with $i = j$) and all other elements of the matrix are 0.

Next, if we evaluate the matrix expression

$$[A][B] - [B][A]$$

we obtain

$$\begin{bmatrix} 0 & 0 & 0 \\ 0 & 0 & 1 \\ 0 & -1 & 0 \end{bmatrix} \begin{bmatrix} 0 & 0 & -1 \\ 0 & 0 & 0 \\ 1 & 0 & 0 \end{bmatrix} - \begin{bmatrix} 0 & 0 & -1 \\ 0 & 0 & 0 \\ 1 & 0 & 0 \end{bmatrix} \begin{bmatrix} 0 & 0 & 0 \\ 0 & 0 & 1 \\ 0 & -1 & 0 \end{bmatrix}$$

$$= \begin{bmatrix} 0 & 0 & 0 \\ 1 & 0 & 0 \\ 0 & 0 & 0 \end{bmatrix} - \begin{bmatrix} 0 & 1 & 0 \\ 0 & 0 & 0 \\ 0 & 0 & 0 \end{bmatrix} = \begin{bmatrix} 0 & -1 & 0 \\ 1 & 0 & 0 \\ 0 & 0 & 0 \end{bmatrix} = [C]$$

Since $[A][B] - [B][A]$ does not equal the null matrix (a matrix of like size containing all zeros), matrix multiplication is not in general commutative. It is left to you to show that matrix multiplication is, however, associative—that is, $([A][B])[C] = [A]([B][C])$.

12.3 Determinants

The preceding discussion was concerned solely with matrix notation for sets of linear equations. We now return to the original problem of solving the equations. In the notation of matrices, the set of equations reads

$$[A]\mathbf{x} = \mathbf{b}$$

where **x** is the set of unknowns. The solution to this equation is then "obviously"

$$\mathbf{x} = \frac{\mathbf{b}}{[A]}$$

Well, not quite. We have defined multiplication of matrices, but division is quite a bit more difficult. For example, how would the rule prohibiting the division of a number by zero translate into the notation of matrices? We shall return to the problem of division of matrices shortly, but first we refer back to the simple problem of two equations in two unknowns for guidance in obtaining the general solution of the equation $[A]\mathbf{x} = \mathbf{b}$.

Determinant of a 2 by 2 Matrix

Starting with

$$a_{11}x_1 + a_{12}x_2 = b_1 \tag{12.12}$$

$$a_{21}x_1 + a_{22}x_2 = b_2 \tag{12.13}$$

we could solve Equation (12.13) for x_2 and substitute that result into Equation (12.12) to obtain an expression for x_1 alone; x_2 could be found in a like manner. The result would be

$$x_1 = \frac{b_1 a_{22} - b_2 a_{12}}{a_{11}a_{22} - a_{21}a_{12}} \tag{12.14}$$

$$x_2 = \frac{b_2 a_{11} - b_1 a_{12}}{a_{11}a_{22} - a_{21}a_{12}} \tag{12.15}$$

Notice that the solutions for both x_1 and x_2 have the same denominator. This combination of coefficients is called the *determinant* of the 2 by 2 coefficient matrix $[A]$. The notation for a determinant is

$$\det[A] = |A| = \begin{vmatrix} a_{11} & a_{12} \\ a_{21} & a_{22} \end{vmatrix}$$

The determinant of the 2 by 2 matrix $[A]$ is a single number that can be evaluated from the matrix $[A]$ by drawing diagonals and then subtracting the products of elements along each diagonal.

$$\begin{vmatrix} a_{11} & a_{12} \\ a_{21} & a_{22} \end{vmatrix} = \begin{vmatrix} a_{11} & a_{12} \\ a_{21} & a_{22} \end{vmatrix} \!\!\!\!\!\! \times \quad = (a_{11}a_{22}) - (a_{21}a_{12})$$

Clearly, if the determinant of $[A]$ is zero, a unique solution is not possible for x_1 and x_2.

◼ Determinant of a 3 by 3 Matrix

The entire process is next repeated for three equations in three unknowns, x_1, x_2, x_3. The third equation is solved for x_3 and is then substituted into the first two equations. The second of these is then solved for x_2, which is then substituted into the first. After considerable algebra, the following expressions for the solutions x_1, x_2, x_3 are obtained:

$$x_1 = \frac{b_1(a_{22}a_{33} - a_{23}a_{32}) - b_2(a_{12}a_{33} - a_{13}a_{32}) + b_3(a_{12}a_{23} - a_{13}a_{22})}{a_{11}a_{22}a_{33} + a_{12}a_{23}a_{31} + a_{13}a_{32}a_{21} - a_{11}a_{23}a_{32} - a_{21}a_{12}a_{33} - a_{31}a_{22}a_{13}}$$

$$(12.16)$$

$$x_2 = \frac{b_1(a_{23}a_{31} - a_{21}a_{33}) + b_2(a_{11}a_{33} - a_{13}a_{31}) + b_3(a_{13}a_{21} - a_{11}a_{23})}{a_{11}a_{22}a_{33} + a_{12}a_{23}a_{31} + a_{13}a_{32}a_{21} - a_{11}a_{23}a_{32} - a_{21}a_{12}a_{33} - a_{31}a_{22}a_{13}}$$

$$(12.17)$$

$$x_3 = \frac{b_1(a_{21}a_{32} - a_{22}a_{31}) + b_2(a_{12}a_{31} - a_{11}a_{32}) + b_3(a_{11}a_{22} - a_{12}a_{21})}{a_{11}a_{22}a_{33} + a_{12}a_{23}a_{31} + a_{13}a_{32}a_{21} - a_{11}a_{23}a_{32} - a_{21}a_{12}a_{33} - a_{31}a_{22}a_{13}}$$

$$(12.18)$$

The results of the three-equations-in-three unknowns problem are clearly much more complicated than were the 2 by 2 solutions. The main point to notice in the solutions is the appearance of the same denominator in all three expressions. Once again this combination of coefficients is called the determinant of the matrix $[A]$, where $[A]$ is now a square 3 by 3 matrix.

The determinant of a 3 by 3 matrix may be evaluated by a procedure somewhat like the evaluation of the 2 by 2 determinant. First the matrix is written out in rows and columns. Next the first two columns are duplicated on the right and diagonal lines drawn as shown below. The determinant is then evaluated as the product of elements along the diagonals, with terms from parallel diagonals grouped. Finally, the value of the determinant is equal to the difference between the two groups of terms.

$$\det[A] = |A| = \begin{vmatrix} a_{11} & a_{12} & a_{13} \\ a_{21} & a_{22} & a_{23} \\ a_{31} & a_{32} & a_{33} \end{vmatrix} \begin{matrix} a_{11} & a_{12} \\ a_{21} & a_{22} \\ a_{31} & a_{32} \end{matrix}$$

$$= (a_{11}a_{22}a_{33} + a_{12}a_{23}a_{31} + a_{13}a_{21}a_{32})$$

$$- (a_{31}a_{22}a_{13} + a_{32}a_{23}a_{11} + a_{33}a_{21}a_{12}) \qquad (12.19)$$

For example,

$$
\begin{vmatrix} 1 & 3 & 2 \\ -2 & 1 & -1 \\ 0 & 1 & 4 \end{vmatrix} = \begin{vmatrix} 1 & 3 & 2 \\ -2 & 1 & -1 \\ 0 & 1 & 4 \end{vmatrix} \begin{matrix} 1 & 3 \\ -2 & 1 \\ 0 & 1 \end{matrix}
$$

$$= (4 + 0 - 4) - (0 - 1 - 24)$$

$$= 25$$

■ ## Determinant of an *n* by *n* Matrix

The solution of four simultaneous equations similarly results in expressions for x_1, x_2, x_3, x_4 that are combinations of the coefficients divided by the determinant of the coefficient matrix $[A]$. Unfortunately, there is no simple method of drawing lines to calculate the determinant of a 4 by 4 matrix. To evaluate the determinant of a square matrix of arbitrary size, it is necessary to introduce a quantity called the *cofactor matrix*, which is denoted as $[A^c]$.

Cofactor Matrix

If a_{ij} is an element of the matrix $[A]$, the *cofactor* of a_{ij}, designated as A_{ij}^c, is defined to be the product of the determinant of what is left of $[A]$ after deleting the *i*th row and *j*th column times the sign $(-1)^{i+j}$. Thus, if

$$
[A] = \begin{bmatrix} 1 & 3 & 2 \\ -2 & 1 & -1 \\ 0 & 1 & 4 \end{bmatrix}
$$

then

$$
A_{11}^c = (-1)^2 \begin{bmatrix} \cdots & \cdots & \cdots \\ \cdots & 1 & -1 \\ \cdots & 1 & 4 \end{bmatrix} = 1(4 + 1) = 5
$$

$$
A_{23}^c = (-1)^5 \begin{bmatrix} 1 & 3 & \cdots \\ \cdots & \cdots & \cdots \\ 0 & 1 & \cdots \end{bmatrix} = -1(1 - 0) = -1
$$

Determinant as a Sum Over Cofactors

It can be shown[2] that the determinant of a square matrix of arbitrary size is given by the equation

$$
\det[A] = |A| = \sum_{j=1}^{n} a_{ij} A_{ij}^c \qquad \text{for any value of } i \tag{12.20}
$$

[2] See C. W. Curtis, *Linear Algebra* (Boston: Allyn and Bacon, 1963); or any textbook on linear algebra.

In Equation (12.20), i may be assigned any value from 1 to n and is usually chosen to be 1 for convenience. Using the matrix above, we find that $A_{11}^c = 5$, $A_{12}^c = 8$, and $A_{13}^c = -2$, so that

$$|A| = a_{11}A_{11}^c + a_{12}A_{12}^c + a_{13}A_{13}^c$$
$$= 1(5) + 3(8) + 2(-2) = 25$$

For example,

$$\begin{vmatrix} 5 & -3 & 12 & 2 \\ 6 & 4 & 8 & 6 \\ 3 & -1 & 8 & -1 \\ 4 & 2 & 12 & 4 \end{vmatrix} = \begin{bmatrix} \boxed{5} & \cdots & \cdots & \cdots \\ \cdots & 4 & 8 & 6 \\ \cdots & -1 & 8 & -1 \\ \cdots & 2 & 12 & 4 \end{bmatrix} - \begin{bmatrix} \cdots & \boxed{-3} & \cdots & \cdots \\ 6 & \cdots & 8 & 6 \\ 3 & \cdots & 8 & -1 \\ 4 & \cdots & 12 & 4 \end{bmatrix}$$

$$+ \begin{bmatrix} \cdots & \cdots & \boxed{12} & \cdots \\ 6 & 4 & \cdots & 6 \\ 3 & -1 & \cdots & -1 \\ 4 & 2 & \cdots & 4 \end{bmatrix} - \begin{bmatrix} \cdots & \cdots & \cdots & \boxed{2} \\ 6 & 4 & 8 & \cdots \\ 3 & -1 & 8 & \cdots \\ 4 & 2 & 12 & \cdots \end{bmatrix}$$

$$= 5(24) - (-3)(160) + 12(-16) - 2(-104) = 616$$

The 4 by 4 determinant is thus expressed as a sum over four 3 by 3 determinants. A 5 by 5 determinant would be written as five 4 by 4 determinants, each in turn written as four 3 by 3 determinants. Clearly, the labor involved in evaluating a determinant increases dramatically with the size of the determinant.

Properties of Determinants

Some useful properties of determinants are listed below without proof.[3]

> **1.** A determinant is identically zero if
>   **a.** All the elements of any one row (or one column) are zero.
>   **b.** The elements of one row are identical to the elements (in the same order) of another row. The same rule applies to columns.
>   **c.** Any one row is proportional to another row. The same rule applies to columns.
> **2.** If all the elements of a row (or column) are multiplied by a constant c, the value of the determinant is then multiplied by the same constant.
> **3.** Any two rows (or any two columns) may be interchanged, and the value of the determinant merely changes sign.

---

[3] Each of these properties can be proved using the expression for a determinant given in Equation (12.20).

4. Adding a constant multiple of one row to a different row does not alter the value of the determinant. The same rule applies to columns.
5. Replacing rows by columns, that is, $a_{ij} \rightarrow a_{ji}$ for all i, j, does not alter the value of the determinant.

Thus, the determinant

$$
\begin{vmatrix}
1 & 0 & 1 \\
3 & 1 & 2 \\
4 & 1 & 3
\end{vmatrix}
$$

is "obviously" zero. This result can be seen by replacing row 3 by $(\text{row}_3) - 1(\text{row}_2)$. This replacement does not alter the value of the determinant and results in

$$
\begin{vmatrix}
1 & 0 & 1 \\
3 & 1 & 2 \\
1 & 0 & 1
\end{vmatrix}
$$

This determinant has two identical rows and is therefore zero.

How does this discussion of determinants relate to the original problem of solving simultaneous equations? Clearly, if the determinant of the coefficient matrix is zero, a solution of the equation $[A]\mathbf{x} = \mathbf{b}$ (probably) does not exist. Additionally, the ability to evaluate determinants of arbitrary size enables us to state the solution to many simultaneous linear equations in terms of an algorithm known as Cramer's rule.

12.4 Cramer's Rule

If a set of simultaneous linear equations is written in the form

$$
[A]\mathbf{x} = \mathbf{b}
$$

where $[A]$ is an n by n matrix, $\mathbf{b}$ is a column vector of n elements, and $\mathbf{x}$ is a column vector containing the n unknowns x_i, then the kth element of $\mathbf{x}$ is given by

$$
x_k = \frac{|B(k)|}{|A|} \quad \text{for } k = 1 \text{ to } n \tag{12.21}
$$

where $|\ |$ denotes a determinant and the matrix $[B(k)]$ is obtained from the matrix $[A]$ by replacing the kth column of $[A]$ by the column vector $\mathbf{b}$. For example,

$$[A]\mathbf{x} = \mathbf{b}$$

$$\begin{bmatrix} 3 & 1 & -1 \\ 1 & 2 & 1 \\ -1 & 1 & 4 \end{bmatrix} \begin{bmatrix} x_1 \\ x_2 \\ x_3 \end{bmatrix} = \begin{bmatrix} 2 \\ 3 \\ 9 \end{bmatrix} \tag{12.22}$$

The determinant $|A|$ is easily evaluated to be $|A| = 13$. To evaluate x_1, x_2, and x_3 by Cramer's rule, we must next evaluate the three determinants

$$|B(1)| = \begin{vmatrix} 2 & 1 & -1 \\ 3 & 2 & 1 \\ 9 & 1 & 4 \end{vmatrix} \qquad |B(2)| = \begin{vmatrix} 3 & 2 & -1 \\ 1 & 3 & 1 \\ -1 & 9 & 4 \end{vmatrix}$$

$$= 26 \qquad\qquad\qquad = -13$$

$$|B(3)| = \begin{vmatrix} 3 & 1 & 2 \\ 1 & 2 & 3 \\ -1 & 1 & 9 \end{vmatrix}$$

$$= 39$$

Cramer's rule then gives the solution as

$$\begin{bmatrix} x_1 \\ x_2 \\ x_3 \end{bmatrix} = \begin{bmatrix} 2 \\ -1 \\ 3 \end{bmatrix}$$

which can be verified by substituting back into Equation (12.22):

$$3x_1 + 1x_2 - 1x_3 = 3(2) + 1(-1) - 1(3) = 2 = b_1$$

$$1x_1 + 2x_2 + 1x_3 = 1(2) + 2(-1) + 1(3) = 3 = b_2$$

$$-1x_1 + 1x_2 + 4x_3 = -1(2) + 1(-1) + 4(3) = 9 = b_3$$

As a second example, you should obtain the solution to the equations,

$$\begin{bmatrix} 1 & -3 & 1 \\ -3 & 1 & 1 \\ 1 & 1 & -3 \end{bmatrix} \begin{bmatrix} x_1 \\ x_2 \\ x_3 \end{bmatrix} = \begin{bmatrix} 2 \\ 1 \\ 3 \end{bmatrix}$$

The result is

$$\begin{bmatrix} x_1 \\ x_2 \\ x_3 \end{bmatrix} = \begin{bmatrix} -\frac{7}{4} \\ -2 \\ -\frac{9}{4} \end{bmatrix} = -\frac{1}{4} \begin{bmatrix} 7 \\ 8 \\ 9 \end{bmatrix}$$

Cramer's rule is the most popular method of solving simultaneous equations in introductory algebra. It is easy to remember and easy to use, provided the number of equations is no larger than three. For larger sets of equations the repeated evaluation of large determinants becomes hopelessly tedious. At this point you may have noticed that the word *tedious* is a buzzword to signal the introduction of a FORTRAN code to replace the hand calculation. Indeed, Cramer's rule can be coded to handle any number of simultaneous equations. Such a code has two essential elements: First, a FORTRAN function, say,

```
FUNCTION DET(A,N)
REAL A(N,N)
   . . .
   . . .
DET = . . .
RETURN
END
```

is required to evaluate the determinant of an n by n matrix $[A]$. Such a function is not terribly difficult to construct, but it is not easy either. Second, we must be able to form the matrix $[B(k)]$ by replacing the kth column of $[A]$ by the column vector **b**, without destroying $[A]$ and then call the function DET(B(K),N). The bookkeeping required to keep track of all the index switching is formidable. You might try to write such a code for fun. However, a much more efficient and transparent procedure for solving simultaneous equations will be discussed in Section 12.5.

The primary reason for bringing up Cramer's rule at all is that it clearly shows that to obtain a solution of the matrix equation $[A]\mathbf{x} = \mathbf{b}$, we must *divide* by the determinant of $[A]$. Thus, if $|A| = 0$, a solution may not exist.

Since the components of the solution vector x_k are determined from

$$x_k = \frac{|B(k)|}{|A|}$$

clearly if $|A| = 0$, the only way a solution can exist is if all the determinants $|B(k)|$ are likewise zero. (See Problem 12.6.) All of the determinants $|B(k)|$ would be zero if, for example, the vector **b** is proportional to one of the columns of $[A]$. However, for an arbitrary right-hand-side vector, no solution exists for a set of equations with a coefficient matrix $[A]$ that has a determinant equal to zero. The set of equations is then called *singular*.

IF $|A| = 0$, the matrix $[A]$ is called *singular*.

Often it is just as bad if $|A|$, even though not zero, is extremely small. In this case the results may be invalidated by round-off errors. We shall return to this situation in more detail in Chapter 16. The set of equations with a coefficient matrix that has a "small" determinant is labeled *ill-conditioned*. An obvious question is, "Small compared to what?"

One criterion might be to compare $|A|$ with the average of all the elements a_{ij}. If the elements of $[A]$ were typically of the order 10^{-18}, then a determinant of the order 10^{-16} could not be considered small.

So then, when solving a set of simultaneous linear equations, everything rides on the value of $|A|$. We shall shortly see that if $|A| \neq 0$, it is possible to construct a totally different matrix (call it $[A^{-1}]$) such that

$$[A][A^{-1}] = [A^{-1}][A] = [I]$$

where $[I]$ is the identity matrix. This matrix $[A^{-1}]$ is then the multiplicative inverse of the matrix $[A]$ and defines the operation of matrix division mentioned earlier.

Consider once again the set of equations written in matrix form:

$$[A]\mathbf{x} = \mathbf{b}$$

If the matrix $[A^{-1}]$ exists and is known, the solution of this equation is then trivial. Simply multiply both sides by $[A^{-1}]$ to obtain

$$[A^{-1}][A]\mathbf{x} = [A^{-1}]\mathbf{b}$$
$$[I]\mathbf{x} = [A^{-1}]\mathbf{b}$$

and the solution vector is then given by the equation,

$$\mathbf{x} = [A^{-1}]\mathbf{b}$$

The operation of matrix division thus consists of determining the matrix $[A^{-1}]$. The procedure for doing this will be a simple extension of the most common method of solving simultaneous equations on a computer — the Gauss–Jordan method.

12.5   Gauss–Jordan Method of Solving Simultaneous Linear Equations

Perhaps the most straightforward method of solving sets of linear equations is simply to add multiples of one equation to the others in a way that introduces zero coefficients in the matrix $[A]$. This is the procedure we began with at the beginning of this chapter. This process, recast in an extremely systematic algorithm, is known as the *Gauss–Jordan method* and is the most common procedure for obtaining computer solutions to systems of linear simultaneous equations.

Development of the Gauss–Jordan Algorithm

To understand the Gauss–Jordan method in the context of a simple example, we once again return to the solution of the two equations that opened this chapter.

$$3x - 1y = 7 \qquad \text{Equation}\ \boxed{1}$$

$$2x - 4y = -2 \qquad \text{Equation}\ \boxed{2}$$

We next wish to replace Equation $\boxed{2}$ by Equation $\boxed{1}$ $+ c\,\boxed{2}$ where the factor c is chosen in such a way that the terms in, say, x cancel. In order to make the choice of this factor more transparent, we rewrite the two equations, first "normalizing" Equation $\boxed{1}$ by dividing through by the coefficient of x so that the coefficient of x becomes 1.

$$x - \tfrac{1}{3}y = \tfrac{7}{3} \qquad \text{Equation}\ \boxed{1}$$

$$2x - 4y = -2 \qquad \text{Equation}\ \boxed{2}$$

Next replace Equation $\boxed{2}$ by $\left(\boxed{2} - 2\,\boxed{1'}\right)$, that is,

$$\boxed{2'} = \left(\boxed{2} - 2\,\boxed{1'}\right)$$

$$= (2x - 4y) - 2(x - \tfrac{1}{3}y) = -2 - 2(\tfrac{7}{3})$$

$$= -\tfrac{10}{3}y \qquad\qquad = -\tfrac{20}{3}$$

and the two equations now become

$$x - \tfrac{1}{3}y = \tfrac{7}{3} \qquad \text{Equation}\ \boxed{1'}$$

$$-\tfrac{10}{3}y = -\tfrac{20}{3} \qquad \text{Equation}\ \boxed{2'}$$

Equation $\boxed{2'}$ is then normalized by dividing through by the coefficient of y to obtain

$$x - \tfrac{1}{3}y = \tfrac{7}{3} \qquad \text{Equation}\ \boxed{1'}$$

$$y = 2 \qquad \text{Equation}\ \boxed{2''}$$

The final step consists of replacing Equation $\boxed{1'}$ by $\boxed{1'}$ $+ c\,\boxed{2''}$ with c chosen so as to eliminate the coefficient of y. This replacement is clearly $\boxed{1'} \to \boxed{1'}$ $+ \tfrac{1}{3}\,\boxed{2''}$. The result is then

$$x + 0 = 3 \qquad \text{Equation}\ \boxed{1''}$$

$$y = 2 \qquad \text{Equation}\ \boxed{2''}$$

This procedure is obviously very laborious, but it is one that can be easily generalized to larger sets of equations. For example, consider the solution of a three-equations-in-three-unknowns problem written in matrix form as

$$\begin{array}{cc} [A] & \mathbf{b} \end{array}$$

$$\begin{bmatrix} 2 & -1 & 3 \\ 1 & -2 & 2 \\ 3 & 2 & -3 \end{bmatrix} \begin{bmatrix} 9 \\ 3 \\ -2 \end{bmatrix}$$

The solution vector $\mathbf{x}$ has been omitted since we will be concerned only with operations on the coefficients in the equations.

The procedure starts by writing down side by side the elements of the coefficient matrix and the right-hand-side vector as a so-called augmented matrix. (Straight lines will be used to delineate the matrix, since the sequence of operations that follows will proceed vertically down the page.)

First Pass

Step 1   In the first pass the first row is called the *pivot row* and the leftmost element, a_{11}, is called the *pivot element,* or simply the pivot. Step 1 consists of normalizing the pivot row (row 1) by dividing all of the elements of that row by the pivot element, $a_{11} = 2$.

$$\begin{vmatrix} 1 & -\frac{1}{2} & \frac{3}{2} & \frac{9}{2} \\ 1 & -2 & 2 & 3 \\ 3 & 2 & -3 & -2 \end{vmatrix}$$

Step 2   Next, add multiples of the pivot row (here row 1) to every other row in turn with the factor chosen so that the elements of the pivot column (here column 1) becomes zero.

$$\begin{vmatrix} 1 & -\frac{1}{2} & \frac{3}{2} & \frac{9}{2} \\ 0 & -\frac{3}{2} & \frac{1}{2} & -\frac{3}{2} \\ 0 & \frac{7}{2} & -\frac{15}{2} & -\frac{31}{2} \end{vmatrix} \begin{matrix} \\ \leftarrow \text{row}_2 - \text{row}_1 \\ \leftarrow \text{row}_3 - 3\text{row}_1 \end{matrix}$$

Second Pass

Step 1   The pivot row is now row 2, and the pivot element is $a_{22} = -\frac{3}{2}$. Normalization of row 2 yields

$$\begin{vmatrix} 1 & -\frac{1}{2} & \frac{3}{2} & \frac{9}{2} \\ 0 & 1 & -\frac{1}{3} & 1 \\ 0 & \frac{7}{2} & -\frac{15}{2} & -\frac{31}{2} \end{vmatrix}$$

Step 2   Add multiples of the pivot row, row 2, to rows 1 and 3 to obtain zeros in the pivot column, that is, force $a_{12} = a_{32} = 0$.

$$\begin{vmatrix} 1 & 0 & \frac{4}{3} & 5 \\ 0 & 1 & -\frac{1}{3} & 1 \\ 0 & 0 & -\frac{19}{3} & -19 \end{vmatrix} \begin{matrix} \leftarrow \text{row}_1 + \frac{1}{2}\text{row}_2 \\ \\ \leftarrow \text{row}_3 - \frac{7}{2}\text{row}_2 \end{matrix}$$

Third Pass

Step 1   Normalize row 3 by dividing by $a_{33} = -\frac{19}{3}$.

$$\begin{vmatrix} 1 & 0 & \frac{4}{3} & 5 \\ 0 & 1 & -\frac{1}{3} & 1 \\ 0 & 0 & 1 & 3 \end{vmatrix}$$

Step 2   The final step consists of forcing the elements of the present pivot column to be zeros.

$$\begin{vmatrix} 1 & 0 & 0 & 1 \\ 0 & 1 & 0 & 2 \\ 0 & 0 & 1 & 3 \end{vmatrix} \begin{matrix} \leftarrow \text{row}_1 - \frac{4}{3}\text{row}_3 \\ \leftarrow \text{row}_2 - \frac{1}{3}\text{row}_3 \\ \\ \end{matrix}$$

Thus, the original set of equations has become

$$
\begin{bmatrix} 1 & 0 & 0 \\ 0 & 1 & 0 \\ 0 & 0 & 1 \end{bmatrix} \begin{bmatrix} x_1 \\ x_2 \\ x_3 \end{bmatrix} = \begin{bmatrix} 1 \\ 2 \\ 3 \end{bmatrix}
$$

or simply

$$
\begin{bmatrix} x_1 \\ x_2 \\ x_3 \end{bmatrix} = \begin{bmatrix} 1 \\ 2 \\ 3 \end{bmatrix}
$$

This procedure, though laborious, is extremely straightforward. You should attempt several problems of this type by hand calculation.

Row Switching

It would appear that we are now ready to construct a FORTRAN code to implement the above algorithm for solving simultaneous equations. But there is a potential problem. What if the current pivot element is zero or extremely small? Dividing by the pivot will then cause the method to fail. For example, in the solution of the set of equations

$$
\begin{bmatrix} 0 & -6 & 9 \\ 7 & 0 & -5 \\ 5 & -8 & 6 \end{bmatrix} \begin{bmatrix} x_1 \\ x_2 \\ x_3 \end{bmatrix} = \begin{bmatrix} 3 \\ 1 \\ 4 \end{bmatrix}
$$

the very first pivot is zero and thus row 1 cannot be normalized. The remedy is

> If the current pivot element is zero (or very small), switch the position of the entire pivot row with any row *below* it and continue.

Switching the positions of row 1 and row 2 in the above problem yields

$$
\begin{bmatrix} 7 & 0 & -5 \\ 0 & -6 & 9 \\ 5 & -8 & 6 \end{bmatrix} \begin{bmatrix} x_1 \\ x_2 \\ x_3 \end{bmatrix} = \begin{bmatrix} 1 \\ 3 \\ 4 \end{bmatrix}
$$

Notice that when switching rows the elements of the right-hand-side vector **b** must be switched as well. Also notice that the positions of the solution vector x_i *have not* been switched. If you write out the three equations represented by each of the above matrix equations, you will find that the two sets of equations are the same. This means that the ultimate solution of the set of equations by the Gauss–Jordan method will yield the values for $x_1, x_2, \ldots$, in sequence, regardless of whether rows have or have not been switched.

The result of the Gauss–Jordan method applied to the above matrix equation is

$$\begin{vmatrix} 1 & 0 & 0 \\ 0 & 1 & 0 \\ 0 & 0 & 1 \end{vmatrix} \begin{array}{c} \frac{6}{17} \\ -\frac{1}{17} \\ \frac{5}{17} \end{array}$$

The bookkeeping associated with recording all the potential row switching can be complex. However, once these techniques for row switching have been incorporated into a program, a slight refinement can be added to the basic algorithm that will significantly improve the accuracy of the overall method. The fact that it is essential to switch rows if the current pivot is extremely small or zero to avoid round-off errors suggests that to improve the accuracy, rows should be switched in *every* pass, bringing the row with the largest element in the pivot column to the current pivot position.[4] This refinement, with variations, is employed in all "professionally written" Gauss–Jordan codes.

This brings us to a cardinal rule of matrix calculations on a computer. When solving "real" problems involving matrices, you should always try to take advantage of the "canned" matrix routines in the computer library. Because the methods are fairly standard and usually independent of the particular problem, it is usually a mistake to write your own codes to perform the basic operations of matrix algebra. This is in contrast with root-solving problems, in which the method must be carefully tailored to the problem at hand, and thus it is frequently best to write your own root-solving codes.

One final point: When using the Gauss–Jordan method to obtain a solution of a set of equations, it appears that the solution was obtained without ever dividing by the determinant of the coefficient matrix. Of course, there is an implicit division by $|A|$, but it is hidden somewhere in all the arithmetic. In fact it can be shown that the value of the determinant of the coefficient matrix is equal to the product of the pivot elements. For example, the three pivot elements obtained in the examples at the start of this section were 2, $-\frac{3}{2}$, and $-\frac{19}{3}$. And the value of the determinant

---

[4] The rules for deciding precisely which row (or column) to move into the pivot position are complex. Any row could be multiplied by, say, 10^{10} without affecting the solution at all, yet it could affect the pivoting strategy. Usually a separate array is used to store the maximum elements of each row individually, and the elements of the pivot column, divided by their corresponding maximum element, are compared when deciding which row to switch. Of course, since rows and not columns represent equations, it would make more sense to move the largest element of an equation to the pivot position, that is, switch columns. This type of rearrangement does, however, reorder the x_i's. Switching *both* rows and columns to maximize the pivot is rarely employed even though the accuracy would be enhanced.

is computed to be 19, which is equal to the product of these pivots. The FORTRAN code based on the Gauss–Jordan method can therefore easily be adapted to include an additional parameter that returns the value of the determinant of the coefficient matrix $[A]$.

■ FORTRAN Code for the Gauss–Jordan Method

In violation of the above suggestion to avoid writing your own codes for basic matrix operations, a short FORTRAN code to solve simultaneous linear equations using the Gauss–Jordan method is given in Figure 12-1. This code does not include any row switching and is intended mainly to illustrate the basic structure of the algorithm.

The subroutine GAUSS in Figure 12-1 assumes that the coefficient matrix $[A]$ is a square N by N matrix and that it has been previously dimensioned in the calling program as an ND by ND matrix, where $N \leq ND$. This distinction is very important and was discussed earlier in Section 7.5.

The code also requires the value of the elements of the right-hand-side vector b_i and returns the elements of the solution vector x_i. Both the coefficient matrix $[A]$ and the right-hand-side vector b_i are destroyed

Figure 12-1
FORTRAN code for
the Gauss–Jordan
method

```
      SUBROUTINE GAUSS(A,B,X,ND,N,DET)
*
*   GAUSS will solve the equation [A]x = b for the solution
*   vector x() given the matrix A and the right-hand-side vector
*   b provided no zero pivots are encountered.  The algorithm
*   does not use any row switching to maximize pivots.  Also,
*   the matrix A and the vector b are destroyed.
*
*   NOTE: ND is the size of the array A as dimensioned in the
*         calling program; N is the size of the array as
*         it is used in this subroutine.  ND must be greater
*         than or equal to N.
*-----------------------------------------------------------------
*  Variables
*
      INTEGER ND, N, IPV
      REAL A(ND,ND),B(ND),X(ND),DET,PIVOT,FCTR
*
*   A()   --  Coefficient matrix, destroyed by GAUSS
*   B()   --  Right-hand-side vector, also destroyed
*   X()   --  Solution vector
*   DET   --  Determinant of A computed by GAUSS
*   PIVOT --  Current pivot element
*   FCTR  --  A factor used in GAUSS elimination
*   ND    --  Size of arrays as dimension in calling program
*   N     --  Size of arrays as used in GAUSS
*   IPV   --  Labels the current pivot row and the current
*                pass number
*-----------------------------------------------------------------
```

Figure 12-1
(concluded)

```
*          The determinant is the product of the pivots
*
           DET = 1.0
*
*          Execute N passes, labeled by IPV
*
           DO 4 IPV = 1,N
*
*             If the pivot is small, the code terminates
*
                 PIVOT = A(IPV,IPV)
                 IF(ABS(PIVOT) .LT. 1.E-5)THEN
                     WRITE(*,10)IPV,IPV,PIVOT
                     PAUSE 'FATAL ERROR in GAUSS - small pivot'
                     RETURN
                 ENDIF
                 DET = DET*PIVOT
*
*             Normalize the pivot row by dividing across by pivot
*
                 DO 1 J = 1,N
                     A(IPV,J) = A(IPV,J)/PIVOT
     1           CONTINUE
                 B(IPV) = B(IPV)/PIVOT
*
*             Replace row-IROW with row-IROW + factor*row-IPV with
*             the factor chosen to get zero in the pivot column
*
                 DO 3 IROW = 1,N
                     IF(IROW .NE. IPV)THEN
                         FCTR = A(IROW,IPV)/PIVOT
                         DO 2 ICOL = 1,N
                             A(IROW,ICOL)=A(IROW,ICOL) - FCTR*A(IPV,ICOL)
     2                   CONTINUE
                         B(IROW) = B(IROW) - FCTR*B(IPV)
                     ENDIF
     3           CONTINUE
     4       CONTINUE
*
*          The solution vector is now contained in the vector B
*
           DO 5 I = 1,N
               X(I) = B(I)
     5     CONTINUE
           RETURN
*----------------------------------------------------------------
    10     FORMAT(/,
         + T5,'===============ERROR IN GAUSS=================',/,
         + T5,'|   GAUSS has failed due to a small pivot    |',/,
         + T5,'|          A(',I2,',',I2,') = ',E9.2,T49,'|',/,
         + T5,'| is smaller than the supplied limit (1.E-5)|',/,
         + T5,'============Program Terminated===============')
           END
```

by the subroutine, so if they are needed later in a program, a copy must be made before the subroutine GAUSS is used.

The key section of the code is the line redefining the element A(IROW, ICOL). The effect of this statement is that the element of row IROW that is in the pivot column—that is, ICOL = IPIV—is replaced by zero. Rewriting this line in an algebraic notation yields

$$a_{rc} \rightarrow a_{rc} - \frac{a_{rp} a_{pc}}{a_{pp}}$$

where r, c, and p are the indices for the row, column, and pivot counters. Thus, the element in the pivot column, $c = p$, is replaced by

$$a_{rp} \rightarrow a_{rp} - \frac{a_{rp} a_{pp}}{a_{pp}} = 0$$

The determinant, which is the product of the pivot elements, is also returned by the subroutine. This code is suitable for most matrix problems provided no zero pivots are encountered. If the matrix [A] is quite large, this code is susceptible to significant round-off errors. Of course, the seriousness of round-off error problems also depends on the word-length characteristic of your computer. A Gauss–Jordan subroutine that computes the inverse of a matrix and that employs a limited pivoting strategy is given in Figure 12-6.

12.6   Matrix Inversion by the Gauss–Jordan Method

The inverse of a matrix [A] is a matrix [A⁻¹] that satisfies the equations

$$[A][A^{-1}] = [A^{-1}][A] = [I]$$

Of course, the matrix [A⁻¹] exists only if the determinant of [A] is nonzero. The inverse of [A] can be determined by a simple variation of the Gauss–Jordan method of Section 12.5. The idea is quite simple and is most easily seen via demonstration with a typical 3 by 3 matrix problem. Consider the three independent matrix equations

$$[A]\mathbf{x}^{(1)} = \mathbf{b}^{(1)}$$

$$[A]\mathbf{x}^{(2)} = \mathbf{b}^{(2)}$$

$$[A]\mathbf{x}^{(3)} = \mathbf{b}^{(3)} \tag{12.23}$$

In each equation the coefficient matrix [A] is the same, but the three solution vectors $\mathbf{x}^{(i)}$ will be different depending on the choices for the three right-hand-side vectors $\mathbf{b}^{(i)}$. These are next specified as

$$\mathbf{b}^{(1)} = \begin{bmatrix} 1 \\ 0 \\ 0 \end{bmatrix} \quad \mathbf{b}^{(2)} = \begin{bmatrix} 0 \\ 1 \\ 0 \end{bmatrix} \quad \mathbf{b}^{(3)} = \begin{bmatrix} 0 \\ 0 \\ 1 \end{bmatrix} \tag{12.24}$$

and the three Equations (12.23) are solved by the Gauss–Jordan method for a particular 3 by 3 matrix $[A]$ resulting in values for the solution vectors $\mathbf{x}^{(i)}$ that satisfy

$$[A]\begin{bmatrix} x_1^{(1)} \\ x_2^{(1)} \\ x_3^{(1)} \end{bmatrix} = \begin{bmatrix} 1 \\ 0 \\ 0 \end{bmatrix} \qquad [A]\begin{bmatrix} x_1^{(2)} \\ x_2^{(2)} \\ x_3^{(2)} \end{bmatrix} = \begin{bmatrix} 0 \\ 1 \\ 0 \end{bmatrix} \qquad [A]\begin{bmatrix} x_1^{(3)} \\ x_2^{(3)} \\ x_3^{(3)} \end{bmatrix} = \begin{bmatrix} 0 \\ 0 \\ 1 \end{bmatrix}$$

These three equations are then suggestively grouped as

$$[A]\left(\begin{bmatrix} x_1^{(1)} \\ x_2^{(1)} \\ x_3^{(1)} \end{bmatrix}\begin{bmatrix} x_1^{(2)} \\ x_2^{(2)} \\ x_3^{(2)} \end{bmatrix}\begin{bmatrix} x_1^{(3)} \\ x_2^{(3)} \\ x_3^{(3)} \end{bmatrix}\right) = \left(\begin{bmatrix} 1 \\ 0 \\ 0 \end{bmatrix}\begin{bmatrix} 0 \\ 1 \\ 0 \end{bmatrix}\begin{bmatrix} 0 \\ 0 \\ 1 \end{bmatrix}\right)$$

But the square array on the right is the identity matrix I_3, and thus the square array on the left must be the inverse of matrix $[A]$; that is, the solution of Equations (12.23) with the choices Equations (12.24) for the vectors $\mathbf{b}^{(i)}$ generates three solution vectors $\mathbf{x}^{(i)}$, which are the respective *columns* of the inverse matrix. This means that the inverse of an n by n matrix can be obtained by n applications of the Gauss–Jordan method with the right-hand-side vectors $\mathbf{b}^{(i)}$ chosen to be n component generalizations of Equations (12.24).

Moreover, the elements of the coefficient matrix determine the numerical operations of the Gauss–Jordan, and since the matrix $[A]$ is the same for all n equations, a little thoughtful contemplation suggests that *all* n computations could be executed *simultaneously*. This process is demonstrated below for a 3 by 3 matrix.

First the matrix $[A]$ to be inverted and the identity matrix of $[I]$ of like size are written side by side. For example,

$$\left|\begin{array}{rrr|rrr} 2 & -1 & 0 & 1 & 0 & 0 \\ -1 & 2 & -1 & 0 & 1 & 0 \\ 0 & -1 & 2 & 0 & 0 & 1 \end{array}\right|$$

Next the Gauss–Jordan method is carried out as before with the addition that when replacing rows, all the elements of a row in both $[A]$ and in $[I]$ are affected.

First Pass

Step 1

$$\left|\begin{array}{rrr|rrr} 1 & -\frac{1}{2} & 0 & \frac{1}{2} & 0 & 0 \\ -1 & 2 & -1 & 0 & 1 & 0 \\ 0 & -1 & 2 & 0 & 0 & 1 \end{array}\right| \leftarrow \text{Normalize pivot row}$$

Step 2

$$\left|\begin{array}{ccc|ccc} 1 & -\frac{1}{2} & 0 & \frac{1}{2} & 0 & 0 \\ 0 & \frac{3}{2} & -1 & \frac{1}{2} & 1 & 0 \\ 0 & -1 & 2 & 0 & 0 & 1 \end{array}\right| \leftarrow \text{Replace row}_2 \text{ by row}_2 + \text{row}_1$$

Second Pass

Step 1

$$\left|\begin{array}{ccc|ccc} 1 & -\frac{1}{2} & 0 & \frac{1}{2} & 0 & 0 \\ 0 & 1 & -\frac{2}{3} & \frac{1}{3} & \frac{2}{3} & 0 \\ 0 & -1 & 2 & 0 & 0 & 1 \end{array}\right| \leftarrow \text{Normalize pivot row}$$

Step 2

$$\left|\begin{array}{ccc|ccc} 1 & 0 & -\frac{1}{3} & \frac{2}{3} & \frac{1}{3} & 0 \\ 0 & 1 & -\frac{2}{3} & \frac{1}{3} & \frac{2}{3} & 0 \\ 0 & 0 & \frac{4}{3} & \frac{1}{3} & \frac{2}{3} & 1 \end{array}\right| \begin{array}{l} \leftarrow \text{row}_1 + \frac{1}{2}\text{row}_2 \\ \\ \leftarrow \text{row}_3 + \text{row}_2 \end{array}$$

Third Pass

Step 1

$$\left|\begin{array}{ccc|ccc} 1 & 0 & -\frac{1}{3} & \frac{2}{3} & \frac{1}{3} & 0 \\ 0 & 1 & -\frac{2}{3} & \frac{1}{3} & \frac{2}{3} & 0 \\ 0 & 0 & 1 & \frac{1}{4} & \frac{1}{2} & \frac{3}{4} \end{array}\right| \leftarrow \text{Normalize pivot row}$$

Step 2

$$\left|\begin{array}{ccc|ccc} 1 & 0 & 0 & \frac{3}{4} & \frac{1}{2} & \frac{1}{4} \\ 0 & 1 & 0 & \frac{1}{2} & 1 & \frac{1}{2} \\ 0 & 0 & 1 & \frac{1}{4} & \frac{1}{2} & \frac{3}{4} \end{array}\right| \begin{array}{l} \leftarrow \text{row}_1 + \frac{1}{3}\text{row}_3 \\ \\ \leftarrow \text{row}_2 + \frac{2}{3}\text{row}_3 \end{array}$$

The contention is then that the matrix on the right in the last step is the inverse of the original matrix; that is,[5]

$$[A^{-1}] = \begin{bmatrix} \frac{3}{4} & \frac{1}{2} & \frac{1}{4} \\ \frac{1}{2} & 1 & \frac{1}{2} \\ \frac{1}{4} & \frac{1}{2} & \frac{3}{4} \end{bmatrix} = \frac{1}{4}\begin{bmatrix} 3 & 2 & 1 \\ 2 & 4 & 2 \\ 1 & 2 & 3 \end{bmatrix}$$

To verify this we simply multiply $[A][A^{-1}]$ to obtain

$$[A][A^{-1}] = \frac{1}{4}\begin{bmatrix} 2 & -1 & 0 \\ -1 & 2 & -1 \\ 0 & -1 & 2 \end{bmatrix}\begin{bmatrix} 3 & 2 & 1 \\ 2 & 4 & 2 \\ 1 & 2 & 3 \end{bmatrix}$$

---

[5] The multiplication of a matrix by a simple number as in $c[A]$ is defined to mean that every element of the matrix is to be multiplied by the number c.

The product of these two matrices is itself a matrix, which will be called
[C]. For example, the row 1, column 1 element of [C] is obtained by multiplying row 1 of [A] by column 1 of [A^{-1}] element by element and summing:

$$c_{11} = \frac{1}{4}[2 \quad -1 \quad 0]\begin{bmatrix} 3 \\ 2 \\ 1 \end{bmatrix}$$

$$= \frac{1}{4}[2(3) + (-1)(2) + 0(1)] = 1$$

In a like manner the nine elements of the product are found to be

$$[A][A^{-1}] = \begin{bmatrix} 1 & 0 & 0 \\ 0 & 1 & 0 \\ 0 & 0 & 1 \end{bmatrix}$$

Once the inverse of the matrix [A] is known, the solution of the set
of equations

$$\begin{array}{ccc} [A] & \mathbf{x} & = \mathbf{b} \end{array}$$

$$\begin{bmatrix} 2 & -1 & 0 \\ -1 & 2 & -1 \\ 0 & -1 & 2 \end{bmatrix}\begin{bmatrix} x_1 \\ x_2 \\ x_3 \end{bmatrix} = \begin{bmatrix} 1 \\ 2 \\ 3 \end{bmatrix} \tag{12.25}$$

is simply given by

$$\begin{array}{ccc} \mathbf{x} & = & [A^{-1}] & \mathbf{b} \end{array}$$

$$\begin{bmatrix} x_1 \\ x_2 \\ x_3 \end{bmatrix} = \frac{1}{4}\begin{bmatrix} 3 & 2 & 1 \\ 2 & 4 & 2 \\ 1 & 2 & 3 \end{bmatrix}\begin{bmatrix} 1 \\ 2 \\ 3 \end{bmatrix} = \frac{1}{4}\begin{bmatrix} 3+4+3 \\ 2+8+6 \\ 2+4+9 \end{bmatrix} = \begin{bmatrix} \frac{5}{2} \\ 4 \\ \frac{7}{2} \end{bmatrix} \tag{12.26}$$

Notice that if the original set of equations is altered by changing
only the right-hand-side vector, the same inverse matrix may be used to
obtain the solution. Thus,

$$\begin{array}{ccc} [A] & \mathbf{x} & = \mathbf{c} \end{array}$$

$$\begin{bmatrix} 2 & -1 & 0 \\ -1 & 2 & -1 \\ 0 & -1 & 2 \end{bmatrix}\begin{bmatrix} x_1 \\ x_2 \\ x_3 \end{bmatrix} = \begin{bmatrix} 1 \\ 1 \\ 1 \end{bmatrix}$$

has a solution vector **x**

$$\begin{array}{ccc} \mathbf{x} & = & [A^{-1}] & \mathbf{c} \end{array}$$

$$\begin{bmatrix} x_1 \\ x_2 \\ x_3 \end{bmatrix} = \frac{1}{4}\begin{bmatrix} 3 & 2 & 1 \\ 2 & 4 & 2 \\ 1 & 2 & 3 \end{bmatrix}\begin{bmatrix} 1 \\ 1 \\ 1 \end{bmatrix} = \begin{bmatrix} \frac{3}{2} \\ 2 \\ \frac{3}{2} \end{bmatrix}$$

This situation is a common one in engineering and science problems. The coefficient matrix [A] remains constant, and the equations are solved for a variety of right-hand-side vectors **b**. The code for a subroutine MINV that computes the inverse of an n by n matrix is given in Figure 12-6.

12.7 Relative Speed and Accuracy of the Various Matrix Algorithms

We have seen that a 5 by 5 determinant can be evaluated by expanding in terms of its five cofactor determinants, each a 4 by 4 determinant. This suggests that evaluating a single nth-order determinant requires $\mathcal{O}n!$ multiplications.[6] Therefore a solution of n simultaneous linear equations using Cramer's rule will require $\mathcal{O}(n + 1)!$ multiplications. So, if you have a FORTRAN code that will solve five equations in five unknowns using Cramer's rule with an execution cost of 10 cents, the bill for solving 10 equations would be roughly $5,500. And since round-off errors accumulate with each arithmetic operation, it is very likely that the numbers obtained will be incorrect. Solving large numbers of equations by Cramer's rule is clearly impractical.

This situation is typical of all tasks that require solving simultaneous equations on a computer. The number of arithmetic operations required to obtain a solution grows very rapidly with the number of equations n, with a corresponding growth in the execution-time costs, memory costs, and round-off error accumulation.

The Gauss–Jordan method requires roughly $n^3/3$ multiplications.[7] Thus, for this method the cost comparison between the $n = 5$ and $n = 10$ cases would be a modest increase of from 10 cents to 80 cents.

Efficient codes for obtaining the inverse of a matrix using the Gauss–Jordan method require only about three times the total number of arithmetic operations needed to obtain a single-solution vector. Thus, if a solution is required for more than a few right-hand-side vectors, it may be prudent to solve for the inverse matrix directly. Moreover, the only sure way to test for round-off errors in the method requires the calculation of $[A^{-1}]$.

In the solution of a matrix equation of order n by the Gauss–Jordan method, where n is 100 or greater, round-off error will be a serious concern that cannot be ignored. For example, solving 100 equations on a computer with eight-figure accuracy will yield results that are at best ac-

---

[6] Since addition is ordinarily much faster on a computer, we will consider only multiplication and division to obtain order-of-magnitude execution-time estimates.

[7] K. S. Kunz, *Numerical Analysis* (New York: McGraw-Hill, 1957).

curate to only two significant figures. The programmer may then be forced to use double-precision variables, which will drive up the execution cost significantly. A second alternative is to employ an iterative solution procedure, such as the Gauss–Siedel method described in Section 12.8. Errors in one step of an iterative method are usually corrected in the next step, and so round-off errors are rarely a concern. Unfortunately, this advantage is frequently offset by a slow convergence rate, as we shall see.

The severity of round-off error problems in a Gauss–Jordan calculation can be determined by computing the inverse of the coefficient matrix $[A^{-1}]$, then performing the multiplication $[A][A^{-1}]$ and examining the product, which should be the identity matrix. If any off-diagonal term is significantly different from zero or any diagonal term is significantly different from one, the reason is probably due to round-off error.

12.8   Iterative Techniques for Solving Simultaneous Equations

The matrices encountered in science and engineering problems almost always belong to one of two categories: (1) small to moderately large *dense* matrices, or (2) large and *sparse* matrices.

A sparse matrix is one in which most of the elements are zeros. Such matrices are frequently encountered in certain methods of solving differential equations. Often a sparse matrix will consist of diagonal elements plus nonzero elements only to the immediate left or right of the main diagonal, such as

$$[C] = \begin{bmatrix} 4 & -1 & 0 & 0 & 0 \\ -1 & 4 & -1 & 0 & 0 \\ 0 & -1 & 4 & -1 & 0 \\ 0 & 0 & -1 & 4 & -1 \\ 0 & 0 & 0 & -1 & 4 \end{bmatrix} \tag{12.27}$$

This matrix is called a *banded* matrix, as it has two "bands" of −1's on either side of the main diagonal. Sparse banded matrices that arise in physical problems can often be truly enormous; the order being thousands or even hundreds of thousands. Solving such a set of equations by the Gauss–Jordan method would not only be very likely impossible due to round-off error and storage considerations, it would be extremely inefficient as well. The procedure would spend an inordinate amount of time multiplying by zeros. The Gauss–Jordan method is only suitable for relatively small ($n \le 100$) matrices that contain few zeros (i.e., dense). Alternative procedures must be developed for the remaining class of matrices. To minimize the danger of round-off errors, an iterative procedure would seem to be a likely candidate.

■ Gauss–Siedel Iterative Procedure

A popular iterative technique, much like the method of successive substitution used to find roots of equations, is the Gauss–Siedel iteration method. The method is fairly simple and is most easily illustrated by means of an example. The matrix equation

$$[A]\mathbf{x} = \mathbf{b}$$

where $[A]$ is a square matrix of order 3 is shorthand for the three equations

$$a_{11}x_1 + a_{12}x_2 + a_{13}x_3 = b_1 \tag{12.28}$$

$$a_{21}x_1 + a_{22}x_2 + a_{23}x_3 = b_2 \tag{12.29}$$

$$a_{31}x_1 + a_{32}x_2 + a_{33}x_3 = b_3 \tag{12.30}$$

If *none* of the diagonal elements of the coefficient matrix $[A]$ are zero, we can formally solve Equation (12.28) for x_1, Equation (12.29) for x_2, and Equation (12.30) for x_3 to obtain

$$x_1 = \frac{b_1 - a_{12}x_2 - a_{13}x_3}{a_{11}} \tag{12.31}$$

$$x_2 = \frac{b_2 - a_{21}x_1 - a_{23}x_3}{a_{22}} \tag{12.32}$$

$$x_3 = \frac{b_3 - a_{31}x_1 - a_{32}x_2}{a_{33}} \tag{12.33}$$

Of course, this is not much of a solution, since to obtain values for x_1, x_2, and x_3 on the left, we need to know the values of x_1, x_2, and x_3 on the right. However, it does suggest the next best thing—a solution by iteration.

We begin with an initial guess for the unknowns, say, $x_1^{(0)}, x_2^{(0)}, x_3^{(0)}$; using these values in the expressions on the right, we then compute a new set of values, $x_1^{(1)}, x_2^{(1)}, x_3^{(1)}$.[8] This procedure is then continued until the difference between successive solution vectors is sufficiently small.

The Gauss–Siedel method is a minor variation of this scheme. It requires less storage and usually will converge more rapidly. The idea is always to use the most recently computed values for the variables. Thus, once $x_1^{(1)}$ has been computed, this value is used in the next equation for $x_2^{(1)}$ in place of $x_2^{(0)}$, and so on.

$$x_1^{(1)} = \frac{b_1 - a_{12}x_2^{(0)} - a_{13}x_3^{(0)}}{a_{11}} \tag{12.34}$$

$$x_2^{(1)} = \frac{b_2 - a_{21}x_1^{(1)} - a_{23}x_3^{(0)}}{a_{22}} \tag{12.35}$$

---

[8] The procedure of using one set of x_i's as an initial guess and then holding these values fixed while a second set is computed is known as *fixed-point* or *Jacobi iteration*. It is less efficient than the Gauss–Siedel technique that follows and is important mainly in the theoretical analysis of convergence proofs.

$$x_3^{(1)} = \frac{b_3 - a_{31}x_1^{(1)} - a_{32}x_2^{(1)}}{a_{33}} \tag{12.36}$$

Notice that there is never a need to store both the old and the new values of the components of the solution vector. Once an element of the vector $\mathbf{x}$ is computed, it is subsequently used in all equations that follow. Thus, only one storage location is required for each element. The FORTRAN statements that implement these operations would be

```
X(1) = (B(1) - A(1,2)*X(2) - A(1,3)*X(3))/A(1,1)
X(2) = (B(2) - A(2,1)*X(1) - A(2,3)*X(3))/A(2,2)
X(3) = (B(3) - A(3,1)*X(1) - A(3,2)*X(2))/A(3,3)
```

For an arbitrary number of equations these statements would be rewritten in terms of DO loops.

Convergence

The proof of the convergence of a multivariable iterative procedure is beyond the scope of this text. The result, however, is very simple:

> If the coefficient matrix is *diagonally dominant*, the Gauss–Siedel iteration procedure is *guaranteed* to converge for *any* initial guess for the solution vector.

Of course, the better the initial guess, the more rapidly the method will converge.

A diagonally dominant matrix is one in which the magnitude of the element on the diagonal in each row is larger than the sum of the magnitudes of all the other elements in that row; that is, for each $i = 1, n$,

$$|a_{ii}| > \sum_{\text{all } j \neq i} |a_{ij}|$$

If the matrix does not meet this rather stringent definition of diagonal dominance, the Gauss–Siedel method may still converge, particularly if the largest elements of the matrix are located on the diagonal. In other words, the requirement that the matrix be diagonally dominant is a sufficient condition for convergence, but it is not a necessary condition.

If a set of equations does not possess diagonal dominance in its present form, it is frequently possible to rearrange the set so that the coefficient matrix is diagonally dominant. For example, if the Gauss–Siedel method is applied to the set of equations

$$\begin{bmatrix} 1 & 4 & 1 \\ 4 & 1 & 0 \\ 0 & 1 & 4 \end{bmatrix} \begin{bmatrix} x_1 \\ x_2 \\ x_3 \end{bmatrix} = \begin{bmatrix} 2 \\ 1 \\ 3 \end{bmatrix} \tag{12.37}$$

(see also Problem 12.14), the method will diverge for any initial guess not equal to the exact solution. However, interchanging the first and second rows yields

$$
\begin{bmatrix} 4 & 1 & 0 \\ 1 & 4 & 1 \\ 0 & 1 & 4 \end{bmatrix} \begin{bmatrix} x_1 \\ x_2 \\ x_3 \end{bmatrix} = \begin{bmatrix} 1 \\ 2 \\ 3 \end{bmatrix}
\tag{12.38}
$$

which is obviously diagonally dominant and thus convergence is assured. The most common criterion to use in deciding whether or not a sufficiently accurate solution vector has been attained is to test the percentage change in each component of x from one iteration to the next; that is, defining

$$
\Delta_i = \frac{|x_{i,\text{new}} - x_{i,\text{old}}|}{x_{i,\text{old}}}
$$

the test could be that *every* Δ_i be less than some small quantity ε; a less stringent test might be that the average of all the Δ_i's be less than ε. In some cases only a few of the many variables have important physical significance, and the convergence test may then be written to check successive changes in only those variables.

■ FORTRAN Code for an Iterative Gauss–Siedel Subroutine

The FORTRAN code for a Gauss–Siedel algorithm applied to N linear simultaneous equations is given in Figure 12-2. The subroutine contains the following features:

1. The coefficient matrix is assumed to be a square N by N matrix that is dimensioned as an ND by ND matrix in the calling program. As in the Gauss–Jordan subroutine, N must be less than or equal to ND.
2. It is assumed that the first N elements of the solution vector X are supplied in the call as the initial guess.

Figure 12-2 ———
Subroutine
implementing the
Gauss–Siedel
method

```
          SUBROUTINE GAUSDL(A,B,ND,N,X,IMAX,EPS,IPASS)
*
*    GAUSDL is a Gauss-Siedel iteration algorithm to solve the
*    matrix equation [A]x = b.   The maximum number of iterations
*    is IMAX, and a successful termination is achieved when the
*    successive fractional changes in all the x's are less than
*    EPS. The number of equations is N, and the starting values
*    for the x's are assumed equal to the values initially con-
*    tained in the array x when the subroutine is called.   ISTOP
*    is a success flag, (ISTOP = 1 (success), 0 (failure).
*-----------------------------------------------------------------
```

Figure 12-2
(continued)

```
* Variables
*--
      INTEGER N,ND,IMAX,IPASS,ISTOP
      REAL A(ND,ND),B(ND),X(ND),EPS,RMSDV,XOLD,DEV
*
*       A()   --  Coefficient matrix dimensioned as ND by ND
*                 in the calling program
*       B()   --  Right-hand-side vector
*       X()   --  Solution vector; as input, it contains the
*                 initial guess
*       EPS   --  Convergence criterion; successful if all
*                 fractional changes in X < EPS
*       IMAX  --  Limiting number of iterations
*       XOLD  --  Previous value of X(I)
*       DEV   --  Fractional change in X(I)
*       RMSDV --  Root-mean-square deviation in the x's
*       IPASS --  Iteration counter
*       ISTOP --  Success(1)/failure(0) flag
*------------------------------------------------------------------
*     First check whether A is diagonally dominant
*
      DO 2 IROW = 1,N
         SUM = 0.
         DO 1 ICOL = 1,N
            IF(ICOL .NE. IROW)THEN
               SUM = SUM + ABS(A(IROW,ICOL))
            ENDIF
 1       CONTINUE
         IF(ABS(A(IROW,IROW)) .LT. SUM)THEN
            WRITE(*,10)IROW
         ENDIF
 2    CONTINUE
*------------------------------------------------------------------
* Computation
*
      DO 6 IPASS = 1,IMAX
         ISTOP = 1
         RMSDV = 0.0
*
*        Solve equation number IEQ for x(ieq)
*
         DO 5 IEQ = 1,N
            SUM  = 0.0
            XOLD = X(IEQ)
            DO 4 J = 1,N
               IF(J .NE. IEQ)THEN
                  SUM = SUM + A(IEQ,J)*X(J)
*
*                 Check for zero diagonal elements
*
               ELSE IF(A(IEQ,IEQ) .EQ. 0.)THEN
                  WRITE(*,11)IEQ,IEQ
                  PAUSE 'FATAL ERROR in GAUSDL - Zero pivot'
                  RETURN
               ENDIF
 4          CONTINUE
            X(IEQ) = (B(IEQ) - SUM)/A(IEQ,IEQ)
```

Figure 12-2
(concluded)

```
                               IF(XOLD .NE. 0.)THEN
                                   DEV = (X(IEQ) - XOLD)/XOLD
                               ELSE
                                   DEV = X(IEQ)
                               ENDIF
        *
        *          If any of the deviations are greater than EPS,
        *          success has not yet been acheived
        *
                   IF(ABS(DEV) .GT. EPS)ISTOP = 0
                   RMSDV = RMSDV + DEV*DEV
        5      CONTINUE
               RMSDV = SQRT(RMSDV/N)

        *
        *          Iteration Ipass is complete.  Test for success
        *
               IF(ISTOP .EQ. 1)THEN
        *
        *              If ISTOP = 1 through all eqs., success achieved
        *
                   RETURN
               ENDIF
        6  CONTINUE
        *
        *      Excessive iterations path
        *
               WRITE(*,12)RMSDV
               PAUSE 'Non-convergence in GAUSDL'
        *-------------------------------------------------------------
        * Formats
        *
        10  FORMAT(/,
           + T5,'========WARNING FROM GAUSDL===========',/,
           + T5,'| Row ',I3,' is NOT diagonally dominant.|',/,
           + T5,'========Program Continues=============')
        *
        11  FORMAT(/,
           +T5,'==========ERROR IN GAUSDL===================',/,
           +T5,'|Diagnonal element, A(',I3,',',I3,') is zero',T48,'|',
           +/T5,'===========Program Terminated===============')
        *
        12  FORMAT(/,
           + T5,'=============FAILURE IN GAUSDL=================',/,
           + T5,'| GAUSDL has failed due to excessive iterations|',/,
           + T5,'| Latest Rms-dev = ',F10.4,T52,'|',/,
           + T5,'===========Program Terminated=================')
               END
```

3. The subroutine first checks for diagonal dominance. If the matrix is not diagonally dominant, a warning message is printed.
4. If any of the diagonal elements of the coefficient matrix are zero, the subroutine prints a diagnostic and stops.
5. The convergence criterion is that *all* of the percentage changes in the components of the solution vector must be less than a programmer-supplied quantity EPS.

6. The maximum number of iterations is limited to IMAX. In the likely event that the procedure has not converged in IMAX iterations, the subroutine prints the average percentage change in the components of X and a warning message, and stops.

This FORTRAN code is used in the example calculation of the next section.

Numerical Example of the Gauss–Siedel Method

The Gauss–Siedel algorithm applied to the diagonally dominant set of Equations (12.38) with an initial guess of zero for all the components of x results in the values in Table 12-1.

The results of the same calculation on the same set of equations except not arranged in a diagonally dominant form are given in Table 12-2. After only a few iterations it is clear that the calculation is diverging.

12.9 Miscellaneous FORTRAN Codes Relating to Matrices

Product of Two Square Matrices

If $[A]$ and $[B]$ are square matrices of order n, the elements of the product matrix $[C] = [A][B]$ are given by the equation

$$c_{ij} = \sum_{k=1}^{n} a_{ik} b_{kj} \qquad (12.39)$$

Table 12-1
Results of Gauss–Siedel iteration if the coefficient matrix is diagonally dominant

i	x_1	x_2	x_3	Average Δ_i
0	0.00	0.00	0.00	
1	0.25	0.44	0.64	0.44
2	0.14	0.30	0.674	0.13
3	0.174	0.288	0.6780	0.018
4	0.1780	0.2860	0.6785	0.0023
5	0.17850	0.28575	0.67856	0.00027
6	0.17856	0.28572	0.678570	0.000034
7	0.178570	0.285715	0.6785713	0.000006
$\vdots$	$\vdots$	$\vdots$	$\vdots$	
∞	5/28	2/7	19/28	

Table 12-2
Gauss-Siedel method applied to a nondiagonally dominant matrix

i	x_1	x_2	x_3
0	0.0	0.0	0.0
1	2.0	−7.0	2.5
2	27.5	−109.0	28.0
3	410.0	−1639.0	410.5
4	6147.5	−24589.0	6148.0

A subroutine that computes and returns the product matrix is given in Figure 12-3.

Output of a Square Matrix

Constructing the code to label the rows and columns of a matrix simultaneously and to print the contents neatly is a tedious chore. To relieve you of this task, Figure 12-4 shows a short subroutine that will print a matrix. This subroutine will accommodate a square matrix of size 10 by 10 or smaller. A sample of the output is shown in Figure 12-5.

FORTRAN Subroutine to Compute the Inverse of a Matrix

The scientific software library at your computing center will have stored on a disk file an efficient and accurate subroutine to compute the inverse of a matrix. You should seek out the instructions required to access that code. In the unlikely event that such a code is not available, a less efficient code that employs only a limited pivoting strategy is given in Figure 12-6. This code was constructed to be easy to read and should give satisfactory results for most matrices of modest size.

Summary

With the notation of matrices it is possible to symbolically manipulate n simultaneous equations in n independent unknowns. The coefficients of each equation are written as successive rows of the matrix, creating a square array of elements labeled by rows and columns. The right-hand-side elements of each equation are grouped together into a matrix consist-

Figure 12-3
Subroutine to
multiply two
matrices

```
      SUBROUTINE PROD(A,B,C,N,ND)
      REAL A(ND,ND),B(ND,ND),C(ND,ND)
*
*     The three matrices are of size n by n but are
*     dimensioned in the calling program as nd by nd.
*
*     For all rows and columns of C, execute the sum.
*
      DO 2 I = 1,N
      DO 2 J = 1,N
         C(I,J) = 0.0
         DO 1 K = 1,N
            C(I,J) = C(I,J) + A(I,K)*B(K,J)
1        CONTINUE
2     CONTINUE
      RETURN
      END
```

Figure 12-4
Subroutine to print
a matrix

```
        PROGRAM MTXPRT
        PARAMETER (N = 4)
        REAL A(N,N),B(N,N),C(N,N)
        DATA ((A(I,J),J=1,N),I=1,N)/1.,2.,3.,4.,
       +                           1.,1.,1.,2.,
       +                           2.,1.,1.,1.,
       +                           4.,3.,4.,1./
        DATA ((B(I,J),J=1,N),I=1,N)/1.,0.,1.,0.,
       +                           0.,1.,0.,1.,
       +                           1.,0.,1.,0.,
       +                           0.,1.,0.,1./
        CALL PROD(A,B,C,N,N)
        CALL PRINT(A,N,N)
        CALL PRINT(B,N,N)
        CALL PRINT(C,N,N)
        STOP
        END
*===================================================
        SUBROUTINE PRINT(A,N,ND)
        REAL A(ND,ND)
        CHARACTER DASH*8,BLANK*8
        DATA DASH,BLANK/'-------|','        |'/

        WRITE(*,10)    (     J,J=1,N)
        WRITE(*,11)    ( DASH,J=1,N)
*       WRITE(*,11)    (BLANK,J=1,N)
        DO 1 I = 1,N-1
        WRITE(*,12)I,(A(I,J),J=1,N)
        WRITE(*,11)    (BLANK,J=1,N)
    1   CONTINUE
        WRITE(*,12)N,(A(N,J),J=1,N)
        WRITE(*,11)    ( DASH,J=1,N)

   10   FORMAT(/, T5,'|',10(2X,I3,2X,'|'))
   11   FORMAT(  T5,'|',10A8)
   12   FORMAT(I3,T5,'|',10(F7.3,'|'))
        RETURN
        END
*===================================================
        SUBROUTINE PROD(A,B,C,N,ND)
*           [See Figure 12-3]
```

ing of a single column of n rows. A column matrix is also known as a vector. The n independent unknowns are grouped similarly, and the complete set of equations is written as

$$[A]x = b$$

where the elements of $[A]$, x, and b are a_{ij}, x_i, and b_i, respectively. The ith equation of the set would then be

$$\sum_{j=1}^{n} a_{ij}x_j = b_i$$

Multiplication of square matrices is defined similarly. Given two n by n matrices $[A], [B]$, the product $[A] \times [B]$ is an n by n matrix whose elements

Figure 12-5

Output from subroutine in Figure 12-4

	1	2	3	4
1	1.000	2.000	3.000	4.000
2	1.000	1.000	1.000	2.000
3	2.000	1.000	1.000	1.000
4	4.000	3.000	4.000	1.000

	1	2	3	4
1	1.000	0.000	1.000	0.000
2	0.000	1.000	0.000	1.000
3	1.000	0.000	1.000	0.000
4	0.000	1.000	0.000	1.000

	1	2	3	4
1	4.000	6.000	4.000	6.000
2	2.000	3.000	2.000	3.000
3	3.000	2.000	3.000	2.000
4	8.000	4.000	8.000	4.000

Figure 12-6

Subroutine to compute the inverse of a matrix

```
      SUBROUTINE MINV(A,AINV,ND,N,DET)

*  MINV computes the inverse of the square n by n matrix A.  The
*  matrix is destroyed in the process.  The determinant is calcu-
*  and returned as DET.  If DET is zero, the calculation is termi-
*  nated and a diagnostic printed.  The inverse of A is returned
*  in matrix AINV.
*
*  A standard Gauss-Jordan elimination algorithm is used.  The
*  rows are rearranged in each pass to use the maximum available
*  pivot.
*-------------------------------------------------------------------
* Variables
*
      INTEGER ND,N,IPASS
      REAL A(ND,ND),AINV(ND,ND),DET,FCTR
*
*  A()    --  Matrix whose inverse is desired; dimensioned as nd
*             by nd in the calling program and is of n by n here
*  AINV()--   Returned as the inverse of A.  Dimensioned same as A
*  DET   --   Computed determinant of A
*  ND    --   Dimension size of A
*  N     --   Local size of A
*  IPASS --   Labels the currrent pivot row
*-------------------------------------------------------------------
```

Figure 12-6
(continued)

```
* Initialization
*
      DET = 1.0
*
*     Initially store the identity matrix in AINV.  After
*     the last pass, AINV will contain the inverse of A.
*
      DO 1 I = 1,N
      DO 1 J = 1,N
         IF(I .EQ. J)THEN
            AINV(I,J) = 1.0
         ELSE
            AINV(I,J) = 0.0
         ENDIF
    1 CONTINUE
*----------------------------------------------------------------
* Computation
*
      DO 7 IPASS = 1,N
*
*        For each pass, first find maximum element
*        in pivot column
*
         IMX = IPASS
         DO 2 IROW = IPASS,N
            IF(ABS(A(IROW,IPASS)) .GT. ABS(A(IMX,IPASS)))THEN
               IMX = IROW
            ENDIF
    2       CONTINUE
*
*        Interchange all elements of row IPASS and row IMX
*        in both A and AINV.  Note, however, that row IMX
*        must be below the current pivot row and the first
*        part of A has already been replaced by 0's and 1's.
*
         IF(IMX .NE.IPASS)THEN
            DO 3 ICOL = 1,N
               TEMP             = AINV(IPASS,ICOL)
               AINV(IPASS,ICOL) = AINV(IMX,ICOL)
               AINV(IMX,ICOL)   = TEMP
               IF(ICOL .GE. IPASS)THEN
                  TEMP          = A(IPASS,ICOL)
                  A(IPASS,ICOL) = A(IMX,ICOL)
                  A(IMX,ICOL)   = TEMP
               ENDIF
    3       CONTINUE
         ENDIF
*
*        The current pivot is now A(IPASS,IPASS), and the
*        determinant is the product of the pivots
*
         PIVOT = A(IPASS,IPASS)
         DET   = DET*PIVOT
*
         IF(DET .EQ. 0.)THEN
            WRITE(*,10)
            PAUSE 'FATAL ERROR in MINV - zero determinant'
            RETURN
         ENDIF
```

Figure 12-6
(conclued)

```
*
*       Step 1 -- Consists of normalization; dividing the pivot
*                 row by the pivot element
*
        DO 4 ICOL = 1,N
            AINV(IPASS,ICOL) = AINV(IPASS,ICOL)/PIVOT
            IF(ICOL. GE. IPASS)THEN
                A(IPASS,ICOL) = A(IPASS,ICOL)/PIVOT
            ENDIF
  4     CONTINUE
*
*       Step 2 -- Replace each row by that row plus a multiple of
*                 the pivot row to get a zero in the pivot column
*
        DO 6 IROW = 1,N
            IF(IROW .NE. IPASS)THEN
                FCTR = A(IROW,IPASS)
                DO 5 ICOL = 1,N
                    AINV(IROW,ICOL) = AINV(IROW,ICOL) -
     +                               FCTR*AINV(IPASS,ICOL)
                    A(IROW,ICOL)=A(IROW,ICOL)-FCTR*A(IPASS,ICOL)
  5             CONTINUE
            ENDIF
  6     CONTINUE
  7 CONTINUE
    RETURN
*-------------------------------------------------------------
 10 FORMAT(/,T5,'=======ERROR IN MINV==========',/,
     +          T5,'|  The matrix is singular    |',/,
     +          T5,'=====Program Terminated=======')
    END
```

correspond to taking the ith row of the first matrix ($[A]$), multiplying, element by element, by the jth column of the second matrix ($[B]$) and summing the results.

$$[C] = [A] \times [B] \rightarrow c_{ij} = \sum_{k=1}^{n} a_{ik} b_{kj}$$

Matrix division is defined in terms of the multiplicative inverse of a matrix. Given a square n by n matrix $[A]$, if a second matrix, $[A^{-1}]$, can be found that satisfies the equation $[A^{-1}] \times [A] = I_n$, where I_n is the identity matrix consisting of a square n by n array with 1's down the diagonal and 0's elsewhere, then division is defined as

$$[B] \div [A] \equiv [B] \times [A^{-1}]$$

and the solution of $[A] \times \mathbf{x} = \mathbf{b}$ becomes simply $\mathbf{x} = [A^{-1}]\mathbf{b}$.

The inverse of a square matrix $[A]$ will always exist if the determinant of the matrix is nonzero. A matrix with a determinant equal to zero is called singular. The determinant of $[A]$ is defined as

$$\det[A] = |A| = \sum_{j=1}^{n} a_{ij} A_{ij}^c \qquad \text{for any value of } i$$

where A_{ij}^c is the ith row, jth column element of the cofactor matrix of $[A]$. The elements of the cofactor matrix, A_{ij}^c, are in turn defined to be equal to the determinant of $[A]$ after deleting row i and column j and multiplying by the sign $(-1)^{i+j}$. Simpler methods of evaluating $|A|$, involving adding or subtracting groups of terms, are possible if $n = 2$ or 3.

The solution of the equation $[A]\mathbf{x} = \mathbf{b}$ may also be expressed in terms of determinants by means of Cramer's rule, which reads,

$$x_k = \frac{|B(k)|}{|A|} \qquad k = 1 \text{ to } n$$

where $[B(k)]$ is a matrix obtained from $[A]$ by replacing the kth column of $[A]$ by the elements of the column vector $\mathbf{b}$. Cramer's rule is not practical for matrices larger than 3 by 3.

The most common procedure used to obtain a computer solution of the matrix equation $[A]\mathbf{x} = \mathbf{b}$ is the Gauss–Jordan method. This method consists of n passes through the set of n equations starting with the first. In pass p, the pth row is called the pivot row and the element a_{pp} is the pivot element. The pivot row is then normalized by dividing through by a_{pp}, thereby placing a 1 in this position. Next, a multiple of the pivot row is added in turn to each row below the pivot row with the factor chosen so as to replace the element in the pivot column by zero. Once all the passes have been completed, the original matrix will be replaced by the identity matrix and the set of right-hand-side terms, b_i, will be replaced by the set of solutions, x_i.

The Gauss–Jordan method may also be used to solve for $[A^{-1}]$ by replacing the vector $\mathbf{b}$ above by the set of column vectors that comprise the identity matrix of order n. The determinant of $[A]$ will be equal to the product of the successive pivot elements of this process. The efficiency and accuracy of the method can be greatly improved by row switching; that is, in each pass, replacing the current pivot row by a row below that has a larger element in the pivot column.

The Gauss–Siedel method is an iterative procedure for solving $[A]\mathbf{x} = \mathbf{b}$ and is especially useful when the matrix $[A]$ is relatively large and contains many zero elements. For matrices such as these, the method of Gauss–Jordan is prone to round-off errors that can substantially limit the accuracy of the results. The method of Gauss–Siedel consists of formally rewriting the n equations by solving the ith equation for x_i. Then, starting with a guess for the complete set of elements x_i, these values are inserted into the expressions on the right and a new set of values computed. The process is repeated until the changes in successive sets of x's are sufficiently small. The speed of convergence of the method is highly dependent on the quality of the initial guess elements; however, eventual convergence is guaranteed if the set of equations is diagonally dominant; that is, if each diagonal element is greater in magnitude than the sum of the magnitudes of all remaining elements of that row.

Problems

12.1 Given the two matrices

$$[A] = \begin{bmatrix} 1 & -1 & 1 \\ -1 & 1 & -1 \\ 1 & -1 & 1 \end{bmatrix} \qquad [B] = \begin{bmatrix} 0 & 1 & 1 \\ -1 & 0 & 1 \\ -1 & -1 & 0 \end{bmatrix}$$

evaluate the following:
a. $[A] + [B]$
b. $[A]^2$, that is, $[A][A]$
c. $[A][B] - [B][A]$

12.2 Given the two matrices

$$[A] = \begin{bmatrix} 0 & -2 & 1 \\ -2 & 1 & -2 \\ 1 & -2 & 0 \end{bmatrix} \qquad [B] = \begin{bmatrix} -4 & -2 & 3 \\ -2 & -1 & -2 \\ 3 & -2 & -4 \end{bmatrix}$$

a. Evaluate $[A][B]$.
b. From the result of part a, determine $[B^{-1}]$.
c. Using the result for $[B^{-1}]$, solve the equation $[B]\mathbf{x} = \mathbf{b}$ where $\mathbf{b}$ is given below. Verify that the solution is correct

$$\mathbf{b} = \begin{bmatrix} 1 \\ -3 \\ 1 \end{bmatrix}$$

12.3 Evaluate the following determinants:

a. $\begin{vmatrix} 1 & 2 \\ 2 & 3 \end{vmatrix}$
b. $\begin{vmatrix} 1 & 0 & 1 \\ 0 & 1 & 2 \\ 1 & 2 & 3 \end{vmatrix}$
c. $\begin{vmatrix} 1 & 0 & 0 & 2 \\ 0 & 1 & 0 & 1 \\ 0 & 0 & 1 & 2 \\ 2 & 1 & 2 & 3 \end{vmatrix}$

12.4 The following determinants are all zero. Justify this statement without explicitly evaluating each determinant.

a. $\begin{vmatrix} 1 & 2 \\ 2 & 4 \end{vmatrix}$
b. $\begin{vmatrix} 1 & 2 & 3 \\ 3 & 2 & 1 \\ 4 & 4 & 4 \end{vmatrix}$
c. $\begin{vmatrix} 1 & 0 & 1 & 0 \\ 0 & 1 & 0 & 1 \\ 1 & 1 & -1 & -1 \\ 2 & -1 & 1 & -2 \end{vmatrix}$

12.5 Solve the matrix equation

$$\begin{bmatrix} 0 & 4 & 4 \\ -4 & 0 & 4 \\ -4 & -4 & 1 \end{bmatrix} \begin{bmatrix} x_1 \\ x_2 \\ x_3 \end{bmatrix} = \begin{bmatrix} 4 \\ 4 \\ 1 \end{bmatrix}$$

by using Cramer's rule. Verify your solution.

12.6 The matrix

$$[A] = \begin{bmatrix} 0 & 2 & 2 \\ -2 & 0 & 2 \\ -2 & -2 & 0 \end{bmatrix}$$

is singular (i.e., $|A| = 0$). Use Cramer's rule to determine the value of α for which there is a solution of the equation $[A]x = b$, where

$$b = \begin{bmatrix} 2 \\ 2 \\ \alpha \end{bmatrix}$$

For this value of α is the solution *unique*?

12.7 Solve the following matrix equations by Gauss–Jordan elimination. Verify the solution.

a. $\begin{bmatrix} 1 & 2 & 0 \\ 2 & 1 & 2 \\ 0 & 2 & 1 \end{bmatrix} \begin{bmatrix} x_1 \\ x_2 \\ x_3 \end{bmatrix} = \begin{bmatrix} 1 \\ 7 \\ -1 \end{bmatrix}$

b. $\begin{bmatrix} 5 & -1 & 5 \\ 0 & 2 & 0 \\ -5 & 3 & -15 \end{bmatrix} \begin{bmatrix} x_1 \\ x_2 \\ x_3 \end{bmatrix} = \begin{bmatrix} 1 \\ -2 \\ 7 \end{bmatrix}$

c. $\begin{bmatrix} 2 & 0 & 1 \\ 1 & 0 & 1 \\ 0 & -2 & 0 \end{bmatrix} \begin{bmatrix} x_1 \\ x_2 \\ x_3 \end{bmatrix} = \begin{bmatrix} 2 \\ 2 \\ 4 \end{bmatrix}$ Beware of zero pivots!

12.8 Determine the inverse matrix of each of the matrices below by using the method of Gauss–Jordan elimination.

a. $\begin{bmatrix} 3 & 0 & 1 \\ 0 & 5 & 0 \\ -1 & 1 & -1 \end{bmatrix}$ b. $\begin{bmatrix} 1 & 1 & 1 & 1 \\ 0 & 1 & 1 & 1 \\ 0 & 0 & 1 & 1 \\ 0 & 0 & 0 & 1 \end{bmatrix}$ c. $\begin{bmatrix} 2 & 0 & 1 \\ 1 & 0 & 1 \\ 0 & -2 & 0 \end{bmatrix}$

12.9 Write the FORTRAN code for a subroutine CHECK(A, N, EPS) that will determine whether or not an n by n matrix $[A]$ is the identity matrix. If the test is affirmative, the subroutine will print a verification and return. If the test fails, a diagnostic is printed and the routine will stop. The form of the test is to verify that for all elements of the matrix $[A]$,

For nondiagonal elements, $(i \neq j)$: $|a_{ij}| < $ EPS
For diagonal elements, $(i = j)$: $|a_{ii} - 1| < $ EPS

12.10 Construct the FORTRAN code for a function subprogram MAXCOL (A, N, IPV, K) that will scan the kth column of the n by n matrix $[A]$ from the IPV row on down and will return the *row* number of the maximum element. For example, if the matrix $[A]$ is

$$[A] = \begin{bmatrix} 3 & 1 & 6 \\ 0 & 5 & 1 \\ 4 & 2 & 2 \end{bmatrix}$$

then MAXCOL(A, 3, 2, 2) would return a value of 2. The maximum element of the second column is 5, which is in row 2.

12.11 Design a FORTRAN subroutine SWITCH(A, B, N, I1, I2) that will interchange the contents of rows i_1 and i_2 of the n by n matrix $[A]$ and the column vector **b**.

12.12 Use the subprograms of Problems 12.10 and 12.11.
   a. Rewrite the FORTRAN code for the subroutine GAUSS of Figure 12-1 to switch rows to maximize the pivot element for each pass.
   b. Test your routine by finding the solutions to the matrix equations of Problem 12.7.

12.13 Rewrite the FORTRAN code for the subroutine GAUSS of Figure 12-1 so that the subroutine will compute the inverse of a matrix $[A]$. The subroutine will return the elements of the inverse in the array $[B]$, and the matrix $[A]$ will be destroyed in the process. Do *not* attempt row switching to maximize pivots; if the current pivot is "small," stop.

12.14 Solve the matrix equation below by the Gauss–Siedel iteration procedure.

$$\begin{bmatrix} 1 & 4 & 1 \\ 1 & 1 & 4 \\ 4 & 1 & 1 \end{bmatrix} \begin{bmatrix} x_1 \\ x_2 \\ x_3 \end{bmatrix} = \begin{bmatrix} 1 \\ -1 \\ 0 \end{bmatrix}$$

   a. Do not switch rows to obtain diagonal dominance. Continue for at least five iterations. Does the solution appear to be converging?
   b. Interchange rows to achieve diagonal dominance and redo the calculation. For both calculations use the same initial guess for the solution vector.

12.15 Construct a FORTRAN function that will examine an n by n matrix and will return the value 1 if the matrix is diagonally dominant and the value 0 if it is not.

12.16 Design a FORTRAN subroutine that will attempt in a single pass to rearrange the rows of a nondiagonally dominant matrix to bring it into a diagonally dominant form. Use the subprograms of Problems 12.10 and 12.11. (It may not be possible to bring a matrix into a diagonally dominant form in a single pass.)

12.17 Solve the following set of *nonlinear* equations by a Gauss–Siedel procedure. (*Note:* Diagonal dominance does not guarantee convergence of nonlinear equations.)

$$4x - y^2 - z^2 = 3$$
$$-x + 4y^2 - z = 2$$
$$-x - y - 4z = 1$$

Start with an initial guess of $x = y = z = 1$ and continue for four or five iterations.

12.18 a. Using the Gauss–Siedel subroutine, solve the equation below, which contains a banded coefficient matrix of order 50. Start with an initial guess for the solution vector of all zeros.

$$
\begin{bmatrix}
8 & -2 & 1 & 0 & \cdots & \cdots & \cdots & 0 \\
-2 & 8 & -2 & 1 & 0 & \cdots & \cdots & 0 \\
1 & -2 & 8 & -2 & 1 & 0 & \cdots & 0 \\
0 & 1 & -2 & 8 & -2 & 1 & \cdots & 0 \\
\cdots & \cdots & \cdots & \cdots & \cdots & \cdots & \cdots & \cdots \\
\cdots & \cdots & \cdots & \cdots & \cdots & \cdots & \cdots & \cdots \\
\cdots & \cdots & 1 & -2 & 8 & -2 & 1 & 0 \\
\cdots & \cdots & 0 & 1 & -2 & 8 & -2 & 1 \\
\cdots & \cdots & 0 & 0 & 1 & -2 & 8 & -2 \\
\cdots & \cdots & 0 & 0 & 0 & 1 & -2 & 8
\end{bmatrix}
\begin{bmatrix}
x_1 \\ x_2 \\ x_3 \\ x_4 \\ \cdots \\ \cdots \\ x_{47} \\ x_{48} \\ x_{49} \\ x_{50}
\end{bmatrix}
=
\begin{bmatrix}
1 \\ 1 \\ 1 \\ 1 \\ 1 \\ 1 \\ 1 \\ 1 \\ 1 \\ 1
\end{bmatrix}
$$

b. Since the matrix contains a great many zeros, the general Gauss–Siedel subroutine is not very efficient. Construct a more compact program by solving the equations directly as

$$x_1 = (1 + 2x_2 - x_3)/8$$
$$x_2 = [1 + 2(x_3 + x_1) - x_4]/8$$
$$\vdots$$

$$x_i = [1 + 2(x_{i-1} + x_{i+1}) - (x_{i-2} + x_{i+2})]/8 \qquad \text{for } i = 3, 48$$

$$\vdots$$

$$x_{49} = [1 + 2(x_{48} + x_{50}) - x_{47}]/8$$
$$x_{50} = (1 + 2x_{49} - x_{48})/8$$

using DO loops in an obvious manner. Compare the execution times for the two solutions.

F

Programming
Assignment

Civil Engineering: Fluid Flow Through a Plumbing Network

When designing a system for transporting fluid from one point to another, the engineer is frequently faced with the task of incorporating a new pipe into an existing and complicated maze of pipes, pumps, and valves. Adding an additional pipe anywhere in the system will change the rate of fluid flow in all pipes in the system in a complicated way. However, in a simple modeling of the network, the relationships between the flows in the different parts of the system can be represented by a set of linear equations that are then solved using the methods of Chapter 12. The ideas used to establish these equations can be summarized by three rules:

Rule 1

Junction equation

At a junction of two or more pipes, the amount of fluid flowing into the junction must equal the amount of fluid flowing out of the junction. This rule is a statement of the conservation of matter. Thus, for the junction

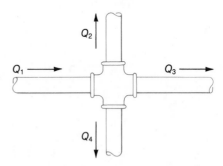

$$Q_1 = Q_2 + Q_3 + Q_4.$$

Rule 2

Linear pressure drop

The pressure drop a fluid experiences when flowing through a pipe is due to the friction with the walls of the pipe.

The fluid flow is classified as either turbulent or laminar. Turbulent flow is extremely complicated and will not be treated in this problem.[1] Laminar flow is very slow, even flow through the pipe. For this case the pressure drop across a length of pipe is given by the equation

$$\Delta P = \frac{8\eta L}{\pi R^4}Q = KQ \qquad\qquad (F.1)$$

where ΔP = Pressure drop (N/m^2)
η = Fluid viscosity (kg/sec-m)
L = Pipe length (m)
R = Pipe radius (m)
Q = Flow rate (m^3/sec)
K = Effective resistance (kg/sec-m^4)

Rule 3

Loop equation

If the total pressure drop is computed as the sum of the pressure drops of pipes connected in a series, then the pressure drop around any closed loop must be zero. (*Note:* When traversing a pipe *against* the direction of flow, the pressure across the length of pipe will increase; that is, the pressure drop ΔP is negative.)

Thus, in Figure F-1, proceeding around the loop containing pipes 1 through 6 and assuming the direction of flow is as drawn, we have

$$\Delta P_1 + \Delta P_2 + \Delta P_3 - \Delta P_4 - \Delta P_5 - \Delta P_6 = 0$$

In addition, rule 1, conservation of flow, requires that

$$Q_1 = Q_2 = Q_3$$
$$Q_4 = Q_5 = Q_6$$
$$Q_{in} = Q_{out} = Q_1 + Q_4 = Q_3 + Q_6$$

---

[1] Unfortunately, almost all fluid flow in pipes is turbulent and therefore the results of this problem represent only the first step in the solution of a realistic problem. In many cases, the basic features of turbulent flow can be approximated by allowing the effective resistance, K, to be an empirically determined function of the flow rate, Q. The rest of the analysis is then the same as presented here, except that the resulting equations are no longer linear in Q.

Figure F-1
The sum of the
pressure drops
around a closed
loop of pipes is zero

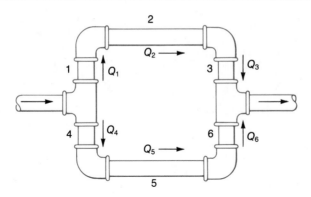

And from rule 2 we have

$$(K_1 + K_2 + K_3)Q_1 = (K_4 + K_5 + K_6)Q_4$$

which may easily be solved to obtain Q_1 in terms of Q_{in} and the pipe resistances.

The purpose of this problem is to apply these rules to compute the flow rates in the very complicated pipe network shown in Figure F-2.

In Figure F-2 the following conditions apply:

1. The resistance of a pipe is $K = (8\eta L)/(\pi R^4)$.
2. The pressure drop across a pipe in the direction of the fluid flow is $\Delta P = KQ$.
3. The pressure at the main pump starts out equal to P_0.
4. The pressure at an open tap is zero.

The problem is analyzed by first writing junction equations for all the junctions, labeled A through I, on the figure.

Junction	Junction Equation
[A]	$Q_1 = Q_2 + Q_3$
[B]	$Q_2 = Q_4 + Q_7$
[C]	$Q_4 = Q_5 + Q_8$
[D]	$Q_5 = Q_6 + Q_9$
[E]	$Q_3 + Q_6 = Q_{10}$
[F]	$Q_8 = Q_{17} + Q_{13}$
[G]	$Q_9 + Q_{17} = Q_{14}$
[H]	$Q_7 = Q_{11} + Q_{12}$
[I]	$Q_{10} = Q_{15} + Q_{16}$

Figure F-2
Schematic of a
complicated
plumbing network

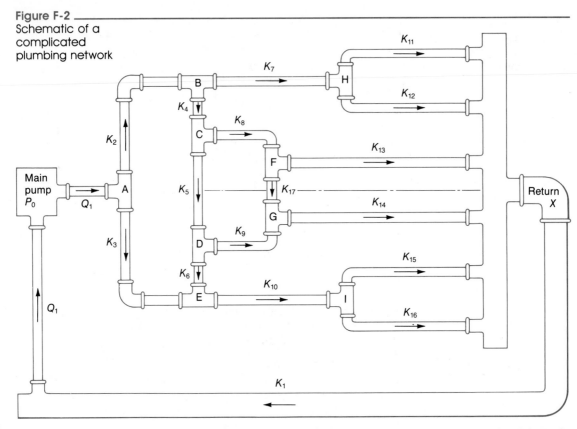

So far we have nine equations in the 17 unknowns (the Q_i). Eight more equations are therefore required for a solution. These are supplied by rule 3 applied to eight arbitrary but independent loops.

Loop	Loop Equation	
[BHXFCB]	$K_7 Q_7 + K_{12} Q_{12} - K_{13} Q_{13} - K_8 Q_8 - K_4 Q_4$	$= 0$
[ABCDEA]	$K_2 Q_2 + K_4 Q_4 + K_5 Q_5 + K_6 Q_6 - K_3 Q_3$	$= 0$
[CFGDC]	$K_8 Q_8 + K_{17} Q_{17} - K_9 Q_9 - K_5 Q_5$	$= 0$
[FXGF]	$K_{13} Q_{13} - K_{14} Q_{14} - K_{17} Q_{17}$	$= 0$
[HXH]	$K_{11} Q_{11} - K_{12} Q_{12}$	$= 0$
[IXI]	$K_{15} Q_{15} - K_{16} Q_{16}$	$= 0$
[ABHXIEA]	$K_2 Q_2 + K_7 Q_7 + K_{12} Q_{12} - K_{16} Q_{16} - K_{10} Q_{10} - K_3 Q_3 = 0$	
[ABHXPA]	$K_2 Q_2 + K_7 Q_7 + K_{12} Q_{12} + K_1 Q_1$	$= P_0$

Notice that the last equation does not equal zero because there is a pump (i.e., a source of pressure increase) within the loop. We now have 17 equa-

Figure F-3
Coefficient matrix for the plumbing network problem (All blank entries are zero.)

[Junction Equations]

	1	2	3	4	5	6	7	8	9	10	11	12	13	14	15	16	17	
1	1	-1	-1															[A] $Q_1 = Q_2 + Q_3$
2		1		-1			-1											[B] $Q_2 = Q_4 + Q_7$
3				1	-1			-1										[C] $Q_4 = Q_5 + Q_8$
4					1	-1			-1									[D] $Q_5 = Q_6 + Q_9$
5			1			1				-1								[E] $Q_3 + Q_6 = Q_{10}$
6								1					-1				-1	[F] $Q_8 = Q_{17} + Q_{13}$
7									1					-1			1	[G] $Q_9 + Q_{17} = Q_{14}$
8							1				-1	-1						[H] $Q_7 = Q_{11} + Q_{12}$
9										1				-1	-1			[I] $Q_{10} = Q_{15} + Q_{16}$
10			$-K_4$				K_7	$-K_8$				K_{12}	$-K_{13}$					Loop [BHXFCB]
11		K_2	$-K_3$	K_4	K_5	K_6												Loop [ABCDEA]
12				$-K_5$				K_8	$-K_9$								K_{17}	Loop [CFGDC]
13													K_{13}	$-K_{14}$			$-K_{17}$	Loop [FXGF]
14											K_{11}	$-K_{12}$						Loop [HXH]
15															K_{15}	$-K_{16}$		Loop [IXI]
16		K_2	$-K_3$				K_7			$-K_{10}$		K_{12}				$-K_{16}$		Loop [ABHXIEA]
17	K_1	K_2					K_7					K_{12}						Loop [ABHXPA]

tions in the 17 unknown flow rates and can proceed to formulate the problem in a matrix form suitable for computer solution. If the equations are written in the form $[A]Q = \mathbf{b}$, the resulting coefficient matrix is shown in Figure F-3 and the right-hand-side vector, $\mathbf{b}$, has components $b_i = 0$ for $i = 1$ to 16 and $b_{17} = P_0$.

Perhaps the most difficult aspect of a problem like this is to ensure that the correct assignments have been made to each of the 289 elements of the coefficient matrix. To do this the coefficient matrix must be printed and carefully scanned to see if any elements have been misplaced. If you can think of any additional internal checks, you can save a great deal of later debugging time by inserting them at the beginning of the problem. In this case several of the checks on the accuracy of the assignments are a consequence of the symmetry of the arrangement of the pipes. You will notice that the pipe arrangement of Figure F-2 is symmetric about the dotted line through the center. Thus, we anticipate that the flows in the upper half and the lower half should be the same. Also, a little thought suggests that the flow through pipes 5 and 17 should be identically zero. If the computed flow rates do not satisfy these symmetry properties, it is likely that an error exists in the coefficient matrix.

Problem Specifics. The program to solve for the flow rates in each of the pipes is then assembled as follows:

1. Construct a data file that contains all the nonzero elements of the coefficient matrix. These elements will be either ± 1 or $\pm K(\text{col})$, where "col" is the column number. The main program will then use a DATA statement to first "zero" the coefficient matrix and then read this file for the nonzero elements.
2. The main program should assign values to the pressure head, P_0, the viscosity, and the length and radii of each pipe by means of a DATA statement. The values of these parameters are listed in Table F-1.
3. Read the data file for the nonzero elements of the coefficient matrix. The solution for the flow rates would then proceed as follows:
   a. Form a copy of the coefficient matrix, ACOPY( ).
   b. Use a subroutine to neatly print the coefficient matrix.
   c. Use the subroutine MINV (Figure 12-6) to compute the inverse of the copy.
   d. Use the subroutine PROD (Figure 12-3) to multiply [A] times [AINV] and store the result in ACOPY. (The matrix ACOPY was destroyed by the subroutine MINV.)
   e. Use a subroutine to check that the product [A]*[AINV] is equal to the identity matrix and to evaluate the average deviation from the identity matrix. This step will check the seriousness of round-off error as well as the accuracy of subroutine MINV.

Table F-1
Parameters for the pipes of the sample problem

Viscosity = η = 0.001 Pa-sec P_0 = 10 kPa (kilo Pascal)		
Pipe No.	R (m)	L (m)
1	0.10	825
2, 3	0.08	226
4, 6	0.06	56
5	0.04	6.3
7, 10	0.06	31
8, 9	0.05	20
11, 12	0.05	20
15, 16	0.05	20
13, 14	0.07	29
17	0.06	8

       f. Obtain the solution for the flow rates from the product
q = [AINV]*b.

       g. Neatly print the input parameters and the flow rates
through the pipes. (*Note:* If the numbers for the flow rate
in a particular pipe turn out to be negative, this means
that the direction of flow is opposite to that assumed in
Figure F-2.)

    4. From the program output verify that the symmetry in the
upper/lower half of the figure is reflected in the computed
results.

    The program to solve this problem is shown in Figure F-4, along
with the computed flow rates. Once this program has been constructed
and tested for accuracy, it can be used to explore various engineering
characteristics of the pipe arrangement. For example, if a blockage occurs
in any of the pipes, it is important to know how the flow in all the remaining pipes will be affected. A blockage can be easily simulated by replacing
the effective resistance in a particular pipe by a very large number. So as

Figure F-4
FORTRAN code for
solving the sample
problem

```
      PROGRAM PLUMB
*
*  This program computes the rate of flow of fluid through a com-
*  plicated network of pipes and pumps.  There are 17 equations in
*  17 unknown flow rates, which are written in matrix form.  The
*  coefficient matrix is [A] and a copy of this matrix is needed
*  because the subroutine MINV that computes the inverse (AINV)
*  also destroys [A].  The effective resistances of each pipe are
*  stored in the array K().  The pressure from the main pump is P0.
*  The product of [A] with its inverse is computed and compared
*  with the identity to determine the effect of round-off error.
*-----------------------------------------------------------------
* Variables
*
      PARAMETER (N=17, N2=17*17, AA = -1.)
      REAL A(N,N),AINV(N,N),ACOPY(N,N),B(N),Q(N),K(N),R(N),L(N),
     +     P0,VISCOS,DET
*
*      A()     --  Coefficient matrix
*      ACOPY() --  Copy of A
*      AINV()  --  Inverse of A
*      B()     --  Right-hand-side vector
*      Q()     --  Solution vector containing the flow rates
*      L()     --  Lengths of the pipes
*      R()     --  Pipe radii (m)
*      K()     --  Effective resistances of the pipes
*      P0      --  Pressure head of the main pump
*      VISCOS  --  Fluid viscosity
*      DET     --  Determinant of A
*      N       --  Size of the matrices
*      AA      --  Symbolic constant (-1.) used in filling A
*-----------------------------------------------------------------
```

Figure F-4 _____
(continued)

```
      * Initialization
      *
            DATA A,B/N2*0.,N*0./
            DATA K
            DATA P0,VISCOS/5000.,.0001/
            DATA L(1),L(2),L(3),L(4),L(6),L(5),L(7),L(10),
           +      L(8),L(9),L(11),L(12),L(15),L(16),L(13),L(14),L(17)
           +      /203.,2*72.5,2*10.0,1.0,2*5.6,6*2.5,2*7.,1.5/
            DATA R(1),R(2),R(3),R(4),R(6),R(5),R(7),R(10),
           +      R(8),R(9),R(11),R(12),R(15),R(16),R(13),R(14),R(17)
           +      /.1,2*.08,2*.06,.04,2*.06,6*.05,2*.07,.06/
            PI = ACOS(-1.)
            DO 1 I = 1,N
                K(I) = 8.*VISCOS*L(I)/PI/R(I)**4
          1 CONTINUE
      *
      * The nonzero elements of the array A are read from a data file.
      * A line of the data file consists of 0 (or 1) followed by the row
      * column element of the nonzero element and the sign of the element.
      * ment. If the first value is zero, the element of A is + or - one.
      * If the first value is one, the element is plus or minus K(row).
      *
            OPEN(7,FILE='PROG6.DAT')
            REWIND (7)
            DO 2 II= 1,200
              READ(7,*,END=3)M,I,J,Z
                IF(M .EQ. 0)THEN
                    A(I,J) = Z
                ELSEIF(M .EQ. 1)THEN
                    A(I,J) = Z*K(J)
                ENDIF
          2 CONTINUE
          3 B(17)     = P0
            DO 4 I = 1,N
            DO 4 J = 1,N
                ACOPY(I,J) = A(I,J)
          4 CONTINUE
            CALL PRINT(A,N,N)
            CALL MINV(ACOPY,AINV,N,N,DET)
            CALL PROD(A,AINV,ACOPY,N,N)
      *
      *     Subroutine check scans the product [A][AINV] to see that is
      *     equal to the identity.  It monitors round-off error.
      *
            CALL CHECK(ACOPY,N,N)
      *
      *     The solution for the flow rates are Q = AINV*B
      *
            DO 6 I = 1,N
                Q(I) = 0.
                DO 5 J = 1,N
                    Q(I) = Q(I) + AINV(I,J)*B(J)
          5     CONTINUE
          6 CONTINUE
            WRITE(*,10)P0,VISCOS,N
            DO 7 I = 1,N
                WRITE(*,11)I,L(I),R(I),K(I),Q(I)
          7 CONTINUE
      *--------------------------------------------------------------
```

Figure F-4
(continued)

```
   10  FORMAT(/,T5,'A calculation of the flow rates in a ',/,
       +          T5,'complicated network of pipes and pumps.',//,
       + T10,'Pressure Head   = ',T30,F7.1,' (N/m^2)',/,
       + T10,'Fluid Viscosity = ',T30,F7.4,' (kg/s-m)',/,
       + T10,'There are ',I3,' flow rates to be computed.',//,
       + T5,'|         |        |        |Effective |  Computed |',/,
       + T5,'|Pipe| Length | Radius |Resistance|Flow  Rate|',/,
       + T5,'| No.|  (m)   |  (m)   |(kg/s-m^4)| m^3/sec  |',/,
       + T5,'|----|--------|--------|----------|----------|')
   *
   11  FORMAT(T5,'| ',I2,T10,'| ',F5.1,T19,'|  ',F4.3,T28,'|  ',
       +           F6.2,T39,'| ',F7.3,T50,'|')
       STOP
       END
*======================================================================
       SUBROUTINE CHECK(A,ND,N)
       REAL A(ND,ND)
       SUM = 0.0
       DO 2 I = 1,N
           DIFF = ABS(A(I,I) - 1.0)
           IF(DIFF .GT. 1.E-4)THEN
               WRITE(*,10)I,I,A(I,I)
           ENDIF
           SUM = SUM + DIFF
           DO 1 J = 1,N
               IF(I .NE. J)THEN
                   DIFF = ABS(A(I,J))
                   IF(DIFF .GT. 1.E-4)THEN
                       WRITE(*,11)I,J,A(I,J)
                   ENDIF
                   SUM = SUM + DIFF
               ENDIF
   1        CONTINUE
   2    CONTINUE
       WRITE(*,12)SUM/N/N
       RETURN
*----------------------------------------------------------------------
   10  FORMAT(T5,'*=====WARNING FROM CHECK=======*',/,
       +      T5,'|  In the product [A][AINV] a  |',/,
       +      T5,'|  diagonal element is not one |',/,
       +      T5,'| A(',I2,',',I2,') = ',F8.6,T36,'|',/,
       +      T5,'*=====Program Continues=======*',/)

   11  FORMAT(T5,'*======WARNING FROM CHECK=======*',/,
       +      T5,'|  In the product [A][AINV] an  |',/,
       +      T5,'|off-diagonal element is not zero|',/,
       +      T5,'| A(',I2,',',I2,') = ',F9.7,T37,'|',/,
       +      T5,'*=====Program Continues=======*',/)

   12  FORMAT(/,T10,'A check on round-off error',/,
       +    T10,'The average deviation from the identity',/,
       +    T10,'matrix in the product [A][AINV] is',/,
       +    T20,'Avg. Dev. = ',E12.5)
       END
*======================================================================
       SUBROUTINE PRINT(A,N,ND)              (See Figure 12-4)
*======================================================================
       SUBROUTINE MINV(A,AINV,ND,N,DET)      (See Figure 12-6)
*======================================================================
```

Figure F-4 _____
(continued)

	1	2	3	4	5	6	7	8	9	10	11	12	13	14	15	16	17
1	1.	-1.	-1.	0.	0.	0.	0.	0.	0.	0.	0.	0.	0.	0.	0.	0.	0.
2	0.	1.	0.	-1.	0.	0.	-1.	0.	0.	0.	0.	0.	0.	0.	0.	0.	0.
3	0.	0.	0.	1.	-1.	0.	0.	-1.	0.	0.	0.	0.	0.	0.	0.	0.	0.
4	0.	0.	0.	0.	1.	-1.	0.	0.	-1.	0.	0.	0.	0.	0.	0.	0.	0.
5	0.	0.	1.	0.	0.	1.	0.	0.	0.	-1.	0.	0.	0.	0.	0.	0.	0.
6	0.	0.	0.	0.	0.	0.	0.	1.	0.	0.	0.	0.	-1.	0.	0.	0.	-1.
7	0.	0.	0.	0.	0.	0.	0.	0.	1.	0.	0.	0.	0.	-1.	0.	0.	1.
8	0.	0.	0.	0.	0.	0.	1.	0.	0.	0.	-1.	-1.	0.	0.	0.	0.	0.
9	0.	0.	0.	0.	0.	0.	0.	0.	0.	1.	0.	0.	0.	0.	-1.	-1.	0.
10	0.	0.	0.	-196.	0.	0.	110.	-102.	0.	0.	0.	102.	-74.	0.	0.	0.	0.
11	0.	451.	-451.	196.	99.	196.	0.	0.	0.	0.	0.	0.	0.	0.	0.	0.	0.
12	0.	0.	0.	0.	-99.	0.	0.	102.	-102.	0.	0.	0.	0.	0.	0.	0.	29.
13	0.	0.	0.	0.	0.	0.	0.	0.	0.	0.	0.	0.	74.	-74.	0.	0.	-29.
14	0.	0.	0.	0.	0.	0.	0.	0.	0.	0.	102.	-102.	0.	0.	0.	0.	0.
15	0.	0.	0.	0.	0.	0.	0.	0.	0.	0.	0.	0.	0.	0.	102.	-102.	0.
16	0.	451.	-451.	0.	0.	0.	110.	0.	0.	-110.	0.	102.	0.	0.	0.	-102.	0.
17	517.	451.	0.	0.	0.	0.	110.	0.	0.	0.	0.	102.	0.	0.	0.	0.	0.

A check on round-off error
The average deviation from the identity
matrix in the product [A][AINV] is
           Avg. Dev. = 0.82328E-06

A calculation of the flow rates in a
complicated network of pipes and pumps.

           Pressure Head   =   5000.0 (N/m^2)
           Fluid Viscosity =   0.0001 (kg/s-m)
           There are 17 flow rates to be computed.

Figure F-4
(concluded)

Pipe No.	Length (m)	Radius (m)	Effective Resistance (kg/s-m^4)	Computed Flow Rate m^3/sec
1	203.0	.100	516.94	6.262
2	72.5	.080	450.73	3.131
3	72.5	.080	450.73	3.131
4	10.0	.060	196.49	0.945
5	1.0	.040	99.47	0.000
6	10.0	.060	196.49	-0.945
7	5.6	.060	110.03	2.186
8	2.5	.050	101.86	0.945
9	2.5	.050	101.86	0.945
10	5.6	.060	110.03	2.186
11	2.5	.050	101.86	1.093
12	2.5	.050	101.86	1.093
13	7.0	.070	74.24	0.945
14	7.0	.070	74.24	0.945
15	2.5	.050	101.86	1.093
16	2.5	.050	101.86	1.093
17	1.5	.060	29.47	0.000

an additional exercise, simulate a blockage in pipe number 8 and rerun the program to determine the new flow rates. Which pipe(s) experience the largest change in their flow rate?

F.2 Programming Problems

Programming Problem F-A: Civil Engineering:
Model of a Stress Calculation for a Bridge

Large computer programs are used in civil engineering to compute the stresses in the supporting elements of a bridge. These computations are usually extremely difficult since the effect of a load on the bridge and the weight of the bridge itself are transmitted to all elements of the bridge and result in a complicated interconnection of stress relations. However, by making enough simplifying assumptions, the problem can be made tractable and employs only the simple essentials of statics that were learned in introductory physics. The bridge design considered here is a seven-element plane truss shown in Figure F-5.

Each element or strut is assumed to be weightless, and all are of length L. They are connected by frictionless pins. There is a load P on the bridge a distance x from the midpoint. To analyze the problem, we must draw a force diagram for each strut and require

$$\sum F_x = 0 \qquad \sum F_y = 0 \qquad \sum \text{torques} = 0$$

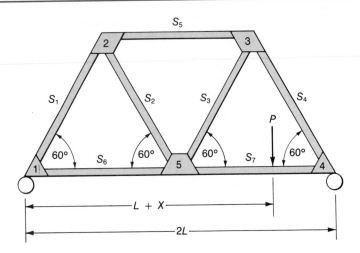

Since all the struts are weightless, the forces on each strut (except S_7) act at
the ends only. The force diagram for strut S_1 is shown in Figure F-6. By
requiring that the sum of the forces equal zero and the sum of the torques
equal zero, we see that $|F_1| = |F_2|$ *and* that the direction of the force must
be parallel to the strut. The force diagram for all struts except S_7 is shown
in Figure F-7. The diagram for S_7 is given in Figure F-8. In Figure F-8 the
forces F_L and F_R have been written in terms of components perpendicular
to the beam (N_L, N_R) and parallel to the beam F_7. Since the sum of the
torques on the strut is zero, we have

$$N_L = \left(1 - \frac{x}{L}\right)P$$

$$N_R = \frac{x}{L}P$$

Next, the forces on the struts can be either compressive or stretching. If
they are *all* drawn as stretching forces, then if the calculation results in a
force that is actually compressive, the computed value of the force will be
negative.

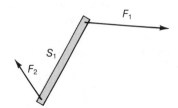

Figure F-7
Force diagram for
struts S_1–S_6

Figure F-8
Force diagram for
strut S_7

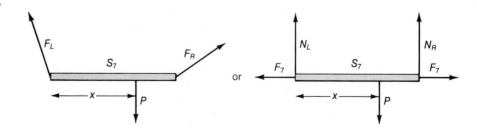

The forces acting on the five pins must likewise be evaluated using force diagrams. The force of a strut on a pin is the negative of the force of the pin on the strut. If the forces exerted by the bridge supports are labeled as σ_L, σ_R, the resulting five force diagrams are as in Figure F-9. Finally, since the torque on the whole bridge is zero, we obtain the relations

$$(2L)\sigma_L = (L - x)P$$

$$\sigma_L = \frac{1}{2}\left(1 - \frac{x}{L}\right)P$$

Figure F-9
Force diagrams for
each of the five
connecting pins in
the bridge section

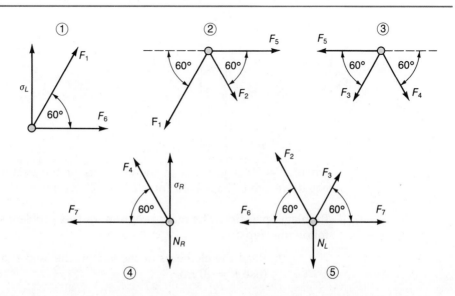

Writing out the x and y equations for the five force diagrams, we obtain the following equations:

1. $F_1 + 2F_6 \qquad\qquad = 0$
2. $F_1 \qquad\qquad\qquad = -S(x, P) \qquad S(x, P) = \dfrac{1}{\sqrt{3}}\left(1 - \dfrac{x}{L}\right)P$
3. $F_1 + F_2 \qquad\qquad = 0$
4. $F_1 - F_2 - 2F_5 \qquad = 0$
5. $F_3 + F_4 \qquad\qquad = 0$
6. $F_3 - F_4 + 2F_5 \qquad = 0$
7. $F_2 - F_3 + 2F_6 - 2F_7 = 0 \qquad$ We need only seven equations.

[Recall that $\cos(60°) = \frac{1}{2}$, $\sin(60°) = \sqrt{3}/2$.] These equations may be written in matrix form as

$$
\begin{array}{ccc}
[A] & \mathbf{F} & = \quad \mathbf{b}_0
\end{array}
$$

$$
\begin{bmatrix}
1 & 0 & 0 & 0 & 0 & 2 & 0 \\
1 & 0 & 0 & 0 & 0 & 0 & 0 \\
1 & 1 & 0 & 0 & 0 & 0 & 0 \\
1 & -1 & 0 & 0 & -2 & 0 & 0 \\
0 & 0 & 1 & 1 & 0 & 0 & 0 \\
0 & 0 & 1 & -1 & 2 & 0 & 0 \\
0 & 1 & -1 & 0 & 0 & 2 & -2
\end{bmatrix}
\begin{bmatrix}
F_1 \\ F_2 \\ F_3 \\ F_4 \\ F_5 \\ F_6 \\ F_7
\end{bmatrix}
=
\begin{bmatrix}
0 \\ -S(x, P) \\ 0 \\ 0 \\ 0 \\ 0 \\ 0
\end{bmatrix}
$$

The problem is then to solve this equation for the forces on the struts.

In a more realistic analysis of the problem, the struts have a weight. This complicates the problem considerably. However, in many circumstances the complications appear only in the vector $\mathbf{b}$ and the coefficient matrix remains the same. The right-hand-side vector you should use for this problem is

$$
\mathbf{b} = \mathbf{b}_0 +
\begin{bmatrix}
-1 \\ 6 \\ -5 \\ 2 \\ 1 \\ 8 \\ 4
\end{bmatrix}
$$

where $P = 50$. The units of the elements of the vector $\mathbf{b}$ are 10^4 N. The equations are to be solved for $x/L = 0, 0.1, \ldots, 1.0$.

Problem Specifics. The main program for this problem should include the following steps:

1. Read the elements of the vector, the load P, and the length L (use $L = 10$ m).

2. Set all the elements of $[A]$ to zero with a DATA statement, then redefine the nonzero elements. Also, since $[A]$ will be destroyed when its inverse is computed, a copy should be made.
3. Use the subroutine MINV or a library subroutine to compute the inverse of the matrix $[A]$ and evaluate $[A][A^{-1}]$.
4. Check that $[A][A^{-1}]$ is indeed the identity matrix.
5. Neatly print **b**, $[A]$, $[A^{-1}]$, $|A|$, and the product $[A][A^{-1}]$.
6. Solve for the forces for $x/L = 0, 0.1, \ldots, 1.0$ and print the results.
7. Determine which of the load positions used results in the maximum stress on strut 5.

Programming Problem F-B: Electrical Engineering: Currents in an Electrical Network

Electrical engineers frequently spend a good bit of their time solving network problems using Kirchoff's laws. Sounds impressive. However, the truth is that anyone can do the most complicated linear network problems with a knowledge of matrix algebra and after a few minutes of instruction in the theory of electrical networks. Consider the network illustrated in Figure F-10.

In the figure the cube has a resistor on each of its 12 edges. The resistors are of known values R_i, $i = 1$ to 12. The eight corners are labeled a through h. A known current I_0 flows into corner a. It then divides among the various wires and eventually flows out again at corner g. The assumed direction of the current in each edge is indicated by arrows.

Figure F-10
Electrical network consisting of resistors on the edges of a cube

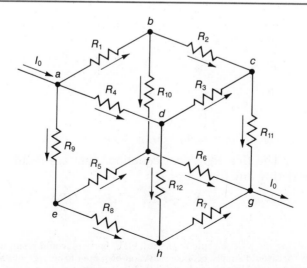

The currents along each edge, I_i, $i = 1$ to 12, are not known and the problem is to solve for them. We will thus need 12 equations. These equations are supplied by Kirchoff's laws:

1. *Junction law.* The sum of all current flowing into a corner must equal the sum of the currents flowing out of the corner (conservation of current).
2. *Ohm's law.* The voltage drop across a resistor R_i (in the direction of the assumed current) is given by the product $V = I_i R_i$. The voltage against the direction of current increases, that is, a negative voltage drop.
3. *Closed-loop rule.* The sum of the voltage drops around a closed loop must be zero; that is, the voltage at a point (the start of a loop) must equal the voltage at the same point (the end of the loop).

For example, the first rule applied to the currents flowing into corner b yields

$$I_1 = I_2 + I_{10} \qquad \text{corner } b$$

And the sum of the voltage drops around the loop labeled *abcda* is

$$V_{ab} + V_{bc} + V_{cd} + V_{da} = 0 \qquad abcda$$

But $V_{ad} = -V_{da} = I_4 R_4$, $V_{ab} = I_1 R_1$, and so on. Thus, using Ohm's law, this relation can be written

$$I_1 R_1 + I_2 R_2 - I_4 R_4 - I_3 R_3 = 0 \qquad abcda$$

These rules are next applied to the cube network to obtain the 12 necessary equations. First the junction rule is applied to seven of the eight corners,[2] resulting in

$$(a) \qquad I_0 = I_1 + I_4 + I_9$$

$$(b) \qquad I_1 = I_2 + I_{10}$$

$$(c) \qquad I_{11} = I_2 + I_3$$

$$(d) \qquad I_4 = I_{12} + I_3$$

$$(e) \qquad I_9 = I_5 + I_8$$

$$(f) \qquad I_6 = I_5 + I_{10}$$

$$(g) \qquad I_0 = I_6 + I_7 + I_{11}$$

The five additional equations that are required are obtained by considering any five loops.

$$abcda \qquad I_1 R_1 + I_2 R_2 - I_4 R_4 - I_3 R_3 = 0$$

---

[2] Applying the junction rule to the full eight corners would result in an additional equation that would simply be a combination of some of the previous seven; that is, the equations would not be independent. Try it and see.

$$abfea \qquad I_1 R_1 + I_{10} R_{10} - I_9 R_9 - I_5 R_5 = 0$$

$$efghe \qquad I_5 R_5 + I_6 R_6 - I_8 R_8 - I_7 R_7 = 0$$

$$adhea \qquad I_4 R_4 + I_{12} R_{12} - I_9 R_9 - I_8 R_8 = 0$$

$$bcgfb \qquad I_2 R_2 + I_{11} R_{11} - I_{10} R_{10} - I_6 R_6 = 0$$

These 12 equations in the 12 unknowns, I_i, the known quantities, I_0, and the resistances, R_i, are next written in matrix form as

$$
\begin{bmatrix}
1 & 0 & 0 & 1 & 0 & 0 & 0 & 0 & 1 & 0 & 0 & 0 \\
-1 & 1 & 0 & 0 & 0 & 0 & 0 & 0 & 0 & 1 & 0 & 0 \\
0 & 1 & 1 & 0 & 0 & 0 & 0 & 0 & 0 & 0 & -1 & 0 \\
0 & 0 & -1 & 1 & 0 & 0 & 0 & 0 & 0 & 0 & 0 & -1 \\
0 & 0 & 0 & 0 & 1 & 0 & 0 & 1 & -1 & 0 & 0 & 0 \\
0 & 0 & 0 & 0 & -1 & 1 & 0 & 0 & 0 & -1 & 0 & 0 \\
0 & 0 & 0 & 0 & 0 & 1 & 1 & 0 & 0 & 0 & 1 & 0 \\
R_1 & 0 & 0 & 0 & -R_5 & 0 & 0 & 0 & -R_9 & -R_{10} & 0 & 0 \\
R_1 & R_2 & -R_3 & -R_4 & 0 & 0 & 0 & 0 & 0 & 0 & 0 & 0 \\
0 & 0 & 0 & 0 & R_5 & R_6 & -R_7 & -R_8 & 0 & 0 & 0 & 0 \\
0 & 0 & 0 & R_4 & 0 & 0 & 0 & -R_8 & -R_9 & 0 & 0 & R_{12} \\
0 & R_2 & 0 & 0 & 0 & -R_6 & 0 & 0 & 0 & -R_{10} & R_{11} & 0
\end{bmatrix}
\begin{bmatrix}
I_1 \\ I_2 \\ I_3 \\ I_4 \\ I_5 \\ I_6 \\ I_7 \\ I_8 \\ I_9 \\ I_{10} \\ I_{11} \\ I_{12}
\end{bmatrix}
=
\begin{bmatrix}
I_0 \\ 0 \\ 0 \\ 0 \\ 0 \\ 0 \\ I_0 \\ 0 \\ 0 \\ 0 \\ 0 \\ 0
\end{bmatrix}
$$

The resistances on the edges of the cube have the values listed below for the three cases to be considered. All resistances are in units of 1000 Ω.

Case 1 $R_i = 3.0$ for all $i = 1,12$

Case 2 $R_1 = 1, R_2 = 2, \ldots, R_{11} = 11, R_{12} = 12$

Case 3 $R_{10} = R_{12} = 1000$, the remaining $R_i = 1$

Also, use $I_0 = 10^{-3}$ A.

Problem Specifics. The main program in your solution should include the following steps:

1. Use a DATA statement to set the coefficient matrix [A] equal to zero and then redefine the nonzero elements. Also, since the matrix [A] will be destroyed when the inverse is computed, form a copy of this matrix.
2. For each of the three cases, compute the inverse matrix $[A^{-1}]$, the determinant $|A|$, and the product $[A][A^{-1}]$.
3. Check that the product $[A][A^{-1}]$ is the identity.
4. Solve for the currents in each resistor.
5. Neatly print $[A]$, $[A^{-1}]$, $[A][A^{-1}]$, $|A|$, R_i, I_0, and the solutions for the currents I_i.

Programming Problem F-C: Calculating a Trajectory with Air Drag

Calculating the trajectory of a projectile requires that we integrate the differential equation $F = ma$. This task is ordinarily formidable, but for some simple forces the problem can be stated in a form appropriate to students just beginning their study of calculus. We first need to review some of the formulas derived in Chapter 10 for the numerical derivatives of functions.

The first derivative of a function $y(t)$ can be approximated by the central difference expression [Equation (10.45)] as

$$\frac{dy}{dx}\bigg|_{t_1} = y_1' \approx \frac{[y(t_1 + \Delta t) - y(t_1 - \Delta t)]}{2\Delta t}$$

where Δt is assumed to be very small. If we designate the equally spaced points along the t axis as t_0, $t_1 = T_0 + \Delta t$, $t_2 = t_0 + 2\Delta t$, and so on, and the values of the function at these points as $y_2 = y(t_2)$), this equation can be written more succinctly as

$$y'(t_n) \approx \frac{y_{n+1} - y_{n-1}}{2\Delta t} \tag{F.2}$$

Similarly, the central difference expression for the second derivative [Equation (10.46)] is

$$y''(t_n) \approx \frac{y_{n+1} - 2y_n + y_{n-1}}{(\Delta t)^2} \tag{F.3}$$

We will use these two equations to solve for the trajectory of a bullet shot straight up in air.

The equation of motion for an object initially shot straight up and experiencing air drag is given by Newton's second law, $F = ma$, as

$$ma = m\frac{d^2y}{dt^2} = -mg - \gamma v \tag{F.4}$$

where $v = dy/dt = y'$ is the velocity, g is the gravitational acceleration, and γ is the air-drag coefficient. The drag force is always directed opposite to the direction of the velocity. (This linear approximation for the air-drag force is a very rough first approximation to the actual force. If we needed more realistic results, a more complicated drag-force expression would be required.)

Replacing the first and second derivatives in Equation (F.4) by the approximate central difference expressions, we obtain

$$(y_{n+1} - 2y_n + y_{n-1}) = -g(\Delta t)^2 - \frac{\gamma}{2m}(y_{n+1} - y_{n-1})\Delta t \tag{F.5}$$

This is really a series of equations relating the set of unknowns, y_0, $y_1, \ldots, y_n$. This set of simultaneous equations can be solved by the Gauss–

Siedel iterative procedure. We first formally solve the equation with $n = 1$ for y_1, the equation with $n = 2$ for y_2, and so on:

$$y_0 = 0$$

$$y_1 = \frac{1}{2} g \,\Delta t^2 + \frac{1}{4} \frac{\gamma}{m} \,\Delta t(y_2 - y_0) + \frac{1}{2}(y_2 + y_0)$$

$$y_2 = \frac{1}{2} g \,\Delta t^2 + \frac{1}{4} \frac{\gamma}{m} \,\Delta t(y_3 - y_1) + \frac{1}{2}(y_3 + y_1)$$

$$\vdots$$

$$y_{n-1} = \frac{1}{2} g \,\Delta t^2 + \frac{1}{4} \frac{\gamma}{m} \,\Delta t(y_n - y_{n-2}) + \frac{1}{2}(y_n + y_{n-2})$$

$$y_n = 0 \tag{F.6}$$

Ordinarily, when computing a trajectory the starting information is the initial position (y_0) and the initial velocity (v_0). However, in this case all we are given is the value of the drag coefficient and the time of flight (T). Thus, we begin with the information that at $t = 0$, the projectile starts at $y_0 = 0$ and that after T seconds it returns to earth ($y_n = 0$). We next need to compute *all* the intervening points, y_i, for $i = 1, n - 1$. To do this we guess values for $y_1, y_2, \ldots, y_{n-1}$ and insert these values in the right side of Equation (F.6) and compute improved estimates. This process is repeated until the average change in the y values from one iteration to the next is less than some prescribed tolerance EPS.

Problem Specifics. The program to solve this problem should contain the following elements:

1. Write a subroutine GSIEDL(Y, N, T, IMAX, ITER, EPS, DRAG, FAIL) that will start with a given set of values of the Y array, the time of flight T, and the drag coefficient DRAG and successively apply Equations (F.6). The maximum number of iterations is IMAX, and the actual number is returned as ITER. If the subroutine is successful, the parameter FAIL is returned as 0. The convergence criteria should be based on the average difference in y values from one iteration to the next. The subroutine should compute a running sum of the changes and compute the following average deviation:

$$\Delta = \frac{1}{N - 1} \sum_{i=1}^{N-1} |y_i^{\text{new}} - y_i^{\text{old}}|$$

If $\Delta <$ EPS after a complete iteration, the calculation is successfully terminated.

2. Write a subroutine GUESS(Y, N, T) that will compute a reasonable first guess for the y values. Since the trajectory can be

easily determined if there is no air drag, use these values for the initial set of y values. The equation for the trajectory with zero air drag is

$$y(t) = \frac{1}{2} gt(T - t)$$

3. The main program should call the two subroutines above to compute the trajectory and, if successful,
   a. Determine the maximum height of the trajectory and the time when this point is reached.
   b. Estimate the initial velocity.
   c. Compare these values with the same quantities for zero drag.
4. Repeat the calculation with a drag force twice as large. Are the results what you expected?
5. For input parameters use DRAG = 8.E-5, m = 0.003, N = 10, T = 25 sec, IMAX = 250, and EPS = 0.1.

Least Squares Curve Fitting

13.1 Introduction

We have all done laboratory experiments that resulted in lengthy tables of data. These data were then plotted on graph paper, and from the appearance of the resulting curves we were supposed to arrive at some wise conclusions. Consider the typical freshman physics lab experiment of dropping a ball in air and measuring the distance it falls as a function of the time elapsed from the point of release. The data are collected as a set of points (t_i, y_i), where y_i is the distance the ball has fallen at the time t_i. If the data are graphed as y_i versus t_i^2, the result may be similar to that shown in Figure 13-1.

The estimated errors in t^2 are indicated by ⊢⊖⊣, and the estimated errors in the y values are indicated by ⌀. A line has been drawn through the data points and the conclusion might be, "within error, the data are consistent with the assumption that $y \propto t^2$"; that is, a straight-line fit to the data seems valid. However, numerous lines could have been drawn, all going more or less through the data. So which is the best line? There also appears to be a slight waviness to the data. Might not some function other than a straight line provide a better fit to the experimental points? Clearly the principal criterion that is being imposed when a line is sketched through the data is that both the number of points that do not fit on the line and the size of the discrepancies of those away from the line be a minimum. To be more precise, consider the set of three points and the possible straight-line fits to these points illustrated in Figure 13-2. The magnitudes of the vertical distances of the three points to line A are (d_1, d_2, d_3), and (d_1', d_2', d_3') are the vertical distances to line B. Line A would be judged a better fit since the sum $(d_1 + d_2 + d_3)$ is less than $(d_1' + d_2' +$

Figure 13-1 _____

Distance fallen as a
function of time
squared

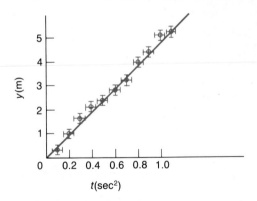

d'_3). The line of best fit would then be defined as the one that minimized the sum of the magnitudes of the deviations.[1]

   In this chapter these ideas form the basis for a popular method of optimizing the fit of a function to data, called _least squares analysis_, which is described and developed in Sections 13.2 through 13.4. The theory of least squares is next used to construct a set of equations for the coefficients of a best-fit polynomial of arbitrary degree. These equations can be written in matrix form and solved by the methods of Chapter 12. A brief discussion of the criteria used to establish the validity of fit of a function to data follows. A FORTRAN code implementing a general-purpose least squares fit of a polynomial to data is described in Section 13.7. Finally, in Section 13.10, an alternative procedure is described, called _cubic spline analysis_, which is equivalent to simply "connecting the dots."

████████████ **13.2   Principle of Least Squares Analysis**

The ideas described above for optimizing the fit of a function to data are next cast in the form of a computational algorithm. We begin with the following information:

1. We have the results of an experiment in the form of data pairs (x_i, y_i) that are to be graphed on a two-dimensional plot of y versus x.
2. We also have an idea of how the results should appear; that is, the functional dependence of y on x [namely, $y(x)$] is sug-

_____

[1] It has probably occurred to you that it would perhaps be more reasonable to use perpendicular distances, as drawn below, than vertical distances. However, such an analysis loses whatever advantages it may have in accuracy to the increased complexity of the resulting algebra.

Figure 13-2

Vertical deviations
from two lines

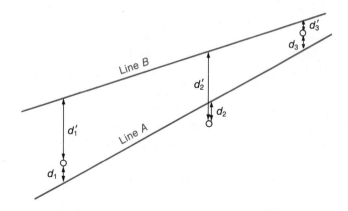

gested by some external considerations. The function that is
used to attempt a fit to the data is known as the model.

If the data points are labeled as $(x_{i,\text{exp}}, y_{i,\text{exp}})$, then the difference between the data and the model is

For the data: Given a *particular* measured value of $x_{i,\text{exp}}$, the
corresponding value of y is $y_{i,\text{exp}}$.

For the model: Given *any* x, in particular $x_{i,\text{exp}}$, the
corresponding model value of y is $y(x_{i,\text{exp}})$.

To put it concisely,

$y(x_{i,\text{exp}})$ is what the quantity *should be* (the model).

$y_{i,\text{exp}}$ is what the quantity *is* (experimental value).

It is the difference between these two values that is to be minimized. The deviation of the model from the data for the ith point is defined as

$$d_i = y(x_{i,\text{exp}}) - y_{i,\text{exp}} \tag{13.1}$$

Since the sign of d_i is not important, we next define a function E, which is
the sum of the squares of the deviations of the N data points.

$$E = \sum_{i=1}^{N} d_i^2 = \sum_{i=1}^{N} [y(x_{i,\text{exp}}) - y_{i,\text{exp}}]^2 \tag{13.2}$$

The next step is to select the model. The simplest model is to assume a linear relation between x and y.

$$y(x_{i,\text{exp}}) = a_0 + a_1 x_{i,\text{exp}} \qquad \text{linear model} \tag{13.3}$$

This expression is then inserted into Equation (13.2), and the task is then
to minimize the function

$$E = \sum_{i=1}^{N} (a_0 + a_1 x_{i,\text{exp}} - y_{i,\text{exp}})^2 \tag{13.4}$$

to obtain the best line. But minimize with respect to what? Recall that we want to vary the *line* to obtain a minimum value for E. Thus, the parameters to vary are the slope (a_1) and the intercept (a_0) of the line. In other words, E is a function of the two variables a_0 and a_1 (not x, y). Also, a function of two variables is represented by a surface in space rather than a curve.

13.3 Minimum or Maximum of a Function of Two Variables

A local minimum or maximum of a function of a single variable $f(x)$ is a point on the curve of f versus x at which the tangent line has zero slope. To determine the point of extremum (minimum or maximum), we simply find a value of x such that $df/dx = 0$ (see Figure 13-3).

To find the extremum of a function of two variables $F(x, y)$, we must find a point on the surface where the slopes of *all* possible tangent lines drawn at that point have zero slope. In other words, the tangent plane at the point of an extremum must be parallel to the xy plane (see Figure 13-4).

The problem is how to determine the point on the surface that has a horizontal tangent plane. One way to proceed is to consider just one variable at a time. For a fixed value of y, say $y = y_c = $ constant, $F(x, y_c)$ is then a function of a single variable x and is represented in Figure 13-4 by the dashed curve resulting from the cut through the surface by the plane $y = y_c$. The slope of the tangent *line* to the dashed curve is then $dF(x, y_c)/dx$, and the extremum on this curve is obtained by finding a value of x such that

$$\frac{dF(x, y_c)}{dx} = 0$$

Figure 13-3
Local extremum of a function of a single variable

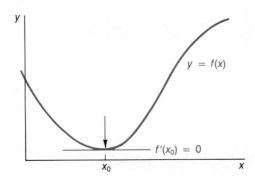

Figure 13-4
Surface $z = F(x, y)$
is cut by the plane
$y = y_c$

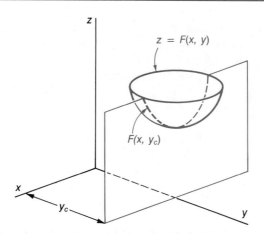

Notice that this equation is an equation in one variable x and the constant y_c. If we choose a different value y_c, a different dashed curve results and a different value for the extremum will be obtained.

We next introduce a new type of derivative, the *partial derivative*

$$\frac{\partial F(x, y)}{\partial x} = \begin{array}{l} \text{The ordinary derivative of } F(x,y) \text{ with} \\ \text{respect to } x, \text{ but } y \text{ is treated} \\ \text{as if it were just another constant.} \end{array}$$

Thus, if $F(x, y) = 3x^2y + y^3$, then

$$\frac{\partial F}{\partial x} = 6xy \qquad \frac{\partial F}{\partial y} = 3x^2 + 3y^2$$

Using this definition we can then express the condition that the slopes of tangent lines in both the x and y directions be simultaneously zero as

$$\frac{\partial F(x, y)}{\partial x} = 0 \qquad \text{Zero slope in the } x \text{ direction for a given } y$$

$$\frac{\partial F(x, y)}{\partial y} = 0 \qquad \text{Zero slope in the } y \text{ direction for a given } x$$

Since the slopes in both the x and y directions are zero, the slope of any combination of these two directions is also zero, and thus these conditions determine the point of a horizontal tangent plane. Solving both of these equations simultaneously for the unknowns x and y will determine the minimum or maximum point of a function of two variables.[2]

---

[2] It is also possible that the equations will specify a "saddle point," that is, a maximum along the x direction and a minimum along the y direction, or vice versa. This possibility is ordinarily rather remote in physical problems and will be ignored.

13.4   Minimization of the Sum of the Squared Deviations

The sum of the squares of the deviations of the data points from a straight line is given in Equation (13.4). The function E is a function of the two variables a_1, the slope of the line, and a_0, the intercept. To determine the minimum of $E(a_0, a_1)$, the two equations

$$\frac{\partial E(a_0, a_1)}{\partial a_0} = 0 \qquad \frac{\partial E(a_0, a_1)}{\partial a_1} = 0$$

must be solved simultaneously for the values a_0, a_1.

To apply the first of these equations to the function of Equation (13.4),

$$E(a_0, a_1) = \sum_{i=1}^{N} (a_0 + a_1 x_{i,\exp} - y_{i,\exp})^2$$

we will need the following properties of the derivative:

1. $\dfrac{d}{dx} \Sigma(\ ) = \Sigma \dfrac{d}{dx}(\ )$

2. $\dfrac{d}{dx}(\ )^2 = 2(\ )\dfrac{d}{dx}(\ )$

3. $\dfrac{\partial}{\partial a_0}(a_0) = 1$

4. $\dfrac{\partial}{\partial a_1}(a_1 x_{i,\exp}) = x_{i,\exp}$

We thus obtain

$$\frac{\partial E(a_0, a_1)}{\partial a_0} = \sum_{i=1}^{N} \frac{\partial}{\partial a_0}(a_0 + a_1 x_{i,\exp} - y_{i,\exp})^2$$

$$= 2 \sum_{i=1}^{N} (a_0 + a_1 x_{i,\exp} - y_{i,\exp}) \frac{\partial a_0}{\partial a_0} = 0 \qquad (13.5)$$

Next, Equation (13.5) is simplified by using the following definitions:

$$\sum_{i=1}^{N} a_0 = \underbrace{(a_0 + a_0 + \cdots + a_0)}_{N \text{ terms}} = Na_0 \qquad (13.6)$$

$$\sum_{i=1}^{N} a_1 x_{i,\exp} = a_1 \sum_{i=1}^{N} x_{i,\exp} \equiv a_1 \Sigma x \qquad (13.7)$$

$$\sum_{i=1}^{N} y_{i,\exp} \equiv \Sigma y \qquad (13.8)$$

Thus, the first condition for the minimum may be written as

$$(N)a_0 + (\Sigma x)a_1 = \Sigma y \qquad (13.9)$$

The second condition for minimum of $E(a_0, a_1)$ is handled in similar manner:

$$\frac{\partial E(a_0, a_1)}{\partial a_1} = \sum_{i=1}^{N} \frac{\partial}{\partial a_1} (a_0 + a_1 x_{i,\text{exp}} - y_{i,\text{exp}})^2$$

$$= 2 \sum_{i=1}^{N} (a_0 + a_1 x_{i,\text{exp}} - y_{i,\text{exp}}) \frac{\partial(a_1 x_{i,\text{exp}})}{\partial a_1}$$

$$= 2 \sum_{i=1}^{N} [a_0 x_{i,\text{exp}} + a_1 (x_{i,\text{exp}})^2 - x_{i,\text{exp}} y_{i,\text{exp}}] = 0 \qquad (13.10)$$

This equation may be written more concisely as

$$(\Sigma x) a_0 + (\Sigma x^2) a_1 = \Sigma xy \qquad (13.11)$$

where the following definitions have been used:

$$\sum_{i=1}^{N} (x_{i,\text{exp}})^2 \equiv \Sigma x^2 \qquad (13.12)$$

$$\sum_{i=1}^{N} (x_{i,\text{exp}})(y_{i,\text{exp}}) = \Sigma xy \qquad (13.13)$$

The two simultaneous equations, Equations (13.9) and (13.11), are linear in the unknowns a_0 and a_1 and can be written in matrix form as

$$\begin{array}{ccc} [A] & \mathbf{a} = & \mathbf{c} \end{array}$$

$$\begin{bmatrix} N & \Sigma x \\ \Sigma x & \Sigma x^2 \end{bmatrix} \begin{bmatrix} a_0 \\ a_1 \end{bmatrix} = \begin{bmatrix} \Sigma y \\ \Sigma xy \end{bmatrix} \qquad (13.14)$$

This matrix equation can be solved using the Gauss–Jordan method of Chapter 12. The solution will yield the values for the coefficients a_0 and a_1, which then specify the least squares best-fit line.

$$y(x) = a_0 + a_1 x$$

However, since the problem involves only two equations in two unknowns, using the general procedures of Chapter 12 would be overkill. The equations are more conveniently solved by hand. When solving these two equations by hand, it is common to rewrite the problem and its solution in terms of average values of the data elements defined in the following way:

$$\langle x \rangle = \text{Average of } x\text{'s} = \frac{\Sigma x}{N}$$

$$\langle y \rangle = \frac{\Sigma y}{N}$$

$$\langle xy \rangle = \frac{\Sigma xy}{N}$$

$$\langle x^2 \rangle = \frac{\Sigma x^2}{N} \qquad (13.15)$$

Also define

$$D_{xx} = \langle x^2 \rangle - \langle x \rangle \langle x \rangle \qquad (13.16)$$

$$D_{xy} = \langle xy \rangle - \langle x \rangle \langle y \rangle \qquad (13.17)$$

The solution of Equation (13.14) by Cramer's rule yields

$$a_1 = \text{slope} = \frac{D_{xy}}{D_{xx}} \qquad (13.18)$$

$$a_0 = \text{intercept} = \langle y \rangle - a_1 \langle x \rangle \qquad (13.19)$$

■ Example of Least Squares Best-Fit Line

The data listed in Table 13-1 are used to compute the line that minimizes the squares of the deviations from the line. From these data we first compute the following quantities:

$$\Sigma x = 45.4 \qquad \qquad \Sigma y = 103.8$$
$$\Sigma x^2 = 370.4 \qquad \qquad \Sigma xy = 819.4$$
$$\langle x \rangle = 4.54 \qquad \qquad \langle y \rangle = 10.38$$
$$\langle x^2 \rangle = 37.04 \qquad \qquad \langle xy \rangle = 81.94$$
$$D_{xx} = 16.43 \qquad \qquad D_{xy} = 34.81$$
$$a_1 = \text{slope} = 2.119 \qquad a_0 = \text{intercept} = 0.7598$$

The best-fit line is then

$$y(x) = 0.7598 + 2.119x$$

and the model prediction for $x = 13.0$ (the last experimental x value) is $y(13.0) = 28.31$ compared with the actual experimental value of 29.0.

■ Least Squares Fit of an Exponential Function

Frequently a theory will suggest a model other than a straight line as the best interpretation of the data. A common functional form for the model is the exponential function.

$$F(t) = \alpha e^{\beta t} \qquad (13.20)$$

In this equation the dependent variable is F and the independent variable is t. If this expression for the model is inserted into Equation (13.4) and the

Table 13-1
Data used in a linear least squares fit

i	1	2	3	4	5	6	7	8	9	10
$x_{i,\text{exp}}$	−0.3	0.4	1.1	1.4	3.3	5.0	5.2	7.1	9.2	13.0
$y_{i,\text{exp}}$	0.2	2.0	3.1	4.0	7.0	11.0	13.0	14.5	20.0	29.0

derivatives with respect to the two parameters α and β are set equal to zero, the resulting equations are

$$\frac{\partial E(\alpha, \beta)}{\partial \alpha} = 2 \sum_{i=1}^{N} e^{\beta t_i}(\alpha e^{\beta t_i} - F_i) = 0 \tag{13.21}$$

$$\frac{\partial E(\alpha, \beta)}{\partial \beta} = 2\alpha \sum_{i=1}^{N} t_i e^{\beta t_i}(\alpha e^{\beta t_i} - F_i) = 0 \tag{13.22}$$

These are two equations in two unknowns but they are *nonlinear* equations in the variables α and β and therefore cannot be written in matrix form. The procedures of Chapter 12 are thus of no help in solving the equations. Nonlinear problems are almost always extremely difficult to solve.

A different approach is to attempt a change of variables to a model that is *linear* in the new parameters. In the present instance the specific form of the appropriate change of variables becomes apparent if we take the natural logarithm of Equation (13.20).

$$\ln(F) = \ln(\alpha e^{\beta t})$$

$$= \ln(\alpha) + \ln(e^{\beta t})$$

$$= \ln(\alpha) + \beta t \tag{13.23}$$

We next introduce two variables (X, Y) in place of (t, F) and two parameters (a_0, a_1) in place of (α, β) defined by the relations

$$X = t \qquad Y = \ln(F) \tag{13.24}$$

$$a_0 = \ln(\alpha) \qquad a_1 = \beta \tag{13.25}$$

In terms of these variables, Equation (13.23) becomes

$$Y(X) = a_0 + a_1 X \tag{13.26}$$

and the ordinary linear least squares analysis may then be applied to the problem.

In summary, if an exponential model, $F(t) = \alpha e^{\beta t}$, is to be used to interpret the set of data points (t_i, F_i), the data set is first replaced by the data set (X_i, Y_i), where the relation between (t, F) and (X, Y) is given in Equations (13.24). Next, the ordinary linear least squares analysis is applied to the set (X_i, Y_i), and the parameters a_0 and a_1 are computed. Finally, the original parameters, α, β, are calculated from the known values of a_0, a_1 by using Equations (13.25). Specifically,

$$\alpha = e^{a_0} \qquad \beta = a_1 \tag{13.27}$$

The result of this analysis is a set of parameters that minimizes the squared deviations of $\ln(F)$ from $\ln(\text{data})$. This method of linearization of the exponential model function is ordinarily a satisfactory approximation to the more difficult problem of minimizing the squared deviations of F directly. Several problems of this type are included in the Problems section at the end of the chapter.

◼◼◼◼◼◼ **13.5   Least Squares Fit of a Polynomial**

Next consider the problem of fitting a parabola to a data set by means of the least squares approach. In this case the model is a general quadratic of the form

$$y(x) = a_0 + a_1 x + a_2 x^2 \qquad (13.28)$$

Inserting this function into the expression for the sum of the squared deviations, Equation (13.2), yields

$$E(a_0, a_1, a_2) = \sum_{i=1}^{N} [a_0 + a_1 x_{i,\exp} + a_2 (x_{i,\exp})^2 - y_{i,\exp}]^2 \qquad (13.29)$$

Notice that E is now a function of three variables, a_0, a_1, and a_2, and the minimization criterion is then the set of equations

$$\frac{\partial E}{\partial a_0} = 0 \qquad \frac{\partial E}{\partial a_1} = 0 \qquad \frac{\partial E}{\partial a_2} = 0 \qquad (13.30)$$

Evaluating these three derivatives, setting them equal to zero, and simplifying the equations yields the following set of three equations:

$$N a_0 + (\Sigma x) a_1 + (\Sigma x^2) a_2 = \Sigma y$$
$$(\Sigma x) a_0 + (\Sigma x^2) a_1 + (\Sigma x^3) a_2 = \Sigma xy$$
$$(\Sigma x^2) a_0 + (\Sigma x^3) a_1 + (\Sigma x^4) a_2 = \Sigma x^2 y$$

which can be written in matrix form as

$$\begin{bmatrix} N & \Sigma x & \Sigma x^2 \\ \Sigma x & \Sigma x^2 & \Sigma x^3 \\ \Sigma x^2 & \Sigma x^3 & \Sigma x^4 \end{bmatrix} \begin{bmatrix} a_0 \\ a_1 \\ a_2 \end{bmatrix} = \begin{bmatrix} \Sigma y \\ \Sigma xy \\ \Sigma x^2 y \end{bmatrix} \qquad (13.31)$$

The coefficients of the parabola are calculated using the techniques of Chapter 12, once all of the sums that appear in the coefficient matrix and the right-hand-side vector have been evaluated. Again, each of the sums involves only experimental quantities and all are from $i = 1$ to $i = N$.

The least squares procedure can easily be generalized to handle the problem of fitting a polynomial of degree n to the data. Thus, if the model function is

$$y(x) = a_0 + a_1 x + a_2 x^2 + \cdots + a_n x^n = \sum_{i=0}^{n} a_i x^i \qquad (13.32)$$

the coefficients of the polynomial are determined by solving the matrix equation

$$
\begin{bmatrix}
N & \Sigma x & \Sigma x^2 & \cdots & \Sigma x^n \\
\Sigma x & \Sigma x^2 & \Sigma x^3 & \cdots & \Sigma x^{n+1} \\
\Sigma x^2 & \Sigma x^3 & \Sigma x^4 & \cdots & \Sigma x^{n+2} \\
\vdots & \vdots & \vdots & \vdots & \vdots \\
\Sigma x^n & \Sigma x^{n+1} & \Sigma x^{n+2} & \cdots & \Sigma x^{2n}
\end{bmatrix}
\begin{bmatrix}
a_0 \\ a_1 \\ a_2 \\ \vdots \\ a_n
\end{bmatrix}
=
\begin{bmatrix}
\Sigma y \\ \Sigma xy \\ \Sigma x^2 y \\ \vdots \\ \Sigma x^n y
\end{bmatrix}
\tag{13.33}
$$

■ Example of a Polynomial Least Squares Fit to Data

The data listed in Table 13-2 will be used to obtain first a linear least squares fit. The best-fit parabola to the data will then be calculated. For the linear fit ($n = 1$), Equation (13.3) becomes

$$
\begin{bmatrix} N & \Sigma x \\ \Sigma x & \Sigma x^2 \end{bmatrix}
\begin{bmatrix} a_0 \\ a_1 \end{bmatrix}
=
\begin{bmatrix} \Sigma y \\ \Sigma xy \end{bmatrix}
$$

$$
\begin{bmatrix} 9 & 18 \\ 18 & 51 \end{bmatrix}
\begin{bmatrix} a_0 \\ a_1 \end{bmatrix}
=
\begin{bmatrix} 208.6 \\ 565.45 \end{bmatrix}
$$

Solving this matrix equation yields

$$
\begin{bmatrix} a_0 \\ a_1 \end{bmatrix}
=
\begin{bmatrix} 3.411 \\ 9.883 \end{bmatrix}
$$

Thus, the best-fit line to the data is

$$
y(x) = 3.411 + 9.883x
$$

To fit a parabola to the data we again use Equation (13.33) with $n = 2$.

$$
\begin{bmatrix}
N & \Sigma x & \Sigma x^2 \\
\Sigma x & \Sigma x^2 & \Sigma x^3 \\
\Sigma x^2 & \Sigma x^3 & \Sigma x^4
\end{bmatrix}
\begin{bmatrix} a_0 \\ a_1 \\ a_2 \end{bmatrix}
=
\begin{bmatrix} \Sigma y \\ \Sigma xy \\ \Sigma x^2 y \end{bmatrix}
$$

$$
\begin{bmatrix}
9 & 18 & 51 \\
18 & 51 & 162 \\
51 & 162 & 548.25
\end{bmatrix}
\begin{bmatrix} a_0 \\ a_1 \\ a_2 \end{bmatrix}
=
\begin{bmatrix} 208.6 \\ 565.45 \\ 1790.82 \end{bmatrix}
$$

Table 13-2
Data used in a linear and a quadratic least squares fit

i	1	2	3	4	5	6	7	8	9
$x_{i,\exp}$	0.0	0.5	1.0	1.5	2.0	2.5	3.0	3.5	4.0
$y_{i,\exp}$	4.90	8.50	14.2	17.0	22.0	26.0	32.0	39.0	45.0

The solution for a_0, a_1, a_2 is obtained by either the Gauss–Jordan method or Cramer's rule and yields

$$\begin{bmatrix} a_0 \\ a_1 \\ a_2 \end{bmatrix} = \begin{bmatrix} 5.321 \\ 6.609 \\ 0.819 \end{bmatrix}$$

The best-fit parabola is then

$$y(x) = 5.321 + 6.609x + 0.819x^2$$

The least squares best-fit line and parabola are compared with the data in Figure 13-5. From the figure it appears that the parabolic fit is slightly better. If the calculation were continued, you would find that the fit of a cubic function to the data would be better still and an eighth-degree polynomial would fit the data exactly. The reason for this is that the eighth-degree polynomial contains nine unknown parameters $(a_1, i = 0,8)$, which are determined by using the nine data points. This is analogous to nine equations in nine unknowns, and the parameters can be uniquely determined without resorting to a least squares procedure.[3]

So it would seem that the best procedure is to fit N data points with a polynomial of degree $n = N - 1$. The resulting least squares fit would be exact, but in what sense would it be a valid interpretation of the

Figure 13-5

Comparison of a best-fit line and parabola with the data

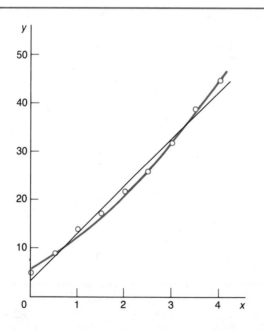

[3] See also the discussion of the Lagrange interpolation polynomial in Section 10.4.

data? The answer to this question is usually found deep in advanced statistics courses. However, it is important that we have at least a cursory understanding of this situation if we are to draw any conclusions from the results of a least squares fit of a polynomial to experimental data.

13.6 Validity of Fit

To decide whether a least squares straight line is an adequate fit to the data, some information about the experimental errors in the data is required. Experimental errors are often indicated on a graph by error bars, $\mathbb{I}$, or by following the data item by the magnitude of the estimated error preceded by a ± sign. Thus, the experimental value of y could be represented as 17.32 ± 0.07, indicating that the actual value of y could be anywhere in the range 17.25 to 17.39. In the discussion that follows, it is assumed that the errors are in the dependent variable (y) only and that the independent variable (x) values are exact.

Let's begin with a few commonsense ideas regarding validity of fit and error bars. In Figure 13-6 three possible curve fits to the data have been drawn. Clearly the line is a poor fit to the data, whereas the parabola appears to be an adequate fit; that is, within error, the parabola roughly goes through all the data points. The third curve, which exactly fits the data, is certainly not justified by the data. We cannot assume that the actual values of y are at the center of the error bars. Any value of y within the range of the error bar is just as acceptable as another. Forcing the model function to fit the y values exactly has introduced numerous wiggles in the curve that are unlikely to be representative of the actual physical phenomena. The third curve thus *overfits* the data.

Figure 13-6
Three possible
curve fits to
experimental data

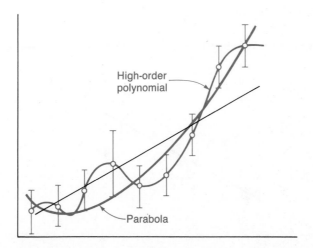

Another common situation, especially in introductory laboratory courses, is for students to overestimate the size of the experimental error in order to ensure that the data, within error, fall on a straight line. Thus, an instructor presented with the results in Figure 13-7 would immediately conclude that the indicated error bars are wrong. The instructor expects to see scatter of the data about the straight line; and the size of the scatter should be approximately the same as the size of the error. Since the data are very nearly linear, the actual experimental error is probably quite small.

The essential idea then in determining whether a particular functional fit to the data is poor, adequate, or an overfit is to compare the deviations of the curve from the actual data with the size of the experimental error. The deviations of the data from the curve (i.e., the scatter) are expected to be the same order of magnitude as the experimental error.

We next define a quantity called χ^2 (chi-squared) by the equation

$$\chi^2 = \sum_{i=1}^{N} \frac{[y(x_{i,\exp}) - y_{i,\exp}]^2}{(\Delta y_{i,\exp})^2} \tag{13.34}$$

where $y(x_{i,\exp})$ is the best-fit model function evaluated at the experimental value of $x = x_{i,\exp}$, then $y_{i,\exp}$ is the measured value of y, and $\Delta y_{i,\exp}$ is the magnitude of the error in the value of $y_{i,\exp}$. The sum is over all N data points. Since each term in the sum is expected to be of order 1, the computed value of χ^2 should be of order N. Thus, if χ^2 is much greater than N, the deviations from the curve are larger than predicted by the error bars and the curve is therefore judged to be a poor fit. If χ^2 is much less than N, indicating deviations much smaller than the anticipated scatter, the curve is possibly an overfit (or the errors are wrong).

A goal of statistics courses is to restate the above much more precisely and to define what is meant by "much greater than" and "much less than." For our purposes these ideas require only a slight refinement.

First consider the situation of fitting a line to only two data points. Since two points uniquely determine a line, the deviations are then

Figure 13-7
Example of
erroneously large
error bars

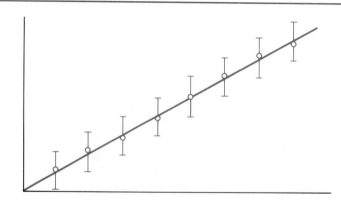

zero and $\chi^2 = 0$, not 2. Similarly, three points determine a parabola, four a cubic, and so on. It would thus appear that the hypothesis that $\chi^2 \simeq N$ should be amended to $\chi^2 \simeq N - g$, where g is the number of parameters in the model function. To summarize, if

$$\chi^2 \begin{cases} \gg (N - g) \to \text{Poor fit} \\ \sim (N - g) \to \text{Adequate fit} \\ \ll (N - g) \to \text{Overfit} \end{cases}$$

13.7 FORTRAN Code for a Polynomial Least Squares Curve Fit

The code to fit a polynomial of degree n to a set of data points must first assemble the square coefficient matrix and the right-hand-side vector given in Equation (13.33). The solution for the coefficients of the polynomial is then obtained by the standard Gauss–Jordan techniques of Chapter 12. Because least squares curve fitting is often but a single part of a larger analysis of the data, the FORTRAN code in Figure 13-8 is written in the form of a subroutine.

In the subroutine the N experimental data pairs are assumed to be stored in the arrays X,Y. The degree of the polynomial that is fit to the data is NP. Thus, NP = 1 is a linear fit, NP = 2 is a parabola, and so on. The number of parameters to be determined in the fitting polynomial is NP + 1. The coefficient matrix of Equation (13.33) is a square matrix of size $(NP + 1)$ by $(NP + 1)$ of the form

$$\begin{bmatrix} N & d_1 & d_2 & \cdots & \cdots & d_{NP} \\ d_1 & d_2 & d_3 & \cdots & \cdots & d_{NP+1} \\ d_2 & d_3 & d_4 & \cdots & \cdots & d_{NP+2} \\ \vdots & \vdots & \vdots & \vdots & \vdots & \vdots \\ d_{NP} & d_{NP+1} & d_{NP+2} & \cdots & d_{2NP-1} & d_{2NP} \end{bmatrix}$$

where

$$d_k = \sum_{i=1}^{N} (x_{i,\text{exp}})^k \tag{13.35}$$

The right-hand-side vector is of the form

$$\mathbf{b} = \begin{bmatrix} b_1 \\ b_2 \\ \vdots \\ b_{NP} \end{bmatrix}$$

Figure 13-8

FORTRAN code for a least squares polynomial fit to data

```
         SUBROUTINE LSTSQR(X,Y,NDATA,A,NP,ICHI,DY)
*--
* The arrays x(), y() are input to the subroutine and contain the
* experimental data.  The array a() is the primary output and con-
* tains the coefficients of the best-fit polynomial of degree NP.
* The number of data points is NDATA.  The least squares best-fit
* polynomial is of the form
*
*        y(x) = a(0) + a(1)x + a(2)x^2 + ... + a(np)x^(np)
*
* and is written as a separate subfunction.
*
* Also, if ICHI = 1, a value of chi-squared is computed and is
* printed.  To compute chi-squared, the experimental errors for
* each of the y values are required and are supplied in the array
* dy().  If all of the errors are the same and equal to, say, Z,
* simply assign dy(0) = -Z.  The subroutine will then use the
* value +Z for all errors.
*
* The subroutine requires a separate matrix-inverting subroutine.
* The routine MINV of Chapter 12 is used here.  The highest-degree
* polynomial that can be handled is NP = 10.
*
* The coefficient matrix is of the form
*
*   | Ndata    d(1)    d(2)    d(3)    ...     ...    d(np)   |
*   |                                                        |
*   |  d(1)    d(2)    d(3)    d(2)    ...     ...   d(np-1)  |
*   |                                                        |
*   |  d(2)    d(3)    d(4)    d(5)    ...     ...   d(np-2)  |
*   |    .       .       .       .       .       .      .    |
*   |    .       .       .       .       .       .      .    |
*   |    .       .       .       .       .       .      .    |
*   |  d(np)  d(np+1) d(np+2)   ...     ...     ...   d(2np)  |
*
*   where d(n) = Sum[x(i)^n]
*-------------------------------------------------------------------
* Variables
*
         INTEGER NDATA,NP,FAIL
         REAL X(NDATA),Y(NDATA),AC(11,11),AINV(11,11),B(11),CHI2,
     +        D(20),DET,DY(NDATA)A(0:NP)
*
* X(),Y() -- Experimental data                    [INPUT]
* DY()    -- Expemental errors in y values.       [INPUT]
* NDATA   -- Number of data points                [INPUT]
* NP      -- Degree of polynomial fit             [INPUT]
* AC()    -- Coefficient matrix (See above.)
* AINV()  -- Inverse of AC
* B()     -- Right-hand-side vector of the form SUM[x(i)^n * y]
* D()     -- Elements of AC (see above)
* DET     -- Determinant of AC
* CHI2    -- Chi-squared coefficient of fit
*            (For adequate fit CHI2 = NDATA - NP - 1)
* FAIL    -- Success/failure flag.  If 0, success, if 1, failure
*-------------------------------------------------------------------
```

Figure 13-8
(continued)

```
*  Initialization
*
*      First compute the elements of the d() array
*
       FAIL = 0
       DO 2 K = 1,2*NP
           D(K) = 0.0
           DO 1 I = 1,NDATA
               D(K) = D(K) + X(I)**K
   1       CONTINUE
   2   CONTINUE
*
*      Next, assign values to the elements of the coefficient
*      matrix, noting AC(row,col) = d(row + col -2)
*
       AC(1,1) = NDATA
       DO 3 I = 1,NP+1
       DO 3 J = 1,NP+1
           K = I + J - 2
           IF(K .NE. 0)THEN
               AC(I,J) = D(K)
           ENDIF
   3   CONTINUE
*
*      The right-hand-side vector is of the form SUM[x(i)^n*y]
*
       DO 5 K = 1,NP+1
           B(K) = 0.
           DO 4 I = 1,NDATA
               IF(K .EQ. 1)THEN
                   TERM = Y(I)
               ELSE
                   TERM = Y(I)*X(I)**(K-1)
               ENDIF
               B(K) = B(K) + TERM
   4       CONTINUE
   5   CONTINUE
*----------------------------------------------------------------
*  Computation
*
*      Solve the matrix equation by finding the inverse
*
       CALL MINV(AC,AINV,11,NP+1,DET)
*
*      If the determinant is zero - routine FAILS, singular matrix.
*      If very small, print a warning, ill-conditioned matrix.
*
       IF(DET .EQ. 0.0)THEN
           FAIL = 1
           WRITE(*,10)DET
           PAUSE 'FATAL ERROR in LSTSQR - singular matrix'
           RETURN
       ELSE IF(ABS(DET) .LT. 1.E-6)THEN
           WRITE(*,11)
       ENDIF
*
*      The coefficients of the best-fit polynomial are A() = AINV*B
*
```

Figure 13-8 _____
(concluded)

```
                  DO 7 I = 1, NP+1
                     A(I-1) = 0.0
                     DO 6 J = 1, NP+1
                        A(I-1) = A(I-1) + AINV(I,J)*B(J)
      6              CONTINUE
      7           CONTINUE
      *
      *           Compute chi-squared if required
      *
                  IF(ICHI .EQ. 1)THEN
                     IF(DY(1) .LT. 0.)THEN
                        E = -DY(1)
                        DO 8 I = 1,NDATA
                           DY(I) = E
      8                 CONTINUE
                     ENDIF
      *
      *              The theoretical value of y is given by the best-fit
      *              polynomial, which is separately coded as YTHEO
      *
                     CHI2 = 0.0
                     DO 9 I = 1,NDATA
                        CHI2 = CHI2 + (YTHEO(X(I),NP-1,A)-Y(I))**2/DY(I)**2
      9              CONTINUE
                     WRITE(*,12)CHI2,NDATA-NP-1
                  ENDIF
                  RETURN
      *-----------------------------------------------------------
      * Formats
      *
      10  FORMAT(/,
        +  T5,'*===========ERROR IN LSTSQR===============*',/,
        +  T5,'|    The coefficient matrix is SINGULAR    |',/,
        +  T5,'| Computation fails -- program terminated. |',/,
        +  T5,'*=========================================*')
      *
      11  FORMAT(/,

        +  T5,'*========WARNING FROM LSTSQR===============*',/,
        +  T5,'| The coefficient matrix is ill-conditioned|',/,
        +  T5,'| The determinant = ',E9.2,T49,'|',/,
        +  T5,'*========Program continues================*')
      *
      12  FORMAT(/,T5,'The computed chi-squared is ',F10.5,' whereas',
        +       /,T5,'an adequate fit should have   ',I3,/)
                  END
```

where

$$b_k = \sum_{i=1}^{N} (y_{i,\exp})(x_{i,\exp})^{k-1} \tag{13.36}$$

The first task of the subroutine is then to construct the elements of the arrays $D(K), B(K)$. The elements of the matrix $[A]$ are then expressed in terms of array D by noting that the matrix elements along the diagonals are all identical. Thus, $A_{14} = A_{23} = A_{32} = A_{41} = D(3)$, or, in general,

$$A_{ij} = D(i + j - 2) \qquad \text{and} \qquad A_{11} = N$$

The polynomial that is constructed from the coefficients returned by the subroutine is given in Figure 13-9.

13.8 Example of a Least Squares Polynomial Fit

As an example of curve fitting to experimental data, consider the following freshman laboratory experiment. The experiment consists of measuring the cooling curve of an initially hot shiny copper cylinder—that is, measuring temperature versus time. The hypothesis is that the graph of $(T - T_0)$ versus time should be approximately exponential, where T_0 is the known room temperature. The independent variable is t (time in minutes). The model function is thus

$$[T(t) - T_0] = \alpha e^{\beta t} \tag{13.37}$$

As was done in Section 13.4, to apply a *linear* least squares analysis we must change variables by defining

$$y_{i,exp} = \ln(T_i - T_0) \qquad x_{i,exp} = t_i$$
$$a_0 = \ln(\alpha) \qquad\qquad a_1 = \beta \tag{13.38}$$

Taking the logarithm of Equation (13.37), the hypothesis now reads

$$y_{i,exp} = a_0 + a_1 x_{i,exp}$$

Computing the coefficients a_0, a_1, then, is equivalent to fitting a straight line to $\ln(T - T_0)$. This process will be extended to next successively fitting a parabola, a cubic, and so on to $\ln(T - T_0)$.

To determine which polynomial fit is most appropriate to the data, we require information on the magnitude of the errors for each

Figure 13-9
FORTRAN code for
the best-fit
polynomial

```
        FUNCTION YTHEO(Z,N,C)
*
*   YTHEO is the theory or model fit to the data.  It is in the
*   form of a polynomial in z of degree n.  The coefficients of
*   the polynomial, c(i), are computed by the subroutine LSTSQR.
*-------------------------------------------------------------------
        REAL C(0:N),Z,SUM
        SUM = C(0)
        DO 1 I = 1,N
            SUM = SUM + C(I)*Z**I
    1   CONTINUE
        YTHEO = SUM
        RETURN
        END
```

value of $y_{i,\,exp}$. It is known that the experimental error in each of the temperature measurements is approximately $\Delta T \simeq 0.8°$ C. The errors in the corresponding values of y are determined by

$$y \pm \Delta y = \ln(T \pm \Delta T)$$

$$= \ln\left[T\left(1 \pm \frac{\Delta T}{T}\right)\right]$$

$$= [\ln(T)] + \left[\ln\left(1 \pm \frac{\Delta T}{T}\right)\right] \tag{13.39}$$

Thus,

$$\pm\Delta y = \ln\left(1 \pm \frac{\Delta T}{T}\right) \tag{13.40}$$

But $\Delta T/T$ is much less than 1, and so Equation (13.40) may be approximated by

$$\pm\Delta y = \ln\left(1 \pm \frac{\Delta T}{T}\right)$$

$$\simeq \pm\frac{\Delta T}{T} \tag{13.41}$$

(see also Equation 10.27). Thus,

$$\Delta y = \frac{\Delta T}{T} = \frac{0.8}{T}$$

The experimental data are listed in Table 13-3. The results of a series of polynomial fits

$$y_{model} = a_0 + a_1x + a_2x^2 + \cdots + a_nx^n$$

are given in Table 13-4 where χ^2 is also computed for each polynomial fit. From the values of χ^2 we would infer that the quadratic fit is the most appropriate.

13.9 Limitations of the Least Squares Procedure

The Least Squares Problem May Be Ill-Conditioned

The underlying premise of a least squares fit to experimental data is that the data can be summarized by a relatively smooth model function that is linear in the parameters; that is, a polynomial of modest degree. With large computers available, it is tempting to fit polynomials of higher and higher degree to improve the fit. Such an exercise is risky. Not only will a polynomial of high degree induce spurious wiggles in the curve if forced through the data, but the least squares analysis also becomes ill-conditioned for large n, the degree of the model polynomial, resulting in rapidly

Table 13-3
Experimental
cooling-curve data

i	t_i (min)	$(T_i - T_0)$ (°C)	$y_{t,exp}$ $[\ln(T_i - T_0)]$
1	0.01	178.0	5.182
2	1.0	173.4	5.156
3	2.0	169.4	5.132
4	3.0	165.0	5.106
5	4.0	160.8	5.080
6	5.0	157.0	5.056
7	6.0	153.3	5.032
8	7.0	149.9	5.010
9	8.0	146.0	4.984
10	9.0	142.8	4.961
11	10.0	139.7	4.939
12	11.0	135.8	4.911
13	12.0	133.0	4.890
14	13.0	130.6	4.872
15	14.0	127.6	4.849
16	15.0	124.1	4.821
17	16.0	121.2	4.797
18	17.0	118.3	4.773
19	18.0	115.5	4.749
20	23.0	105.5	4.659
21	28.0	94.8	4.552
22	33.0	85.0	4.443
23	38.0	76.4	4.336
24	48.0	61.1	4.113
25	53.0	55.2	4.011
26	58.0	50.0	3.912
27	63.0	45.2	3.811

Table 13-4
Results of a succession of polynomial fits to the cooling-curve data (number of parameters in the model function is g)

g	$N - g$	χ^2	a_0	a_1	a_2	a_3	a_4	a_5
2	25	94.9	5.15949	−0.21685				
3	24	24.5	5.17295	−0.23464	0.00300			
4	23	10.5	5.17913	−0.24953	0.00996	−0.00079		
5	22	7.8	5.18490	−0.27318	0.03008	−0.00621	0.00045	
6	21	6.2	5.18298	−0.26124	0.01472	0.00085	−0.00087	0.00009

escalating round-off errors. The instability of the least squares method for large n can be seen as follows.

The elements of the coefficient matrix in Equation (13.33) are of the form Σx^k, where $k = 1, \ldots, 2n$. To obtain a rough estimate of these terms, we assume that the Nx values are equally spaced between 0 and 1. Then if N is large, $dx \approx 1/N$ or

$$\Sigma x_i^k \approx \int_0^1 x^k (N\,dx) = N\frac{x^{k+1}}{k+1}\bigg|_0^1 = \frac{N}{k+1} \tag{13.42}$$

Thus, the matrix in Equation (13.33) is approximately

$$[A] = \begin{bmatrix} N & \dfrac{N}{2} & \dfrac{N}{3} & \cdots & \dfrac{N}{n+1} \\[2mm] \dfrac{N}{2} & \dfrac{N}{3} & \dfrac{N}{4} & \cdots & \dfrac{N}{n+2} \\[2mm] \dfrac{N}{3} & \dfrac{N}{4} & \dfrac{N}{5} & \cdots & \dfrac{N}{n+3} \\[2mm] \vdots & \vdots & \vdots & \vdots & \vdots \\[2mm] \dfrac{N}{n+1} & \dfrac{N}{n+2} & \dfrac{N}{n+3} & \cdots & \dfrac{N}{2n+1} \end{bmatrix}$$

and the determinant of $[A]$ is

$$|A| = N^{n+1} \begin{vmatrix} 1 & \dfrac{1}{2} & \dfrac{1}{3} & \cdots & \dfrac{1}{n+1} \\[2mm] \dfrac{1}{2} & \dfrac{1}{3} & \dfrac{1}{4} & \cdots & \dfrac{1}{n+2} \\[2mm] \dfrac{1}{3} & \dfrac{1}{4} & \dfrac{1}{5} & \cdots & \dfrac{1}{n+3} \\[2mm] \vdots & \vdots & \vdots & \vdots & \vdots \\[2mm] \dfrac{1}{n+1} & \dfrac{1}{n+2} & \dfrac{1}{n+3} & \cdots & \dfrac{1}{2n+1} \end{vmatrix}$$

The common factor N^{n+1} in each term of the determinant of $[A]$ can be a very large number depending on N. But the remaining determinant, which is independent of the number of points, is a very rapidly diminishing function of n, the degree of fit. Some values of this determinant are given below.

n	Determinant
0	1.0
1	0.0823
2	0.000463
3	1.653×10^{-7}
4	3.75×10^{-12}
5	5.37×10^{-18}
6	4.84×10^{-25}
7	2.74×10^{-33}
8	9.72×10^{-43}
9	2.17×10^{-53}

Clearly, a least squares fit of a polynomial of even modest degree may involve the solution of a matrix equation in which the coefficient matrix is ill-conditioned. There are thus compelling reasons for not pushing a least squares analysis beyond a third- or fourth-degree polynomial.

Nonlinear Least Squares Analysis

Very frequently nature is unwilling to generate data that can be nicely summarized by simple polynomials or exponentials. For example, the model function suggested by a theory may be nonlinear in its parameters and not readily rewritten as linear by a change of variables, such as

$$y(x) = \alpha \sin(\beta t)$$

An expression like this can be inserted in the equation for $E(\alpha, \beta)$ [Equation (13.2)] and the derivatives with respect to α and β computed to find the minimum of the squared deviations. Since these equations are nonlinear in α and β, a completely different approach must be developed for their solution. The procedures of Chapter 12 were conceived to solve iteratively *one* nonlinear equation in one unknown. These algorithms can be extended to solve iteratively several simultaneous equations in several unknowns. The idea, not suprisingly, is to start with a Taylor series expansion of a function of two or more variables. However, this topic is beyond the scope of this book. If you are interested you can find an accessible discussion in R. H. Pennington, *Computer Methods and Numerical Analysis* (Toronto: Macmillan, 1970).

The least squares analysis of this chapter is based on the idea of optimizing the fit of model functions that are expressed in terms of polynomials of varying degree. A different approach is to rephase the discussion, replacing a model function

$$y_{\text{model}}(x) = a_0 + a_1 x + \cdots + a_n x^n$$

with a model function of the form

$$y_{\text{model}}(x) = a_0 g_0(x) + a_1 g_1(x) + \cdots + a_n g_n(x)$$

where the functions $g_n(x)$ are a special class of so-called orthogonal functions. This analysis, although not complicated, requires a detour into the study of orthogonal functions and will not be considered here. (An example of fitting with one class of orthogonal functions can be found in Programming Assignment H-C.)

13.10 Cubic Spline Fits*

Often it is best to abandon the attempt to use least squares analysis to fit a simple function to complex data and simply to "connect the dots" by draw-

---

*This section contains more advanced material and may be omitted without a loss of continuity.

ing a smooth curve through the data using a French curve or a drafter's spline (a flexible elastic bar). This procedure is especially appropriate if the points are not experimental values but are simply representative points of a physical structure such as an airplane wing. If we want the computer to duplicate the work of a drafter, the prime concern is that the function smoothly pass through each of the points with a minimum of intermediate wiggles. The exact nature of the function is unimportant. This process is obviously very important in computer graphics applications.

Cubic Splines

The most common procedure is to fit each segment of two points $(x_i \leftrightarrow x_{i+1})$ with a cubic that passes through both points and then connect all of the segments into a smooth curve. Thus, if the combined fitting curve is called $F(x)$, then $F(x)$ is represented by n segments $[f_i(x), i = 0, n - 1]$, each of which can be written as

$$f_i(x) = a_i + b_i(x - x_i) + c_i(x - x_i)^2 + d_i(x - x_i)^3 \qquad (13.43)$$

for $x_i \leq x \leq x_{i+1}$ and $i = 0, n - 1$.

Each of the segments contains four parameters that must be determined by imposing four conditions on each segment. Two of these are obviously that the function segment must pass through the points $(x_i, y_i), (x_{i+1}, y_{i+1})$,

$$y_i = F(x_i) = f_i(x_i) = a_i$$

$$y_{i+1} = F(x_{i+1}) = f_i(x_{i+1}) = a_i + b_i \Delta x_i + c_i \Delta x_i^2 + d_i \Delta x_i^3$$

where Δx_i is the width of the ith interval, $\Delta x_i = (x_{i+1} - x_i)$.

Two additional conditions are required. These will be requirements on the "smoothness" of the overall function at the connections (knots) between the segments. Mathematically, the conditions will be that the slopes of two adjoining segments must match at the knots.

$$f'_{i-1}(x_i) = f'_i(x_i) \qquad \text{for } i = 1, n$$

$$f'_i(x_{i+1}) = f'_{i+1}(x_{i+1}) \qquad \text{for } i = 0, n - 1$$

These relations are illustrated graphically in Figure 13-10.

Applying these four conditions to determine the coefficients of the cubic segments is straightforward but involves considerable algebra because the latter two conditions have introduced adjoining segments (along with their unknown coefficients) into the problem. The details of the solution for the coefficients is given in M. H. Schultz, *Spine Analysis* (Englewood Cliffs, N.J.: Prentice-Hall, 1973). The results are given below.

Figure 13-10
Combined fitting
function $F(x)$ is a
combination of
smoothly joined
cubic segments

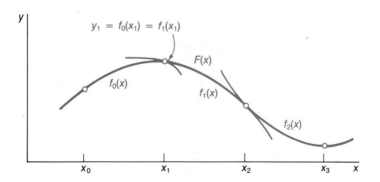

$$y_1 = f_0(x_1) = f_1(x_1)$$

Coefficients of the Cubic Spline Segments

$$a_i = y_i$$

$$b_i = y'_i$$

$$c_i \Delta x_i = \frac{\Delta y_i}{\Delta x_i} - y'_i - d_i \Delta x_i^2$$

$$d_i \Delta x_i^2 = y'_{i+1} + y'_i - 2\frac{\Delta y_i}{\Delta x_i} \tag{13.44}$$

where Δy_i is the first forward difference [Equation (10.35)], $\Delta y_i = y_{i+1} - y_i$), and y'_i is the slope (i.e., the derivative) of the curve at point i. If the values of the derivative of the fitting function are known, the coefficients of the cubic segments are then readily computed from Equations (13.44).

Ordinarily, the derivative of the fitting function is not known at each point and the data consist of only the pairs (x_i, y_i). For such cases a separate computation must be carried out to first obtain the y'_i for $i = 0, n$.

Computation of the Slopes at the Knots

Since there are $n + 1$ unknown quantities y'_i, we will require $n + 1$ additional conditions. Most of these can be supplied by requiring that the second derivative of each segment match the adjoining segments at the knots; that is,

$$f''_{i-1}(x_i) = f''_i(x_i) \qquad \text{for } i = 1, n - 1 \tag{13.45}$$

Two additional requirements are

$$f''_0(x_0) = 0$$

$$f''_{n-1}(x_n) = 0 \tag{13.46}$$

which are equivalent to allowing the drafter's spline to be free and straight at both ends of the curve.

Applying these conditions to our cubic segments yields

$$2c_{i-1} + 6d_{i-1}\Delta x_{i-1} = 2c_i \qquad \text{for } i = 1, n \qquad (13.47)$$

Inserting the earlier expressions for c_i and d_i, we obtain a single equation relating the y' at the adjoining points.

To simplify the results, from this point on we will assume equally spaced points, $\Delta x_i = \text{constant} = \Delta x$. The more general case is described in Schultz. The resulting equations are

$$\frac{1}{3}y'_{i+1} + \frac{4}{3}y'_i + \frac{1}{3}y'_{i-1} = \frac{\Delta y_{i-1}}{\Delta x} + \frac{\Delta y_i}{\Delta x} \qquad \text{for } i = 1, n-1 \qquad (13.48)$$

These are $n - 1$ relations in the $n + 1$ unknowns y'_i, $i = 0, n$. The two relations in Equation (13.46) are used to specify y'_0 and y'_n.

$$y'_0 = \frac{3}{2}\frac{\Delta y_0}{\Delta x} - \frac{1}{2}y'_1$$

$$y'_n = \frac{3}{2}\frac{\Delta y_{n-1}}{\Delta x} - \frac{1}{2}y'_{n-1} \qquad (13.49)$$

If we next designate the quantities $\Delta y_i/\Delta x$ as h_i, Equations (13.48) and (13.49) may be rewritten as

$$y'_0 = \frac{3}{2}h_0 - \frac{1}{2}y'_1$$

$$y'_i = \frac{3}{4}(h_i + h_{i-1}) - \frac{1}{4}(y'_{i+1} + y'_{i-1})$$

$$y'_n = \frac{3}{2}h_{n-1} - \frac{1}{2}y'_{n-1} \qquad (13.50)$$

where

$$h_i \equiv \frac{y_{i+1} - y_i}{\Delta x}$$

Equations (13.50) are written in a form suitable for a Gauss–Siedel iterative solution. The FORTRAN code to solve these equations is given in Figure 13-11. This code can be easily generalized to accommodate unevenly spaced points.

Once the quantities y'_i have been computed, we can return to Equations (13.44), compute the entire set of coefficients of the cubic segments, and have the computer graph the function. As an example, this procedure is applied to the wildly oscillating set of points shown in Figure 13-12.

Figure 13-11
FORTRAN
subroutine to
compute the
coefficients of a
cubic spline fit to
equally spaced
data

```
      SUBROUTINE SPLINE(X0,XN,Y,N,EPS,IMAX,A)
*--
*  SPLINE computes the coefficients of the cubic segments, A(),
*  to fit the N+1 data points Y() over the interval X0 to XN.  The
*  data are assumed to be equally spaced.
*
*  The computation requires determining the first derivatives of
*  the fitting function at each point.  This is accomplished by a
*  Gauss-Siedel iteration procedure starting with a central diff-
*  erence approximation as the initial guess for the derivatives.
*  (Subroutine GSIEDL, included below, is used for this purpose.)
*
*  The Gauss-Siedel solution is terminated successfully when the
*  root-mean-square deviation of the set of values for the deriva-
*  tives DY() from the previous set is less than the user supplied
*  EPS.  The subroutine then computes the coefficients A() and
*  returns.
*
*  The solution fails if not successful in KMAX iterations.  The
*  maximum number of data points the code can handle is 51.
*----------------------------------------------------------------
*  Variables
*
      REAL X0,XN,Y(0:N),DY(0:50),H(0:50),A(0:3,0:N),
     +     DX,SUM,TERM,EPS
      INTEGER IMAX
*
*  X0,XN  --  x interval from X0 to XN
*  Y()    --  Equally spaced data points
*  DX     --  x-spacing of the data points
*  EPS    --  Convergence criterion on the rms deviation of the
*             DY() from one iteration to the next
*  DY()   --  First derivatives of the cubic segments at the data
*             positions.  The main part of the subroutine concerns
*             the solution for these quantities.
*  IMAX   --  Maximum number of iterations allowed
*  H()    --  Secant segments (Y(I+1) - Y(I))/DX
*  A()    --  Computed coefficients of the cubic segments A(K,I) is
*             the coefficient of X**K in the Ith segment.  The Ith
*             segment runs from X(I) to X(I+1).
*----------------------------------------------------------------
*  Initialization and Initial Guess for DY()
*
      DX = (XN - X0)/N
*
*  Use central difference expressions for the DY() at all interior
*  points.  At left and right ends, use forward or backward diff-
*  erences respectively.
*
      DY(N) = (-3.*Y(N) + 4.*Y(N-1) - Y(N-2))/2./DX
      DY(0) = (-3.*Y(0) + 4.*Y(1)   - Y(2))  /2./DX
      H(0)  = (Y(1) - Y(0))/DX
      DO 1 I = 1,N-1
         DY(I) = (Y(I+1) - Y(I-1))/2./DX
         H(I)  = (Y(I+1) - Y(I))/DX
    1 CONTINUE
*
*----------------------------------------------------------------
```

Figure 13-11
(continued)

```
*   The Gauss-Siedel Solution for the DY()'s
*
      CALL GSIEDL(N,H,EPS,ITER,IMAX,DY)
*------------------------------------------------------------------
*   The DY()'s have been successfully computed. Next compute A().
*
      DO 4 I = 0,N-1
         A(0,I) = Y(I)
         A(1,I) = DY(I)
         A(3,I) = (DY(I+1) + DY(I) - 2.*H(I))/DX**2
         A(2,I) = (H(I) - DY(I))/DX - A(3,I)*DX
    4 CONTINUE
      RETURN
      END
*==================================================================
      FUNCTION YSPLIN(X,A,B,N,C)
*
*   This function computes the model value of Y for the i-th
*   cubic segment using the coefficients of the cubic segments
*   computed in the subroutine SPLINE. (i.e. C(K,I))
*
      REAL X,XI,YSPLIN,A,B,C(0:3,0:N)
      DX = (B-A)/N
*
*           The Ith segment is determined as
*
      I = (X-A)/DX
*
*           But be careful, if X = B => i = N - 1
*
      IF(X .GE. B)I = N - 1
*
*           The segment begins at XI
*
      XI = A + I*DX
      YSPLIN = C(0,I)
      DO 1 K = 1,3
         IF ((X-XI) .NE. 0.0)THEN
            YSPLIN = YSPLIN + C(K,I)*(X - XI)**K
         END IF
    1 CONTINUE
      RETURN
      END
*==================================================================
      SUBROUTINE GSIEDL(N,H,EPS,ITER,IMAX,DY)
*
* GSIEDL iteratively solves Equations (13.50) for the first der-
* ivatives of the cubic spline fitting function.  The maximum
* number of iterations is IMAX, and convergence is acheived when
* the average deviation of one set of results from the previous
* set is less than EPS.  The vector h() is the computed first
* forward differences of the data. The solution is returned in
* the array DY. ITER is the actual number of iterations.
*------------------------------------------------------------------
```

Figure 13-11
(concluded)

```
          REAL DY(0:N),H(0:N),EPS,DEV,TERM
*
          DO 2 ITER = 1,IMAX
             SUM = 0.0
*
*         Solve the N+1 equations for the DY(I) and also let
*         TERM = |DYNEW(I) - DYOLD(I)|.  SUM is then the average
*         deviation from one iteration to the next.
*
             DY(0) = -.5*DY(1) + 1.5*H(0)
             SUM = 0.0
             DO 1 I = 1,N-1
                TERM = -.25*(DY(I+1)+DY(I-1)) + .75*(H(I)+H(I-1))
                DX   = ABS(DY(I) - TERM)
                SUM  = SUM + DX
                DY(I) = TERM
    1        CONTINUE
             DY(N) = -.5*DY(N-1) + 1.5*H(N-1)
*
             SUM = SUM/N
*
*            Test for convergence.
*
             IF(SUM .LT. EPS)THEN
*
*            Convergence has been acheived.
*
                RETURN
             ENDIF
    2     CONTINUE
*
*      Excessive Iterations Path
*
          WRITE(*,10)SUM,DY
          RETURN
*------------------------------------------------------------
   10  FORMAT(/,T10,'*===========ERROR IN SPLINE=============*',/,
      +           T10,'| Calculation of derivatives has failed |',/,
      +           T10,'| to converge.  The latest rms deviation|',/,
      +           T10,'| was ',E10.4,T50,'|',/,
      +           T10,'| The last set of dy/dx is given below   |',/,
      +           T10,'*=========Program Continues=============*',/,
      +    T3,(2X,7E10.3))
*------------------------------------------------------------
          END
```

Summary

The most common procedure to optimize the fit of a function to a set of data points is least square analysis. Least squares analysis consists in first postulating a particular model function containing a number of parameters to represent the data. Next, the parameters of the function are determined by minimizing the sum of the squared deviations of the model

Figure 13-12

Cubic spline fit to
nonsmooth data

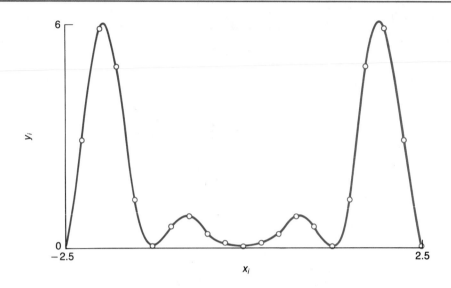

from the data. A popular choice for the model function is a polynomial of
degree n

$$y(x) = a_0 + a_1 x + a_2 x^2 + \cdots + a_n x^n$$

The $n + 1$ coefficients of the polynomial are then the parameters to be determined by optimizing the fit to the given set of N data points. This is
accomplished by constructing a function E, which is the sum of the
squares of the deviations of the polynomial evaluated at a data point from
the actual data point.

$$E = E(a_0, a_1, \ldots, a_n) = \sum_{i=1}^{N} [y(x_{i,\exp}) - y_{i,\exp}]^2$$

The minimum of E is specified by requiring that the partial derivatives of
E with respect to each of the a_i be zero,

$$\frac{\partial E}{\partial a_i} = 0 \quad \text{for } i = 0, n$$

These $n + 1$ equations are then solved for the $n + 1$ unknown coefficients
a_i by first writing the equations in matrix form as $[A]\mathbf{a} = \mathbf{b}$, where

$$[A] = \begin{bmatrix} N & \Sigma x & \Sigma x^2 & \cdots & \Sigma x^n \\ \Sigma x & \Sigma x^2 & \Sigma x^3 & \cdots & \Sigma x^{n+1} \\ \Sigma x^2 & \Sigma x^3 & \Sigma x^4 & \cdots & \Sigma x^{n+2} \\ \vdots & \vdots & \vdots & \vdots & \vdots \\ \Sigma x^n & \Sigma x^{n+1} & \Sigma x^{n+2} & \cdots & \Sigma x^{2n} \end{bmatrix} \quad \text{and} \quad \mathbf{b} = \begin{bmatrix} \Sigma y \\ \Sigma xy \\ \Sigma x^2 y \\ \vdots \\ \Sigma x^n y \end{bmatrix}$$

and where the sum is over the N data points (x_i, y_i). The solution for the a's is then obtained by standard matrix methods.

For linear fits to data these equations are usually replaced by

$$a_1 = \frac{D_{xy}}{D_{xx}} \qquad a_0 = \langle y \rangle - a_1 \langle x \rangle$$

where

$$D_{xy} = \langle xy \rangle - \langle x \rangle \langle y \rangle \qquad D_{xx} = \langle x^2 \rangle - \langle x \rangle^2$$

and $\langle \, \rangle$ designates the average of the quantity over the N data points.

The validity of a model fit to data is expressed in terms of the quantity χ^2 (chi-squared), which is defined as

$$\chi^2 \equiv \sum_{i=1}^{N} \left(\frac{[y(x_{i,\exp}) - y_{i,\exp}]^2}{\Delta y_{i,\exp}^2} \right)$$

where $(x_{i,\exp}, y_{i,\exp})$ are the data, $y(x)$ is the fitting function, and $\Delta y_{i,\exp}$ is the experimental error in the ith data point. $\chi^2 \approx N$ indicates an adequate fit to data, whereas $\chi^2 \gg N (\chi^2 \ll N)$ indicates a poor fit (an overfit) to the data.

Using a function other than a polynomial as the fitting function will result in a set of nonlinear simultaneous equations for which matrix methods are unsuitable. Often, a change of variables can be found that will result in a model function of the new variables that is linear in the parameters. For example, the fit of $(x_{i,\exp}, y_{i,\exp})$ to an exponential, $y(x) = \alpha e^{\beta x}$, is accomplished by rewriting the problem as instead a fit of $[x_{i,\exp}, \ln(y_{i,\exp})]$ to $F(x) = a_0 + a_1 x$, with $a_0 = \alpha$ and $a_1 \equiv \ln(\beta)$.

Finally, an alternative to fitting a single function to the entire set of data is to use cubic segments that are smoothly connected at each data point. This procedure, known as cubic spline curve fitting, is more complex than least squares analysis; however, there are situations when a smooth fit is more important than a particular choice of a model and so a FORTRAN implementation of the spline method is given in Figure 13-11.

Problems

13.1 Determine the value of d that minimizes the sum of the squared deviations from the numbers $(4, 3, 6, 1, 2)$ and then evaluate the minimum sum of the squared deviations

$$E = (4 - d)^2 + (3 - d)^2 + (6 - d)^2 + (1 - d)^2 + (2 - d)^2$$

Verify that with this value of d the sum of the deviations (not squared) is zero.

13.2 Evaluate the following partial derivatives:

a. $\dfrac{\partial}{\partial a}(a^2 b + 4xe^a)$

b. $\dfrac{\partial}{\partial c}\left[\sum_{i=1}^{N}(c^2 x_i^2 - y_i)\right]$

c. $\dfrac{\partial}{\partial b}\left\{\sum_{i=1}^{N}[y(x_i) - y_i]^2\right\}$ where $y(x) = e^{bx}$

13.3 Use the data set to answer parts a–e:

i	1	2	3	4	5	6
x_i	1.0	2.0	3.0	4.0	5.0	6.0
y_i	0.0	3.0	2.0	5.0	4.0	7.0

a. Determine the intercept (a_0) and the slope (a_1) of the least squares best-fit line.

b. Plot the data on graph paper, draw the best-fit line by eye, and then draw the least squares line $y(x) = a_0 + a_1 x$.

c. Explain why the two lines differ by such a large amount.

d. Which line do you think is more accurate—that is, which results in the smaller deviations? (Be careful in defining what is meant by deviations.)

e. Interchange the x and y values in the table and determine the least squares line ($x = b_0 + b_1 y$) once more. Explain why the latest line is not the same as the previous least squares line.

13.4 Fit the data below first to a straight line and then to a parabola. For each case compute the resulting value of the minimum of the sum of the squared deviations—that is, Equation (13.2).

i	1	2	3	4	5	6	7	8
x_i	−2.0	−1.0	0.0	1.0	2.0	3.0	4.0	5.0
y_i	−33.0	−24.0	−15.0	−3.0	10.0	24.0	39.0	55.0

13.5 The amount of a particular radioactive element decreases with time according to the equation $N(t) = N_0 e^{-\lambda t}$ where $N(t)$ is the number of atoms left at time t if the original number at $t = 0$ is N_0. The decay constant is λ. The half-life of the decay is defined to be $\tau = \ln(2)/\lambda$. The data below have been measured for a particular type of radioactive hydrogen atom. Fit the data to an equation of the form $N(t) = \alpha e^{\beta t}$ and determine the half-life and the original number of atoms present.

i	1	2	3	4	5
t (months)	0.0	10.0	20.0	40.0	80.0
N	1.41×10^{18}	1.35×10^{18}	1.29×10^{18}	1.17×10^{18}	9.72×10^{17}

13.6 Fit the data below to an equation of the form $y = \alpha x^{\beta}$. (*Hint:* Take the logarithm of this equation to suggest a linear model.)

i	1	2	3	4	5	6
x_i	1.0	2.0	3.0	4.0	5.0	6.0
y_i	1.0	3.3	7.2	13.0	20.0	28.0

Once you have obtained the best-fit values of α and β, compare the theoretical results with the data.

13.7 According to the Stefan–Boltzmann law, the total energy radiated per second, R, from a hot object varies as the absolute temperature to the fourth power according to

$$R = \sigma(T^4 - T_0^4)$$

where T_0 is the room temperature (K) and σ is called the Stefan–Boltzmann constant. From the data below determine a value for σ by fitting a line $y = a_0 + a_1 x$ to the data where $y_i = R_i$ and $x_i = T_i^4$. The accepted value of σ is $\sigma = 5.670 \pm 0.003 \times 10^{-8}$ W/m^2 = K^4.

i	1	2	3	4	5	6
T	300.0	350.0	400.0	450.0	500.0	550.0
R	40.0	430.0	1050.0	1920.0	3150.0	4750.0

13.8 Fit a line, a parabola, and a cubic to the data below and for each fit compute χ^2 using an error in each of the y values of $\Delta y \simeq \pm 0.5$. What is your conclusion?

i	1	2	3	4
x_i	0.0	0.5	1.0	2.0
y_i	3.6	5.0	7.4	13.6

13.9 Graph the data below, including error bars, and fit the following functional form selecting the most appropriate from the values of chi-squared determined for each. Plot each of the three theoretical curves.

i	1	2	3	4	5
x_i	0.0	0.5	1.0	1.5	2.0
y_i	3.4	6.0	13.3	25.7	51.5
Δy_i	±0.4	±0.5	±0.5	±0.7	±0.9

13.10 The purpose of this problem is to carry out the procedures for fitting a cubic spline by a hand calculation through three equally spaced points. The three points are

i	0	1	2
x_i	−2	1	4
y_i	15	3	9

Thus, $d = x_{i+1} - x_i = 3$ and $h_0 = (y_1 - y_0)/d = -4, h_1 = (y_2 - y_1)/d = 2$.
a. Write Equations (13.50) in matrix form and solve for the quantities y_i'. You should get

$$\begin{bmatrix} y_0' \\ y_1' \\ y_2' \end{bmatrix} = \frac{1}{4}\begin{bmatrix} 5h_0 - h_1 \\ 2h_0 + 2h_1 \\ -h_0 + 5h_1 \end{bmatrix} = \begin{bmatrix} -\frac{11}{2} \\ -1 \\ \frac{7}{2} \end{bmatrix}$$

b. Use these values and Equations (13.44) to compute the coefficients of the *two* cubics drawn between the adjacent pairs of points. You should obtain

$$f_0(x) = y_0 + \frac{(x - x_0)}{4d}(-5y_0 + 6y_1 - y_2) + \frac{(x - x_0)^3}{4d^3}(y_0 - 2y_1 + y_2)$$

$$= \tfrac{1}{6}(x^3 + 6x^2 - 21x + 32)$$

$$f_1(x) = y_1 + \frac{(x - x_1)}{2d}(y_2 - y_0) + \frac{3(x - x_1)^2}{4d^2}(y_2 - 2y_1 + y_0)$$

$$- \frac{(x - x_1)^3}{4d^3}(y_2 - 2y_1 + y_0)$$

$$= \tfrac{1}{6}(-x^3 + 12x^2 - 27x + 34)$$

13.11 Determine the cubic spline fit through just *two* points (x_0, y_0); (x_1, y_1).
   a. First, using Equations (13.50), show that $y_0' = y_1' = h_0(y_1 - y_0)/(x_1 - x_0)$.
   b. Then, by using Equations (13.44), determine the coefficients of the cubic and show that the "cubic" is simply a straight line:

$$y(x) = y_0 + h_0(x - x_0)$$

G

Programming Assignment

Sample Program

Chemistry/Chemical Engineering:
Empirical Heat Capacities of Gases

The specific heat of a substance is a measure of the heat energy that must be added in order to raise the temperature of 1 kilogram of the substance 1 K. If the proportionality constant relating heat added (ΔQ) to increase in temperature (ΔT) is measured at a constant pressure, the result is called c_p, the specific heat at a constant pressure.

$$c_p = \frac{\Delta Q}{\Delta T}$$

The measured values of the specific heat of all common gases have been extensively tabulated and are of vital concern to the engineer when designing any apparatus or system that deals with heat transfer in gases. Both mechanical engineers (e.g., combustion, heat transfer) and chemical engineers (thermodynamics of chemical processes in gases) use tables of c_p versus T in their work.

It is usually more convenient to have on hand a simple equation that summarizes limited portions of the tables. It has been found that the following equation quite accurately duplicates the actual c_p values for some gases:

$$c_p(T) = a + bT + cT^2 + \frac{d}{T^2} \tag{G.1}$$

The temperature T is in Kelvin, and the four parameters, a, b, c, d, are determined by a best fit of the equation to the experimental values. Notice that this model function, because of the d/T^2 term, is not a polynomial fit. This fact can be easily rectified by a change of variables. Multiplying Equation (G.1) by T^2 suggests the change of variables $y(T) \rightarrow T^2 c_p(T)$, or

$$y(T) = d + aT^2 + bT^3 + cT^4 \tag{G.2}$$

This equation is now a polynomial (minus a linear term) that is to be fit to the data. How do we incorporate the missing term in the model function into our theory? There is no shortcut. Equation (G.2) is inserted into the equation for the sum of the squared deviations, Equation (13.2)

$$E(d, a, b, c) = \sum_{i=1}^{N} [(d + aT_i^2 + bT_i^3 + cT_i^4) - (T_i^2 c_{p,i})]^2 \tag{G.3}$$

531

The condition for a minimum of this function is that the four equations

$$\frac{\partial E}{\partial d} = 0 \qquad \frac{\partial E}{\partial a} = 0 \qquad \frac{\partial E}{\partial b} = 0 \qquad \frac{\partial E}{\partial c} = 0$$

are solved simultaneously. By evaluating these derivatives and simplifying the resulting equations in a manner similar to that in Chapter 12, we easily obtain the following matrix equation for the coefficients:

$$\begin{bmatrix} N & \Sigma T^2 & \Sigma T^3 & \Sigma T^4 \\ \Sigma T^2 & \Sigma T^4 & \Sigma T^5 & \Sigma T^6 \\ \Sigma T^3 & \Sigma T^5 & \Sigma T^6 & \Sigma T^7 \\ \Sigma T^4 & \Sigma T^6 & \Sigma T^7 & \Sigma T^8 \end{bmatrix} \begin{bmatrix} d \\ a \\ b \\ c \end{bmatrix} = \begin{bmatrix} \Sigma c_p T^2 \\ \Sigma c_p T^4 \\ \Sigma c_p T^5 \\ \Sigma c_p T^6 \end{bmatrix} \qquad (G.4)$$

The problem then is to use the values of c_p versus T in Table G-1 to compute the sums in Equation (G.4) and then to solve the matrix equation for the parameters a, b, c, d. Since the matrix differs from the ordinary least squares polynomial fit, the subroutine LSTSQR of Figure 13-8 will have to be amended.

If the experimental errors in the c_p values are $\Delta c_p = \pm 3$ J/kg-K, compute χ^2 and comment on the validity of the overall fit to the data.

Duplicate the entire calculation, this time first adding $+\Delta c_p$ to the first, third, fifth, and so on c_p values and $-\Delta c_p$ to the second, fourth, sixth, and so on c_p values. The resulting change in the parameters should give some indication of the sensitivity of the parameters to the experimental error in c_p.

▬ Sample Program Solution

The FORTRAN code for solving this problem is given in Figure G-1. The required alterations to the subroutine LSTSQR are trivial enough that

Table G-1

Specific heat versus temperature for carbon dioxide. The pressure is constant at 7.0×10^5 N/m². The error in the c_p values is ± 15 J/kg-K.

i	T (°C)	c_p (J/kg-K) ($\times 10^3$)
1	170	1.101
2	225	1.110
3	275	1.123
4	330	1.136
5	390	1.153
6	445	1.170
7	500	1.185
8	555	1.200
9	610	1.216
10	670	1.230
11	725	1.243
12	775	1.256
13	830	1.268
14	1100	1.318
15	1390	1.354
16	1670	1.373

Figure G-1
FORTRAN program
to curve fit the heat
capacity of a gas

```
        PROGRAM SEVEN
*--
*  This program executes a least squares best-fit calculation of a
*  model function of the form
*
*             Cp(T) = a + bT + cT^2 + d/T^2
*
*  to the experimental specific heat values for a gas over a broad
*  range of temperatures but at a constant pressure.  Multiplying
*  the model function by T**2 yields a polynomial of degree 4 but
*  missing the linear term.  The subroutine LSTSQR is altered to
*  adjust to this change.
*
*  Additionally, the experimental error in the data, dC, is used to
*  to compute chi-squared to test the validity of the model fit.
*
*  Finally, each data point is altered by Cp(T) => Cp(T) +/- dC and
*  the entire calculation is repeated to determine the sensitivity
*  of the parameter values to experimental error.
*-------------------------------------------------------------------
* Variables
*
        INTEGER KRUN,NDATA
        PARAMETER (NDATA = 16)
        REAL T(NDATA),CP(NDATA),Y(NDATA),DY(NDATA),DC,AC(4,4),CHI2,
     +      COEF(0:3),P0,A,B,C,D
        CHARACTER NAME*15
*
*  T()   -- Temperature (deg-K)                           [INPUT]
*  CP()  -- Specific heat at constant pressure (T/kg/K)   [INPUT]
*  NDATA -- Number of data points                         [INPUT]
*  DC    -- Constant error in the CP values               [INPUT]
*  P0    -- Pressure at which data obtained (N/m**2)       [INPUT]
*  NAME  -- Name of the gas                               [INPUT]
*  Y()   -- T**2 times the CP values
*  DY()  -- Computed error in Y, i.e. DC*T**2
*  AC()  -- Coefficient matrix of the least squares analysis
*  COEF()-- Coefficients of the best-fit polynomial
*  A,B   -- Same as COEF(). More familiar names for
*  C,D      the parameters
*  KRUN  -- The calculation is performed twice (KRUN = 1,2)
*-------------------------------------------------------------------
* Initialization
*
        DATA T / 170., 225., 275., 330., 390., 445., 500., 555.,
     +          610., 670., 725., 775., 830.,1100.,1390.,1670./
        DATA CP/1101.,1110.,1123.,1136.,1153.,1170.,1185.,1200.,
     +          1216.,1230.,1243.,1256.,1268.,1318.,1354.,1373./
        DATA P0,DC /7.E5,2.5/
        DATA NAME /'Carbon Dioxide'/
        WRITE(*,10)NAME,P0,DC
        DO 1 I = 1,NDATA
           WRITE(*,11)I,T(I),CP(I)
    1   CONTINUE
*-------------------------------------------------------------------
```

Figure G-1
(continued)

```
* Computation
*
*   Fill in the arrays for y and the errors and convert T to Kelvin
*   [Note:  Since we require Sum[T**8] and these could easily cause
*           a floating point overflow, we scale the temperatures
*           down by a factor of 1000.  The values printed are scaled
*           back up by an appropriate factor.]
*
      DO 2 I = 1,NDATA
         CP(I) = CP(I)
         T(I)  = T(I) + 273.16
         T(I)  = T(I)/1000.
         Y(I)  = CP(I)*T(I)**2
         DY(I) = DC*T(I)**2
   2  CONTINUE
*
*   Call the amended subroutine LSTSQR to compute the coefficients
*   of the model polynomial
*
      DO 4 KRUN = 1,2
         CALL LSTSQR(T,Y,NDATA,COEF,3,1,CHI2,DY)
         IF(KRUN .EQ. 1)THEN
            WRITE(*,12)CHI2,NDATA-5
            A = COEF(1)
            B = COEF(2)
            C = COEF(3)
            D = COEF(0)
            WRITE(3,13)A*1.E-6,B*1.E-9,C*1.E-12,D
*
*         Alter the data for the second calculation
*
            DO 3 I = 1,NDATA
               IF(I/2*2 .EQ. I)THEN
                  Y(I) = Y(I) - DY(I)
               ELSE
                  Y(I) = Y(I) + DY(I)
               ENDIF
   3        CONTINUE
         ELSE
            A = ABS((A-COEF(1))/A)*100.
            B = ABS((B-COEF(2))/B)*100.
            C = ABS((C-COEF(3))/C)*100.
            D = ABS((D-COEF(0))/D)*100.
            WRITE(*,14)CHI2,COEF(1)*1.E-6,COEF(2)*1.E-9,
     +            COEF(3)*1.E-12,COEF(0),A,B,C,D
         ENDIF
   4  CONTINUE
      STOP
*------------------------------------------------------------------
* Formats
  10  FORMAT(//,
     +T5,'A calculation of the parameters in an empirical formula'/
     +T5,'for the specific heat of ',A15,          '.  The data are '/
     +T5,'at a constant pressure of ',E9.2, ' N/m^2 and the error'/
     +T5,'in the Cp values is a constant ',E9.2,      ' J/kg/K.',//,
     +T10,'The input data are',//,
     +T10,' I    Temp.    Cp  ',/,
     +T10,'---   ------   -------')
*
```

Figure G-1
(concluded)

```
   11 FORMAT(T11,I2,T16,F5.0,T24,F5.0)
 *
   12 FORMAT(/,
    +T5,'The primary calculation has chi-squared = ',F7.1,/,
    +T5,'while a satisfactory fit would have a value of ',I2)
 *
   13 FORMAT(/,T5,'The computed parameters are ',//,
    + T10,'    A          B          C          D      ',/,
    + T10,'---------- ---------- ---------- ----------',/,
    + T10,4(E10.4,1X))
 *
   14 FORMAT(/,
    +T5,'The calculation to test the parameter sensitivity has',/,
    +T5,'a chi-squared of ',F7.1,//,
    +T5,'This calculation uses the same data with the error',/,
    +T5,'alternately added or subtracted from each point. The',/,
    +T5,'new values for the coefficients are listed below. ',/,
    +T5,'Beneath each value is its percentage change. '/
    +T10,'    A          B          C          D      ',/,
    +T10,'---------- ---------- ---------- ----------',/,
    +T10,4(E10.4,1X),/,
    +T10,4('(',F7.2,'%)',1X))
      END
 *=================================================================
      SUBROUTINE LSTSQR(X,Y,NDATA,A,NP,ICHI,CHI2,DY)
 *=================================================================
      FUNCTION YTHEO(Z,N,C)
 *=================================================================
      SUBROUTINE MINV(A,AINV,ND,N,DET)
 *=================================================================
```

this subroutine is not listed. The results of the program are given in Figure G-2.

G.2 Programming Problems

Programming Problem G-A: Aerodynamics: Free Fall in Air

Several times in earlier examples we have used the results of a relatively simple experiment—measuring the distance of fall versus time for an object released in air. Typically, the trajectory is photographed while illuminated by a rapidly flashing light. The positions of the images on the film are then used to determine the distance of fall at regular time intervals. The results for one run of such an experiment are given in Table G-2 and are graphed in Figure G-3.

From the graph it can be seen that the functional dependence of position on time is complicated. The data start out parabolic in appearance and end up being very nearly a straight line. The straight-line portion of the curve is a result of the ball reaching its terminal velocity; that is, $dy/dt =$

Figure G-2
Output from
program in
Figure G-1

A calculation of the parameters in an empirical formula
for the specific heat of Carbon Dioxide . The data are
at a constant pressure of 0.70E+06 N/m^2 and the error
in the Cp values is a constant 0.25E+01 J/kg/K.

The input data are

I	Temp.	Cp
1	170.	1101.
2	225.	1110.
3	275.	1123.
4	330.	1136.
5	390.	1153.
6	445.	1170.
7	500.	1185.
8	555.	1200.
9	610.	1216.
10	670.	1230.
11	725.	1243.
12	775.	1256.
13	830.	1268.
14	1100.	1318.
15	1390.	1354.
16	1670.	1373.

The primary calculation has chi-squared =   10.7
while a satisfactory fit would have a value of 11

The computed parameters are:

A	B	C	D
0.8836E-03	0.4660E-06	-.1106E-09	0.5063E+01

The calculation to test the parameter sensitivity has
a chi-squared of   19.2

This calculation uses the same data with the error
alternately added or subtracted from each point. The
new values for the coefficients are listed below.
Beneath each value is its percentage change.

A	B	C	D
0.8491E-03	0.5098E-06	-.1249E-09	0.9750E+01
(3.90%)	(9.39%)	(12.94%)	(92.59%)

constant. If we attempt to fit a polynomial to this curve by a least squares
analysis, neither a parabola nor a line will be suitable over the entire range
of data. The apparent solution is to use a parabolic fit over the first part
and a straight-line fit over the last part. The problem is then where to
make the break. This can be determined in the following way.

Table G-2

Fall distance versus time for a Styrofoam ball

Index	t_i (sec)	y_i (cm)	Index	t_i (sec)	y_i (cm)
1	0.2650	16.55	18	0.6900	109.00
2	0.2900	18.85	19	0.7150	116.60
3	0.3150	21.68	20	0.7400	124.40
4	0.3400	25.00	21	0.7650	132.20
5	0.3650	28.90	22	0.7900	140.10
6	0.3900	33.36	23	0.8150	148.10
7	0.4150	36.07	24	0.8400	156.20
8	0.4400	43.06	25	0.8650	164.30
9	0.4650	48.51	26	0.8900	172.40
10	0.4900	54.30	27	0.9150	180.60
11	0.5150	60.29	28	0.9400	189.70
12	0.5400	66.53	29	0.9650	197.90
13	0.5650	73.26	30	0.9900	206.00
14	0.5900	80.69	31	1.0150	214.20
15	0.6150	87.12	32	1.0400	223.30
16	0.6400	94.15	33	1.0650	231.50
17	0.6650	101.60			

Figure G-3

Fall distance versus time

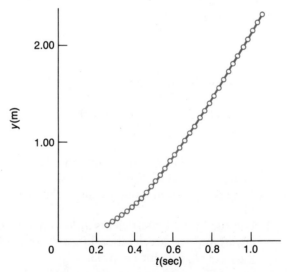

There are 33 data points. Fit the first six with a parabola and determine the coefficients a_0, a_1, a_2 [see Equation (13.33)]. Then fit the final $33 - 6 = 27$ points with a straight line and determine the coefficients of the line b_0, b_1. Print all the coefficients along with the sum of the squared deviations,

$$E_6 = \sum_{i=1}^{6} [(a_0 + a_1 t_i + a_2 t_i^2) - y_i]^2 + \sum_{i=7}^{33} [(b_0 + b_1 t_i) - y_i]^2 \qquad (G.5)$$

Next repeat the calculation with the break at point number 7; that is, fit the first 7 points with a parabola and the last 26 with a line. Continue this up to a break point at point number 22. The calculation with the smallest value of E gives the best fit by this method.

Finally, for the overall optimum fit, print the terminal velocity.

Problem Specifics. The complete program to solve this problem should contain the following elements:

1. Create a data file containing the experimental values.
2. For NC (cut point) = 7 to 22
   a. Construct the matrices

   $$[A] = \begin{bmatrix} NC & \Sigma t & \Sigma t^2 \\ \Sigma t & \Sigma t^2 & \Sigma t^3 \\ \Sigma t^2 & \Sigma t^3 & \Sigma t^4 \end{bmatrix} \qquad [B] = \begin{bmatrix} N - NC & \Sigma't \\ \Sigma't & \Sigma't^2 \end{bmatrix}$$

   and the right-hand-side vectors

   $$\mathbf{c} = \begin{bmatrix} \Sigma y \\ \Sigma ty \\ \Sigma t^2 y \end{bmatrix} \qquad \mathbf{d} = \begin{bmatrix} \Sigma'y \\ \Sigma'ty \end{bmatrix}$$

   where

   $$\Sigma \equiv \sum_{i=1}^{NC} \qquad \Sigma' \equiv \sum_{i=NC+1}^{N}$$

   b. Solve the two matrix equations by using the matrix subroutine MINV of Figure 12-4. Store the coefficients of the parabola and the line for this value of NC [e.g., A(I, NC), B(I, NC)].
   c. Evalute E(NC) for this value of NC.
3. Determine the overall minimum of the set of values E(NC). Print a neat table of E(NC), A(I, NC), B(I, NC) for NC = 7, 22. Tag the optimum value in the table with a label OPTIMUM FIT.
4. Use the best-fit coefficients a_i, b_i to determine the velocity (dy/dt) and the acceleration (d^2y/dt^2), and print a table of $y_{i,\exp}$, $y_{i,\text{theory}}$, vel_i, acc_i for $i = 1, 33$.

Programming Problem G-B: Record Times for the Mile Run

Very frequently in least squares data fitting, the assumed model function, $y(x)$, cannot be forced to resemble a straight line or a polynomial by a change of variables. As a result, the equations that determine the minimum of the squared deviations are nonlinear in the parameters and an iterative procedure must be used in place of the ordinary matrix tech-

Table G-3
Record times for
the mile run since
1865

i	Year	Time	i	Year	Time	i	Year	Time
1	1864	4:56	14	1913	4:14.4	27	1954	3:58.0
2	1865	4:36.5	15	1913	4:14.1	28	1957	3:57.2
3	1868	4:29.0	16	1915	4:12.6	29	1958	3:54.5
4	1869	4:28.9	17	1923	4:10.4	30	1962	3:54.4
5	1874	4:26.0	18	1931	4:09.2	31	1964	3:54.1
6	1875	4:24.5	19	1933	4:07.6	32	1965	3:53.6
7	1880	4:23.2	20	1934	4:06.8	33	1966	3:51.3
8	1882	4:21.4	21	1937	4:06.4	34	1967	3:51.2
9	1882	4:19.4	22	1942	4:06.2	35	1975	3:49.5
10	1884	4:18.4	23	1943	4:02.6	36	1979	3:49.0
11	1894	4:18.2	24	1944	4:01.6	37	1980	3:48.8
12	1895	4:17.0	25	1945	4:01.4	38	1981	3:47.3
13	1911	4:15.4	26	1954	3:59.4	39	1985	3:46.3

Figure G-4
Decrease in the
record time for the
mile run since 1865

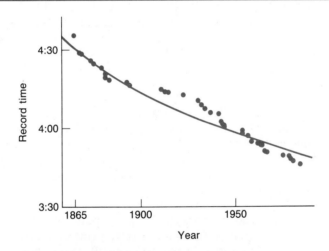

niques. For example, the record times for the mile are listed in Table G-3
and graphed in Figure G-4.

From the graph it appears that the record times are decreasing in
an exponential fashion. But the curve is not asymptotic to zero as t approaches infinity but rather approaches a fixed number somewhat below
4 minutes. Thus, we might attempt to fit the data to a model equation of
the form

$$R(t) = R_0(1 + e^{-\alpha t}) \tag{G.6}$$

where $R(t)$ is the record time, t is the year measured from 1865, and the
parameters are R_0, the asymptote, and the decay constant α. For large val-

ues of t the expression approaches R_0, which we expect to be ≈ 4 min. Since Equation (G.6) will result in nonlinear equations for R_0 and α, an alternate method of solution must be developed.

If we define

$$y = \ln\left[\frac{R(t)}{R_0} - 1\right] \tag{G.7}$$

Equation (G.6) may be written as

$$y = -\alpha t \tag{G.8}$$

Inserting this model function into the expression for $E(R_0, \alpha)$, the sum of the squared deviations, yields

$$E = \sum_{i=1}^{n} (\alpha t_i + y_i)^2 \tag{G.9}$$

which is to be minimized by solving $\partial E / \partial \alpha = 0$ for the value of α. [*Note:* The values of y_i, computed from Equation (G.7) are all negative.] The result is

$$\alpha = -\frac{\Sigma ty}{\Sigma t^2} \tag{G.10}$$

Unfortunately, to carry out the summations we first need to know the values of R_0 to be used in Equation (G.7). We have encountered situations similar to this frequently when solving nonlinear equations. The remedy then was often an iterative approach to a solution. Here, an iterative procedure is likewise suggested and could be constructed along the following lines:

1. Read the data $[t_i, R(t_i)]$, compute the set of values y_i from Equation (G.7), and neatly print in a table.
2. Choose an initial guess for R_0. Note that since the logatithm of a negative number is undefined, Equation (G.7) requires that R_0 be smaller than the minimum value of $R(t)$ in the data.
3. Determine α from Equation (G.10).
4. Compute a *new* value of R_0 by using Equation (G.6). For example,

$$R_{0,\text{new}} = \frac{1}{N} \sum_{i=1}^{n} \frac{R(t_i)}{1 + e^{-\alpha t_i}} \tag{G.11}$$

5. If the change in R_0 is less than 10^{-5}, stop; otherwise return to the second step and repeat.

The output of the program should consist of values for α, R_0, the number of iterations required, and the final value for the average deviation defined as

$$\Delta = \left(\frac{E}{N}\right)^{1/2}$$

Finally, use the computed values of α and R_0 to determine the precise day and time that the time of 3:40 will be recorded.[1]

---

[1] The times in Table G-3 are given as minutes:seconds. All the times used in computation must be converted to decimal minutes, whereas all times that are printed should be converted to the form minutes:seconds.

Numerical Integration

Introduction

The integration of a function of a single variable can be thought of as either the opposite of differentiation—that is, the antiderivative—or as the area under a curve. Antiderivatives are ordinarily discussed in depth in a calculus course. Here we will concentrate instead on the less analytic, more visual approach of interpreting[1] a definite integral as an area. That is, the integral of the function $f(x)$ from $x = a$ to $x = b$, designated as

$$I = \int_a^b f(x)\, dx$$

will be evaluated by devising schemes for measuring the area under the graph of the function over this interval. (See Figure 14-1.) This method of evaluating an integral lends itself so naturally to numerical computation that the most effective way to understand the process of integration is to learn the numerical approach first and later have these ideas reinforced by the more formal concepts of the antiderivative.

Another reason for studying numerical integration at this stage is that it is a so-called stable process; it almost always works. In contrast, numerical differentiation studied in Chapter 10 and defined by a relation like

$$\frac{df}{dx} = \lim_{\Delta x \to 0} \left[\frac{f(x + \Delta x) - f(x)}{\Delta x} \right]$$

is inherently unstable. As we attempt to evaluate this expression for smaller and smaller values of Δx, the problems of round-off error (sub-

---

[1] This interpretation defines regions where the function falls below the x axis to have *negative* area. Thus, the area "under" the sine function from $\theta = 0$ to $\theta = 2\pi$ is zero.

542

Figure 14-1
Integral as an area
under a curve

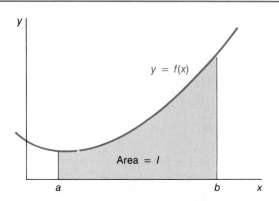

tracting numbers of about the same magnitude) and division by zero will
complicate the computation for even the simplest functions. Numerical integration, on the other hand, consists of expressing the area as the sum of
areas of smaller segments, a procedure that is relatively safe from such
computational difficulties.

Finally, it is unfortunately true that many, perhaps most, of
the integrals that occur in actual engineering or science problems cannot
be expressed in any closed form. For example, an integral as innocent
appearing as

$$I = \int_b^a e^{-x^2} dx$$

is of this type and the only way that it can be evaluated is numerically. To
formally integrate a function—that is, to obtain a closed expression for
the answer—often takes considerable training and experience. Dozens of
"tricks" must be learned and understood. On the other hand, the procedures of numerical integration are few in number, all quite easy to understand and remember. As in many earlier numerical procedures, we begin
by replacing the function over a limited range by straight-line segments.
The interval $x = a$ to $x = b$ is divided into subintervals or panels of size
Δx, the function is replaced by line segments over each subinterval, and
the area under the function is then approximated by the area under the
line segments. This is the trapezoidal rule approximation for an integral
and is described in the next section. The next order approximation is to
replace the function by parabolic segments and is known as Simpson's
rule. Extrapolating the ideas in these two methods to arbitrary order results in the Romberg algorithm for numerical integration, the most popular and accurate procedure for evaluating an integral using equally spaced
subintervals.

A different class of integration techniques, known as Gaussian
quadrature, permits the size of the subintervals to vary in such a way as to

optimize the accuracy of the approximation. These highly efficient, but more complex techniques, are briefly described in Section 14.6.

Suggestions for evaluating improper integrals (integrals with infinite limits or with singular integrands) are then summarized in Sections 14.7 and 14.8. Finally, the evaluation of double integrals in a FORTRAN program requires special care and is treated in Section 14.9.

14.2 Trapezoidal Rule

An approximation to the area under a complicated curve is obtained by assuming that the function can be replaced by simpler functions over a limited range. A straight line, the simplest approximation to a function, is the first to be considered and leads to what is called the *trapezoidal rule*.

The area under the curve $f(x)$ from $x = a$ to $x = b$ is approximated by the area beneath a straight line drawn between the points (x_a, f_a) and (x_b, f_b) (see Figure 14-2). The shaded area is then the approximation to the integral and is the area of a trapezoid, which is

$$I = \text{(average value of } f \text{ over interval)} \text{ (width of interval)}$$

or

$$I = \tfrac{1}{2}(f_a + f_b)(b - a) \equiv T_0 \tag{14.1}$$

This is the trapezoidal rule for one panel, identified as T_0.

Formula for the Trapezoidal Rule for *n* Panels

To improve the accuracy of the approximation to the area under a curve, the interval is next divided in half and the function approximated by

Figure 14-2
Approximating the area under a curve by a single trapezoid

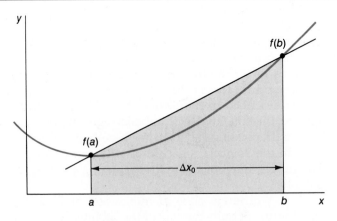

straight-line segments over each half. The area in this case is approximated by the area of two trapezoids (see Figure 14-3).

$$I \simeq T_1 = [\tfrac{1}{2}(f_a + f_1)\Delta x_1] + [\tfrac{1}{2}(f_1 + f_b)\Delta x_1]$$

or

$$T_1 = \frac{\Delta x_1}{2}(f_a + 2f_1 + f_b) \qquad (14.2)$$

where

$$\Delta x_1 = \frac{(b - a)}{2}$$

$$f_1 = f(x = a + \Delta x_1)$$

Notice that when adding the areas of the trapezoids, the sides at f_a and f_b are sides of only the first and last trapezoid, whereas the side at f_1 is a side of two trapezoids and thus "counts twice," explaining the factor of 2 in Equation (14.2).

Furthermore, the two-panel approximation, T_1, can be related to the one-panel results, T_0, as

$$T_1 = \frac{T_0}{2} + \Delta x_1 f_1 \qquad (14.3)$$

To increase the accuracy further, the interval is simply subdivided into a large number of panels. The result for n panels is clearly

$$I \simeq T_n = \frac{1}{2}\Delta x_n \left(f_a + 2\sum_{i=1}^{n-1} f_i + f_b \right) \qquad \text{Trapezoidal rule} \qquad (14.4)$$

Figure 14-3
Two-panel approximation to the area

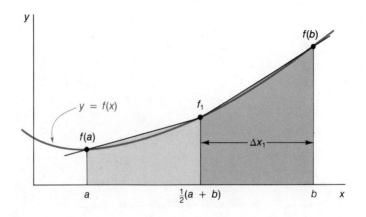

where $\Delta x_n = (b - a)/n$ and f_i is the function evaluated at each of the interior points,

$$f_i = f(x = a + i\Delta x_n)$$

The reason for the extra factor of 2 in Equation (14.4) is the same as in the two-panel example.

Alternate Form of the Trapezoidal Rule Equation

Equation (14.4) was derived assuming that the widths of all the panels are the same and equal to Δx_n. However, equal panel widths are not required in the derivation, and the equation can easily be generalized to a partition of the interval into unequal panels of width $\Delta x_i, i = 1, \ldots, n - 1$. However, for reasons to explained a bit later, we will not only restrict the panel widths to be equal but the number of panels to be a power of 2—that is,

$$n = 2^k$$

The number of panels is n, the order of the calculation will be called k, and the corresponding trapezoidal rule approximation will be labeled as T_k. Thus, T_0 is the result for $n = 2^0 = 1$ panel. The situation for $k = 2$ or $2^2 = 4$ panels is illustrated in Figure 14-4. In the figure the width of a panel is $\Delta x_2 = (b - a)/2^2$, and the value of the $k = 2$ trapezoidal rule approximation is

$$T_2 = \frac{\Delta x_2}{2}[f_a + 2f(a + \Delta x_2) + 2f(a + 2\Delta x_2) + 2f(a + 3\Delta x_2) + f_b]$$

(14.5)

However, since $2\Delta_2 = \Delta x_1$ we see that

$$f(a + 2\Delta x_2) = f(a + \Delta x_1)$$

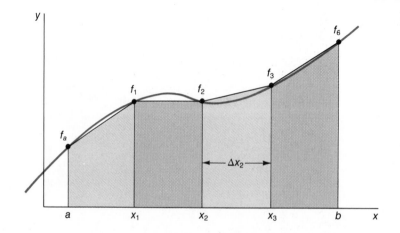

Figure 14-4
Four-panel
trapezoidal
approximation, T_2

and $f(a + \Delta x_1)$ was already determined in the previous calculation of T_1 [Equation (14.3)]. The point is that by successively doubling the number of panels in each stage, the only new information we require to proceed to the next order trapezoidal rule approximation is the evaluation of the function at the *midpoints* of the current intervals.

To exploit this fact further, Equations (14.2) and (14.3) can be used to rewrite Equation (14.5) in the form

$$T_2 = \frac{\Delta x_1}{4}[f_a + 2f(a + \Delta x_1) + f_b] + \Delta x_2[f(a + \Delta x_2) + f(a + 3\Delta x_2)]$$

$$= \frac{T_1}{2} + \Delta x_2[f(a + \Delta x_2) + f(a + 3\Delta x_2)]$$

This equation can easily be generalized to yield

$$T_k = \frac{1}{2}T_{k-1} + \Delta x_k \sum_{\substack{i=1 \\ \text{odd only}}}^{n-1} f(a + i\Delta x_k) \tag{14.6}$$

where

$$\Delta x_k = \frac{b - a}{2^k}$$

The procedure for using Equation (14.6) to approximate an integral by the trapezoidal rule is then:

1. Compute T_0 by using Equation (14.1).
2. Repeatedly apply Equation (14.6) for $k = 1, 2, \ldots$ until sufficient accuracy is obtained.

Example of a Trapezoidal Rule Calculation

To illustrate the ideas of this section, we use the integral

$$I = \int_1^2 \left(\frac{1}{x}\right) dx$$

The function $f(x) = 1/x$ can of course be integrated analytically to give $\ln(x)$, and since $\ln(1) = 0$, the value of the integral is $\ln(2) = 0.69314718$. The trapezoidal rule approximation to the integral with $b = 2$ and $a = 1$ begins with Equation (14.1) to obtain T_0.

$$T_0 = \frac{1}{2}\left(\frac{1}{1} + \frac{1}{2}\right)(2 - 1) = 0.75$$

Repeated use of Equation (14.6) then yields

$$k = 1 \qquad \Delta x_1 = \frac{1}{2}$$

$$T_1 = \frac{T_0}{2} + \frac{1}{2}\left[f\left(1 + \frac{1}{2}\right)\right] = \frac{0.75}{2} + \frac{1}{2}\left(\frac{1}{1.5}\right)$$

$$= 0.708333$$

$$k = 2 \qquad \Delta x_2 = \frac{1}{4}$$

$$T_2 = \frac{T_1}{2} + \frac{1}{4}\left(\frac{1}{1.25} + \frac{1}{1.75}\right)$$

$$= 0.6970238$$

$$k = 3 \qquad \Delta x_3 = \frac{1}{8}$$

$$T_3 = \frac{T_2}{2} + \frac{1}{8}\left(\frac{1}{1.125} + \frac{1}{1.375} + \frac{1}{1.625} + \frac{1}{1.875}\right)$$

$$= 0.69412185$$

Continuing the calculation through $k = 5$ yields

k	T_k
0	0.75
1	0.70833
2	0.69702
3	0.69412
4	0.69339
5	0.693208
⋮	⋮
Exact	0.693147...

The convergence of the computed values of the trapezoidal rule is not particularly fast, but the method is quite simple.

14.3 Simpson's Rule Approximation for an Integral

The trapezoidal rule is based on approximating the function by straight-line segments. To improve the accuracy and the convergence rate of the method, an obvious direction to take would be to approximate the function by parabolic segments in place of straight lines; that is, use the next term in a Taylor series expansion of the function. This idea results in an approximation for the integral known as *Simpson's rule*, the simplest example of which is illustrated in Figure 14-5. To uniquely specify a parabola requires three points, and so the lowest-order Simpson's rule has two panels.

To proceed, we need to know the area under a parabola drawn through three points. Note that the corresponding step in the derivation of the trapezoidal rule was trivial: the area under a line through two points is simply $\Delta x(f_a + f_b)/2$. Here we must first derive the expression for the area under a parabola.

■ Area under a Parabola Drawn through Three Points

A general parabola can be written as

$$y(x) = c_0 + c_1(x - x_0) + c_2(x - x_0)^2$$

If we have three equally spaced points, x_0, $x_1 = x_0 + \Delta x$, and $x_2 = x_0 + 2\Delta x$, and are given the corresponding values of y at these points (namely, y_0, y_1, and y_2), we can force the parabola to pass through the given points by requiring that

$$y(x = x_0) \equiv y_0 = c_0$$

$$y(x = x_1) \equiv y_1 = c_0 + c_1\Delta x + c_2\Delta x^2$$

$$y(x = x_2) \equiv y_2 = c_0 + c_1 2\Delta x + c_2 4\Delta x^2$$

or

$$\begin{bmatrix} y_0 \\ y_1 \\ y_2 \end{bmatrix} = \begin{bmatrix} 1 & 0 & 0 \\ 1 & 1 & 1 \\ 1 & 2 & 4 \end{bmatrix} \begin{bmatrix} c_0 \\ c_1\Delta x \\ c_2\Delta x^2 \end{bmatrix} \tag{14.7}$$

Figure 14-5
Two-panel
Simpson's rule
approximation to
an integral

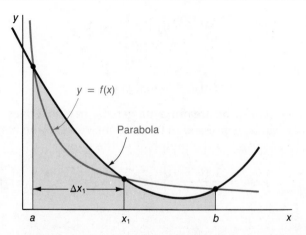

The inverse of this matrix can be found by using the subroutine MINV of Figure 12-6. The result is

$$
\begin{bmatrix} 1 & 0 & 0 \\ 1 & 1 & 1 \\ 1 & 2 & 4 \end{bmatrix}^{-1} = \begin{bmatrix} 1 & 0 & 0 \\ -\frac{3}{2} & 2 & -\frac{1}{2} \\ \frac{1}{2} & -1 & \frac{1}{2} \end{bmatrix}
$$

Thus, the coefficients of the parabola may be expressed in terms of the given points as

$$
\begin{bmatrix} c_0 \\ c_1 \Delta x \\ c_2 \Delta x^2 \end{bmatrix} = \begin{bmatrix} 1 & 0 & 0 \\ -\frac{3}{2} & 2 & -\frac{1}{2} \\ \frac{1}{2} & -1 & \frac{1}{2} \end{bmatrix} \begin{bmatrix} y_0 \\ y_1 \\ y_2 \end{bmatrix} \tag{14.8}
$$

Next, the area under the parabola from x_0 to x_2 is given by

$$
\text{Area} = \int_{x_0}^{x_2} y(x)\, dx = c_0(x_2 - x_0) + \tfrac{1}{2}c_1(x_2 - x_0)^2 + \tfrac{1}{3}c_2(x_2 - x_0)^3
$$

$$
= 2c_0 \Delta x + 2c_1 \Delta x^2 + \tfrac{4}{3}c_2 \Delta x^3
$$

$$
= \tfrac{2}{3}\Delta x[3c_0 + 3c_1 \Delta x + 4c_2 \Delta x^2]
$$

$$
= \tfrac{2}{3}\Delta x[3 \quad 3 \quad 4]\begin{bmatrix} c_0 \\ c_1 \Delta x \\ c_2 \Delta x^2 \end{bmatrix} \tag{14.9}
$$

where the result is written as a product of a row vector times a column vector in the last line. If we now use the result of Equation (14.8), the expression for the area becomes

$$
\text{Area} = \tfrac{2}{3}\Delta x[3 \quad 3 \quad 4]\begin{bmatrix} 1 & 0 & 0 \\ -\frac{3}{2} & 2 & -\frac{1}{2} \\ \frac{1}{2} & -1 & \frac{1}{2} \end{bmatrix}\begin{bmatrix} y_0 \\ y_1 \\ y_2 \end{bmatrix}
$$

$$
= \tfrac{2}{3}\Delta x[\tfrac{1}{2} \quad 2 \quad \tfrac{1}{2}]\begin{bmatrix} y_0 \\ y_1 \\ y_2 \end{bmatrix}
$$

$$
= \tfrac{1}{3}\Delta x[y_0 + 4y_1 + y_2] \tag{14.10}
$$

Thus, the area under a general parabola over the interval $x = a$ to $x = b$ can be expressed in terms of the value of the parabola at the left and right ends and at the midpoint of the interval.

$$
\text{Area} = \frac{1}{3}\frac{(b-a)}{2}\left[y(x=a) + 4y\left(x = \frac{a+b}{2}\right) + y(x=b) \right] \tag{14.11}
$$

Equation (14.11) is then the starting point of the derivation of Simpson's rule in the same way that Equation (14.1) is the basis of the trapezoidal rule derivation.

■ Derivation of the Simpson's Rule Approximation

If the curve $f(x)$ drawn in Figure 14-5 is approximated by a parabola drawn through the three points $f_a, f_b,$ and the value of $f(x)$ at the midpoint of the interval, f_{mid}, the first-order Simpson's rule approximation is obtained.

$$k = 1 \qquad n = 2^1 \text{ panels} \qquad \Delta x_1 = \frac{b - a}{2}$$

$$S_1 = \tfrac{1}{3}\Delta x_1 [f_a + 4f(a + \Delta x_1) + f_b]$$

The next level of approximation is to halve the interval width and partition the interval into four panels, as shown in Figure 14-6. The area under the function $f(x)$ is then approximated as the area under the two parabolas drawn through the two sets of points (f_a, f_1, f_2) and (f_2, f_3, f_b). Since the area under a single parabola is given by Equation (14.11), the area under the two parabolas is

$$S_2 = \tfrac{1}{3}\Delta x_2[(f_a + 4f_1 + f_2) + (f_2 + 4f_3 + f_b)]$$
$$= \tfrac{1}{3}\Delta x_2[f_a + 4(f_1 + f_3) + 2f_2 + f_b] \qquad (14.12)$$

Figure 14-6
Second-order Simpson's rule approximation is the area under two parabolas

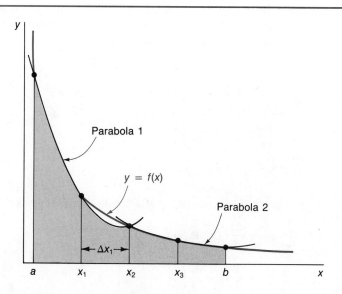

where

$$\Delta x_2 = \frac{b - a}{2^2}$$

and

$$f_i = f(x = a + i\Delta x_2)$$

This procedure can be extended to 8, 16, 32, and so on panels. The result is a rather simple generalization of Equation (14.12) and for $n = 2^k$ panels is:

$$S_k = \tfrac{1}{3}\Delta x_k \left[f_a + 4 \sum_{\substack{i=1 \\ \text{odd only}}}^{n-1} f(a + i\Delta x_k) + 2 \sum_{\substack{i=2 \\ \text{even only}}}^{n-2} f(a + i\Delta x_k) + f_b \right]$$

Simpson's rule

(14.13)

where

$$\Delta x_k = \frac{b - a}{2^k}$$

Equation (14.13) is an extremely popular method of evaluating integrals of functions that are smooth, and rightly so. As we shall see later in the chapter, Simpson's rule converges nicely in most instances and it is relatively easy to use. Also, Equation (14.13) can easily be adapted to handle an odd number of unevenly spaced points and is the most common method for estimating the integral of experimentally obtained data.

Relationship between Simpson's Rule and the Trapezoidal Rule

Because both the trapezoidal rule [Equation (14.6)] and Simpson's rule [Equation (14.13)] employ the values of the function evaluated at the same points, the two formulas should be related. If we collect the relevant equations for $k = 0$ and 1, we have

$$T_0 = \frac{1}{2}\Delta x_0(f_a + f_b)$$

$$T_1 = \frac{T_0}{2} + \Delta x_1 f_1$$

$$S_1 = \frac{1}{3}\Delta x_1[f_a + 4f_1 + f_b]$$

Since $\Delta x_0 = 2\Delta x_1$, we can write the last equation as

$$S_1 = \frac{\Delta x_0}{6}(f_a + f_b) + \frac{4}{3}\Delta x_1 f_1$$

$$= \frac{1}{3}T_0 + \frac{4}{3}\left(T_1 - \frac{1}{2}T_0\right)$$

or

$$S_1 = T_1 + \frac{T_1 - T_0}{3}$$

For $k = 2$ the equations are

$$T_1 = \Delta x_2(f_a + 2f_2 + f_b)$$
$$T_2 = \tfrac{1}{2}\Delta x_2[f_a + 2(f_1 + f_2 + f_3) + f_b]$$
$$S_2 = \tfrac{1}{3}\Delta x_2[f_a + 4(f_1 + f_3) + 2f_2 + f_b]$$

where $f_i = f(x = a + i\Delta x_2)$.

Using these expressions you can easily verify that

$$S_2 = T_2 + \frac{T_2 - T_1}{3}$$

In fact, using the general expressions for T_k [Equation (14.6)] and for S_k [Equation (14.13)], this result can be generalized to

$$S_k = T_k + \frac{T_k - T_{k-1}}{3} \tag{14.14}$$

This important result provides a convenient alternative method of obtaining the results of Simpson's rule: First compute the trapezoidal rule values through order k, then use Equation (14.14) to generate the Simpson's rule values likewise through order k. Notice that by this method, once the trapezoidal rule values are obtained, the function itself is not evaluated at any additional points.

■ Example of Simpson's Rule as an Approximation to an Integral

Again consider the integral

$$I = \int_1^2 \frac{1}{x}\,dx$$

Using Equation (14.13) first for $k = 1$ yields

$$k = 1 \qquad n = 2^1 = 2 \qquad \Delta x_1 = \frac{b - a}{2} = \frac{1}{2}$$

$$S_1 = \frac{1}{3}\left(\frac{1}{2}\right)\left[1 + 4\left(\frac{1}{1.5}\right) + \frac{1}{2}\right]$$
$$= 0.6944444$$

Repeating for $k = 2$,

$$k = 2 \qquad n = 2^2 = 4 \qquad \Delta x_2 = \frac{1}{4}$$

$$S_2 = \frac{1}{3}\left(\frac{1}{4}\right)\left[1 + 4\left(\frac{1}{1.25} + \frac{1}{1.75}\right) + 2\left(\frac{1}{1.5}\right) + \frac{1}{2}\right]$$

$$= 0.69325397$$

Continuing the calculation, we obtain the values listed in Table 14-1. For comparison, results are also included for the same integral obtained in the previous section by the trapezoidal rule. Clearly, Simpson's rule converges much faster than the trapezoidal rule, at least for this example.

The Simpson's rule values could also have been computed directly from the trapezoidal rule numbers by using Equation (14.14). For example,

$$S_2 = \frac{1}{2}(0.69702) + \frac{(0.69702) - (0.70833)}{3}$$

$$= 0.69325$$

<hr>

14.4   Beyond Simpson's Rule

Higher-level integration algorithms are next obtained by approximating the function $f(x)$ by interpolating polynomial segments with the degree of the polynomial now chosen to be 3, 4, 5, and so on. What results is an entire class of numerical integration techniques collectively called Newton–Cote's formulas. The trapezoidal rule and Simpson's rule are the first two of these formulas. To obtain the next formula in the set, a fourth-order polynomial, $y_4(x)$, is fit through the points associated with a four-panel partition ($k = 2, n = 2^2$) of the interval $x = a$ to $x = b$, and the integral $\int y_4(x)\,dx$ is used as the next level approximation to $\int f(x)\,dx$. For eight panels, two fourth-degree segments are used, and so on. The formula that follows from this procedure is called *Boole's rule*. Boole's rule is similar to

Table 14-1
Trapezoidal and Simpson's rule results for the integral $I = \int_1^2 dx/x$

Order k	Number of Panels n	T_k	S_k
0	1	0.75	—
1	2	0.7083	0.6944
2	4	0.69702	0.69325
3	8	0.69412	0.69315
4	16	0.69339	0.6931466
5	32	0.693208	0.6931473
6	64	0.693162	0.6931472

but more complicated than the equations for the trapezoidal rule and Simpson's rule and is not included here. (See, however, Problem 14.9.) Instead, let us consider how a higher-level algorithm such as Boole's rule relates to the earlier equations for the trapezoidal and Simpson's rules.

If the partitioning of the interval proceeds as before into $2, 4, 8, \ldots$ panels, the values of the function that enter Boole's rule will be the same set that was used in both Simpson's and the trapezoidal rule. It should then be possible to relate the Boole's calculation to the previous estimates in a manner similar to Equation (14.14). This is in fact possible, and, if the Boole's kth-order result is labeled as B_k, yields

$$B_k = S_k + \frac{S_k - S_{k-1}}{15} \tag{14.15}$$

Thus, once a table of Simpson's rule values has been determined, the improved Boole's rule results can easily be computed. For example, a third column can be added to the values in Table 14-1 in the evaluation of the integral

$$I = \int_1^2 \frac{1}{x} dx = \ln(2) = 0.6931471806\ldots$$

as shown in Table 14-2. The Boole's rule values are an improvement over the Simpson's rule and the trapezoidal rule estimates. The easiest way to obtain the more accurate Boole's rule results is to first generate a table of trapezoidal rule estimates through order k, then use Equation (14.14) to determine the Simpson's rule values, and then apply Equation (14.15) to generate the Boole's rule numbers.

You can probably see the pattern emerging in this analysis. The next step would be to fit the eight-panel partition with an eighth-degree polynomial, $y_8(x)$, approximate the area under the curve $f(x)$ by the area under successively more and more polynomial segments, and label the kth-order such approximation as, say, C_k. Finally, this higher-degree estimate is related to the previous area estimates B_k, S_k, and T_k. The result of

Table 14-2
Column of Boole's rule values is added to Table 14-1

Order k	Number of panels n	T_k	S_k	B_k
0	1	0.75	—	—
1	2	0.7083	0.6944	—
2	4	0.69702	0.69325	0.69317
3	8	0.69412	0.693154	0.693149
4	16	0.69339	0.693146	0.6931472
5	32	0.693208	0.69314721	0.693147181
6	64	0.693162	0.6931471842	0.69314718054

Exact 0.6931471806...

this formidable but straightforward exercise is that the higher-degree approximations C_k are related to the Boole's rule results by

$$C_k = B_k + \frac{B_k - B_{k-1}}{63} \tag{14.16}$$

The limit suggested by the sequence of integration algorithms

$$T_k \to S_k \to B_k \to C_k \to \cdots$$

is known as *Romberg integration*[2] or Richardson extrapolation to the limit.

14.5 Romberg Integration

The first step in unifying the previous numerical integration algorithms is to define a new notation, T_k^m, where the subscript k labels the order of the approximation (n = number of panels = 2^k) and m will now identify the *level* of the integration algorithm, that is,

$m = 0$ Trapezoidal rule

$$T_0^0 = T_0$$

$$T_1^0 = T_1$$

$$\vdots$$

$$T_k^0 = T_k$$

$m = 1$ Simpson's rule

$$T_k^1 = S_k$$

$m = 2$ Boole's rule

$$T_k^2 = B_k$$

$m = 3$

$$T_k^3 = C_k$$

etc.

Equations (14.14), (14.15), and (14.16) rewritten in terms of these quantities become

$$T_k^1 = T_k^0 + \frac{1}{3}(T_k^0 - T_{k-1}^0)$$

$$T_k^2 = T_k^1 + \frac{1}{15}(T_k^1 - T_{k-1}^1)$$

$$T_k^3 = T_k^2 + \frac{1}{63}(T_k^2 - T_{k-1}^2)$$

---

[2] The proof of the Romberg algorithm, however, follows a different path. See S. Kuo, *Computer Applications of Numerical Methods* (Reading, Mass.: Addison-Wesley, 1972).

The generalization of these results leads to the equation for the Romberg algorithm:

$$T_k^{m+1} = T_k^m + \frac{T_k^m - T_{k-1}^m}{4^{m+1} - 1} \qquad \text{Romberg equation} \qquad (14.17)$$

The importance of this equation lies in the fact that under normal conditions quite accurate results may be obtained for the integral of a reasonably smooth[3] function with little more work than is applied in obtaining the trapezoidal rule estimates.

Constructing Romberg Tables

The procedure is to start with the one-panel trapezoidal rule value

$$T_0 \to T_0^0 = \tfrac{1}{2}(b - a)(f_a + f_b)$$

then increase the *order* of the calculation (increment k from 0 to 1) by using Equation (14.6):

$$T_k = \tfrac{1}{2}T_{k-1} + \Delta x_k \sum_{\substack{i=1 \\ \text{odd only}}}^{n-1} f(a + i\Delta x_k)$$

Next increase the *level* of the algorithm (i.e., from trapezoidal to Simpson's) by using Equation (14.17). These ideas can be collected together in the form of a triangular table

T_0

$T_1 \quad S_1$

$T_2 \quad S_2 \quad B_2$

$T_3 \quad S_3 \quad B_3 \quad C_3$

$T_4 \quad S_4 \quad B_4 \quad C_4 \ldots$

or in terms of the symbols T_k^m,

m	0	1	2	3	4
k					
0	T_0^0				
1	T_1^0	T_1^1			
2	T_2^0	T_2^1	T_2^2		
3	T_3^0	T_3^1	T_3^2	T_3^3	
4	T_4^0	T_4^1	T_4^2	T_4^3	T_4^4

An increase in accuracy is achieved by increasing the number of panels (stepping down in the triangle) or by increasing the level of the al-

---

[3] "Smooth" means that the function must be continuous over the interval and all of its derivatives must be finite in that interval; that is, the function must be expandable as a Taylor series in this region.

gorithm (stepping across horizontally in the triangle). The chief advantage of the method is that the function is evaluated only in obtaining the elements of the first column, the trapezoidal rule results.

Convergence and Accuracy

The Romberg procedure is terminated when the numbers along the diagonal of the triangle no longer change significantly. To be more precise, we must analyze the algorithm more carefully for potential problems. In determining the first set of trapezoidal rule elements, only addition and subtraction of terms is involved, and so we expect the potential for round-off error problems to be minimal. However, when determining the higher-level approximations, subtraction of numbers of like size occurs (i.e., $T_k^m - T_{k-1}^m$) and round-off error will eventually limit the accuracy of these terms. It is essential to have some sort of indicator that will tell us when round-off error begins to be a problem. To this end we rewrite Equation (14.17) in a slightly different form for two values of k,

$$(4^{m+1} - 1)T_k^{m+1} = 4^{m+1}T_k^m - T_{k-1}^m$$

$$(4^{m+1} - 1)T_{k-1}^{m+1} = 4^{m+1}T_{k-1}^m - T_{k-2}^m$$

and subtract:

$$4^{m+1}(T_k^m - T_{k-1}^m) - (T_{k-1}^m - T_{k-2}^m) = (4^{m+1} - 1)(T_k^{m+1} - T_{k-1}^{m+1})$$

$$(14.18)$$

Since the terms on the right side of Equation (14.18) correspond to a higher level of approximation, we expect the right side of the equation to approach zero. We next define

$$R_k^m = \frac{1}{4^{m+1}} \frac{T_{k-1}^m - T_{k-2}^m}{T_k^m - T_{k-1}^m} \tag{14.19}$$

and from Equation (14.19), R_k^m should approach the limit

$$R_k^m \to 1$$

Notice that three values of T_k^m are required to determine each R_k^m.

Clearly the quantity R_k^m is extremely susceptible to round-off error problems when successive calculations of T_k^m are nearly the same. A satisfactory flag of a problem is when R_k^m begins to differ significantly from 1.

Formulas exist that give estimates of the magnitude of the errors involved in all of the integration algorithms discussed so far. All of these error estimates require that the third, fourth, or higher derivatives of the function be evaluated on the interval and that the maximum value of this derivative on the interval be estimated. This estimation is usually a difficult task and requires much more effort than simply allowing the computer to run longer, keeping an eye out for round-off errors and divergences. The error estimate equations are particularly important in convergence proofs but are rarely used in actual computations.

Example Calculation Using the Romberg Algorithm

To illustrate the Romberg method we return to the integral

$$I = \int_1^2 \frac{1}{x} dx = \ln(2) = 0.6931471806\ldots$$

The results through $m = 4$ are listed in Table 14-3.

The values of the quantities R_k^m defined by Equation (14.19) are listed in Table 14-4. Notice that in this instance the presence of a divergent value for the error flag R_k^m does not indicate a failure of the calculation but rather marks a limit beyond which accuracy will not increase with further computation. Thus, continuing the calculation beyond the $k = 6, m = 3$ step does not add to the accuracy of the result.

FORTRAN Code for Romberg Integration

The FORTRAN code for a function subprogram that employs the Romberg algorithm to approximate the integral of a function is given in Figure 14-7. The function follows the procedure used in the previous section in obtaining the numbers in Tables 14-3 and 14-4.

First, the one-panel (0th-order) trapezoidal rule value is computed. Next, Equation (14.6) is used to compute the next-order trapezoidal rule approximation that is one step down the first column of the triangle.

Table 14-3
Results of a Romberg integration of $\int_1^2 dx/x$

k \ m	0	1	2	3	4
0	0.75				
1	0.70833	0.694444			
2	0.6970238	0.6932540	0.69317460		
3	0.69412185	0.69315453	0.693147901	0.693147478	
4	0.69339120	0.693147653	0.693147194	0.693147183	0.6931471808
5	0.693208208	0.693147210	0.6931471808	0.6931471806	0.6931471806
6	0.693162439	0.693147182	0.6931471805	0.6931471806	0.6931471806

Header of table: T_k^m

Table 14-4
Quantities R_k^m monitor round-off error in the previous Romberg table

k \ m	0	1	2	3	4
0	—				
1	—	—			
2	0.921	—	—		
3	0.974	0.748	—	—	
4	0.993	0.904	0.590	—	—
5	0.998	0.971	0.818	0.460	—
6	1.000	0.991	0.941	∞	∞

Header of table: R_k^m

Figure 14-7 _____

FORTRAN code
for a function
that implements
the Romberg
integration
algorithm

```
      FUNCTION ROMBRG(F,A,B,KMX,EPS,IPRNT,IFAIL)
*--
* ROMBRG integrates the function f(x) from x=a to x=b.  The ele-
* ments of the Romberg table are stored in T(K,M), where K de-
* notes the order and M labels the level of the approximation,
* that is, the number of panels, n = 2**k, and M=0 => trapezoidal
* rule, M=1 => Simpson's rule, and so on.  The calculation is
* terminated successfully when successive diagonal elements dif-
* fer by less than the user-supplied tolerance, EPS.  Round-off
* error is monitored by computing the quantity, R(K) which should
* be close to 1.  If significantly different from 1, the calcula-
* tion is halted, a message printed, and the most recent value
* returned. The calculation is continued through a maximum user
* supplied order, KMX. If the desired accuracy is not achieved
* after order KMX, a diagnostic message is printed and the
* latest, most accurate value is returned. If IPRNT=1, the com-
* plete Romberg table is printed before any return. If IFAIL = 1,
* the proceedure has failed.
*=====================================================================
* Variables
*--
      DOUBLE PRECISION T(0:15,0:15),R(0:15)
      CHARACTER FLAG*3
      INTEGER K,M,NPTS,KMX,IPRINT
      REAL    DX,A,B,EPS,SUM,FRACT
*
*     A,B    -- Integration interval             [INPUT]
*     EPS    -- Convergence tolerance            [INPUT]
*     KMX    -- Maximum order of the calculation [INPUT]
*     IPRNT  -- Print flag, if 1 print tables    [INPUT]
*     T(,)   -- Elements of the Romberg table
*     R(,)   -- Table of round-off error flags
*     K      -- Current order of the calculation
*     M      -- Current level of the calculation
*     NPTS   -- Current number of sampling points
*     SUM    -- Sum of interior function values
*     FRACT  -- Fractional change in diagonal elements
*     IFAIL  -- If zero, no errors detected
*--------------------------------------------------------------------
* First compute the 0-th order/one panel trapezopidal rule value
*
      DX = (B-A)
      T(0,0) = 0.5*DX*(F(A) + F(B))
      R(0)   = 1.
      R(1)   = 1.
      IF(IPRNT .EQ. 1)THEN
         WRITE(*,10)(I,I=0,KMX)
         WRITE(*,11)' Order',('--------|',I=0,KMX)
         WRITE(*,12)0,T(0,0)
         WRITE(*,'(T7,''|--------|'')')
      ENDIF
*
*        Next, for order K = 1 through KMX
*
      DO 5 K = 1,KMX
*
*        Compute the next order trapezoid rule value; that is,
*        step down the 1st column of the table by halving the
*        intervals and doubling the number of sampling points.
*
```

Figure 14-7
(continued)

```
                        NPTS = 2**K
                        DX   = DX/2.
     *
     *         Sum the function at all odd points, that is, the
     *         midpoints of the previous intervals.
     *
                        SUM = 0.0
                        DO 2 I = 1, NPTS-1, 2
                            SUM = SUM + F(A+I*DX)
          2        CONTINUE
     *
     *         The next-order trapezoid rule is given by
     *
                        T(K,0) = T(K-1,0)/2 + DX*SUM
     *
     *         Next step across the table, M = 1,2, ..., K
     *
                        KSTOP = K
                        DO 3 M = 0, K-1
                            T(K,M+1) = T(K,M) + (T(K,M)-T(K-1,M))/(4.**(M+1)-1)
          3        CONTINUE
                        ROMBRG  = T(K,K)
                        IF(IPRNT .EQ. 1)THEN
                            WRITE(*,12)K,(T(K,M),M=0,K)
                            WRITE(*,11)'        ',('---------|',I=0,K)
                        ENDIF
     *
     *         Test for errors or success in this pass
     *
                        IFAIL = 0
                        IF(K .GE. 2)THEN
                            FRACT = (T(K,K) - T(K-1,K-1))/T(K,K)
                            IF(ABS(FRACT) .GT. EPS)THEN
                                R(K)   = (T(K-1,K-2) - T(K-2,K-2))/
          +                             (T(K  ,K-2) - T(K-1,K-2))/(4.**(K-1))
                                IF(ABS(LOG(ABS(R(K)))) .GT. 2.)THEN
                                    WRITE(*,13)K,R(K),FRACT,T(K,K)
                                    IFAIL = 1
                                    RETURN
                                ENDIF
                            ELSE
                                RETURN
                            ENDIF
                        ENDIF
          5    CONTINUE
     *
     *   In KMX passes, the calculation has failed to obtain a
     *   sufficiently accurate value.  Print a warning.
     *
              WRITE(*,14)KMX,FRACT,ROMBRG
              IFAIL = 1
              RETURN
     *----------------------------------------------------------------
     * Formats
     *--
         10  FORMAT(/,T5,'The Romberg table',//,
              + T9,'Level =>',/,
              + T7,'|',7(3X,I2,4X,'|'))
```

Figure 14-7
(concluded)

```
*--
 11  FORMAT(A6,'|',7A10)
*--
 12  FORMAT(2X,I2,T7,'|',7(F9.6,'|'))
*--
 13  FORMAT(/,
    + T5,'*============ERROR in ROMBERG===============*',/,
    + T5,'| In pass ',I2,' the calculation was halted ',T50,'|',/
    +,T5,'| due to round-off error. The round-off error|',/,
    + T5,'| flag is ',E7.1,'. The latest fractional',T50,'|',/,
    + T5,'| change in diagonal terms = ',E7.1,T50,'|',/,
    + T5,'| The value returned = ',F12.8,T50,'|',/,
    + T5,'*===============IFAIL = 1====================*')

 14  FORMAT(/,
    + T5,'*============ERROR in ROMBERG===============*',/,
    + T5,'| ROMBRG has failed due to excessive iterations*',/,
    + T5,'| After ',I2,' passes, sufficient accruacy was not |',/
    +,T5,'| acheived.  The latest fractional change was  |',/,
    + T5,'| R = ',E7.1,T52,'|',/,
    + T5,'| The value returned was ',F12.8,T52,'|',/,
    + T5,'*=================IFAIL = 1==================*')
     END
```

After incrementing the order by $k \rightarrow k + 1$, Equation (14.17) is used to step across from the first column ($m = 0$) to the diagonal column ($m = k$). If the fractional change in two successive elements along the diagonal of the triangular Romberg table differs by less than the user-supplied tolerance, EPS, the function returns with the most recent and most accurate value for the integral.

Additionally, round-off error is monitored using Equation (14.19) to compute the quantity R_k^m. If it differs significantly from 1, the calculation is halted.

14.6 Gauss Quadrature

All numerical integration techniques, and for that matter most numerical procedures of any kind, are based on the following idea: a complicated function may be approximated over a small enough interval by polynomials of varying degree, and then the differentiation, integration, or whatever operation on the original function is replaced by the same operation on the simpler polynomial. The procedures of numerical integration that we have discussed so far—the trapezoidal rule, Simpson's rule, and Romberg integration—are examples of this idea. Romberg integration is the theoretical optimum procedure that can be applied to an arbitrary smooth function over a finite interval that contains no singularities (points where the function approaches infinity) *provided* that the calculation is restricted to *evenly* spaced points. If the constraint of evenly spaced points is removed, a new class of numerical integration algorithms may be developed, known collectively as *Gauss quadrature algorithms*. (Quadrature is the technical name for numerical integration.)

Derivation of a Simple Gauss Quadrature Procedure

Each of the various numerical integration methods discussed—for example, trapezoidal, Simpson's, Boole's—approximates the integral $\int f(x)\,dx$ by a sum of function evaluations at equally spaced points multiplied by so-called weight factors ω_i.

$$\int_a^b f(x)\,dx \simeq \sum_{i=0}^n \omega_i f(x_i) \tag{14.20}$$

where $x_i = a + i\Delta x_k$, and the weights are specified by the particular type of integration algorithm. For example, the trapezoidal rule has a set of weights $\omega_i = \frac{1}{2}(1, 2, 2, \ldots, 2, 2, 1)\Delta x$, that is,

$$\int_a^b f(x)\,dx \simeq \Delta x_k \frac{1}{2}(f_0 + 2f_1 + 2f_2 + \cdots + 2f_{n-1} + f_n) \quad \text{Trapezoidal}$$

The set of weights for Simpson's rule is $\omega_i = \frac{1}{3}(1, 4, 2, 4, \ldots, 2, 4, 2, 4, 1)\Delta x$, that is

$$\int_a^b f(x)\,dx \simeq \Delta x_k \frac{1}{3}(f_0 + 4f_1 + 2f_2 + \cdots + 4_{n-1} + f_n) \quad \text{Simpson's}$$

The set of multiplicative weight factors were determined by fitting successively higher-degree polynomials to segments of the function.

The great mathematician and scientist Carl Friedrich Gauss suggested that the accuracy of the computational algorithm could be significantly improved if the positions of the function evaluations as well as the set of weight factors were left as parameters to be determined by optimizing the overall accuracy. By this he meant that the procedure should be *exact* when applied to polynomials of as high a degree as possible. If the approximation employs function evaluations at, say, n points, the procedure has $2n$ parameters to be determined (the x_i and the factors ω_i). Since a general polynomial of degree N has $N + 1$ coefficients, the Gauss procedure with n points is required to be exact for any polynomial of degree $N = 2n - 1$ or less.

The Gauss quadrature algorithms are usually stated in terms of integrals over the interval -1 to 1. For such an integral we would anticipate that, from symmetry, the sampling points and the weights would be the same for $\pm x$. Thus, the form of the algorithm is

$$\int_{-1}^1 f(x)\,dx \approx \omega_0 f(0) + \sum_{i=1}^k \omega_i[f(x_i) + f(-x_i)] \qquad \text{for odd } n, k = \frac{(n-1)}{2}$$

$$\approx \sum_{i=1}^k \omega_i[f(x_i) + f(-x_i)] \qquad \text{for even } n, k = \frac{n}{2}$$

$$\tag{14.21}$$

The remaining task is to determine the parameters ω_i, x_i such that the approximation is of optimum accuracy in the sense discussed above.

For example, in the case of two sampling points, the parameters are ω_1, x_1, and these are determined by requiring that Equation (14.21) is *exact* whenever $f(x)$ is a polynomial of degree 3 or less. Applying this condition successively to the functions $1, x, x^2, x^3$, results in the following four relations:

$$\int_{-1}^{1} 1 \, dx = 2 = \omega_1[1 + 1]$$

$$\int_{-1}^{1} x \, dx = 0 = \omega_1[x_1 - x_1]$$

$$\int_{-1}^{1} x^2 \, dx = \tfrac{2}{3} = \omega_1[x_1^2 + x_1^2]$$

$$\int_{-1}^{1} x^3 \, dx = 0 = \omega_1[x_1^3 - x_1^3]$$

Thus, $\omega_1 = 1$ and $x_1^2 = \tfrac{1}{3}$. Equation (14.21) for $n = 2$ now reads

$$\int_{-1}^{1} f(x) \, dx \approx f\left(x = \frac{1}{\sqrt{3}}\right) + f\left(x = \frac{-1}{\sqrt{3}}\right) \tag{14.22}$$

You should verify that this remarkably simple approximation does indeed give the exact result for the integral of any polynomial of degree 3 or less.

If the function $f(x)$ is not a polynomial of degree 3 or less, the result of the $n = 2$ Gauss quadrature expression, Equation (14.22), will only be an approximation to the actual integral. The accuracy of the approximation will depend on how much the function $f(x)$ resembles polynomials of degree 3 or less. For example, consider the integral

$$I = \int_{-1}^{1} \cos(x) \, dx = [\sin(x)]|_{-1}^{1} = 1.6829\ldots$$

The Gauss approximation to this integral is

$$I \approx \cos\left(-\frac{1}{\sqrt{3}}\right) + \cos\left(\frac{1}{\sqrt{3}}\right) = 1.6758$$

Higher-Order Gauss Quadrature Procedures

To improve the accuracy of the approximation given in Equation (14.22), the number of sampling points is increased from 2 to $3, 4, \ldots$. For each choice of n, the number of points, the weight factors ω_i, and the position of the sampling points x_i must be determined by requiring that the approximation be exact for polynomials of degree $N \leq 2n - 1$. These have

Table 14-5

Sampling points and weight factors for Gauss quadrature

$$I = \int_{-1}^{1} f(x)\, dx \approx \sum_{i=1}^{n/2} \omega_i[f(x_i) + f(-x_i)] \qquad \text{if } n \text{ is even}$$

$$\approx \omega_0 f(0) + \sum_{i=1}^{(1/2)(n-1)} \omega_i[f(x_i) + f(-x_i)] \qquad \text{if } n \text{ is odd}$$

n	i	x_i	ω_i
2	1	0.5773502692	1.0
3	0	0.0	0.8888888889
	1	0.7745966692	0.5555555556
5	0	0.0	0.5688888889
	1	0.5384693101	0.4786286705
	2	0.9061798459	0.2369268850
10	1	0.1488743390	0.2955242247
	2	0.4333953941	0.2692667193
	3	0.6794095683	0.2190863625
	4	0.8650633667	0.1494513492
	5	0.9739065285	0.0666713443
20	1	0.0765265211	0.1527533871
	2	0.2277858511	0.1491729865
	3	0.3737060887	0.1420961093
	4	0.5108670020	0.1316886384
	5	0.6360536807	0.1181945320
	6	0.7463319065	0.1019301198
	7	0.8391169718	0.0832767416
	8	0.9122344283	0.0626720483
	9	0.9639719273	0.0406014298
	10	0.9931285992	0.0176140071

been determined and tabulated for $n = 2$ through 95.[4] An abbreviated table of the weights and sampling points for several values of n is given in Table 14-5.

Applying the Gauss Quadrature to Integrals with a Range Other Than −1 to 1

For integrals that are over an x range that differs from −1 to 1, a change of variables must first be effected before the Gauss quadrature procedures of

---

[4]M. Abramowitz and I. Stegun, *Handbook of Mathematical Functions*, National Bureau of Standards reprint, (New York: Dover, 1965).

the previous section can be employed. For example, if the integral is from a to b,

$$I = \int_a^b f(x)\,dx$$

the change of variable would be

$$x = \left(\frac{b-a}{2}\right)\xi + \left(\frac{b+a}{2}\right) \tag{14.23}$$

so that when $\xi = 1$, $x = b$, and when $\xi = -1$, $x = a$.

The idea then is first to transform the variable x to ξ and the integral is then replaced by an integral from -1 to 1 in ξ. For example, the integral

$$I = \int_0^2 \sin(x)\,dx$$

is first rewritten in terms of ξ defined by the transformation,

$$x = \xi + 1$$
$$dx = d\xi$$

to give

$$I = \int_{-1}^1 \sin(\xi + 1)\,d\xi$$

This integral may then be numerically integrated by the Gauss quadrature procedure using the weights and sampling points given in Table 14-5. The result for the $n = 5$ point calculation is then

$$I \approx \omega_0 f(0) + \omega_1[f(x_1) + f(-x_1)] + \omega_2[f(x_2) + f(-x_2)]$$
$$= 0.237[\sin(0.906 + 1) + \sin(-.906 + 1)]$$
$$\quad + 0.479[\sin(0.538 + 1) + \sin(-.538 + 1)] + 0.569\sin(1.0)$$
$$= 1.4161467 \quad \text{Exact answer} = 1.0 - \cos(2) = 1.4161468\ldots$$

14.7   Improper Integrals

An integral is said to be *improper* (or *singular*) if (a) one or both of the limits are infinite or (b) the integrand becomes unbounded ("blows up") for any values of the integration variable within the interval of integration. In both cases, the occurrence of infinity in either the limits or the integrand may cause the integral to diverge. As with infinite summations, there are a variety of tests that can be used to determine whether or not an improper integral converges. And, just as with summations, if a numerical value is required, convergence though necessary is not always sufficient to permit an accurate computation. Infinities in any form will cause problems in a numerical calculation, and therefore special techniques must be developed to evaluate even convergent improper integrals.

Integrals with Infinite Limits

In order for the integral

$$I = \int_a^\infty f(x)\, dx$$

to have meaning, that is converge, clearly the function $f(x)$ must approach zero for large x. This situation is analogous to that faced in Chapter 4 when summing an infinite series. The evaluation of the infinite integral proceeds similarly. We simply integrate far enough out along the x axis until we are satisfied that the remainder of the integral will contribute only an insignificant amount.

   If the integrand $f(x)$ is largest near the beginning of the interval, one procedure is to break the interval [a to ∞] into *four* parts, say,

$$I = \int_0^\gamma f(x)\, dx + \int_\gamma^{3\gamma} f(x)\, dx + \int_{3\gamma}^{9\gamma} f(x)\, dx + \int_{9\gamma}^\infty f(x)\, dx$$

$$= I_1 + I_2 + I_3 + I_4 \tag{14.24}$$

The value of γ is chosen so that the interval [a to γ] contains the dominant part of the integral; that is, the region where $f(x)$ is the largest. If the sequence of inequalities

$$I_1 \gg I_2 \gg I_3$$

is satisfied, and I_3 is very small, we are probably justified in neglecting the last term, I_4, which cannot be integrated numerically anyway. The first three integrals can be approximately integrated by any of the methods discussed so far in this chapter.

Numerical Example of an Integral with an Infinite Upper Limit

Consider the integral

$$I = \int_0^\infty x^2 e^{-x^2}\, dx$$

This integral can be found in tables of definite integrals and the result is $\sqrt{\pi}/4$. The integrand is tabulated below for various values of x.

x	$f(x) = x^2 e^{-x^2}$
0.0	0.0
0.5	0.195
1.0	0.368
1.5	0.237
2.0	0.073
4.0	0.000002
8.0	1.03×10^{-26}

Since the integrand falls to zero so rapidly beyond $x = 2.0$, we might try a partition like the following:

$$\int_0^\infty x^2 e^{-x^2}\,dx = \int_0^2 + \int_2^6 + \int_6^{18} + \int_{18}^\infty$$

$$= I_1 + I_2 + I_3 + I_4$$

$$= 0.422725056486 + 0.020388560464 + 1.2 \times 10^{-26} + ?$$

$$= 0.4431136169 \quad \text{Exact answer} = 0.443113463\ldots$$

The above integrals were evaluated using a 10-point Gauss quadrature and the numerical values for the weights and sampling points found in Table 14-5.

Asymptotic Replacements

A procedure similar to that of the previous section is to approximate the integrand by a simpler function for the portion of the integral where x is large. For example, consider the function

$$f(x) = \frac{x^2}{e^2 - 1}$$

and the integral

$$I = \int_0^\infty f(x)\,dx$$

First, since $e^0 = 1$, it may appear that the integrand diverges near the origin. However, using the series expression for e^x (namely $e^x = 1 + x + \cdots$), we see that $f(x = 0) = 0$.[5]

Second, for very large values of x, $e^x \gg 1$, and therefore it is a good approximation to replace $f(x)$ in this region by the simpler expression

$$f(x) \to x^2 e^{-x} \qquad \text{for large } x$$

and this expression can be integrated *analytically*. Since $e^{10} = 22026.5$, the approximation

$$I = \int_0^\infty \frac{x^2}{e^x - 1}\,dx$$

$$\simeq \int_0^{10} \frac{x^2}{e^x - 1}\,dx + \int_{10}^\infty x^2 e^{-x}\,dx$$

$$= I_1 + I_2$$

---

[5] In a situation such as this it would be prudent to include in the FORTRAN code for the function $f(x)$ a statement of the form

```
IF(X .EQ. 0.0)F = 0.0
```

rather than attempt to compute a value that may result in 0.0/0.0.

should be valid to better than five significant figures. The first integral is done numerically; the second can be done analytically. The results, again using a 10-point Gauss quadrature, are

$$I_1 = 2.3985748995$$

$$I_2 = 0.0055387914$$

$$I \simeq I_1 + I_2 = 2.40411369$$

Numerous other techniques, such as change of variables, can be developed to handle integrals with infinite limits. Most of these tricks are acquired through experience and will not be discussed here.

Singularities in the Integrand

As odd as it may seem, even though a function is infinite for some value of x, the area under the function over an interval containing this point may still be finite. The integral

$$I = \int_0^1 \frac{dx}{(1 - x^2)^{1/2}}$$

is such an integral.

Obviously, the computer will be unable to obtain a value for this integral since the integrand approaches infinity as $x \to 1$. The standard procedure is to rewrite the integral in a form that eliminates the singularity by changing variables.[6] For example, if we make the replacement

$$x \to \sin(\theta)$$

$$dx \to \cos(\theta)\, d\theta$$

$$1 - x^2 \to \cos^2(\theta)$$

and when

$$x = 0 \to \theta = 0$$

$$x = 1 \to \theta = \pi/2$$

the above integral may be written as

$$I = \int_0^{\pi/2} \frac{\cos(\theta)\, d\theta}{\cos(\theta)} = \frac{\pi}{2}$$

Again, these change-of-variable tricks come mostly from experience and are not an appropriate concern of an elementary text.

---

[6] It may not be possible to avoid the singularity by any change in variables. This situation usually indicates that the integral is itself divergent (i.e., infinite) as can be verified by replacing the integrand by its asymptotic form near the singular point and integrating the simpler expression over the interval containing the point. If the simpler integral still diverges, the original integral does as well.

■ 14.8 Double Integrals

■ Interpretation of a Double Integral

Occasionally the solution of a problem in engineering or science will require the evaluation of a double integral of the form

$$I = \int_c^d \int_a^b f(x, y)\, dx\, dy \tag{14.25}$$

For example, the total force of a stream on the side of a dam is a sum of the pressure at a point on the dam times an infinitesimal area element, summed over the entire area of the dam. The dam illustrated in Figure 14-8 has a height h and a width w and thus the total force on the dam is

$$\text{Force} = \int_0^h \int_0^w P(x, y)\, dx\, dy$$

The procedure for evaluating a double integral is to first evaluate the innermost integral [in Equation (14.25) this is the integral over dx]. The result of this first integration is then a function of y; that is,

$$I = \int_c^d \int_a^b f(x, y)\, dx\, dy = \int_c^d g(y)\, dy$$

where

$$g(y) = \int_a^b f(x, y)\, dx$$

Figure 14-8
Force on the infinitesimal area element $dx\,dy$ is $P(x, y)\,dx\,dy$

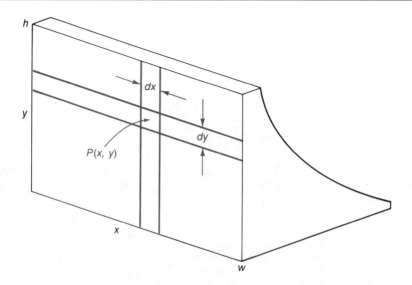

For example, the pressure on the dam is a function of position and is given by

$$P(x, y) = \rho g(h - y)$$

where ρ is the density of water (10^3 kg/m^3) and g is the gravitational acceleration (9.8 m/sec^2). The first integral then yields, for a dam with vertical sides,[7]

$$g(y) = \int_0^w \rho g(h - y)\, dx = \rho g(h - y)x \big|_0^w$$

$$= \rho g w(h - y)$$

and the total force is then

$$\text{Force} = \int_0^h \rho g w(h - y)\, dy$$

$$= \rho g w(hy - \tfrac{1}{2}y^2) \big|_0^h$$

$$= \tfrac{1}{2}\rho g w h^2$$

■ FORTRAN Code to Evaluate Double Integrals

To construct a FORTRAN code to evaluate a double integral, the programmer would simply mimic the actions of the previous section. Assuming that we have an adequate function subprogram[8] to evaluate a single integral of a function, the code might be as indicated in Figure 14-9.

Notice that since the function subprogram GAUSQD expects a function of a *single* variable, the function $f(x, y)$ is finessed into appearing as such a function by introducing the function FF(X) and passing the value of the variable y through a common block.

The logical structure of this code is perfectly valid; however, if you attempt to execute the program, it will fail. The fault is not with the logic of the program but in the basic structure of FORTRAN itself. FORTRAN forbids one subprogram from calling itself either directly or indirectly. In our program, the first reference to the subprogram GAUSQD in the main program will in turn reference the function G(Y), which will then itself call GAUSQD. Thus, GAUSQD is in effect referencing GAUSQD, which is not allowed. You may wish to attempt to execute this program;

---

[7] The integration limits of the inner integral may themselves be a function of the outer variable. Thus, if the sides of the stream are not vertical, the width of the dam will not be a constant but will be a function of the height above the stream bottom.

[8] I will use a function subprogram GAUSQD(F, A, B, K) that employs the weights and sampling points of Table 14-5 to approximate numerically the integral of $f(x)$ from $x = a$ to $x = b$ using k sampling points. We could just as well have used the function ROMBRG of Figure 14-7.

Figure 14-9 _____

The logical structure of a FORTRAN program to evaluate the double integral

$$\int_0^1 \int_0^1 f(x, y)\, dx\, dy$$

This program contains an execution error.

```
            PROGRAM MAIN
      *
      *     [warning: this code contains an error.]
      *
            EXTERNAL G
            ANSWR = GAUSQD(G,0.,1.,10)
            WRITE(*,*)'double integral = ',ANSWR
            STOP
            END
      *============================================
            FUNCTION G(Y)
            COMMON/Y/YY
            EXTERNAL FF
            YY = Y
            G  = GAUSQD(FF,0.,1.,10)
            RETURN
            END
      *============================================
            FUNCTION FF(X)
            COMMON/Y/Y
            FF = F(X,Y)
            RETURN
            END
      *============================================
            FUNCTION F(X,Y)
            F = ...
            RETURN
            END
      *============================================
            FUNCTION GAUSQD(FNC,A,B,K)
            ...
            ...
            END
```

$$\text{Answer} = \int_0^1 g(y)\, dy$$

$$g(y) = \int ff(x)\, dx$$

$ff(x) = f(x, y)$ with y passed to the function via COMMON

but be warned: tracing the ultimate error in the execution of the program can be extremely difficult. This problem is an example of one of the most subtle errors in FORTRAN, especially troublesome because the problem lies in the language itself.

Not surprisingly, there is no easy solution to the problem. The function GAUSQD must not reference the function GAUSQD. Two distinct functions must be used. One remedy might be simply to use two identical copies of the function and rename them GAUSQD and GAUSQF. Once these changes are made, the program will execute smoothly.

14.9   Conclusion

Several topics in numerical integration have not been mentioned in this chapter. One of these is how to integrate highly oscillatory functions. Special techniques have been developed to handle such functions, but they are specialized and beyond the scope of this text. Also, the Gauss quadrature procedure has several variations to accommodate functions that resemble quantities other than polynomials. Again, these procedures are specialized and not sufficiently relevant to include here.

Despite these omissions, the material in this chapter is not merely an introduction to numerical integrations. The procedures and algorithms detailed here are suitable for most problems you will encounter. Most professional engineers and scientists include the methods of this chapter among their skills; only a small percentage need (or know) more.

Summary

The integral of $f(x)$ from $x = a$ to $x = b$, written as $\int_a^b f(x)\, dx$, is evaluated numerically by computing the area under the curve $f(x)$ over the specified range of x. The procedures for estimating this area consist of partitioning the interval $a \le x \le b$ into n panels of width $\Delta x_i (i = 1, n)$, and approximating the function $f(x)$ over each panel by a simpler function.

The trapezoidal rule results from replacing the function $f(x)$ by straight-line segments over the panels Δx_i. The approximate value for the integral is then given by the formula

$$\int_a^b f(x)\, dx \approx \frac{1}{2}\left(f_a + f_b + 2 \sum_{i=1}^{n} f(x_i)\, \Delta x_i \right) \quad \text{Trapezoidal rule}$$

If the panels are of equal size *and* the number of panels is $n = 2^k$, where k is a positive integer, the trapezoidal rule approximation is then labeled as T_k and satisfies the equation

$$T_k = \frac{1}{2} T_{k-1} + \Delta x_k \sum_{\substack{i=1 \\ \text{odd}}}^{n-1} f(a + i \Delta x_k)$$

where

$$\Delta x_k = \frac{(b - a)}{2^k}$$

In the next level of approximation the function $f(x)$ is replaced by $n/2$ parabolic segments over pairs of equal-size panels $\Delta x = (b - a)/n$ and results in the formula for the area known as Simpson's rule:

$$\int_a^b f(x)\, dx \approx \frac{1}{3} \Delta x \left(f_a + f_b + 4 \sum_{\substack{i=1 \\ \text{odd}}}^{n-1} f(a + i \Delta x) + 2 \sum_{\substack{i=2 \\ \text{even}}}^{n-2} f(a + i \Delta x) \right)$$

Simpson's rule

If the number of panels is again $n = 2^k$, the Simpson's rule approximation of order k, S_k, can be related to the trapezoidal rule value of the same order by

$$S_k = T_k + \frac{T_k - T_{k-1}}{3}$$

The approximation technique known as Romberg integration is merely a generalization of the equation above, obtained by replacing the function $f(x)$ by higher-order polynomials. The result is

$$T_k^{m+1} = T_k^m + \frac{T_k^m - T_{k-1}^m}{(4^{m+1} - 1)} \qquad \text{Romberg equation}$$

where m characterizes the "level" of the approximation: $m = 0$ for the trapezoidal rule, $m = 1$ for the Simpson's rule, and so on. Romberg integration is the optimum procedure for integrating an arbitrary function if the panel widths are constrained to be of equal size.

Relaxing the condition that the panel widths be of equal size results in a set of integration techniques known as Gauss quadrature. The simplest form of Gauss quadrature consists of evaluating the function at n *sampling* points, x_i, and multiplying the function value at each sampling point by a *weight* factor, ω_i. If there are n sampling points, the $2n$ parameters $(x_i, \omega_i, i = 1, n)$ are determined by requiring that the procedure be exact for an arbitrary polynomial of degree $N = 2n - 1$. The weights and sampling points are computed for an integration interval $-1 \le x \le +1$ and are listed in Table 14-5. For other intervals, say $a \le x \le b$, a change of variables, $x = \frac{1}{2}(b - a)t + \frac{1}{2}(b + a)$ is first required to replace the interval $a \le x \le b$ by the standard $-1 \le x \le +1$. The algorithm is then

$$I = \int_{-1}^{1} f(x)\, dx \approx \sum_{i=1}^{n/2} \omega_i [f(x_i) + f(-x_i)] \qquad \text{if } n \text{ is even}$$

$$\approx \omega_0 f(0) + \sum_{i=1}^{\frac{1}{2}(n-1)} \omega_i [f(x_i) + f(-x_i)] \qquad \text{if } n \text{ is odd}$$

Since Gauss quadrature does not require the value of the function at the end points of the interval, it is often suitable to use for integrals that are convergent but whose integrands are undefined at the end points.

Improper integrals are those that contain infinities either in integration limits or values of the integrand at points within the region of integration. The procedure to handle an infinite upper limit is to partition the complete interval $0 \le x \le \infty$ into four subintervals as

$$\int_0^\infty = \int_0^\gamma + \int_\gamma^{3\gamma} + \int_{3\gamma}^{9\gamma} + \int_{9\gamma}^\infty$$

for some γ chosen so the first three integrals, which can be evaluated numerically, are progressively smaller, with the third negligible compared with the previous two. This result then suggests that the last integral may be neglected.

If a convergent integral has an integrand that diverges at a point, the integral is likewise improper and must be evaluated with special techniques. Often a change of variables can be found that will remove the singularity. Otherwise, the function can be replaced by its asymptotic form as it approaches the singularity, and the problematic part of the integral is done *analytically* over a small interval containing the singularity. The remaining part of the integral can be done numerically.

Double integrals are easily evaluated in FORTRAN provided the programmer takes care to avoid a structure wherein the integration module indirectly references itself. This situation can be corrected by including in the complete program two differently named but otherwise identical copies of the integration function code.

Problems

14.1 Evaluate the integrals below by using the trapezoidal rule in the following way:
   a. Evaluate T_0 for one panel by using Equation (14.1).
   b. Compute T_1 using the value of T_0 and Equation (14.6).
   c. Continue the calculation through T_4.
   Collect your results in the form of a table. (Be careful: errors in one step will carry over into the next.)

		Exact Result
(1)	$\int_0^8 x^2\, dx$	$170\frac{2}{3}$
(2)	$\int_0^8 x^4\, dx$	6553.6
(3)	$\int_0^1 xe^{-x}\, dx$	$1 - 2/e = 0.2642411175\ldots$
(4)	$\int_0^{\pi/2} x\,\sin(x)\, dx$	1.0
(5)	$\int_0^1 (1 + x^2)^{3/2}\, dx$	$1.567951962\ldots$
(6)	$\int_0^1 e^{-x^2}\, dx$	$0.74682404\ldots$

14.2 Calculate the two-panel and the four-panel Simpson's rule results, S_1, S_2, for the same integrals attempted in Problem 14.1 using Equation (14.13).

14.3 Calculate S_1 through S_4 for the integrals attempted in Problem 14.1 using the trapezoidal rule results and Equation (14.14).

14.4 Complete the entire Romburg table for the integrals attempted in Problem 14.1 using the trapezoidal rule values and Equation (14.17).

14.5 From any of the Romberg tables you constructed in Problem 14.4 compute a table of round-off error flags, R_k^m, by using Equation (14.19).

14.6 Evaluate each of the integrals below by the method of Section 14.7. After selecting an appropriate partition of the x axis, compute the integral segments numerically using (1) the Romberg algorithm with $k = 3$, and (2) the Gauss quadrature procedure with three-point sampling.

Exact Result

a. $\int_0^\infty xe^{-x}\,dx$ 1.0

b. $\int_0^\infty x^2 e^{-x}\cos(x)\,dx$ $-\frac{1}{2}$

c. $\int_0^\infty xe^{-x}\sin(x)\,dx$ $\frac{1}{2}$

14.7 Use the fact that for large values of x the integrand of the integral below can be approximated by a simpler function and that part of the integral may then be done in closed form, and the remaining part may be done numerically. Choose the cut point carefully.

$$\int_0^\infty \frac{dx}{(e^x + x)}$$

14.8 The integral

$$\int_0^1 \ln(x)\,dx$$

has a singularity as $x \to 0$. Find the change of variables that enables you to rewrite this integral as

$$-\int_0^\infty te^{-t}\,dt$$

which may then be evaluated by the methods of Problem 14.6.

14.9 A general fourth-degree polynomial can be written as

$$y(x) = c_0 + c_1(x - x_0) + c_1(x - x_0)^2 + c_2(x - x_0)^3 + c_3(x - x_0)^4$$

a. Show that if this polynomial is forced to pass through the five points (x_i, y_i), $i = 0, 4$, where the x values are equally spaced $[x_1 = x_0 + \Delta x, x_3 = x_0 + 3\Delta x,$ etc.], the relation between the coefficients and the given points is

$$
\begin{bmatrix} y_0 \\ y_1 \\ y_2 \\ y_3 \\ y_4 \end{bmatrix}
=
\begin{bmatrix}
1 & 0 & 0 & 0 & 0 \\
1 & 1 & 1 & 1 & 1 \\
1 & 2 & 4 & 8 & 16 \\
1 & 3 & 9 & 27 & 81 \\
1 & 4 & 16 & 64 & 256
\end{bmatrix}
\begin{bmatrix} c_0 \\ c_1 \Delta x \\ c_2 \Delta x^2 \\ c_3 \Delta x^3 \\ c_4 \Delta x^4 \end{bmatrix}
$$

b. Use subroutine MINV in Figure 12-6 to obtain the inverse of this matrix and thus express the coefficients in terms of the given points y_i.

c. Show that the area under the quartic from $x = x_0$ to $x = x_4$ is

$$\text{Area} = \frac{4}{15}\Delta x[15c_0 + 30c_1\Delta x + 80c_2\Delta x^2 + 240c_3\Delta x^3 + 768c_4\Delta x^4]$$

$$= \frac{4}{15}\Delta x[15 \quad 30 \quad 80 \quad 240 \quad 768]\begin{bmatrix} c_0 \\ c_1\Delta x \\ c_2\Delta x^2 \\ c_3\Delta x^3 \\ c_4\Delta x^4 \end{bmatrix}$$

d. Use the result of part b to show that the area may be written as

$$\text{Area} = \frac{2}{45}\Delta x[7y_0 + 32y_1 + 12y_2 + 32y_3 + 7y_4]$$

e. Explicitly write out the Simpson's rule approximations S_1, S_2 and show that $B_2 \equiv \frac{1}{15}(16S_2 - S_1)$, Boole's rule of order 2, gives the same result.

14.10 Derive the values of the weights and sampling points for a three-point Gauss quadrature.

14.11 Write a subroutine GAUSQD that will approximate an integral using a 10-point sampling. Use the sampling points and weight factors given in Table 14-5. Test this subroutine by evaluating the integrals of Problem 14.1.

14.12 Using a suitable root-solving subroutine and the subroutine GAUSQD of Problem 14.11, return to Problem 5.20 and complete the problem by finding the root of the given function. This function has one positive root near $x = 0.5$.

H
Programming
Assignment

H.1 Sample Program

Mechanical/Aeronautical Engineering:
Shear Force on an Airplane Wing

An airplane wing is acted upon by a wide variety of loads, and each load must be carefully analyzed to determine the safety and performance of the wing. The net shear force at the base of the wing is the total upward force of the wing on the body or fuselage of the plane. This force in turn is a sum of all upward forces on the wing itself. These forces depend, in a complicated way, on the physical properties of the wing and other parameters concerned with flight, such as air speed.

The simplified wing structure to be used in this problem is illustrated in Figure H-1. The net shear force at the base of the wing is the sum of the upward pressure on the point (x, y) times the infinitesimal area $dx\, dy$, summed over the entire area of the wing:

$$aS = \int_0^L dx \int_{e_b}^{e_f} P(x, y)\, dy \tag{H.1}$$

where L is the length of the wing, e_f is the leading (front) edge of the wing, and e_b is the trailing (back) edge of the wing.

The inner integral over y results in a function of x only, so the stress S could also be expressed as

$$S = \int_0^L G(x)\, dx$$

where

$$G(x) = \int_{e_b(x)}^{e_f(x)} P(x, y)\, dy \tag{H.2}$$

Notice that unlike the example problem in Section 14.8, the integration over the inner variable (here y) is not between constant limits. As you can see from Figure H-1, the y integration slice extends from the back edge to the front edge, and each edge is itself a function of x.

Problem Specifics. If the wing width is ω and if we define $x_0 \equiv L - \omega$, the equations for the front and back edges of the wing are

$$e_f(x) = \omega \qquad\qquad \text{if } 0 \le x \le x_0$$

$$= \frac{1}{3}\omega\left\{1 + 2\left[1 - \left(\frac{x - x_0}{\omega}\right)^{1/2}\right]\right\} \qquad \text{if } x_0 \le x \le L \tag{H.3}$$

579

Figure H-1

Top and front view of an airplane wing. The approximate form of the lift force as a function of x is also indicated.

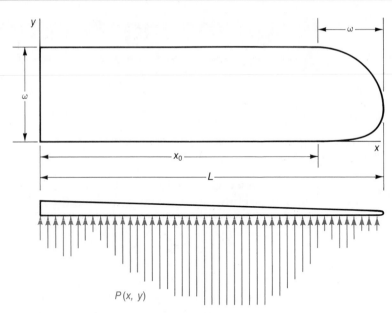

$$e_b(x) = 0 \qquad\qquad\qquad \text{if } 0 \le x \le x_0$$

$$= \frac{1}{3}\omega\left\{1 + \left[1 - \left(\frac{x - x_0}{\omega}\right)^{1/2}\right]\right\} \qquad \text{if } x_0 \le x \le L \qquad (H.4)$$

The wing is subject to the following upward pressure at a point (x, y):

$$P(x,y) = \frac{P_0}{L^8\omega^2}[x^2(x - L)^2(x - 3)^2(x - x_0)^2][y(\omega - y)e^{-(\frac{y}{4} - \frac{\omega}{6})^2}] \qquad (H.5)$$

with $P_0 = 6 \times 10^8 \text{ n/m}^2$.

Details. The FORTRAN program to compute the net force on the wing contains the following main items:

1. The main program will integrate the function $G(x)$ [Equation (H.2)] from $x = 0$ to $x = L$ using the Romberg algorithm. (See Figure 14-7.)
2. The function $G(x)$ will integrate a function $Px(y)$ from $y = e_b(x)$ to $y = e_f(x)$, also using a Romberg algorithm; however, the reference to this integration subprogram must be to a renamed second copy of the function ROMBRG. (See Section 14.8.)
3. The Function $Px(y)$ is simply the function $P(x, y)$ written as a function of a single variable, y.
4. The complete program will contain function subprograms for the functions $e_f(x)$, $e_b(x)$, and $P(x, y)$, and two copies, with different names, of the Romberg code.

5. A key feature of the program, in addition to the prescription for a double integration, is the use of several common blocks and EXTERNAL statements.

The complete program along with the computed output is shown in Figure H-2.

H.2 Programming Problems

Programming Problem H-A: Nuclear Engineering: Shielding a Nuclear Reactor (Integration of Noisy Data)

In a nuclear reactor the fuel, uranium with enriched amounts of a fissionable isotope ^{235}U, is burned by capturing a free neutron on a ^{235}U nucleus, whereupon it splits roughly in half, releasing considerable energy in the form of kinetic energy of the fragments. High-energy neutrons and gamma rays are also produced. Some of these neutrons are used to keep the reaction going, but most will escape the reactor core. Because this intense and penetrating radiation is harmful to people and can cause considerable damage to equipment, it is vital to surround the reactor core with adequate material called *shielding* to prevent the radiation from escaping. The shielding material is usually concrete or water.

To design a protective shield, we must have a measure of the total number of "prompt" neutrons released per second during the reactor's

Figure H-2
FORTRAN code and output from the shear-force-on-an-airplane-wing problem

```
      PROGRAM TSTR
*--
*  This program integrates the lift force on an airplane wing over
*  the entire area of the wing to obtain the total shear force on
*  the fuselage.  As a test case, a lift force is given by the
*  function P(x,y) for 0 < x < WL, and Eb < y < Ef.  WL is the
*  length of the wing and Eb, Ef are functions of x that define the
*  back and front profiles of the edges of the wing, respectively.
*
*  For each value of x, the integration over y is done by the Rom-
*  berg method using function ROMBRG of Figure 14-7.  To accomplish
*  this the function P(x,y) must be finessed into appearing as a
*  function of a single variable, y.  This is done in function
*  PX(y).  The other independent variable, x, is passed via a
*  common block.  The function G(x) does the actual integration
*  over y for a given x by calling the ROMBRG algorithm.
*
*  The final result for the total force is then the integral of
*  G(x) from x = 0 to x = WL which is evaluated by means of a
*  second copy of the Romberg algorithm called ROMBRF.
*
*  The convergence criteria and the maximum levels are the same for
*  both integrations: EPS = 1.E-4 and KMX = 6.  The only parameters
*  are the wing length, WL = 16.25 (m), the width, w = 2.2 (m), and
*  the force constant, P0 = 6,000 N.
*--------------------------------------------------------------------
```

Figure H-2 _____
(continued)

```
*
      COMMON/PARAM/W,XO,WL
      EXTERNAL G
      W  = 2.2
      WL = 16.25
      XO = WL-W
      PO = 6000.
      S = ROMBRF(G,0.,WL,6,1.E-4,1,IFAIL)
      WRITE(*,10)S*PO,WL,W
  10  FORMAT(/,
     +   T5,'The value of the total shear force on the fuselage '
     +,/,T5,'          is SHEAR = ',F12.1,' newtons',//,
     +   T5,'The wing has a length of ',F5.2,'m',/,
     +   T5,'          and a width of ',F5.2,'m')
      STOP
      END
*================================================================
      FUNCTION EF(X)
*
*  The equation for the leading edge (front) of the wing
*----------------------------------------------------------------
      COMMON/PARAM/W,XO,WL
      IF(X .LT. XO)THEN
         EF = W
      ELSE
         EF = W/3.*(1.+2.*SQRT(1. - ((X-XO)/W)**2))
      ENDIF
      RETURN
      END
*================================================================
      FUNCTION EB(X)
*
*  The equation for the trailing edge (back) of the wing
*----------------------------------------------------------------
      COMMON/PARAM/W,XO,WL
      IF(X .LT. XO)THEN
         EB = 0.
      ELSE
         EB = W/3.*(1.-1.*SQRT(1. - ((X-XO)/W)**2))
      ENDIF
      RETURN
      END
*================================================================
      FUNCTION P(X,Y)
*--
*  The equation for the lift force on the wing as a function of
*  position (x,y) on the wing.
*----------------------------------------------------------------
      COMMON/PARAM/W,XO,WL
      P      = X*X*(X-WL)**2*(X-3.)**2*(X-14.05)**2*Y*(W-Y)*
     +          EXP(-(Y/4.-W/6.)**2)/WL**8/W/W*100000.
      RETURN
      END
*================================================================
```

Figure H-2
(concluded)

```
      FUNCTION PX(Y)
*--
*  Since ROMBRG expects a function of a single variable, the
*  function for the lift force, P(x,y) is rewritten as Px(y)
*  with the value of x passed through a common block.
*----------------------------------------------------------------
      COMMON/XX/XX
      X = XX
      PX = P(X,Y)
      RETURN
      END
*================================================================
      FUNCTION G(X)
*--
*  For a particular value of x, this function integrates the lift
*  force over the y values from the back edge (Eb(x)) to the front
*  edge (Ef(x)).  Notice that the current value of x is also placed
*  in the common block to be passed to the function Px(y).
*----------------------------------------------------------------
      COMMON/XX/XX
      EXTERNAL PX
      XX = X
      A  = EB(X)
      B  = EF(X)
      G  = ROMBRG(PX,A,B,6,1.E-4,0,IFAIL)
      RETURN
      END
*================================================================
      FUNCTION ROMBRF(F,A,B,KMX,EPS,IPRNT,IFAIL)
*================================================================
      FUNCTION ROMBRG(F,A,B,KMX,EPS,IPRNT,IFAIL)
          [An identical copy renamed ROMBRG]
```

The Romberg Table

Order	Level => 0	1	2	3	4	5
0	0.0000					
1	240.5874	320.7832				
2	150.0450	119.8642	106.4696			
3	156.0098	157.9981	160.5404	161.3987		
4	156.6018	156.7992	156.7193	156.6586	156.6400	
5	156.6298	156.6391	156.6284	156.6270	156.6268	156.6268

The value of the total shear force on the fuselage
        is SHEAR =   939760.9 newtons

The wing has a length of 16.25 m
              and a width of 2.20 m

operation.[1] The source strength of the reactor core will be labeled S (neutrons/sec). The approximate thickness of the concrete shield can then be computed from the equation

$$D = \frac{Se^{-\mu t}}{4\pi R^2} F \tag{H.6}$$

where

> D = Amount of radiation that penetrates the shield, called the *dose rate* (units are rem/hr). The maximum dose is about 0.1 rem over a 24-hour period
> μ = Effective removal coefficient for concrete (units are m^{-1})
> t = Thickness of the concrete shield
> R = Distance of observer from the reactor
> F = Dose rate (converts neutrons/m^2-sec to rem/hr)

This equation can be solved for the concrete thickness and yields

$$t = \frac{1}{\mu} \ln\left(\frac{SF}{4\pi R^2}\right) \tag{H.7}$$

The problem is to determine the source strength S experimentally and then to use reasonable values for the other parameters to compute the shielding thickness. The measurements consist of the number of neutrons emitted per second at a particular energy; the energy is then scanned from zero up to some maximum value. An illustration of how the results of such a measurement might appear is given in Figure H-3, and the data are listed in Table H-1. The most distinctive feature of the data is the large amount of scatter in the count rates. This scatter could be caused by relatively large experimental error associated with the particular equipment used, or it could be a reflection of some inherent random features of the actual phenomena. In either case it would appear that the integral of these data, that is, the area under the "curve" represented by the data, could not possibly yield a very accurate or reliable value. However, consider a bit more carefully exactly what it is that we are attempting—namely, to evaluate the area under a curve. Presumably, the data are a representation of that curve with a lot of random "noise," or scatter, superimposed. If the noise on the curve is indeed random, we would expect that when summed it should average out to approximately zero; that is, the integral of just the noise component of the data will be roughly zero if the noise is indeed random. Thus, it is possible that the integral of these data may yield a number significantly more accurate than the individual points themselves. To achieve such a result, we must proceed carefully.

One approach is to first "smooth" the data or to fit the entire set with a continuous function and then integrate the resulting function. This would be a mistake. Smoothing or curve fitting necessarily removes information from the data while perhaps making the analysis more tractable. A

---

[1] Since the fission fragments are frequently radioactive, additional "delayed" neutrons are often released in their decay. Delayed neutrons represent only about ½ percent of the total neutrons released. Moreover, because their energy is always much less than the prompt neutrons, they are not very significant in the design of the shielding of the core.

Figure H-3
Neutron count rate as a function of energy in MeV's[2]

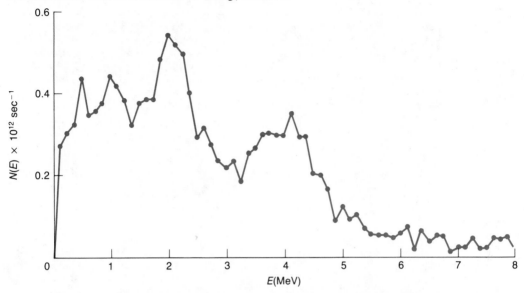

far better approach would be to use the raw data and then simply apply a numerical code to sum the points in either a Romberg or Gauss-quadrature approach. Of course, for either of these methods we need to have data points at prescribed values of x_i. If this is not possible, small segments of the data can be interpolated to estimate the appropriate value to use for a particular x. In the data listed in Table H-1, there are conveniently 65 points, equally spaced along the horizontal axis, and thus we can immediately employ a Romberg procedure with KMAX = 6. By monitoring the "convergence" of the procedure, we can get an estimate of the accuracy of the result, again assuming that the error is random.

Details. Write a FORTRAN code to use the Romberg algorithm of Figure 14-7 to integrate the data of Table H-1. From the variation in the last two diagonal elements, the program should estimate the accuracy of the integral. Finally, use Equation (H.7) to compute the appropriate thickness of the reactor shielding. Additional parameters required in this problem are as follows:

Penetration Dose Limit (rem/hr)	Dose Rate Conversion Factor	Distance from Core	Concrete Removal Rate
D	F	R	μ
0.004	1.43	10 m	8.6 m^{-1}

---

[2] The units of MeV (million electron volts) are standard in nuclear physics and are related to more common SI units by 1 MeV = 1.602×10^{-25} J.

Table H-1

Neutron count rate data $N(E)$ as a function of E to be used in Programming Problem H-B. The E values are equally spaced with a step size of 0.125 MeV from $E = 0$ to $E = 8$ MeV.

E(MeV)	$N(E) \times 10^{12}$ sec^{-1}	E(MeV)	$N(E) \times 10^{12}$ sec^{-1}
0.000	0.664	4.125	3.618
0.125	2.842	4.250	3.023
0.250	3.125	4.375	3.038
0.375	3.347	4.500	2.093
0.500	4.515	4.625	2.037
0.625	3.548	4.750	1.690
0.750	3.638	4.875	0.900
0.875	3.875	5.000	1.252
1.000	4.577	5.125	0.952
1.125	4.338	5.250	1.087
1.250	3.924	5.375	0.770
1.375	3.259	5.500	0.618
1.500	3.867	5.625	0.560
1.625	3.965	5.750	0.593
1.750	3.967	5.875	0.517
1.875	4.996	6.000	0.582
2.000	5.664	6.125	0.767
2.125	5.355	6.250	0.204
2.250	5.139	6.375	0.697
2.375	4.115	6.500	0.416
2.500	2.987	6.625	0.556
2.625	3.249	6.750	0.541
2.750	2.817	6.875	0.156
2.875	2.404	7.000	0.270
3.000	2.206	7.125	0.255
3.125	2.398	7.250	0.516
3.250	1.875	7.375	0.226
3.375	2.608	7.500	0.238
3.500	2.733	7.625	0.523
3.625	3.096	7.750	0.450
3.750	3.137	7.875	0.551
3.875	3.073	8.000	0.271
4.000	3.054		

Extra Problem

The following extension of this problem examines more carefully the effects of noisy data on the accuracy of a computation. It also features a function that generates random numbers.

The data of Table H-1 were generated by first computing the count rate from an approximate theoretical expression,

$$N(E) = 0.453e^{-1.04E} \sinh(\sqrt{2.47E}) \qquad \text{if } E \leq 4.0 \text{ MeV}$$

$$= 1.75e^{-0.75E} \qquad \text{if } E > 4.0 \text{ MeV} \qquad \text{(H.8)}$$

then adding two distribution functions representing particular abundant sources of neutrons at energies of 2.1 and 4.0 MeV,

$$N_a(E) = 0.2e^{-5(E-2.1)^2} \qquad N_b = 0.2e^{-2(E-4.0)^2} \qquad \text{(H.9)}$$

Finally, each computed value of the count rate, N_k, was multiplied by the factor

$$1 + 0.3[RAN(K) - 0.5] \tag{H.10}$$

and added to a term simulating background noise of the form

$$\text{Background} = \tfrac{1}{2}(0.3)|RAN(K) - \tfrac{1}{2}| \tag{H.11}$$

where RAN(K) is a FORTRAN function that will return a different "random" number between 0 and 1 for each value of the integer k. Even though this function *is not* a standard FORTRAN intrinsic function, most FORTRAN installations have such a function in their systems. You should determine the precise name and characteristics of the function available on your system. If you do not have a random-number function available, try the one in Figure H-4. (*Note:* Satisfactory random-number functions

Figure H-4
Example of a simple random-number generator

```
          PROGRAM RANTST
          SUM = 0.
          K = 1
          WRITE(*,*)' Test of random number generator'
          WRITE(*,'(T5,A,T10,A,T20,A)')'I','Seed','Random No.'
          DO 3 ICALL = 1,10
             S = RAN(K)
             WRITE(*,'(T4,I2,T7,I7,T20,F9.7)')ICALL,K,S
             SUM = SUM + S
        3 CONTINUE
          SUM = SUM/10.
          WRITE(*,*)'Average = ',SUM
          STOP
          END
*=========================================================
          FUNCTION RAN(K)
*
* A simple random-number generator.  Note, that the func-
* tion changes the value of K that will be used in the
* next call.  The choices for M, IA, IC are from D. E.
* Knuth, The Art of Computer Programming, vol.2, Addison-
* Wesley,  1981.
*
          PARAMETER (M = 243000, IA = 4561, IC = 51349)
          K   = MOD(K*IA+IC,M)
          RAN = K/(1.*M)
          RETURN
          END
```

Test of random number generator		
I	seed	Random No.
1	55910	0.2300823
2	149859	0.6167037
3	242248	0.9969053
4	23477	0.0966132
5	209946	0.8639753
6	195055	0.8026955
7	74204	0.3053662
8	239793	0.9868025
9	4222	0.0173745
10	110891	0.4563416
Average =	0.5372860	

must be written in machine language, so the FORTRAN function in Figure H-4 should be used only for amusement, not serious computations.)

Problem Specifics. Write a program to study the effects that random noise superimposed on a function will have on the integral of that function. The program should include the following steps:

1. Use Equations (H.8) and (H.9) to generate a set of data with random noise superimposed. The results should be written to a data file.
2. Write a FORTRAN program to read the data file and then integrate the data and estimate the error in the integral.
3. Change the factor 0.3 in Equations (H.10) and (H.11) representing 15% scatter first to 0.1 and then to 0.6 and rerun the calculation. Do your estimates of the accuracy of the integral scale accordingly?

Programming Problem H-B: Mechanical Engineering/Physics:
Total Heat Radiation from a Hot Bar

An important equation in the history of science is the expression for the energy radiated per unit area by a hot object as a function of the temperature of the object *and* the wavelength of the emitted radiation. This equation is known as *Planck's radiation law* and is given by

$$R(\lambda,T) = \frac{a}{\lambda^5}(e^{\frac{b}{\lambda T}} - 1)^{-1} \quad \text{where} \quad a = 3.7415 \times 10^{-4} \text{ W-}\mu\text{m}^2 \quad \text{(H.12)}$$
$$b = 14{,}388 \ \mu\text{m-K}$$

and λ is expressed in micrometers ($1 \ \mu\text{m} = 10^{-6}$ m) and the temperature is in Kelvin ($T_{\text{Kelvin}} = T_{\text{Celsius}} + 273$). This equation is graphed in Figure H-5 for several temperatures as a function of λ. The visible portion of the radiation spectrum is from 0.4 μm to 0.7 μm. This equation reproduces the familiar phenomenon that as an object gets hotter it will first glow red, then yellow, then white; that is, as the temperature gets hotter, the peak of the curve, representing the major portion of the emitted radiation, shifts to lower and lower wavelengths (red $\approx$ .65 μm, yellow $\approx$ .57 μm). The peak of the curve occurs at a value of λ_{max} given by the equation

$$\lambda_{\text{max}} = \frac{2878}{T} \quad \text{(H.13)}$$

where λ is again in μm and T and in K. The total energy radiated at a particular temperature is then the area under the curve times the total surface area of the radiating object. Thus, if we have a hot bar at a temperature T_0 and if the bar is 1 m long and has a circular cross-section of radius 0.01 m, the area of the bar is $2\pi \times 10^{10} \ \mu\text{m}^2$ and the total energy radiated is given by the integral

$$E = 2\pi 10^{10} \int_0^\infty R(\lambda,T_0) \ d\lambda \quad \text{(H.14)}$$

Figure H-5

Heat energy radiated as a function of wavelength of the emitted radiation for three temperatures. Note that the maximum of the curve is determined by Equation (H.13).

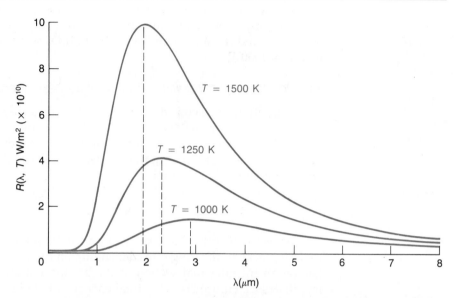

This integral is clearly difficult to do analytically. Moreover, because of the infinite upper limit and the complicated structure of the function, it is also difficult to do numerically. Since the function falls off so rapidly, we could replace the upper limit of infinity by, say $10\lambda_{max}$, where λ_{max} is given by Equation (H.13). The lower limit is also a problem. When λ is zero or very small, the exponential function in Equation (H.12) can very easily generate a floating-point overflow condition. (See also the discussion in Section 5.6.) To avoid this condition we will have to carefully program the FORTRAN function representing the integrand. The point is, if λ is very small or zero or if $b/(\lambda T)$ is very large, the function $R(\lambda,T)$ should be set equal to zero. In the illustration below, WL is the wavelength, λ, in micrometers.

```
FUNCTION R(WL,T)
  IF(WL .EQ. 0.)THEN
     R = 0.
  ELSE
     ARG = 14388.0/WL/T
     IF(ARG .GT. 65.)THEN
        R = 0.
     ELSE
        BOT = (WL**5)*(EXP(ARG) - 1.)
        R   = 3.7415E-4/BOT
     ENDIF
  ENDIF
  RETURN
END
```

Before continuing on to the main problem, you should attempt to integrate $R(\lambda,T)$ using this function and the Romberg integration function of Figure 14-7 for a temperature of 729 K. The convergence criterion should be $1.E - 4$ and the maximum level should $IMX = 9$. The correct answer is then $E \approx 1000W$.

Heat Radiated by a Bar with a Temperature Dependent on Position

In the situation to be considered here, the bar is heated at one end only, so that the temperature will be a function of the position along the bar. If the hot end of the bar is held at a temperature of T_{hot} and the opposite end is held at a temperature of T_{cold}, the temperature across the length of the bar will be given by the equation

$$T(x) = T_{cold} + (T_{hot} - T_{cold})\frac{x}{L} \qquad \text{(H.15)}$$

where L is the length of the bar. Thus, different sections of the bar will be radiating heat at differing rates depending on their temperature. If we isolate on an infinitesimal section of the bar located at a position x and of length dx (see Figure H-6), the total energy radiated by this small segment is then

$$E(x)\, dx = \left\{ 2\pi10^{10} \int_0^\infty R[\lambda,T(x)]\, d\lambda \right\} dx$$

and the energy radiated by the entire bar is the sum of the contributions from all the infinitesimal segments. In the limit that $dx \to 0$, this sum becomes the integral over x from $x = 0$ to $x = L$.

$$E_{tot} = 2\pi10^{10} \int_0^L dx \int_0^\infty R[\lambda,T(x)]\,d\lambda \qquad \text{(H.16)}$$

or

$$E_{tot} = \int_0^L E(x)\, dx$$

where

$$E(x)\, dx = \left\{ 2\pi10^{10} \int_0^{10\lambda_{max}} R[\lambda,T(x)]\,d\lambda \right\} dx \qquad \text{(H.17)}$$

Problem Specifics. The complete program to compute the total energy radiated along the full length of the bar should include the following main items:

1. Write a function subprogram $RR(\lambda)$ that is simply a copy of the function $R[\lambda,T(x)]$ but has only a single variable in its argument list. The other variable (x) should be passed to the function by means of a labeled common block. Note that the

Figure H-6
Temperature distribution along a bar heated at one end. The ends of the bar are held at temperatures 300 K and 1,300 K, respectively, and the radiation emanating from the slice of width *dx* is computed using Equation (H.17).

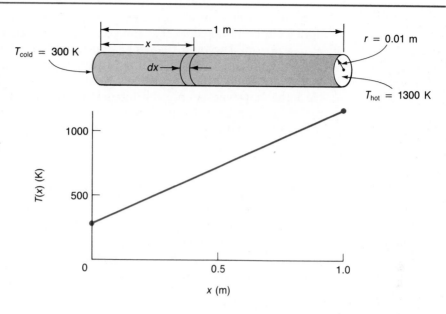

function $R(\lambda,T)$ will in addition call the function for the temperature, $T(x)$. Use $T_{hot} = 1{,}300$ K and $T_{cold} = 300$ K.

2. Write a function subprogram $E(x)$ that calls the Romberg function of Figure 14.7 to integrate $RR(\lambda)$ from $\lambda = 0$ to $\lambda = 25\lambda_{max}$. The convergence criterion should be $\varepsilon = 10^{-4}$ and use KMAX $= 8$. Unless there are problems, this function should not print any elements of the Romberg table.

3. The main program will call a second renamed copy of the Romberg function to execute the integral over x from $x = 0$ to $x = L$. For this integral use $\varepsilon = 10^{-4}$ and KMAX $= 8$. (See also the program layout for the double-integration example in Section 14.8.) The program should neatly print the parameters and the result. You may wish to print the Romberg table for the x integration. Notice that the result will be simply in watts. Finally, redo the calculation with a constant temperature across the bar equal to the average bar temperature. Do you get the same temperature? Explain.

Once you have programmed the above, it is an easy matter to use this program to answer a variety of other questions. For example, an incandescent light bulb is designed so that the peak of its radiation curve is at about $\lambda_{max} \approx .5$ μm. The bulb filament temperature can then be estimated by means of Equation (H.13). The total wattage of the bulb is then the integral of $R(\lambda,T)$ over the complete range of λ's. The energy delivered in visible light, however, is only the integral from $\lambda = 0.4$ μm to $\lambda = 0.7$ μm. Adapt your program to compute the percentage of total energy delivered in the visible range.

Programming Problem H-C: Geology, Petroleum Engineering: Shape of the Earth, Curve Fitting with Legendre Polynomials

Frequently we are faced with the task of fitting a set of data to a given curve. If we wish to fit to polynomials, the least squares procedures of Chapter 13 are adequate; however, it is sometimes preferable to fit to a different class of functions. For example, the functions listed below are called *Legendre polynomials* and are defined for $-1 \leq x \leq 1$.

$$P_0(x) = 1$$
$$P_1(x) = x$$
$$P_2(x) = \tfrac{1}{2}(3x^2 - 1)$$
$$P_3(x) = \tfrac{1}{2}(5x^3 - 3x)$$
$$P_4(x) = \tfrac{1}{8}(35x^4 - 30x^2 + 3)$$
$$P_5(x) = \tfrac{1}{8}(63x^5 - 70x^3 + 15x)$$
$$\vdots$$

$$P_{m+1}(x) = \frac{2m + 1}{m + 1} x P_m - \frac{m}{m + 1} P_{m-1} \tag{H.18}$$

The idea then is to express an arbitrary function of x over the interval $-1 \leq x \leq 1$ as an expansion in these P_m functions.

$$f(x) = \sum_{m=0}^{N} a_m P_m(x) \tag{H.19}$$

where the coefficients in the expansion are a_m and are yet to be determined.
The advantage is expanding in Legendre polynomials is that these functions were designed to satisfy the following orthogonality condition:

$$\int_{-1}^{1} P_m(x) P_m(x) \, dx \begin{cases} = 0 & \text{if } m \neq m' \\[2mm] = \dfrac{2}{2m + 1} & \text{if } m = m' \end{cases} \tag{H.20}$$

For example,

$$\int_{-1}^{1} P_2(x)P_1(x)\,dx = \int_{-1}^{1} \frac{x}{2}(3x^2 - 1)\,dx$$

$$= \left(\frac{3}{8}x^4 - \frac{1}{4}x^2\right)\Bigg|_{-1}^{1} = 0$$

$$\int_{-1}^{1} P_2(x)P_2(x)\,dx = \int_{-1}^{1} \frac{1}{4}(3x^2 - 1)^2\,dx$$

$$= \frac{1}{4}\int_{-1}^{1}(9x^4 - 6x^2 + 1)\,dx$$

$$= \frac{1}{4}\left(\frac{9}{5}x^5 - 2x^3 + x\right)\Bigg|_{-1}^{1}$$

$$= \frac{1}{4}\left(\frac{18}{5} - 4 + 2\right) = \frac{2}{5}$$

We can use this fact to solve Equation (H.14) for the unknown coefficients in the expansion, a_m. First multiply both sides of Equation (H.14) by $P_m(x)$ and then integrate over x from -1 to 1.

$$\int_{-1}^{1} P_m'(x)f(x)\,dx = \sum_{m=0}^{N} a_m \int_{-1}^{1} P_m(x)P_{m'}(x)\,dx$$

Now, because of the orthogonality property of the P_m's, *every* term in the sum over m on the right is zero *except* the single term when $m = m'$. Thus,

$$\int_{-1}^{1} f(x)P_m'(x)\,dx = a_{m'}\frac{2}{2m' + 1}$$

or since m' was an arbitrary value, the coefficients can be expressed as

$$a_m = \frac{2m + 1}{2}\int_{-1}^{1} f(x)P_m(x)\,dx \tag{H.21}$$

Thus fitting the expansion to a function consists of the evaluation of the integrals for the coefficients a_m.

Problem Specifics. Geologists and petroleum engineers use precise measurements of the earth's gravitational field to aid them in their search for oil and other minerals. The gravitational force varies slightly depending on the density of the local land masses. However, the gravitational force also varies due to the fact that the earth is not a perfect sphere. Thus, knowledge of the precise shape of the earth is important in understanding the results of such measurements.

Three centuries ago Isaac Newton predicted that the earth should exhibit a slight bulge at the equator due to its rotation. He was able to

Table H-2

Earth radii at various latitudes. The angle θ is measured in degrees, with the North Pole at $\theta = 0$. The quantity $x = \cos \theta$. The values of x are equally spaced from $x = -1$. to $x = 1$. in steps of $\frac{1}{8}$. The values for $R(\theta)$ are inferred from the satellite measurements of the gravitational field.

$x = \cos \theta$	θ (degrees)	$R(\theta)$ (km)
-1.000	180.000	6357.41
-0.875	151.045	6358.19
-0.750	138.590	6360.43
-0.625	128.682	6363.78
-0.500	120.000	6367.75
-0.375	112.024	6371.71
-0.250	104.478	6375.07
-0.125	97.181	6377.31
0.000	90.000	6378.07
0.125	82.819	6377.26
0.250	75.522	6375.03
0.375	67.976	6371.69
0.500	60.000	6367.75
0.625	51.318	6363.80
0.750	41.410	6360.44
0.875	28.955	6358.19
1.000	0.000	6357.39

quite accurately estimate the magnitude of the bulge, but it was not until the advent of satellite measurements that precise measurements of the deviation of the earth from a perfect sphere were readily available. One way to express the results is to allow the earth's radius to be a function of polar angle, θ, measured from the North Pole. Table H-2 lists some approximate values for the earth's radius for 17 values of θ from $\theta = 0$ (North Pole) to $\theta = 180°$ (South Pole). You can readily notice that there is indeed a slight (about 20 km) bulge at the equator. In addition, you can see that there is a very slight asymmetry between the northern and southern hemispheres. The earth is slightly pear-shaped. The problem then is to obtain an expansion of $R(x)$ in terms of the Legendre polynomials above. The form of the expansion will be

$$R(x) = R_{\text{avg}} + \sum_{m=1}^{m_{\max}} a_m P_m(x) \qquad \text{where } x \equiv \cos \theta \qquad \text{(H.22)}$$

This is accomplished by using the Romberg algorithm (Figure 14.7) to evaluate the integral in Equation (H.21) for the coefficients in the expansion. In this case the function $f(x)$ is represented by the values of $R_i = R(x_i)$ for $i = 0$ to 16. Thus, the level of the Romberg integration will be KMAX = 4, $2^4 = 16$. Your program should print the computed values for a_m, $m = 0, \ldots, 5$ along with an estimate of the accuracy. (Use $\varepsilon = .2$ in the call to ROMBRG.) Once the coefficients have been obtained, the program should construct a table comparing the actual values R_i with the values computed by means of Equation (H.22).

Numerical Solutions to Differential Equations

15.1 Introduction

The solution of differential equations is not ordinarily an appropriate topic for an elementary text. With that said, let me explain why the material in this chapter is worth your time, effort, and attention. First of all, the solution of differential equations by numerical methods is where the action is. Not only are a vast number of problems in engineering and science expressible in terms of differential equations, but the numerical procedures for their solution on a computer are currently improving both in accuracy and efficiency. These modern methods are far too complex to be relevant here. However, the more standard procedures, sufficiently distilled, can be understood by a novice. The topics up to this point have been serious descriptions of the modern methods used by practicing engineers and scientists; the material of this chapter is intended merely as an introduction. I hope you will see a more thorough discussion in later courses in numerical analysis.

The second and more important reason for risking your confusion and frustration is that the best way to understand what a differential equation is and what is meant by a solution to a differential equation is to learn how to solve one by numerical means. The numerical procedures of this chapter are based on the familiar notion of approximating a function by a simpler function, such as a line, over short segments and are generally easier to understand than many of the analytical methods you will encounter in calculus.

Before beginning the description of techniques for solving differential equations, we will briefly summarize the basic properties of first- and second-order differential equations along with several examples from physical phenomena. Then we will take a quick look at the various sources of computational error that are unavoidably in every algorithm.

Each of the numerical techniques for solving first-order differential equations described in this chapter is based on a stepping procedure that combines information about the solution at a specific point with the information contained in the given differential equation to predict the solution one step further along the axis of the independent variable. The prototype for stepping techniques is the method of Euler, described in Section 15.4. The refinements of this algorithm include the midpoint method, Heun's method, and the Runge–Kutta method and are discussed next. Finally, techniques for extending any of these methods to apply to second-order equations or to boundary-value problems are given in Sections 15.8 and 15.9.

15.2 Meaning of a Differential Equation

Any equation that relates an independent variable x, a dependent variable $y(x)$, and the first derivative $y'(x) = dy/dx$ is called a *first-order differential equation*. Any first-order differential equation can be written formally as

$$y' = f(x, y) \tag{15.1}$$

Solving a differential equation involves finding a *function* $y(x)$ such that Equation (15.1) is satisfied. This process is fundamentally different from finding the root of an equation; that is, finding a single value of x such that $f(x) = 0$. A few examples of differential equations and their solutions follow.

Examples of Differential Equations and Their Solutions

1. The simplest differential equation is

$$y'(x) = \frac{dy(x)}{dx} = 0$$

The solution, by inspection, is

$$y(x) = \text{constant} \quad \text{Any constant}$$

The proposed solution is verified by simply inserting back into the original differential equation.

2. An equation that is not as simple is

$$y' + ax = 0 \tag{15.2}$$

This equation is commonly solved by writing $y' = y/dx$ so that

$$dy + ax \, dx = 0$$

$$\int dy = -a \int x \, dx$$

$$y(x) = -\frac{a}{2}x^2 + \text{constant}$$

Again, you can verify that this is a solution of Equation (15.2) by differentiating. Notice that we have solved Equation (15.2) not for a single value of y but for a complete function $y(x)$. And the function obtained is a valid solution for *any* value of the undetermined constant.

The appropriate value of the constant for a particular problem can be determined only by some additional information expressed in terms of boundary conditions. For example, we may be given the value of y for a particular value of x, say, $y(x = 6) = 0$. Then using the general form of the solution, we can use this information to determine the value of the unknown constant:

$$y(x = 6) = 0 = -\frac{a}{2}(6^2) + \text{constant}$$

or

$$\text{constant} = 18a$$

Thus, the solution for this equation plus the particular auxiliary condition is

$$y(x) = -\frac{a}{2}x^2 + 18a$$

3. In more complicated first-order differential equations, the difficulty in obtaining closed-form expressions for the solution $y(x)$ increases dramatically. In fact, the arbitrary first-order differential equation generally has no closed-form solution and the only alternative then is a numerical solution in the form of a table of values of x and $y(x)$. For example, the innocent-looking equation

$$y' + xy = 1$$

has no closed-form solution.

A second-order differential equation is one similar to Equation (15.1) but that generally contains the second as well as the first derivative of $y(x)$:

$$y'' = f(x, y, y') \tag{15.3}$$

Higher-order differential equations are defined analogously.

Examples of Physical Phenomena Described by Differential Equations

Many problems in all fields of science and engineering can be expressed in terms of relations between the rates of change of the variables. A few examples follow.

1. *Melting rate.* The melting rate of a snowball is roughly proportional to its surface area; that is,

$$\frac{d(\text{volume})}{dt} \propto \text{surface} \tag{15.4}$$

And since for a sphere

$$V = \tfrac{4}{3}\pi r^3 \qquad S = 4\pi r^2$$

we have

$$S = (36\pi)^{1/3} V^{2/3}$$

and the proportionality in Equation (15.4) may be expressed as

$$\frac{dV}{dt} = -kV^{2/3}$$

The proportionality constant is chosen to be negative because the volume decreases with time. This equation can be integrated by grouping the V terms on one side of the equation and the t terms on the other.

$$\int \frac{dV}{V^{2/3}} = -k \int dt$$

Using the relation $\int x^c \, dx = x^{c+1}/(c+1)$, the solution is then

$$3V^{1/3} = -kt + C_0$$

where C_0 is an as yet undetermined constant. If we are told that at time $t = 0$ the volume is known to be $V(t = 0) = V_0$, the constant C_0 must have the value $C_0 = 3(V_0)^{1/3}$, so that

$$V(t) = (V_0^{1/3} - \tfrac{1}{3}kt)^3$$

and the snowball disappears ($V \to 0$) when $t = 3V_0^{1/3}/k$ sec.

2. *Radioactive decay.* If there are N radioactive atoms in a sample at time t, the number of decays expected per second at that time is proportional to the number of such atoms present. Thus, the number of radioactive atoms at time t, $N(t)$ decreases by an amount dN/dt where

$$\frac{dN(t)}{dt} \propto N(t)$$

or

$$\frac{dN(t)}{dt} = -kN(t)$$

where once again the proportionality constant is chosen to be negative because $N(t)$ is decreasing. The solution is obtained as before by arranging the different variables on opposite sides of the equation and integrating:

$$\int \frac{dN}{N} = -k \int dt$$

$$\ln(N) = -kt + C$$

Since $e^{\ln(N)} = N$, we obtain

$$N = e^C e^{-kt}$$

The integration constant C could be specified by, for example, the additional information that at time $t = 0$ the number of radioactive atoms is known to be $N(t = 0) = N_0$, or

$$N(t) = N_0 e^{-kt}$$

3. *Simple harmonic motion.* In mechanics, problems are expressed in terms of forces. And since $F = ma$, where the acceleration a is the second derivative of position with respect to time, d^2x/dt^2, these problems amount to solving a second-order differential equation. Of course, most forces encountered in the real world are extremely complicated. However, if x is small we can use a Maclaurin series approximation for $F(x)$ and write

$$F(x) \simeq F_0 - kx + \cdots$$

where F_0 and k are constants. The term F_0 is ordinarily ignored since it represents a constant force and can only add uninteresting constant acceleration motion. The equation $F = ma$ then results in

$$m\frac{d^2x}{dt^2} \simeq -kx \tag{15.5}$$

This is a second-order differential equation; that is, it depends on the variables (t, x, x', x''). The analytical solution of this equation is

$$x(t) = C_1 \sin\left(\sqrt{\frac{k}{m}}t\right) + C_2 \cos\left(\sqrt{\frac{k}{m}}t\right)$$

where C_1, C_2 are as yet undetermined integration constants. Notice that since a second-order equation must be integrated twice to obtain a solution, there are two constants of integration. You can verify that this is the solution to the original differential equation by differentiating twice and plugging back into Equation (15.5).

Second-order differential equations are generally much more difficult to solve and obtain closed-form expressions for the solutions than are first-order equations. However, we can always reduce a higher-order differential equation to a series or set of first-order equations by introducing superfluous variables in the following manner. If we introduce the variable v, the velocity, by the relation $v = dx/dt$ and then note that $a = dv/dt$, the second-order equation, Equation (15.5), may be expressed as two first-order equations:

$$m\frac{dv}{dt} = -kx$$

$$\frac{dx}{dt} = v$$

The introduction of the new variable v has indeed reduced the single second-order equation to two first-order equations. But these equations are *coupled;* that is, they cannot be solved independently. The same variables appear in both equations. However, if we have a tried-and-true method of solving first-order equations, it may not be difficult to adapt this method to equations of any order by the above procedure.

The main objective of this chapter is to explain the various methods that can be used to obtain solutions to first-order differential equations. Any such equation can be written in the form

$$\frac{dy(x)}{dx} = f(x, y) \tag{15.6}$$

15.3   Computational Errors: A Question of Trade-Offs

The procedures of this chapter are intended to obtain approximate numerical solutions to Equation (15.6) in the form of a table of values of y corresponding to values of x in some interval $a \le x \le b$. Although the details of one algorithm may differ substantially from another, the underlying idea to all the methods is the same: partition the x interval into a finite number of points, x_i, then, knowing the value of y at some starting value of x, say, $y(x_0) = y_0$, compute the value of the dependent variable y at the next x value by some approximation procedure. This process is repeated for all the x values in the partitioned interval; that is, knowing (x_i, y_i) + approximation algorithm $\rightarrow [x_{i+1}, y_{i+1}]$. Clearly, the smaller the step size, the more accurate will be the computed values of successive y values. The computational errors in such methods are of thee types: discretization, truncation, and round-off.

Discretization Errors

If the step size from x_i to x_{i+1}, that is, Δx_i, were allowed to approach zero, all of the algorithms would be exact. Of course, an infinitesimal step size would imply an infinite number of steps to span the x interval, thus rendering any algorithm computationally useless. The fact that the step size we use in a numerical algorithm is not truly infinitesimal will generate errors in each step. These errors can often be estimated theoretically to be, say, $\mathcal{O}(\Delta x)^2$ or $\mathcal{O}(\Delta x)^3$, and so on. Alternatively, the accuracy of the calculation can be monitored by noting the changes in the computed results when the step size is reduced from Δx_i to $\frac{1}{2}\Delta x_i$. Reducing the step size will improve the theoretical accuracy of the results at the expense of more steps and consequently more arithmetic operations.

Truncation Errors

One method that can be used to get from point y_i to y_{i+1} is to assume that the function $y(x)$ can be approximated by a straight line over the interval x_i to x_{i+1}. This approximation is equivalent to retaining only the first two terms in a Taylor expansion of the function $y(x)$ and may be adequate if the function is smooth enough and if the step size is small enough. Truncation errors can be reduced by improving the basic approximation for the function—for example, by including quadratic terms. In general this will result in an algorithm that is more complicated and that requires more arithmetic operations per cycle.

Round-Off Errors

Every arithmetic operation involving real numbers executed by the computer results in a loss of accuracy due to the finite nature of the computer word. If the basic computer word is 10 digits or so, the loss of the last digit is inconsequential in one multiplication or addition. However, if the computation requires tens or hundreds of millions of arithmetic operations to obtain a result, round-off error becomes a serious concern and will often invalidate a result even though it is based on sound analytical procedures. The more arithmetic there is to be done in an algorithm, the greater will be the associated round-off error. Thus, round-off error will generally *increase* with a smaller step size or with an improved higher-order algorithm.

In developing a numerical solution to a differential equation, we must keep the various types of computation errors in mind. For all procedures there is an *optimum* step size that minimizes the overall error; that is, either a larger or a smaller step size will result in an increase in the overall numerical error. This topic will be discussed in more detail in Chapter 16.

15.4   Euler's Method

Numerical procedures for solving the differential equation $y' = f(x, y)$ are classified as either one-step or multistep algorithms. A one-step method uses the most recently computed value for y at the position x_n—that is, y_n—and values of the function $f(x, y)$ evaluated at this point or possibly at points in the following interval x_n to $x_n + \Delta x$ to estimate the next value of y—that is, y_{n+1}. A multistep algorithm uses the current value of y_n plus one or more previously computed values from preceding steps. Not surprisingly, the multistep methods are usually more accurate and more efficient than the one-step methods. But a price is paid for this increased accuracy and efficiency: these algorithms are generally much more complicated to code, and, because information from several previous steps is required, they are difficult to start. In this chapter we deal almost exclusively with single-step algorithms; however, a short discussion of a relatively simple multistep procedure is discussed in Section 15.7.

The simplest one-step method is called *Euler's method* and is based on the definition of the derivative:

$$\frac{dy}{dx} \simeq \frac{y(x + \Delta x) - y(x)}{\Delta x}$$

In the rest of this chapter, $y(x_i)$ will denote the exact value of the solution at the position x_i, and y_i will be the computed value. Since Δx is finite, the above equation is equivalent to the first two terms of a Taylor series expansion:

$$y(x_i + \Delta x) \simeq y(x_i) + \frac{dy}{dx} \Delta x$$

And since the original differential equation reads $dy/dx = f(x, y)$, we arrive at the computational algorithm

$$y_{i+1} = y_i + f_i \Delta x \tag{15.7}$$

where f_i represents the function $f(x, y)$ evaluated at the point (x_i, y_i). Euler's method is illustrated graphically in Figure 15-1.

Just as in Chapter 10, where Taylor series were described, Equation (15.7) simply replaces the function $y(x)$ at the point x_i by a straight line with the same slope as the tangent line at that point. If this approximation is not particularly good [e.g., if Δx is not small enough or if $y(x)$ is rapidly changing], then the calculated value for y_{i+1} will not be very accurate. The subsequent point, y_{i+2}, which depends upon the values calculated for y_{i+1}, will be even worse. The error will accumulate for subsequent points. Despite the obvious inadequacies of Euler's method, its compelling simplicity makes it useful as a starting point for the development of more sophisticated procedures for solving differential equations. Even though Euler's

Figure 15-1
Euler's method for
computing the step
from y_i to y_{i+1}

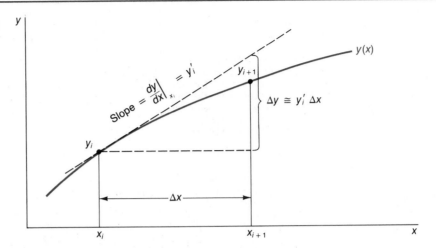

method is rarely used in a serious solution of a problem, the FORTRAN code implementing it is given in the next section and is applied to several example differential equations in order to better convey the shortcomings of the procedure and to suggest improvements.

FORTRAN Code for Euler's Method

A FORTRAN code to solve the differential equation $y' = f(x, y)$ by using the approximation of Equation (15.7) would require the following components:

1. A function subprogram F(X,Y) for the derivative $y' = f(x, y)$.
2. A specified interval $a \leq x \leq b$ and the number of subdivisions N of this interval; that is, $\Delta x = (b - a)/N$.
3. The starting value of $y(x)$; that is, $y(x = a) = y_0$.

The code is quite simple and is given in Figure 15-2. The accuracy of the code could be tested by doubling the value of N and monitoring the change in the computed values. This procedure may require excessive computer time and expense. Also remember that although the fine-grain calculation can be used to judge the accuracy of the course-grain results, it tells us nothing about the accuracy of the fine-grain calculation itself.

From Equation (15.7) it is evident that the truncation error in a single step of Euler's method is proportional to $(\Delta x)^2$, the next term in the Taylor series. After completing the N steps in the interval, the accumulated error will be of order $O(N(\Delta x)^2)$. Since $\Delta x = (b - a)/N$, the total accumulated error incurred in Euler's method will be of order $O(\Delta x)$; that is, the error in the procedure is linear in Δx. The method is a so-called first-order procedure.

Figure 15-2

FORTRAN code for
Euler's method

```
      SUBROUTINE EULER(X,Y,N,A,B,F)
*--
*   EULER integrates the differential equation y' = f(x,y)
*   using the Euler stepping method.  The interval is x = a
*   to x = b and a total of n steps are computed.  Is is
*   assumed that the starting value of y, that is, y(0), is
*   already stored in the array Y().  The function subpro-
*   gram f(x,y) must be usersupplied.
*-------------------------------------------------------------
      REAL X(0:N),Y(0:N),A,B,DX,F
      X(0) = A
      DX   = (B - A)/N
      DO 1 I = 0,N-1
          X(I+1) = X(I) + DX
          Y(I+1) = Y(I) + F(X(I),Y(I))*DX
    1 CONTINUE
      RETURN
      END
```

Example Calculations Using Euler's Method

As an example of the application of Euler's method, the results for the simple test equation

$$y' = y(x) \qquad y(x = 0) = 1.0 \tag{15.8}$$

have been tabulated. The analytical solution to this differential equation is $y(x) = e^x$. The results of the Euler integration for a variety of step sizes are presented in Table 15-1.

Also included in Table 15-1 and positioned below each of the computed numbers is the percentage difference between the computed values and the exact analytical result. Notice that as the step size is dimin-

Table 15-1

Computed solutions to $y' = y$ with $y(0) = 1$ using Euler's method. The interval $x = 0$ to $x = 1$ is broken into N panels and the computed result is compared with the exact solution $y(x) = e^x$. The values in parentheses are the actual error expressed in percentage.

x	N = 10	N = 100	N = 1,000	N = 10,000	Exact
0.0	1.000000	1.000000	1.000000	1.000000	1.000000
0.2	1.210000	1.220190	1.221281	1.22139	1.2214028
	(0.93)	(0.10)	(0.010)	(0.0013)	
0.4	1.464100	1.488864	1.491527	1.491794	1.4918247
	(1.86)	(0.20)	(0.020)	(0.0005)	
0.6	1.771561	1.816697	1.821572	1.822062	1.8221188
	(2.77)	(0.30)	(0.030)	(0.0018)	
0.8	2.143589	2.216715	2.224650	2.225449	2.2255409
	(3.68)	(0.40)	(0.039)	(0.0062)	
1.0	2.593743	2.704814	2.71692	2.718143	2.7182818
	(4.58)	(0.50)	(0.049)	(0.0104)	

ished by a factor of 10, the fractional error also decreases by about the same factor. In addition, the accumulated error after marching across the entire interval is roughly $\frac{1}{2}\Delta x$. Both these observations are consistent with our prediction that Euler's method is a first-order procedure in Δx.

The above example yielded a very smooth and simple function over the interval $x = 0$ to $x = 1$ and yet it required on the order of 10,000 steps to obtain satisfactory results. Since the error in the calculation decreased uniformly with a decrease in the step size, we can conclude that the source of the error is not round-off error but is rather a reflection of the inadequacies of the basic algorithm. If the solution were more rapidly varying over the interval, an even smaller step size would be required. Eventually, reducing the step size to achieve satisfactory accuracy will be offset by the growth in the round-off errors due to the increased amount of arithmetic. Even more important, if the function appearing on the right of the differential equation were much more complicated, calling this function tens of thousands of times can be quite expensive. Improvements in Euler's method are urgently needed.

15.5 Improvements to Euler's Method

The simplest and most direct improvements to Euler's method are based on the following observation:

> In Euler's approximate algorithm for estimating the next value of y (i.e., y_{i+1}), the function is approximated by a straight line with the same slope as the tangent to the curve at the *left* end of the interval. However, much better results are usually obtained if, instead, the slope of the tangent drawn at the *middle* of the interval is used for the approximating straight line.

This idea, which is illustrated in Figure 15-3, forms the basis for two modifications to Euler's method: the midpoint method and Heun's method. Both of the new methods use an algorithm of the form

$$y_{i+1} = y_i + f_{i+1/2}\Delta x \tag{15.9}$$

where $f_{i+1/2}$ represents the slope of the function $y(x)$ at the midpoint of the interval x_i to x_{i+1}. The two methods differ in how this slope is estimated.

Midpoint Method

Equation (15.9) can be implemented by first estimating y at the midpoint of the very first interval using Euler's method:

$$y_{1/2} \approx y_0 + \tfrac{1}{2}\Delta x f(x_0, y_0)$$

Figure 15-3
Approximating the function $y(x)$ by a straight line using the slope at the midpoint of the interval

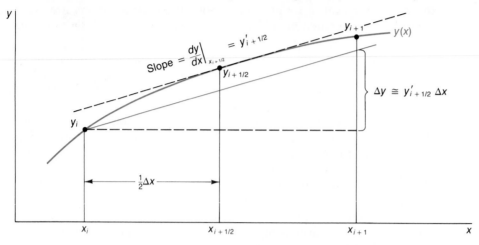

The slope at the midpoint is then approximately $f(x_{1/2}, y_{1/2})$, where $x_{1/2} = x_0 + \frac{1}{2}\Delta x$. The first step would consist of

$$y_1 \approx y_0 + f(x_{1/2}, y_{1/2})\Delta x$$

The procedure is then repeated across the entire interval.

$$y_{i+1/2} \approx y_i + \tfrac{1}{2}f(x_i, y_i)\Delta x$$

$$y_{i+1} \approx y_i + f(x_{i+1/2}, y_{i+1/2})\Delta x$$

It can be shown that the accumulated error, not including round-off error, in this method is proportional to $(\Delta x)^2$; that is, the midpoint method is a second-order method. The procedure goes by a variety of names and is also called the improved polygon method or the second-order Runge–Kutta method.

The method is based on the Euler equation

$$y_{i+1} \approx y_i + f(x_i, y_i)\Delta x$$

Equations of this type are called *predictor* equations. They use currently known information, in this case the value of y and the slope at the left end of the interval, to predict the next value of y.[1]

We could also estimate the next value of y by using the slope at the *right* end of the interval as

$$y_{i+1} \approx y_i + f(x_{i+1}, y_{i+1})\Delta x \tag{15.10}$$

In this equation, however, to compute a value for y_{i+1} we must already have a value for y_{i+1}. This situation suggests a solution by iteration, that is, by guessing y_{i+1} and inserting it into Equation (15.10) and iterating the

---

[1] Predictor-like equations are also commonly referred to as *open* equations.

equation several times. This type of equation is called a *corrector* equation.[2] Equations of this type will be used in the next section for a slightly different improvement to Euler's method. But first let us investigate the successes and limitations of the midpoint method by comparing it to the simple Euler method.

The FORTRAN code for the midpoint method is given in Figure 15-4 and is used once again to solve the test equation

$$y' = y(x) \qquad y(0) = 1.0$$

The results are compared with the previous Euler method results in Table 15-2. Notice that for every calculation the midpoint method is significantly more accurate and that the actual error is indeed proportional to $(\Delta x)^2$.

Heun's Method

A slightly different approach to estimate the slope of the function at the middle of the interval is to average the slopes on the left and the right ends. More specifically, first estimate the change in y using the known slope on the left end of the interval:

$$\Delta y_L = f(x_i, y_i) \Delta x$$

Figure 15-4
FORTRAN code for the midpoint method

```
      SUBROUTINE MDPNT(X,Y,N,A,B,F)
*--
*   MDPNT integrates the differential equation y' = f(x,y)
*   using the approximate slope in the middle of the in-
*   terval to estimate each step.  The interval is x = a to
*   x = b and a total of n steps are computed.  It is as-
*   sumed that the starting value of y, that is, y(0), is
*   already stored in the array Y(). The function subpro-
*   gram f(x,y) must be usersupplied.
*-----------------------------------------------------------
      REAL X(0:N),Y(0:N),A,B,DX,F,XMID,YMID
      X(0) = A
      DX   = (B - A)/N
      DO 1 I = 0,N-1
          XMID  = X(I) + .5*DX
          YMID  = Y(I) + F(X(I),Y(I))*.5*DX
          X(I+1) = X(I) + DX
          Y(I+1) = Y(I) + F(XMID,YMID)*DX
    1 CONTINUE
      RETURN
      END
```

[2]Corrector-like equations are also known as *closed* equations.

Table 15-2

Comparison of the Euler method and the midpoint method applied to the equation $y' = y$ with $y(0) = 1$

x	N	Euler	Midpoint
0.0		1.000000	1.000000
0.2	10	1.210000	1.221025
		(0.93)	(0.031)
	100	1.220190	1.221399
		(0.10)	(0.00032)
	1,000	1.221281	1.221402
		(0.01)	(0.00006)
0.4	10	1.464100	1.490902
		(1.86)	(0.062)
	100	1.488864	1.491815
		(0.20)	(0.00062)
	1,000	1.491527	1.491825
		(0.02)	(0.00014)
0.6	10	1.771561	1.820429
		(2.8)	(0.093)
	100	1.816697	1.822101
		(0.30)	(0.00094)
	1,000	1.821572	1.822119
		(0.03)	(0.00044)
0.8	10	2.143589	2.222789
		(3.7)	(0.12)
	100	2.216715	2.225512
		(0.40)	(0.0013)
	1,000	2.224650	2.225541
		(0.039)	(0.0007)
1.0	10	2.593743	2.714081
		(4.6)	(0.15)
	100	2.704814	2.718237
		(0.50)	(0.0016)
	1,000	2.716920	2.718281
		(0.05)	(0.0009)

Then estimate the slope on the right using $y_{i+1} \approx y_i + \Delta y_L$ as

$$\Delta y_R \approx f(x_{i+1}, y_i + \Delta y_L) \Delta x$$

and average the two values to obtain

$$y_{i+1} = y_i + \tfrac{1}{2}(\Delta y_L + \Delta y_R)$$

Notice that this is equivalent to

One Application of a Predictor Equation

$$y_{i+1} = y_i + f(x_i, y_i) \Delta x$$

Plus One Iteration of a Corrector Equation

$$y_{i+1} = y_i + \tfrac{1}{2}[f(x_i, y_i) + f(x_{i+1}, y_{i+1})]\Delta x$$

This procedure is illustrated graphically in Figure 15-5.

This method is also known as *Heun's method*. The procedure is quite easy to code; a FORTRAN subroutine implementing Heun's method is given in Figure 15-6. This method is also an example of a second-order

Figure 15-5

Heun's method approximates the slope at the middle of the interval by averaging the slope on the left and right ends

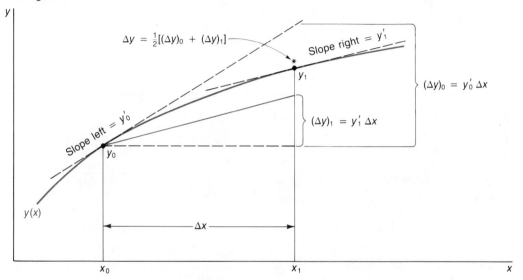

Figure 15-6

FORTRAN code for Heun's method

```
                SUBROUTINE HEUN(X,Y,N,A,B,F)
*--
*   HEUN integrates the differential equation y' = f(x,y) by
*   using the average of the slopes on the right and the left
*   of each interval to compute the size of the step.  The
*   interval is x = a to x = b, and a total of n steps are
*   computed. It is assumed that the starting value of y,
*   that is, y(0), is already stored in the array Y().  The
*   function subprogram f(x,y) must be usersupplied
*-----------------------------------------------------------
        REAL X(0:N),Y(0:N),A,B,DX,F,DYL,DYR
        X(0) = A
        DX   = (B - A)/N
        DO 1 I = 0,N-1
           X(I+1) = X(I) + DX
           DYL  = F(X(I),Y(I))*DX
           YR   = Y(I) + DYL
           DYR  = F(X(I+1),YR)*DX
           Y(I+1) = Y(I) + .5*(DYL + DYR)
    1   CONTINUE
        RETURN
        END
```

Runge–Kutta algorithm, which is described in more detail in Section 15.6. Using Heun's method on the test equation $y' = y$, $y(0) = 1.0$, generates exactly the same results as obtained with the midpoint method which merely verifies that the Huen's method is also second order. However, to illustrate the differences between the two methods, the solutions to a more challenging differential equation,

$$y' = x^{-2} - \frac{y}{x} - y^2 \qquad y(1) = -1$$

have been tabulated. This rather difficult-looking equation was designed to have the simple solution $y = -1/x$, as can be easily verified by substitution.

The results of Table 15-3 show that each of the three methods has problems obtaining an accurate solution to this equation. First, Eulers'

Table 15-3

Comparison of Euler's, the midpoint, and Heun's methods for the equation $y' = x^{-2} - y/x - y^2$ with $y(1) = 1$. The exact solution is $y = -1/x$.

x	N	Euler	Midpoint	Heun
2.0	100	−0.4431393 (11.)	−0.4999067 (0.019)	−0.4955571 (0.89)
	1,000	−0.4941867 (1.2)	−0.5000036 (0.0007)	−0.4999569 (0.009)
	10,000	−0.4994822 (0.10)	−0.5000634 (0.015)	−0.5000632 (0.015)
4.0	100	−0.1406942 (44.)	−0.2498078 (0.077)	−0.240679 (3.7)
	1,000	−0.2371561 (5.1)	−0.2500106 (0.0042)	−0.2499114 (0.036)
	10,000	−0.2488636 (0.46)	−0.2501709 (0.066)	−0.2501704 (0.066)
6.0	100	−0.0357536 (79.)	−0.1663784 (0.17)	−0.1529608 (8.2)
	1,000	−0.1477902 (11.)	−0.1666853 (0.012)	−0.1665361 (0.078)
	10,000	−0.1649533 (1.0)	−0.1669317 (0.15)	−0.1669310 (0.15)
8.0	100	0.0094963 (108.)	−0.1246159 (0.31)	−0.1072828 (14.)
	1,000	−0.1008258 (19.)	−0.125028 (0.024)	−0.1248288 (0.14)
	10,000	−0.1227277 (1.8)	−0.1253642 (0.29)	−0.1253633 (0.29)
10.0	100	0.0294094 (129.)	−0.0995204 (0.48)	−0.0786997 (21.)
	1,000	−0.0713108 (29.)	−0.1000369 (0.038)	−0.0997880 (0.21)
	10,000	−0.0971789 (2.8)	−0.1004636 (0.47)	−0.1004623 (0.47)

method, except for the calculation with 10,000 points, is unsatisfactory. Keep in mind that in an actual situation we will not have an exact solution with which to compare our results. We can only estimate the error of the *previous* calculation by comparing it with the most recent. Thus, at $x = 4.0$, with $N = 1,000$, the result is $y(4) = -0.23716$, whereas the $N = 10,000$ calculation yields $y(4) = -0.24886$. Therefore, without knowing the exact result, we can with confidence accept only two-digit accuracy in the $N = 10,000$ results. Even this would be suspect if there is indication of round-off error. Fortunately, since we know that Euler's method is a first-order method, we can monitor the accuracy of the calculation and see if it is indeed progressing linearly to a result. Since the step size is reduced by a factor of 10 from one line to the next and since the actual error is reduced by approximately the same factor, we conclude that round-off error is not yet a serious concern. These results were obtained on a machine with single precision and an eight-digit computer word.

The increase in accuracy in the midpoint method is very dramatic. Also, the actual error from the $N = 100$ to the $N = 1,000$ calculation is reduced by roughly a factor of 100, as expected. However, the calculation deteriorates as the computation is pushed to $N = 10,000$, obviously due to round-off error. This deterioration can be seen in the computed results even without the aid of an exact solution by noticing, for example, in the $y(6)$ results from $N = 100$ to $N = 1,000$, that the change is in the fourth digit. The next calculation should be approximately one hundred times more accurate. Therefore, we expect a change in the sixth digit, whereas the results again yield changes in the fourth digit. The remedy is either to redo the calculation with double precision or to resort to an algorithm of higher order. (The midpoint method is of order 2.)

Heun's method, though significantly less accurate for this equation than the midpoint method, is also seen to yield satisfactory results for the $N = 100$ and $N = 1,000$ calculations and to deteriorate in the $N = 10,000$ case.

The reason round-off error has so severely impacted our results can be seen from the nature of the solution. The exact solution is $y(x) = -1/x$, which decreases as x increases across the interval, whereas the round-off error is inexorably increasing. Eventually the two will be approximately the same size and all accuracy will be lost. These same considerations are required in evaluating all numerical solutions to differential equations even if much more elaborate algorithms are used.

Most well-written computer codes to solve a differential equation constantly monitor the accuracy of a calculation and will adjust the step size accordingly. Thus, the program should simultaneously compute one step and two half-steps. If the two results differ by more than some user-supplied tolerance, the step size is reduced and we try again. Also, if the two solutions agree by more than the required accuracy, the step size can be increased. Although this will tend to lengthen the computer code, it should be considered as an addition to a working code to improve the efficiency.

The procedures introduced in this section, the midpoint method and Heun's method, are meant as relatively simple introductions to the two basic ideas for solving differential equations. Using the same ideas, but retaining more terms in a Taylor series expansion, more complicated but higher-order algorithms can be developed (see Section 15.6). You should try to fully understand the second-order methods of this section. But you should use the fourth-order methods of Section 15.6 when you actually attempt to numerically solve differential equations.

15.6 Method of Runge–Kutta

The elementary refinements of the basic Euler method were based on the idea that using the average slope of the tangent over an interval to extrapolate a function to the next point should result in greater accuracy. The method of Runge–Kutta carries this a bit further. The slope that is used in the linear extrapolation is taken to be a *weighted* average of the slope at the left end of the interval and some intermediate point. Thus, the algorithm reads

$$y_{i+1} = y_i + f_{ave}\Delta x$$

where f_{ave} is determined by the equation

$$f_{ave} = af_i + bf_{i'}$$

where a, b are the "weights" and f_i is the function evaluated at the point x_i, and $f_{i'}$ is the function evaluated at some intermediate point defined as

$$f_{i'} = f(x_i + \alpha\Delta x, y_i + \beta f_i \Delta x)$$

where the two parameters α, β specify the position of the intermediate point.

Runge and Kutta used this form of the algorithm with the four parameters chosen to optimize the accuracy of the computed result. The parameters are not totally free parameters. By expanding the function $f(x, y)$ in a Taylor series expansion (in two variables!), they were able to obtain the following constraint equations on the parameters:

$$a + b = 1$$

$$\alpha b = \beta b = \tfrac{1}{2}$$

These are three equations in the four unknown parameters and thus there is still some freedom in how the parameters are chosen. The particular choice of parameters

$$a = 0 \qquad b = 1 \qquad \alpha = \beta = \tfrac{1}{2}$$

will result in an algorithm that is identical to the midpoint method discussed earlier. And a different choice of parameters, namely,

$$a = b = \tfrac{1}{2} \qquad \alpha = \beta = 1$$

yields Heun's algorithm.

Both of these computational algorithms are known as second-order Runge–Kutta procedures, meaning that the accumulated truncation error is proportional to $(\Delta x)^2$ in either method.

Fourth-Order Runge–Kutta Algorithm

By including more sampling points in the interval, the basic Runge–Kutta method can be improved to a procedure that has an accumulated truncation error proportional to $(\Delta x)^4$—that is, a fourth-order method. The determination of the many parameters is once again partially given by comparing with a two-variable Taylor series expansion and involves considerable algebra. The results are simply quoted here:

$$y_{i+1} = y_i + \tfrac{1}{6}[\Delta y_0 + 2\Delta y_1 + 2\Delta y_2 + \Delta y_3] \tag{15.11}$$

where

$$\Delta y_0 = f(x_i, y_i)\,\Delta x$$
$$\Delta y_1 = f(x_i + \tfrac{1}{2}\Delta x, y_i + \tfrac{1}{2}\Delta y_0)\,\Delta x$$
$$\Delta y_2 = f(x_i + \tfrac{1}{2}\Delta x, y_i + \tfrac{1}{2}\Delta y_1)\,\Delta x$$
$$\Delta y_3 = f(x_{i+1}, y_i + \Delta y_2)\,\Delta x \tag{15.12}$$

You can easily show that for the special case where the function $f(x, y)$ is a function of x *only*, the above procedure amounts to an integration of $\int f(x)dx$ by the Simpson's rule approximation; that is,

$$y_{i+1} = y_i + \frac{\Delta x/2}{3}\left[f(x_i) + 4f\left(x_i + \frac{\Delta x}{2}\right) + f(x_{i+1})\right] \tag{15.13}$$

The classical fourth-order Runge–Kutta algorithm is by far the most popular method for obtaining numerical solutions to differential equations. It is very easy to code and, except for especially perverse differential equations, is very stable and accurate. The method is self-starting, and the step size can easily be adjusted in the middle of a calculation to accommodate a function that is rapidly varying. There are other, more modern, methods that are more difficult to code but that are occasionally preferred over the Runge–Kutta methods since they require fewer function evaluations and are thus a bit more efficient. One class of these modern numerical techniques, the use of so-called *predictor-corrector* equations; is briefly described in Section 15.7. A second class, representing more recent progress in the solution of differential equations, is based on replacing the Taylor series approximation to a function by an approximation that is a ratio of polynomials. These methods are beyond the scope of this text but are described in W. H. Press *et al.*, *Numerical Recipes*, Cambridge University Press, 1986.

■ Numerical Comparison of the Fourth-Order Runge–Kutta Method with the Previous Methods for the Test Equation $y' = -y$

The solution of the differential equation

$$y' = -y \qquad y(0) = 1$$

is $y(x) = e^{-x}$. As x increases, the solution decreases exponentially while the accumulated errors will be monotonically increasing, eventually becoming larger than the function itself. This particular equation should then be a sensitive test of the stability of the various methods. The equation is solved over the interval $x = 0$ to $x = 10$ for a variety of step sizes and by the three basic procedures covered thus far: the midpoint method, Heun's method, and the fourth-order Runge–Kutta method. The results are presented in Table 15-4. Once again the actual percentage errors are listed below the computed values.

Table 15-4

Fourth-order Runge–Kutta algorithm compared with previous second-order methods when applied to the test equation $y' = x^2 - y/x - y^2$. The exact solution is $y = -1/x$. The actual percentage error is in parentheses.

x	N	$R - K - 4$	Midpoint	Heun
2.0	10	−0.4954183 (0.9)	−0.4722222 (5.6)	−0.3750000 (25.)
	100	−0.4999962 (0.0007)	−0.4999067 (0.019)	−0.4955571 (0.89)
	1,000	−0.4999993 (0.0002)	−0.5000036 (0.0007)	−0.4999569 (0.0087)
4.0	10	−0.2403551 (3.9)	−0.1976348 (21.)	−0.0578327 (77.)
	100	−0.2499921 (0.003)	−0.2498078 (0.077)	−0.2406790 (3.7)
	1,000	−0.2499980 (0.0009)	−0.2500106 (0.0042)	−0.2499114 (0.036)
6.0	10	−0.1525216 (8.5)	−0.0976343 (41.)	0.0275639 (116.)
	100	−0.1666548 (0.007)	−0.1663784 (0.17)	−0.1529608 (8.2)
	1,000	−0.1666645 (0.0006)	−0.1666853 (0.012)	−0.1665361 (0.078)
8.0	10	−0.1067407 (14.)	−0.0459672 (63.)	0.0529426 (142.)
	100	−0.1249841 (0.013)	−0.1246159 (0.31)	−0.1072828 (14.)
	1,000	−0.1249984 (0.0002)	−0.1250280 (0.024)	−0.1248288 (0.14)
10.0	10	−0.0780762 (22.)	−0.0162717 (84.)	0.0587540 (159.)
	100	−0.0999801 (0.020)	−0.0995204 (0.48)	−0.0786997 (21.)
	1,000	−0.0999990 (0.0004)	−0.1000369 (0.038)	−0.0997879 (0.21)

15.7   Predictor-Corrector Methods

Consider once again the two equations

$$y_{i+1} = y_i + f_{i+1/2}\Delta x \quad \text{Midpoint method (predictor equation)} \tag{15.14}$$

$$y_{i+1} = y_i + \tfrac{1}{2}(f_i + f_{i+1})\Delta x \quad \text{Heun's method (corrector equation)} \tag{15.15}$$

Higher-order versions of these equations can be used to construct highly efficient computational procedures known as *predictor-corrector methods*. Again, the idea is to use the predictor equation to estimate a value of y at the next step. This value is then inserted in the right-hand side of the corrector equation, and this equation is iterated two or three times to improve the value of y.

A popular choice for a set of higher-order predictor-corrector equations is from Milne.[3] This set is given here without a proof:

$$y_{i+1} = y_{i-3} + \tfrac{4}{3}\Delta x(2f_i - f_{i-1} + 2f_{i-2}) \quad \begin{array}{l}\text{Predictor equation}\\\text{(Milne method)}\end{array} \tag{15.16}$$

$$y_{i+1} = y_{i-1} + \tfrac{1}{3}\Delta x(f_{i+1} + 4f_i + f_{i-1}) \quad \begin{array}{l}\text{Corrector equation}\\\text{(Milne method)}\end{array} \tag{15.17}$$

You will notice that predictor-corrector methods are difficult to start. For example, to use the Milne method, the initial point y_0 and the first three computed values, y_1, y_2, y_3, will be required before the predictor equation can be used.

15.8   Second-Order Differential Equations

As discussed in Section 15.2, a second-order differential equation like Newton's second law, $F = m\, d^2y/dt^2$, can be rewritten as two coupled first-order equations by introducing the superfluous variable $v = dy/dt$.

$$m\frac{dv}{dt} = F(t, y, v)$$

$$\frac{dv}{dt} = v \tag{15.18}$$

These two equations can then be solved by any of the methods we have developed for first-order equations. However, we must carefully rewrite any

---

[3] See W. E. Milne, *Numerical Calculus* (Princeton, N.J.: Princeton University Press, 1949). The predictor equation was obtained by fitting a cubic (four parameters) through the points $(f_{i-3}, f_{i-2}, f_{i-1}, f_i)$ and then integrating

$$\int_{x_{i-3}}^{x_{i+1}} y'\, dx = y_{i+1} - y_{i-3} = \int f(x, y)\, dx \simeq \int (\text{cubic})\, dx$$

Clearly the corrector equation is based on a similar integration using Simpson's rule [see Equation (14.13)].

of the algorithms that we have chosen to solve the equations so that both equations are solved *simultaneously;* that is, in the above example, for each time step $t_i \rightarrow t_{i+1}$, both a new value of y_{i+1} and a new v_{i+1} are computed.

Of course, to start the calculation initial values of *both* y and v will be required. If both of the dependent variables (y,v) are specified at the *same* value of the independent variable t, the problem is called an *initial-value* problem.[4] For *any* other form of the specifications for y and v, the problem is called a *boundary-value* problem. The typical starting conditions for an initial-value problem are $y(t = 0) = y_0$, $v(t = 0) = v_0$; examples of specifications for a boundary-value problem might be $[y(t = 0) = y_0, v(t = 10) = v_{10}]$ or $[y(t = 0) = y_a, y(t = 10) = y_b]$. In general, numerical solutions to boundary-value problems are substantially more difficult to obtain than the solution to a corresponding initial-value problem. In this section we will be concerned exclusively with initial-value problems; procedures for solving boundary-value problems are discussed in Section 15.9.

Applying these ideas more formally to the general second-order initial-value problem,

$$y'' = F(x, y, y')$$

$$y(x_0) = y_0, \qquad y'(x_0) = v_0$$

suggests the following replacements:

Let $y_a = y,$ $y_a' = y_b$ $\begin{cases} y_a(0) = y_0 \\ y_b(0) = v_0 \end{cases}$ (15.19)

$\qquad\quad y_b = y'$ $y_b' = F(x, y_a, y_b)$

If we have in hand a satisfactory procedure for solving the equation $y' = f(t, y)$, say the subroutine MDPNT of Figure 15-4, it is then a straightforward exercise to adapt this code to solving both Equations (15.19) simultaneously.

FORTRAN Code to Solve Two Simultaneous Differential Equations Using a Fourth-Order Runge–Kutta Algorithm

It is relatively easy to adapt any of the methods described so far to solve two simultaneous differential equations of the form of Equations (15.19). We merely have to compute increments in both y_a and y_b for each step in the independent variable x. As was mentioned earlier, it is most common to use the fourth-order Runge–Kutta method when a moderately accurate solution is desired. For this reason such a subroutine has been included in Figure 15-7. Once again, to use this subroutine to solve two differential

---

[4] Even if we specify both $v(t)$ and $y(t)$ at the *end* of the time interval, the problem is still classified as an initial-value problem. In this case the solution is obtained by using a negative time step and marching backward across the interval.

Figure 15-7
Subroutine to solve two simultaneous differential equations using the fourth-order Runge–Kutta method. The solutions are returned in *y* and the user must supply the two right-hand-side functions, f_1 and f_2, for the two differential equations.

```
SUBROUTINE RKTWO(Y,N,A,B,F1,F2)
INTEGER N
REAL Y(2,0:N),A,B,X,DX,XH,Y1,Y2,DY1,DY2,
+     DY10,DY20,DY11,DY21,DY12,DY22,DY13,DY23
DX = (B-A)/N
X  = A
DO 1 I = 0,N-1
    XH   = X + .5*DX
    Y1   = Y(1,I)
    Y2   = Y(2,I)
    DY10 = F1(  X,       Y1,       Y2)*DX
    DY20 = F2(  X,       Y1,       Y2)*DX
    DY11 = F1(  XH,Y1+.5*DY10,Y2+.5*DY20)*DX
    DY21 = F2(  XH,Y1+.5*DY10,Y2+.5*DY20)*DX
    DY12 = F1(  XH,Y1+.5*DY11,Y2+.5*DY21)*DX
    DY22 = F2(  XH,Y1+.5*DY11,Y2+.5*DY21)*DX
    DY13 = F1(X+DX,   Y1+DY12,   Y2+DY22)*DX
    DY23 = F2(X+DX,   Y1+DY12,   Y2+DY22)*DX
    DY1  = (DY10 + 2.*DY11 + 2.*DY12 + DY13)/6.
    DY2  = (DY20 + 2.*DY21 + 2.*DY22 + DY23)/6.
    Y(1,I+1) = Y(1,I) + DY1
    Y(2,I+1) = Y(2,I) + DY2
    X = X + DX
1   CONTINUE
RETURN
END
```

equations, we are attempting to find two complete functions, labeled as $y_{1,i}$ and $y_{2,i}$, over the interval $x = a$ to $x = b$. To start the procedure you must supply the two initial values for the y's that are stored in the array Y, that is, $y(1,0)$ and $y(2,0)$, as well as the FORTRAN code for the two right-hand-side functions $f_1(x, y_1, y_2)$, $f_2(x, y_1, y_2)$. Finally, these functions must be declared as EXTERNAL in the calling program.

Examples of Solutions of Coupled Differential Equations

In this section the subroutine of Figure 15-7 is used to solve two problems involving coupled differential equations. The first example is a continuation of the $F = ma$ problem.

Position versus Time of a Projectile, Including Air Drag

If an object is thrown straight up, the trajectory is determined by solving Newton's second law, $F = ma$, where the force on the object is given as

$$F = -mg - \lambda v^2 \qquad \text{if } v > 0$$
$$= -mg + \lambda v^2 \qquad \text{if } v < 0 \qquad (15.20)$$

That is, the air-drag force λv^2 is always directed opposite to the direction of the velocity.

The initial conditions for an object that is thrown straight up are

$$y_a(0) = y(t = 0) = y_0$$

$$y_b(0) = v(t = 0) = v_0$$

For this problem we will use $y_0 = 0$, $v_0 = 20$ m/sec, and the coefficient of the drag force will be taken as $\lambda = 0.1$ kg/m. The two functions that must be supplied are then

$$f_a(t, y_a, y_b) = a = \frac{1}{m}F = -g - \frac{v}{|v|}\frac{\lambda}{m}v^2$$

$$f_b(t, y_a, y_b) = v = y_b$$

The results of the calculation over the time interval $t = 0$ to $t = 10$ sec are shown in Figure 15-8.

Before leaving this example I should point out the significance of what has been done. A large fraction of the problems of engineering and science are expressed in terms of the forces acting between atoms, or support beams, or machine parts, or any number of other possibilities. The computer code to solve the equation $F = ma$ frees engineers and scientists from the less productive labor of finding solutions to an equation and enables them to spend more time on the "loftier" ideas concerning the principles or assumptions involved in setting up the problem.

Figure 15-8
Computed trajectory of an object thrown straight up and subject to air drag

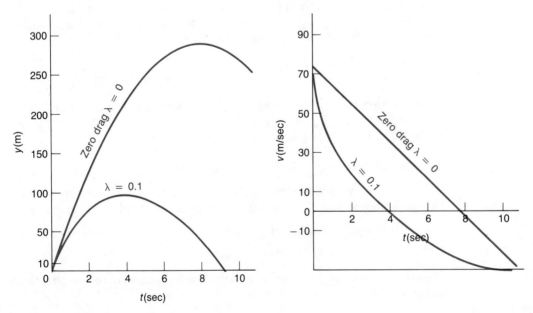

Coupled Differential Equations: Predator-Prey Problem

In the previous example a second-order differential equation was rewritten as two *coupled* first-order equations. This is not the only way that coupled equations can arise. Frequently a physical problem will be specified in terms of numerous variables and a variety of relations among the variables. Often the relations are differential equations. One example of a problem of this type is the predator-prey problem.

The predator-prey problem is an attempt to understand how two or more species compete with each other in a limited environment with limited resources. This is a very complicated problem, and as with all complicated problems in science and engineering, we begin by replacing the original problem, which we cannot solve, by a simpler but similar one that we can solve. In solving the easier problem we usually gain some information that will lead to the next refinement of the model.

First, we consider a single species, say, foxes, in an infinite environment, with an instant maturation period. If we start with more than two foxes, the rate of increase of the population is likely to be proportional to the number of foxes now present.

$$\frac{dN_f}{dt} \propto N_f$$

or

$$\frac{dN_f}{dt} = G_f N_f$$

where G_f is the growth rate of the fox population. This is the same equation that was used to describe radioactive decay in Section 15.2. Since G_f is positive, the solution is a growing exponential.

$$N_f(t) = N_0 e^{G_f t}$$

If the environment is finite—for example, an island—we might expect that there is a maximum number of foxes that can be supported, M_f. This number could be included in the model as

$$\frac{dN_f}{dt} = G_f N_f(t)\left[1 - \frac{N_f(t)}{M_f}\right] \tag{15.21}$$

so that the growth rate approaches zero as the population approaches the limit of the population, M_f. The solution of this differential equation is sketched in Figure 15-9. There are problems with the model already. You might expect the population to first overshoot the maximum before some foxes begin to die off; that is, we expect to see some oscillations at the top of the curve of $N_f(t)$ versus t. This refinement is left out for now; perhaps you can think of a way of including it later.

Figure 15-9
Effect of a
population upper
bound on the
growth of a species

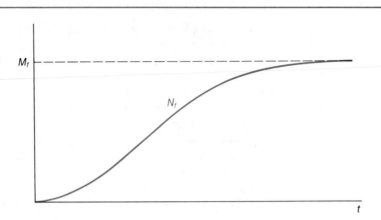

The next refinement is to introduce a second species (rabbits) to
the environment. An equation similar to Equation (15.21) will describe the
population of the rabbits. At this point the populations are controlled by
two uncoupled equations that can be solved independently. Of course, the
rabbit and fox populations are not independent; there is competition between the two species. To put it bluntly, the fox population will benefit at
the expense of the rabbit population. A new competition term must be
added to the equations for both N_f and N_r.

The competition term will reflect the idea that the growth rate of
each species will depend on the likelihood of two members of different
species meeting; that is, the term will be proportional to the product $N_f N_r$.
The equations for the growth rates now read

$$\frac{dN_f}{dt} = G_f N_f \left(1 - \frac{N_f}{M_f}\right) + A_f N_f N_r \tag{15.22}$$

$$\frac{dN_r}{dt} = G_r N_r \left(1 - \frac{N_r}{M_r}\right) + A_r N_f N_r \tag{15.23}$$

If the coefficient A is positive, the species will benefit from the encounter
(i.e., foxes eat rabbits), and conversely, if the coefficient is negative. Equations (15.22) and (15.23) are known as the *Lotka–Volterra equations*.

Before solving these two equations, one more simple refinement
will be added. Since the foxes depend heavily on the rabbits for food, but
not the reverse, we would expect this situation to be reflected in the maximum number of foxes; that is, the upper limit of the fox population will be
less if there is a scarcity of rabbits. This hypothesis for M_f is sketched in
Figure 15-10.

If $N_r > 10N_f$, then $M_f = M_f$

If $N_r \leq 10N_f$, then $M_f \rightarrow \frac{1}{2}\left[1 + \exp\left(1 - \frac{10N_f}{N_r}\right)\right]M_f \tag{15.24}$

Figure 15-10
The upper limit of the fox population is generalized to include a dependence on a diminished abundance of rabbits

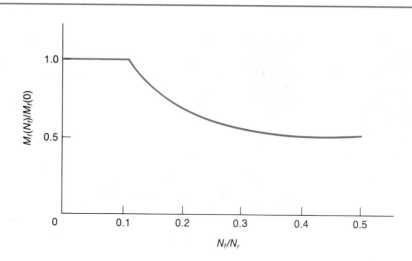

Finally, some of each species will be fortunate enough to avoid starvation and being eaten and will die a natural death after a normal life span; that is, there will be a decrease in the population now, at time t, that will be proportional to the number of the species alive at time $t - t_0$, where t_0 is the life span of the species.

Numerous additional refinements could be added to this model; but let us go directly to the numerical solution. The correction due to the finite life span is ignored because it makes the FORTRAN code too long.

The FORTRAN code to solve Equations (15.22) and (15.23) used the subroutine RKTWO of Figure 15-7. All that is additionally required is the code for the main calling program, the two function subprograms for the derivative functions, and some reasonable estimates for all of the parameters. The FORTRAN code for the derivative functions is given in Figure 15-11. The values used for the parameters are given in the figure and the computed populations of both species are graphed versus time in Figure 15-12.

Of course, in actual situations the comparison of computed results with experiment is very difficult, since there are seldom only two species and the factors controlling the populations are much more numerous, complicated, and perhaps poorly understood than those discussed here. However, Equations (15.22) and (15.23) are a start; building from these, extremely complicated "word population forecasting" codes have been constructed. Their validity is of course no better than the assumptions that were built into the code, as is also the case in the rabbit-fox problem.

The two example calculations of this section illustrate how two very dissimilar problems can be cast in terms of coupled first-order differential equations and solved by almost identical means. However, remember that these examples are inadequate to convey the enormous variety of

Figure 15-11 _____

FORTRAN code to compute the populations of rabbits and foxes by solving the Lotka–Volterra equations. The values are written to a data file, and this file is then read and graphed in Figure 15-12.

```
      PROGRAM RABFOX
      PARAMETER (N = 1000)
      REAL P(2,0:N)
      EXTERNAL DRABDT,DFOXDT
      COMMON/FOX/GF,AF,XF
      COMMON/RAB/GR,AR,XR
      DATA P(1,0),P(2,0)/10.,4./
      GR = 0.05
      GF = 0.02
      AR = -.0004
      AF = 0.0001
      XR = 4000.
      XF =  250.
      OPEN(8,FILE='RABFOX.OUT')
      CALL RKTWO(P,N,0.,250.,DRABDT,DFOXDT)
      DX = 250./N
      DO 1 I = 0,N
        WRITE(*,'(T2,F5.1,T10,F9.2,T20,F9.2)')I*DX,
     +             P(1,I),P(2,I)
   1  CONTINUE
      STOP
      END
*=================================================================
      FUNCTION DFOXDT(T,R,F)
      COMMON/FOX/GF,AF,XF
*
*   The growth rate of the fox population.  The parameters
*   are:
*     GF = the basic growth rate
*     AF = competition factor for fox encounters with rabbits
*     XF = maximum no. of foxes.
*     R  = current no. of rabbits
*     F  = current no. of foxes
*     T  = current value of time (in days)
*    XXF = adjusted maximum value of foxes when there are
*          few rabbits
*-----------------------------------------------------------------
      XXF = XF
      IF(R .LE. 10.*F)XXF = .5*XF*(1. + EXP(1. - 10.*F/R))
      DFOXDT = GF*F*(1. - F/XXF) + AF*F*R
      RETURN
      END
*=================================================================
      FUNCTION DRABDT(T,R,F)
*
*   The growth rate of rabbits.  The parameters have meanings
*   analogous to those in the above function
*
      COMMON/RAB/GR,AR,XR
      DRABDT = GR*R*(1. - R/XR) + AR*R*F
      RETURN
      END
*=================================================================
      SUBROUTINE RKTWO(Y,N,A,B,F1,F2)
*        ...         ...
      END
```

Figure 15-12
Rabbit and fox
populations as a
function of time

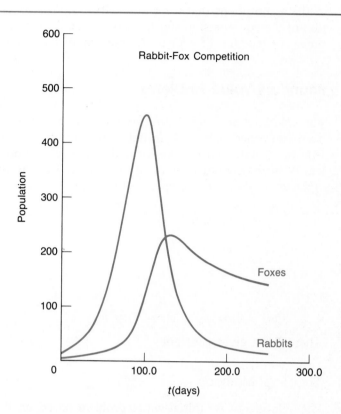

problems in all branches of science and engineering that can also be cast in a similar form and solved by the methods of this chapter.

The primary reason for the tremendous progress in the physical sciences and engineering in the last several centuries is that we have learned to express problems in terms of tightly phrased mathematical equations and then solve or manipulate these equations in place of the original phenomena. The solution of the abstract equations, once done, understood, and tested, is then used to understand the original problem and any other physical phenomena that can be phrased in a mathematically similar structure. The trick is to be sufficiently fluent in mathematics to recognize two dissimilar problems as being mathematically similar. Newton's second law and the competition of rabbits and foxes appear totally unrelated, yet both can be expressed in terms of second-order differential equations and solved by identical means. To a scientist or engineer, once the phenomena are approximately described in terms of equations, understanding the phenomena reduces to a tested recipe for the solution of the equations. These phenomena and any other that are described by similar equations are then understood completely, within the limitations of the assumptions that went into setting up the problem, with the solution of the equations. In short, coding a problem for solution on the computer is a true test of your understanding of the problem.

15.9   Boundary-Value Problems

The solutions of coupled differential equations given to this point have been concerned only with initial-value problems. Boundary-value problems are usually much more difficult. Recall that a boundary-value problem is ordinarily one in which the additional constraints are specified at *different* values of the independent variable. For example,

$$\frac{dv}{dt} = \frac{1}{m} F(t, y, v)$$

$$\frac{dy}{dt} = v$$

with

$$y(t = 0) = y_0 \qquad y(t = T) = y_T$$

where T is a given constant.

"Shooting" Methods

The solution of an initial-value problem based on the above equations started with the values for y_0, v_0 and then proceeded to step along the t axis, computing successive value of y_i, v_i along the way. In the problem above, however, we have a dilemma: we have no starting value for v. We might try guessing a value for v_0, then march across the t interval to $t = T$, and finally check whether $y(t = T)$ is indeed equal to the given condition y_T. In the likely event that it is not, we would alter the original guess for v_0 and start over.

If all this sounds vaguely familiar, rather like root solving, it was intended so, for in this case we are searching for a single number, the missing initial condition, v_0. Thus, the task is to phrase the current problem in terms of the root-solving techniques of Chapter 11. Remember that the "variable" is v_0. Therefore, the function whose root we seek must be zero for a value of v_0 that ultimately results in $y(t = T) = y_T$.

First recall the structure of the subroutine to solve two simultaneous differential equations:

```
SUBROUTINE RKTWO(Y,N,A,B,F1,F2)
```

Next consider the rather odd function shown in Figure 15-13. This function is zero when the boundary condition is satisfied, that is, $y_1(t = T) =$

Figure 15-13 _____

```
      FUNCTION F(X)
        COMMON/INITL/T0,Y10,Y20,A,B
        COMMON/ENDPT/Y1F
        REAL Y(2,0:100)
        EXTERNAL F1,F2
*
*   Y1F is the given endpoint of the first variable y1,
*   whereas y20 is not yet known.  The number of panels
*   is n, and the solutions are stored in y.  The variable
*   x is going to be a guess for the missing value y20.
*
        Y20 = X
        CALL RKTWO(Y,100,A,B,F1,F2)
        F = Y1(N) - Y1F
        RETURN
      END
```

y_T, and the search variable is in our case $x = y_2(0)$. All that remains is to use an appropriate root-solving subroutine, say the secant method, to solve the problem. You are most likely aware that the solution will require solving the entire initial-value problem perhaps hundreds of times; that is, each call to the function F(X) solves a complete initial-value problem. Thankfully, more efficient means exist for some problems. But for moderately small problems, and if the computer time is not excessive, the above method is adequate.

This procedure for solving boundary-value problems is called *shooting*, in an obvious analogy to trajectory problems. Most other methods for solving boundary-value problems are handled in a similar fashion; that is, the problem is converted into a search for the equivalent initial-value problem.

▬ Finite Difference Methods

A different approach is to use the expression for first and second derivatives given in Chapter 10 and to rewrite the differential equation in terms of y_i, y_{i+1}, y_{i-1}, and so on. For example, the second derivative can be approximated by the central difference expression, Equation (10.46),

$$y''(x_i) \approx \frac{y_{i+1} - 2y_i + y_{i-1}}{\Delta x^2}$$ Central difference equation for second derivative (15.25)

These equations for $i = 0,\ldots, n$ are written in matrix form and the entire set is solved for the unknowns $\{y_i\}$. See Programming Problem F-C for an explicit example.

■■■■■■■   **15.10   Conclusion**

All of the procedures in this chapter, most of the numerical methods in this text, and a great many of the numerical procedures developed in the last two centuries have at their core the Taylor series; that is, replacing a function over a limited range by a simpler polynomial expressed in terms of derivatives of the complicated function seems to be the idea that has driven numerical analysis for most of its history. However, more recently a different approach has been gaining acceptance — the Pade approximation. This approximation to a funciton replaces the function not by a power series like the Taylor series but rather by a function composed of one polynomial divided by another polynomial. The reason that such an expansion is desirable is to be found in the theory of complex variables and is beyond the scope of this text. However, this idea has been found to be extraordinarily successful when applied to many areas of numerical analysis, and you will no doubt encounter it in later courses. If you are interested, see the discussion of rational function interpolation in W. H. Press et al., *Numerical Recipes*, Cambridge University Press, 1986.

■■■■■■■   **Summary**

A differential equation is a set of conditions on the derivatives of a function plus conditions on the value of the function at specified points (called initial conditions or boundary conditions) sufficient to uniquely determine the function. Thus, the differential equation

$$y''(x) = y(x)$$

$$y(0) = 1, y'(0) = 0$$

means: determine a complete function that is equal to its own second derivative and that has the value 1 when $x = 0$. Since the solution to a differential equation is always itself a function, a numerical solution usually involves tracing out the function by starting at the known value and stepping in the independent variable. The procedures described in this chapter are summarized below.

Before we start, several terms must be defined:

- *Convergence rate.* Each of the methods will generally converge to the solution with an error proportional to $(\Delta x)^n$, where Δx is the step size in the independent variable. The order of convergence is then n.
- *Stability.* For some methods and under certain circumstances, a small change in the starting values can result in a very large change in the solution. Such methods are called unstable and are very prone to round-off error problems.
- *Initial values.* If a differential equation is of order n (the highest derivative is the nth), then the function and its first

$n - 1$ derivatives must be specified at the same value of the independent variable to begin a stepping procedure. A differential equation of this type is called an initial-value problem, and the starting values are called initial conditions. All other forms of conditions on the values of the function, for example, specifying the function at both ends of an interval, are called boundary conditions. First-order equations are always initial-value problems.

- *Notation.* A step size is indicated by Δx; the computed values of the solution at $x = x_i$ are labeled y_i; a first-order differential equation is written as $y'(x) = f(x, y)$; and f_i represents $f(x, y)$ evaluated at the point (x_i, y_i).

The stepping procedures for first-order differential equations are listed below:

Euler's Method

Convergence rate: First order in Δx

Stability: Very stable

Characteristics: Euler's method is useful primarily for demonstration purposes and should not be used for a serious solution to any problem.

Algorithm:

$$y_0 = \langle\text{given initial condition at } x_0 = a\rangle$$

For $i = 0$ to $n - 1$

$$x_{i+1} = a + i\Delta x$$

$$y_{i+1} = y_1 + f(x_i, y_i)$$

Midpoint Method

Convergence rate: Second order in Δx

Stability: Stable for most differential equations

Characteristics: For each step, the value of the slope at the middle of the interval is estimated and used to compute Δy.

Algorithm:

$$y_0 = \langle\text{given initial condition at } x_0 = a\rangle$$

For $i = 0$ to $n - 1$, compute

$$x_{\text{mid}} = x_i + \tfrac{1}{2}\Delta x$$

$$y_{\text{mid}} = y_i + \tfrac{1}{2}f(x_i, y_i)\,\Delta x$$

$$x_{i+1} = x_i + \Delta x$$

$$y_{i+1} = y_i + f(x_{\text{mid}}, y_{\text{mid}})\,\Delta x$$

Heun's Method

Convergence rate: Second order in Δx

Stability: Stable for most differential equations

Characteristics: Heun's method is similar to the midpoint method. The difference is that instead of estimating the midpoint values, the value of y' used is an average of the values on the left and right sides of the interval.

Algorithm:

$$y_0 = \langle \text{given initial condition at } x_0 = a \rangle$$

For $i = 0$ to $n - 1$

$$x_{i+1} = y_i + \Delta x$$

$$\Delta y_L = f(x_i, y_i)\Delta x$$

$$\Delta y_R = f(x_{i+1}, y_i + \Delta y_L)$$

$$\Delta y = \tfrac{1}{2}(\Delta y_L + \Delta y_R)$$

$$y_{i+1} = y_i + \Delta y$$

Predictor-Corrector Methods (Milne's Method)

Convergence rate: Third order in Δx

Stability: Frequently unstable. Ordinarily a fourth-order method is preferable.

Characteristics: Milne's method is among the simplest examples of predictor-corrector equations and is useful as a demonstration of the method.

Algorithm: To start the procedure, the first three values of the solution must be obtained in addition to the initial condition y_0. This requires a separate calculation, usually using a fourth order Runge–Kutta procedure.

$$y_0 = \langle \text{given initial condition at } x_0 = a \rangle$$

Compute y_1, y_2, y_3

For $i = 0$ to $n - 1$

$$x_{i+1} = x_i + \Delta x$$

$$y_{i+1} = y_{i-3} + \tfrac{4}{3}(2f_i - f_{i-1} + 2f_{i-2})\Delta x \qquad \text{Predictor equation}$$

For each value of i apply three iterations of the corrector equation.

$$y_{i+1} = y_{i-1} + \tfrac{1}{3}(f_{i+1} + 4f_i + f_{i-1})\Delta x \qquad \text{Corrector equation}$$

The next category of equations are second-order differential equations. If the two conditions on the solution are both specified at the same value of the independent variable, the problem is an initial-value-type problem and is solved by rewriting the second-order equation as two coupled first-order equations with the introduction of a superfluous variable, v:

$$\begin{pmatrix} y'' = f(x, y, y') \\ y(x_0) = y_0, y'(x_0) = v_0 \end{pmatrix} \text{ let } \begin{matrix} y_a = y \\ \xrightarrow{} \\ y_b = y' \end{matrix} \begin{pmatrix} y_a' = y_b & y_a(x_0) = y_0, f_a = y_b \\ y_b' = f_b(x, y_a, y_b), y_b(x_0) = v_0 \end{pmatrix}$$

These equations are then solved simultaneously, usually using a fourth-order Runge–Kutta procedure:

Method of Runge–Kutta (Fourth Order)

Convergence rate: Fourth order in Δx

Stability: Stable for most differential equations

Characteristics: The fourth-order Runge–Kutta is by far the most popular algorithm for solving initial-value problems either of first or second order. The procedure outlined here is the suggested technique for second-order equations.

Algorithm:

$$y_0^a, y_0^b = \langle\text{initial conditions on the two functions at } x = x_0\rangle$$

For $i = 0$ to $n - 1$

$$x_{\text{mid}} = x_i + \tfrac{1}{2}\Delta x$$

$$x_{i+1} = x_i + \Delta x$$

$$\Delta y_0^a = f_a(x_i, y_i^a, y_i^b)\Delta x \qquad\qquad \Delta y_0^b = f_b(x_i, y_i^a, y_i^b)\Delta x$$

$$\Delta y_1^a = f_a(x_{\text{mid}}, y_i^a + \tfrac{1}{2}\Delta y_0^a, y_i^b + \tfrac{1}{2}\Delta y_0^b)\Delta x$$

$$\Delta y_2^a = f_a(x_{\text{mid}}, y_i^a + \tfrac{1}{2}\Delta y_1^a, y_i^b + \tfrac{1}{2}\Delta y_1^b)\Delta x$$

$$\Delta y_3^a = f_a(x_{i+1}, y_i^a + \Delta y_2^a, y_i^b + \Delta y_2^b)\Delta x$$

$$\Delta y^a = \tfrac{1}{6}(\Delta y_0^a + 2\Delta y_1^a + 2\Delta y_2^a + \Delta y_3^a)$$

$$y_{i+1}^a = y_i^a + \Delta y^a \qquad\qquad \Delta y_{i+1}^b = y_i^b + \Delta y^b$$

Analogous equations for the quantities $\Delta y_1^b, \ldots, \Delta y^b$

If the conditions on the solution are specified at different values of the independent variable, the problem is a boundary-value problem and is ordinarily much more difficult to solve. One approach, called *shooting,* attempts to convert the problem into a search for a set of appropriate initial conditions.

For example, if the problem is first rewritten as coupled first-order equations, as above, and the conditions on the solution are not specified at the same value of x, the problem is a boundary-value problem. For example,

$$\begin{pmatrix} y_a' = f_a(x, y_a, y_b), & y_b' = f_b(x, y_a, y_b) \\ y_a(x_0) = Y_0 & y_a(x_1) = Y_1 \end{pmatrix}$$

But in this case, the value of y_b at the initial point, that is, $y_b(x_0)$, is not given. The method of shooting is then to guess a value of $y_b(x_0)$, say V_0, solve the now initial-value problem from x_0 to x_1, and then see if the computed value for $y_a(x = x_1)$ is indeed equal to Y_1. If not, the initial guess for V_0 is improved and the calculation repeated. This algorithm can be expressed in terms of a search for the root of a function of V_0 that will be zero when $y_a(x_1) = Y_1$.

Problems

15.1 Solve the following differential equations by arranging the terms in each variable on opposite sides of the equation using $y' = dy/dx$ into a form

$$M(x)\,dx = N(y)\,dy$$

and integrating. In each case determine the value of the integration constant by imposing the extra condition. Verify that your solution is indeed a solution of the original equation.

a. $y'y = x$ $\qquad$ $y(2) = 4$
b. $xy' = 2y$ $\qquad$ $y(2) = 4$
c. $y' = 2y$ $\qquad$ $y(0) = 1$
d. $L\dfrac{dI(t)}{dt} + RI(t) = 0$ $\qquad$ $I(0) = 2$ $\qquad$ $L = 0.001, R = 50$
e. $N(t) = k\dfrac{dN(t)}{dt}$ $\qquad$ $N(0) = N_0$ $\qquad$ $k = \text{constant}$

15.2 Replace the following differential equations by two (or more) first-order differential equations by introducing new variables. Be sure to rewrite the extra conditions in terms of the new variables.

a. The equation describing the oscillations in time of the charge $Q(t)$ on the plates of a capacitor placed in an electric circuit containing the capacitor (capacitance, C) and a coil (inductance, L) is

$$L\frac{d^2Q(t)}{d^2t} + \frac{1}{C}Q(t) = 0 \qquad Q(0) = Q_0, \left.\frac{dQ}{dt}\right|_{t=0} = 0$$

b. The equation for the steady-state heat conduction through a large flat slab with a temperature-dependent heat conductivity ($\lambda = \lambda_0 + \alpha T$) is given below. The solution describes the temperature $T(x)$ as a function of x through the slab.

$$\frac{d}{dx}\left[(\lambda_0 + \alpha T)\frac{dT}{dx}\right] = 0 \qquad T(0) = 5, \left.\frac{dT}{dx}\right|_{x=0} = 1$$

c. The equations

$$a_x = \frac{d^2x}{dt^2} = -k\frac{x}{r^3}$$

$$a_y = \frac{d^2y}{dt^2} = -k\frac{v}{r^3}$$

with

$$r = (x^2 + y^2)^{1/2} \qquad \text{and} \qquad k = Gm_1$$

determine the orbital motion of one object about another when the force acting between the two is the gravitational force. The constant G is the gravitational force strength (6.6720×10^{-11} N-m^2/kg^2), and m_1, m_2 are the masses of the two objects. The initial conditions are

$$x(0) = -2.0 \times 10^7 \text{ m} \qquad \left.\frac{dx}{dt}\right|_0 = 0$$

$$y(0) = 0 \qquad \left.\frac{dy}{dt}\right|_0 = 5000 \text{ m/sec}$$

$$m_1 = m_{\text{earth}} \qquad m_2 = 10 \text{ kg}$$

$$= 5.97 \times 10^{24} \text{ kg}$$

15.3 Solve the following equations with the help of a calculator using Euler's method. Carry out five steps using the indicated step size and compare with the exact solution.

Equation	Initial Condition	Δx	Exact Solution
a. $y' = -y/x$	$y(1) = 1.0$	0.1	$y(x) = 1/x$
b. $y' = -y^2$	$y(1) = 1.0$	0.1	$y(x) = 1/x$
c. $y' = -y/x$	$y(1) = 1.0$	-0.1	$y(x) = 1/x$
d. $y' = x + y$	$y(0) = 0$	0.4	$y(x) = e^x - 1 - x$

15.4 Solve the differential equations of Problem 15.3 using the midpoint method.

15.5 Write a program to use Heun's method to twice solve the differential equation $y' = -y$, $y(0) = 1$ and determine $y(0.2)$; first with a step size of $dx = 0.01$ and then with $dx = 0.02$. If we call the two computed values of y at $x = 0.2$, y_1 and y_2, respectively, the latter should be less accurate since a larger step size was used. The program should then compute the ratio

$$R = \frac{y_2 - y_{ex}}{y_1 - y_{ex}}$$

which is a measure of how the accuracy of the procedure depends on a reduction of step size by half. If the method is "linear," we expect the accuracy to improve by a factor of 2; if "quadratic," the factor should be 4; and so on. Equating R to 2^p, determine the approximate order p of this calculation.

15.6 Show that the two choices for the parameters a, b, α, β given in Section 15.6 do indeed result in algorithms identical to the midpoint and Heun's method, respectively.

15.7 a. Write a FORTRAN subroutine MDPT4 that will use the midpoint method to solve *four* simultaneous coupled differential equations.
  b. Test this code by solving Problem 15.2c. (Use $N = 1,000$ and integrate from $t_0 = 0$ to $t_0 = 50,000$ sec.)

15.8 Carry out one step in detail using the fourth-order Runge–Kutta algorithm of Section 15.6 applied to the initial-value problem

$$y' = \left(\frac{y}{x}\right) + 2\left(\frac{y}{x}\right)^2 \qquad y(1) = -\frac{1}{2} \qquad y_{exact} = -\frac{x}{2 + 2\ln(x)}$$

15.9 a. Write a general-purpose FORTRAN subroutine to solve a single differential equation using the fourth-order Runge–Kutta algorithm of Section 15.6.
  b. Test the code by solving the following differential equation for $1 \le x \le 3$.

$$y' = 4x - \frac{2y}{x} \qquad y(1) = 1 \qquad y_{exact} = x^2$$

15.10 Show that if $y' = f(x)$, that is, f is a function of x only, then
  a. Equation (15.14) is equivalent to simply integrating the differential equation by means of the trapezoidal rule.
  b. Equation (15.17) is equivalent to simply integrating the differential equation by means of Simpson's rule.

15.11 Alter the rabbit-foxes problem to account for the natural death of both species, as described in Section 15.8.

15.12 Apply the predictor-corrector method using Equations (15.14) and (15.15) and carry out two steps applied to the equation

$$y' = -2xy^2 \qquad y(1) = 1 \qquad y_{exact} = \frac{1}{x^2}$$

Start with a step size of $\Delta x = 0.01$, compute y_0 and y_1 from the exact solution, and use these values and the predictor equation, (15.14), to estimate y_2. Then apply the corrector equation, (15.15), twice to improve the estimate of y_2. Then move on to calculate y_3.

15.13 Solve Problem 15.12 using the predictor-corrector method of Milne [Equations (15.16) and (15.17)].

15.14 Write a complete FORTRAN program to implement the predictor-corrector method using Equations (15.14) and (15.15). The main program should use an appropriate method to first compute y_1 in order to get the procedure started and then call a subroutine to apply the predictor-corrector equations and obtain a solution. Test the code on the equation given in Problem 15.12.

15.15 Write a complete FORTRAN program to implement the predictor-corrector method using the Milne equations, (15.16) and (15.17). The main program should use an appropriate method (fourth-order Runge–Kutta) to first compute y_1, y_2, y_3 in order to get the procedure started and then call a subroutine MILNE to apply the predictor-corrector equations and obtain a solution. Test the code on the equation given in Problem 15.12.

15.16 The differential equation describing heat conduction in Problem 15.2b is specified as an initial-value problem. It is more common to specify the temperature at two points on the slab and solve the differential equation to obtain $T(x)$ for the remaining x values. The conditions then might be

$$T(0) = T_0 = 0 \qquad T(x = 10) = T_{10} = 100$$

With these conditions the equation becomes a boundary-value problem. Set up the FORTRAN code that will use the subroutine RKTWO of Figure 15-7 and a root solver, say SECANT, to obtain the solution of the differential equation in the manner of Section 15.9.

Error
Analysis

16.1 Introduction

Conventionally, a discussion of error analysis precedes the study of the various numerical methods we have covered to this point. However, there are several compelling reasons for postponing this particular topic until last. First, particularly for novices, it is important to develop a feel for how numerical procedures work and to acquire experience in correcting computational problems as they arise before attacking the complicated and subtle job of predicting and verifying the accuracy of a calculation.

But perhaps just as important is the impression most students have that error analysis is terribly tedious and boring. The description of significant figures and round-off error, which is usually first encountered in a freshman physics laboratory, is often felt to be a monotonous, even painful, experience. Instead of taking advantage of the enthusiasm of novices and their desire to involve themselves in laboratory work, a detour into a study of all the things that can go wrong in analyzing data often is less productive than the instructor had hoped. After the experiment is finished or after a calculation has been completed is certainly not the appropriate time to begin to be concerned about experimental or numerical errors. But it most definitely is a point at which those errors can be better appreciated. At this stage of your study of numerical methods I am sure you would agree that the importance of a valid estimate of the total errors involved in a numerical solution cannot be overemphasized. Frequently the error estimate is more valuable than the actual answer. If your computed results are to be of any value whatsoever, you must be able to justify your confidence in them by some kind of validity check. Of course, there is no way to be 100 percent sure of any result. But the prudent engineer will have carried out every reasonable test before submitting a solution to a problem, and the estimate of the uncertainty of the results should always be part of the solution.

The numerical error in a computation has been an incidental concern in most of the example programs to this point. We are aware of the deleterious effects that a finite computer word length can have on a variety of calculations. And we have seen that retaining too few terms in a Taylor series when approximating a function can often invalidate a calculation. The purpose of this chapter is to summarize these error considerations and, where possible, to suggest remedies.

The study of errors in numerical computation is a vast and complex field that is seldom studied in isolation and is usually tacked onto the analysis of individual problems. The discussion in this chapter is by no means comprehensive; however, it should be adequate to at least begin an error analysis of the problems you face in the future.

16.2   Review of Definitions Relating to Error Analysis

Significant Figures

The numbers used in mathematics are exact. For example,

$$\tfrac{5}{7} = 0.714285714285714\ldots$$

$$\pi = 3.1415926536\ldots$$

$$e = 2.7182818285\ldots$$

where ... indicates that the number continues indefinitely either by repeating a pattern of digits (714285 in the case of $\tfrac{5}{7}$) or by never repeating any such pattern, as in the case of e and π. The numbers used to represent physical quantities are never exact. A number that represents a measured physical quantity is also used to reflect the quality of the measurement itself. For example, measuring the temperature with a common household thermometer can at best result in a determination of the temperature to $\pm\tfrac{1}{2}°$ C. A measured temperature could be 27.5° C, indicating that the measurement has determined three figures with some uncertainty in the last digit. The same temperature measured by a more accurate laboratory thermometer may result in a value of 27.500° C, indicating that in this measurement five digits have been determined with a presumed error in the last digit. The first measurement has three significant figures and the second has five. Explicitly writing trailing zeros on a quantity usually means that these zeros are intended to be significant figures. On the other hand, *leading* zeros are never counted as significant figures. A standard convention for indicating how many digits are of significance in a measured quantity is to write the numbers in scientific notation—for example, 2.75×10^1 and 2.7500×10^1 for the two measured temperatures.

Next, if the temperatures are converted to Kelvin by adding 273.16, the second measurement of the temperature would be written as 3.0066×10^2, again indicating five significant digits. This number would not, however, be a realistic representation of the less accurate measurement. After all, simply converting from Celsius to Kelvin cannot increase the accuracy or the number of significant digits in the result. To reflect the three-figure accuracy of the measured quantity, the result is *rounded* to 3.01×10^2 K.

Furthermore, when two numbers are combined in the arithmetic operation of multiplication or division, the result cannot have more significant figures than *any* of the numbers that enter into the expression. This of course means that the result will at best have the same number of significant digits as the *least* accurate number used. Numerical constants that are part of an arithmetic expression will be assumed to have an infinite number of significant digits or at least the number corresponding to the word length of the computer.

Relative and Absolute Error

If the error in a temperature measurement is ±0.5° C out of a measured value of 27.5° C, the result is then represented as $T = 27.5 \pm 0.5°$ C. The error in the measurement has the units of temperature and is called the *absolute* error. Another way to express the size of the error in the measured value is to indicate the size of the error relative to the actual measured value. This result may be expressed as a fraction as $|\Delta T|/T = 0.5/27.5 = 0.02$ and is then called the *fractional* or *relative* error. Another common usage is to express this result as a percentage, say 2%, indicating that the temperature measurement is correct to 2 parts in 100. Also, notice that since there is only *one* significant figure in the absolute error (0.5° C) it would be inconsistent to retain more in the relative error.

Addition of Errors as a Result of Arithmetic Operations

> When adding (or subtracting) two numbers, both of which have experimental errors, the *absolute* error of the result is the *sum* of the *absolute* errors of each of the original numbers.

$$T_1 = 27.5 \pm 0.5° \text{ C}$$

$$T_2 = 36.445 \pm 0.005° \text{ C}$$

$$T_1 + T_2 = 63.945 \pm 0.505° \text{ C} = 63.9 \pm 0.5° \text{ C}$$

A digital position in a result of addition or subtraction is a significant figure *only* if the same digital position is a significant figure in *all* of the terms involved. Thus, even though T_2 has significant digits in the 10^{-3} position, the result of adding or subtracting T_1 is rounded to the 10^{-1} position since this number contains significant digits only to the tenths position.

The same absolute error results from a subtraction.

$$T_2 - T_1 = 8.945 \pm 0.505° \text{ C} = 8.9 \pm 0.5° \text{ C}$$

Notice that even though the less accurate number has three significant figures, the result of the subtraction has only two. This is because the error is in the first digit after the decimal and representing the result as 8.94 would incorrectly suggest significance to the last digit. This is an important example of how significant figures can be lost as a result of subtracting two numbers of like size.

> When multiplying (or dividing) two numbers, both of which have experimental errors, the *relative* error of the result is the *sum* of the *relative* errors of each of the original numbers.

You can easily see this result by symbolically writing the product of two numbers as

$$(T_1 \pm \Delta T_1)(T_2 \pm \Delta T_2) = \left[T_1\left(1 \pm \frac{\Delta T_1}{T_1}\right)\right]\left[T_2\left(1 \pm \frac{\Delta T_2}{T_2}\right)\right]$$

$$= (T_1 T_2)\left[1 \pm \left(\frac{\Delta T_1}{T_1} + \frac{\Delta T_2}{T_2}\right) + \frac{\Delta T_1 \Delta T_2}{T_1 T_2}\right]$$

Since the last term in the brackets is much smaller than the first two terms, the relative error in the product can be identified as $(\Delta T_1/T_1 + \Delta T_2/T_2)$. Thus,

$$(27.5 \pm 2\%)(27.500 \pm 0.02\%) = 756.25 \pm 2.02\% = 756 \pm 2\%$$

Error in a Function $f(x \pm \Delta x)$

If we assume that the error Δx in a number x is much smaller than the number, an arbitrary function of $x \pm \Delta x$ may then be expanded in a Taylor series as

$$f(x \pm \Delta x) \simeq f(x) \pm f'(x)\Delta x + \cdots$$

Thus, the error in the function is roughly $f'(x) \Delta x$. For example, if a number plus its error is represented as $T + \Delta T$, then the corresponding absolute error in the logarithm of the number is[1]

$$\ln(T + \Delta T) = \ln(T) + \Delta[\ln(T)] = \ln(T) + \frac{1}{T}\Delta T$$

---

[1] Recall that the derivative of the logarithm is
$$\frac{d}{dT}\ln(T) = \frac{1}{T}$$

That is, the *absolute* error in the logarithm of a number is the same as the relative error in that number. (We have seen this result before in Section 13.8.) Similarly, the error in $(T + \Delta T)^4$ is $4T^3 \Delta T$.

Finally, all of the considerations of error in numbers referred to experimental error. But the numbers used in computations are likewise only approximate values limited by the word length of the computer, and so each of the concerns that are allotted to experimental values must simultaneously be given to all computed quantities as well.

16.3   Types of Error

The types of errors present in most computations can be separated into four classes:

1. *Round-off error.* Caused by the finite word length of the computer and, except for being much smaller, has the same characteristics as experimental error.
2. *Discretization error.* Basically, the result of using calculus equations that assume $\Delta x \to 0$, while the smallest Δx used in the calculation is finite. These errors will diminish as $\Delta x \to 0$.
3. *Truncation errors.* Usually refer to the approximation of a function by a straight line or a parabola over a limited interval. As with discretization errors, if the interval is reduced the errors should decrease. Also, the errors can be reduced by increasing the level of the approximation by, for example, replacing a linear approximation by a parabolic approximation.
4. *Experimental error.* Measurement error present in all data that are submitted for analysis. The numerical methods used to analyze the data may have the effect of amplifying or diminishing the experimental error.

We have encountered each of these errors at various points in this text. Here we will look at each type individually and discuss how to recognize impending problems and how to minimize them.

16.4   Round-Off Errors

Ordinarily, the easiest error to spot and one that can be the most troublesome is round-off error. Typically, problems with round-off error are caused by a dramatic loss of significant figures when either numbers of similar size are subtracted or an elementary arithmetic operation is repeated hundreds of thousands of times, each time the round-off error accumulating inexorably.

Figure 16-1

Square inscribed within a unit circle

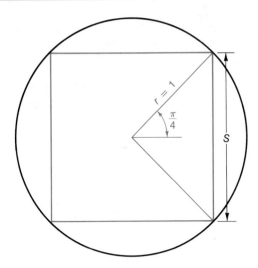

Calculation of π

One of the earliest calculations of π was done by Archimedes, who compared the (unknown) circumference of a circle with the (known) circumference of a regular polygon inscribed within the circle. If the circle has a unit radius and a square is inscribed within the circle, as drawn in Figure 16-1, the length of one side of the square is[2]

$$S = 2 \sin\left(\frac{\pi}{4}\right) = 2\left(\frac{1}{\sqrt{2}}\right) = \sqrt{2} \tag{16.1}$$

Thus, the circumference is $4S = 4\sqrt{2}$. This is then the first approximation for the circumference of the unit circle (i.e., 2π). If we next label this approximation for π as the kth-order approximation, p_k, where $k = 2$ and the number of sides of the inscribed polygon is $n = 2^k$, then the equation for P_k for arbitrary k is

$$\pi \approx p_k = \frac{n}{2}[2\sin(\theta_k)] = 2^k \sin(\theta_k) \tag{16.2}$$

where the angle is given by $\theta_k = \pi/n = \pi/2^k$.

Doubling the number of sides—that is, $k \rightarrow k + 1$—then yields

$$p_{k+1} = 2(2^k) \sin(\tfrac{1}{2}\theta_k) \tag{16.3}$$

(See Figure 16-2.) Equations (16.2) and (16.3) can be related using the trigonometric identity

---

[2] Of course, Archimedes did not have trigonometric functions available. His calculation is all the more impressive for this reason.

Figure 16-2
Doubling the
number of sides
improves the
approximation for
π

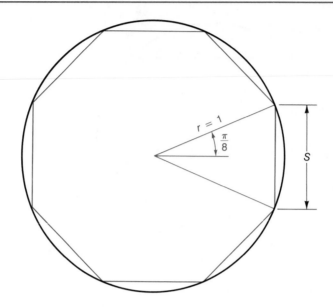

$$\sin^2\left(\frac{\theta}{2}\right) = \frac{1}{2}[1 - \cos(\theta)]$$

$$= \frac{1}{2}\{1 - [1 - \sin^2(\theta)]^{1/2}\} \tag{16.4}$$

which then yields

$$p_{k+1} = \sqrt{2}\,(2^k)\left\{1 - \left[1 - \left(\frac{p_k}{2^k}\right)^2\right]^{1/2}\right\}^{1/2} \tag{16.5}$$

Starting with $k = 2$, $p_2 = 2\sqrt{2}$, we can apply this equation repeatedly to obtain ever-improved estimates for π by using inscribed polygons with ever more sides. Thus, for $k = 3$ (8 sides) we obtain

$$p_3 = \sqrt{2}\,(4)\left\{1 - \left[1 - \left(\frac{2\sqrt{2}}{4}\right)^2\right]^{1/2}\right\}^{1/2}$$

$$= \sqrt{2}\,(4)\left[1 - \frac{1}{\sqrt{2}}\right]^{1/2}$$

$$= 3.0614675\ldots$$

Using a pocket calculator it is relatively easy to generate the higher approximations for π that are listed in Table 16-1. If we assume that we do not know the correct value of π, we can use the most recently computed value in the table to estimate the accuracy of the previous table entry. Thus, the third calculation ($k = 4$) suggests that at best only the

Table 16-1

Calculation of π using Equation (16.3). Digits judged to be significant are in boldface.

k	n	$\pi \approx p_k$
2	4	2.8284271248
3	8	3.0614674589
4	16	3.1214451525
5	32	3.1365484904
6	64	3.1403311479
7	128	3.1412772578
8	256	3.1415137813
9	512	3.1415737570
10	1024	3.1415862735
11	2048	3.1415946179
12	4096	3.1416613714
13	8192	3.1419288372
14	16384	3.1429961472
15	32768	3.1429961472
16	65536	3.1429961471
17	131072	3.2105951957
18	262144	3.2105951957
19	524288	3.7072763240
20	1048576	7.4145526840

first two digits of the $k = 3$ calculation are significant and, after rounding the result to 3.1, the rest can be discarded. The digits judged to be significant are set in boldface type.

The calculation then proceeds quite nicely for the next several steps, with the estimated accuracy increasing in every step until the $k = 12$ calculation. In this step the computed value seems to suggest that fewer digits are correct than were correct in the previous step. This turn of events continues, each successive calculation being less accurate than the previous one, until a very strange thing happens in steps 14, 15, and 16. The computed value remains the same for 10 digits out of 11 for three steps. Should we quit here and proudly publish a new value for π accurate to 10 figures?[3] Perhaps not, since the same thing happens at a different value in steps 17 and 18. Thereafter the calculation falls apart completely.

Notice that the most accurate value occurs in step 11, the last step before the onset of the strange behavior. By carefully monitoring the progress of the calculation in each step, we would avoid the embarrassment of incorrectly reporting a result as accurate to 10 figures only to learn that 7 of the 10 figures are in error. Unfortunately, this example illustrates a situation that is more common than it should be. Every day numbers are reported in technical papers that are the result of extensive computation. Frequently, many of these values are slightly to grossly in error and in both cases outside the stated error estimates.

---

[3] This odd feature will occur on most computing devices; where depends on the computer word length and the procedures for executing the arithmetic operations.

If there is any hint that round-off errors are affecting the results in a serious way, the calculation should be repeated using a slightly different starting position or step size.

Causes of Round-Off Error

The characteristic indicator of the onset of round-off error problems is an *increase* in the inaccuracy after successive iterations or after a decrease in the step size. The absence of such an indicator is not a guarantee of no serious round-off error problems, of course, but in most cases this test, if applied with caution, will suffice. Since round-off errors are always present, it would be best to estimate their effects both before and after the calculation. Unfortunately, this is rarely possible or practical. Since round-off errors are essentially a growth of a random "noise" in a calculation, statistical models are often used to estimate the progress of round-off errors through a calculation. These models are frequently successful and interesting; however, they are beyond the scope of this text. Unless your program costs many hundreds or thousands of dollars for each computer run, it is usually most cost-effective simply to run the program more than once with different parameters and watch for anomalous features in the results. Of course, the best advice is to always thoroughly understand the computational algorithm and to use common sense.

The prime candidate for a source of round-off error problems is a calculation that involves repeated subtraction of numbers of comparable size. For example, the Romberg integration algorithm of Chapter 14 used the equation

$$T_k^{m+1} = T_k^m + \frac{(T_k^m - T_{k-1}^m)}{(4^{m+1} - 1)}$$

to repeatedly improve the estimate of an integral. The two quantities in the term $(T_k^m - T_{k-1}^m)$ are possibly very close together and their difference will then suffer serious round-off error problems. Round-off error was monitored by the quantity R_k^m of Equation (14.19). However, the main term in the above equation is T_k^m, which is ordinarily much larger than the correction term, and thus the accuracy of the calculation is only marginally affected. The result is therefore limited by round-off errors but is not in danger of being destroyed by them.

Another situation that can lead to problems concerns the addition of very small terms to a not-so-small sum. This was illustrated in Problem 2.5, where it was pointed out that on any computing device there is a small number, EPS, for which the arithmetic statement

$$1.0 + EPS \rightarrow 1.0$$

is true. For example, on a computer with only a six-digit word length, if the value for TERM were carefully calculated as 3.14159×10^{-4}, the result of 1.0 + TERM would be simply 1.00031 and most of the accuracy of the calculation has been lost. Loss of significant figures in this manner is especially common in the solution of differential equations. The basic operation consists of computing a correction term, $y'\Delta x$, and then adding this small term to the current y value to obtain the next value of y.

$$y_{i+1} = y_i + y_i' \, \Delta x$$

This step is then repeated hundreds or thousands of times to obtain the complete solution. In each step much of the accuracy of the correction term is lost, and then to compound the problem the new, less accurate value of y is used in the next step. It may be surprising that any numerical solutions to differential equations are possible. Of course, most calculations do work and yield accurate results, and even in those cases where the validity of the calculation is in jeopardy due to round-off error the problems can usually be greatly reduced by a simple modification of the code that we will discuss later in this section.

Theoretical Investigation of the Growth of Round-Off Error in the Solution of a Differential Equation

For some differential equations it is possible to determine theoretically the manner of growth of the round-off error in the solution. For example, consider the equation for which the midpoint method of Section 15.5 produced such poor results,

$$y' = -y \qquad \text{with } y(x = 0) = 1$$

which has the analytic solution $y(x) = e^{-x}$—that is, simple exponential decay.

The solution via the midpoint method is obtained by applying the equation

$$y_{i+2} = y_i + y_{i+1}' 2\,\Delta x$$

$$= y_i - y_{i+1} 2\,\Delta x \tag{16.6}$$

Next we attempt to determine the effect of round-off errors in the application of this equation. To make things simple, we will assume that round-off error appears in the first step only and then propagates through the solution. We can simulate this by assuming that the original specification of the condition at $y(x = 0)$ is slightly in error due to round-off or other problems; that is, in place of $y(x = 0) = 1$ we will begin the problem with $y(x = 0) = 1 + \delta$, where δ will represent the slight error in the starting value. The computed values based on this initial condition will be slightly different from the values obtained by starting with $y(x = 0) = 1$ and will be designated as y_i^*. Put another way, with round-off error included, we are actually solving the equation

$$y_{i+2}^* = y_i^* - y_{i+1}^* 2\,\Delta x \qquad \text{with } y_0^* = 1 + \delta \tag{16.7}$$

Defining the difference between the y_i^* values and the true values y_i as

$$\varepsilon_i = y_i^* - y_i \tag{16.8}$$

an equation can be obtained that governs the growth of the error ε_i by subtracting Equation (16.6) from Equation (16.7) to yield

$$\varepsilon_{i+2} = \varepsilon_i - \varepsilon_{i+1} 2\,\Delta x \qquad \text{with } \varepsilon_0 = \delta \tag{16.9}$$

Notice that this equation is of the same form as Equation (16.6), and because we already know that the solution to that equation is $y(x) = e^{-x}$, we might guess that a solution to Equation (16.9) is by analogy

$$\varepsilon_i \propto e^{-x_i} \tag{16.10}$$

This guess can be verified as a solution of Equation (16.9) in the limit of infinitesimal Δx as follows: let $x = x_i$, then $x_{i+2} = x + 2\,\Delta x$, so

$$\varepsilon_i \propto e^{-(x+2\Delta x)} = e^{-x}e^{-2\Delta x}$$

$$\approx e^{-x}(1 - 2\,\Delta x)$$

where the approximation $e^{-2\Delta x} \approx 1 - 2\,\Delta x$ is used in the last step. Using the same approximations, the right-hand side of Equation (16.9) becomes

$$\varepsilon_i - \varepsilon_{i+1} 2\,\Delta x \propto e^{-x} - 2\,\Delta x e^{-(x+\Delta x)}$$

$$= e^{-x}(1 - 2\,\Delta x e^{-\Delta x})$$

$$= e^{-x}[1 - 2\,\Delta x(1 - \Delta x)]$$

$$\approx e^{-x}(1 - 2\,\Delta x)$$

which, to lowest order in Δx, is the same as the result above.

However, $\varepsilon_i = e^{-x_i}$ is not the only solution of Equation (16.9). After a bit of trial and error, you would find that a second function that is also a solution is

$$\varepsilon_i = (-1)^i e^{x_i} \tag{16.11}$$

as can be verified by again substituting into Equation (16.9) and showing that the equation is satisfied for small Δx.

The complete solution is then any linear combination of the two solutions, Equations (16.10) and (16.11),

$$\varepsilon_i = A e^{-x_i} + B(-1)^i e^{x_i} \tag{16.12}$$

where A and B are constants yet to be determined. For example, the extra information for the initial condition on ε_i, that is, $\varepsilon_0 = \delta$, yields

$$\varepsilon_0 = A + B = \delta$$

One additional condition is required to specify both A and B. If we assume that the error in the next step is approximately the same value, $\varepsilon_1 \approx \delta$, we obtain the relation

$$\varepsilon_1 = A e^{-\Delta x} - B e^{\Delta x} = \delta$$

Solving these two equations for A and B and again keeping only first-order terms in Δx, we obtain

$$A = \delta(1 + \tfrac{1}{2}\Delta x)$$

$$B = -\tfrac{1}{2}\delta\Delta x$$

Thus, the approximate expression for the solution of Equation (16.9) for the growth of the error is

$$\varepsilon_i = \delta(1 + \tfrac{1}{2}\Delta x)e^{-x_i} + \tfrac{1}{2}\delta\Delta x(-1)^{i+1}e^{x_i} \qquad (16.13)$$

The first term is approximately δe^{-x_i} and represents normal exponential decay and results from the fact that ε_i satisfies the same equation as y_i, Equation (16.6), which in turn was a result of the original differential equation $y' = -y$. The second term is called a "parasitic" solution since it does not satisfy the original differential equation although it is a solution of the difference equation, Equation (16.6). This term *grows* exponentially with increasing x while the function $y(x)$ is simultaneously decreasing. Thus, even though the coefficient $\delta\Delta x$ multiplying the positive exponential is very small, the error term will likely grow to exceed the diminishing value of $y(x)$. Also, a signature of these error terms is that they are expected to alternate in sign from term to term due to the factor $(-1)^{i+1}$.

The same analysis applied to the equation $y' = y$ generates an error term similar to Equation (16.13). However, in this case the round-off errors are *not* expected to present problems.

Admittedly, the above discussion is not completely rigorous, and perhaps you are less than totally convinced.[4] Yet even approximate theoretical predictions of the growth of error in a numerical solution to an arbitrary differential equation are usually not possible. The reason is that it is not always so easy to obtain a form for the parasitic solution. Thus, in the final appraisal, there is no recipe for the estimation of round-off errors in a general problem. You must use your own common sense, solve the problem more than once, be knowledgeable about the instabilities inherent in the algorithm you are using, and be ever watchful for suspicious anomalous features in the computed results.

Suggestions to Minimize Round-Off Errors

If it is clear to you that the accuracy of your calculation can be adversely affected by round-off error, there are a few remedies that you can try. First, attempt to locate the part of the code that is the major source of the problem. You should look for repeated operations that either subtract

---

[4]The fact that the actual computed results in Chapter 15 do indeed exhibit errors that grow exponentially and that alternate in sign is convincing circumstantial evidence of the validity of the basic approximation of assuming round-off error in the initial assignment $y(x = 0) = 1 + \delta$.

numbers of like size or add small numbers to not-so-small numbers; that is, operations like

$$(T_{k+1} - T_k) \qquad \text{or} \qquad \sum_{1}^{1000} \frac{1}{i^3}$$

are very likely to result in a loss of significant figures.

A suggestion given earlier to partially rectify the problem in the summation example is to sum the terms in reverse order. This will have the effect of accumulating the smallest terms first into a value that is comparable to the magnitude of the larger earlier terms in the sum, thereby avoiding the possibility of encountering operations of the type $1 + \text{EPS} \rightarrow 1$.

Unfortunately, this trick is usually of little use in reducing the round-off error in a differential equation. The solution proceeds by adding very small terms to not-so-small terms, as in

$$y_{i+1} = y_i + y_i' \Delta x$$

but the value of y_{i+1} is required for the next step, so we cannot simply add up the small terms $y_i' \Delta x$ separately. You could declare all the variables required in the calculation to be double precision; however, this will frequently result in prohibitive execution costs.[5] An intermediate approach that is found to be extremely effective and efficient is:

1. Compute the small correction terms $y_i' \Delta x$ in ordinary single-precision arithmetic.
2. Execute the summation of (current term) + (correction term) using a temporary double-precision variable. For example,

```
DOUBLE PRECISION ONE
      ...        ...
EPS = 1.E-8
ONE = 1.D+00
ONE = ONE + EPS
```

The major computation time in a code usually involves calculating the correction term, say EPS, and the only use of double-precision arithmetic is then in the one line employing mixed-mode addition (real + double precision). Because this improvement is so easily implemented and is so effective in reducing round-off error, you should include it in every program that repeatedly adds small terms to not-so-small terms.

Although similar tricks can be employed to reduce the loss of significant figures resulting from subtraction of numbers of like size and still retain an efficient program, the prescription is not as clear and these problems must be resolved on a case-by-case basis.

---

[5] With some compilers double-precision arithmetic is a factor of 8 slower than the same arithmetic operations carried out on ordinary single-precision numbers.

To compute an exact value for e^x or for any other transcendental function requires an infinite number of elementary arithmetic operations or, equivalently, summing an infinite number of terms in the series

$$e^x = 1 + x + \frac{x^2}{2!} + \frac{x^3}{3!} + \cdots$$

Anything short of an infinite number of terms will lead to errors, called *truncation errors*. This example is a special case of the general situation wherein a function $f(x)$ is first written in terms of its Taylor series

$$f(x) = f(a) + f'(a)(x - a) + \frac{1}{2!}f''(a)(x - a)^2 + \cdots$$

and the series is then truncated after a finite number of terms.

As we know, this approximation is the cornerstone of most of numerical analysis. For example, when evaluating the value of the integral of a function $f(x)$ via the trapezoidal rule, the function is replaced by straight-line segments over limited intervals, an approximation equivalent to retaining only the first two terms in the Taylor series. Simpson's rule integration replaces the function with parabolic segments, a better approximation corresponding to retaining an additional term in the series. Thus, for a given step size Δx, Simpson's rule should give more accurate results.

We can obtain more accurate trapezoidal rule results by reducing the step size (discretization error), and in the limit $\Delta x \to 0$, the trapezoidal rule will return exact answers for most functions. However, that is calculus, not numerical analysis. On a computer, as the panel width is reduced the total number of computational operations is increased, and with them the round-off error. Thus, the discretization error and the round-off error are in competition. As the panel width Δx is successively decreased, the accuracy of the calculation will increase for a while but must eventually decrease when the round-off error begins to dominate. As a result, for every problem there is an *optimum* panel width that will minimize the *overall* error. The limitations that round-off errors impose on a calculation are demonstrated in Table 16-2, where the results of a Simpson's rule and a trapezoidal rule calculation are compared. Notice that in this case the most accurate values ultimately obtained by each method are the same. However, Simpson's rule reaches this value much more quickly.

As a general rule, the higher the level of the approximation algorithm, the more accurate *and* the more efficient the resulting computer code. However, this increased accuracy and efficiency must be balanced against the time and effort of coding and debugging the problem. Most of us would ordinarily opt for the simpler solution and merely let the computer run longer to achieve the desired accuracy. But as we have just seen, this may not always be possible due to the accumulation of round-off

Table 16-2
Comparison of the convergence rate and the accuracy of the trapezoidal rule and Simpson's rule approximations to an integral

$$I = \frac{2}{18} \int_0^1 x^{7.5} dx = 1.0$$

Order	Number of Panels	Trapezoidal Rule	Simpson's Rule
1	2	2.1484781802	1.4479709491
2	4	1.3199548051	1.0437804312
3	8	1.0822395608	1.0030012093
4	16	1.0207037628	1.0001918934
5	32	1.0051850155	1.0000120997
6	64	1.0012968108	1.0000008903
7	128	1.0003241897	1.0000001304
8	256	1.0000810660	1.0000000037
9	512	1.0000202060	1.0000000037
10	1024	1.0000050068	1.0000001937
11	2048	1.0000012703	1.0000001304
12	4096	1.0000004470	1.0000000037
13	8192	0.9999996871	1.0000001937
14	16384	1.0000001304	0.9999998771
15	32768	1.0000012703	0.9999999404
16	65536	0.9999988005	0.9999994338

error. In such cases we have no choice but to resort to a fancier, higher-level algorithm. Of course, in those situations in which a high-level approximation can be used with very little additional effort, as in Romberg integration, it is almost unforgivable to use a very coarse algorithm such as the trapezoidal rule. You should notice that one of the best and most efficient means of reducing the effects of round-off errors is to improve the level of the approximation algorithm. This is perhaps best illustrated in the solution of differential equations.

As mentioned earlier, truncation errors are introduced into a solution whenever the Taylor series representing a function is terminated after a few terms. Euler's method, which is based on the approximation

$$y_{i+1} \simeq y_i + y_i' \Delta x$$

is clearly a lowest-order method. The methods can be shown to be equivalent to using the approximation

$$y_{i+1} \simeq y_i + y_i' \Delta x + \tfrac{1}{2} y_i'' \Delta x^2$$

and as we have seen yield consistently better results than the ordinary Euler method.

Again, the fancier numerical methods are not just a matter of esthetics; depending upon the computer and the problem, they are often essential in obtaining a solution.

16.6 Experimental Errors

Many of the calculations you will do in the future will involve either analyzing experimental data or comparing model calculations with experimental numbers. Since each and every measurement includes unavoidable errors, there is yet another source of error to be considered. Of course, experimental errors, unlike round-off error and approximation errors, are something over which numerical analysis has very little control. The minimization of the experimental errors is of prime concern to the experimental scientist or engineer, but as we shall see, the uncertainties in measured quantities are also critically important to the person who wishes to use those numbers in a calculation. It is essential that anyone using numbers resulting from measurements be aware of the quality of those experimental numbers. There are any number of numerical analysis algorithms that will normally proceed smoothly and without problems to an accurate solution but collapse completely when even small experimental errors are introduced. A very instructive example of this is found in the solution of linear algebraic equations.

Amplification of Experimental Errors in Ill-Conditioned Matrix Equations

In the discussion of Cramer's rule in Section 12.4 you were told that a pivotal ingredient in the solution of the matrix equation $[A]\mathbf{x} = \mathbf{b}$ is the evaluation of the determinant of the coefficient matrix $[A]$. If the determinant $|A|$ is zero, then ordinarily no solution is possible; and if $|A|$ is small, the solution may be suspect. In this section we will investigate more carefully the consequences of ill-conditioned equations.

In order to make the discussion as simple as possible, we will consider first only two equations in two unknowns. The extension to larger sets of equations is straightforward. We begin with the following equations:

$$x + 0.8y = 0.2$$
$$2x + 1.6y = 0.5 \tag{16.14}$$

or

$$\begin{bmatrix} 1.0 & 0.8 \\ 2.0 & 1.5 \end{bmatrix} \begin{bmatrix} x \\ y \end{bmatrix} = \begin{bmatrix} 0.2 \\ 0.5 \end{bmatrix}$$

$$[A] \qquad \mathbf{x} \ = \ \mathbf{b} \tag{16.15}$$

The determinant of the coefficient matrix is $|A| = -0.1$, which, for our purposes, will be considered to be small. Nonetheless, since $|A| \neq 0$ a solution of the equation can be obtained either by the Gauss–Jordan technique or by Cramer's rule. The result is

$$\begin{bmatrix} x \\ y \end{bmatrix} = \begin{bmatrix} 1.0 \\ -1.0 \end{bmatrix} \tag{16.16}$$

Next consider the consequences of small experimental errors in the numbers in the right-hand-side vector **b**. For example, if the uncertainty in **b** were 1%, then the acceptable range in the elements of **b** would be

$$\mathbf{b} \pm \Delta\mathbf{b} = \begin{bmatrix} 0.2 \\ 0.5 \end{bmatrix} \pm \begin{bmatrix} 0.0020 \\ 0.0050 \end{bmatrix} = \begin{bmatrix} 0.198 & \leftrightarrow & 0.202 \\ 0.495 & \leftrightarrow & 0.505 \end{bmatrix} \tag{16.17}$$

If we next solve Equation (16.15) using Equation (16.17) as the right-hand-side vector and use the complete range of **b** values that are given, the result is a range of values for the solution vector.

$$\begin{bmatrix} x \\ y \end{bmatrix} = \begin{bmatrix} 0.93 & \leftrightarrow & 1.07 \\ -0.91 & \leftrightarrow & -1.09 \end{bmatrix} = \begin{bmatrix} 1.00 \\ -1.00 \end{bmatrix} \pm \begin{bmatrix} 0.07 \\ 0.09 \end{bmatrix} \tag{16.18}$$

Another way to express this result is to solve the matrix equation

$$[A]\mathbf{x} = \mathbf{b} \pm \Delta\mathbf{b}$$

directly as

$$\mathbf{x} = [A^{-1}](\mathbf{b} \pm \Delta\mathbf{b})$$

Inserting the inverse of the coefficient matrix, which is easily computed, we obtain

$$\begin{bmatrix} -15 & 8 \\ 20 & -10 \end{bmatrix} \left(\begin{bmatrix} 0.20 \\ 0.45 \end{bmatrix} + \begin{bmatrix} \pm 0.002 \\ \pm 0.005 \end{bmatrix} \right) = \begin{bmatrix} 1 \\ -1 \end{bmatrix} + \begin{bmatrix} -15 & 8 \\ 20 & -10 \end{bmatrix} \begin{bmatrix} \pm 0.002 \\ \pm 0.005 \end{bmatrix} \tag{16.19}$$

Special care must be employed when the second term in Equation (16.19) is evaluated. If the *same* sign is used for both of the elements of $\Delta\mathbf{b}$, the result will be ± 0.1 for the error in both elements of the solution vector. However, there is no reason to assume that the errors in b_1 and b_2 are related; thus, the proper procedure is to evaluate the product not as

$$\sum_{j=1}^{2} A_{ij}^{-1} \Delta b_j$$

but rather as

$$\sum_{j=1}^{2} |A_{ij}^{-1} \Delta b_j|$$

That is, in the worst possible case, the errors all add in the same direction. The result is then the same as obtained in Equation (16.18).

The most important feature of this example is the fact that a small 1% error in **b** has been amplified into a 7% error in x and a 9% error in y. If there were also uncertainties in the elements of $[A]$ or if $|A|$ were smaller still, the results would be even worse. To see how this has come about, the same problem is solved once more, graphically.

The two equations

$$x + 0.8y = 0.2$$

$$2y + 1.5y = 0.5$$

can be written as

$$y = -\frac{5}{4}x + \frac{1}{4} \tag{16.20}$$

$$y = -\frac{4}{3}x + \frac{1}{3} \tag{16.21}$$

The intersection of these two lines then determines the single point (x, y) that is simultaneously a solution of both equations. This is shown in Figure 16-3 to be the point $(1, -1)$.

To include the uncertainties in the elements of **b** in the graphical solution, Equation (16.20), for example, would be replaced by

$$y = -\frac{5}{4}x + \left(\frac{1}{4} \pm \frac{1}{400}\right) \tag{16.22}$$

That is, the "thin" line, Equation (16.20), is replaced by a "broad" line that is bounded by

$$y = -\frac{5}{4}x + \frac{101}{400}$$

Figure 16-3
Solution of two simultaneous equations corresponds to the point of intersection of the two curves

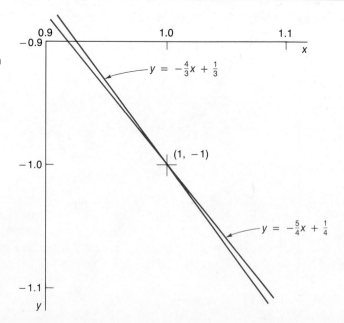

and

$$y = -\frac{5}{4}x + \frac{99}{400}$$

Following the same procedure for the second of the two equations and once again obtaining the solutions by graphing the two lines now with the error included results in the plot of Figure 16-4.

The intersection of the two lines is now represented by the thin diamond-shaped region extending roughly from ($x = 0.93$, $y = -0.91$) to ($x = 1.07$, $y = -1.09$). The reason for the amplification of the 1% error in b into a 7% to 9% error in the solution is now clear. The two equations are very nearly parallel. This is indicated by the small value of the determinant of the coefficient matrix. If the two lines were precisely parallel, one would be simply a multiple of the other with a different intercept (b value) and the determinant would be exactly zero. If the determinant were relatively large, this would suggest that the two lines are approximately perpendicular and therefore the band of values in the intersection region would be much smaller, indicating a well-defined solution. Including round-off errors in the solution will of course only compound the difficulties of solving ill-conditioned problems.

So far we have considered only the possibility of experimental errors in the right-hand-side vector. If there are also errors in the coeffi-

Figure 16-4
Intersection of two lines with error results in an extended region of permissible solutions

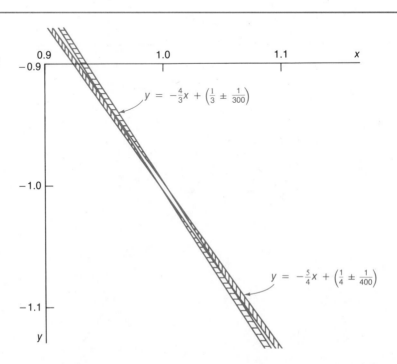

cient matrix, the situation can be much worse. Returning to the original equation,

$$\begin{bmatrix} 1 & 0.8 \\ 2 & 1.5 \end{bmatrix} \begin{bmatrix} x \\ y \end{bmatrix} = \begin{bmatrix} 0.2 \\ 0.5 \end{bmatrix}$$

$$[A] \quad (x) = \quad b$$

you can easily show that if there is a 1% error in the elements of $[A]$, the error in the determinant $|A|$ is then 62%. Since $|A|$ is required in the solution, the final results will be almost meaningless.

The consequences of experimental error in other areas of numerical analysis can be equally dramatic. Keep in mind that experimental error behaves exactly like round-off error except it is ordinarily much larger. Experimental error in the initial conditions of a differential equation can very quickly grow in successive steps to swamp the solution.

16.7 Conclusion

I have postponed this discussion of numerical errors until now for fear of frightening you. You should not get the impression from all this worry about errors that all or most of your calculations are doomed to yield meaningless results or that you must spend 90 percent of your time ferreting out sources of round-off error and devising clever procedures to minimize the amplification of experimental errors. Most computers carry a sufficient number of significant figures and most of the procedures described in this text are sufficiently accurate so that your programs will work smoothly and accurately in the majority of cases. Of course, at each stage in the solution of a problem you should be aware of the potential difficulties that may arise and have some ideas about how to correct them. The problems associated with the various forms of numerical errors are always lurking in the dark corners of a program, and when they do finally appear is when the engineer or scientist really begins to earn his or her pay.

After considerable experience in numerical analysis you may even find the study of error considerations to be interesting—but that is the proper province of a later course in numerical methods.

Problems

16.1 A state legislature, which will be left unnamed, in trying to be helpful to schoolchildren, once defined π to have a value $\frac{22}{7}$. Determine the effect that this foolish action would have on the profits of a manufacturer whose product is sold by volume in cylindrical cans. (That is, can the manufacturer make the cans smaller or larger, and by what percentage?) A better approximation to π is $\frac{355}{113}$. What is the effect of using this value?

16.2 The period of a simple pendulum consisting of a mass at the end of a string of length l is frequently measured to determine the gravitational force at the earth's surface. If the maximum angle of swing, θ, is not large ($\theta \leq 15°$), an accurate expression for the period of oscillation of the pendulum is

$$T = 2\pi \sqrt{\frac{l}{g}\left[1 + \frac{1}{4}\sin^2\left(\frac{\theta}{2}\right)\right]}$$

Ordinarily, the term involving $\sin^2(\frac{\theta}{2})$ is neglected for small angles, an example of truncation error. What is then the size of the fractional error in the measured value of g caused by this truncation error for angles $\theta = 5°$, $10°$, and $15°$?

16.3 Show that if the error in x is Δx (that is, $x \pm \Delta x$) then the resulting fractional error in $f(x) = x^{\frac{1}{10}}$ is approximately

$$\frac{\Delta f}{f} \approx \frac{1}{10}\frac{\Delta x}{x}$$

Demonstrate this numerically for $x = 1024 = 2^{10}$.

16.4 Evaluate approximately the infinite sum

$$\sum_{i=1}^{\infty}\frac{1}{i^2} = \frac{\pi^2}{6}$$

by writing a computer program to sum the first 10,000 terms. Next, redo the summation, but in reverse order. That is, evaluate

$$\sum_{i=10000}^{1}\frac{1}{i^2}$$

Explain why the two summations result in different values and why the second procedure is more accurate.

16.5 Assume that the trapezoidal rule approximation for an integral has an error given by $k(\Delta x)^p$, where Δx is the panel width and k and p are constants.
   a. Use the numerical results for the trapezoidal rule from the first three rows of values in Table 16-2 to determine the values of k and p. [Hint: if the actual error in step 1 was assumed to be $d_1 = k(\frac{1}{2})^p$, and $d_2 = k(\frac{1}{4})^p$, first show that $p = \frac{\ln(d_1/d_2)}{\ln(2)}$.]
   b. Using your computed values for k and p, calculate the estimate of the error in the trapezoidal rule for all successive steps, and compare with the actual error. From these results, determine in which step the trapezoidal rule begins to fail due to round-off error.
   c. Repeat parts (a) and (b) for the Simpson's rule results.

16.6 The matrix

$$[A] = \begin{bmatrix} 0 & -1 & -6 \\ 1 & 0 & 12 \\ 6 & -12 & 1 \end{bmatrix}$$

has a determinant $|A| = 1$ and inverse given by

$$[A^{-1}] = \begin{bmatrix} 144 & 73 & -12 \\ 71 & 36 & -6 \\ -12 & -6 & 1 \end{bmatrix}$$

The solution of the matrix equation $[A]\mathbf{x} = \mathbf{b}$, where

$$\mathbf{b} = \begin{bmatrix} -7 \\ 13 \\ -5 \end{bmatrix}$$

is then easily found to be

$$\mathbf{x} = \begin{bmatrix} x_1 \\ x_2 \\ x_3 \end{bmatrix} = \begin{bmatrix} 1 \\ 1 \\ 1 \end{bmatrix}$$

Show that if there is a 1% error in each of the elements of the vector $\mathbf{b}$, the resulting error in the value of x_1 is approximately ± 20. (or 2000%). What is the error in the elements x_2, x_3?

Summary of FORTRAN Statements ▰▰▰▰
and Grammar Rules ▰▰▰▰

The information contained in this appendix is intended for quick reference. A detailed account of most of the items listed can be found in the text as indicated. For the sake of completeness, several FORTRAN statements are included here that are not described in the text. These are denoted by asterisks.

The following notation is used in this appendix:

[...]	Indicates an optional part of a statement
⟨..⟩	Indicates a list or numerical value that is to be supplied by the programmer
CAPITALS	Indicate FORTRAN statements

FORTRAN statements are entered in columns 7 through 72. Blanks are ignored. A line beginning with a "*" or a "C" in column 1 is ignored by the compiler and is treated as a comment. Any character other than "blank" or zero in column 6 indicates that this line is a continuation of the previous FORTRAN line. Some FORTRAN statements may be given an identifying statement number of 1 to 5 digits in columns 1 through 5.

▰▰▰▰▰▰ **A.1 Procedure Statements**

Statement	Comment
PROGRAM ⟨name⟩ (p. 43)	Defines the program name that is used as an entry point for the program execution. If omitted, the compiler assigns a name.
SUBROUTINE ⟨name⟩ [argument list] (pp. 164*ff*)	The symbolic name defines the main entry point. The subroutine name is not to be assigned a value. The optional argument list contains dummy variable names that can be variables, arrays, dummy procedure names, or alternate return addresses

of the form *⟨statement number⟩.
Multiple ENTRYs and alternate
RETURNs are permitted.

FUNCTION ⟨name⟩ ([argument list])
(p. 173)
The symbolic name defines the main
entry point. If the type of the
function is specified (e.g., REAL
FUNCTION ⟨name⟩), the name must
not appear in a type statement. The
name must be assigned a value
before any RETURN. Control is back
to the referencing program unit
when a RETURN or an END
statement is encountered. Multiple
ENTRY points are permitted, but
alternate RETURNs are not.

Statement functions
(p. 126)
A user-defined, single-statement
computation that is valid only within
the program unit containing the
definition. It is a nonexecutable
statement. The argument list may not
contain an array or a function name.
The statement function name must
not appear in an INTRINSIC or
EXTERNAL statement.

BLOCK DATA [name]
(p. 321)
Variables in labeled common blocks
may be initialized via a BLOCK
DATA program module. Such
variables may not be initialized by
means of ordinary DATA statements.
The BLOCK DATA program module
consists of type and COMMON
statements, and may include SAVE,
IMPLICIT, and PARAMETER
statements. These are then followed
by DATA statements to initialize the
variables in labeled COMMON. No
executable statements are permitted.
The name is optional and if included
should not be used for any other

purpose in the program. There may be only one unnamed BLOCK DATA statement. The structure ends with an END statement.

END	All FORTRAN procedures must have END as their last line. No procedure may reference itself either directly or indirectly.

Argument Lists

Statement	Comment
Actual arguments (pp. 128, 169)	Arguments that appear in the "call" to the subprogram. They can be variable names, expressions, and array names or elements. They cannot contain a statement-function name.
Dummy arguments (pp. 128, 166)	Arguments that appear in the definition of a subprogram. They are associated with the actual arguments when the subprogram is referenced and when it returns. Dummy arguments that refer to arrays must be dimensioned within the subprogram to a size less than or equal to the actual dimensioning. The association with actual arguments is by position in the list, and both the total number and types of variables in both lists must agree. If the dummy argument list contains a procedure name, it must be available at the time of the call. The subprogram must not redefine a dummy argument that is a constant, a name of a function, an expression using operators, or any expression enclosed in parentheses.

A.2 **Specification Statements**

Type-Declaration Statements

Statement	Comment
INTEGER ⟨name list⟩ (p. 34)	Used to define the names of variables, arrays, functions, or dummy procedures to be of type integer. The names in the name list must be separated by commas.
REAL ⟨name list⟩ (p. 34)	Similar to INTEGER, used to define names to be of type real.
CHARACTER[*s], ⟨name[*s_1],...⟩ (pp. 35, 298)	Defines a variable, array, function, or dummy procedure to be of type character. If the optional [*s] is present, each of the elements of the name list is of length s, where s is a positive (unsigned) constant or an asterisk enclosed in parentheses. The latter is used in subprograms for the assigning of dummy argument names to have whatever length the associated actual argument has at the time of the call. Alternately, each name in the name list can be assigned different lengths by using the form ⟨name⟩*s_1, where s_1 is the length of the string and satisfies the same rules as does s. The string lengths (s, s_1) may be variable names only if the variable has been initialized in a previous PARAMETER statement and is enclosed in parentheses.
DOUBLE PRECISION ⟨name list⟩ (p. 313)	Similar to INTEGER and REAL. Used to define names to be of type double precision.

COMPLEX ⟨name list⟩ (p. 314)

Similar to INTEGER and REAL. Used to define names to be of type complex. Complex numbers consist of two real numbers corresponding to the real and imaginary parts. Thus, if C is complex, an assignment statement would be

$$C = (3.0, 4.0)$$

and SQRT(C) would return the complex result

$$SQRT(C) \rightarrow (2.0, 1.0)$$

LOGICAL ⟨name list⟩ (p. 316)

Similar to INTEGER and REAL. Used to define names to be of type logical. Logical variables can have only two values, namely,

$$.TRUE. \qquad .FALSE.$$

(The periods are part of the value.) Thus, if X is of type logical, the expression

$$X = 4 .GT. 7$$

assigns a value of .FALSE. to X.

IMPLICIT ⟨type⟩ $(a_1 - a_2)$ (p. 317)

Used to override or augment the default typing. ⟨type⟩ is any of the above six variable types and a_1, a_2, are single letters. The IMPLICIT statement must precede all statement specifications except PARAMETER. Explicit typing overrides an IMPLICIT specification.

Other Specification Statements

Statement	Comment

PARAMETER (⟨name⟩ = ⟨exp⟩, ...) (p. 319)

Assigns a symbolic name to a constant. ⟨exp⟩ is a constant expression (can be of type character). Any variable name in the expression must have been previously defined in a PARAMETER statement. The parentheses may contain more than one assignment. Variables in one PARAMETER statement may not be redefined in another. Variables initialized in PARAMETER statements may be used in a DATA statement but not in a FORMAT statement.

DATA ⟨name list⟩/⟨value list⟩/[,⟨name list⟩/⟨value list⟩/...]
(p. 152)

Used to initialize variables, arrays, array elements, and substrings at compilation time. DATA statements are nonexecutable and must appear after other specification statements and should appear before the first executable statement. The same name should not appear in two DATA name lists. The values in the value list are assigned, one-to-one, to the elements of the name list, which should agree in type and must agree in total number of elements. The name list may contain an array name and an implied-DO loop (or nested loops) of the form:

$$(A(I), I = ILO, IHI, ISTEP)$$

The values in the limits of the implied DO and in the value list must be constants or named constants defined in a PARAMETER statement. The values in the value list may be repeated by preceding by a positive (unsigned) integer or named integer constant (defined in a PARAMETER statement). Variables in blank COMMON cannot be assigned values with a DATA statement.

DIMENSION ⟨array name⟩(n_d [, n_d, ...])
(p. 248)

Designates a name as an array name and defines the subscript bounds. More than one array can be declared in a single DIMENSION statement. The form of the subscript bound definition, n_d, is either one of the forms

i_{top} Limits are $1, 2, \ldots, i_{\text{top}}; i_{\text{top}} > 0$

$i_{\text{bot}} : i_{\text{top}}$ Limits are $i_{\text{bot}}, i_{\text{bot}} + 1, \ldots, i_{\text{top}}$

If only the upper bound (i_{top}) is given, the default value for i_{bot} is 1. The bounds must be integers or integer expressions. In the initial dimensioning the bounds must be integer constants, whereas in subsequent dimensioning (in subprograms) the bounds can be dummy integer variables or expressions.

EXTERNAL ⟨procedure name⟩
(p. 183)   Used to define a name as representing a user-written, externally defined, subprogram, procedure, or dummy procedure name. More than one name can be declared external in a single EXTERNAL statement. The purpose of the EXTERNAL statement is to allow the name to appear as an actual argument in an argument list. If an intrinsic function name is entered in an EXTERNAL ⟨procedure name⟩ list, the name then refers to a user-written function and the library function can no longer be referenced.

INTRINSIC ⟨function name⟩
(p. 183)   Similar to EXTERNAL, but applies to library functions. All intrinsic function names that appear as actual arguments in an argument list must be declared INTRINSIC. A function cannot be declared both intrinsic and external. Type-conversion functions (e.g., FLOAT, IFIX) and minimum/maximum functions (e.g., MIN, MAX) cannot be used as actual arguments.

COMMON [/blockname/] ⟨name list⟩
(p. 189)   Stores all the variables in the name list together in a block of memory

that can be given a block name. These variables may then be accessed by different program units without using argument lists. As with argument lists, elements in the name list are assigned values by position. Two program units that share data via common blocks must have a COMMON statement with the same block name (or unnamed) and be of identical lengths. More than one block name may be defined in a single COMMON statement. The block name may also be used as a variable name without conflict. If any variable in a common block is of type character, then *all* variables in the block must be of type character. Entries in a labeled common block can be initially defined via a DATA statement only in the BLOCK DATA subprogram. The variables in blank COMMON are automatically saved upon return from a subprogram, whereas those in labeled COMMON *may* not be. (They are saved if the labeled COMMON in the subprogram also appears in the main program.)

(∗)EQUIVALENCE (⟨name list⟩)

Provides for the sharing of the same memory locations by two or more variables, arrays, array elements, or character substrings. When coupled with COMMON statements, the effect of EQUIVALENCE statements can be extremely complex, and use of this statement is not recommended.

SAVE [⟨name list⟩]
(p. 189)

Preserves the value of variables in a subprogram after a RETURN has been executed. The value of the variable may then be referenced in a subsequent call to the subprogram. Dummy variable names, names in a common block, and procedure names must not appear in the name list. A

SAVE statement with no name list will save *all* allowable variables in the subprogram.

(*)ENTRY ⟨entry name⟩[(argument list)]

In addition to the main entry point of a subprogram (the top), the ENTRY statement may be used to begin the subprogram execution anywhere except within a DO loop or an IF-THEN-END IF block. The subprogram is initiated at the alternate entry point by replacing the subprogram name by ⟨entry name⟩ in the referencing line. The argument list in the ENTRY statement should be similar to the argument list in the subprogram definition. ENTRY statements are often used to skip repetitive computations or assignments in a subprogram, such as

```
PROGRAM MANE
   ...       ...
CALL XX(A,M)
   ...       ...
CALL XXMID(B,N)
   ...       ...
END
SUBROUTINE XX(C,L)
DIMENSION C(L)
DO 1 I = 1,L
1 C(I) = 0.0
ENTRY XXMID(C,L)
C(5) = ...
   ...       ...
END
```

▬▬▬ A.3 Assignment and Program Control Statements

Statement	Comment
Assignment statement ⟨variable name⟩ = ⟨expression⟩ (p. 41)	Where ⟨variable name⟩ is the name of a variable or array element. If the expression ⟨expression⟩ on the right is arithmetic, it is first evaluated according to the hierarchy rules and the type of the dominant variable

type, then converted to the type of ⟨variable name⟩ and then assigned to ⟨variable name⟩. If the expression is of type character, the variable name must also be of type character. If the string lengths differ, the expression is either padded with blanks to the right or truncated on the right to match the length of ⟨variable name⟩. If ⟨variable name⟩ is of type logical, then the expression must have a value of either .TRUE. or .FALSE. Multiple assignments of the form A = B = C = D = 5. are not standard FORTRAN 77.

(∗)ASSIGN ⟨statement number⟩ TO ⟨name⟩

In this statement, ⟨statement number⟩ is the statement number of an executable statement or a FORMAT statement, and ⟨name⟩ is the name of an integer variable. This statement is used in conjunction with the ASSIGNED GO TO statement or with WRITE(5, ⟨name⟩)... statements and in general is not recommended.

END
(p. 49)

Used to mark the end of a compilation unit. The END statement can have a statement number. If during execution of the main program the program flow branches to, or encounters, an END statement, the program terminates. The same situation in a subprogram will result in a RETURN. Both are considered poor style.

STOP [tag]
(pp. 49, 86)

The STOP statement terminates the execution of the program wherever it is encountered in a program or subprogram, and the word "STOP" is displayed in the day file or on the terminal screen. The optional [tag] can be a positive integer (of five digits or less) or a character string constant and will be displayed along with STOP. For example,

STOP 'SUCCESSFUL RUN -
                    JOB TERMINATED'
STOP 97

A program may have more than one STOP statement.

PAUSE [tag] (p. 172)	Similar to the STOP statement. This statement causes the program execution to be interrupted and the word "PAUSE" followed by the optional [tag] to be displayed. If the program is being run in batch mode, only the operator at the console can cause the program to continue. In interactive mode, the user enters either "DROP" to terminate or "GO" to continue. Use of this statement is not recommended.

A.4   Flow-Control Statements

Statement	Comment
RETURN [expression] (pp. 167, 174)	A RETURN statement causes the termination of a subprogram procedure and the return to the referencing program or subprogram. RETURN statements may appear only in subprograms. Each subprogram may have more than one RETURN. If the optional alternate return address expression [expression] is omitted, the procedure returns to the next statement in the referencing program unit (the normal situation).
(*)Alternate RETURN	An alternate RETURN (from subroutines only) is effected by including an integer or integer expression following RETURN *and* a sequence of asterisks in the defining subroutine argument list, which will function as dummy address labels and will be associated with the actual statement numbers in the referencing call. Thus RETURN 3

will cause a return to the statement number in the third position in the actual argument list. The statement numbers in the actual argument list must refer to executable statements and be preceded by single asterisks.

```
    PROGRAM MANE
        ...     ...
    CALL CAL(A,B,*1,*3,*7)
    STOP
        ...     ...
  3 C = A + B
        ...     ...
  1 C = A - B
        ...     ...
  7 C = A/B
        ...     ...
    END
    SUBROUTINE CAL(S,T,*,*,*)
        ...     ...
    RETURN 3    ⟨Causes return
                 to statement 7⟩
        ...     ...
    RETURN      ⟨Normal
                 return,
                 executes the
                 STOP⟩
    END
```

CALL ⟨subname⟩ [(argument list)]
(p. 167)

Initiates a transfer of control to the subroutine named ⟨subname⟩. The arguments list contains actual arguments that may be constants, expressions, variable names, array names or elements, procedure names, or an alternate return address in the form *⟨statement number⟩.

CONTINUE
(pp. 81, 102)

The CONTINUE statement is an executable statement that performs no operation and may be placed anywhere among the executable statements. It is most commonly used as the terminus of DO loops. The CONTINUE statement should have a statement number.

GO TO Statements

Statement	Comment
GO TO ⟨statement number⟩ (pp. 18, 85)	*Unconditional GO TO:* Simply transfers control to the statement labeled with ⟨statement number⟩, which must be an integer constant, not a variable name, and correspond to an existing executable statement anywhere in the same program or subprogram. When possible, use of the GO TO should be avoided and replaced with structured FORTRAN.
GO TO (⟨statement number list⟩), ⟨expression⟩ (p. 99)	*Computed GO TO:* The statement number list contains labels of existing executable statements, and ⟨expression⟩ is an integer or integer expression. If ⟨expression⟩ is 1, control transfers to the statement identified by the first number in the list; if ⟨expression⟩ is 2, to the second; and so on. If ⟨expression⟩ is less than 1 or greater than the number of labels in the list, execution continues with the next line of the program after the GO TO.
(*)GO TO ⟨ivar⟩, [(⟨statement number list⟩)]	*Assigned GO TO:* The integer variable ⟨ivar⟩ must have been previously assigned a value by an ASSIGN TO statement. The statement then acts much like the unconditional GO TO if the statement number list is not present and like the computed GO TO if it is. Use of this statement should be avoided.

IF Statements

Statement	Comment
IF(⟨arithmetic expression⟩) s_-, s_0, s_+ (p. 100)	*Arithmetic IF:* The arithmetic expression is evaluated and if negative,

zero, or positive, control is transferred to the executable statement labeled by the statement number $s_-, s_0,$ or s_+, respectively.

IF($\langle$logical expression$\rangle$) $\langle$executable statement$\rangle$
(p. 99)
    Logical IF: The $\langle$logical expression$\rangle$ is evaluated, and if true, the executable FORTRAN statement $\langle$executable statement$\rangle$ is executed; otherwise, the program continues with the next line after the IF. The $\langle$executable statement$\rangle$ cannot be a DO, IF, ELSE, ELSE IF, END or END IF statement.

Block IF Statements

Statement	Comment
IF($\langle$logical expression$\rangle$)THEN (pp. 44, 67)	If the $\langle$logical expression$\rangle$ is true, then the program execution continues with the next line; otherwise, the control branches to the next ELSE or ELSE IF statement if present, or to the END IF, the terminus of the block, if an ELSE or ELSE IF is not present.
ELSE (p. 73)	Marks the beginning of the alternate (false) path of an IF(...)THEN or an ELSE IF(...)THEN statement. The ELSE statement should not have a statement number.
ELSE IF($\langle$logical expression$\rangle$)THEN (p. 77)	The operation of this statement is the same as the IF(...)THEN statement; however, it can only be reached by an evaluation of $\langle$false$\rangle$ in a previous IF(...)THEN or ELSE IF(...)THEN statement. ELSE and ELSE IF statements must be placed within a corresponding IF(...)THEN–END IF block. Block IF structures can be nested; that is, one block IF structure may contain another only if the entire second block

IF is contained within the first. It is permitted to branch to a block IF statement but not permitted to branch to any statement within a block. Each block IF structure can contain several ELSE IF statements but only a single ELSE statement, which must follow all the ELSE IFs in the structure.

END IF (pp. 44, 67)	Marks the end of an IF(...)THEN structure. The END IF statement should not have a statement number. (It is not permitted to GO TO ⟨ENDIF⟩.) Each IF(...)THEN must have a corresponding END IF statement. If the program flow arrives at an END IF statement, the program continues with the next line of the program.

DO-Loop Structures

Statement	Comment
DO ⟨statement number⟩ $a_c = b_{low}, b_{high} [,b_{step}]$ (p. 80)	Marks the beginning of a block of statements that are executed with the value of the counter variable, a_c, set equal to the initial limit, b_{low}. The entire block is then repeated with a_c assigned the value $b_{low} + b_{step}$ (or $b_{low} + 1$ if the optional b_{step} is omitted). This process is repeated until the counter variable exceeds the final limit, b_{high}. The program then continues with the line following the loop terminator. The loop terminator is an executable statement with a statement number ⟨statement number⟩ that occurs after the related DO statement and that is not an IF, GO TO, RETURN, STOP, END, ELSE, or another DO. CONTINUE statements are always recommended as DO terminators. The DO-loop limits, b_{low}, b_{high}, b_{step}, are numerical constants, vari-

ables, or expressions that are converted to the type of the counter a_c before execution of the loop. Generally, a DO loop will execute zero times if $b_{low} > b_{high}$ (if $b_{step} > 0$ or omitted) or if $b_{low} < b_{high}$ and b_{step} is negative. If the loop executes zero times, the counter variable has the value of b_{low}. Transfer out of a loop before completion is permitted and the value of a_c will be its most recent value. Branching into a DO loop that has not yet been initiated is forbidden; however, branching out and then back in is permitted provided the counter variable has not been redefined. This practice, however, is strongly discouraged.

Nested loops
(p. 87)

DO loops can be nested provided one loop is totally contained within the other. Nested loops may share the same terminal line. Branching to a shared terminal statement from an inner loop does not constitute branching out of the inner loop. If a block IF contains a DO loop, the loop must be completely contained within the block.

A.5 FORTRAN File-Directive Statements

Statement	Comment
OPEN(⟨argument list⟩) (pp. 55, 147)	The OPEN statement is used to assign a unit number to an already existing file, to a newly created file, or to alter some properties of existing files. The extensive options permitted in the argument list are explained in Section 4.6. The most common use is to permit a program to access a separate data file or to write output on a disk-stored file. The shortened form is then

```
OPEN(13,FILE='DATAFL',STATUS='OLD')
OPEN(14,FILE='RESULTS',STATUS='NEW')
```

The unit number can be a positive integer (of three digits or less) or an integer constant name initialized in a PARAMETER statement. When a program begins execution, the input and output files are automatically connected to the program and need not be opened. These files may be specified by using an asterisk in place of the unit number in I/O statements.

CLOSE(⟨argument list⟩) (p. 149)

The CLOSE statement is used to disconnect a file from a unit number, enabling that unit to be connected to a different file. The most common form is

```
CLOSE(⟨unit number⟩)
```

or

```
CLOSE(UNIT=⟨unit number⟩)
```

Any file that has been previously opened with a status other than "SCRATCH" (i.e., either "OLD" or "NEW") will automatically be retained on the system after a CLOSE. To disconnect *and* delete the file from the system, the option STATUS = "DELETE" is included in the argument list. SCRATCH files are always automatically deleted upon termination of a program. Also, the system will automatically CLOSE all connected files upon program termination, so this statement is often unnecessary.

(*)INQUIRE(⟨argument list⟩)

FORTRAN 77 permits the user to ascertain the present attributes of a file by means of the INQUIRE statement. This statement is generally used to avoid errors in opening a file or in reading or writing a file. The options available in the argument list are very extensive. If you think you need this statement, a detailed account can be found in Balfour and Marwick or Wagener, listed in the references.

REWIND([UNIT=]⟨unit number⟩)
(p. 149)

The REWIND statement positions a file to the beginning of the file. The file must have been previously opened and assigned a ⟨unit number⟩. A shortened form is

```
REWIND ⟨unit number⟩
```
⟨*no parentheses needed*⟩

The ⟨unit number⟩ is a positive integer (of three digits or less) or an integer constant initialized in a PARAMETER statement.

BACKSPACE ([UNIT=]⟨unit number⟩)
(p. 149)

Similar to REWIND, except the file is only backspaced one record (usually one line). Only sequential files can be backspaced.

ENDFILE([UNIT=]⟨unit number⟩)
(p. 150)

The END FILE statement puts an end-of-file mark on the file connected to ⟨unit number⟩. This is useful when constructing a data file and the "END =" option in the READ statement is anticipated. Only sequential files can be marked with an end-of-file.

A.6 Input/Output Statements

Input/Output Lists

The I/O list (designated in what follows as either ⟨in list⟩ or ⟨out list⟩) is that part of an I/O statement in which the elements to be read or written are specified along with their ordering. The elements of an input list may be variables, array names, or elements, or these items enclosed in an implied-DO loop. The elements of an output list may additionally include constants, arithmetic expressions, character string constants, or references to functions, provided the functions themselves neither cause I/O operations nor alter other elements of the list. A character string constant is a string enclosed in apostrophes—for example, 'THE ANSWER IS'. The appearance of the name only of an array in either an input or an output list will cause the entire array to be read or written in the order in which it is stored. An implied-DO loop in an I/O list is treated as a single element of the list. (For a more detailed description of implied-DO loops see Section 7.4.)

Statement	Comment
READ ([UNIT=]⟨unit number⟩⟨format⟩[,ERR=⟨err-sl⟩] [,END=⟨end-sl⟩])⟨in list⟩ (pp. 18, 222, 237)	The only essential specifications in the READ statement are the input unit number ⟨unit number⟩ and the format specification ⟨format⟩ that specifies the arrangement of the items in the input list ⟨in list⟩. The unit number may refer to any opened file or may be replaced by an asterisk, which is the default specification for the INPUT. The optional specifications, ERR = ⟨err-sl⟩ will cause a transfer to the statement labeled by statement number ⟨err-sl⟩ if an error is encountered during the read; END = ⟨end-sl⟩ will do similarly if an end-of-file mark is encountered. For example,
`READ(5,3)X`	Read from file 5 according to format 3, the value of X.
`READ(*,3,ERR=9)Y`	Read X from file INPUT according to format 3: if error, branch to statement 9.
	Additionally, the format specification ⟨format⟩ may be either the statement number of an existing FORMAT statement, a set of format specifications enclosed in parentheses and delimited before and after by apostrophes, as
	`'(1X,F5.3,/,10X,I5)'`
	or it may simply be a single asterisk, in which case the variables are read without format as list-directed input. List-directed input data elements are separated by commas. For example,
`READ (*,*)X`	Reads X from file INPUT without a format.
WRITE([UNIT=]⟨unit number⟩, ⟨format⟩[ERR=⟨err-sl⟩]⟨out list⟩ (pp. 17, 223, 237)	The meaning of the specifications are the same as in the READ statement ex-

cept that replacing the ⟨unit number⟩ by an asterisk will cause the output to be written to the file OUTPUT. A shortened form of this statement is

PRINT ⟨format⟩ , ⟨out list⟩

for example,

PRINT 6,X Print X according to format 6

PRINT *,X Print X without format specifications

If the ⟨format⟩ = '*' option is used, the elements of the ⟨out list⟩ are written in a format controlled by the compiler.

⟨statement number⟩ FORMAT ((⟨format specification list⟩))

(p. 223)

A FORMAT statement is nonexecutable, must have a statement number, and can appear anywhere within a program unit. The format specification list is a sequence of editing specifications separated by commas and of the form

[*n*]⟨edit-rep.⟩
⟨edit-nonrep.⟩
[*n*](format specification list)

where [*n*] is an optional positive (unsigned) integer repeat constant, ⟨edit-rep.⟩ is a repeatable edit specification, ⟨edit-nonrep.⟩ is a nonrepeatable edit specification, and the last form is a multiple of an entire format specification sublist. For a description of the more common edit specifications see Chapter 6.

References

FORTRAN 77 References

American National Standards Institute. *American National Standard FORTRAN X3.9-1978* (the standard of FORTRAN 77), 1430 Broadway, New York.

Balfour, A., and D. H. Marwick. *Programming in Standard FORTRAN 77.* New York: North Holland, 1979. A comprehensive listing of all features of FORTRAN 77.

Kernighan, B., and P. J. Plauger. *The Elements of Programming Style.* New York: McGraw-Hill, 1974.

Merchant, Michael J. *FORTRAN 77, Language and Style.* Belmont, Calif.: Wadsworth, 1981. A comprehensive treatment of FORTRAN 77 from a nonengineering perspective.

Wagener, Jerold L. *FORTRAN 77.* New York: Wiley, 1980. Contains a more extensive description of the application of data files.

Numerical Methods References

Abramowitz, M., and I. Stegun, eds. *Handbook of Mathematical Functions with Formulas, Graphs, and Mathematical Tables.* National Bureau of Standards. Reprinted by Dover, New York, 1964.

Acton, F. S. *Numerical Methods That Work.* New York: Harper & Row, 1970.

Cheney, W., and D. Kincaid. *Numerical Mathematics and Computing.* Monterey, Calif.: Brooks/Cole, 1980.

Collatz, L. *The Numerical Treatment of Differential Equations.* 3rd ed. Berlin: Springer-Verlag, 1966.

Conte, S. D., and C. deBoor. *Elementary Numerical Analysis.* New York: McGraw-Hill, 1972.

Hornbeck, R. W. *Numerical Methods.* New York: Quantum, 1975.

Milne, W. E. *Numerical Solution of Differential Equations.* New York: Wiley, 1953.

Pennington, R. H. *Introductory Computer Methods and Numerical Analysis.* 2nd ed. London: Macmillan, 1970.

Ralston, A. *A First Course in Numerical Analysis.* New York: McGraw-Hill, 1965.

Schultz, M. H. *Spline Analysis.* Englewood Cliffs, N.J.: Prentice-Hall, 1973.

Southworth, R. W., and S. L. DeLeeuw. *Digital Computation and Numerical Methods.* New York: McGraw-Hill, 1965.

Wilkinson, J. H. *Rounding Errors in Algebraic Processes.* Englewood Cliffs, N.J.: Prentice-Hall, 1963.

Answers and Solutions to Odd-Numbered Problems

Chapter 1

1.1 **a.** $(11)_{10} = 2(5) + 1$
$\quad\quad\quad\quad\quad\quad\quad \llcorner 2(2) + 1$
$\quad\quad\quad\quad\quad\quad\quad\quad\quad \llcorner 2(1) + 0$
$\quad\quad\quad\quad\quad\quad\quad\quad\quad\quad\quad \llcorner 2(0) + 1$
$\quad\quad\quad\quad = 2(2(2(2(0) + 1) + 0) + 1) + 1$
$\quad\quad\quad\quad = 2^4(0) + 2^3(1) + 2^2(0) + 2^1(1) + 2^0(1) = (1011)_2$

b. $(100001)_2$

c. $(100)_{10} = (1100100)_2$

d. $(10.1)_2$

e. $(12.625)_{10}$: $\quad (12)_{10} = (1100)_2$
$\quad\quad\quad\quad\quad 0.625 \times 2 = 1 + .25$
$\quad\quad\quad\quad\quad 0.25 \times 2 = 0 + .50$
$\quad\quad\quad\quad\quad 0.50 \times 2 = 1 + 0$
$\quad\quad\quad\quad\quad\quad (.625)_{10} = (.101)_2$

f. $(0.1)_{10}$: $.1 \times 2 = 0 + 0.2$
$\quad\quad\quad\quad\quad .2 \times 2 = 0 + 0.4$
$\quad\quad\quad\quad\quad .4 \times 2 = 0 + 0.8$
$\quad\quad\quad\quad\quad .8 \times 2 = 1 + 0.6$
$\quad\quad\quad\quad\quad .6 \times 2 = 1 + 0.2$
$\quad\quad\quad\quad\quad .4 \times 2 = 0 + 0.8$
$\quad\quad\quad\quad\quad .8 \times 2 = 1 + 0.6$
$\quad\quad\quad\quad\quad\quad \cdots \quad\quad \cdots$
$\quad\quad\quad\quad (0.1)_{10} = (.0001100110011001100\cdots)_2$

1.3 **a.** $1011 \quad\quad (11)_{10}$ **b.** $1010 \quad\quad (10)_{10}$
$\quad\quad\quad \underline{+\ 11} \ \rightarrow \ \underline{+\ (3)_{10}} \quad\quad \underline{-\ 11} \ \rightarrow \ \underline{-\ (3)_{10}}$
$\quad\quad\quad 1110 \quad\quad (14)_{10} \quad\quad\quad 111 \quad\quad\quad (7)_{10}$

1.5 **a.** Remove all three markers in row 2.

b. No

1.9 **a.** The typing errors detected by the compiler would be

```
D=2A+BC   ***ERROR*** MISSING OPERATOR
  |
```

The line was probably intended to read D = 2*A + B*C.

```
E=D/-A       ***ERROR*** BAD SEQUENCE OF OPERATORS
   |
```

The line was probably intended to read E = D/(−A).

After making these corrections, the program begins execution and asks for values for A, B, and C. After entering the values 1, 2, and 3, the computer signals an execution error:

```
***EXECUTION ERROR*** NO VALUES ASSIGNED TO  C
                      PROGRAM TERMINATED IN LINE 4
```

The remaining error is the missing comma between B and C in the READ statement. Since blanks are ignored, the program proceeded to read a value of 2 for the variable BC, and neither B nor C were ever assigned a value.

b. The following typing errors would be detected by the compiler:

```
X + 1 = Y      should read     Y = X + 1
PRINT X,Y      should read     PRINT *, X,Y
```

`This is a Comment!` must have a "C" or an "*" in column 1. The last line of the program must be END.

Chapter 2

2.1 Using the results of Figure 2-1, we would conclude that both a VAX mainframe computer and an IBM PC carry only about eight significant figures in a real number.

2.3 **a.** The output from an execution on a PC is

```
1.0000E+01
1.0000E+02
1.0000E+03
1.0000E+04
   . . .
1.0000E+36
1.0000E+37
1.0000E+38
***ERROR*** FLOATING POINT OVERFLOW, EXECUTING
IN STATEMENT 3
```

2.5 **a.** 1000.00----   Six significant figures

$$+ \quad .00999999$$

$$\overline{1000.00999999} \rightarrow 1000.00 \quad \text{Retaining only six figures}$$

Thus, EPS = 9.99999E-2.

b. The first 1 million additions will accumulate to 100000.---. Adding 0.1 to this number will not change it if the computer only retains six figures. Thus, the result of the sum is 100,000.0.

c. 1.0E+8 times 1.0E−1 is correctly computed as 1.0E+7.

2.7 **a.** Error. Embedded commas not permitted

b. Error. Decimal points not permitted in exponent

c. None. But base should contain a decimal point

d. None. Valid mixed-mode replacement

e. None. Plus sign in exponent may be omitted

f. Error. Variable name may not begin with a digit

g. None

h. Error. Side-by-side operators, (**) and (−)

i. Error. Negative base to REAL exponent

j. None

k. None. Valid mixed-mode replacement

l. None. But the statement is useless

2.9 **a.** 1.20 **d.** 4.00 **g.** 9 **j.** 27.0
   b. 4 **e.** 1 **h.** 5 **k.** 3
   c. 0 **f.** 1.500 **i.** 4.5

2.11 **a.** X*Y/(Z+1.)   **d.** ACOS(ABS(LOG(X)))
   b. X**(N+1)   **e.** X**(A+B)   or   X**A*X**B
   c. X**.5   or   X**(1./2.)   **f.** (X**A)**B   or   X**(A*B)

Chapter 3 **3.1** **a.** Compilation error. THEN must be on the same line as IF ( ).
   b. OK
   c. OK, but notice that there is no logical path to the PRINT statement.
   d. Compilation error. Both sides of .AND. must be of type logical. Presumably X is of type real.
   e. OK, but the logical phrase can never be true.
   f. OK. Note that "GE" and "LE" are variable names, while ".GE." is a comparison operator.
   g. Compilation error. The statement following IF ( ) must be an executable statement. "A.EQ.0" is a logical expression.
   h. OK
   i. OK. This is the arithmetic IF statement.
   j. Compilation error. "<" is not a valid FORTRAN character. This error will generate several additional error messages.
   k. Compilation error. Each IF ( ) must have its own ENDIF.
   l. Compilation error. DO statements are not allowed after IF ( ).
   m. Compilation error. The equals sign is not permitted within a logical expression. Also, either the "THEN" must be removed or the "B = 5" placed on a different line and followed by an END IF statement.

3.3
```
PROGRAM TRES
REAL AGE
PRINT *,'Enter the age of the person.'
READ *,AGE
IF(AGE .GE. 13. .AND. AGE .LE. 19.)THEN
    PRINT *, 'Teenager'
ELSEIF(AGE .GE. 65.)THEN
    PRINT *, 'Retired'
ENDIF
END
```

3.5 **a.** (16.NE.8 .AND. 2.EQ.4 .OR. 1. .GT.-2.)
   (true .AND. false .OR. true) → (false .OR. true) → true
   b. (2.GT.4 .AND. 1..GT.-2. .OR. 0.EQ.0)
   (false .AND. true .OR. true) → (false .OR. true) → true
   c. ((2.GT.4) .AND. (1.GT.-2.) .OR. 0.EQ.0)
   ((false) .AND. (true .OR. true)) → (false .AND. true) → false
   d. (3.*.0033*EXP(3.) .GT. 2.**3.*.1/3./2./2.)
   (.19885 .GT. .666667) → false

3.7

```
        PROGRAM QDRNT
        REAL THETA,PI
        INTEGER QUAD
        PI = ACOS(-1.)
        PRINT *,'Enter the angle in radians'
        READ  *,THETA
        QUAD = THETA/(.5*PI)
*
* Quad is now the total number of quadrants rotated through.
* Next reduce this to the range 1 - 4, i.e., 11 => 3 etc.
*
        QUAD = QUAD - (QUAD/4)*4 + 1   [or  QUAD = MOD(QUAD,4) + 1]
        PRINT *,'The angle ',THETA,' is in quadrant ',QUAD
        END
```

3.9

```
        PROGRAM PROFIT
        REAL PRICE,TRADE,COMMIS,SALE
        PRINT *,'Enter the sale price and the value of the trade-in'
        READ  *,PRICE,TRADE
        SALE = PRICE - TRADE
        IF(SALE .LT. 200.)THEN
            COMMIS = 0.
        ELSEIF(SALE .LT. 2500.)THEN
            COMMIS = .1*SALE
        ELSE
            COMMIS = 250 + .12*(SALE-250.)
        ENDIF
        PRINT *,'Price = ',PRICE,' Trade-in = ',TRADE
        PRINT *,'   Commission is ',COMMIS
        STOP
        END
```

3.11

```
        PROGRAM INVERT
        REAL X,C
        INTEGER ITER,IMAX
        PRINT *,'Enter the number whose inverse is desired.'
        READ  *,C
        PRINT *,'Now, enter an rough estimate for the inverse of C'
        READ  *,X
    1   IF(C*X .GT. 2.)THEN
            X = .5*X
            GO TO 1
        ENDIF
        PRINT *,'Enter the limit on the number of iterations'
        READ  *,IMAX
        ITER = 0
    2   IF(ABS(1.-C*X) .LT. 1.E-6)THEN
            PRINT *,' The inverse of ',C,' was successfully found'
            PRINT *,' after ',ITER,' iterations to be ',X
        ELSE
            ITER = ITER + 1
            IF(ITER .LT. IMAX)THEN
                X = X*(2.-C*X)
                GO TO 2
            ELSE
                PRINT *,' Program fails to find sufficiently '
                PRINT *,' accurate inverse within ',IMAX,' iterations'
            ENDIF
        ENDIF
        STOP
        END
```

3.13 **a.** The statement X = C/2. should precede the DO loop. As it is, the same value (C/2.) is assigned to X in every step of the loop.

b. The first two PRINT statements should precede the DO loop. The third PRINT will then print the numerical values of the table.

c. The DO loop proceeds in reverse from 1991 to 1971 and thus the step size must be explicitly stated as −1.

Chapter 4 **4.1** **a.** F(X) = 3.*X*X + X − 1.

b. G(X) = A*X*X + B*X + C   or
G(A, B, C, X) = A*X*X + B*X + C

c. R1(A, B, C) = .5*(−B + SQRT(B*B − 4.*A*C))/A

d. H(Y) = EXP(−A*Y) + LOG(SIN(ACOS(−1.)*Y))   or
H(A, Y) = EXP(−A*Y) + LOG(SIN(PI*Y))   With PI previously defined.

4.3
```
PROGRAM SUMS
INTEGER I,IMAX
REAL EPS,ANSWER,TERM
DATA EPS/1.E-4/
IMAX =  a) 1./SQRT(EPS) + 1
        b) (1.+EPS)/2./EPS + 1
        c) -LOG(EPS)/LOG(2.) + 2
        d) -LOG(EPS)/LOG(4.) + 1
ANSWER = 0.0
DO 1 I = 1,IMAX
      TERM = a) 1./I**2
             b) (-1)**(I+1)/(2.*I-1.)
             c) 1./2.**(I-1)
             d) 1./4.**I
      ANSWER = ANSWER + TERM
1 CONTINUE
WRITE(*,*)'Sum = ',ANSWER,' including ',IMAX,' terms.'
STOP
END
```

The computed results are

a. 1.6350820 after 101 terms

b. 0.7855192 after 5001 terms

c. 1.9999390 after 15 terms

d. 0.3333130 after 7 terms

4.5 The infinite product is terminated when $|\text{term} − 1| < \epsilon$.
```
PROGRAM PRODCT
INTEGER I,IMAX
REAL EPS,PROD,TERM
DATA EPS,IMAX/1.E-5,200/
PROD = 1.0
DO 1 I = 1,IMAX
      TERM = (4.*I**2)/(2.*I-1)/(2.*I+1)
      PROD = PROD*TERM
      IF(ABS(TERM - 1) .LT. EPS)THEN
         WRITE(*,*)'After ',I,' terms, product = ',PROD
         STOP
      ENDIF
```

```
      1 CONTINUE
        WRITE(*,*)'After ',IMAX,' terms, the product',
       +          'has not yet converged'
        STOP
        END
```

After 159 terms, product = 1.5683370.

4.7
```
        PROGRAM MKDATA
        REAL X,Y,T,VX,VY,G,DT
        INTEGER I
        DATA G,VX,VY,DT/9.8,10.5,51.0,0.10/
        OPEN (10,FILE='TRAJ.DAT')
        WRITE(10,*)DT,VX,VY
        DO 1 I = 1,100
            T = I*DT
            X = VX*T
            Y = VY*T - .5*G*T**2
            WRITE(10,*)T,X,Y
      1 CONTINUE
        CLOSE (10)
        STOP
        END
```

```
        PROGRAM RDDATA
        REAL X,Y,T,VX,VY,DT,YMAX
        INTEGER I
        OPEN (11,FILE='TRAJ.DAT')
        REWIND (11)
        READ(11,*)DT,VX,VY
        YMAX = 0.
        DO 1 I = 1,100
           READ(11,*)T,X,Y
              IF(Y .GT. YMAX)THEN
                  YMAX = Y
                  TMAX = T
              ENDIF
      1 CONTINUE
        WRITE(*,*)'The peak of the trajectory occurs ',
       +          'at t = ',TMAX,' and equals ',YMAX
        END
```

The peak of the trajectory occurs
at $t = 5.20$ and equals 132.7040.

4.9 a.
```
        PROGRAM REWRIT
        CHARACTER GRADE*1,NAME*10
        INTEGER CLASS, COLEGE,KOLAGE,Q1,Q2,Q3,HW,EXAM,TOTAL,REC,
       +        LINE,IC1,IC2,IC3,K
        REAL PERCNT
        DATA IC1,IC2,IC3,IC4,IC5/5*0/
        OPEN(22,FILE='TWO4.DAT')
        REWIND (22)
        OPEN(33,FILE='A:TWO4.DAM',ACCESS='DIRECT',
       +        FORM='UNFORMATTED',RECL=40)
        READ(22,*)N
        DO 2 I = 1,N
            READ(22,*)NAME,CLASS,COLEGE,Q1,Q2,Q3,HW,EXAM
            IF(COLEGE .EQ. 1)THEN
                IC1 = IC1 + 1
                K   = IC1
            ELSEIF(COLEGE .EQ.2)THEN
                IC2 = IC2 + 1
                K   = IC2
```

```
      ELSEIF(COLEGE .EQ.3)THEN
          IC3 = IC3 + 1
          K   = IC3
      ENDIF
      LINE = 100*(COLEGE-1) + K
      WRITE(33,REC=LINE)NAME,CLASS,COLEGE,Q1,Q2,Q3,HW,EXAM
      READ (33,REC=LINE)NAME,CLASS,COLEGE,Q1,Q2,Q3,HW,EXAM
      WRITE( *,*       )NAME,CLASS,COLEGE,Q1,Q2,Q3,HW,EXAM
2 CONTINUE
  WRITE(*,*        )IC1,IC2,IC3
  WRITE(33,REC=400)IC1,IC2,IC3
  CLOSE (33)
  STOP
  END
```

```
      PROGRAM ASSIGN
      CHARACTER GRADE*1,NAME*10
      INTEGER CLASS,COLEGE,KOLAGE,Q1,Q2,Q3,HW,EXAM,TOTAL
      REAL PERCNT
      OPEN(22,FILE='A:TWO4.DAM',ACCESS='DIRECT',FORM='UNFORMATTED',
     +     RECL=40)
      OPEN(33,FILE='TWO.GRD')
      READ(22,REC=400)IC1,IC2,IC3
      WRITE(33,*)'The final grades for students arranged by college'
      DO 2 COLEGE = 1,3
          WRITE(33,*)'------------------------------------------------'
          WRITE(33,*)'For students in college No.-',COLAGE
          WRITE(33,*)'            Hour quizzes Home Final  Tot.      '
          WRITE(33,*)'Name        1   2   3  work Exam  Pct.  Grade'
          WRITE(33,*)'--------- -- -- -- ---- ---- --- - ---'
          IF(COLEGE .EQ. 1)N = IC1
          IF(COLEGE .EQ. 2)N = IC2
          IF(COLEGE .EQ. 3)N = IC3
          DO 1 I = 1,N
              LINE = 100*(COLEGE-1) + I
              READ(22,REC=LINE)NAME,CLASS,MM,Q1,Q2,Q3,HW,EXAM
*--
*-- Compute letter grade for this student in college = COLEGE
*--
              TOTAL  = Q1 + Q2 + Q3 + HW + 3*EXAM
              PERCNT = TOTAL/700.*100.
              IF(PERCNT .GE. 90.)THEN
                  GRADE = 'A'
              ELSEIF(PERCNT .GE. 80.)THEN
                  GRADE = 'B'
              ELSEIF(PERCNT .GE. 70.)THEN
                  GRADE = 'C'
              ELSEIF(PERCNT .GE. 60.)THEN
                  GRADE = 'D'
              ELSE
                  GRADE = 'F'
              ENDIF
              WRITE(33,*)NAME,Q1,Q2,Q3,HW,EXAM,PERCNT,GRADE
1     CONTINUE
2 CONTINUE
  CLOSE (22)
  CLOSE (33)
  STOP
  END
```

b. If the process converges, $x_0 \rightarrow x_1 \rightarrow r$, so $r^2 + br - a = 0$ and the value of r (the "fixed point") is the solution of this quadratic.

c. $(a,b) = (1,1)$ Converges to $r = 0.6180328$ in 12 iterations.
       $(8,3)$ Converges to $r = 1.7015640$ in 12 iterations.
       $(10.,.01)$ Diverges

4.11   **a.** $f(x) = x^2 + 2x - 15$

i	x_1	x_2	x_3	f_1	f_2	f_3	cross
1	2.80000	2.95000	3.10000	−1.5600000	−0.3974991	0.8099995	R
2	2.95000	3.02500	3.10000	−0.3974991	0.2006254	0.8099995	L
3	2.95000	2.98750	3.02500	−0.3974991	−0.0998421	0.2006254	R
	...	...	...	...	...	...	...
	...	...	...	...	...	...	...
16	3.00000	3.00000	3.00001	−0.0000162	0.0000191	0.0000563	L
17	3.00000	3.00000	3.00000	−0.0000162	0.0000029	0.0000191	L
18	3.00000	3.00000	3.00000	−0.0000162	−0.0000076	0.0000029	R

b. $g(x) = \sin(x) \sinh(x) + 1$

i	x_1	x_2	x_3	f_1	f_2	f_3	cross
1	1.00000	2.50000	4.00000	1.9888980	4.6208790	−42.991799	R
2	2.50000	3.25000	4.00000	4.6208790	−0.3930970	−42.991799	L
3	2.50000	2.87500	3.25000	4.6208790	3.3274150	−0.3930970	R
	...	...	...	...	...	...	...
	...	...	...	...	...	...	...
19	3.22158	3.22159	3.22160	0.0000550	−0.0000221	−0.0000993	L
20	3.22158	3.22159	3.22159	0.0000550	0.0000163	−0.0000221	R
21	3.22159	3.22159	3.22159	0.0000163	−0.0000029	−0.0000221	L

c. $e(x) = \sqrt{(R^2 - x^2)} - x \tan(x)$

i	x_1	x_2	x_3	f_1	f_2	f_3	cross
1	4.00000	4.35000	4.70000	4.5338670	−2.4692450	−370.52332	L
2	4.00000	4.17500	4.35000	4.5338670	2.0803920	−2.4692450	R
3	4.17500	4.26250	4.35000	2.0803920	0.2194996	−2.4692450	R
	...	...	...	...	...	...	...
	...	...	...	...	...	...	...
17	4.27109	4.27109	4.27110	0.0001755	0.0000267	−0.0001097	R
18	4.27109	4.27110	4.27110	0.0000267	−0.0000477	−0.0001097	L
19	4.27109	4.27110	4.27110	0.0000267	−0.0000114	−0.0000477	L

d. $n_a > 16$, $n_b > 19$, $n_c > 16$

Chapter 5

5.1   **a.**
```
SUBROUTINE POLAR(R,THTA,X,Y)
   REAL R,THTA,X,Y
   X = R*COS(THTA)
   Y = R*SIN(THTA)
   RETURN
END
```

b.
```
   PROGRAM CONVRT
   REAL R,THTA,XORIG,YORIG,X,Y
   WRITE(*,*)'Enter original values of x and y'
   READ (*,*)XORIG,YORIG
   CALL VECTOR(XORIG,YORIG,R,THTA)
   CALL POLAR(R,THTA,X,Y)
   WRITE(*,*)'The pair (',XORIG,',',YORIG') converted to polar'
   WRITE(*,*)'and then back to Cartesian yields the pair'
   WRITE(*,*)'(',X,',',Y,')'
   END
   SUBROUTINE VECTOR(X,Y,R,THETA)
     ...
   END
   SUBROUTINE POLAR(R,THTA,X,Y)
     ...
   END
```

5.3 **a.**
```
   SUBROUTINE TRMIN8
   WRITE(*,*)'The program has successfully com',
  +          'pleted the calculation.'
   WRITE(*,*)'  --JOB TERMINATED--'
   STOP
   END
```

b. See above

c. (1) Yes   (2) Yes   (3) No   (4) Yes   (5) Yes

5.5
```
   SUBROUTINE SWITCH(A,B)
   TEMP = A
   A    = B
   B    = TEMP
   RETURN
   END
```

5.7 **a.** $a_n = \dfrac{(2n-1)!}{(n+1)!\,n!} \times \dfrac{1}{2^{4n}(2n+1)}$

b.
```
   SUBROUTINE TERM(N,NUM,DEN)
   INTEGER NUM,DEN,ID
   NUM = 1
   DEN = 2
   DO 1 K = 1,N
       NUM = NUM*(2*K-1)
       DEN = DEN*2*K
1      CONTINUE
   DEN = DEN * 2**(2*N+1)
   DEN = DEN * (2*N+1)
   ID = IGCF(NUM,DEN)
   NUM = NUM/ID
   DEN = DEN/ID
   RETURN
   END
```

c. This program uses the subroutine ADD and the function IGCF in the text.

```
   PROGRAM PI
   INTEGER T1,T2,S1,S2
   DATA S1,S2,T1,T2/0,1,1,2/
```

```
            DO 1 N = 1,4
               CALL ADD (S1,S2,T1,T2,S1,S2)
               CALL TERM(N,T1,T2)
     1      CONTINUE
            WRITE(*,*)'Pi/6 = ',S1,'/',S2
          STOP
          END
```

5.9
```
     SUBROUTINE CHANGE(PAY,COST,TENS,FIVES,ONES,HALFD,
    +                  QUARTR,DIMES,NICKL,CENTS)
     INTEGER TENS,FIVES,ONES,HALFD,QUARTR,DIMES,NICKL,
    +        CENTS,LEFT
     REAL    PAY,COST,CHNG
     CHNG = PAY - COST
     IF(CHNG .LT. 0.)THEN
         WRITE(*,*)'Amount paid is insufficient'
         STOP
     ENDIF
     LEFT  = CHNG
     CENTS = 100.*(CHNG - LEFT) + .01
     TENS  = LEFT/10
         LEFT = LEFT - 10*TENS
     FIVES = LEFT/5
         LEFT = LEFT - 5*FIVES
     ONES  = LEFT
     HALFD = CENTS/50
         LEFT = CENTS- 50*HALFD
     QUARTR= LEFT/25
         LEFT = LEFT - 25*QUARTR
     DIMES = LEFT/10
         LEFT = LEFT - 10*DIMES
     NICKL = LEFT/5
         LEFT = LEFT - 5*NICKL
     CENTS = LEFT
     RETURN
     END
```

5.11 A few examples might be (a) a function that returns the largest root of a quadratic; (b) a function that has different algebraic expressions for different ranges of x, for example, $f(x) = 0$ for $x < 0$, and $f(x) = x^2$ for $x > 0$; or (c) a function that itself calls a subroutine.

5.13 a.
```
     PROGRAM PASCAL
     INTEGER C(0:20,0:20),P
     DO 4 N = 0,20
        C(N,0) = 1
        DO 3 P = 0,N-1
           C(N,P+1) = (N-P)*C(N,P)/(P+1)
     3    CONTINUE
     4  CONTINUE
     DO 6 N = 0,20
        WRITE(*,*)(C(N,P),P=0,N)
     6  CONTINUE
     STOP
     END
```

b. The output has been rearranged in the form of a triangle.

```
                        1
                      1   1
                    1   2   1
                  1   3   3   1
                1   4   6   4   1
              1   5  10  10   5   1
            1   6  15  20  15   6   1
          1   7  21  35  35  21   7   1
        1   8  28  56  70  56  28   8   1
      1   9  36  84 126 126  84  36   9   1
    1  10  45 120 210 252 210 120  45  10   1
```

5.15 a. Error—"I+1". Arithmetic operations not permitted in subroutine definition line.
b. OK
c. Error—"A(X)". Parentheses not permitted within definition line.
d. OK
e. OK
f. OK, but the empty argument list could be omitted for a subroutine.
g. Error. The name of the function (here SUM) must be assigned a value before any return.
h. Error. Subroutine name may not be assigned a value.
i. Error. There is a call to the function named Z within a function of the same name. A function may not call itself.
j. Error. The function is not terminated by an END statement.

5.17 a.
```
SUBROUTINE POLAR(LAT,LONG,A,B)
REAL LAT,LONG,A,B,PI
INTEGER ILAT,ILONG
PI = ACOS(-1.)
ILAT  = LAT
ILONG = LONG
LAT  = ILAT + (LAT - ILAT )*100./60.
LONG = ILONG+ (LONG- ILONG)*100./60.
IF(LAT .GT. 0.)THEN
    A = 90 - ABS(LAT)
ELSE
    A = 90 + ABS(LAT)
ENDIF
IF(LONG .GT. 0.)THEN
      B = LONG
ELSE
      B = 360 - ABS(LONG)
ENDIF
A = A*PI/180.
B = B*PI/180.
RETURN
END
```

b.
```
FUNCTION ANGLE(A1,B1,A2,B2)
C = COS(A1)*COS(A2) + SIN(A1)*SIN(A2)*COS(B1-B2)
ANGLE = ACOS(C)
RETURN
END
```

c.
```
PROGRAM EARTH
CHARACTER*14 NAME1,NAME2
REAL LAT1,LAT2,LONG1,LONG2,R,DIST,A1,A2,B1,B2
R = 3958.89
WRITE(*,*)'Enter the name of the first city ',
+            '(enclosed in quotes)'
READ (*,*)NAME1
WRITE(*,*)'Enter latitude, longitude as ',
+            'specified in problem'
READ (*,*)LAT1,LONG1
WRITE(*,*)'Enter the name of the second city'
READ (*,*)NAME2
WRITE(*,*)'Enter latitude, longitude'
READ (*,*)LAT2,LONG2
   CALL POLAR(LAT1,LONG1,A1,B1)
   CALL POLAR(LAT2,LONG2,A2,B2)
      DIST = R*ANGLE(A1,B1,A2,B2)
WRITE(*,*)'The distance between ',NAME1,' and ',NAME2,
+            ' is ',DIST,' miles.'
STOP
END
```

d. The computed results for all combinations of distances are given in the table below.

	Chicago	LA	Montreal	London	Rio de J	Melbourn	Vladivsk	Johannes
Chicago	0	1697	745	3951	5288	9613	6080	8677
Los Angeles	1697	0	2391	5344	6335	7936	5439	10366
Montreal	745	2391	0	3218	5206	10291	6023	8135
London	3951	5344	3218	0	5925	10496	5242	5767
Rio de Janr	5288	6335	5206	5925	0	8127	11077	4579
Melbourne	9613	7936	10291	10496	8127	0	5714	6341
Vladivostk	6080	5439	6023	5242	11077	5714	0	8168
Johannesbg	8677	10366	8135	5767	4579	6341	8168	0

5.19 a. Error. Only names, not numerical values, permitted in a COMMON statement.

b. Error. COMMON statement must precede all executable statements.

c. OK

d. Error. Numerical values and character variables may not appear in the same common block.

e. Error. A variable may not appear both in the argument list and in the common block.

f. Error. Variable name cannot be repeated in a COMMON block list.

g. OK

h. OK

i. Error. Variable name INTEGER exceeds six characters.

5.21 a.
```
PROGRAM GRAPH
REAL PI
INTRINSIC SIN
   PI = ACOS(-1.)
   CALL PLOT(0.,2*PI,SIN)
   STOP
END
*=======================================
SUBROUTINE PLOT(A,B,F)
   ...    ...
END
```

b. (1)

```
PROGRAM GRAPH
REAL A,B,C,Q,X
Q(X) = A*X*X + B*X + C
   WRITE(*,*)'Enter a,b,c'
   READ (*,*)A,B,C
   CALL PLOT(-10.,10.,Q)
   STOP
END
*======================================
SUBROUTINE PLOT(A,B,F)
   ...   ...
END
```

(2)

```
PROGRAM GRAPH
REAL A,B,C,Q,X
COMMON/COEF/A,B,C
   WRITE(*,*)'Enter a,b,c'
   READ (*,*)A,B,C
   CALL PLOT(-10.,10.,Q)
   STOP
END
*======================================
FUNCTION Q(Z)
REAL C1,C2,C3,Q,Z
COMMON/COEF/C1,C2,C3
   Q(Z) = C1*Z*Z + C2*Z + C3
   RETURN
END
*======================================
SUBROUTINE PLOT(A,B,F)
   ...   ...
END
```

5.23 While you probably predicted that the printed value would be B = 3., the actual value printed will be B = 2. The point is that variables in common or in the argument list are not local. When it is executed, the statement "X = 2." in the function will also cause a change in the value of A in the main program; this change occurs even before the RETURN.

Chapter 6 **6.1** **a.** READ(*,*) or READ *,

b. READ(11,*,END=99)   or insert a trailing data line that can be used as a flag; for example,

```
READ(11,*)A,B,C,D
   IF(A .LT. 0.)THEN     End of data flag is A < 0.
```

c. WRITE(*,'(1X,F9.6)')EXP(ACOS(-1.))
d. Unused FORMAT statements will not cause an error.
e. Formats F, E, I, X, and A may be in the form of multiples; / ,T may not.
f. Examples of when replacing "WRITE" by "READ" will cause a compilation error are

```
READ(*,*,END=99)  →  WRITE(*,*,END=99)        END option not
                                               permitted in
                                               WRITEs

READ *,A,B          →  WRITE *,A,B             Short form
                                               is PRINT *,
```

g. No, FORMAT statements are not executable.

6.3 **a.** Error. Attempt to read IY with an F4.1 format specification
b. Error. Attempt to read Y with an I5, and IX with an F5.1 specification
c. OK, provided that the input numbers are arranged with X, Y, Z on one line and Z on the next line.
d. Error. This format specification is too wide.
e. OK, but notice that the entire format is not used.
f. OK

6.5 **a.** OK
b. OK
c. OK
d. Compilation error. F6.7 not possible.
e. Compilation error. The expression 2E+02 is meaningless as a format specification. Perhaps 2E10.2 was intended.
f. Execution error. Character constants are not permitted in a format that is used for reading values.
g. OK, but if the READ statement were READ(*,4)I, J, A, B the input line would have to be

```
| iiiii    aaa.ajjjjj     bbb.bb
```

h. Compilation error. The slash cannot be preceded by a multiple.
i. OK. However, the inner parentheses are not needed unless the FORMAT statement is repeatedly used in a single READ.

6.7

col no.	1	1	2	2
	1	5	0	5	0	5

a. `1.   2.  .3   2   3`

b. `        0.1E+01  0.2E+01`
`2 3`

c. `0.1E+01   2`
`0.2E+01   3`
`0.3E+00`

d. `1.0  =x`

e.
`1.`

`2.`

`0.`

f. With most compilers, attempts to print reals with an integer format, or viceversa, will result in an execution error.

g. `1.0***  2`
`2.0---  3`
`0.3`

h. `0.333E+00 0.300E+01 0.000E+00`

6.9   a. `WRITE(*,'(/,F7.2)')X,Y,X+Y`
      b. `WRITE(*,'(2(A,F7.2,/))')'x = ',X,'y = ',Y`   or
      `WRITE(*,'(''x = '',F7.2,/,''y = '',F7.2)')X,Y`

6.11
```
      PROGRAM METALS
      CHARACTER METAL*10
      INTEGER   STEP
      REAL      TEMP
      OPEN(27,FILE='MLTDTA')
      REWIND (27)
      I = 0
      WRITE(*,10)
    1 READ(27,11,END=99)METAL,TEMP
        I = I + 1
        WRITE(*,12),I,METAL,TEMP
        IF(TEMP .GT. 1400.)THEN
            WRITE(*,13)'Too high'
        ELSE IF(TEMP .LT. 600.)THEN
            WRITE(*,13)'Too low '
        ENDIF
      GO TO 1
   99 STOP
   10 FORMAT(T4,'       Metal   Melting ',/,
     +       T4,'Number  Type    Temp. ',/,
     +       T4,'------  -----   ------- ',)
   11 FORMAT(A10,F6.0)
   12 FORMAT(T6,I2,1X,A10,1X,F6.1)
   13 FORMAT('+',T28,A)
      END
```

6.13
```
      PROGRAM PERFEC
      INTEGER ITEST
      REAL XI
      WRITE(*,9)
      DO 1 I = 1,100
         XI   = I
         ITEST = XI**(1./3.) + .0001
    *
    * A small number is added to avoid
    * truncation due to round-off.
    *
         IF(ITEST**3 .EQ. I)THEN
             WRITE(*,10)I,ITEST
         ELSE
             WRITE(*,11)I
         ENDIF
    1    CONTINUE
    9    FORMAT(T5,'A list of the integers',/)
   10    FORMAT(T10,I3,' is the cube of ',I3)
   11    FORMAT(T10,I3)
         END
```

6.15 a.
```
   10   FORMAT(T10,' MM        MM ',/,
     +         T10,' MMM      MMM ',/,
     +         T10,' MM M    M MM ',/,
     +         T10,' MM M  M M MM ',/,
     +         T10,' MM  M M  MM ',/,
     +         T10,' MMMM  M  MMMM ')
```

b.
```
 2   FORMAT(T5,'Step      x       y  ',/,
     +        T5,' No.    pos.    pos. ',/,
     +        T5,'----   -------  -------',/,
     +5(T6,I2,T11,F7.2,T20,F7.2,/))
```

c.
```
     PROGRAM ADDER
     CHARACTER ANS*3
     REAL X,SUM
     OPEN(11,FILE='SUM')
     WRITE(*,*)'Do you wish to compute a sum (yes or no)?'
     READ (*,'(A3)')ANS
     IF((ANS.EQ.'YES') .OR. (ANS.EQ.'Yes') .OR.
     +   (ANS.EQ.'yes'))THEN
         WRITE(*,*)'Enter the ten numbers one at a time ',
     +             'at the prompt. '
         SUM = 0.0
         DO 1 I = 1,9
             WRITE(*,*)'Number please'
             READ (*,*)X
             WRITE(11,'(T13,F8.4)')X
             SUM = SUM + X
 1       CONTINUE
         WRITE(*,*)'And the last number'
         READ (*,*)X
         SUM = SUM + X
         WRITE(11,20)X,SUM
     ENDIF
 20 FORMAT(T10,'+',T13,F8.4,/,
     +       T10,'-----------',/,
     +       T10,'=',T12,F9.4)
     END
```

d.
```
     PROGRAM CONVRT
     REAL TIME
     INTEGER HOUR,MIN
     CHARACTER*2 AMPM
     WRITE(*,*)'Enter time'
     READ(*,'(I2,1X,I2,A2)')HOUR,MIN,AMPM
       TIME = HOUR + 60.*MIN
       IF(AMPM .EQ. 'PM')HOUR = HOUR + 12.*60.
       WRITE(*,*)'Elapsed time = ',TIME,' minutes'
     STOP
     END
```

Chapter 7   **7.1**   **a.** OK, has the same effect as REAL M.

b. Error. The lower limit of the array is greater than the upper limit. Also, very poor choice of array name.

c. OK, but the array will require 7! = 5040 memory locations.

d. Error. Variable name INTEGER has seven characters. Again, a poor choice of variable name.

e. OK. The variable is REALX.

f. Error. The index limits must be integers.

g. Error. N is undefined in the first line.

h. Error. Type statement must precede all executable statements.

i. Error. The upper limits are less than the implied lower limits.

j. OK

k. OK

l. Error. The memory allocation for the array R may be declared only once.

7.3
```
SUBROUTINE LRGST(A,N,MINROW,MINCOL)
INTEGER MINROW,MINCOL,IROW,ICOL
REAL A(N,N),AMIN
AMIN = A(1,1)
MINROW = 1
MINCOL = 1
DO 1 I = 1,N
DO 1 J = 1,N
    IF(A(I,J) .LT. AMIN)THEN
        AMIN = A(I,J)
        MINROW = I
        MINCOL = J
    ENDIF
1  CONTINUE
RETURN
END
```

7.5 **a.**
```
SUBROUTINE SWITCH(A,N)
REAL A(N,N),TEMP
DO 2 I = 1,N
    DO 1 J = I+1,N
        TEMP   = A(I,J)
        A(I,J) = A(J,I)
        A(J,I) = TEMP
1     CONTINUE
2 CONTINUE
RETURN
END
```

b.
```
SUBROUTINE PIVOT(A,N,K)
REAL A(N,N),MAX
INTEGER COL,K,MAXROW,ROW
MAX    = A(1,K)
MAXROW = 1
DO 1 ROW = 1,N
    IF(A(ROW,K) .GT. MAX)THEN
        MAXROW = ROW
        MAX    = A(ROW,K)
    ENDIF
1 CONTINUE
DO 2 COL = 1,N
    TEMP            = A(1,COL)
    A(1,COL)        = A(MAXROW,COL)
    A(MAXROW,COL) = TEMP
2 CONTINUE
RETURN
END
```

7.7 Simply replace MIN by MAX and .LT. by .GT.

7.9 In the subroutine, make the following replacements

$$DO\ 2\ PASS = N,2,-1 \rightarrow DO\ 2\ PASS = 1,N-1$$
$$DO\ 1\ I = 1,PASS-1 \rightarrow DO\ 1\ \ I = N-1,PASS,-1$$

7.11
```
      SUBROUTINE PLOT(A,B,F1,F2)
      CHARACTER*1 LINE(0:50),BLANK,STAR,CROS
      REAL X(0:40),Y1(0:40),Y2(0:40),XSTEP,
     +     YMIN,YMAX,RATIO,F1,F2
      INTEGER IC
      DATA BLANK,STAR,CROS,LINE/' ','*','+',51*' '/
*
*  Generate the table of data x(i),y1(i),y2(I)
*
      XSTEP = (B-A)/40.
      X(0)  = A
      Y1(0) = F1(A)
      Y2(0) = F2(A)
      DO 1 I = 1,40
         X(I)  = X(I-1) + XSTEP
         Y1(I) = F1(X(I))
         Y2(I) = F2(X(I))
    1 CONTINUE
*
*  Determine the min/max of the set of y's.
*
      YMIN = Y1(0)
      YMAX = Y1(0)
      DO 2 I = 1,40
         IF(Y1(I) .GT. YMAX)YMAX = Y1(I)
         IF(Y2(I) .GT. YMAX)YMAX = Y2(I)
         IF(Y1(I) .LT. YMIN)YMIN = Y1(I)
         IF(Y2(I) .LT. YMIN)YMIN = Y2(I)
    2 CONTINUE
*
*  Print the overall headings for the y axis
*
      WRITE(*,10)YMIN,YMAX
*
*  Step through the data pairs, position the symbols
*  and print line by line.
*
      DO 3 I = 0,40
         RATIO    = (Y1(I) - YMIN)/(YMAX - YMIN)
         IC1      = 50.*RATIO
         LINE(IC1)= STAR
         RATIO    = (Y2(I) - YMIN)/(YMAX - YMIN)
         IC2      = 50.*RATIO
         LINE(IC2)= CROS
         WRITE(*,11)X(I),(LINE(J),J=0,50)
*
*          Remember to blank out the star to
*          set up for the next line.
*
         LINE(IC1) = BLANK
         LINE(IC2) = BLANK
    3 CONTINUE
      RETURN
*-------------------------------------------------
```

```
* Formats
*
  10  FORMAT(//,T10,'Plots of the functions',/,
      +    T8,'Ymin',T58,'Ymax',/,
      +    T8,F5.2,T58,F5.2,/,
      +    T5,'X',T10,'+',T35,'+',T60,'+',/,
      +    T9,'|',51('-'),'|')
  *
  11  FORMAT(T2,F5.2,T9,'|',51A1,'|')
      END
```

7.13 **a.** Simply insert the lines

$$YMIN = ROUNDR(YMIN)$$
$$YMAX = ROUNDR(YMAX)$$

after the call to the subroutine MINMAX and include a copy of the function ROUNDR.

b. First include an additional integer parameter, SIGN, in the argument list for the function ROUNDR that will cause the function to round up (down) if SIGN is +1 (−1). (See also Problem 5.10.) This can be accomplished by changing the line

$$IC = 2.*(IC + .5)$$

to

$$IC = 2.*(IC + (SIGN + 1.)/2.)$$

Next, insert the following lines after the call to MINMAX in the code for PLOT,

```
SIGN = 1
IF(YMIN .GT. 0.)SIGN = -1
YMIN = ROUNDR(YMIN)
SIGN = 1
IF(YMAX .LT. 0.)SIGN = -1
YMAX = ROUNDR(YMAX)
```

7.15   a. $f(x, y) = \sin(x^2 + y^2)$

```
            a                                                          b
         -1.00                        X                             1.00
          --------------------------------------------------------
   1.00  | 9                9                9                     9
   0.90  |
   0.80  |       9          7      6    6         7      9
   0.70  |     9            6    5            5    6            9
   0.60  |
   0.50  |
   0.40  | 9   7  6          3                    3        6  7   9
   0.30  |
   0.20  |       5                                         5
   0.10  |     6                          0                    6
   0.00  |                              0   0   0
  -0.10  |     6                          0                    6
  -0.20  |       5                                         5
  -0.30  |
  -0.40  | 9   7  6          3                    3        6  7   9
  -0.50  |
  -0.60  |
  -0.70  |     9            6    5            5    6            9
  -0.80  |       9          7         6    6         7      9
  -0.90  |
  -1.00  | 9                9                9                     9
          --------------------------------------------------------
```

The contour plots for (b) and (c) are similar.

7.17 In a square 10-by-10 array there are 10 elements along the diagonal, 45 above the diagonal, and 45 below the diagonal.

```
DATA ( A(I,I),I=1,10)                    /10*1./
DATA ((A(I,J),I=2,10),J=1  ,I-1)/45*2./
DATA ((A(I,J),I=1, 9),J=I+1,10 )/45*0./
```

Chapter 8   **8.1   a.** $C = \boxed{A \quad\quad}$ $E = \boxed{A}$ **e.** $D(2) = \boxed{A\ 1\ 2\ 1\ 2}$

b. $F = \boxed{1\ 2}$ **f.** $D(3) = \boxed{5\ 4\ 3\ 2\ 1}$

c. $D(0)(3{:}4) = \boxed{2\ 3}$ **g.** $C = \boxed{A\ 1\ 2\ 3\ 4}$

d. $D(1)(:) = \boxed{1\ 2\ 3\ 4\ 5}$

8.3
```
PROGRAM FOG
CHARACTER LINE*70
INTEGER NSNTC,NWORD,LEFTWD,RGHTWD,LEFTSN,RGHTSN
DATA NSNTC,NWORD/0,0/
OPEN(9,FILE='VVV.IN')
REWIND(9)
DO 4 NLINE = 1,25
  READ (9,'(A70)',END=99)LINE
  EOL = INDEX(LINE,' ')
  LEFTWD = 1
  LEFTSN = 1
```

```
    2  RGHTWD = INDEX(LINE(LEFTWD:),' ') + LEFTWD
       IF((RGHTWD.GT.LEFTWD) .AND. (LEFTWD.LT.EOL))THEN
             NWORD  = NWORD  + 1
             LEFTWD = RGHTWD + 1
             GO TO 2
       ENDIF
    3  RGHTSN = INDEX(LINE(LEFTSN:),'. ') + LEFTSN
       IF((RGHTSN.GT.LEFTSN) .AND. (LEFTSN.LT.EOL))THEN
             NSNTC  = NSNTC  + 1
             LEFTSN = RGHTSN + 2
             GO TO 3
       ENDIF
    4  CONTINUE
   99  WRITE(*,*)'FOG factors'
       WRITE(*,*)'No. of words     = ',NWORD
       WRITE(*,*)'No. of sentences = ',NSNTC
       STOP
       END
```

If the program reads the problem statement, the output is:

```
FOG factors
No. of words     = 68
No. of sentences =  3
```

8.5
```
    PROGRAM DIREC
    CHARACTER LINE *50,NUMB*8
    OPEN(1,FILE='DIRECTORY')
    REWIND(1)
  1 READ(1,'(A)',END=99)LINE
       MATCH1 = INDEX(LINE,'Jones, James')
       IF(MATCH1 .NE. 0)THEN
             I      = MATCH1 + 12
             MATCH2 = INDEX(LINE(I:),'Jennings') + I
             IF(MATCH2 .NE. I)THEN
                 NPOS = INDEX(LINE,'-')
                 NUMB = LINE(NPOS-3:NPOS+4)
                 WRITE(*,'(A,A)')'No. = ',NUMB
                 STOP
             ELSE
          ENDIF
          GO TO 1
   99 WRITE(*,*)'Not in phone directory'
      END
```

8.7
```
    PROGRAM BIGFAC
    PARAMETER (M=200)
    INTEGER N , L(M)
    CHARACTER DIGIT(M)
    DATA L/M*0/
    OPEN(1,FILE='BIGFAC.OUT')
    L(1) = 1
    PRINT *,'Enter N'
    READ *,N
    DO 2 K = 1,N
       IC = 0
       DO 1 I = 1,M
          L(I) = L(I)*K + IC
          IC   = L(I)/10
          L(I) = L(I) - 10*IC
  1    CONTINUE
```

```
  2 CONTINUE
    CALL IMAGE(L,M,DIGIT)
    WRITE(1,11)(DIGIT(I),I=180,136,-1)
    WRITE(1,11)(DIGIT(I),I=135, 91,-1)
    WRITE(1,11)(DIGIT(I),I= 90, 46,-1)
    WRITE(1,11)(DIGIT(I),I= 45,  1,-1)
    STOP
 10 FORMAT(T3,15(3I1,',')/)
 11 FORMAT(T3,15(3A1,',')/)
    END
    SUBROUTINE IMAGE(L,M,DIGIT)
    CHARACTER VAL(0:9)*1,DIGIT(M)*1
    INTEGER L(M)
    DATA VAL/'0','1','2','3','4','5',
   +         '6','7','8','9'/
    DO 1 I = 1,M
        DIGIT(I) = VAL(L(I))
  1 CONTINUE
    DO 2 I = M,1,-1
      IF(DIGIT(I) .NE. '0')RETURN
      DIGIT(I) = ' '
  2 CONTINUE
    END
```

For example,

$$50 \text{ factorial} = 30,414,093,201,713,378,043,612,$$
$$608,166,064,768,844,377,641,$$
$$568,960,512,000,000,000,000$$

Chapter 9

9.1 **a.** False, but variables assigned values in a PARAMETER statement may only be used after the PARAMETER statement. Thus,

```
        REAL A(N)
        PARAMETER (N=10)
```

would be an error.

b. False

c. True

d. False

e. False

f. False

9.3
```
PROGRAM CSQRT
COMPLEX GUESS,C
REAL DIFF,EPS
INTEGER ITER,IMAX
DATA IMAX,EPS/30,1.E-6/
WRITE(*,*)'Enter a complex number in the form (x,y)'
READ (*,*)C
ITER = 0
```

```
 WRITE(*,*)'Enter a guess for the square root.'
 WRITE(*,*)'The guess must have a non-zero',
+              ' imaginary part.'
 READ(*,*)GUESS
 DO 1 ITER = 1,IMAX
      DIFF = ABS(GUESS*GUESS - C)
      IF(DIFF .LT. EPS)THEN
           WRITE(*,*)'Square root of ',C,' = ',GUESS
           WRITE(*,*)'and ',ITER,'iterations were required.'
           STOP
      ELSE
           GUESS = .5*(GUESS + C/GUESS)
      ENDIF
1 CONTINUE
 WRITE(*,*)'Square root not found in ',IMAX,' iterations'
 END
```

9.5 For I = −1 and I = 0, D has the value ⟨false⟩, whereas E is ⟨true⟩. So the statement

```
The order of AND/OR makes
a difference for
F   .AND. F .OR. T
```

is printed twice.

9.7 **a.** Error. Only constant expressions may appear in PARAMETER statements; ACOS( ) is a function.

b. OK

c. Error. Variables assigned values in a PARAMETER statement cannot be used in place of statement numbers.

d. OK

e. OK

f. Error. The only error is that the variable name STUDENT is seven characters long.

Chapter 10   **10.1**   **a.** $f(x) = (2x - 1)^5$
$$= -1 + 10x - 40x^2 + 80x^3 - 80x^4 + 32x^5$$

b. $f(x) = e^{2x}$
$$= 1 + (2x) + \frac{1}{2!}(2x)^2 + \frac{1}{3!}(2x)^3 + \cdots$$

c. $f(x) = \cos(1 + 2x)$ [Define $C_1 = \cos(1), S_1 = \sin(1)$]
$$= C_1 - S_1(2x) - \frac{1}{2!}C_1(2x)^2 + \frac{1}{3!}S_1(2x)^3 + \frac{1}{4!}C_1(2x)^4 + \cdots$$
$$= C_1\left[1 - \frac{1}{2!}(2x)^2 + \frac{1}{4!}(2x)^4 + \cdots\right] - S_1\left[2x - \frac{1}{3!}(2x)^3 + \cdots\right]$$
$$= C_1\cos(2x) - S_1\sin(2x)$$

d. $f(x) = (1 - x)^{1/2}$
$$= 1 - \frac{x}{2} - \frac{x^2}{8} - \frac{x^3}{16} - \frac{5x^4}{128} - \frac{7x^5}{256} - \cdots$$

e. $f(x) = \ln(1 + x)$

$$= x - \frac{x^2}{2} + \frac{x^3}{3} - \frac{x^4}{4} + \cdots + \frac{x^n}{n} + \cdots$$

The ratio of successive terms is

$$(\text{term})_{n+1}/(\text{term})_n = -x\frac{n}{n + 1}$$

10.3 Taylor series

$$f(x) = f_a + f_a'(x - a) + f_a''\frac{1}{2!}(x - a)^2 + \cdots$$

a. $f(x) = 32x^5 - 80x^4 + 80x^3 - 40x^2 + 10x - 1$

$$= 0 + 0 + 0 + 0 + 0 + 3840\frac{1}{5!}\left(x - \frac{1}{2}\right)^5$$

$$= 32\left(x - \frac{1}{2}\right)^5$$

b. $f(x) = \cos(1 + 2x), a = -\frac{1}{2}$

$$f(x) = 1 - \frac{1}{2!}\left[2\left(x + \frac{1}{2}\right)\right]^2 + \frac{1}{4!}\left[2\left(x + \frac{1}{2}\right)\right]^4 - \cdots$$

$$= 1 - \frac{1}{2!}(2x + 1)^2 + \frac{1}{4!}(2x + 1)^4 - \cdots$$

c. $f(x) = \ln(2 + x), a = -1$

$$f(x) = (x + 1) - \frac{1}{2}(x + 1)^2 + \frac{1}{3}(x + 1)^3 - \cdots$$

10.5 $R_6(\xi) = e^\xi\frac{\xi^6}{6!}$,   for $0 \leq \xi \leq x$

For $x = 0.1$, the maximum of e^ξ with $0 \leq \xi \leq 0.1$ is $e^1 = 1.105\ldots$
Thus,

$$[R_6]_{max} = \left[1.105\frac{x^6}{6!}\right]_{max} = 1.535 \times 10^{-9}$$

The sum of the six terms $= 1.105170917\ldots$ and

$$e^1 = 1.105170918\ldots; |\text{diff}| = 1.5 \times 10^{-9} < R_6$$

For $x = 10.$, $[R_6]_{max} = 3.059 \times 10^6$,
    Sum of first six terms $= 1477.67\ldots$
$$e^{10} = 22026.47\ldots; |\text{diff}| = 2.04 \times 10^4 < R_6$$

10.7 Use the first approximation for e^x in place of z in the second.

$$\ln(e^x) = (e^x - 1) + \mathcal{O}[(e^x - 1)^3]$$

$$= [x + \mathcal{O}(x^2)] + \mathcal{O}[(x + \mathcal{O}(x^2))^2]$$

$$= x + \mathcal{O}(x^2) + [x^2 + x\mathcal{O}(x^2) + \mathcal{O}(x^4)]   [x^2 \gg x\mathcal{O}(x^2) \gg \mathcal{O}(x^4)]$$

$$= x + \mathcal{O}(x^2)$$

10.9 $f(x) = e^{\sin x}$

    a. $f_0 = e^{\sin x}|_0 = 1$

        $f_0' = e^{\sin x} \cos x|_0 = 1$

        $f_0'' = e^{\sin x}[\cos^2 x - \sin x]|_0 = 1$

        $f_0''' = e^{\sin x}[\cos^3 x - 3 \cos x \sin x - \cos x]|_0 = 0$

        $f_0^{iv} = e^{\sin x}[\cos^4 x - 6 \cos^2 x \sin x - 4 \cos^2 + 3 \sin^2 x + \sin x]|_0 = -3$

        So, $e^{\sin x} = 1 + x + \dfrac{1}{2!}x^2 - \dfrac{3}{4!}x^4 + \mathcal{O}(x^5)$

    b. $e^{\sin x} = 1 + \sin x + \dfrac{1}{2} \sin^2 x + \dfrac{1}{6} \sin^3 x + \dfrac{1}{24} \sin^4 x + \mathcal{O}(\sin^5 x)$

$$= 1 + \left[x - \frac{x^3}{6} + \mathcal{O}(x^5) \right] + \frac{1}{2}[\ ]^2 + \frac{1}{6}[\ ]^3 + \frac{1}{24}[\ ]^4 + \mathcal{O}([\ ]^5)$$

$$= 1 + \left(x - \frac{x^3}{6} \right) + \frac{1}{2}\left(x^2 - \frac{x^4}{3} \right) + \frac{1}{6}(x^3) + \frac{1}{24}(x^4) + \mathcal{O}(x^5)$$

$$= 1 + x + \frac{1}{2}x^2 - \frac{1}{8}x^4 + \mathcal{O}(x^5)$$

10.13

x	$\dfrac{d(e^x)}{dx}$		$\dfrac{d^2(e^x)}{dx^2}$	
	Approximate	Exact	Approximate	Exact
0.0	1.00167	1.00000	1.00083	1.00000
1.0	2.72282	2.71828	2.72280	2.71828
2.0	7.07140	7.38906	7.39519	7.38906

Chapter 11   **11.1**

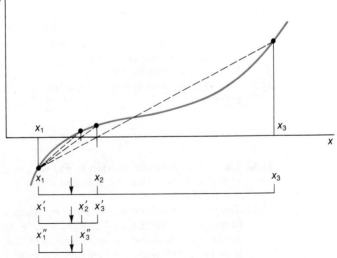

11.3

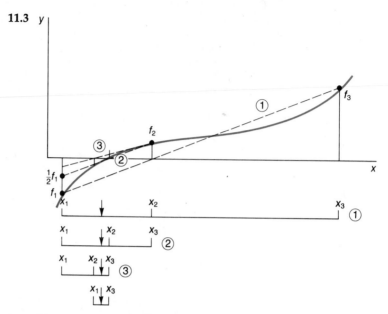

11.5 Newton's method solution for the roots of four of the functions of Problem 11.2.

Initial Guess	Root	Number of Steps
a. 1.5	1.351491	4
b. 2.5	3.000000	4
c. 2.5	2.094552	4
d. 1.5	1.118326	4

11.7 **a.** The function approaches zero but does not change sign near $x = 2.25$, suggesting a root of even multiplicity in this region. The best procedure to use to find the root is Newton's method with a multiplicity factor of 2 or 4.
b. The exact root is at $x = 2.2$.

11.9 Newton's method applied to the function $f(x) = x^n - C$ yields the algorithm:

$$x_1 = x_0 - \frac{x_0^n - C}{nx_0^{n-1}} = \frac{1}{n}\left[(n-1)x_0 + \frac{C}{x_0^{n-1}}\right]$$

11.11 The function can be written as $f(x) = (x - e^{-x})^2$, which has a multiple root at the value of x that is a solution of $x - e^{-x} = 0$, easily found to be $x = 0.567143$.

11.13 The root of the function is found by repeatedly drawing secant lines through the points (x_0, f_0) and $(x_1 = x_0 + \Delta x_0, f_1)$, then finding the root of the line and making the replacement $(x_0, \Delta x_0) \rightarrow (x_1, \Delta x_1)$. This is illustrated below on the function $f(x) = x^2 - 2x + 0.9$.

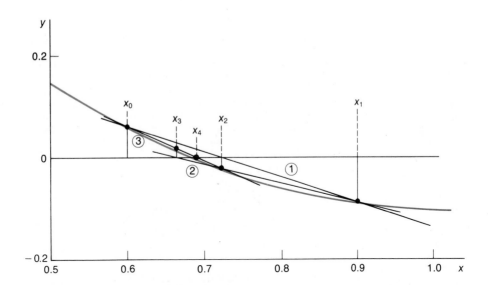

11.15 In each of these subroutines, simply declare all variables except EPS as double precision within the subroutine, including the function names. Additionally, all constants like 1.0 should be replaced, for example, by 1.0D0.

11.17 a. $f(x) = x(x^3 + 6x^2 + 3x - 10) = xg(x)$

Obviously, one root is $x = 0$. The function $g(x)$ has one positive real root and either two or zero negative real roots. Also, $g(-1) = -8$, $g(0) = -10$, $g(1) = 0$. So, the positive root is $x = 1$. If the remaining roots are labeled $-r_3, -r_4$, Newton's relations require

$$\frac{6}{1} = -(1 - r_3 - r_4) \qquad -\frac{10}{1} = (-1)^3 r_3 r_4$$

and the solution of these two equations is $r_3 = 2$, $r_4 = 5$.

b. The function $g(x) = 8x^3 + 12x^2 + 14x + 9$ has zero positive real roots, either three or one negative real roots, and $g(-1) = -1$, $g(0) = 9$. So, one of the three is in the interval -1 to 0. Call this $-r_1$. Assuming there are two remaining real negative roots labeled as $-r_2, -r_3$, Newton's relations require

$$(r_1 + r_2 + r_3) = 3/2 \qquad r_1 r_2 r_3 = 9/8 \qquad \text{(with } 0 \le r_1 \le 1)$$

The maximum of the product of the two numbers with a fixed sum occurs when $r_2 = r_3$, which would imply that $r_2 < 2/3$, so that the product cannot be greater than $9/8$. This contradiction then requires that the remaining two roots be complex.

c. Since both $h(x)$ and $h'(x)$ are zero at $x = 1$, the root is a multiple root. The remaining two roots can be shown to be at $x = \pm i$.

d. Solution similar to **b.**

Chapter 12   **12.1**   **a.** $\begin{bmatrix} 1 & 0 & 2 \\ -2 & 1 & 0 \\ 0 & -2 & 1 \end{bmatrix}$ **b.** $\begin{bmatrix} 3 & -3 & 3 \\ -3 & 3 & -3 \\ 3 & -3 & 3 \end{bmatrix}$ **c.** $\begin{bmatrix} 0 & 0 & 0 \\ 0 & 0 & 0 \\ 0 & 0 & 0 \end{bmatrix}$

12.3   **a.** -1 **b.** -2 **c.** -6

12.5 $(x_1, x_2, x_3) = (0, 0, 1)$

12.7   **a.** $(x_1, x_2, x_3) = (3, -1, 1)$

b. $(x_1, x_2, x_3) = (1, -1, -1)$

c. $(x_1, x_2, x_3) = (0, -2, 2)$

12.9
```
         SUBROUTINE CHECK(A,N,EPS)
         REAL A(N,N)
         DO 1 I = 1,N
         DO 1 J = 1,N
           IF(I .EQ. J.)THEN
             IF(ABS(A(I,J)-1.0) .GT. EPS)THEN
               WRITE(*,*)' The diagonal term',
     +              'A(',I,',',J,')' = ',A(I,J)
               STOP
             END IF
           ELSE
             IF(ABS(A(I,J)) .GT. EPS)THEN
               WRITE(*,*)' The non-diagonal term',
     +              'A(',I,',',J,')' = ',A(I,J)
               STOP
             ENDIF
           ENDIF
       1   CONTINUE
         RETURN
         END
```

12.11
```
         SUBROUTINE SWITCH(A,B,N,I1,I2)
         INTEGER N,I1,I2
         REAL A(N,N),B(N),TEMP
         TEMP = B(I1)
         B(I1) = B(I2)
         B(I2) = TEMP
         DO 1 I = 1,N
           TEMP     = A(I1,I)
           A(I1,I) = A(I2,I)
           A(I2,I) = TEMP
       1   CONTINUE
         RETURN
         END
```

12.13 First replace the right-hand-side vector by an n by n matrix B( ) that is then initialized to equal the identity matrix. Next alter the section of step-1 that divides by the pivot element to read

```
         DO 1 J = 1,N
           A(IPV,J)  = A(IPV,J)/PIVOT
           B(IPV,J)  = B(IPV,J)/PIVOT
       1   CONTINUE
```

and the section of step-2 that replaces row-IROW by row-IROW plus a multiple of the pivot row to read

```
         DO 2 ICOL = 1,N
           A(IROW,ICOL) = A(IROW,ICOL) - FACTOR*A(IPV,ICOL)
           B(IROW,ICOL) = B(IROW,ICOL) - FACTOR*B(IPV,ICOL)
       2   CONTINUE
```

Finally, delete the DO 5 loop entirely. The inverse of the matrix A will be contained in the matrix B.

12.15
```
FUNCTION DIADOM(A,N)
REAL A(N,N),SUM
INTEGER DIADOM
DIADOM = 1
DO 2 I = 1,N
    SUM = 0.
    DO 1 J = 1,N
        IF(J.NE.I)THEN
            SUM = SUM + ABS(A(I,J))
        ENDIF
1       CONTINUE
        IF(ABS(A(I,I)) .GT. SUM)THEN
            DIADOM = 0
            RETURN
        ENDIF
2 CONTINUE
RETURN
END
```

12.17 With an initial guess of $(x, y, z) = (1, 1, 1)$, the system of equations quickly converges to a solution at $(1.015609, 0.761784, -0.694348)$. However, as with any nonlinear problem, several other solutions to the set of equations are possible. The two other real solutions are found at $(51.372, 3.1422, -13.879)$ and $(65.177, -3.589, -15.647)$.

Chapter 13

13.1 The minimum of the function $E(d)$ is obtained at a value of $d_{min} = 16/5$.

13.3 The line that minimizes the deviations in the y direction is then given by

$$y_1(x) = a_1 x + b_1$$

with

$$a_1 = \frac{41}{35} \qquad b_1 = -\frac{3}{5}$$

Interchanging the x and y values and repeating the calculation is equivalent to finding the line that now minimizes the deviations in the x direction,

$$x_2(y) = a_2 y + b_2$$

where

$$a_2 = \frac{41}{59} \qquad b_2 = \frac{63}{59}$$

Rewriting the second equation as $y_2(x)$, the equations for the two best-fit lines are

$$y_1(x) = \frac{41}{35}x - \frac{3}{5}$$

$$y_2(x) = \frac{59}{41}x - \frac{63}{41}$$

These two lines are compared with the data on the sketch that follows. Notice that the two lines are substantially different, indicating that minimizing the deviations in the x direction can yield results quite different from those obtained by minimizing deviations in the y direction.

Also included on the sketch is a best by-eye fit to the data. This line differs substantially from either of the two earlier lines. This is because a best by-eye fit will tend to minimize the *perpendicular*

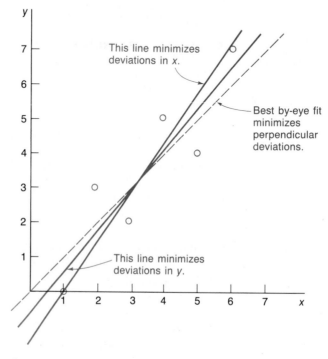

deviations of the data from the line. In the present case the best by-eye fit is superior to either of the least squares fits.

13.5 The model function $N(t) = N_0 e^{-\lambda t}$ is linearized by taking the logarithm of both sides of the equation to yield

$$y(t) = at + b$$

$$= \ln[N(t)]$$

$$= \ln[N_0 e^{-\lambda t}] = -\lambda t + \ln(N_0)$$

A least squares analysis to obtain a and b yields $a = -4.67654$, $b = 41.7922$, and these in turn determine the values of λ and N_0 to be

$$\lambda = -a = 4.6765 \qquad N_0 = e^b = 1.413\text{E}+18$$

13.7 The Stefan–Boltzmann law is used as the model function. To linearize this equation we make the identifications

$$y(x) = ax + b$$
$$= R(T) = \sigma(T^4 - T_0^4)$$

Thus,

$$y(x) = R(T) \qquad x = T^4 \qquad a = \sigma \qquad b = -\sigma T_0^4$$

The result of the least squares analysis for a and b is

$$a = 5.657 \times 10^{-8} = \sigma \qquad b = -407.9845 = -\sigma T_0^4$$
$$T_0 = [407.9845/\sigma]^{1/4} = 291.4\,\text{K} = 18.24°\,\text{C}$$

i	T_i	R_i	$R_{\text{model}}(T_i)$
1	300.0	40.0	50.26
2	350.0	430.0	440.96
3	400.0	1050.0	1040.28
4	450.0	1920.0	1911.86
5	500.0	3150.0	3127.83
6	550.0	4750.0	4768.80

13.9 Linear, quadratic, and exponential fits to the data yield.

Linear Fit $[y_1(x) = a_0 + a_1 x]$

$$a_0 = -3.200$$
$$a_1 = 23.180$$

Quadratic Fit $[y_2(x) = b_0 + b_1 x + b_2 x^2]$

$$b_0 = 4.24571$$
$$b_1 = -6.40286$$
$$b_2 = 14.77143$$

Exponential Fit $[y_3(x) = \alpha e^{\beta x}]$

Let $Y(X) = c_0 + c_1 X$

$$= \ln[y(x)] = \beta x + \ln(\alpha)$$

So, $Y_i = \ln(y_i)$, $X_i = x_i$, $\beta = c_1$, $\ln(\alpha) = c_0$. The results for c_0, c_1 are then

$$c_1 = 1.37807 \qquad c_0 = 1.18021$$
$$\alpha = e^{c_0} = 3.25504 \qquad \beta = c_1 = 1.37806$$

The three model fits are compared with the data in the following table. Beneath each computed value is the deviation from the data point.

i	x_i	y_i	Linear $y_1(x_i)$	Quadratic $y_2(x_i)$	Exponential $y_3(x_i)$
1	0.0	3.4	−3.200 $\langle -6.60 \rangle$	+4.2462 $\langle -0.846 \rangle$	+3.255 $\langle -0.145 \rangle$
2	0.5	6.0	8.390 $\langle +2.390 \rangle$	4.7371 $\langle -1.263 \rangle$	6.483 $\langle +0.483 \rangle$
3	1.0	13.3	19.980 $\langle +6.680 \rangle$	12.6143 $\langle -0.6857 \rangle$	12.914 $\langle -0.386 \rangle$
4	1.5	25.7	31.570 $\langle +5.870 \rangle$	27.8770 $\langle +2.1770 \rangle$	25.721 $\langle +0.021 \rangle$
5	2.0	51.5	43.160 $\langle -8.340 \rangle$	50.5261 $\langle -0.9739 \rangle$	51.231 $\langle -0.269 \rangle$

Sum of squared deviations	197.907	8.4689	0.476
Chi-squared	629.77	23.58	1.75

Thus, the only adequate fit of the three is the exponential fit.

13.11 For a cubic drawn through just two points, $i = 0$ only, $d = (x_1 - x_0)$, and $h_0 = h = (y_1 - y_0)$.

a. The Z_i values are determined first by using Equations (13.50).

$$Z_0 = \frac{1}{2}(3h - Z_1) \qquad Z_1 = \frac{1}{2}(3h - Z_0)$$

which can be solved to yield $Z_0 = Z_1 = h$.

b. Next, Equations (13.44) are used to determine the four coefficients of the cubic function drawn through the two points. (*Note: $i = 0$ for all equations.*)

$$a_{00} = y_0$$

$$a_{10} = y_0' = h = (y_1 - y_0)/(x_1 - x_0)$$

$$a_{30}d^2 = (y_0' + y_1') - 2h = 2h - 2h = 0$$

$$a_{20}d = h - y_0' - a_{30}d^2 = h - h - 0 = 0$$

Thus, the equation for the cubic is

$$f(x) = a_{00} + a_{10}(x - x_0) + a_{20}(x - x_0)^2 + a_{30}(x - x_0)^3$$

$$= y_0 + \frac{y_1 - y_0}{x_1 - x_0}(x - x_0)$$

which is obviously just a straight line drawn through the two points (x_0, y_0) and (x_1, y_1).

Chapter 14   **14.1**   **a.** Evaluate $T_0 = \frac{1}{2}\Delta x_0(f_a + f_b)$

b. $T_1 = \frac{T_0}{2} + \Delta x_1 f(a + \Delta x_1)$

c. $T_k = \frac{1}{2}T_{k-1} + \Delta x_k \sum_{\substack{i=1 \\ \text{odd only}}}^{n-1} f(a + \Delta x_k)$

for the functions and intervals given.

	T_0	T_1	T_2	T_3	T_4
(1)	256.0	192.0	176.0	172.0	171.0
(2)	16384.0	9216.0	7232.0	6724.0	6597.0
(3)	0.18393	0.24360	0.25904	0.26293	0.26392
(4)	1.23370	1.05303	1.01295	1.00322	1.00080
(5)	1.91421	1.65588	1.59002	1.57347	1.56933
(6)	1.68393	0.73137	0.74298	0.74587	0.74658

14.3   Simpson's rule values can be computed directly from the trapezoidal rule numbers using the relation

$$S_{k+1} = T_{k+1} + (T_{k+1} - T_k)/3$$

The results for the functions of Problem 14.1 are

	S_1	S_2	S_3	S_4
(1)	$170\frac{2}{3}$	$170\frac{2}{3}$	$170\frac{2}{3}$	$170\frac{2}{3}$
(2)	$6826\frac{2}{3}$	$6570\frac{2}{3}$	$6554\frac{2}{3}$	$6553\frac{2}{3}$
(3)	0.26349	0.26419	0.26424	0.26424
(4)	0.99281	0.99959	0.99998	1.00000
(5)	1.56977	1.56808	1.56796	1.56795
(6)	0.74718	0.74686	0.74683	0.74682

14.5   The tables of the round-off error monitors, R_k^m, given by Equation (14.19) for each of the functions in Problem 14.1 follow.

(1) $f(x) = x^2$, $a = 0$, $b = 8$

$R_2^0 = 1.0$; the rest are 0/0

(2) $f(x) = x^4$, $a = 0$, $b = 8$

k	R_k^0	R_k^1
2	0.903	
3	0.976	1.000

(3) $f(x) = xe^{-x}$, $a = 0$, $b = 1$

k	R_k^0	R_k^1	R_k^2
2	0.9659		
3	0.9912	0.9646	
4	0.9978	0.9909	0.9672

(4) $f(x) = x \sin(x)$, $a = 0$, $b = \pi/2$

k	R_k^0	R_k^1	R_k^2
2	1.1270		
3	1.0296	1.1050	
4	1.0073	1.0246	1.0933

(5) $f(x) = (1 + x^2)^{3/2}$, $a = 0$, $b = 1$

k	R_k^0	R_k^1	R_k^3
2	0.9807		
3	0.9951	0.9785	
4	0.9988	1.0040	−1.3409

(6) $f(x) = e^{-x^2}$, $a = 0$, $b = 1$

k	R_k^0	R_k^1	R_k^2
2	1.0210		
3	1.0076	0.6943	
4	1.0019	0.9815	4.0638

14.7   The integrand $(e^x + x)^{-1}$ approaches e^{-x} for large x. To see how accurate such a replacement might be, we first construct a table of both quantities as a function of x.

x	$(e^x + x)^{-1}$	e^{-x}
0.0	1.000000	1.000000
1.0	0.268941	0.367879
2.0	0.106507	0.135335
4.0	0.017065	0.018316
8.0	0.000335	0.000335

Thus, the approximation

$$\int_0^\infty \frac{dx}{(e^x + x)} \simeq \int_0^9 \frac{dx}{(e^x + x)} + \int_9^\infty e^{-x}\,dx$$

should be accurate to about five significant figures. The first integral must be done numerically. The Gauss quadrature with $k = 10$ sampling points was used. The result for the first integral is

$$I_1 = 0.806160570$$

The second integral can be done analytically, and the result is

$$I_2 = e^{-9} = 0.00012341$$

So the approximate value of the integral is

$$I \simeq 0.806284$$

14.9 **b.** The inverse of the matrix is

$$[A^{-1}] = \begin{bmatrix} 1 & 0 & 0 & 0 & 0 \\ 1 & 1 & 1 & 1 & 1 \\ 1 & 2 & 4 & 8 & 16 \\ 1 & 3 & 9 & 27 & 81 \\ 1 & 4 & 16 & 64 & 256 \end{bmatrix}^{-1} = -\frac{1}{24} \begin{bmatrix} 24 & 0 & 0 & 0 & 0 \\ -50 & 96 & -72 & 32 & -6 \\ 35 & -104 & 114 & -56 & 11 \\ -10 & 36 & -48 & 28 & -6 \\ 1 & -4 & 6 & -4 & 1 \end{bmatrix}$$

and thus

$$\begin{bmatrix} c_0 \\ c_1 \Delta x \\ c_2 \Delta x^2 \\ c_3 \Delta x^3 \\ c_4 \Delta x^4 \end{bmatrix} = [A^{-1}] \begin{bmatrix} y_0 \\ y_1 \\ y_2 \\ y_3 \\ y_4 \end{bmatrix}$$

c. Area $= \displaystyle\int_{x_0}^{x_4} y(x)\, dx$

$$= c_0(x_4 - x_0) + \frac{1}{2}c_1(x_4 - x_0)^2 + \frac{1}{3}c_2(x_4 - x_1)^3 + \frac{1}{4}c_3(x_4 - x_0)^4$$

$$+ \frac{1}{5}c_4(x_4 - x_0)^5$$

$$= c_0 4\,\Delta x + 8c_1\,\Delta x^2 + \frac{64}{3}c_2\,\Delta x^3 + 64c_3\,\Delta x^4 + \frac{1024}{5}c_4\,\Delta x^5$$

e. $S_1 = \dfrac{(x_2 - x_0)}{3}[y_0 + 4y_2 + y_4]$

$S_2 = \dfrac{(x_1 - x_0)}{3}[y_0 + 4y_1 + 2y_2 + 4y_3 + y_4]$

thus $\dfrac{1}{15}[16S_2 - S_1] = \dfrac{4}{15}\Delta x[7y_0 + 32y_1 + 12y_2 + 32y_3 + 7y_4]$

14.11

```
     FUNCTION GAUS10(F,A,B)
*
*  F   -- Function to be integrated, supplied elsewhere in the
*         program
*  A,B -- x-interval of integration
*  S() -- Gaussian evaluation points
```

```
*  W() -- Weight factors
*  Z   -- The integral over x from a to b is transformed to an
*            integral over z from -1 to +1.
*
      REAL    F,A,B,Z,S(0:4),W(0:4)
      DATA (S(M),M=0,4)/-.9739065285,-.8650633667,-.6794095683,
     +                  -.4333953941,-.1488743390/
      DATA (W(M),M=0,4)/ .0666713443, .1494513492, .2190863625,
     +                   .2692667193, .2955242247/
*------------------------------------------------------------------
      SUM = 0.0
      DO 3 M = 0,4
         XMINUS =  (B-A)*.5*S(M)  +  0.5*(B+A)
         XPLUS  = -(B-A)*.5*S(M)  +  0.5*(B+A)
         TERM   = W(M)*(F(XMINUS) + F(XPLUS))*(B-A)*0.5
         SUM    = SUM + TERM
    3 CONTINUE
      GAUS10   = SUM
      RETURN
      END
```

The percentage errors when using this function to integrate the functions of Problem 14.1 are:

a. 0.000009   **d.** 0.000024
b. 0.000015   **e.** 0.000015
c. 0.0   **f.** 0.000016

Chapter 15   **15.1**   **a.** $y(x) = \sqrt{x}$ **d.** $I(t) = 2e^{-50000t}$
                     b. $y(x) = x^2$ **e.** $N(t) = N_0 e^{t/k}$
                     c. $y(x) = e^{2x}$

15.3   Euler's method applied to a variety of differential equations.
        a. $y' = -y/x$, $y(1) = 1.0$, $\Delta x = 0.1$
                 $\langle$exact solution, $y(x) = 1/x\rangle$

i	x_i	$y(x_i)$ Exact	$y(x_i)$ Euler	Fractional Difference
0	1.0	1.000000000	1.000000000	0.00000
1	1.1	0.909090909	0.900000000	0.01000
2	1.2	0.833333333	0.818181818	0.01818
3	1.3	0.769230769	0.750000000	0.02500
4	1.4	0.714285714	0.692307692	0.03077
5	1.5	0.666666667	0.642857143	0.03571
6	1.6	0.625000000	0.600000000	0.04000
7	1.7	0.588235294	0.562500000	0.04375
8	1.8	0.555555556	0.529411765	0.04706
9	1.9	0.526315789	0.500000000	0.05000
10	2.0	0.500000000	0.473684211	0.05263

b. $y' = -y^2$, $y(1) = 1.0$, $\Delta x = 0.1$

⟨exact solution, $y(x) = 1/x$⟩

i	x_i	$y(x_i)$ Exact	$y(x_i)$ Euler	Fractional Difference
0	1.0	1.000000000	1.000000000	0.00000
1	1.1	0.909090909	0.900000000	0.01000
2	1.2	0.833333333	0.819000000	0.01728
3	1.3	0.769230769	0.751923900	0.02250
4	1.4	0.714285714	0.695384945	0.02646
5	1.5	0.666666667	0.647028923	0.02946
6	1.6	0.625000000	0.605164280	0.03174
7	1.7	0.588235294	0.568541899	0.03348
8	1.8	0.555555556	0.536217910	0.03481
9	1.9	0.526315789	0.507464946	0.03582
10	2.0	0.500000000	0.481712878	0.03657

c. $y' = -y/x$, $y(1) = 1.0$, $\Delta x = -0.1$

⟨exact solution $= y(x) = 1/x$⟩

i	x_i	$y(x_i)$ Exact	$y(x_i)$ Midpoint	Fractional Difference
0	1.0	1.0000000	1.0000000	——
1	0.9	1.1111111	1.0999999	0.01000
2	0.8	1.2500000	1.2222222	0.02222
3	0.7	1.4285714	1.3749999	0.03750
4	0.6	1.6666667	1.5714285	0.05714
5	0.5	2.0000000	1.8333332	0.08333
6	0.4	2.5000000	2.1999998	0.11999
7	0.3	3.3333333	3.7499995	0.17499
8	0.2	5.0000000	5.4999978	0.44999
9	0.1	10.0000000	10.9999900	0.99999
10	0.0	∞	——	——

d. $y' = x + y$, $y(1) = 0.0$, $\Delta x = 0.4$

⟨exact solution $= y(x) = e^x - 1 - x$⟩

i	x_i	$y(x_i)$ Exact	$y(x_i)$ Midpoint	Fractional Difference
0	0.0	0.0000000	0.0000000	——
1	0.4	0.0918267	0.0000000	1.0000
2	0.8	0.4255409	0.1600000	0.6240
3	1.2	1.1201169	0.5440000	0.5154
4	1.6	2.3530324	1.2416000	0.4723
5	2.0	4.3890561	2.3782400	0.4581
6	2.4	7.6231764	4.1295360	0.4583
7	2.8	12.6446467	6.7413504	0.4669
8	3.2	20.3325302	10.5578906	0.4807
9	3.6	31.9982344	16.0610468	0.4981
10	4.0	49.5981500	23.9254655	0.5176

15.5 $y_1 = 0.8187422$
$y_2 = 0.8187342$
$y_{ex} = e^{-.2} = 0.8187308$
$R = 3.35088$
$p = 1.74$

15.7 a.

```
          SUBROUTINE MDPT4(X,Y,N,A,B,F1,F2,F3,F4)
*
*  MDPT4 integrates the four coupled differential equations
*     y1' = f1(x,y1,y2,y3,y4) ...  y4' = f1(x,y1,y2,y3,y4)
*  using the approximate slope in the middle of the interval
*  to estimate each step.  The interval is x = a to x = b and
*  a total of n steps are computed.  It is assumed that the
*  starting values of all 4 y-s, that is (y(i,0), i=1,4), are
*  stored in the array y().  The function subprograms f1(),
*  ..., f4() must be usersupplied.
*================================================================
          REAL X(0:N),Y(4,0:N),A,B,DX,F1,F2,F3,F4,XMID,Y1,Y2,Y3,Y4
          X(0) = A
          DX   = (B-A)/N
          DO 1 I = 0,N-1
            XMID = X(1) + 0.5*DX
            Y1 = Y(1,I) + F1(XMID,Y(1,I),Y(2,I),Y(3,I),Y(4,I))*.5*DX
            Y2 = Y(2,I) + F2(XMID,    Y1,Y(2,I),Y(3,I),Y(4,I))*.5*DX
            Y3 = Y(3,I) + F3(XMID,    Y1,    Y2,Y(3,I),Y(4,I))*.5*DX
            Y4 = Y(4,I) + F4(XMID,    Y1,    Y2,    Y3,Y(4,I))*.5*DX
            Y(1,I+1) = Y(1,I) + F1(XMID,Y1,Y2,Y3,Y4)*DX
            Y(2,I+1) = Y(2,I) + F2(XMID,Y1,Y2,Y3,Y4)*DX
            Y(3,I+1) = Y(3,I) + F3(XMID,Y1,Y2,Y3,Y4)*DX
            Y(4,I+1) = Y(4,I) + F4(XMID,Y1,Y2,Y3,Y4)*DX
            X(I+1) = X(I) + DX
1         CONTINUE
          RETURN
          END
```

b. Using the following associations:

$$t_i = X(I)$$

$$x_i = Y(1,I) \qquad (v_x)_i = Y(2,I)$$

$$y_i = Y(3,I) \qquad (v_y)_i = Y(4,I)$$

The subroutine MDPT4 is used to compute the orbit beginning with the conditions of Problem 15.2. The results are graphed below.

30,000
(km)

−30,000
−40,000

40,000
(km)

15.9

```
PROGRAM FTN9
PARAMETER (N=500)
REAL X,Y(0:N),A,B,F
EXTERNAL F
DATA Y(0),A,B/1.,1.,3./
CALL RKFOUR(Y,N,A,B,F)
DO 1 I = 0,N,10
    WRITE(*,10)I,1.+I*DX,Y(I),(1.+I*DX)**2
1   CONTINUE
10  FORMAT(T2,I3,T6,F5.3,T15,F9.6,T26,F12.8)
END
FUNCTION F(X,Y)
  F = 4.*X - 2.*Y/X
  RETURN
END
*=======================================================
SUBROUTINE RKFOUR(Y,N,A,B,F)
INTEGER N
REAL Y(0:N),A,B,X,DX,XH,Y1,DY1,DY10,DY11,DY12,DY13,F
DX = (B-A)/N
X  = A
DO 1 I = 0,N-1
    XH   = X + .5*DX
    Y1   = Y(I)
    DY10 = F(  X,        Y1)*DX
    DY11 = F(  XH,Y1+.5*DY10)*DX
    DY12 = F(  XH,Y1+.5*DY11)*DX
    DY13 = F(X+DX,    Y1+DY12)*DX
    DY1  = (DY10 + 2.*DY11 + 2.*DY12 + DY13)/6.
    Y(I+1) = Y(I) + DY1
    X = X + DX
1   CONTINUE
RETURN
END
```

15.11 If the life span of a rabbit is RLS and that of a fox is FLS, we need to reduce the population now, at time t_i, by the number of individuals born between $(t_i -$ life span$)$ and $(t_i -$ life span$) + dt$. If the time step is DX and the current step is I, we need to know the birth rate in step I$-$(RLS/DX) for rabbits and I$-$(FLS/DX) for foxes. Thus, in the Runge–Kutta subroutine, the following lines need to be added immediately after the DO loop.

```
IF(I .GT. RLS/DX)THEN
    K = I - RLS/DX
    Y1(I) = Y1(I) - GR*Y1(K)*DX
    IF(Y(I) .LE. 0.)Y1(I) = 0.01
ENDIF
IF(I .GT. FLS/DX)THEN
    K = I - FLS/DX
    Y2(I) = Y2(I) - GF*Y2(K)*DX
    IF(Y(I) .LE. 0.)Y2(I) = 0.01
ENDIF
```

where GR and GF are the growth rates of rabbits and foxes, respectively.

15.13 To start the procedure we need values for y_1, y_2, y_3 in addition to the given value for y_0. If we use the exact solution to compute these quantities we may then use the Milne equations to compute y_4 and y_5. The results are then:

i	x_{i+1}	y_{i+1} from Predictor Equation	Corrector Equation Applied Three Times
3	1.040	0.92455623253	
			0.92455621212
			0.92455621238
			0.92455621238
4	1.050	0.90702949675	
			0.90702947765
			0.90702947789
			0.90702947789

15.15 Assuming values for y_i, $i = 0,3$ have already been computed in the main program, the following subroutine will solve a differential equation $y' = f(x, y)$ using the Milne method.

```
SUBROUTINE MILNE(A,B,N,Y,F)
REAL X,DX,A,B,F,Y(0:N)
DX = (B-A)/N
DO 2 I = 3,N-1
    Y(I+1) = Y(I-3) + 4.*DX/3.*(2.*F(X(I),Y(I)) -
+            F(X(I-1),Y(I-1)) + 2.*F(X(I-2),Y(I-2)))
    DO 1 ITER = 1,3
        Y(I+1) = Y(I-1) + DX/3.*(F(X(I+1),Y(I+1)) +
+                4.*F(X(I),Y(I)) + F(X(I-1),Y(I-1)))
1       CONTINUE
2   CONTINUE
    RETURN
    END
```

Chapter 16   **16.1** Since the legislated value of π is 0.04% greater than the actual value, the manufacturer can reduce the volume of cans by this same fraction and still claim to have the stated volume. Thus, the radius of the cans will be reduced by a factor of $r' = \sqrt{1.0004}$, $r \approx 1.0002r$, or by 0.02%. The fraction, $\frac{355}{113}$ is a much more accurate approximation, allowing the manufacturer to decrease the can radius by only a factor of 1.00000004.

16.3 Rewriting the approximation $f(x \pm \Delta x) \approx f(x) \pm f'(x)\Delta x$ as

$$\frac{f(x \pm \Delta x) - f(x)}{f(x)} = \frac{\Delta f}{f} \approx \pm \frac{f'(x)}{f(x)}\Delta x$$

and using $f(x) = x^{1/10}$, we obtain

$$\frac{\Delta f}{f} \approx \frac{1}{10}\frac{\Delta x}{x}$$

Numerically, $(1024 \pm 1\%)^{-1} \approx 2 \pm 0.1\%$

16.5 Using first rows 1 and 2 of Table 16-2 to compute values of k and p for the trapezoidal rule results, repeating this for rows 2 and 3, and averaging the two sets of values, we obtain the following expression for the approximate error.

Trapezoidal rule: $\varepsilon \approx 4.4(\Delta x)^{1.9}$

Applying the same technique to the Simpson's rule values we obtain:

Simpson's rule: $\varepsilon \approx 6.0(\Delta x)^{3.6}$

For the remaining table elements, the fractional differences between the actual error and that predicted by the equations above are computed and listed below:

i	$\lvert (\Delta \varepsilon / \varepsilon) \rvert_{\text{Trap}}$	$\lvert (\Delta \varepsilon / \varepsilon) \rvert_{\text{Simp}}$
3	0.02	0.08
4	0.07	0.29
5	0.14	0.45
6	0.19	0.51
7	0.24	0.12
8	0.30	0.69
9	0.34	1.27
10	0.39	2389.4
11	0.42	—
12	0.24	—
13	0.98	—
14	2.08	—
15	111.3	—
16	—	—

The Simpson's rule values begin to fail in step 10, and the trapezoidal rule values begin to fail in step 15.

Index

FORTRAN-Coded Mathematical Procedures